Expressions in
Canadian Native Studies

Expressions in Canadian Native Studies

Edited by
Ron F. Laliberte, Priscilla Settee, James B. Waldram, Rob Innes,
Brenda Macdougall, Lesley McBain, F. Laurie Barron

University Extension Press
Saskatoon, Saskatchewan

Cover art: Dean Whitebear
Cover design: Eyecatcher Graphics and Design, Saskatoon, SK
Managing editor: Perry Millar
Copy editor: Allison Muri
Indexer: Noeline Bridge
Layout: Marla Ramsay

Printed and bound in Canada by Houghton Boston

Canadian Catalogue in Publication Data

Main entry under title:

Expressions in Canadian native studies

    Includes index.
    ISBN 0-88880-411-3

1. Native people—Canada.* I. Laliberte, Ron. F.

E78.C2E867 2000   **971'.00497**   **C00–920142–4**

To order copies of this book contact U-Learn
phone: (306) 966-5565
fax: (306) 966-5567
mail: Room 125, 117 Science Place
     Saskatoon, SK S7N 5C8
e-mail: u.learn@usask.ca

Dedication

This book is dedicated to the memory of F. Laurie Barron, a founding member of the Department of Native Studies at the University of Saskatchewan: scholar, colleague, and friend.

Table of Contents

Challenging the Past

Challenging the Present—Looking to the Future

Documents

Guide to Critical Reading and Writing

Preface

The artwork on the cover of this book, *Return of the Buffalo* by the Saskatchewan artist Dean Whitebear, symbolizes the belief by some in the North American Aboriginal community that education is the new buffalo. Until the late nineteenth century, the buffalo was of central importance in the survival and cultural development of the Aboriginal people of the northern plains and prairie. Government policy and the signing of treaties, combined with settlement of the land, in effect removed the Aboriginal people from their source of life. The changes that Aboriginal people were forced to confront are reflected in the scholarship and issues that arose in the discipline of Native Studies, particularly as new Aboriginal scholars began to take their place in the academy. This book recognizes, in various ways, the challenges this new discipline brings to the academy and the many issues that are arising. Underlying all the articles, however, is the fight for acknowledgment of Aboriginal ways of knowing and self-identity, of bringing forth an absent history and knowledge.

The book was developed because of a void in the field of Native Studies in which critical perspectives on the most important issues were absent, including critical interpretations offered by Aboriginal scholars. It was clear that it was time to bring Aboriginal scholarship to the forefront and in a manner that would be accessible to students. While the primary goal has been to produce a useable text for university-level courses, a secondary goal was to bring together articles that would be relevant for researchers and of interest to the general reading audience.

Native Studies remains a dynamic field in which the contributions of both Aboriginal and non-Aboriginal scholars are valued as part of the ongoing dialogue. In recent years there has been an enormous growth in literature authored by Aboriginal scholars, and the editors decided to weight the book in favour of these because of both a need and demand. As a result, scholars from different fields and from different regions of the country have intentionally been brought together to give this collection an interdisciplinary and national feel.

An effort has also been made to have this book reflect the "state of the field," a debate underlying Aboriginal scholarship. Some argue that research and writing in the field adhere to traditional scholarly methodology, where literature is surveyed and assessed, and argument is built on the foundation of previous scholarship and research. Others challenge this traditional Western scholarly model and argue it is equally valid to draw directly from the Aboriginal tradition, to use stories or the teachings of Elders, for example. These are seen as authentic social and historical materials that allow the writer's voice to speak with greater freedom.

The articles in the book reflect this debate. A number are by Aboriginal and non-Aboriginal scholars whose work reflects the scholarly tradition. Other articles are written by established or emerging Aboriginal scholars and are a greater blend of the scholarly and Aboriginal traditions. We have also included speeches, a section on the five treaties in Saskatchewan drawn from a larger publication, writing from newspapers and popular journals, some stories, and government documents. We believe that the selection of scholarly argument, the new voices, and the diverse other materials represent an important dialectic in the field.

The articles and stories in the book are divided into five sections: Beginnings, Challenging Native Studies, Expressions in Native Identity, Challenging the Past, and Challenging the Present—Looking to The Future. The essays within each section speak in differing ways about the struggle of Aboriginal people to create, on their own terms, a space for themselves in both the academy and Canadian society. Using a variety of tones ranging from humour to anger, the articles also reflect the state of the Native Studies discipline, the concerns of various Aboriginal communities, and the complexities of the issues that Aboriginal peoples confront daily. Another section provides documents or excerpts from documents that have had a major impact on the lives of Aboriginal people in Canada. It is readily apparent to those in the field of Native Studies that, while the existence of these documents is widely known in the Aboriginal and non-Aboriginal communities, few have ready access to them or have ever been afforded the opportunity to see for themselves what they contain.

Finally, two guides to critical reading and writing have been included to assist readers in interpreting the material.

Readers may notice inconsistencies with regard to capitalization, for example "Aboriginal" and "aboriginal" and other terminology. A conscious decision was made to respect the preference of the individual authors rather than enforcing a consistent vernacular throughout the book. These types of inconsistencies again reflect the dynamic nature of a field in which consensus has yet to emerge on many key points.

In conclusion, we hope that as the discipline of Native Studies changes and evolves, the book will be a touchstone for readers and that the articles will provide a foundation for further thought and discussion.

We would like to acknowledge funding assistance from the University of Saskatchewan, the Native Studies Department, and the Indigenous Peoples Program in the Extension Division (both at the University of Saskatchewan). Bertram Wolfe from the University Extension Press provided editorial advice at the beginning of the project, and Perry Millar guided the book through to press. The following individuals— Ron Bourgeault, Peggy Brizinski (Peggy Martin McGuire), Maria Campbell, Tom Flanagan, Joyce Green, Margaret A. Jackson, Ted Moses, and Arthur J. Ray—and the following organizations—Gabriel Dumont Institute, the Saskatchewan Office of the Treaty Commissioner, and Indian Country Communications—all kindly agreed to allow reprinting of previously published work without charge.

This book is dedicated to the memory of F. Laurie Barron, a founding member of the Department of Native Studies at the University of Saskatchewan, who passed away just months before the book was completed. A man of deep commitment to the field of Native Studies and to his students, Laurie was a friend, a mentor, and a colleague whom we will miss.

The Editors

Tribal Distributions In and Near Canada at Time of Contact

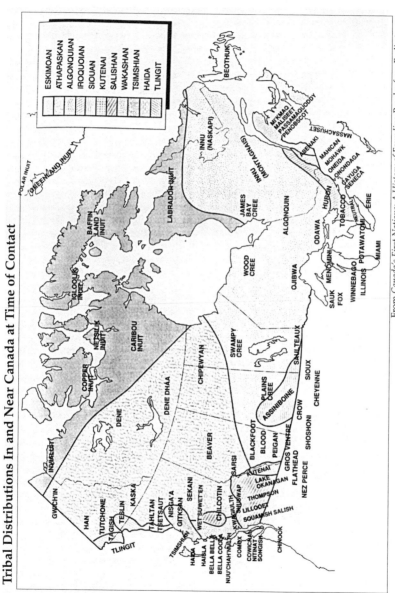

From *Canada's First Nations: A History of Founding Peoples from Earliest Times* by Olive Patricia Dickason. Copyright © 1992 Olive Patricia Dickason. Reprinted by permission of Oxford University Press Canada.

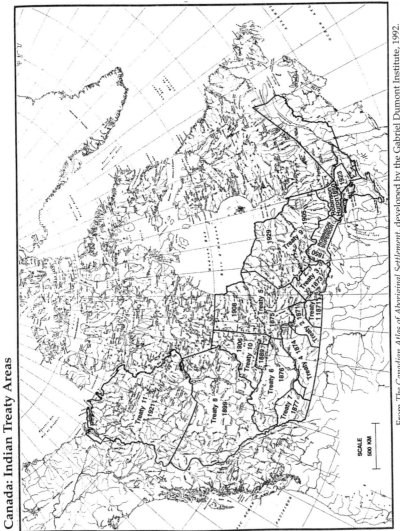

Canada: Indian Treaty Areas

From *The Canadian Atlas of Aboriginal Settlement*, developed by the Gabriel Dumont Institute, 1992. Reprinted with permission of the Gabriel Dumont Institute of Métis Studies and Applied Research Inc.

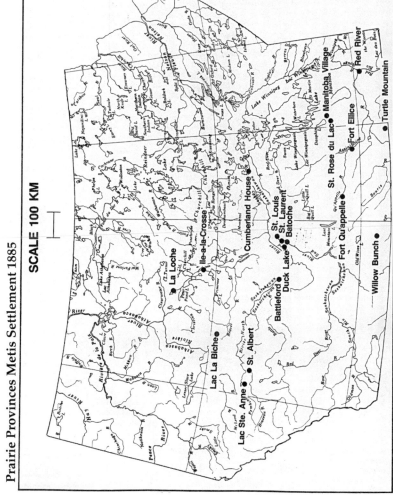

Prairie Provinces Metis Settlement 1885

SCALE 100 KM

From *The Canadian Atlas of Aboriginal Settlement*, developed by the Gabriel Dumont Institute, 1992.
Reprinted with permission of the Gabriel Dumont Institute of Métis Studies and Applied Research Inc.

Saskatchewan: Indian Treaty Areas

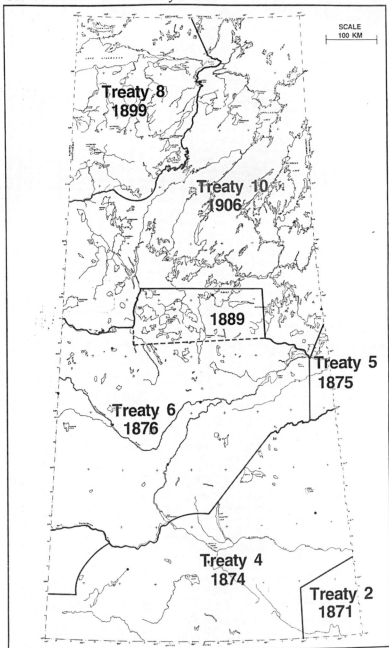

From *The Canadian Atlas of Aboriginal Settlement*, developed by the Gabriel Dumont Institute, 1992.
Reprinted with permission of the Gabriel Dumont Institute of Métis Studies and Applied Research Inc.

Beginnings

Creation Stories

Edward Benton-Banai

Edward Benton-Banai lives in Wisconsin and is a cultural and educational resource/consultant.

The Ojibway Creation Story

*B*oo-zhoo´ (hello), my name is Mishomis. I am an Ojibway Indian. I live here in my cabin on the forested shores of Madeline Island. Madeline Island is in Lake Superior and is part of a group of islands now called the Apostle Islands. It is not far from the city of Ashland, Wisconsin. Many years ago, my Ojibway ancestors migrated to this area from their original homeland on the eastern shores of North America. Now the Ojibways and their offshoots are spread from the Atlantic coast, all along the St. Lawrence River, and throughout the Great Lakes region of this country. Madeline Island was the final stopping place on this great migration. Here, the Waterdrum of the traditional Midewiwin Lodge sounded its voice loud and clear. Its voice travelled far over the water and through the woodlands. Its voice attracted the many bands of the Ojibway until this island became the capital of the Ojibway nation.

From the *Mishomis Book* (Saint Paul: Red School House, 1988). Published with permission of the author and Indian Country Communication, Inc.

The *Mishomis Book* with all fifteen chapters or the *Mishomis Color Book* series (first five chapters) for children are available from Indian Country Communications, Inc., 7831N Grindstone Lane, Hayward, Wisconsin, USA 54843. For more information on these and other products they may be reached at (715) 634-5226 or at <indiancountrynews.com>. Mr. Benton-Banai may be contacted at 12616 Lilly Pad Lane, Hayward, Wisconsin, USA 54843.

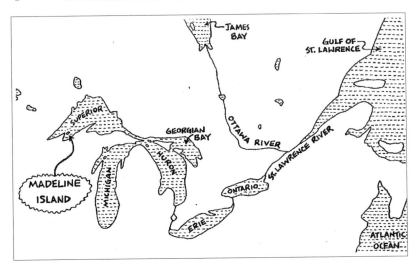

It has been many years since the Waterdrum has sounded its voice here. This Waterdrum that I have beside me was handed down from my grandfathers. I am preparing this place to be a place of rebirth for traditional Indian ways. I am preparing myself so that I might remember the teachings of my grandfathers. I would like to give these teachings to you. I believe that, together, we can begin the journey back to find what many of our people left by the trail. This will be a journey to rediscover a way of life that is centred on the respect for all living things. It will be a journey to find the centre of ourselves so that we can know the peace that comes from living in harmony with powers of the Universe. I do not believe in isolating myself in the memories of the past. I do believe that with the teachings of yesterday we can better prepare ourselves for the uncertainties of tomorrow.

I hope you will take these words that I seek to put down and use them in a good way. Use them to teach your children about the way life has developed for the Native people of this country. Use them to redirect your life to the principles of living in harmony with the natural world.

I would like to tell you an account of how man was created on this Earth. This teaching was handed down by word of mouth from generation to generation by my ancestors. Sometimes the details of teachings like this were recorded on scrolls made from *Wee´-gwas* (birchbark). I am fortunate to be the keeper of several of these scrolls. They will help me remember some of the details of what I give to you.

When Ah-ki´ (the Earth) was young, it was said that the Earth had a family. Nee-ba-gee´-sis (the Moon) is called Grandmother, and Gee´-sis (the Sun) is called Grandfather. The Creator of this family is called

Gi´-tchie Man-i-to´ (Great Mystery or Creator).

The Earth is said to be a woman. In this way it is understood that woman preceded man on the Earth. She is called Mother Earth because from her come all living things. Water is her life blood. It flows through her, nourishes her, and purifies her.

On the surface of the Earth, all is given Four Sacred Directions—North, South, East, and West. Each of these directions contributes a vital part to the wholeness of the Earth. Each has physical powers as well as spiritual powers, as do all things.

When she was young, the Earth was filled with beauty.

The Creator sent his singers in the form of birds to the Earth to carry the seeds of life to all of the Four Directions. In this way life was spread across the Earth. On the Earth the Creator placed the swimming creatures of the water. He gave life to all the plant and insect world. He placed the crawling things and the four-leggeds on the land. All of these parts of life lived in harmony with each other.

Gitchie Manito then took four parts of Mother Earth and blew into them using a Sacred Shell. From the union of the Four Sacred Elements and his breath, man was created.

ANI	NISHINA	ABE
From whence	lowered	the male of the species

All tribes came from this Original Man. The Ojibway are a tribe because of the way they speak. We believe that we are nee-kon´-nis-ug´ (brothers) with all tribes; we are separated only by our tongue or language.

Today, the Ojibways cherish the Megis Shell as the Sacred Shell through which the Creator blew his breath. The Megis was to appear and reappear to the Ojibway throughout their history to show them the Path that the Creator wished them to follow. Some Ojibway Indians today wear the Megis or Cowrie shell to remember the origin of man and the history of their people.

There are a few people in each of the tribes that have survived to this day who have kept alive their teachings, language, and religious ceremonies. Although traditions may differ from tribe to tribe, there is a common thread that runs throughout them all. This common thread represents a string of lives that goes back all the way to Original Man.

Today, we need to use this kinship of all Indian people to give us the strength necessary to keep our traditions alive. No one way is better than another; I have heard my grandfathers say that there are many roads to the High Place. We need to support each other by respecting and honouring the "many roads" of all tribes. The teachings of one tribe will shed light on those of another.

It is important that we know our native language, our teachings, and our ceremonies so that we will be able to pass this sacred way of living on to our children and continue the string of lives of which we are a living part.

Mi-gwetch´ (thank you)!

Original Man Walks the Earth

*B*oozhoo, I have more Ojibway stories to tell you. These *e-ki-na-ma´-di-win´* (teachings) have been handed down to me by my Grandfathers. In the last story we learned of how Original Man was created and lowered to the Earth by the Creator, Gitchie Manito.

After Original Man was placed on the Earth, he was given instructions by the Creator. He was told to walk this Earth and name all the *o-way-se-ug´* (animals), the plants, the hills, and the valleys of the Creator's *gi-ti-gan´* (garden).

Original Man had no name of his own yet. Later, people would refer to him as Anishinabe and, still later, Way-na-boo´-zhoo. But at this early time, he who had no name would name all the Creation.

As Original Man walked the Earth, he named all of the *ni-bi´* (water). He identified all the rivers, streams, ponds, lakes, and oceans. He learned that there were rivers that ran underground. These are the veins of Mother Earth. Water is her lifeblood. It purifies her and brings food to her.

Original Man also named all the parts of the body. He even named the *o-kun-nug´* (bones) and organs inside the body.

While Original Man was carrying out the instructions given to him by the Creator, he noticed that the Earth had four seasons. All life was part of a never-ending cycle.

The plants were given new life in the spring. With the coming of summer, they blossomed and bore the seeds for the next generation. Some of the plants produced fruits.

In the fall season, the leaves of many of the plants turned from green to many spectacular colours. The leaves gradually fell to the ground as the *gee-zhi-gad-doon´* (days) got shorter and the *dee-bee-kad-doon´* (nights) got colder.

In winter, the cold winds of the Gee-way´-din (North) brought the purifying snows that cleansed Mother Earth. Some of the plants died and returned their bodies to their Mother. Other plants fell into a deep sleep and awoke only when Grandfather Sun and the warm winds of the Zha-wa-noong´ (South) announced the coming of spring.

As Original Man travelled the Earth he identified what fruits were good to eat and what was not to be eaten. As he went, he found that some *o-gee'-bic-coon'* (roots) were good for food. Others were good for *mush-kee-ki'* (medicine). Some roots could be used to make dyes of different colours and flavourings for food. Other roots could be used as a strong thread in sewing and in making tools.

As he walked, Original Man walked with the animals. He named them as he went. He noted that some animals were good *we-sin'-ni-win'* (food) and medicine. He noticed that each type of animal had its own individual kind of wisdom. He did not know that all of these plants and animals would play an important part for all the people that would be coming to live on the Earth at a later time.

Original Man travelled everywhere. There was not one plant, animal, or place that was not touched by him.

In his travels, Original Man began to notice that all the animals came in pairs and they reproduced. And yet, he was alone.

He spoke to his Grandfather the Creator and asked, "Why am I alone? Why are there no other ones like me?"

Gitchie Manito answered, "I will send someone to walk, talk, and play with you."

He sent Ma-en'-gun (the wolf).

With Ma-en'-gun by his side, Original Man again spoke to Gitchie Manito, "I have finished what you asked me to do. I have visited and named all the plants, animals, and places of this Earth. What would you now have me to do?"

Gitchie Manito answered Original Man and Ma-en'-gun, "Each of you are to be a brother to the other. Now, both of you are to walk the Earth and visit all its places."

So, Original Man and Ma-en'-gun walked the Earth and came to know all of her. In this journey they became very close to each other. They became like brothers. In their closeness they realized that they were brothers to all of the Creation.

When they had completed the task that Gitchie Manito asked them to do, they talked with the Creator once again.

The Creator said, "From this day on, you are to separate your paths. You must go your different ways.

"What shall happen to one of you will also happen to the other. Each of you will be feared, respected, and misunderstood by the people that will later join you on this Earth."

And so Ma-en'-gun and Original Man set off on their different journeys.

This last teaching about the wolf is important for us today. What the Grandfather said to them has come true. Both the Indian and the wolf have come to be alike and have experienced the same thing. Both of them mate for life. Both have a Clan System and a tribe. Both have had their land taken from them. Both have been hunted for their *wee-nes´-si-see´* (hair). And both have been pushed very close to destruction.

We can tell about our future as Indian people by looking at the wolf. It seems as though the wolf is beginning to come back to this land. Will this prove that Indian people will cease to be the "Vanishing Americans?" Will Indian people emerge to lead the way back to natural living and respect for our Earth Mother?

The teaching about wolf is important for another reason. From the wolf came the *ah-ni-moosh-shug´* (dogs) that are friends to our people today. They are brothers to us much like wolf was a brother to Original Man. Because Gitchie Manito separated the paths of wolf and man, and since our dogs today are relatives of the wolf, we should never let dogs be around our sacred ceremonies. To do so would violate the Creator's wishes and endanger the lives of those participating in the ceremony. So also, dogs are not supposed to be around places where ceremonial objects are stored. Some tribes today honour dogs in special ceremonies. This is done to recognize the special brotherhood that existed between wolf and Original Man.

It is from the sacrifices that Original Man made in naming all of the Creation that our Naming Ceremonies today are taken. For this ceremony, a medicine person is asked by the father and mother of a child to seek a name for their young one. This seeking can be done through fasting, meditation, prayer, or dreaming. The Spirit World might speak to the medicine person and give a name for the young child.

At a gathering of family and friends, the medicine person burns an offering of Tobacco and pronounces the new name to each of the Four Directions. All those present repeat the name each time it is called out.

In this way the Spirit World comes to accept and recognize the young child with the new name. It is said that prior to the Naming Ceremony, the spirits are not able to see the face of the child. It is through this naming act that they look into the face of the child and recognize him as a living being. Thereafter, the Spirit World and all past relatives watch over and protect this child. They also prepare a place in the Spirit World that this living being can occupy when his life on Earth is at an end.

At this ceremony the parents of the child ask four women and four men to be sponsors for the child. It is a great honour to be asked to fill this position. After the child is given a name, each of the sponsors stands and proclaims a vow to support and guide this child in his development. In this way a provision is made by which the child will always be cared for.

Through this Naming Ceremony that was started by Original Man continuity is given to the lives of the people who would come to inhabit the Earth.

Today, we should use these ancient teachings to live our lives in harmony with the plan that the Creator gave us. We are to do these things if we are to be the natural people of the Universe.

Challenging
Native Studies

What Is Native Studies?

Peter Kulchyski

A non-Native, Peter Kulchyski attended a government-run residential high school in northern Manitoba. He is Head of Native Studies at the University of Manitoba and is engaged in research on Aboriginal rights, social theory, and cultural politics in northern Canada. He co-authored with Frank Tester Tammarniit: Inuit Relocation in the Eastern Arctic 1939–1963, *is co-editor with Don McCaskill and David Newhouse of* In the Words of Elders: Aboriginal Cultures in Transition, *and editor of* Unjust Relations: Aboriginal Rights in Canadian Courts.

> *"to keep our culture alive is just like saying thank you to our grandfathers..."*
>
> Paul Wright, Begade Shuhtagot'ine elder

Native Studies *is the setting right of names*, the righting of names as much as the writing of names. In any study that deserves to be called Native Studies, there will be no un-named, so-called Native informants. There will be no un-named elders. The words of elders and other sources of information are attributed, so that the names of these knowledgeable people can take their place besides the names of the non-Native authorities so carefully cited in scholarly practice. Place names will also be righted, so that the inscriptions on the land developed over centuries by First Nations may once again be read, the stories once again told. The names of the First Nations themselves— Inuit instead of Eskimo, Gwi'chin instead of Loucheaux, Innu instead of Montagnais—will be returned by them, to them. There are many forces, practices, powers, and implications to this righting of names. Native Studies plays a role in, and may be nothing more than, the careful calculation, the deliberate, cautious, but necessary practice of righting names.

As a result, *Native Studies may be seen at the outset as an ethical attitude.* Native Studies is structured around an ethical approach and an ethical call, the call of Aboriginal peoples for justice, the call to name forms of oppression, to search out mechanisms that will respond to the call, the call that demands redress, the call for the righting of names. There is no way to work within the field of Native Studies while ignoring this call; there is no way to avoid taking an ethical stance. The protocols of Native Studies—how to address an elder, how to listen to an elder, what names to deploy, what forms of respect to show others and one-self, what silences to keep—these all emerge from painstaking experience in research and discussion and constitute an ethical relation. Native Studies is an intellectual or scholarly practice that questions and presupposes the questioning of an ethical attitude.

Native Studies involves the creation, recognition, or legitimization of new knowledge and new forms of knowledge. It is a scholarly enterprise, though it is not confined to academic units called Native Studies, First Nations Studies, Aboriginal Studies, Native American Studies, Inuit Studies, and the like. Native Studies programs, wherever they exist and whatever they are called, involve an attempt to support the production of a specific form of knowledge regarding Aboriginal peoples. To a certain extent, it is possible to characterize this form of knowledge as knowledge that comes from within, rather than from outside of, an Aboriginal culture, although this characterization creates almost as many difficulties as it alleviates.

Description of a culture from within involves placing a greater priority on the categories and forms that structure the culture itself, rather than exclusive reliance on a set of categories and analytical devices produced externally. Such an emphasis or priority dramatically shifts the terrain of research, which again is why Native Studies most critically involves a reconfiguration of the ethical relation between the investigating subject and her or his community. Researchers in Native Studies cannot allow themselves to sit comfortably on the principle that they have an academic freedom to pursue whatever inquiry they are inclined towards. Nor can they avoid thinking through difficult ethical questions by assuming their work is in the interest of an objective science that will benefit humanity as a whole. Rather, those engaged in Native Studies find themselves working within and working through the ethical beliefs of the First Nations of which they are members, or with whom they study or work. Appropriate to the face-to-face circumstances (and ethics!) of most First Nations, this ethical approach involves the researcher in a set of daily challenges, constant questioning, and rigorous self-questioning.

For this reason, Native Studies fits uneasily within the institutions of professional scholarly inquiry. The university is premised on the unfettered search for knowledge, and takes as self-evident the axiom that academic freedom is a precondition to this search. Academic freedom is valued by those engaged in the project of Native Studies, since they, for example, refuse to set themselves up as mouthpieces in support of particular Aboriginal political leaders—who indeed may require challenging—and since they have as much independence of thought as anyone else engaged in scholarly practice. But the respect for academic freedom is not unqualified, is not an absolute value; within Native Studies the limits of academic freedom are constantly being broached. Native Studies involves a twofold responsibility: meeting the demands of the academic community as well as meeting the demands of the Aboriginal communities. This means on the one hand that Native Studies, even in its most esoteric or abstract modes, is rarely an "ivory tower" exercise divorced from the real, daily concerns of Aboriginal peoples. And it means on the other hand that Native Studies involves an embodied and insistent questioning of some of the most basic principles of contemporary academic inquiry, including the limits of the principle of academic freedom.

In this regard, *Native Studies may be seen as part of a broader movement within academia to question the now dominant standards for inquiry that were laid down in large measure by the western Enlightenment tradition.* A variety of challenges to the notion of a universal "man" who would continue to "progress" through the application of his rational powers have in the last few decades gained force within the humanities and social sciences. Feminists, anti-racists, and those involved in the struggle for decolonization have thrown the notion of a universal "man" into question, finding for the most part that where such a figure is presupposed it usually, on closer scrutiny, has been found to be a figure bound by values embedded in racial, class, and gender privilege. The concept of "culture" has itself gained an extraordinary status in twentieth century social thought, in part to displace the concept of "race" and the notion of "humanities" that were a legacy of Enlightenment thought. The notion of universal reason has also been questioned, as other forms of knowledge such as narrative knowledge come to illustrate how impoverished instrumental thinking has become. Native Studies itself represents one trajectory of this challenge, not a desire to entirely dismiss the values and approaches of the dominant paradigm, but rather to carefully work through them, never satisfied to accept their underlying principles at face value.

It can be said that *Native Studies involves an active, ongoing reconfiguration of the relation between universities and Aboriginal communities*, a reconfiguration that reflects the broader changes in relations between Aboriginal peoples and non-Native peoples in contemporary society. Hence, it is an aspect of the dialogue between Aboriginal and non-Native peoples and to some extent is one of the areas where the form of that dialogue is being invented. Native Studies is not confined to departments that have taken the name: as a form of inquiry it can take place in any academic unit. Similarly, scholars employed in Native Studies departments may engage in research that reflects the protocols of their own disciplinary backgrounds, and they may not necessarily be engaged in the project of carrying forward the dialogue that comprises Native Studies. That dialogue itself may be produced by Native peoples or by non-Native peoples who follow the protocols, forms, ethical principles, and methods that are developing within the field.

It is the purpose of this article to provisionally enunciate some of these emerging protocols, to add some detail to this general characterization of Native Studies. Given how new the field is, the discussion will necessarily be hesitant, itself subject to some degree of speculation. However, even with such a short history, there is one point I will confidently pose at the outset: *in Canada at least, Native Studies represents the best of its university system*. It is where the most interesting scholarly discussions are taking place. It is resolutely anti-elitist in impulse. It is vibrant, active, engaged. It moves both inside and outside the boundaries of the academy. It is insistently questioning and self-questioning. It challenges the institutional form of the very institutions that house it. It deals with questions of critical urgency to the nation as a whole. It never gains the opportunity for self-satisfaction and intellectual rest. It is an intellectual invention indigenous to Canada inasmuch as the intellectual practice, where it gained an institutional form, usually did so as a result of the struggles of students and faculty to support a distinct form of inquiry.

Native Studies is the development of a new language. To a great extent, Native Studies is a dialogue. But in order for the dialogue to take place, and as it does so, new terms, new forms, new grammatical constructions come to structure the conversation. Developing a new language means inventing new concepts, taking older terms and adapting them or investing them with a new critical charge, questioning long-standing ideas embedded in the language as it exists. This, too, is part of the process of righting names. It may be that within the academy a dynamic has developed where each scholarly generation engages in a process of purging language of the ethnocentric, culturally biased ideas of its predecessors; Native Studies is involved in a process of questioning the conceptual field within which Aboriginal peoples have been constrained. Ultimately, since Native Studies is not solely a critical project but of necessity is an affirmative and constructive one as well, this means it must offer new concepts or reinvigorate old ones. For example, the concept of "pre-history" that structures so much of archaeological conceptual practice is wholly unsatisfactory from the perspective of Native Studies, implying as it does that history begins with the arrival of Europeans, that Aboriginal peoples themselves did not have history.

Though the practice of developing a specialized language has only begun, it is now possible to discuss a series of terms that have a particular critical meaning within the field. For example, the whole set of notions around what is called *traditional knowledge* have taken on extraordinary urgency within Native Studies. To a great extent, Native Studies involves legitimization and exploration of the vast corpus of traditional knowledge associated with Aboriginal peoples. Traditional knowledge is the knowledge of the cultural traditions of an Aboriginal people; it can take an enunciated form, as in the teaching of the Great Law of the longhouse peoples, or it can be implicit in the manner in which people live their lives, make decisions, and so on. If this provisional definition is accepted, then it becomes possible to distinguish something called *indigenous knowledge* as the knowledge a particular Aboriginal people have developed in their present circum-stances that is built upon their past. The way hunters can find seals near ice floes, in this view, would be traditional knowledge. How to shoot the seal so that it remains floating would be indigenous knowledge. Both forms of knowledge are unique to, in this instance, Inuit, and both are of great concern in the practice of Native Studies. *Local knowledge*, in this schema, is the knowledge associated with a particular territory of land and water, a form of knowledge that comes with a lengthy period of occupancy. Local knowledge can be traditional or indigenous; it may even be possessed by non-Native peoples who have acquired it through a long or intensive relation to a particular territory. Both indigenous knowledge and traditional knowledge are forms of knowing associated with Aboriginal peoples, though they may be disseminated or transmitted to others. There are some forms of traditional knowledge that involve deeply held spiritual beliefs, which may only be passed on to practitioners within the spiritual tradition: Native Studies is a search for knowledge that respects such constraints as part of its ethical stance.

The patterns of thinking laid down by the Enlightenment that were absorbed into Western thought emphasized progressive thought, the accumulation of knowledge and the destruction of traditional "fetters" to human advancement. There was certainly a point in history when this form of reason had to struggle against overwhelming and oppressive constraints. However, it is now ascendant to the point where at least some of its weaknesses are evident and some of its own practices oppressive. There is an emerging view, which can be associated with Native Studies, that traditional knowledge has much greater value than was once assumed and that the repetition of knowledge may be as important as its accumulation.

Another term that gains its own inflection within Native Studies is *culture* itself. Cultural studies, as it is broadly practised, has come in the last few decades to replace an older form of inquiry called the "humanities" within academia. Native Studies, to a great extent, can be seen as a version of Cultural studies that deals with the cultures of Aboriginal peoples in co-operation or conflict with the cultures of the dominant society. *Culture* itself has become too unwieldy a term, and it is best to distinguish between popular culture, mass culture, high culture, and elite culture. Popular culture is that which is produced and consumed by culturally distinct groups of people. Mass culture is produced by specialized individuals for a market, and it is wholly in the realm of commodity production. Elite culture is the specialized culture of the wealthy and powerful. High culture is art, the cultural products that gain a venerated status usually because of the strength, vitality, complexity, or richness of the cultural text. Any of these can be of concern to Native Studies; what is characterized as traditional culture would here be seen as a variety of popular culture.

The concern of Native Studies with culture is not of the order of a reclamation or "saving" project. The concern is not to document the last remaining vestiges of disappearing peoples. Rather the concern of Native Studies is to document, critically examine, and sometimes celebrate the cultural practices of living Aboriginal peoples. Hence, Native Studies is less concerned with material culture (the objects produced by a people) than with ensuring that the skills to produce the material culture continue to be passed on. Native Studies does not want culture preserved behind glass or taken out on special days; it looks to culture as a vital part of everyday life. It is in this sense that Native Studies is more concerned with the living culture as it is practised today than with the traces of the culture as it was practised in some so-called *pristine* past, wherever that is located. Hence, if an object has a spiritual value to a people, in Native Studies showing respect for that spiritual value is a better way of maintaining the culture than preserving, documenting, and venerating the object itself. In its own institutional practices Native Studies attempts to at least respect, and to some extent embody, the cultural and spiritual values and practices of Aboriginal peoples. This sometimes means Native Studies becomes a de-institutionalizing part of the academic institution.

The final term to review in this provisional lexicon is *elders*. Elders have a special value within the discipline of Native Studies, as keepers or holders of the traditional, indigenous, and local knowledges that concern us. Elders are highly respected Aboriginal individuals, usually of an advanced age, who may have knowledge of life on the land, of ancient stories, of aspects of society such as law, decision making, and clan systems; they may also be respected for their knowledge of how to maintain the core values of their people in contemporary times. While knowledge is what can be repeated, accumulated, and disseminated, analyzed and debated, elders are respected for something that escapes all of this: their wisdom. They help us understand what a good life may be, how to be good, how to heal ourselves and help others. In this manner elders' capabilities go far beyond the realm of the concerns of Native Studies, or indeed of any academic enterprise. Native Studies does not follow the practice of other social sciences, where the so-called *native informant* is usually unnamed. Within Native Studies elders are cited as authorities, their words subject to close reading and therefore always properly attributed and recognized, as one way of paying them respect, a vital aspect of the protocols that inform inquiry in the field.

Although Native Studies involves the production of a language appropriate to the conversation it has undertaken, there is another critical dimension of language that cannot be ignored. The teaching of Aboriginal languages is usually a feature of academic programs in Native Studies for very good reason. Much of the traditional knowledge is structured into the languages themselves. Native Studies recognizes the extent to which culture is bound to language, and as part of the project of supporting living culture, strongly endorses and commits resources to ensuring that Aboriginal languages continue. The approach, for the most part, to language instruction in Native Studies has not been to follow the protocols of professional linguists. Usually, Native

Studies language instructors speak their Aboriginal language as a "mother tongue," while having the support of professional training. They frequently stress the conversational side of language instruction. Again, the concern is not that the language become an esoteric aspect of one's cultural armoury; rather that the language is heard in the play-grounds and grocery stores as a part of everyday life.

Native Studies is a lack of discipline. It is sometimes called multidisciplinary, on the assumption that practitioners in the field come from different academic backgrounds and bring some of these differences together. Among the fields most prominent are history, anthropology, sociology, political studies, geography, literary studies, and philosophy. But Native Studies is more than the sum of some combination of these different academic parts, involving as it does a distinct ethical trajectory. It would be more accurate to characterize Native Studies as interdisciplinary, a new form of knowledge that falls into the gap of existing approaches, somewhere between history and anthropology, for example. My own preference is to characterize it more precisely as a lack of discipline, an attempt to develop knowledge that is not "disciplined," not constrained by the methodologies, theories, values, and impulses traditionally associated with a specific discipline. Rather it is charged with an ethical impulse that of necessity constantly challenges boundaries, even those it provisionally establishes for its own purposes. Characterizing Native Studies as lacking discipline does not mean it lacks rigour or careful thought, certainly not an "anything goes" attitude for those who are sensitive to the caution embedded in the protocols associated with the area of inquiry, but rather Native Studies is a critical challenge to the existing constraints of disciplined thought.

Native Studies represents a working through of historical trauma. History is a critical part of Native Studies, since recognition of the past is a necessary step in the process of constructing a better conversation between Natives and non-Natives. The history of Canada takes on dramatically different meanings when it is taught within Native Studies. History is not seen as an inevitable march of progress or triumphal procession, but rather is seen as an extraordinarily painful series of conflicts between Aboriginal peoples and newcomers. The history of Canada for its aboriginal inhabitants is a history of struggle. If different nations are characterized by specific historically traumatic events, which the nation then attempts to find ways of forgetting, repressing, ignoring, or working through, in Canada's case the history of its First Nations in conflict with European colonial powers would be the most important Canadian historical "moment." For many years this aspect of Canadian history was largely ignored and sometimes deliberately suppressed, but in the last few decades it has returned to command the attention of historians. While the first six decades of this century saw the production of an enormous Canadian scholarship on the fur trade, for example, in the last few decades it has been almost impossible to engage in serious scholarship on the subject without centring what had earlier been marginalized and nearly forgotten: the critical place of Aboriginal peoples in the trade.

Native Studies involves its own approach to history, not just in the centring of Aboriginal peoples as subjects, but in methodological techniques. Where Native Studies engages in historical scholarship, it does so with a much greater recognition of the importance of the oral record, of the testimonies of Aboriginal people whether recorded on archival documents or recorded by the historian. Historical scholarship of this form has been called *ethnohistory*. Native Studies as an historical enterprise borrows from recent historical scholarship where "cultural history" has become an important branch of history in the last few decades, to a certain extent as an offshoot of social history, though also influenced by contemporary anthropology. These developments in existing disciplines are particularly suitable to the new work being undertaken in Native Studies, where cultural history is a central focus of inquiry.

In a politically charged field such as Native Studies, the historian usually does not find a great deal of distance from the historical material she or he works with. Whether the historian in this arena of study likes it or not, the work usually has direct implications for how contemporary grievances will be understood and dealt with. This makes the lot of the historian in the field particularly fraught, though at the same time unusually rewarding. Native Studies scholars with a historical bent are almost by definition public intellectuals, and their work has enormous currency. The historian's ends, arguably, have as much to do with working through the historical trauma—and their own relationship to it—as a disinterested search for facts and new interpretations. The historian in Native Studies has stepped across a chasm and must question her or his own narrative practices, sources of evidence, reasons for pursuing a particular topic, and techniques of inquiry with as much rigour as the material itself is questioned.

Native Studies is a turn in social science towards the qualitative. Knowledge generated by social science research techniques is a crucial aspect of Native Studies. Since Native Studies involves questions of public concern, which in turn often involve debates over approaches to policy, such debates can be guided by solid social science research. The most useful social science-oriented research follows the protocols of Native Studies. As a social science, Native Studies pays greater attention to qualitative research than does inquiry in most social sciences; it does not dispense with quantitative data but is rarely solely led by that form of research and argument. Sometimes, the statement of one elder can have an equal weight as evidence as a whole set of data and can provide a much more compelling argument.

Many Aboriginal communities, particularly in the mid- and far north, are so small that quantitative data have questionable value for formal analysis. Furthermore, many of the standard social science quantitative tests have been produced from a culturally biased perspective and are not relevant, or lead to skewed data when applied to Aboriginal communities. Finally, there are whole areas of life, for example hunting, which is of central importance to Aboriginal people, that do not easily translate into numerical values. Although some very creative work has been done to achieve such a translation, it is still common for hunters to be treated as "unemployed" in much official statistical analyses. This has frequently led to culturally biased arguments produced by social scientists, sometimes generating justifiable resentment from Aboriginal communities.

This is not to say that Native Studies scholars inclined to social science do not engage in quantitative research. Quite the contrary, they might lead the way in developing culturally appropriate data-collecting tests, methods, and results. However, such scholars usually give greater attention to interpretive strategies, to qualitative research methods, and to participatory and other forms of community-based research. They do not begin with a presupposition that their "scientific" approach shelters and exempts them from the necessity of opening themselves up to the possibility that a community may have knowledge that surpasses their own. This broader approach obviously has an impact on the outcomes of the research, which may also borrow more heavily on narrative form in communicating results.

Since the concept of culture has a critical urgency, anthropological inquiry, particularly ethnography, is the most relevant of the social sciences and has the potential to come closest to the research approaches and strategies adopted in Native Studies. It is possible to argue that the forms of anthropological inquiry that have emerged out of the last decade of self-questioning within the discipline of professional anthropology overlap significantly with the protocols of Native Studies. Anthropology has had to come to terms with its colonial past and present; to the extent that it has done so, it has come to have a set of ethical concerns that parallel those centred in Native Studies. To the extent that it has not done so, it continues to play a role in the colonial subjugation of First Nations. We can specify the difference between Native Studies and anthropology as a matter of temporality: *Native Studies involves scholars in the temporalities of Aboriginal cultures.* This implies working with Aboriginal peoples for extended durations, perhaps a lifetime, rather than coming to know a culture through the anthropological practice of year-long field work. It involves an immersion in the pace of life, in the temporal spell of an Aboriginal community or elder, and a commitment to some places and that some times embodies that temporality.

Geography, which is centrally concerned with space and place, also has a special importance to Native Studies. The righting of place names, a rewriting or reinscribing of maps, is one aspect of Aboriginal peoples' quest for justice. Geography is also concerned with contemporary forms of land use and has produced valuable work in this area. The forms of inquiry developed in recent geographical research—for example, geographical information systems—have been eagerly put to use by many Aboriginal communities.

All these intellectual practices associated with Native Studies are political, inasmuch as the lives and very survival of Aboriginal peoples is itself a political question and struggle, and inasmuch as in a secular world of generalized commodity production, culture itself is saturated with politics. In a social field so steeped in colonial history and so influenced by the colonial structures that continue to exist, as Cindy Gilday once said, "when an Indian breathes, it's politics."

As Native Studies comes into its own, it resembles none of the various disciplines that contribute to it, it comes to represent a whole that is more than the sum of its parts. *In large measure, Native Studies, properly understood, is a storytelling practice and comes to resemble forms of narrative knowledge.* The narratives can be traditional tales of tricksters and law-givers and place names handed down over centuries, or life stories of relocation to large urban centres or short but powerful moral fables or histories of dispossession and struggle, or descriptions of ancient ideals of justice. The forms of these narratives, the manner in which they are told as well as the multiple meanings enfolded within, comprise much of the substance of thought and inquiry within Native Studies. In this sense, Native Studies can be seen as an interpretive practice, a mode and an ethics of reading that depends upon an exploded concept of text.

As a teaching practice, Native Studies within post-secondary institutions usually involves a dual mandate. On the one hand, it works to provide Aboriginal students with the skills and knowledge they require to assist their communities and realize their own individual potential and goals. This frequently involves Native Studies acting as a mechanism that provides access to post-secondary institutions for Aboriginal students (although many do not require such assistance) as well as acting as an institutional home to those same students. On the other hand, Native Studies is concerned with drawing attention and awareness of non-Native students to the cultures, histories, and experiences of First Nations. As a result, *the teaching and learning of Native Studies is itself an intellectual challenge and intellectual experience of the first order, as many of the issues around identity, cultural, and spiritual integration, appropriation, and colonialism on are staged in the dynamics of classroom interaction.* For those who open themselves to its ethical challenge, Aboriginal or non-Native, Native Studies can never be easy. It will involve demanding and sometimes exhaustive constant self-questioning and a constant process of being questioned. At its best these dynamics frequently make for a profoundly rich intellectual experience, where the knowledge presented, the form of the knowledge presented, and the contextual nature of the discussion in which these happen are all inextricable aspects of the teaching and learning.

Within the field of Native Studies, my own trajectory of thought has been, in concert with a few other scholars, to forge an articulation or conversation between the discourse of Native Studies and the discourse of contemporary critical theory. Contemporary currents in social and political thought, variously characterized as post-modernism, post-structuralism, post-colonial theory, feminism, cultural Marxism, have much to learn from and much to offer Aboriginal peoples. Critical theory has concerned itself in recent years with problems of identity formation, knowledge transmission, cultural boundaries, power relations, the nature of texts, close reading practices, gendering processes, commodification of culture, dissident sexualities and sexual orientations, and a host of other conceptual issues of strategic relevance to the field of Native Studies. The histories, cultures, and experiences of Aboriginal peoples offer both a challenge to emerging orthodoxies within critical theory as well as a fruitful field of inquiry within which the value and relevance of an approach, its insights and limits, may be explored.

In Canada, Native Studies is in a moment of intellectual ferment and is an area of intellectual inquiry that has gained confidence even as it remains insistently self-questioning. Native Studies throws almost everything into doubt: the limits of academic freedom, the nature and structure of the university, the responsibilities of the intellectual, the value of knowledge gained by academic forebears painstakingly through years of research, the naming practices that ground the symbolic structures of colonialism, the powers and repetitions enunciated in institutional dynamics including teaching, the limits of its own practice. This is no groundless, academic exercise, though. It has and gives itself an urgency inasmuch as it is part of a broader process and a broader challenge posed by the continued existence and persistence of Aboriginal peoples in contemporary Canada. Somehow, and in some way, material and social structures will have to change far more than they have if the call of Aboriginal peoples is going to be heard. Native Studies has a role to play in this and is in large measure defined by that role. *In Canada, Native Studies is an intellectual working towards a post-colonial space.*

Bibliographic Note

This article concerns itself primarily with Native Studies in Canada. The terms "Native," "Aboriginal," and "First Nations" are used interchangeably to describe the Inuit, Indian, or Métis descendants of Canada's first inhabitants. The opening quote comes from research I conducted with Paul Wright and Gabe Etchinelle in the western NWT in the summer of 1997. The Cindy Gilday quote is from *Living Arctic* (Vancouver: Douglas and McIntyre 1987, 236) by Hugh Brody. The substance of this essay is drawn from a wide variety of theoretical and applied readings. The critique of the Enlightenment and the centring of rational "man" as a category are explored in Max Horkheimer and Theodor Adorno's *Dialectic of Enlightenment* (New York: Seabury Press, 1972). On questions related to the concept of culture and the ethics of cross-cultural research, the anthropologist Clifford Geertz in *The Interpretation of Cultures* (New York: Basic Books, 1973) and *Works and Lives* (Stanford: Stanford University Press, 1988) provides much food for thought. For a discussion of the questions from a historian's perspective, Dominick LaCapra's *History and Criticism* (Ithaca: Cornell University Press, 1985) and *Representing the Holocaust* (Ithaca: Cornell University Press, 1994) have remarkable resonance in the field of Native Studies, particularly around the conceptual framing of trauma in history, though I also borrow the cultural typology largely from him. On questions of narrative, the stories and analyses of Angela Sidney, Kitty Smith, and Annie Ned and the discussions of them by Julie Cruikshank, in her *Life Lived Like a Story* (Vancouver: UBC Press, 1990) are enormously rich and in my view embody the best principles of a Native Studies approach.

Similarly, *Killing the Shamen* (Waterloo ON: Penumbra Press, 1991) by Chief Thomas Fiddler and James R. Stevens uses narrative form and the oral record in a manner that I consider representative of Native Studies. Among the more prominent post-colonial theorists, Gayatri Chakravorty Spivak's *Outside in the Teaching Machine* (New York: Routledge, 1993) raises questions that overlap with a wide range of considerations discussed in this reading. *In the Words of the Elders*, edited by Peter Kulchyski, Don McCaskill, and David Newhouse (Toronto: University of Toronto Press, 1998) contains an editor's introduction that provides an overview of the history of Native Studies in Canada and also attempts to embody as a text some of the principles enunciated above.

Indigenous Studies:

Negotiating the Space Between Tribal Communities and Academia

Neal McLeod

Neal McLeod, from the James Smith Cree First Nation, is currently writing his dissertation entitled Cree Narrative History. In addition to teaching at the Saskatchewan Indian Federated College in the Department of Indian Studies, Neal is a practising poet and painter.

In the last thirty years, the discipline of Indigenous Studies has struggled for a place within the university structure in both Canada and the United States. Before this time, there were very few Indigenous people in Canada who participated in the life of universities, and the process to bring Indigenous philosophies and histories into the university setting has been very difficult. Frequently, Indigenous scholars working within academia have felt pressures both from their home communities and academia. There are pressures from home communities to be accurate with cultural information as well as respect, at least on some level, existing taboos. On the other hand, academia puts forward its own set of standards such as the assertion of "objectivity" and the use of supporting written documentation. Ideally, Indigenous scholars help to extend knowledge and history from their communities into academia. In this paper, I will examine the efforts of Indigenous scholars to negotiate the space between tribal communities and academia.

John A. Price wrote in 1978 that, during the emergence of the field of Indigenous Studies, there was "an increasing awareness on the part of Native people that academic methods can be used to foster an ethnic cultural renaissance" (1). Undoubtedly, the massive move of Aboriginal people to the cities in the 1960s contributed to the awareness that universities could be a way of transmitting Indigenous knowledge and history. However, the move to the cities and the move to universities are merely the latest changes, which have been ongoing since time immemorial.

In moving into positions in academic institutions, there is the real possibility for Indigenous scholars to become assimilated by the system. While "education" is often seen as a vehicle for helping to improve the lives of Indigenous people, it can actually contribute to the loss of Indigenous culture. Many minority scholars have difficulty within the system because of the pressure to adopt the paradigms of the mainstream culture. Howard Adams criticizes Indigenous people who "have internalized the consciousness of the colonizer as their own consciousness" (44). In *Keeping the Faith*, Cornell West describes the pressures that exist for minority scholars to adopt the consciousness of the mainstream society. Unless Indigenous Studies adopts Indigenous paradigms and uses Indigenous languages, it will become nothing more than a vehicle to assimilate Indigenous people. Without the use of these alternative paradigms, the work done would merely duplicate the work of other departments.

Indigenous Studies should help empower Indigenous people and be a forum for the articulation of Indigenous stories and languages, a vehicle for Indigenous people to describe themselves on their own terms. For too long, Indigenous stories have been ignored and marginalized within this country. It is indeed timely that the various departments and programs have emerged and continue to develop. The process of Indigenous people giving voice to their lives and world view will be therapeutic on one level and, on another level, will allow for the internalization of colonization to abate to some extent.

I use the term Indigenous Studies for a variety of reasons. First, it is an inclusive term, as it does not artificially separate "Indian" and "Métis." The artificial line between these two groups is largely the creation of the Indian Act. Furthermore, the use of the term Indigenous is descriptive of the people and culture encompassed in the discipline and implies a relationship to a specific piece of land developed over a period of time. This relationship has been manifested in ceremonies, songs, and narratives. Also, the term Indigenous Studies is useful as it broadens the possible discourse of the discipline. More and more, the term Indigenous is being used to refer the hundreds of millions of other Indigenous peoples throughout the world. By engaging with the experiences of these peoples, I think that we are in a better position to understand our own experience.

While Indigenous Studies should seek to articulate and expand Indigenous paradigms, it must also help to revitalize Indigenous languages. It is unfortunate that the place of Indigenous languages is minimal in some Indigenous Studies departments. Without knowledge of Indigenous languages, there is really no way of understanding in a holistic way the life-world of Indigenous people, and the task of articulating Indigenous paradigms becomes impossible. Language, as our old people tell us, and as many people in other cultures have known, is the vehicle for the transmission of ideas and world views. In an interview, John B. Tootoosis, an important twentieth-century Cree leader, says he believes: "Language is power." Language guides a people and helps to create a space wherein tribal memories linger.

One of the largest obstacles to Indigenous people articulating their stories and paradigms has been the notion of "objectivity." By "objectivity," I mean a detached and abstract perspective. Adams notes that Indigenous history has often been denigrated under the rubric of "objectivity": "The most common argument is that Aboriginal writing lacks documentation, authenticity, or methodology, and therefore, credibility" (Adams 34). The authority of interpreting and articulating Indigenous history and world views seems to stem from the use of written documents and accepted mainstream paradigms. Thus, much Indigenous writing has been dismissed as biased and subjective: "Academics discredit Aboriginals' historical perspectives as 'myth' or 'advocacy', and thus denigrate the works of Indian and Metis historians" (Adams 31). In contrast to this, mainstream scholars are often given interpretative authority because of their use of written documents and also because they and their families are and were not participants in the events and stories described. Thus, it is believed a certain measure of "objectivity" is achieved.

As Indigenous people we are often told not to write in the first person, again in the name of the venerated "objectivity. A detached, abstract mode of writing dominates English-speaking scholarship. However, within this model, human experience is often distorted and becomes disjointed. Detached scientific modes of explanation are often seen to be the benchmark of truth, but such an assumption does much to displace Indigenous narratives.

Many Indigenous scholars have embraced European methodologies in the struggle to articulate Indigenous experience and history. Undoubtedly, there is much to be learned from such an incorporation of these methodologies, but they are alien and their adoption has often been uncritical. For instance, the excessive use of Marxism by Indigenous scholars such as Howard Adams distorts the original experience of the participants of historical events. Jack Forbes writes that "we have sometimes seen the adoption of new tribal ideologies that mirror European ideals more than they reflect our authentic heritage" (20). While the use of methodologies such as Marxism can be informative, one must also be fully cognizant of the tensions between this methodology, which favours a highly secularized form of explanation, and Indigenous paradigms, which stress a belief in Manito (the all spirit).

Indigenous Studies needs to sort out problems of discursive authority. Non-Indigenous people have for a long time been taken to be the "experts" with regard to issues involving Indigenous people. This has undermined the agency of Indigenous people, both historically and in the present. Within this discursive rubric, the authority of discourse for Indigenous narratives rests with people who subscribe to this methodology and who have been accredited by mainstream institutions. Now, with the emergence of Indigenous Studies, Indigenous people are no longer merely the objects of study, but rather are the subjects and creators of our own narratives.

For example, sometimes so called "experts" really have no appreciation of tribal knowledge. They often write from a secular point of view. I would contend that the heart of Indigenous Being (world view) is in prayers and ceremonies. While some of these prayers and ceremonies should not be talked about directly in the classroom, we should be aware of and stress their importance to Indigenous Being. Ernest Tootoosis, the younger brother of John Tootoosis, was heavily involved in the cultural revitalization of the 1970s, and he stressed the importance of spirituality in Indigenous self-description.

I think that at this stage, the voice of Indigenous people still is not being fully articulated within the spaces of Indigenous Studies departments. Real representation by Indigenous people is often only superficial. But it is not that Indigenous people are necessarily being excluded from these positions. The point is that it is only recently that Indigenous people have begun to get Ph.D.s. Undoubtedly, over time more and more Indigenous people will teach and assume positions of increasing responsibility in Indigenous Studies departments. It is only recently that Indigenous people have begun to get Ph.D.s and as Roxanne Dunbar Ortiz notes, "The principle reason for the instability of Native American Studies programs in universities is the lack of qualified Indian faculty to develop academically viable curricula and research" (7). As more and more Indigenous people begin to teach and assume positions of greater responsibility in Indigenous Studies departments, their increased involvement will bring stability to the situation.

However, it becomes increasing difficult to negotiate the ground between Indigenous knowing and the requirements of the academy. Some years ago, I was approached to help develop a class on Indigenous philosophy. In retrospect, I see the whole process was a subtle form of colonialism. My views and culture were not important to the person who had solicited my help. Rather, I believe I was asked to help in order to legitimate his project. Processes such as these illustrate how superficial the involvement of Indigenous people with the academy can be. My presence was not really necessary, as he thought, because the legitimacy of voice rested with him and not with Indigenous people.

Indigenous Studies must squarely address this question of legitimacy of voice. Many interests must be balanced in order to do justice to the material and for Indigenous Studies to flourish. Ideally, there should be a variety of voices engaged with the development and articulation of Indigenous Studies. Such a multilayered conversation will ensure a fuller description. A pluralism of interpretation, while keeping in mind past problems, should be the goal of Indigenous Studies. Such pluralism would include, but not be limited to, gender difference, ethnic diversity, and differing stances and interpretations of ceremonies honouring the Indigenous world view. However, while such pluralism is desirable, there clearly has to be a rethinking of the colonial tendencies that still exist in Indigenous Studies departments in the universities.

Undoubtedly, "expertise" in European techniques is useful, and many Indigenous people are pursuing university degrees in an effort to help their communities. Ortiz argues that Indigenous scholars may be "essential for the nation-building process of Indian tribes" (7). Indeed, one of the points of the general bylaws of the Canadian Indian/Native Studies Association stresses the importance of "professional development" as a way for those who have acquired post-secondary education to keep abreast of new ideas, both Western and Indigenous. In this way these individuals can return to their communities or professions and introduce them for debate or integrate them into programs in which they are working.

To have meaningful Indigenous Studies, we have to have Indigenous story-tellers and elders in our departments. Indeed, one of the reasons that people wanted Indigenous Studies established was because they saw how Indigenous history and paradigms had been excluded. Forbes discusses the role of elders in the creation of D-Q University in California: "The elders and other grassroots people were closely involved in all our efforts at both D-Q University and in Native American Studies at the University of California, Davis, campus" (13). The institution thus reflected the wishes and desires of the people it purported to represent. All too often, academic institutions do not value the words and advice of Indigenous people themselves, but rather are concerned only with interpretation and representation as the institutions see fit. In this and similar ways, the expertise that was developed in the department drew heavily from traditional Indigenous paradigms.

Furthermore, Indigenous Studies can assist in the transcription of traditional tribal stories. In doing so expertise can be drawn from Indigenous storytellers and from linguistics. If stories are transcribed, the generations yet unborn will be able to learn from them. Indigenous Studies can thus serve a role in the revitalization of Indigenous cultures.

In addition to transcribing Indigenous stories today, Indigenous scholars also work with documents that were recorded in the distant past. Missionaries, for example, worked actively among the fur traders and in many instances began to record Indigenous languages and history in works such as *The Jesuit Relations* (Mealing 1997) and the texts of George Nelson (Brown and Brightman 1988), a fur trader who worked in northern Manitoba amongst the Crees and Ojibway. While some of the authors of these documents tried to be fair, they undoubtedly distorted Indigenous experience to some extent because of their interpretative location, that is, their European, outside point of view. Emma Laroque, in "On the Ethics of Publishing Historical Documents," stresses that these texts must be studied with a certain degree of suspicion.

People working in the field of Indigenous Studies need to critically study texts. Approaching the interpretation of texts with a certain degree of suspicion is a useful strategy developed by feminist scholars. In applying the strategy the reader keeps in mind the possible inter-pretative distortion of the original document while at the same time trying to extract value and meaning that is still useful in the text itself. Forbes suggests: "When using European sources, we must of course, be prepared to challenge them, that is, subject them to textual criticism" (20). Thus, an understanding of texts can be supplemented through criticism, a criticism that now includes Indigenous world views and languages.

William N. Fenton advocates a similar approach in what he calls "upstreaming." Fenton uses the term "upstreaming" to describe the activity of "ethnohistory" (Butterfield, Washburn and Fenton 21). His methodology rests on the central assumption that "major patterns of culture remain stable over a long period of time" (Butterfield et al. 21) and knowledge we have in the present can be used as a foil to further reconstruct the past. For example, when we contrast present-day understanding of history and religious ceremonies gleaned from the historical records, with traditional stories of the same event, our contemporary knowledge enriches and reinforces the understanding we hold of the story. If we use this ethnohistorical approach, we will be in need of raw data such as is found in ethnology and oral history collections. Fenton's monumental work *The Great Law and the Longhouse* (1998) represents the culmination of a lifetime of application of ethnohistorical methodology. By using the languages and stories of the longhouse, Fenton offers us rich insights into the way the contemporary Iroquois people experience and understand the world, an understanding enriched by their knowledge (expressed in their terms through stories and language) of their past.

I would like to extend Fenton's concept of upstreaming. I think that it lends itself to the creation of interdisciplinary projects (which Fenton argues for) but also moves beyond the limitations of the disciplines themselves. By applying upstreaming we can retrieve Indigenous narratives on their own terms and incorporate Indigenous paradigms, which will make the description of Indigenous history and experience more holistic.

In the effort to construct a fuller understanding of Indigenous history and experience, there needs to be an ongoing dialogue between Indigenous communities and the academic community. I think that sometimes we, as Indigenous scholars, find ourselves trapped between the demands of our communities and the academic community. We have to try to find a way to "indigenize" the classroom and the study of Indigenous people.

Vine Deloria's notion of Master Scholar does much to link these two communities together. Deloria envisioned an advisory body that would "lead to some nationally recognized committee, board of council that can speak on matters of importance to Indians and scholars alike" ("Commentary" 17). The purpose of Master Scholars is to make the act of writing about Indigenous people a communal act. All too often there has been an exploitation of Indigenous knowing by outsiders, and these people have tried to present themselves as authentic. Here I think of Chief Red Fox, man who claimed to be the nephew of Crazy Horse, and Grey Owl, the Englishman Archie Belany. People doing research in Indigenous studies need to be accepted on two levels: 1) by the community that is being described in research, and 2) by the academic community. In this scenario, the Master Scholar, whose "academic accomplishments are impeccable" (Deloria, "Intellectual

Self-Determination" 17), would have his or her research validated by both communities. However, I would like to take this one step further. Ideally, there should be an overlap between the academy and Indigenous communities, and that overlap can be found in the Indigenous scholars in academia.

This can be illustrated in a practical way. John B. Tootoosis notes the importance of his own education in the 1970s: he learned to read English, which allowed him to fight for Cree rights. He also stressed that the schools, which were run by churches, were a part of a larger process of colonization: "The Church was supporting the domination ... [and] the brainwashing in those residential schools." He called the negative aspects of the schools "the price that had to be paid" in order to have the tools to fight back.

With the acquisition of an "education" by some, interpreters for dealing with the non-Indigenous world were no longer provided. However, many did not receive an education or only had a partial education, and Tootoosis speaks of the position of the old people after the imposition of the reserve system: "after they settled down on reservations they had no interpreters to express themselves with." Without interpreters, the voices of Indigenous people were nearly silent. Today, the new generation of educated Indigenous academics can interpret—for both their communities and the larger world—their new knowledge gained from research in Indigenous studies, just as interpreters once translated English for Indigenous people. They will be able to speak for themselves and their people. Thus the Indigenous academics will be needed as "academic interpreters," "experts" who can describe Indigenous history for Indigenous people.

Once the importance of Indigenous paradigms is established, it becomes important to try to define these paradigms. Robert Allen Warrior (1996), Forbes (1998), and Elizabeth Cook-Lynn (1997) write of a Native American intellectual tradition. The use of the term intellectual stands in contrast to earlier notions that Indigenous people of North America did not have any valid world views. The use of the term intellectual also perhaps adds legitimacy to the work of Indigenous scholars; however, the term is also borrowed from the mainstream society.

In the old days, people would refer to themselves as storytellers and spiritual leaders, and I am not sure that many of them would have referred to themselves as intellectuals. The word intellectual has a long, burdened history in Western thought. It comes from the Latin word *intellectus*: the action of understanding or comprehension, which infers the use of the mind. The mind, or intellect, however, is only one part of the human experience. Other essential parts for human understanding are the body and the spirit. The word intellectual distorts the more holistic approach found in Indigenous paradigms. Also, as Deloria points out, the choice of the word tends to divorce the people in question from social action and from their identities as Indians: "People are trading their personal identity as an Indian for a professional identity and in effect siding with their profession. They place maintaining their status in their work above their allegiance to their people" ("Intellectual Self-Determination and Sovereignty" 30). I think that what Deloria is intimating is similar to the point made earlier, namely that there is the distinct danger of assimilating within the university structure.

Ideally, Indigenous Studies should seek to articulate Indigenous stories through academic channels and not the other way around. Whether it is implicit or not, all stories are founded upon some basis of authority. For instance, much of the accepted scholarship concerning Indigenous people rests upon written and archival records that have, generally speaking, been created by the mainstream society. I fear that by adopting an identity of "Native American intellectual" one is taking a step towards submerging one's tribal identity for one sanctioned by the mainstream society. The legitimacy of oral history and communal Indigenous knowing have been continually undermined. To fully realize the potential of Indigenous Studies, we need to use our own world views, our own languages and our own ways of transmitting information.

As mentioned before, "objective" modes of description can distort Indigenous history and experience. If scholars continue to undermine the importance of oral history and continue to claim that Indigenous world views are from the stone age, then Indigenous Studies is doomed to fail. This is not to say that such criticism should not exist. All that I want to say is that there has to be a core of people who do believe, both in theory and practice, in the power and legitimacy of Indigenous paradigms.

A second point made earlier suggested that one of the central tasks of Indigenous Studies should be the deconstruction of "objectivity," and the emerging field of Indigenous Studies should stress "lived," local experience through the utilization of stories. Perhaps one way in which we can make Indigenous Studies lively and vibrant is by trying to use some of the techniques that have worked so well in tribal contexts. In my teaching, I share many of the stories that my father or other family members and friends have told me. I then ask my students to imagine that they are participants in the story being described. For instance, I ask them: "How would you feel in this particular situation? What would you do? What in your life is similar to this story? By using such a straightforward technique, "history" becomes a living, holistic experience wherein students become active participants. This model of teaching stresses the importance of "lived" experience and orientates the class-room towards an openness to Indigenous narratives.

Nimosôm (my grandfather), John R. McLeod, used a similar technique when he addressed groups of non-Indigenous people. Noel Dyck, a long-time friend of Nimosôm, noted that it was the stories of his (Nimosôm's) life, and those that he heard from his grandmother, Kêkêhk-iskwêw (Hawk Woman), Betsy McLeod, that he drew upon in "his public acts of remembering" (Dyck 132). As I remember Nimosôm, and indeed as I spend time listening to Old Ones today, I realize there is a moral imperative to the stories being told. The stories are told to transform understanding that has been distorted.

Nimosôm told stories of what he knew based on his life experience, which is in contrast to a more "objective" mode of scholarship. Further-more, he told stories in which he, or his ancestors, were participants. Knowledge within this paradigm comes from what you have seen and what you have internalized. Dyck writes that Nimosôm "began by telling his listeners that since he only had a grade-three education he could only speak about things that had happened to him, things that he knew about" (Dyck 136). Dyck calls this approach "a traditional Cree genre" (138). Furthermore, one of the fundamentals of this approach is an open-endedness. Dyck writes that Nimosôm "never said what the point of his stories were; he forced the listeners to discover this for them-selves" (138). Indeed, this is one of the traditional Cree narrative techniques. The reason that the meaning is left open is that each person will bring certain experiences into the hearing of the story. Also, by leaving it open, the listener is given a chance to internalize the meaning. The story becomes real only once it has been internalized. I prefer to think of Nimosôm more as a story-teller and someone who tried to be a good human being rather than merely as an "intellectual."

Indigenous experience should be the foundation of Indigenous Studies. If Indigenous paradigms and experience are subverted, then the colonization that has occurred in a large historical context will simply be duplicated in the university setting. Rather, Indigenous Studies should seek to heal and transform through the telling of stories.

In the Old Days, Kêhte-âyak (Elders) would lecture young people. At the start of the lecture, they would stick a knife in the ground. They would say, "If you don't like what I am saying, you can stab me with this." I understand this as a metaphor. What they meant, at least the way that I understand it, is that if someone didn't like what the old person was saying, a listener could "kill" their words. Perhaps, in a different sense, the Elder was saying the young people had to make sense of the words and stories themselves by weaving the stories into their own lives in order to make sense of them. This is what Nimosôm tried to do through "his public remembering."

We should see the university and Indigenous Studies departments as places where we can adapt and reshape Indigenous Being. We have to breathe new life into our stories if they are to survive and remain parts of a vital, living culture. We have to interpret our traditions in light of new experiences.

The creation and existence of Indigenous Studies presents many challenges, not the least of which is the transmission and translation of knowledge from traditional tribal environments to academic settings. As people involved and interested in the emergence of Indigenous Studies, we have to constantly ask questions about the direction that things are going in and about the changes to Indigenous knowing that occur once it is brought into the classroom. For instance, the context of the classroom is often an artificial environment in the sense that we usually do not know each other personally. This differs substantially from a tribal context, but as I have suggested, it is possible to come to terms with the new context.

I present as many stories as possible to my students, but I always encourage them to make sense of the stories for themselves. I think that as teachers of Indigenous Studies we have to be extremely careful of trying to avoid dogmatism. The task of teaching should be to transform consciousness, not merely to impose consciousness. While I share stories with my students, I also encourage them to ignore the stories if they find no meaning in them.

It would be a mistake to think of the creation of Indigenous Studies departments as the beginning of Indigenous knowing. Indeed, Indigenous knowing would exist with or without Indigenous Studies. Undoubtedly, there will always be those who will see the university as a place of assimilation, and there will be Indigenous people who will dismiss the possibility and enterprise of Indigenous Studies. I think that, instead of trying to argue with these people and trying to convince them that they are wrong, we should use their critiques as a way of keeping Indigenous Studies grounded. I think that Indigenous Studies has a great deal of potential in helping Indigenous Being survive into the next century. However, I think that, ideally, Indigenous Studies should be an extension of pre-existing knowledge, rather than something in and of itself.

Works Cited

Adams, Howard. *A Tortured People: The Politics of Colonization*. Penticton, BC: Theytus Books, 1995.

Brown, Jennifer S. H. and Robert Brightman, eds. *"The Orders of the Dreamed": George Nelson on Cree and Northern Ojibwa Religion and Myth, 1823*. Winnipeg: University of Manitoba Press, 1988.

Butterfield, L.H., Wilcomb E. Washburn, and William N. Fenton. *American Indian and White Relations to 1830, Needs and Opportunities for Study*. New York: Russell and Russell, 1971/1957.

Canadian Indian/ Native Studies Association. "Statement of Objectives." 1984.

Cook-Lynn, Elizabeth. "American Indian Intellectualism and the New Indian Story." *Natives and Academics: Researching and Writing about American Indians*. Ed. Devon A. Mihesuah. Lincoln and Lincoln: University of Nebraska Press, 1997.

Deloria, Vine Jr. "Intellectual Self-Determination and Sovereignty: Implications for Native Studies and for Native Intellectuals." *Wicazo Sa Review* 13.2 (1998): 25–31.

_____. "Commentary: Research, Redskins, and Reality." *The First Ones: Readings in Indian/ Native Studies*. Ed. Miller, David. Senior editor. Carl Beal, James Dempsey and R. Wesley Heber. Piapot: Saskatchewan Indian Federated College Press, 1992. 15–19.

Dunbar Ortiz, Roxanne. "Developing Indian Academic Professionals." *Wicazo Sa Review* 1.1: 5–10.

Dyck, Noel. "Negotiating the Indian 'Problem'." *The First Ones: Readings in Indian/ Native Studies*. Ed. Miller, David. Senior editor. Carl Beal, James Dempsey and R. Wesley Heber. Piapot: Saskatchewan Indian Federated College Press, 1992. 132–139.

Fenton, *William N. The Great Law and the Longhouse: A Political History of the Iroquois Confederacy*. Norman: University of Oklahoma Press, 1998.

Forbes, Jack D. "Intellectual Self-Determination and Sovereignty: Implications for Native Studies and for Native Intellectuals." *Wicazo Sa Review* 13.1: 11–23.

Laroque, Emma. *"On the Ethics of Publishing Historical Documents." "The Orders of the Dreamed": George Nelson on Cree and Northern Ojibwa Religion and Myth, 1823*. Eds. Jennifer S.H. Brown and Robert Brightman. Winnipeg: University of Manitoba Press, 1988. 199–203.

Price, John A. *Native Studies: American and Canadian Indians*. Toronto: McGraw-Hill Ryerson Limited, 1978.

Tootoosis, John. Interview: Murray Dobbin. Date of Interview. September 7, 1977, Poundmaker Reserve. Saskatchewan Provincial Archives A1178. Transcription: Neal McLeod.

Warrior, Robert Allen. *Tribal Secrets*. Minneapolis: University of Minnesota Press, 1996.

West, Cornell. *Keeping the Faith: Philosophy and Race in America*. New York: Routledge, 1993.

Challenging Eurocentric History

Howard Adams

Born and raised in the Métis community of St. Louis, SK, Howard Adams has been a high school counsellor and teacher, and a Professor in the Faculty of Education at the University of Saskatchewan and in the Native American Studies Department at the University of California, Davis. He has also been an activist and leader in the Indian and Métis civil rights movement. Until his death in 2001, he continued to be an activist and writer.

The tragedy of North American Natives and many other Indigenous peoples is their alienation from their past. The history assigned to them is not that of their authentic culture or people. What is taught to them is "Western" history, more specifically western European history, a history that has been used to capture and control their minds, often by outright fabrication or suppression of facts. Such fabricated and distorted history has been an important factor in the development of colonial consciousness. The concepts of Indian "backwardness" and western European "superiority" that have dominated the world for so long are now recognized by many as deliberate distortions. The notions of western European superiority in the fields of science and technology go back to the Renaissance.

The history of northwestern European superiority took centuries to create. It emerged not from real events, but from myths fabricated primarily by explorers, governments, and historians who procured technological information from the Eastern world. At the beginning of the Crusades, the Eastern world, that is, the Arabic world, was the intellectual and material centre of the most advanced civilizations. By the end of the Crusades that centre had shifted to the West, with "new" learning imported from Eastern medicine, chemistry, astronomy, geography, mathematics, and architecture. The formation of western European culture took place during the tenth to the thirteenth centuries, and this development is reflected in modern historiography.

During the medieval period, western Europe was the now the cultural and economic centre of power in the world. It was a mix of Christianity, feudalism, and barbarity. One way western European countries sought to consolidate their power were to wage "holy wars" in the Middle East. R.T. Naylor claims that, "The purpose of the Crusades was to roll back the limits of Arab influence... and to control the major trade routes" (4). The Roman Catholic Church promoted the Crusades in the hope that they would strengthen western Europe. As a result, the countries of western Europe became the base for a merchant trade economy. The Crusades served to transmit materials critical to the emerging Western economy from the Eastern world to Europe. Naylor notes that, "the result was an enormous stimulus to the shipping business, to manufacture of iron and woolen products, to the growth of military and naval power" (5). At the same time, the Crusades resulted in the overthrow of both the Byzantine and Arab empires and totalitarian monarchies arose in the European nations to take absolute power. This movement led to expansionism and the conquest of civilizations throughout the world by a few western European nations.

The western Europeans looted all the inventions and technology from the Middle Eastern and Asian countries. The compass and gunpowder proved to be their most valuable bounty. Although Europeans were not the inventors, they must be credited with the skill of plundering inventions from other civilizations, integrating them into Western society as their own, and using these inventions and technologies for further scientific development. This assisted them in creating European dominance in the world, out of which a Eurocentric ideology emerged. Such plundering was a major stimulus towards advancing European trade, expansionism, and intellectual thought. Although Europeans considered themselves to be Christian, in addition to plundering, they looted, and killed. Their social and cultural life was immoral, anarchistic, and crude. They lacked compassion and a sense of humanity that led to the subjugation of the Native peoples of other continents. According to the Native Studies scholar, Ward Churchill, the "European conquest of the Western Hemisphere [that Columbus] set off is greatly analogous to the celebration of the glories of nazism and Heinrich Himmler"(81). Churchill claims that "a hermispheric population estimated to have been as great as 125 million was reduced by something over 90 percent" (1). He observes:

The people had died in their millions of being hacked apart with axes and swords, burned alive and trampled under horses, hunted as game and fed to dogs, shot, beaten, stabbed, scalped for bounty, hanged on meathooks and thrown over the sides of ships at sea, worked to death as slave labourers, intentionally starved and frozen to death during a multitude of forced marches and internments. (81)

These kinds of atrocities demonstrate the true nature of those European invaders who had internalized the Eurocentric mentality. By 1500, white supremacy was deeply ingrained in European explorers and Eurocentric myths were so extensively developed that they seriously debased Aboriginal civilizations in the New World. Since the rise of Europe most European historians believe in some form of the theory of "the European miracle" (Blaut 2). In his analysis of the theory of the autonomous rise of European superiority the renowned geographer J.M. Blaut, in *The Colonizer's Model of the World*, draws a parallel between "European superiority" and "the European miracle." The European miracle or European superiority point of view was expressed by reporters, historians, sailors, and others who were reporting back to the people in their home nations in Europe and were interpreting what they had seen in the New World in accordance with a belief in European superiority (or miracle).

It is puzzling why stereotypes such as cannibals, headhunters, and scalpers were created by Eurocentric writers. However, we know from documentary evidence that scalping was practised by the English and French colonizers. Churchill writes, "Even after the final defeat of France in 1763,... scalp hunts continued almost unabated" (185). He claims that "there is no doubt that [generalized] scalp-taking... was due to barbarity of White men rather than the barbarity of Red men .... The earliest confirmed English bounty for scalps rather than whole heads dates from 1694" (180–181).

According to the eminent scholar Samir Amin, early intellectuals invented a unique, eternal western Europe that was based on selective constructs and myths, such as racism, conquest, and genocide. The early stages of western European history had to be fabricated so as to obscure its own primitiveness. Writers created a distinctive Eurocentric history comprised of a white supremacist ideology and culture that eventually became the capitalist culture and ideology.

However, this modern ideology came relatively late in history. According to Amin, it emerged after the three centuries that spanned the Renaissance through to the Enlightenment. By that time it had expressed itself as a particularly European, rationalist, and secular ideology. History is a matter of looking back in the European tunnel of time and trying to decide what happened, when, and why. Blaut claims that until 1492 the older form of history ignored the non-European world (5). However, after this date, Europe and its colonial settlements were the centres of struggles: in Europe struggles for religious and economic power; in the colonial settlements struggles, to suppress the culture of Indigenous peoples and seize their wealth and knowledge. Northern Europe expressed itself as a unique European, rationalist, and secular ideology. Any comments about non-European history were largely related to European colonial activities. This Eurocentric dimension of the dominant ideology invented the "eternal West" that became the well-known version of "Western" capitalist history, which adheres to pseudo-scientific rules. As a result early scholars disregarded the history of most of central and eastern Europe.

Eurocentrism assumes that there is only one view of the human race: the superiority of white people. Since the European invasion of North America, the Western world's Eurocentric interpretation has dominated almost all printed matter in Western society, particularly educational materials. It has shaped the consciousness of North American Natives in the way they perceive and understand themselves and the world. Eurocentric history is a political interpretation of the world-based colonization and Euro-America's blind faith in its own racial superiority. It embraces the premises of western Europe, which encourage Natives' complicity in their own oppression.

Academics write history from their own particular frame of reference and experience. Generally, historians assume that their versions of history are objective and credible. According to most historians, North American Natives have no history because almost nothing is known about them before European conquest. In Canada, schooling is Eurocentric from primary grades to university, and there is little opportunity for counter-cultural thought or non-Eurocentric training in most curricula. The general spectrum of Canadian history is remarkably similar. The facts are the same; it is the interpretation of the facts and the Eurocentric-based subjective, personal discussions that vary.

Since subjective history does not adhere to scientific rules, it can ignore precise or objective truth and embrace conceptual notions, such as European superiority. However, this subjectivity is cloaked in the guise of rationalist principles and objectivity. Because Aboriginal academic space is empty, European historians exploit it to further what become imperialistic caricatures of history. For example, the policy and writings of the Catholic missionary orders, which held immense temporal and ecclesiastical authority, rationalized their subjugation and oppression of Aboriginal peoples. It is the nature of subjective history that it is only justifiable or credible in terms of the values of the mainstream culture, in this case, Eurocentric culture. Thus Eurocentric history can be considered a semi-popular opinion. This subjective or fabricated history of the Aboriginal population has been continuously reproduced in almost all publications over several centuries. Eurocentrism is a departure from objective reality. It is the colonizer's method of creating a consensus of views that distort history and create racial stereotypes in order to secure the dominant position of the colonizer's rule.

During the Renaissance three forces, mercantilism, Christianity, and racism, combined and the *outcome* was powerful Eurocentric myths or narratives. Although historians traditionally interpret the Renaissance as the pivotal period that ushered progressive and rationalist philosophies into Western culture, in reality it marks the birth of a colonial and white supremacist ideology that formed the foundation of European imperialism. A narrow perception of the world distorted Western thought to the extent that "social theory produced by capitalism gradually reached a conclusion that the history of Europe was exceptional... because it could not have been born elsewhere" (Amin 105). Eurocentrism formed the ideological basis for colonial and economic dominance of Indigenous nations that created horrific human disasters in every conquered land. In other words, European states conquered and devastated Indigenous societies, and established a system of oppression and colonization that remains to the present time.

Modern Western interpretations of history are rooted in the ideology of European domination and subjugation of colonial nations. Armed with gunpowder and military technology plundered largely from Asia and the Middle East, Europeans seized Native territories. Britain, France, Portugal, and Spain carried out the most extensive holocausts in the history of mankind. When Natives served no economic purpose, they were either herded elsewhere or slaughtered—sometimes whole populations were slaughtered, as were the Beothuk Indians in New-foundland. Imperialism was the vicious destroyer of everything Native; its weapons were Christianity, political intrigue, imprisonment, and germ warfare.

Ronald Wright, a prominent author on conquests of Indigenous peoples in the Americas, claims that in the 1700s England as well as other imperial European nations of northwestern Europe were actively engaged in germ warfare. Lord Jeffrey Amherst, who successfully captured Louisbourg in 1758 and Monteal in 1760 from the French, secured his place in history as an organizer of modern germ warfare on North American Indians. Wright documents the comments of James Adair, an Irish trader and writer who lived with the Cherokees, who observed the psychological effects of the disease: "[Indian] survivors were deranged... some shot themselves, others cut their throats" (Wright 103). Amherst supported this tactic. He stated: "'Infect the Indians with sheets upon which smallpox patients have been lying...'" (Wright 136). Churchill concurs that England was indeed using biological warfare to eradicate Native populations.

Western European colonial powers espoused the same basic goals to justify the exploration and settlement of the New World. The imperialist nation-states agreed that "cross and crown"—church and king—legitimized the invasion and takeover of the Americas. While missionaries were undermining Indigenous civilizations in the name of God, European merchants were accumulating private and public wealth through trade, and enhancing national and personal prestige and power through colonization. In fact, the ideals and interests of missionaries and private companies were one and the same; religion subdued the Natives for economic advantage and paved the way for national expansion. The missionary orders fought to protect their own profit property and wealth. For example, the Jesuits unilaterally appropriated Native land, to be exact 900,000 acres (Myers 17). European documentation from that period can be considered little more than fictions designed to justify European land theft by England and France and rupturing the lives of Indian and Métis tribes. "The European conquest of the Americas has been termed one of the darkest moments of human history," wrote Alvin Josephy, a prominent American historian. "No one will ever know how many Indians... were enslaved, tortured, debauched and killed" (277). Josephy maintains that "the colonization of America resulted in the physical extermination of the Indigenous population" (38). The Indians were driven from their territory, and European immigrants were brought in to settle on the Indian land.

To ensure that God's (that is the church's) goals were protected, the sixteenth century saw priests design colonial charters, royal edicts, and colonial public law. Europeans set up policies allowing them to commit atrocities against Native peoples with impunity. Native peoples had no legal recourse to protect their land or their homes from European plunderers. According to the Europeans,

Natives were subhuman, so Indigenous occupancy did not constitute human residence. The Europeans claimed they had "discovered" vacant land and therefore were free to claim it as their own. This sham has evolved into today's bewildering array of land claims and the attendant judicial games that respond to these claims and continue to deal unjustly with Native peoples. The political structure was designed to place all authority, privileges, and even the most basic human rights exclusively within the colonizer's domain. Short of warfare, the Natives had no options except ultimately to sign treaties in which they had little control over the terms. However, the ruling imperialists were allowed to use violence freely because it was in the "public" interest to do so. This legitimized state abuse has continued to the present day.

During the nineteenth century, western European colonizers increased cultural racism by extending Eurocentrism in the academic literature of the social sciences. Western publications are based on colonial assumptions using western European philosophy as the norm. Thanks to the unethical and imperial practices of European scientists and academics, Indigenous peoples have been stereotyped as backward and lazy, indolent and thoughtless, and their culture characterized as stagnant and devoid of civility or creativity. These stereotypes persist today and continue to exploit Aboriginals in all aspects of their daily lives. Racist views have been held by European writers and probably by the vast majority of the white citizentry who considered populations outside Europe inferior and very likely uncivilized. It was held with certainty that "these people were naturally inferior to Europeans, naturally less brave, less freedom-loving, less rational, and so on, and progress for them depended on acceptance of European domination" (Blaut 20).

Popular school texts concerning North American Aboriginals exhibit Eurocentrism that applauds the efforts and works of the ruling class. Because Eurocentric models of behaviour incorporate competition and individual achievement, it is not surprising that a commonly held notion among many Canadians is that Native peoples, as individuals, prefer to live on welfare.

Consistent with the self-image as "world conqueror" is the western European self-proclaimed mandate to save the world with its "special" qualities and knowledge that oblige it to shoulder the burden of guiding those less fortunate. This is the arrogant presumption in the western European self-image. The current work of Euro-Canadian academics and journalists serves the corporate establishment by sustaining the same widespread Eurocentric bias in the production and dissemination of distorted history. However, recently a few non-Aboriginal historians have produced favourable interpretations of Aboriginal history that are non-Eurocentric.

Today, Eurocentrism serves to create a consensus among the population that accepts free enterprise ideology and the racial stereotypes. It is, in other words, an interpretation of Indian, Métis, and Inuit peoples designed to ensure their subjugated position. It denies them their own history and their participation in a transformed Western society. Euro-Canadian academics treat the Natives as marginal, and thus do not recognize their contributions.

Aboriginal history cannot be understood without understanding "white settler" colonialism and its ideology. Eurocentric British colonizers were instrumental in shaping Canada's demographic development to their political and economic advantage. As a rule, the colonial British government brought a large population of white immigrants to the colonies, ensuring the dominance of western Europeans. After Confederation, the Canadian industrialists and the British imperialists developed the country through specific policies still colonial in spirit under which the Canadian government also brought in and settled European immigrants on Native land. However, before bringing the settlers to Canada, the imperial governments, Britain and Canada, had to remove the entire Aboriginal population from their territory and eradicate all claims to it. Using British and Canadian military forces, the Macdonald Conservative government waged prolonged war against the Métis and Indians during the middle and later 1800s. At the end of these genocidal wars almost all Aboriginal peoples were driven from their home territory, imprisoned in Manitoba Stoney Mountain prison, or killed—several by public hanging in the main streets of the cities of Regina and North Battleford. After 1885, the year the Métis were crushed at Batoche, it was deemed safe to bring in the European immigrants to Canada.

The Conservative government passed the Dominion Lands Act in 1872—two years after Prime Minister Macdonald had savagely driven the Métis from their land in the Red River and granted 160 acres to any white settler. According to Valerie Knowles, England "was sending chartered shiploads of the 'deserving' poor of Great Britain to Canada" (71). By 1914, the "'Army next to God' had assisted 150,000 such people to emigrate to Canada... [and] the Dominion government was paying the Army bonuses for 'agriculturalists' who soon became industrial workers" (Knowles 71). During the latter part of the nineteenth century, western Canada became an agricultural region. To expand agricultural production, land was allocated for western Europeans, who served as markets in North America for British industrial products. This homestead scheme again took land from the Natives and made it available to European immigrants who then became purchasers of farm machinery and other manufactured goods. Native labourers were no longer needed, so they were assigned to reserves.

When conducting research for their books, Eurocentric historians usually claim to have studied previously unexamined government documents. But one does not require much historical knowledge to realize that most government documents are far from being objective accounts. Although considered to be correct information they are opinions of imperialist officials, written from the point of view of their own Eurocentric ideology to provide the establishment, that is, senior bureaucratic officials, the required documented "proof" that upholds the dominant Eurocentric ruling-class perspective. Not recognizing their own Eurocentrism or that of the government officials, academics discredit Natives' historical writings as absolute "myth" or "advocacy." For example, in an influential book *The Birth of Western Canada* (1936), the historian George Stanley, composes a contradictory account of a matter between the halfbreeds and the federal government in which his use of language is pejorative in his discussion of the halfbreeds:

> The half-breeds ... were doomed to economic absorption. Neither their racial consciousness, nor their primitive economy was strong enough to maintain the separate identity of the half-breed nation in the midst of overwhelming white immigration and a competitive nineteenth-century civilization. Herein lay the basic cause of the half-breed rising in 1869.... Resistance was therefore inevitable. (18)

Clearly Stanley portrays and blames the halfbreeds for the forthcoming rebellion, and the federal government is not to blame for the resultant terrorizing and slaughter in the suppression of the resistance in the Red River colony by the Métis. This despite the fact that they have systematically overwhelmed and suppressed the Métis culture. This account by Stanley is a fabrication formulated in his imagination because the issue between the halfbreeds and the federal government prior to 1869 had not been settled. This is typical of the distortions of history that result in fictions created by academics misrepresenting the authentic historical circumstances in order to preserve the integrity of the ruling class colonizer. Most white historians are obviously unaware of their entrenched biases and subjectivity and are, without exception, the strongest advocates of white ruling-class ideology.

In western Canadian historical writing, the Métis uprising at Batoche is said to be due exclusively to Riel. Such theorizing allows authors to focus on a personality while largely ignoring the socio-economic and political dynamics that shaped this history. According to Sealey the most profound change after the insurrection of 1869–70 was the social humiliation of the Métis (63). The Métis at Red River were persecuted by the victorious Canadians who were openly contemptuous of anyone "papist" or French or a Breed. As a result about half of the Red River Métis left Manitoba during the 1870s to seek a freer life elsewhere.

Misrepresentation and intrigue are shown by Don Mclean in his description of the role of one of the Métis negotiators Lawrence Clarke:

> It seems that Clarke was trying to deny his role as the Métis representative in Ottawa. His efforts matched those of the Federal Government in hiding the official and unofficial roles he played in creating the resistance [of 1869–70].
>
> Clarke's actions ... resulted in a series of incidents pointing to Clarke's engineering of a resistance.... Clarke's information and confirmation of the results of his statement justified the Government's decision to send troops north [to the Red River]. The timing of the [Federal] troop movements [confirmed that] ... [t]he Métis could now be accused of starting the whole affair. (62–63)

This passage clearly illustrates the methods of intrigue and deception used by the ruling class. In terms of his own writing, Mclean reveals the mentality of historians. He states later that Indian Commissioner Edgar Dewdney, appointed in 1879 with broad discretionary powers, "was not aware of any causes of discontent [in the Red River turbulence]" (63). It is hard to understand how anyone could conclude that Dewdney, a diligent and attentive administrator, could make such a sanctimonious and deceptive statement in all honesty and good faith. After all, he was the federally appointed Governor of the North West Territories and was fully informed and knowledgeable of both sides of the issues of the resistance struggles. This article with Mclean's conclusions about Dewdney is an example of the writing of Eurocentric historians and is used by them to disguise the real purposes of the white European establishment.

In Eurocentric societies, racist beliefs constitute the official criteria to determine the "objective" situation. Historians working within the Euro-Canadian systems do not have to prove western European superiority; it is taken for granted. This assumption remains implicit in their historical analyses, particularly those dealing with Native populations. Generally, academics claim that the oppression of Métis during the Red River Resistance, however severe, was not sufficiently provocative as to require armed uprising against the state. Many historians omit or misrepresent the deceitful and covert actions of John A. Macdonald and his cabinet, which failed to reveal the facts of their torturous and genocidal operations both in the Red River resistance and the Battle of Batoche because such an analysis would expose the imperialists' exploitation of the Natives. The Eurocentric concept held that the Native population had two options: assimilation or death.

Perhaps one of the most crucial issues about Eurocentric publications is the support they receive from government institutions and the media. The state and its governments, universities, and media believe that it is in their best interest to maintain the status quo. For example, most fellowships and private foundation grants support proposals from academics who uphold the Eurocentric ideology, including the stereotypes of racial minorities. At the same time, very few grants are given to Native scholars and teachers who produce publications that present an Aboriginal perspective. This may not be a startling revelation about Canadian society, but it does suggest the nature of Eurocentrism and how establishment foundations provide support.

The state ensures its supremacy by preventing non-Eurocentric historians, especially Natives, from gaining wide exposure to counter-consciousness interpretations of Aboriginal history. Canadian publishers readily provide establishment historians with a forum for their Eurocentric historical perspectives, while obstructing an empirical analysis of Native history. Unfortunately, white supremacy writing appeals to the mainstream audience because it harmonizes with racist stereotypes. For the most part publishers will not alienate their white audience by challenging the familiar stereotypes of Natives. Fortunately, there are a few small publishers who are not Eurocentric.

Indigenous scholars of newly independent Third World countries, such as those in Africa, were the first to challenge Eurocentrism, and gradually, the scholars of Africa took control of the interpretation of their past. The Eurocentric histories of African people were not only irrelevant but also were gross distortions of the Aboriginal heritage and culture. In North America, documents that are consistent with establishment thinking have been accepted for generations as authentic historical sources without critical scrutiny. For example, *The Jesuit Relations* diaries, which were portrayed for centuries as unquestionable, "deified" statements, are today regarded as little more than myth by numerous historians whose perspective of history is either Eurocentric or counter-culture.

Eurocentric interpretations create a false consciousness among the colonized. Eurocentrism does not allow for alternatives and thereby deceives Native people into believing that their history can be acquired only through the colonizer's institutions. Rather than critically attacking their oppressor's dogma, the Native elite, particularly Native professors, teachers, doctors, and judges who receive patronage and glory from the colonizer, have accepted historical distortions to an alarming extent. Many Natives are intellectual captives and have become collaborators with the oppressor, and some Native academics write Indian and Métis history with a strictly Eurocentric interpretation.

Criticism of the colonizer does not occur spontaneously. Instead, many of the oppressed elite want to be like the colonizer, or even worse, they wish to be the colonizer. In some cases, this desperate desire leads Native people to become more passionate Eurocentrics than the average white supremacist who takes his or her privileged position for granted. Some Native writers do not offer new insights into Native history; instead they entrench their own subjugation and colonization. Not surprisingly, their publications are made highly visible by the academic community, which endorses them with little, if any, critical examination.

Ideally, Aboriginals, not Euro-Canadian academics, should research Native culture. Indigenous institutions must be staffed by scientists who grew up in Native societies and, therefore, identify themselves with the future well being of Native nations. This, however is no small task; Canada is imbued with semi-apartheid philosophies that make it difficult to develop a counter-consciousness. Aboriginals have to dispel the pervasive stereotypes and destroy all encrustations of colonial mentality that repress them. This must occur before they can develop a non-Eurocentric interpretation of Indigenous history. It demands a critical analysis that emphasizes Native consciousness, life experiences, and resistance struggles.

White academics, primarily western European historians and anthropologists, for too long have owned the past, particularly that of Native nations. Although soldiers, missionaries, and merchants were the initial forces that colonized Natives, the continuing psychological processes of dehumanization and inferiorization ensure their subjugated status. Therefore, it is from that base that Native decolonization must begin. The racist Eurocentric pattern established by the first colonizers will be broken only when the colonized reclaim their history. Third World scholars who are not rewriting their history demonstrate that

Native history can be properly interpreted only by Natives because other scholars and authors do not have the colonized consciousness to express the authentic socio-political values and orientations of Native society. Only Aboriginals who have experienced colonization can understand the nuances of Native customs, spirituality, and traditions, which include unspoken assumptions and significant meanings that permeate Native communities.

Métis and Indian history is both a movement and a discipline challenging Eurocentrism. Intrinsic to that history is a people's sense of resistance and struggle that emerges from a growing counter-consciousness and realization that they have suffered injustices and oppressive inequalities because of their race and colonization. Authentic Native history must confront the inequalities in the judicial, economic, and political realms; however, in order to do this one should examine the processes and structures that promote Eurocentrism. Métis history, for example, is much more than Riel, and finally, there are Native accounts of Métis' positive contributions to Canada's development.

Eurocentric history is more than a glorification of western Europe's past and a denigration of Native people. It is an aspect of imperialism, a mechanism designed to suppress resistance and to prevent the Native population from developing a counter-consciousness to Western Europe's culture. Within the context of imperialism, Natives are unique in that they are a distinct class and race, a nation of Indigenous peoples within a capitalist state who have a different consciousness of history. The force of life of the Native has been principally that of Indigenous nationalist liberation struggles for land and autonomy while the written history ignores the reality of that fight.

As an Aboriginal historian, I am deeply concerned by the incredible lack of authentic Aboriginal historical writing. By muffling the voices of protest or simply by ignoring them, the corporate ruling class hopes to keep Natives out of sight. Our histories are dismissed or marginalized while our impoverishment and subjugation increases. Our struggle for liberation should expand and advance in all dimensions.

Works Cited

Amin, Samir. *Eurocentrism*. New York: Monthly Review Press, 1989.

Blaut, J.M. *The Colonizer's Model of the World*. New York: Guilford Press, 1993.

Josephy, Alvin. *The Indian Heritage of America*. New York: Bantam, 1969.

Lussier, Antoine S. and Bruce Sealey. *The Other Natives*. Winnipeg: Manitoba Métis Federation Press, 1978.

Mclean, Don. "Lawrence Clarke: Architect of Revolt." *Canadian Journal of Native Studies*, 3:1 (1983).

Myers, Gustavus. *A History of Canadian Wealth*. Toronto: Lewis and Samuel, 1972.

Naylor, R.T. *Canada in the European Age*. Vancouver: New Star Books, 1987.

Wright, Ronald. *Stolen Continents*. Toronto: Penguin, 1992.

Expressions in
Native Identity

How Native Is Native if You're Native?

Drew Hayden Taylor

A prolific Ojibway playwright and writer from the Curve Lake First Nation, Drew Hayden Taylor has had over forty-seven productions of his plays, has written for four television series, has published ten books, and has a column in four newspapers. He recently completed direction of an NFB documentary on Native humour, is working on a proposed Native comedy show for CBC, has another book coming out in fall 2000, and in May had two plays open, one in Winnipeg and one in Tulsa, Oklahoma.

Within the growing and diverse Native community, there seems to be an ongoing ideological battle raging, one that seems to have reversed itself from what was practised decades ago. When I was growing up, I remember that the more "Native" you looked, i.e., dark skinned with prominent Aboriginal features, the lower you were on the social totem pole (no cultural appropriation of West Coast symbolism intended). White was in and Native people (and no doubt many other ethnic people) tried to look it, dress it, and act it. Those who didn't were often made fun of. Being dark was no lark. In the Caucasian world, people whose family history included a drop or two of Native blood bent over backwards to keep the scandal a secret. The skeletons in those closets would thrill anthropologists and museums the world over.

These days, it's a completely different ball game. Native is in. The darker you are, the more you are embraced and the more Indian you are thought to be. The lighter your skin, the more difficult it sometimes is to be accepted by your Aboriginal peers (and the non-Native world). White is no longer right. And heaven forbid that a person from the dominant culture, who happens to have some barely-remembered ancestor who tickled toes and traded more than some furs and beads with a Native

All articles by Drew Hayden Taylor reprinted with permission of the author.

person, should let a conversation slip by without mentioning that at least four of the 46 chromosomes in his body don't burn in the summer sun.

But it's often more than simply how you look. It's how you think, act, where you live, and point with your lower lip. Consequently, something more representational of the existing philosophical schism is the difficult question of determining "what makes a Native a Native?" What set of qualifications or characteristics will allow an individual to speak as a Native person, or have an opinion representative of the larger Indigenous population? Sure as hell beats me. But as sure as there's a hundred "Xena—Warrior Princess" Web sites on the Net, there's a vast number of "experts" existing in this world eager to tell you what defines a Native and more than happy to tell you whether you fit into that category. Personally, I think it must be so great to have all the answers. My ambition in life is to be such an expert. I have done the necessary amount of research. God (or Creator) knows my bluish-green eyes have allowed me a unique entry into such discussions. Drew Hayden Taylor—Aboriginal Attitude and Attributes Assessor (DHT-AAAA).

One such example of the broad spectrum of Aboriginal acceptance involves the world of education. Many reserves and Native educational organizations are constantly encouraging and extolling the virtues of education on the youth. Yet, these communities also believe that the more educated you become, the less "Native" you will be. They scorn and disdain those who want to or have gone through the educational process. Evidently, knowledge and learning deprives individuals of their cultural heritage. I must have missed that in the sweat lodge.

Conversations with Elders and traditional teachers have convinced me that this is not a traditional teaching. Many Elders urge and encourage the pursuit of education. In fact, the two worlds of tradition and scholastics can, and often do, travel the same roads, albeit one on horseback and the other on a vintage 1953 Indian Scout motorcycle. In fact, those who are often wary of formal education are usually locked somewhere between both worlds, neither traditional nor particularly well-educated. Unfortunately, it is their own insecurity that is being presented—thus proving the need for educated Native psychologists.

Another example on the flip side involves the disquieting story a Native educator told me of a reserve education counsellor in a southern Ontario community. Practically every year, this person would ask at least one on-reserve and who knows how many off-reserve students, "Why should you continue going to university?" She would then strongly hint that this student almost owes it to the community to quit school, thus saving the reserve money. So if some students on the reserve are being urged not to go to university, but all the money is being reserved for them to go, where is all this money going? That is what is called the I-don't-know-if-I-should-go-to-school-or-stay-home-and-collect-welfare-or-possibly-scratch-out-a-living-telling-students-what-to-do Paradox.

I have a column jokingly called *The Urbane Indian* that runs in a Regina publication. I was telling this to a Native woman at a meeting and she asked me what urbane meant. I told her it was similar to sophisticated, refined or knowledgeable. She thought for a moment before responding, "I hope I never get like that." Evidently being suave and debonair (or as we say on the reserve, swave and debone her) is not a Native characteristic worth having.

There are also those who believe the more successful you are, the less Native you are considered. If you have money, toys, a nice house, two accountants, and a vague idea where the Caribbean is, then you are obviously not one of the Indigenous people. I remember reading an interview with a successful prairie businessman who was looked down upon by his brethren because he had made a financial success of his life. He rationalized it by saying, "if being Indian means being poor, then I don't necessarily want to be Indian." It was a harsh statement indicating the man did not think there was a middle ground. I know many successful Aboriginal people who are every bit as "Native" as those who still subsist on Kraft Dinner and drive 1974 Dodge pickups.

A friend of mine severely criticized another friend because she had made the decision to live in the city, while friend number one moved back to the reserve. Friend number one felt that one could only be Native, or really be called an Aboriginal person, within the confines of those artificial borders. Even though friend number one had moved back home in his mid-thirties, having never lived on the reserve and having grown up in urban environments, I think he officially considered himself, finally, to be an Indian. Taking all this into consideration, I guess it means the only true "Native" people are uneducated, poor people with poor vocabularies who live on reserves. Yikes.

As clichéd as it may sound, I think everybody has his or her own unique definition of what being Native means. Very few of us exist in the world our grandparents lived in, where their definition was no doubt far from ours. And this definition will no doubt further evolve in the coming Millennium. My career as a DHT-AAAA will have to wait because I don't have all the answers. I don't know the boundaries and necessary factors for such important decisions as these. To tell you the truth, I don't even care anymore.

I do know one thing though. Passing judgments on other people isn't a particularly Aboriginal thing to do. I know this because an eagle came to me in my dreams, along with a coyote and a raven. They landed on the tree of peace, smoked a peace pipe, ate a baloney sandwich, played some bingo, then told me so.

That should shut them up.

What to Believe?

Drew Hayden Taylor

Every once in a while, something happens in most people's lives that makes them wonder about what they believe, what they don't believe, what they should believe, and what they're afraid to believe. Oddly enough, my believability dilemma originated from something as obscure as the new *Tarzan and The Lost City* movie, if you can believe it.

In this rather mediocre film, Tarzan, the all-powerful white demi-god, races through the jungle trying to save the local Indigenous people and the lost city of Opar from vicious and greedy white men who are a combination of explorers, archaeologists, and self-confessed representatives of civilization. How many times have we heard that before? After getting over the obvious cultural déjà-vu, there happened within the movie several sequences that made me laugh and shake my head in artistic disbelief.

Assisting Tarzan in his noble quest is the chief of the local tribe, who also happens to be the shaman/medicine man possessing some very interesting power. He has the ability to suddenly appear out of nowhere as a swarm of bees that covers the unconscious cobra-bitten Tarzan, hiding him from the evil white people. At various other times in the movie—after saving Tarzan from the venom with a single touch—this man turns himself into a giant cobra (evidently a lot of cobras in Africa). He is impervious to bullets. They just pass through him with barely a ripple. He also creates entire living warriors out of a single inch-long bone fragment.

Putting aside a basic assumption that a people with such a bag of cool tricks up their collective sleeve wouldn't need the help of Tarzan (whose name, by the way, translates as "White Skin" in great ape language), the movie set up a disturbing question.

As I rolled my eyes and groaned during the bee sequence, my friend, who is also Native had a substantially different reaction. She shrugged and said, "it's shape-shifting. Our people have it too. I can believe it." There it was. I was scoffing at this Hollywoodized adventure story, with the clichéd and mysterious wise man from deepest, darkest Africa, forgetting that shape shifting and other such manifestations such as these have long been part of Aboriginal legend and lore.

It put me in a position of trying to figure out, for the first time in a long time, what I actually believe in. Not just about Native (or African for that matter) shape shifting, but Christianity and everything. It's just that in our upbringing in this twentieth century, the stories of shape shifting and other spiritual beliefs have been relegated to quaint children's stories of stories from a long time past—in much the same way that a vast majority of the country feels about most religious stories of miraculous events. Then every once in a while, you meet somebody who really believes. It's not a story, it's not a legend. It's a reality.

Several years ago I was sitting in a kitchen in northern Ontario late one night, talking with six or eight people, most from Manitoulin Island, and most of them women. And through one route or another, the topic turned to the fabled Mimiquashug, the little hairy people of the water. They're a mythical (and I use the term loosely) people who live in the rocks and cracks around large bodies of fresh water. They travel the water in stone canoes and are very hard to catch a glimpse of.

One after another, each woman related stories of the Mimiquashug. Who in their community had seen one, how they had seen them, why they had seen them? It was an evening of Mimiquashug stories. Except it wasn't stories, any more than listening to people talk about relatives or their recent adventures at the Bingo are simply stories. The tone, the language, the feeling of the conversation told me these women not only believed in the Mimiquashug but also considered them a part of everyday life. It was like talking about old friends who come to visit every other year or so.

It's not that I didn't believe in them. It's just that I never took the time to actually think about them, or shape shifters, or any of the other wonderful and exciting aspects of Native spirituality, on a personal level. I'm feeling a bit of a spiritual emptiness. When you don't know what you believe, or how much to believe, it can be a bit of a downer.

I once read an interview with a Native judge who was receiving an award. Recently in the news there had been articles about a community banishing a lawbreaker. The punishment for his offences was to spend time alone on an island, in accordance with traditional teachings. The Native judge was asked how he felt about the resurgence of this form of punishment, and he responded by saying that he respected the decisions of this community but he still preferred the Queen's law. He felt it was a better, more objective system.

To each his (or her) own.

Though still plagued by particular questions and a certain amount of skepticism inherent in living in the dominant culture, I've decided to believe rather then disbelieve. Positive is always better than negative. The glass is half full, not half empty. Maybe nobody can definitively prove the existence of the Mimiquashug, or shape shifters (though if anybody wants to try it will more than likely be white people). But the whole point is, they don't have to. I can't prove I have relatives I see every other year. I don't want to. It's nobody's business but my own.

Besides, I want to see if the mighty Tarzan can paddle a stone canoe.

The "Dating" Game: Who Should Date Who in the Native Community

Drew Hayden Taylor

The last time I was in Edmonton I got asked it again. It's a question I find myself getting asked quite frequently, as if I am the spokesperson for all Native men in Canada (if I am, I want a better salary). And to tell you the truth, it's getting annoying. This time it happened on a radio talk show hosted by a Native woman. Logically, it is always a Native woman who asks this question.

"Why is it that Native men, when they reach a certain level of success and power, end up dating and marrying only white women and not Native women?"

Often they point to Ovide Mercredi, Graham Greene, Tom Jackson, etc. as examples. All well-known, prosperous men whose partners are of the Caucasian persuasion. This is a question and issue that is of specific interest to many Native women, who regard this practice as a rejection of them, and the destruction of Native society.

Many Aboriginal nations are either entirely or directly matriarchal, or have elements involving strong female interaction embedded in the culture. There is a belief that women are the protectors and teachers of the culture, especially when it comes to raising children. So when a non-Native woman enters the scene, it can disrupt what some see as the continuing cycle of cultural preservation.

But understanding that, is their question still a valid one? True, you go to many functions and social gatherings where the intelligentsia or successful Aboriginal gather and it does seem like the majority of the Native men do sport non-Native spouses. Jordan Wheeler, Native writer for *Sixty Below* and *The Rez* (whose wife by the way is a lovely Native woman) blames it on the circles in which "prosperous" Native people are forced to socialize.

Since there are more "successful" white people than Native people, relatively speaking, and more "prominent" (again I use the term loosely) Native males than females the individuals one is likely to meet, interact with, and develop relationships with will have a mathematical probability of being non-Native females. Unfortunate, but true.

However, I do seriously doubt this is the only reason. Life is not that simple. Some who like to dabble in amateur (or not so amateur) sociological examination believe there is a deeply subconscious (or maybe not so deep) belief that a non-Native girlfriend is a symbol of success, of achievement in both white and Native society. Or then there's the theory that white women are just easier to find in the dark. I don't know which is the correct answer, or even it there is an answer. One could say that maybe two people just fall in love, but for reasons I've quoted above, this issue has taken on a political taint.

If snuggling with people of no definable Native heritage is a crime, then it is one I am guilty of. Rightly or wrongly, I am a graduate of the "colour-blind school of love." But taking into account the last four girlfriends I have had, I've noticed a disturbing trend developing in my personal life, one that, on the surface, may lend credence to the argument.

One of the first serious relationships I ever had was with a Native woman, then some time afterward I fell in love with a woman who was a half-breed like myself, then I found myself with a Filipino woman (still technically a visible minority but not Native and not Caucasian), and then finally, I spent several years with a white woman. If this trend keeps up, my next woman will either be an albino or alien.

To the best of my knowledge, none of these relationships were politically or socially motivated. I'm not that bright or ambitious. They just developed as most relationships do. You see each other in a room, make eye contact, you mumble to yourself "oh please God, please," and the rest I'll leave to your imagination.

One older Native woman, a strong proponent of Native men marrying Native women, even verbally chastised me for dating a white girl, urging me to break up with her and start seeing a Native women she had just recently met. Even though her three daughters had married, had children by, or were dating white men, I was at fault here. The irony of the situation was not lost on me.

This begs a different consideration to the original dating question. Why is it never questioned when successful Native women marry white men (i.e., Buffy Ste. Marie, or Tantoo Cardinal)? Granted, the ratio is substantially different but still I think it is a valid issue. I even posed that question to the hostess on the radio show. She looked at me blankly for a moment before answering "I don't know. I don't have an answer for that."

And is it only the white culture that's at question here? The issue of the dominant culture absorbing and sublimating the much smaller Aboriginal culture? What about, for argument's sake, Black people? There was no noticeable reaction to my relationship with my Filipino girlfriend, and in fact many people jokingly commented that she looked more Native than I did. What about Asians, both South (the real "Indians!") and East? And if you really want to throw a wrench into the works, what about the Sami, the Aboriginal people of Scandinavia, otherwise known as the Laplanders? They all have blonde hair and blue eyes but are recognized as an Indigenous people. I've been claiming to be half Sami, half Ojibway for years.

And does this question only relate to procreative couples? What about the gay and lesbian relationships? I've never heard of any grief being given or received over an inter-racial relationship in either community. It all gets so confusing.

So I sit here, a single man, afraid to pick up the telephone and call somebody. For, depending on who I phone, I will no doubt be making a very important and major political statement. I just want somebody to go to the movies with.

The Erotic Indian:
A Contradiction in Terms?

Drew Hayden Taylor

Native sexuality. Now there's something you don't hear about much. Sensuality within the Native community seems to be oddly nonexistent if you observe much of the pop culture that surrounds us. Culturally speaking, Native people do not automatically spring to mind when it come to affairs of the heart, or other organs. Unlike other cultures, for instance, Latins, Italians and the French, to name a few, Indians do not share a reputation for romance and love.

Now this in itself is odd when you take into consideration that fifty percent of the over one million people in Canada who claim some form of Native ancestry are under thirty years old. Though we were once tragically thought of as "the vanishing Indian," there has been an amazing population explosion in Native communities across the country. So either Aboriginal scientists have mastered the difficult science of cloning more than sheep and cows, or somebody out there is doing something a hell of a lot more interesting than hunting deer. (Perhaps a game one Elder referred to as "hiding the pickerel.")

Whoever is generating this fifty percent population explosion is obviously not paying attention to pop culture. Or as one mother of four on the reserve put it, "See what happens when you don't have cable?"

Historically, Native people were not generally viewed as potential love partners, except if you read the voluminous amount of historical romances with characters such as Iron Horse or White Wolf, with muscles bulging (amongst other things). Pocahontas, the first and ultimate Indian Princess, was perhaps one of the only symbols of love to break this wall. But keep in mind that in reality, she was only thirteen years old, while her beau, John Smith, was actually around thirty. There's a word for that kind of love.

The term "Indian Princess" is in itself an odd phrase, since most Native cultures never had an established royalty or nobility. The only possible exception might be the Two-Spirited community (also known as gay and lesbians) where "God save the Queen" takes on a whole new meaning.

Now this brings up an interesting question. We as Native people are aware of our own sensuality. Is it important to make the dominant culture aware of it too, to further enlighten them as to the wonderful and myriad aspects of Aboriginal culture, or should we be content to share our little amorous secrets only amongst ourselves and revel in it, and by doing this, maintain a reputation for stoicism and be perceived as sexually uninterested?

And of course in North American culture there is a fine line between expressing sensuality and exploiting it. Several years ago I went to Hawaii and saw to my amazement in almost every tourist and souvenir store a calendar titled "The Girls of Hawaii." Inside the magazine, beginning every month was a topless Polynesian girl smiling benevolently out at the viewer.

At first I was stunned. And then I realized I was stunned, and I couldn't figure out why I was stunned. After all, I had seen photographs of nude women before. I am a man of the world. Then it hit me: it was the cultural representation I perceived—or better yet, the presentation of the culture as well as the women that was being used to sell the calendar. No different perhaps than "Bushwomen of the Kalahari" wet T-shirt contests. I found myself offended. And no doubt part of the shock was also trying to imagine some poor soul trying to develop and promote this same type of calendar here in Canada. "Indian Princesses of Canada" with page after page of scantily clad Aboriginal women, no doubt in buckskin bikinis, holding a new born fawn or frolicking about on some glacier, freezing their you-know-whats off.

But I could not helping thinking how unlikely this seemed. For one thing, I cannot foresee the Aboriginal women of Canada (not to mention most Native men with a traditional background) allowing such a thing to be developed and marketed. Politically, spirituality, and ethically, there would be too much to overcome and I believe the repercussions would be formidable, to say the least. Besides, it would be a very "American" thing to do.

During the last half decade or so, there have been two popular actresses carving a career out of the American porn industry. They have gone by the names of Jeannette Littledove and Hyapatia Lee. Both have used their Native heritage to market themselves extensively. *Hyapatia* is supposedly a Cherokee word and she is quoted as saying, in reference to her Native heritage and beliefs, "why tear down a tree to build a church when you can simply worship the tree?" As a Native person, I don't remember ever worshipping a tree. Not even a bush. But then again, I don't get out much. In fact, if my memory is correct, didn't the Druids of ancient Europe have a thing for oak trees and mistletoe?

On the cover of a recent issue of *Blueboy*, a skin magazine for gay men, was a tall, good-looking, obviously Native man, complete with the prerequisite bone choker. The caption beneath this almost naked Aboriginal: "Indian Summer—Hung Like Crazy Horse." He obviously must have been Ojibway.

In the December issue of *Playboy*, two of the women "featured" claim and offer up their Aboriginal heritage for the public. And coincidentally, one of them is the cover girl, Danielle House, the former Miss Canada International who lost her crown last year for punching out her ex-boyfriend's new girlfriend. Inside she proudly asserts her Inuit—do not call her Eskimo—background and her ambition is to be the spokesmodel for the Canadian Fur Association. "It's my heritage and I'm proud of it," she says. Oddly enough, she wasn't wearing any fur in the layout. I know, I looked.

The other "naked Native" is playmate Karen McDougal who proudly handles a dog team and sleigh stark naked except for the fur boots and hat. Evidently the Inuit have been doing it all wrong all this time. She credits her Cherokee grandfather for her high cheekbones. She has cheekbones?

While *Playboy* and porn are not the best examples of Native sexuality, it does illustrate the point that being the Erotic Indian seems to be a marketable product now. Something as private and personal as a person's, and a culture's own passionate practices is in fact becoming part of the monster known as pop culture.

Just one thing, please no Pocahontas blow-up dolls.

Mixed-Race Urban Native People:

Surviving a Legacy of Policies of Genocide

Bonita Lawrence

Bonita Lawrence is a mixed-race urban Native person of Mi'kmaq heritage. She is currently an Assistant Professor at the Institute of Women's Studies, Queen's University, Kingston ON.

Introduction

Who am I? Where do I belong? For people of mixed-race Native heritage, these questions can trouble and trail them through a lifetime. It's no accident that so many Native people are urban and mixed-race and don't speak their Native languages. Below, I will explore some of the findings of a study I conducted in 1998 with thirty individuals of mixed-race Native heritage living in Toronto. The study suggests that urban mixed-race Native people should be seen as survivors of a range of deliberate policies created by the Canadian government to abolish Native culture. These policies, genocidal[1] in their implications, have included residential schooling, the removal of Indian status from Native women who married non-status or non-Native men, and the widespread adoption of Native children into white families that began in the 1960s. Such policies forced great numbers of Native people to leave their communities. Once they had moved to the cities, they faced enormous pressures to leave Native culture behind. Many did so, in order that their children would not face the racism that they faced. For their children, however, the aftermath of these pressures brought to bear on their parents and grandparents has been a sense of alienation from Native culture, a struggle to regain the Native status that their parents may have lost, a need to learn as much as they can about their communities of origin, and a desire to be as active as possible in the urban Native community. From the perspectives of the communities who suffered the loss of their children to residential schools and adoption agencies, and the constant "bleeding off" of women and children who lost status because they moved to the cities, the effects of these policies has been incalculable damage to culture and heritage.

While a range of government policies have been instrumental in separating tremendous numbers of Native people from their communities over the past fifty years, it is also important to recognize that these policies of forced assimilation are not new—they originated during the earliest days of Canada's existence as a settler colony on Native land. Native peoples' identities have been influenced by these policies long before the policies of residential schooling and the enforced removal of Native children from their families and their subsequent adoption into non-Native families were put into effect. In a sense, it is impossible to understand mixed-race urban Native identity without looking at the whole subject of Native identity, and how it has historically been shaped by government definitions of who is Indian and who is not.

With these issues in mind, my study also focuses on those who left their communities, the pressures they faced to do so, and the range of processes they were subjected to within the dominant society that continuously worked to diminish their abilities to remain connected with culture and heritage. I will, therefore, begin by briefly exploring some of the experiences that are particular to urban Native people. The common thread connecting their experiences to those remaining in their communities—a history of policies designed to eliminate "the Indian problem" by eliminating Native peoples as distinct groups— will be examined next. Finally, I will discuss the contemporary circumstances that urban mixed-race Native people face, their efforts to reconnect with culture and heritage, and the issues they face in connection to those who live in First Nations communities.

The Family Histories of Urban Mixed-Race Native People

For my research, I conducted lengthy, in-depth interviews with twenty-two women and eight men on the subject of their identities—beginning with my own friends, and then interviewing *their* friends, moving outwards from the circle until I had found thirty people to interview. I interviewed far more women than men, simply because I know far more Aboriginal women then men. And yet I did not want to make the investigation only about Native women. My reasons were twofold. First of all, it seemed I would get a broader range of possible responses from interviewing both men and women. Secondly, and more importantly, in doing this research, I was troubled by the absence of Native people in my academic department, and at University of Toronto in general. When I began my research as a graduate student there were no Native faculty members at my university and, in general, very few Aboriginal people in North America writing sociological theory from Native perspectives. Because of this, I was aware that my research on Native identity was treading on new ground, and yet there were no other Aboriginal academics to consult with about the implications of undertaking work that questions aspects of Native identity in a non-Native environment. Indeed, much of the existing academic work by Aboriginal people, primarily from the United States, has suggested that it is dangerous to explore Native identity in an academic setting where there are no other Native people present to ensure that Aboriginal perspectives will be well represented. I was therefore keenly aware that I was speaking from an absent space in academia where Native voices had not been represented. Because of this, I could not simply explore the experiences of half the population— I had to look at the circumstances facing Native people as a whole.

Almost one-third of the people I interviewed were status Indians, mostly Ojibway and Mohawk people whose families came from nearby reserves. Another one-third were Métis people from western Canada. The rest were non-status Native people from Indigenous Nations all over the Americas—mostly from what is now Canada but including American Indians and South American Indigenous peoples. All of them were mixed-race of white and Native heritages, but one person was also of African American background while another had a Japanese father and a Passamaquoddy mother. We talked about their family histories, their experiences of belonging and not belonging, and their opinions about what was important for maintaining a strong sense of Native identity.

The family histories of all of the participants bespoke a similar story. Each family had undergone many painful experiences of violence, all of which had the effect of separating them from their communities or from silencing Native cultural expression within their families. Almost half the people I interviewed had parents and grandparents who had attended residential schools. For many of these individuals, becoming urbanized began when grandparents or parents never returned home after residential school had succeeded in breaking their ties to their communities. Several individuals came from families so devastated by alcoholism and sexual abuse because of residential schooling and racism that for years they had struggled to disown any connection to a Native identity at all. One-quarter of the people I interviewed had had some experience with the loss of close family members—their parents, siblings, or children—to provincial childcare authorities, either temporarily or permanently. For five of these individuals, the fact that their Native parents or grandparents were adopted as children signalled the end of their family's connection to their Native community of origin.

My research also uncovered a number of ways in which the individuals I interviewed have been blocked from reclaiming their heritage by what amounts to unofficial policies of deliberately erasing the Native heritage of those who left their communities behind. For example, I interviewed one participant whose mother's name was removed from her band list by the Indian agent when she was taken away to residential school. The mother, an orphan, lived at the school from the age of five to the age of twenty-one, and never returned to her community. Her daughter has struggled since then to have her mother's name rein- stated posthumously on the band list, simply as a means of asserting that this was her mother's heritage. The woman herself, as the daughter of a Métis man, has been rejected as a member of her mother's community.

Another individual had a grandmother whose name was arbitrarily changed by nuns while she was in residential school. It took years, and costly legal fees before the descendents of this woman could trace their ancestry back beyond the name change to find the grandmother's First Nation—where they are not accepted as members.

Other individuals spoke of having ancestors whose Native origins were obscured by being labelled as "French" by priests when they married French men.[2] A number of participants came from families who faced difficulties regaining their status due to technicalities beyond their control, such as being denied access to their adoption records so they could not enter a claim for Indian status or having their grandparents' birth records misplaced from official records or destroyed in church fires. Many of these individuals come from families who now do not think they are entitled to consider themselves "Native."

In addition to these experiences of individual removal from home, community, and official classification as "Indian," were incidences of *collective* removal. Individuals from as far away as southern Chile and eastern New Brunswick all described how settler violence forced their ancestors off their land. One woman spoke of how her band, which two centuries earlier had been forced from their land in New Brunswick into what is now the United States, had been so decimated that only fifty-six people remained when the band reformed and launched a land claim in the 1970s. This woman, whose family has always lived in Canada, is a federally recognized American Indian and member of the Passamaquoddy tribe of Maine, but because of different legislation controlling Native identity in Canada, she is not recognized as Indian in Canada.

Several of the western Métis came from families who had fled to the United States to escape persecution in Canada after the 1885 rebellion. These individuals spoke of their families' struggles as landless Métis forced to live in white urban centres. Attempting to distance themselves from their Native identity in the face of the relentless racist violence they faced was, for many, a necessary step to ensure basic survival.

What this bald listing of details cannot impart is the pain that these official and unofficial policies of removal and erasure have caused to those who experienced them. For two of the adoptees, their Native parents were arbitrarily listed on their birth records as non-Native, which considerably delayed their abilities to trace their parents. One adoptee was only successful in finding the identity of her Native parent a short time after his dead body was found in the streets of the northern community where he lived. He had suffered a heart attack but nobody stopped to help him because they assumed he was just a drunk Indian— he was therefore left to die in the street. Had she not been delayed from finding him by having her knowledge of his identity obscured, she might have had a chance to know him prior to his death—and indeed, perhaps he might not have died alone on the street. The other individual whose Native origins were deliberately obscured also could not track down her mother until years after her mother's death.

The effects of the removal of children, on both the individuals and the families where children have been removed, are clearly intergenerational. One individual described how his father and all his aunts and uncles were removed from their mother because provincial authorities suspected that she was working as a prostitute. The children were for the most part placed in reform schools and all grew up troubled, violent, and alcoholic. This legacy of violence and alcoholism has shaped the lives of the grand-children as well, who struggle with their own addictions and who have never tried to return to their grandmother's community because they know that they will not be accepted there after two generations of removal. This legacy extends also to the children and grandchildren of the survivors of residential schools. A number of individuals spoke of their parents' alcoholism after residential school, including one woman whose mother has been missing for a decade and is presumed murdered. The effects of such losses on the lives of some of the participants were profound and palpable.

The reality of illegal adoptions, the "sale" of Indian children, and the all-too-casual removal of Native children into temporary foster care was also spoken about by a few of the participants. One individual described how her mother was sold from the Navajo Nation to a Saskatchewan family where she grew up as a farm labourer, until her parents were able to find her.[3] The emotional scarring that this woman carried from her childhood was later visited upon her daughter, who was forbidden any expression of Navajo culture in her childhood, due to her mother's internalized self-hatred. Another woman spoke of the damage to the fabric of her family during childhood because the hospital's nuns had taken her sister away from her mother at birth and place the baby in foster care with a white family. The nuns wanted to force her unwed mother to marry; if the mother refused, they were going to make the daughter a ward of the state. The pressure on the woman to marry the children's father forced the family to relocate far from the support of extended family, so that the father could find enough work to support the family. This relocation caused years of chaos in the family home. Meanwhile, the trauma of being willfully removed from her family and placed in foster care for no reason other than racism remains with the daughter who was fostered out so arbitrarily.

Almost unnoticed initially in these stories of individual and family suffering and alienation from community and culture was the constant mention of loss of Indian status. The Métis people described how status Indian grandmothers "became" Métis by marrying Métis fathers. Others spoke of living off-reserve for generations and of never having *had* status. Others described their mothers' losing and regaining status, or losing status themselves for marrying non-Natives. When these separate instances were added up, I discovered that *nineteen* out of thirty individuals came from families where one or both grandparents had had Native status; however, only twelve of these individuals had status themselves, and only five would be able to pass status on to their children. For all but eight of the nineteen people, loss of status had separated their families from their reserves for good. Other western Métis, although they were from families who were dark-skinned, Cree-speaking and indistinguishable from Cree Indians in any way other than status, had never been granted status for a variety of reasons and so had always been designated "Métis." These individuals suffered from racism, and yet lacked the treaty rights to education, health care, or off-season hunting, which would have made their lives significantly better. From the interviews, it appeared that being deprived of, or losing, Indian status was one of the central methods by which Native peoples historically were removed from their communities, the primary source not only of their livelihood but of their identity.

The cumulative picture of profound loss that these small- and large-scale official and unofficial policies have created in the lives of the people who lived them—loss of identity, loss of familial connections, loss of access to parents or children, loss of any sense of rootedness in community, and most profoundly, loss of knowledge of language and culture—must be taken into consideration. The participants of my study are all survivors of policies designed one way or another to destroy their distinct identities as Native people and to erase all records of their existence. These experiences mark urban mixed-race people as survivors of particular policies of cultural genocide. The effect of this continuous pressure to remove Native people from their communities is that once removed, they begin to sever all the ties that bind these individuals to their sense of their own identity as Native people.

However it is also clear that most of these processes, implemented in the past few decades, are part of a larger picture. From the earliest days of Canada's establishment as a settler colony, it has implemented policies of classification and control of Indianness that have been frankly genocidal in intent. Duncan Campbell Scott, Deputy Superintendent of Indian Affairs in the mid-nineteenth century, described the goals of his enfranchisement[4] policy as follows:

> I want to get rid of the Indian problem…. After one hundred years of being in close contact with civilisation it is enervating to the individual or to a band to continue in that state of tutelage, when he or they are able to take their positions as British citizens or Canadian citizens, to support themselves and stand alone. That has been the whole purpose of Indian education and advancement since the earliest times… Our object is to continue until there is not a single Indian in Canada that has not been absorbed into the body politic, and there is no Indian question, and no Indian department. (Scott, quoted in Miller 207)

It is clear that from the start legislation created to define and restrict Indianness has been created with this goal: to control Native people, with the ultimate object their assimilation and disappearance as peoples. Below I will explore the history of legislation controlling Native identity.

Historical Definitions of Indianness

To be federally recognized as a status Indian in Canada, an individual must be able to comply with strict standards of government regulation. The effect of having Native identity so highly regulated by a body of laws such as the Indian Act is that our ways of understanding Native identity are, in a sense, shaped by these various laws. The Indian Act, in this respect, is much more than a set of regulations that have controlled every aspect of Indian life for over a century. It provides ways of understanding Native identity, organizing a conceptual framework that has shaped contemporary Native life in ways that now are so familiar as to almost seem "natural." To treat the Indian Act merely as a set of policies to be repealed, or even as a genocidal scheme, which we can simply choose not to believe in, ignores how having the identity of colonized people classified by colonial government regulations can strongly influence their understand of their identity. The practices dictated by the Indian Act—in particular, the manner in which Native women for over a century lost their Indian status if they married white men, and how "halfbreeds" (now called "Métis") have been excluded from any recognition as Indian—in many cases now seem normal or even "natural" in most Native communities.[5] We now behave as if the different categories of Nativeness, such as status Indian, non-status and Métis, have always existed—instead of recognizing that these categories were created by the settler government to divide us.

Why was the settler government of the colony then known as Upper Canada so intent on controlling Native identity? The primary reason seems to have been to control the widespread intermarriage between Native women and white men, which was a feature of every region where the fur trade existed. On a deeper level, these definitions then controlled who would have access to Native land and who would have the rights of white settlers, including the right to inherit their property.

Legislation defining who was Indian was first put into place in 1850. In that year, the newly unified Province of Canada passed legislation to "protect the lands and property of Indians" within the colony. This legislation, designed to reinforce the settlers' rights to land within the existing colony by restricting Indians to specific territories within it, had one feature that set the terms through which further treaties would be negotiated with the Province of Canada. For the first time, this legislation defined who was to be considered "Indian": anybody who was reputed to have Indian blood and to be living with a band, anyone married to such a person, anyone residing with Indians either of whose parents was Indian, and anyone adopted as a child by Indians and still living with them (Miller 109–110). The truly significant feature of this legislation was that until that point, no European settler government had ever claimed the authority to define who was or was not a member of an Indigenous nation. Prior to this, the Indigenous nations had officially been recognized as "foreign powers" equal in stature to the colonial government (Milloy 56).

The timing of this legislation was crucial. In 1850, the newly unified Province of Canada was engaged in the first step of its expansion into what is now Northern Ontario, through negotiating the Robinson-Huron and Robinson-Superior treaties. These treaties marked the first time that Native peoples were able to negotiate the mandatory setting aside of reserve lands as part of treaty negotiations (Dickason, *Canada's First Nations*, 255). From that point, it was clearly in the interests of the settler government to gain some form of control over who could be defined as Indian, that is, over who would have the right to have reserve land set aside and who could safely be ignored as irrelevant to the process. As Canada expanded onto the western plains, ever more stringent standards were set over who would be recognized as Indian and who would be classified as "mixed blood" and left out of the treaty process.

Within the existing Province of Canada (at that point consisting of what is now southern Ontario and southern Quebec), the laws created to regulate Native identity helped to appease the anxieties of European settlers about how to assert control social control over the colony when faced with the presence of large numbers of mixed-bloods who had inhabited the region since the days of the Great Lakes fur trade. Globally, the European colonial settlements that developed on other peoples' lands have always been obsessed with how to maintain colonial control. Rigidly asserting differences between "Europeans" and "Natives" was the primary means through which they sought to create white social solidarity and cohesion among groups of European settlers who had little else in common but the fact that they weren't Indigenous to the lands they were occupying. The very existence of settler societies therefore has always depended on maintaining the strictest racial apartheid, on emphasising racial difference, white superiority and "Native" inferiority (Stoler 53). This practice flies in the face of the actual origins of French and English settlements in North America—which began with displaced and often marginal white men, whose success with trade and often their very survival depended on their ability to marry into Indigenous families, and who in many cases had few loyalties to Europe and empire. Because of this, in the early days of the fur trade and French and English settlement, the boundaries between who should be considered "European" and who should be considered "Native," and by what means, were not always clear. In the east coast French colonies, for example, the manner in which Acadians not only intermarried with Mi'kmaq people but began to adopt their ways of life was troubling to colonial authorities, who began to pass laws that restricting intermarriage—and prevented Native wives and children from inheriting European family fortunes.[6]

For English settlers, the fact that by 1830 there were over fifty Métis communities surrounding their settlements (RCAP, Vol.1, Sect. 6.2: 150) made it difficult for them to maintain clear boundaries between colonizers and colonized. Social control depended on being able to clearly identify who was white, with the rights to land and citizenship, and who was Native, without those rights. Clearly, if the mixed-race children of white men who married Native women were to inherit their fathers' property, they had to be legally classified as white. As a result, in 1869, the *Gradual Enfranchisement Act* was passed, which stipulated that any Native woman who married a non-Native would lose her Indian status and any right to band membership. It was this statute that, for the first time, created the legal categories of "status Indian" and "non-status Indian" (Miller 114). Prior to this, Canada's definition of who was Indian involved a loose, general, non-restrictive definition. Such legislation, however, could not allow for the kind of control that could make a person born Native (and her offspring) legally white. In order to do this, "Indianness" had to be legally codified, to make it a category that could be granted or withheld, according to the needs of the settler society. This legislation was incorporated into the Indian Act of 1876 and all subsequent revisions, until 1985. As a result, for 116 years, the Indian Act removed the Native status of all Native women who married white men, and, particularly after 1951, forced them to leave their communities.[7] Creating the legal category of "status Indian" enabled the settler society to create the fiction of a Native person who was by law no longer Native, whose offspring could be considered white. Because of the racist patriarchal framework governing white identities, European women who married Native men were considered to have stepped outside the social boundaries of whiteness. They became, officially, status Indians.

This legislation removing Indian status from Native women who married white men also had the affect of removing the status of any Native women who married a non-status Indian man, including anybody who was Métis, American Indian, or Canadian non-status Indian. In this way, countless individuals with little intermarriage in their families became non-status Indians or were classified as "halfbreeds."

The results, for Native communities, of this long-term gender discrimination have been disastrous. The majority of the 25,000 Indians who lost status and were forced to leave their communities between 1876 and 1985 did so because of gender discrimination in the Indian Act. With their loss of status, not only this 25,000 people but also their children and grandchildren, were lost to their communities of origin. Estimates of the Indigenous population in Canada at the time of European contact range from two million to six million, but by the time Bill C-31, which ended this discrimination, was passed in 1985, there were only 350,000 status Indians left in Canada (Holmes 8).[8]

After over a century of gender discrimination in the Indian Act, the idea that it is somehow acceptable for Native women to lose status for marrying non-status or non-Native men has become a normalized aspect of Native life in many communities. As a result, the very notion of which Native people should even be considered to *be* "mixed race" is highly shaped by gender. Because Native men who married white women were allowed to bring these women onto reserves and raise their children as Native children, the family histories of many on-reserve Native people have routinely included the presence of white women married to Native men, as well as (in some cases) the children of Native women who had babies by white men but were not married to them.[9] These experiences have not been seen, or theorized, as "mixed-race" experiences. The children of a Native father and a white mother have never had to leave their communities.[10] Native reserves, particularly those adjacent to white settlements, may have grown progressively mixed-race under these circumstances—but they have not been *called* mixed-race communities, and on-reserve mixed-race families have therefore not been externalized *as* mixed-race people. It has been the children of Native mothers and white or Métis fathers who have been forced through loss of Indian status to become urban Indians, and who, in their Native communities of origin, are often regarded as outsiders because they *have* been labelled as "not being Indian" (implicitly because they are mixed race and grew up in an urban environment).

Gender has thus been crucial to determining not only who has been able to stay in Native communities but also who has been called "mixed-race" and externalized because of this. In this respect, gender discrimination in the Indian Act has shaped what we think about who is Native, who is "mixed-blood," and who is entitled to access to Indian land. These beliefs are only rendered more powerful by the strongly protectionist attitudes towards preserving Native culture as it is lived on reserves at present, where outsiders may be seen as profoundly threatening to community identity.

Legislated control of Native identity not only happened along the lines of gender, however. A central aspect of how Native identity has been controlled in Canada has been to externalize those who are considered mixed-blood from Indianness—as part of a project to further control and limit who could be included in treaty-signing and who would have land set aside for them. When Canada passed the *Gradual Enfranchisement Act* in 1869, a blood quantum requirement was added for the first time to the definition of an Indian. After 1869, the only people eligible to be considered Indian were those who had at least one-quarter Indian blood (Dickason, *Canada's First Nations*, 251). With the expansion of Canada into the western regions of the continent, however, officials in the Indian Affairs, in negotiating treaties with the new Nations they encountered, began the practice of exerting much more stringent controls over who would be accepted as Indian. As a result, when the Indian Act was created in 1876, it contained a provision that for the first time excluded anybody who was not considered to be "pure Indian" from Indianness. It stated:

> no half-breed head of a family (except the widow of an Indian, or a half-breed who has already been admitted into a treaty) shall… be accounted an Indian, or entitled to be admitted into any Indian treaty. (Canada, Indian Act, Section 3, 1876. R.S.C., 1951, quoted in Waldram 281)

But who was "Indian" and who was "half-breed"? These distinctions have to a tremendous extent been *created* by colonial categories, as well as being regulated by them. While many Métis communities have had extremely different histories and have been culturally distinct from status Indian communities, in some instances the differences between "Indians" and so-called "halfbreeds" have been quite minor. Most Native bands have had mixed-race members, and marriages between halfbreeds and treaty Indians have always been a reality. Many people of Native heritage have been eligible for either treaty or Métis scrip, and the extent to which they chose one or the other has depended on a broad range of factors.[11] In some cases, whole families were split, with some family members opting to "become" Métis while others opted to "become" status Indians.[12] It has been the Indian Act which has played the largest role not only in *creating* the separate category of "halfbreed" in regions where no such concept existed, but in forcibly excluding mixed-race people from Native communities, thereby externalizing them from "Indianness."

It is, therefore, important to recognize that the process of differentiating between "Indians" and "halfbreeds" did not necessarily conform either to actual racial blood quantum or to individual self-identification. In the fifty year interval during which the numbered treaties one to eleven were negotiated with Native bands across western Canada and the subarctic, treaty commissioners in each location set up tables where potential halfbreeds were to present themselves, individual by individual, to be judged *what* they were by white officials. In a context where racial mixing was frequently difficult to determine, factors such as lifestyle, language, and residence were employed (Waldram 281). Thus ascribed, an individual became, irrevocably, "Indian" or "halfbreed" (as did their descendants). Many Native families who were away when registration was first carried out never made treaty lists and ended up being classified as halfbreeds. Indeed, whole bands that were absent during treaty signing similarly lost any chance of acquiring Native status and became, de facto, "halfbreed" communities. In other parts of Canada, where the treaties did not expressly separate "halfbreeds" from "Indians" in the way that the numbered treaties in western Canada did, such individuals were usually considered to be "non-status Indians."

The government frequently sought to "winnow out" from Indianness all who could be claimed to be Métis. In 1879, the Indian Act was amended to enable individuals to withdraw from treaty, to take scrip and be counted as Métis (Hatt 197). Because of the wide-spread destitution on the newly created Indian reserves, and because halfbreed money scrip could immediately be cashed, a rush to leave treaty status on the part of some bands, regardless of ancestry, ensued, until regulations were created that ensured that individuals who "led the mode of life of Indians" were not to be granted discharge from treaty (Hatt 197). In rare cases, individuals known to be half or three-quarters Indian, were said to be following "an Indian way of life," and were destitute and prevented by hunting regulations from living off the land, were allowed to be taken into treaty (Coates and Morrison 259). The numbered treaties were thus crucial to the project of forcibly identifying and segregating "halfbreeds" from "Indians," regardless of how individuals saw themselves.

If the preceding history clarifies anything, it is that both "Indian" and "Métis" identities have been shaped to a phenomenal extent by discriminatory legislation in the Indian Act. In this sense, to view these groups solely as the products of entirely different histories and the bearers of entirely different destinies belies the common origins of both groups, as members of Aboriginal nations who faced colonization pressures in different ways, or who were classified in different ways by colonial legislation. Treaty Indians and the Métis—like status and non-status Indians in general—represent two very distinct sides of a common history. Status Indians have been removed from most of their traditional territory and confined to reserves, but the Métis have been forcibly excluded from any membership in Native communities. Thus they have been externalized from Indianness, deprived of their rights as Aboriginal peoples, and given little option but to pursue an entirely separate path to empowerment.

Contemporary Mixed-Race Urban Native People

As the previous section demonstrates, for over 150 years, Native people's understanding of their own identities has been strongly affected by these government policies controlling who should be considered Indian and who should not. This long history of government control has been central to policies designed to eliminate the presence of Native people in Canada, and still shapes how many of us see "Indianness" today. Moreover, for urban Native people, especially if we are of mixed ancestry, the images of "Indianness" that are presented to us in mainstream culture, and the maze of academic assumptions about what "Indianness" is, often encourages us to hold a yardstick to our lives and our families' lives by way of measuring to what extent we should be considered "really" Native. How Native do we look? Do we have status or not? Do we speak our language? How much do we know about our culture? In essence, *how much* Native we can be said to be.

In a sense, to even talk about mixed-race urban Native identity, then, may seem as if it is simply falling into this trap, which the white society sets so well for us: weighing and measuring "Indianness" to see how well we fit. Many people have responded to the phenomenal divisions created by government classification and control of Native identity have created by insisting simply that "we are all Native people—the differences between us are not important." While this is a valuable step, it often ignores the experiences of many Native people who are mixed-race and urban and who need to explore the ways that we *don't* fit, for example, the way that we are often challenged to explain our difference or our exclusion from some circles. On the other hand, insisting we are all Native people erases the power differences between those Native people who can pass as white and those who cannot avoid regularly facing racism for *looking* Native. However, ultimately this stance ignores the very real differences in entitlement that exist between status Indians and those who are non-status, and to a growing extent, those that are urban and those that are reserve-based.

The family histories, for example, demonstrated that there were broad differences between people who came from families who had been mixed-race for more than one generation and those who were first generation mixed-race. For urban people whose families had been mixed-race for a generation , Native identity was silenced in such profound ways that the children and grandchildren of these families were permanently uncertain as to who they were and where they came from. These individuals, in returning to the Native community, often had to negotiate between family members who no longer identified as Native and communities which expected anybody who identified as Native to be "100% Indian" in blood and experience. The label "wannabee" was most often applied to these individuals.

There were also differences between those whose families had been mixed-race before they left the reserve and those who had only inter-married with whites after becoming urbanized. It was clear from some peoples' histories that their parents had occupied positions of authority in Native communities because they were light skinned. One individual, whose light-skinned mother taught school in fly-in Native communities, described being brought up to avoid other Native children and to only play with the white girl whose parents ran the store on the reserve.

Differences in experiences between status Indians and Métis people in western Canada were also occasionally discussed in the interviews. One Métis individual, despite the racism he suffered while growing up in the white society, saw Métis people as much better off than status Indians because they did not have to go to residential school. Another individual described how her dark-skinned Métis mother, in the face of the alcoholism, and physical and sexual abuse that she faced in the urban Métis ghetto of the western town she grew up in, envied status Indians because they could get away from violence and alcoholism in the community by going away to school.

It is clear that although mixed-race urban Native people share a common legacy of bearing the brunt of policies designed to remove our Native identities, we are positioned differently depending on our family histories, our appearance, and whether or not we have Indian status. Below, I will explore some of these differences and their significance.

Appearance

Twelve out of the thirty people I interviewed were indistinguishable in appearance from white people, in their own eyes and in the eyes of most observers. About a third of the people were very dark, and did not even appear to *be* mixed-race. The remainder were people who looked non-white but not necessarily Native. As urban Native people, surrounded by a non-Native society which sees "Indianness" solely as a matter of race, appearance has been crucially important to the people I interviewed, especially those who are adoptees or who grew up in families where Native identity has been denied. Peoples' experiences with having an appearance that did not fit their identity differed. These experiences bordered on the tragic in the case of two white-looking individuals whose parents had been adopted off-reserve, were never reunited with their families, and did not bother attempting to reconnect with their communities of origin because they knew they would simply be turned away as "white people." For another white-looking woman the experience was surreal when she was arrested with a group of other Native people, all of them charged with being drunk and disorderly, and she was pulled from the cell, released, and lectured by a paternalistic white police chief about the dangers of "hanging around with Indians." Of the individuals who had grown up in families that disregarded their Native heritage, the darker individuals spoke with pleasure of how validating it was to join the urban community, and how, in particular, the elders there were a source of strength to them, for seeing them as *really* being Native. By comparison, the white-looking individuals who had grown up alienated from their communities spoke of how devastating it was when urban elders ignored and rejected them. This seemed, to them, to be the ultimate expression that they weren't *really* Native. Most of the white-looking people simply described routine daily experiences of alternate rejection and affirmation, of coming from Native environments where they were known and trusted into other Native environments where they were viewed with suspicion and hostility, of how wearying it was to negotiate the same reactions day after day, year after year, and how difficult they found it at times to maintain a sense of trust around other Native people in the face of such ever-changing circumstances. A few people deliberately limited their contact with other Native people and worked in non-Native environments to avoid rejection for looking too white.

This was much more common with white-looking women than white-looking men. While the groups are too small and not balanced enough in numbers to be statistically sound, the fact that each of the six white-looking men I interviewed was working in the Native community, while three of the five white-looking women spoke of not fitting into the Native community and chose to work in white environments instead, suggests that white-looking Native women might find it more difficult to negotiate a place in the Native community than their male counterparts. One woman, a brilliant student, spoke of her decision to not go into law, because it struck her that it was difficult enough for a Native woman in law without having to constantly face hostility for being a Native woman lawyer who looked white. By comparison, one of the white-looking men was a lawyer and while he saw his appearance as something needing constant negotiation, he never saw it as a career barrier.

Gender disparity also existed around poverty and wealth in other respects. Of the poorest and least-educated people I interviewed, the least-educated man (a white-looking individual with a grade six education and a criminal record) was a thriving artist and activist who made his living producing small movies and doing public speaking. However, the three least-educated women (all with Grade eleven education and with no criminal records) were on welfare and struggled with depression and a strong sense of marginalization (including two of the white-looking women).

A similar gender difference existed with respect to the issue of choice of partner. While all of the white-looking women I interviewed mentioned that Native men did not seem to want them because they were too white looking, only one out of six white-looking men made this comment.

Because most of the white-looking individuals I interviewed witnessed the racism that darker siblings or parents faced every day, they were often quite clear that looking white protected them from racism in ways they could not ignore, even though it made it more difficult for them to negotiate their daily lives within the urban Native community. Most of the people I interviewed, however, did not have much sense of the extent of the daily privilege they enjoyed from having white skin. They were aware that they were not targeted for racist hostility—but they did not have much sense of how much easier it was to rent an apartment, apply for a bank loan or a job in the mainstream society, or deal with the government bureaucracy. Their concerns about not fitting in within the Native community at times appeared to overshadow their awareness of the fact that their lives were made much easier by virtue of *not* looking Native. Darker-skinned Native people, on the other hand, sometimes acknowledged that they saw white-looking people who reclaimed their Native identity as purely self-serving. They referred to the fact that the presence of numbers of white-looking Native people working in the Native community only lessens opportunities for the darker Native people, who not only have to compete against white people for jobs in the mainstream society, but also have to compete against white-looking individuals in the Native community as well.

On a daily basis, many individuals in the Toronto Native community are attempting to disregard the importance of looking Indian in the interest of overcoming dominant-culture stereotypes about who is a "real" Indian and who is not. My study, however, suggests that these attempts are not taking into account the ongoing racism in Canadian society which continues to so bitterly oppress people who *look* Native. It may be that having white-looking people identify with their Native heritage provides opportunities for these individuals to promote Native empowerment from a position of relative strength. However, unless divisions related to appearance are actually respectfully addressed, in different settings, the different circumstances that white-looking and dark Native people face will continue to be unspoken.

A different but related issue is cultural differences. Two of the dark-skinned people I interviewed spoke of how they are often made unwelcome, not because of their appearance but because they are too *culturally* different. Both women—an African-Cherokee from the United States and a Mapuche woman from Chile—spoke of how they are seen as too "multicultural" in the urban Native community in Toronto. It appears that people who are mixtures of Native and white (particularly if the white background is Anglo-Canadian) are more easily accepted in the urban community than those who are Native and Black or who are Native in appearance but whose first languages is Spanish or another non-Indigenous language rather than English. Because the future generation of urban Native people in Toronto will probably be increasingly multiracial, given the high rates of contemporary intermarriage between people of colour and Native people, it will be an important issue for Native people to consider. As people of multiple cultural backgrounds, and whose non-Native heritages are from all around the world, struggle to create new, hybrid Native identities that still affirm their connections to Indigenous communities, the next decade will probably signify a radical shift in our understandings of what it means to be urban Native people.

Status

While divisions between those who look Native and those who look white appear to be negotiable among the people I interviewed, the issue of being status or non-status or Métis represented a fundamental division that could not be surpassed. Everybody I interviewed asserted loftily, as if it was all too obvious, that status had *nothing* to do with whether one is a Native person or not. At the same time, almost everybody, when pressed, admitted that they did feel status Indians *were* "more Native" than non-status Indians or Métis. The status Indians I interviewed frequently indicated their determination that they would only have children with partners who would enable them to pass their status on to their children. They expressed the view that status was the only thing protecting Native people from genocide. The non-status Indians and Métis, on the other hand, saw the divisiveness that status creates as being the greatest weakness that Native people face.

One issue that became clear throughout the interviews was the incredibly diverse range of experiences Native people have had with respect to status. Some of the people I interviewed had had multiple experiences of gaining and losing status in their family (for example, losing it through a grandfather being enfranchised, regaining it when a mother married a status Indian, and losing it themselves on marrying a non-Native prior to 1985). Some individuals came from families where, of different siblings with the same parents, some were status and some non-status, depending on whether their mothers were married to their fathers at time of birth. Two could not regain status because their grandfathers had been born in the United States, where their families had fled to escape persecution after the 1885 North West Rebellion. One woman was a federally recognized American Indian whose band originally came from Canada but had been pushed south by Loyalist settlers. In Canada, where her family had always lived a stone's throw from the reserve boundaries, which ended at the American border, she was considered non-status. A number of individuals could not regain status because of the second-generation cut off with Bill C-31.

In surveying the participants' experiences, it becomes clear that Indian status has, for many people, been granted or removed in a purely arbitrary fashion. However, among the people I interviewed, status (in conjunction with band membership) remains a fundamental dividing line between experiences of Indianness, marking clear divisions around entitlement and non-entitlement, despite the attempts by each individual I interviewed to minimize its importance through statements such as "status has nothing to do with who is Native." The fact that urban Native people, who are struggling valiantly to make their own definitions of who is Native and who is not, do not seem able to easily come to terms over the issue of status suggests that government regulation of Native identity has far more power over different groups than is frequently acknowledged. Status is more than a matter of "believing in" government categories or not—it is, above all (along with band membership) the fundamental determinant over who has access, or who should have access, to whatever fragments of land still remain in Indian hands. Every government action with respect to Native people—whether it is a funding decision, a change in policy, or a response to a land claim—enhances divisions on the basis of status. Clearly it is not enough to simply say "status has nothing to do with being Indian" as a means of overcoming divisions—when, in fact , those divisions are about entitlement, particularly to funding but also to land.

The Future

With all the people I interviewed, a major concern was the future of urban Native people. Most individuals felt that in addition to strengthening knowledge of culture and building a strong urban infrastructure of Native organizations to service the needs of the community, building closer ties to reserve communities were important. For many of the individuals, this reflected their own feelings about being urban, and their own, personal relationship to their community of origin—their understanding of the extent to which they would be able to attempt to undo past losses through rebuilding ties or relearning their language, for example. The conversation returned, again and again, to the manner in which so many urban Native people no longer have known familial connections to their Native communities of origin. How can we work to rebuild our Indigenous nations when as urban people we do not have membership in any First Nation? And why is the current network of over 600 tiny "matchbook" size First Nations, currently occupying less than one percent of the traditional landmass, generally seen as the only viable expression of nation-building? What about the growing numbers of urban Native who have no communities to return to?

In the discussions about the future, the issue of developing new forms of nation-building was discussed. Some individuals felt that all urban non-status individuals should join the Métis nation as an advocacy group, while at the same time working towards being "adopted" back into their home communities in order to rebuild cultural connections. Others were angry about not having their status reinstated, or having band membership denied them and felt that regaining the membership their mothers had lost in the communities was the primary direction for empowerment. From the discussions, however, it emerged that a number of individuals recognized that there is no "going back" for many of us—we cannot rebuild ourselves as "full-blooded traditionalists" in the communities that our parents or grandparents were separated from. The notion of embracing different forms of nation-building—such as revitalizing the traditional confederacies, which were the forms of political organization at the time of colonization—is only beginning to be explored. Adopting traditional forms of governance, those ways of living in a community that preceded Indian Act divisions and worked well for thousands of years, was felt to be the most promising route to take out of the government-regulated divisions among Native people. On the other hand, individuals also highlighted the fact that without a deep understanding of how these divisions have been imposed on us, there is a danger that these rebuilt or new forms of organization will develop the same divisions as before, restricting citizenship only to those with Indian status, as the present Indian Act system does. Nevertheless, if urban and non-status Native people make strong efforts to embrace these ancient and alternative political frameworks, it could do much to strengthen these more traditional organizations, to the empowerment of all of us.

Wel'alioq! Um sed nogumak. (Thank you! All my relations.)

Endnotes

[1] The term "genocide" is not used lightly or casually. The meaning of the term, as coined by Raphael Lemkin in 1944, during the discussions leading to the United Nations Genocide Convention, was given as follows: "Generally speaking, genocide does not necessarily mean the immediate destruction of a nation, *except when* accomplished by mass killing of all the members of a nation. It is intended rather to signify a coordinated plan of different actions aimed at destruction of the essential foundations of the life of national groups, with the aim of annihilating the groups themselves. The objective of such a plan would be disintegration of the political and social institutions, of culture, language, national feelings, religion, and the economic existence of national groups, and the destruction of personal security, liberty, health,

dignity, and the lives of individuals belonging to such groups...
Genocide has two phases: one, destruction of the national pattern of
the oppressed group: the other, the imposition of the national pattern
of the oppressor" (Lemkin quoted in Churchill 12–13). The United
Nation's 1948 Convention on Punishment and Prevention of the Crimes
of Genocide (UN GOAR Res. 260A (iii) 9 December 1948, effective 21
January 1951) delineates five categories of action that are deemed genocidal
when directed against an identified "national, ethnical, racial or
religious group" and therefore criminal under international law. Only
one of these involves outright killing (U.N. Doc. E/A.C.25/S.R. 1–28,
quoted in Churchill 14):

A.   Killing members of the group.
B.   Causing serious bodily or mental harm to members of the group.
C.   Deliberately inflicting on the group conditions of life calculated
     to bring about its physical destruction in whole or in part.
D.   Imposing measures intended to prevent births within the group.
E.   Forcibly transferring children of the group to another group.

[2] According to Peterson and Brown, this was a common practice
in Acadia and New France for generations (Peterson and Brown 8).

[3] Little is known of the phenomenon of selling people, but some
investigation into the practice is taking place.

[4] This paper will go on to describe the blood quantum restrictions
and gender restrictions created by the Gradual Enfranchisement Act,
later preserved in subsequent versions of the Indian Act. However,
the whole topic of enfranchisement—governmental legislation that at
different times encouraged or forced various Native peoples to give
up their Indian status in exchange for Canadian citizenship and the
abandoning of any collective rights or band membership—will not be
explored. While enfranchisement was the linchpin of governmental
policies aimed at destroying Native peoples as distinct groups in
Canada, generalized resistance to voluntary enfranchisement was so
strong that the numbers of individuals who gave up their Indian status—
even during the years when it was legal to compulsorily enfranchise individuals—have always remained relatively low. This is particularly
noticeable when compared to the numbers of individuals who lost
status because of gender discrimination (Holmes 4).

[5] It is important, however, to take into account the fact that Métis
identity historically has been more than a matter of government
classification. Some mixed-blood communities have had extremely
different histories and have been very distinct culturally from reserve
communities; they have also asserted their goals and needs as such.

In other instances, however, the differences between "Indians" and "halfbreeds" have been quite minor, and distinctions between them have been created quite arbitrarily by government classification and regulation of Native identity. For an exploration of the range of identities adopted by mixed-race Native peoples, see Peterson and Brown.

[6] A number of European French families attempted to challenge the inheritance of Quebec fortunes by Native wives and children, and some were successful. Meanwhile, in 1735, an edict was passed which required the consent of the governor or commanding officer for all mixed marriages in New France to be considered legal, while another edict restricted the rights of Native women to inherit their French husband's property (Dickason, "From 'One Nation' in the Northeast," 28).

[7] Prior to 1951, at least some recognition was given to the needs of Native women who were deserted or widowed. Native women who lost their status were no longer legally Indian, and no longer formal band members, but they were not considered to have the full rights that enfranchised women had. These women were often issued informal identity cards, known as "red tickets," which identified them as entitled to shares in treaty monies, and informally recognized their band membership to the extent that some of them were able to live on the reserve. However, the 1951 enfranchisement provisions compulsorily enfranchised all women who married non-status or non-Native men. This meant that they not only lost band membership, reserve residency, or any property they might have held on reserve but also access to any treaty monies or band assets, a process referred to by Mr. Justice Laskin as "statutory banishment." The 1951 Indian Act amendments thus actually increased discrimination against Native women, despite the trend towards greater egalitarianism in the rest of Canadian society (RCAP, Vol. 1, Sect. 9: 301–302).

[8] It is impossible to do a "before and after" comparison of these figures. At the time the Gradual Enfranchisement Act was passed in 1869, "Canada" consisted of southern Ontario and Quebec, and parts of the Maritimes. Furthermore, Native women began to have their status removed well before any census of the number of status Indians in these regions was taken. What might be informative, however, is to take into account the various estimates of pre-contact populations and compare this to the 1985 figures. While Olive Dickason, relying on Russell Thornton's figures that estimate 7 million to 8 million Native people north of Mexico in pre-Columbian times (Thornton 22–25), suggests that the Canadian land mass was home to approximately 2 million Native people on contact (Dickason, *Canada's First Nations*, 63),

Henry F. Dobyns has estimated that 18 million people existed north of Mexico at the time of contact (Dobyns 342–43). Taking the conservative estimate that only one-third of this population lived in what is now Canada, the figures still suggest a population of 6 million Native people in Canada at the time of contact, compared to the 350,000 people who were recognized as "Indian" in Canada in 1985. The population estimates of Thornton and Dobyns are based on extensive studies by what is known as the "Berkeley School" of anthropologist, whose methods include exhaustive examination of church and governmental archives listing tribute, baptismal and marriage records, historical documents, and studies of environmental carrying capacities of specific regions.

[9] Under Section 12(2), of the pre-1985 Indian Act, "illegitimate" children of status Indian women could also lose status if the alleged father was known to not be a status Indian and if the child's status as an Indian was "protested" by the Indian agent. This legislation was removed in 1985 (Holmes 4).

[10] However, a child of a Native father, a white paternal grand-mother, and white mother had to leave at the age of 21. Until 1985, Section 12(1)(a)(iv) of the Indian Act, known as the "double mother" clause, removed status from children when they reached the age of 21 if their mother and paternal grandmother did not have status before marriage (Holmes 4)

[11] For example, the churches played a role in influencing their parishioners in their choice of identity. Because church missions received government grants based on a per capital enrollment of treaty Indians in their schools, they generally encouraged their parishioners to take treaty rather than scrip (Harrison, 1985:76).

[12] Coates and Morrison describe one example of the mutability of categories of "Indian" and "halfbreed," within the family of Marguerite Bouvier. Born in Winnipeg in 1854, both she and her son Michel received scrip as Métis, but her three daughters took treaty as Indians (Coates and Morrison 258–9).

Works Cited

Churchill, Ward *Indians Are Us? Culture and Genocide in Native North America*. Toronto: Between the Lines, 1994.

Coates, K.S. and W. R. Morrison. "More Than a Matter of Blood: The Federal Government, the Churches and the Mixed Blood Population of the Yukon and the Mackenzie River Valley, 1890–1950." *1885 and After: Native Society in Transition*. Ed. F. Laurie Barron and James B. Waldram. Regina, Saskatchewan: University of Regina, Canadian Plains Research Centre, 1986. 253–278.

Dickason, Olive Patricia. *Canada's First Nations: A History of Founding Peoples from Earliest Times*. Toronto: Oxford University Press, 1992.

_____ ."From 'One Nation' in the Northeast to 'New Nation' in the Northwest: A Look at the Emergence of the Métis." *The New Peoples: Being and Becoming Métis in North America*. Ed. Jacqueline Peterson and Jennifer S. H. Brown. Winnipeg: University of Manitoba Press, 1985. 19–36.

Dobyns, Henry F. *Their Number Become Thinned: Native American Population Dynamics in Eastern North America*. Knoxville: University of Tennessee Press, 1983.

Harrison, Julia D. *Métis: People between Two Worlds*. Vancouver/Toronto: The Glenbow-Alberta Institute in association with Douglas & McIntyre, 1985.

Hatt, Ken. "The North-West Rebellion Scrip Commissions, 1885-1889." *1885 and After: Native Society in Transition*. Eds. Laurie Barron and James B. Waldram. Regina, Saskatchewan: University of Regina, Canadian Plains Research Centre, 1986. 189–204.

Holmes, Joan. *Bill C-31—Equality or Disparity? The Effects of the New Indian Act on Native Women*. Background Paper, Canadian Advisory Council on the Status of Women, 1987.

Lemkin, Raphael. *Axis Rule in Occupied Europe*. Concord, NH: Carnegie Endowment for International Peace/Rumford Press, 1944.

Miller, J. R. *Skyscrapers Hide the Heavens: A History of Indian-White Relations in Canada*. Toronto: University of Toronto Press, 1989.

Milloy, John S. "The Early Indian Acts: Developmental Strategy and Constitutional Change." *As Long as the Sun Shines and the Water Flows: A Reader in Canadian Native History*. Ed. Ian A. L. Getty and Antoine S. Lussier. Vancouver: University of British Columbia Press, 1983. 56–63.

Peterson, Jacqueline and Jennifer S. H. Brown. "Introduction." *The New Peoples: Being and Becoming Métis in North America*. Eds. Jacqueline Peterson and Jennifer S. H. Brown. Winnipeg: University of Manitoba Press, 1985. 3–18.

Royal Commission on Aboriginal Peoples (RCAP). *For Seven Generations: Report of the Royal Commission on Aboriginal Peoples*. Ottawa: Government of Canada, 1996.

Stoler, Ann. "Carnal Knowledge and Imperial Power: Gender, Race and Morality in Colonial Asia." *Gender at the Crossroads: Feminist Anthropology in the Post-Modern Era*. Ed. Micaela di Leonardo. Berkeley: University of California Press, 1991. 51–101.

Thornton, Russell. *American Indian Holocaust and Survival: A Population History Since 1492*. Norman: University of Oklahoma Press, 1987.

Waldram, James. "The 'Other Side': Ethnostatus Distinctions in Western Subarctic Native Communities." *1885 and After: Native Society in Transition*. Ed. F. Laurie Barron and James B. Waldram. Regina, Saskatchewan: University of Regina, Canadian Plains Research Centre, 1986. 279–95.

The Formalization of Métis Identities in Canadian Provincial Courts

Chris Andersen

Chris Andersen is a Ph.D. candidate in Sociology and a Professor in the School of Native Studies at the University of Alberta. His research focuses on Aboriginal identities in the courts and treatment of sentencing circles by the courts.

What does it mean to be Métis[1] in the eyes of the provincial courts in present-day Canada? What are the boundaries of Métis identities in contemporary Canadian society, and in particular in the judges' reasoning in their court decisions? How are Métis identities thought to differ from "whitestream"[2] Canadian identities, and perhaps more importantly, from those of First Nations peoples? Through an examination of several court cases and their appeals, this article explores how Canadian provincial courts are interpreting Métis rights, federally recognized in the Constitution Act of 1982. It also examines and Métis histories, which over-emphasize their Red River roots, in ways that limit when, where, and especially how they are able to hunt, fish, and engage in other traditional resource extraction activities.

The legal reasoning in current judges' decisions reflects Eurocentric understandings about Aboriginality (see Andersen; Denis). This is part of a "cultural hierarchy" where whitestream Canadian culture is placed at the top and Aboriginal cultures are placed somewhere beneath. In this hierarchy, the rights of Métis are placed below those of Indians. Although the courts are moving in the direction of granting Indians commercial resource rights, that is, the right to sell what they kill or catch (see *R. v. Marshall*, 1999; *R v. Gladstone*, 1996), they have granted only *some* Métis substance rights, that is, the right to hunt and fish for food. Granting subsistence rights is a strategy forwarded by Métis defence lawyers. And, until the most recent Métis court case, *R. v. Powley*, 1999; 2000, judges have accepted the word of defendants that they were, in fact Métis. Instead of demonstrating their "Métis-ness," Métis defendants have based their defense on trying to prove that, even though they might not consider themselves to be Indian, they live enough "like an Indian" to be considered Indians because they live a traditional lifestyle. On the other hand, treaty Indians are granted the right to hunt and fish regardless of lifestyle and do not have to demonstrate that they live "like an Indian."

The first section of this article includes a brief discussion of the idea of "race" from which "mixed blood" identities are derived. The links between the concept of race, colonialism, and the various forms of colonial governance that exercised power over the Indigenous peoples are also briefly discussed. The second section focuses more specifically on how Métis histories have been constructed, particularly the tendency of academic research to over-emphasize the link between Métis identities and the general population of the Red River settlement, an area roughly situated in and around Winnipeg, where the Métis made up roughly two thirds of the population. If, however, Métis settlements beyond the Red River settlement are included, a picture of diverse Métis communities emerges, which is in many ways as diverse as First Nations communities. The third section is a chronological overview of the case law regarding Métis hunting and fishing court challenges and pays particular attention to the importance of the concept of a subsistence lifestyle for judges when making their decisions about the validity of Métis defendants' claims. The article concludes with a discussion of the *Powley* decisions in Ontario. These are the most recent decisions regarding Métis hunting and fishing rights and are the first cases to move away from the strategy of Métis attempting to prove they live like Indians to a fuller consideration of what it means to be Métis.

"Race" and Modernity

It is important to understand the concept of race and its legacy in court decisions. To talk about "mixed blood" identities, such as those of the Métis discussed here, requires us to buy into ideas about race. To put it plainly, in order to see a particular person or group as "mixed," there must be some agreement that there are "pure" or "real"[3] races from which these mixed identities are born—such as "white" and "Indian." As a result, we in the "modern" world—and especially western societies—have a tendency to link race to identity, because our societies are founded on this very agreement. This is not necessarily an unreasonable linkage to make. For example, statistics continually demonstrate that people who self-identify as Aboriginal (that is, identify with a "race") in Canada are more likely to fall into a low socio-economic level and on average to have a low life expectancy and low educational qualifications (Royal Commission on Aboriginal Peoples, 1996, vol. 1). Race, then, is used as a defining marker by nation states in the census, for example, for such categories as income, life expectancy, education, or fertility rates. It is important to keep in mind, though, that there is *no such thing as race*. It is, at best, an abstract category that is used for various types of political and cultural purposes. For example, the idea that "black" is a race is absurd when one looks at all the different countries and cultures that may see themselves as "black" as only one part of their identity. However, the belief that race does exist has profound effects because it conjures up very singular or narrow ranges of stereotypes. When racialized stereotypes are used, there are power structures at play that raise the stakes for the consequences of these stereotypes.

What are stereotypes? Racialized stereotypes have a number of characteristics. First, they function by "get[ting] hold of the few 'simple, vivid, memorable, easily grasped and wide widely recognized' characteristics about a person, *reduc[ing]* everything about the person to those traits, *exaggerat[ing]* and then *simplify[ing]* them, and *fix[ing]* them without change or development to eternity... *stereotyping reduces, essentializes, naturalizes and fixes 'difference'*" (Hall 258, Hall's emphasis). Second, stereotypes tend to exclude by building communities or boundaries and expelling anything that does not belong (Hall 258). This is often structured—especially in situations of great power inequalities (a normal feature of racial stereotypes)—through binary oppositions: white versus black (or "red"); civilized versus primitive; modern versus traditional; commercial enterprises versus subsistent economies; innovative versus lazy; progressive versus stagnant; adult versus child. All these binary oppositions were—and continue to be—constructed in the context of a racial hierarchy. This hierarchy has had the effect of solidifying barriers between Indigenous and non-Indigenous people by denying Indigenous communities an equal "playing field" in the new, modern world. Moreover, these racialized ideologies were used by the colonizers to justify the rampant alienation of Indigenous communities from traditional lands. Through war, the pretense of treaty signing, or by simply declaring a portion of geographical territory as *terra nullius*, colonial governments "legally" cleared the way for settlement and large-scale exploitation of resources.

Why are these racialized stereotypes important in the context of this article? They are important because perceptions about the binary opposition of Aboriginal versus whitestream culture(s) are deeply embedded in legal understandings about Indigenous cultures in general and, more specifically, Métis rights. Racialized stereotypes shape the strategies used by defense attorneys and the evidence considered relevant by the judges. Where does this concept of race, and its stereotypes, come from? Well, race is strongly tied to the concept of modernity. Modernity signalled the beginning of new types of social relationships and is often linked to the growth of capitalism and the industrial revolution in Europe. It often worked by building a hierarchy of civilization(s), fixing itself at the top, and putting others beneath it. These binarisms are the heart of modernity, and it reveals how it modernity "sees" itself, especially in relation to "the past."

One of the main ways through which this past is viewed and visited by us today is through the lens of colonialism. Colonialism is fundamentally rooted in racial assumptions about those who were colonized and those who did the colonizing (see Culhane, Green, Said, and Stoler). The colonization processes treat Aboriginals as lazy or stupid *or* romanticized them as raven-haired warriors, and in order to deal with the Aboriginal population, colonial governments historically established policies and instruments such as the 1876 Indian Act or the Scrip Commissions (Tough). Even today, everyday practices still exist, such as the increased likelihood of Aboriginal defendants being denied bail, or non-Native school children making fun of Native students for not speaking "proper" English, that are responsible for, and directly involved in, supporting certain social, legal, and cultural structures (whitestream Canadian ones) at the expense and silencing of others.

For a couple hundred years at least, these ideologies, institutions, and practices anchored diverse colonial projects—those aspects of colonial governance that emerged from the differential between the policies and the actual practice. These projects penetrated distant, exotic locales, such as the area now known as Canada, and the policies ensured the continued extraction of the enormous material wealth crucial to the advancement of global imperial aggression (Blaut, and Wolf). Despite their diversity, colonial projects by the European colonial powers left a legacy of institutions and practices that tend to reflect the "colonizers' model of the world" (Blaut; Francis; Said, *Orientalism*). Maintaining the colonizers' world view (for example, seeing the British or European-Canadian citizen as "superior" to the Indian) required bureaucrats to think about, write about, and make public policies based on the idea that there were essential differences between those doing the colonizing, "us," and those subjected to colonization, "them" (Culhane; Green; Said, *Culture and Imperialism*; Stoler; Young). For example, a number of authors have noted the extent to which "Aboriginal world views" are said to differ from those of whitestream Canadians (for example, Denis; Ross; Murray and Sinclair; Royal Commission on Aboriginal Peoples). Aboriginals, these authors note, are said to live in a different world and on a different time-space continuum from whitestream Canadians, one filled with the mystical and the spiritual, and one that holds a deep connection to the land while understanding this land to be a living, breathing, sentient being. This is one stereotype and, to a certain extent, is implicit in the idea of "living an Indian mode of life"—an idea suggesting that, historically, Aboriginal communities lived a subsistence mode of life, with none of the commercial processes currently villainized by Aboriginals. It is these stereotypes that are now being challenged in contemporary court cases.

But closer examination of the facts does not support this colonial view. Far from being an accurate assessment of Aboriginal life, the "Indian" or Métis known to most Canadians may well be an invention of the European (see Burkhofer or Francis). Francis, for example, actually argues that "Indians, as we think we know them, do not exist. In fact, there may well be no such thing as an "Indian" (4). Who is this "Indian" being criticized? On the one hand, it is true that traditional Native cultures did contain some of the characteristics mentioned above. On the other hand, however, Indian and Métis communities were also deeply involved in the fur trade and fur trade posts, and had a strong, commercial side to their culture[4] (see Ray or Tough). Thus, these stories about being "one with the land" are only part of the story. But they are the part that is most easily understood and eagerly accepted by non-Natives, because they fit the stereotypes about Natives that we read about, watch on television and in movies, and pass on to others on a daily basis.

In virtually all modern nation-states, through time and repeated official "telling," these historical stories have turned into essential, taken-for-granted truths about what it means to be Aboriginal. In turn, these stories function to determine the parameters for gauging Aboriginal authenticity in Canada today. And the courts—perhaps more so than other social institutions—are one of the main ways in which this authenticity is defined and measured. For example, in the next section it can be seen that Métis culture is generally understood to be a mixture of Indigenous and European influences—hence the term *Métis* (from Old French *metis*, "mixed"). What is lost in this discussion, however, is that by virtue of contact, *all* Aboriginal cultures in Canada are a mixture of Indigenous and European cultures. Just as "colonial" communities borrowed liberally from the Indigenous communities, any Indigenous nation or community south of the border of Nunavut, the Northwest Territories, and the Yukon that was touched by the fur trade contains both white and pre-contact Indigenous facets in their cultures, such as Christianity, pots, axes, guns, fur trapping supplies, flour, to name a few. However, while all Aboriginal cultures exhibit this mixture of the "traditional" and the "modern," only the Métis are forced to *prove* their "traditionality," and therefore, only the Métis are forced to squeeze themselves into the stereotypes described above.[5]

The Histories of the Métis

The fact that it is necessary to define Métis identity and their rights reflects the origins of Métis peoples in the fur trade society prevalent between late seventeenth and late nineteenth century Canada (see Foster and Tough). Beginning sometime in the late 1600s, anywhere there was a well-established fur trading post, there was a catalyst for a Métis population. As Frank Tough put it in his expert testimony in *R. v. Morin & Daigneault* (1995; discussed later),

> [t]he Métis people have their origins in the Indian population. It comes from the fur trade, the union and creation of families with white fur traders or employers of fur trade companies and Indian women because in the sort of economy that was created, trade relations or economic relations were greatly encouraged by kin relations. (Transcript of Proceedings, Vol. III, 1995: 498)

So, liaisons between European fur traders and Native women were crucially important for advancing fur trade alliances (see Brown, *Strangers in Blood*, and Van Kirk). These liaisons led to new and separate identities that were further entrenched by collectively sharing in the hardships of the harsh, icy winter climate in the fur-trading north, an area isolated from both Indian bands and colonial communities. Initially, the offspring of the early liaisons between fur traders and Indian women tended to be re-absorbed into the mother's culture— that is, these children thought of themselves and were viewed by others as Indians (see Van Kirk and Brown, "Linguistic Solitudes and Changing Social Categories"). However, as the fur trade grew and as these offspring began intermarrying amongst themselves, they began to take on new cultural traits and new identities. They were no longer white, nor were they Indian—they were distinctly *Métis*.

The offspring of these alliances have variously been called Homeguard Indians, countryborn, Rupertslanders, *apeetagosan*, *bois-brûlé*, halfbreeds, and perhaps most famously, Métis (see Brown, "Linguistic Solitudes and Changing Social Categories"). Métis individuals and communities held various positions in the fur trade, from trappers to traders to freighters to buffalo hunters to merchants (Tough). However, Métis communities were in some ways as diverse as those of First Nations. Except for the work of the historian John Foster, most historians do not adequately acknowledge this fact, whether in terms of work considered classic to the field (for example, Giraud's *The Métis in the Canadian West* or Stanley's *The Birth of Western Canada: A History of the Riel Rebellions*) or work in a more contemporary context (Ens; Flanagan; Sprague). As a result, more often than not, the legacy of the Métis is tied to the Red River basin area in southern Manitoba, and to the writings and career of Louis Riel. As a political leader of these Métis, Riel led a Métis rebellion in the Red River settlement in 1869 and was hanged for treason in 1885 after leading a second rebellion in Saskatchewan against the Canadian government. So deeply have the Red River-Riel links pervaded the Métis literature that researchers have referred to the lack of any broader research regarding Métis diversity as "Red River myopia" (Nicks and Morgan).

There is no doubt that the Red River society was a cultural and political centre of the Métis during the fur trade years (Ens; Flanagan; Stanley; Sprague; Taylor). It served as one of the key hubs of the northern fur trade and as a centre for the commercial buffalo robe market to the south. The Métis dominated the Red River community and helped ensure the entry of Manitoba as a province into Canadian confederation. This community also served as a primary crucible for the expansion and maintenance of Métis culture across the country and into the United States. Research has, however, examined the racial and cultural ambivalence of Métis communities outside the Red River basin in northwestern Ontario (see Peterson) and in communities situated on the far reaches of the historical fur trade circuits in northern Saskatchewan, Alberta, and Northwest Territories (see Tough). In the case of the Great Lakes area around what is now northwestern Ontario, Peterson suggests that "[t]he eighteenth and nineteenth centuries saw a host of Métis intermarriages linking the dominant lineages of the Great Lakes communities," such that "a population estimate of ten thousand to fifteen thousand residents of Métis communities south and west of Lake Superior and Huron seems a plausible estimate" (63). Similarly, in his expert testimony in the *Powley* decision (discussed later), Arthur Ray, a historical geographer, suggests that "absolutely by the turn of the 19th century, you have Métis communities sprinkled throughout the Great Lakes... you have some coalescing of people together into small communities taking place" (*R. v. Powley*, 1999, Excepts From Trial Volume II: 202).[6] Peterson argues that many of the "new people" of Red River were actually transplanted inhabitants from Great Lakes communities (64). This recognition of the historical footprints of Métis communities outside of Red River has been acknowledged in a recent court case (*R. v. Powley*, 2000; 1999; discussed below), which adopted a genealogical and historical approach to defining Métis.

On the other hand, the Métis living in the northern reaches of the fur trade routes were a different story. Although there was a strong Métis presence in these regions, neither these individuals nor the communities were unconditionally Métis or Indian. That is, they were mixed and were often viewed as one or the other depending on the individual's and community's position in the fur trade, and the observer's position and knowledge. Indeed, what it meant to be Métis or Indian was, in some cases, a fairly open question. For example, when some of the Scrip Commissions travelled to Native communities, up to one-third of those receiving Scrip had previously been included in a treaty. Between 1885 and 1887, at least thirty percent of the Scrip issued went to "Treaty halfbreeds" ("Indians" withdrawing from treaty in order to apply for scrip) (Canada Sessional Papers). So, through a small bookkeeping adjustment, suddenly they were "Métis."

The identities that we see today are nowhere near as historically solid as they are made out to be. Whether you were Métis or Indian might change from family to family—or from year to year—thus there was an incredible amount of flux in these identities in some of these communities. As Tough argues, there are "very general patterns in terms of economic roles and what terms that might be used like Native, Métis, Indian, but they're not frozen, and they're in flux, they're very dynamic" (*R. v. Morin & Daigneault*, Transcript of Proceedings, Vol. III: 505). He goes on to quote James A.J. McKenna, the Treaty 10 Commissioner, who suggests that it was "'difficult to draw a line of demarcation between those who class themselves as Indians and those who elected to be treated as half-breeds. Both dress alike and *follow the same mode of life'"* Tough continues, "What it means to me [is] that whatever legal categories he was administering did not have social[,] cultural or economic[ally] separate expression" (Transcript of Proceedings, Vol. III: 575—emphasis added). Tough ends his testimony by quoting McKenna again, who stated that "'the term "Indian" is meant to include half-breed as well, and one term might include them both for it has been repeatedly stated to the commissioner that there are few, if any, pure-bred Indians in existence at the present times, referring especially to those living in the north.'" Tough added, "there's still a kind of common usage, an interchangeability of the terms" (Transcript of Proceedings, Vol. III: 592).

This very brief discussion of Métis histories has highlighted several features of historical Métis identities. First, Métis identities are synonymous with the fur trade. They are not confined just to Red River, even though that geographical area was undoubtedly a cultural and economic hub. Nor are they confined to the influence of Louis Riel. The Métis circulated throughout all aspects of fur trade society. They were important trappers, hunters, and suppliers and played an important role in moving freight and furs over the vast waterways on which the fur trade economy depended (Tough). Secondly, historically speaking, to be Métis or Indian meant different things to different people: depending on where one lived and what one's job was, one would have varying connections to the land and differing ideas about what being Métis meant. In the same way that being Canadian today means different things to different people, this would apply no less to historical Métis identities. Does this historical cultural diversity finds its ways into the court's decisions?

Métis Identities and the Courts

Before discussing the place of a defendant's lifestyle in a judge's decision, it is helpful to briefly discuss the symbolic value and organizational structure of the court system in Canada. The rule of law in both the legislature and the courts holds a tremendous legitimacy in modern nation-states such as Canada where it is the basis of governance (Aylward; Hunt). In fact, the rule of law, enshrined in such documents as the Charter of Rights and Freedoms, is seen as the triumph of modern rationality (formal rules and regulations) over the irrationality (an Aboriginal chief's decisions, supposedly made on a whim) of "primitive" societies (Culhane; Fitzpatrick; Hunt; Weber). Law plays an important role in determining the range of activities that we can legally engage in, and in doing so it is an important influence for regulating the types of lives we can and are encouraged to lead.

In addition, we live in a legal culture and are surrounded every day by media images of crime and criminality. Sensational court cases and decisions, such as the O.J. Simpson case in Los Angeles or the Karla Homolka case in Ontario, are followed by and hotly debated in the newspapers, news magazines, on talk shows, on the radio, in the universities, and often, with friends and acquaintances. The legitimacy of the courts themselves is rarely questioned—only particular aspects of unpopular or controversial decisions. And, despite the fact that virtually none of us have formal legal training or direct contact with the court apparatus, we live in the shadow of its judgments. It has this further impact on our lives because of the importance we attach to its symbolic value: how we believe it operates (McCormick 4).

The Court Structure

The Canadian court apparatus itself is comprised of a combination of federal and provincial "systems," and is fundamentally hierarchical in nature. Peter McCormick suggests technical jargon often used to describe the court process can be avoided by keeping in mind a few basic principles of Canada's court system: that less serious cases are routed towards higher volume and quicker outcome courts; that less frequent, more serious cases are routed to lower volume courts to give them more attention; that court of appeals are used to correct errors in lower court decisions while ensuring decisional equality among the court cases in the jurisdiction (that similar crimes get similar sentences, for example); and that a more general and ultimately binding court of appeal serves to promote a more general uniformity in decisions across the country (McCormick 23). Decisions delivered from a higher level of court always supersede those of a lower court, and appeals are always made from the lower to higher level, with the Supreme Court of Canada having the ultimate and final decision-making power. Thus the appeal court judges in the discussion below are ruling on decisions made in the lower courts.

Formalizing Hunting and Fishing Rights in the Courts

Before discussing the court cases, it is important to keep in mind that the Métis involved in these cases are actively choosing to take their fight to the courts. However, it is not the only route they could have chosen. For example, the largest land-based collective of Métis in Canada, the Métis Settlements in Alberta, has favoured what they call a "results-based" approach and stayed away from language of constitutional rights. They deal directly with the provincial government of Alberta rather than fight through the courts. Part of the 1990 Métis Settlements agreement set aside indefinitely a lawsuit launched by them against the Alberta government regarding resources taken out of settlement lands without adequate compensation (see Bell). In addition, urban-based Métis organizations have fought for the right to build, shape, and deliver government policies in their communities through their own organizations, such as the Métis Child and Family Services Society in Alberta. Instituting a court case is just one of several different strategies pursued by Métis individuals or communities to formalize their rights and shape their identities.

In discussing the following court cases, the "full evidence" (all the documents entered into court as evidence) of the cases is not used, rather only material contained in the published decisions is drawn on. Published accounts of court cases are an excellent way of determining the judicial reasoning of the case. What this means is that, of all the documents entered into court, the evidence used in the published decision represents what the judge thought was relevant or noteworthy enough to be included in the final decision. This selection reveals underlying ideas about what the judges understand to be the issues of the case, and more importantly, what pieces of evidence they thought were irrelevant.

There have been an increasing number of Métis hunting and fishing cases to come before the Canadian courts in recent years. Most, although not all, have been in western Canada. In a nutshell, the decisions in these court cases have consistently recognized that Métis people in Alberta, Saskatchewan, and Ontario (the evidence is conflicting in Manitoba) have an Aboriginal right to hunt and fish for subsistence purposes. This means no commercial hunting or fishing and no forestry or mineral extraction. The lower provincial courts along with Supreme Court of Canada have generally avoided the issue of commercial rights—as have Métis defence strategies. In the hunting and fishing cases, the judges generally took the word of the defendants (as did the Crown prosecutors) that they were Métis and have instead looked for evidence that the Métis defendants lived like "Indians," even though they may not see themselves as Indians. And what exactly does "living like an Indian" mean in the courts? The courts have concentrated on finding evidence of the defendant's "traditional" lifestyle. In other words, they looked for evidence that hunting and fishing was the principle way by which the defendant(s) and their families' food requirements were met, and that there were no commercial facets to the hunting and fishing. This is what "living like an Indian means," and the reason it is so damaging to the Métis defendants is that it totally ignores the last 300 years of their fur trade history.[7]

In one of the earliest cases to deal with Métis hunting rights, *R. v. Pritchard*, 1971, the defendant, George Pritchard, was found on occupied Crown land in possession of a deer carcass in closed season. The defence argued that although Pritchard was not an Indian as defined in the Indian Act, he was "born on an Indian reserve and… his family had always been known as Indians" (Slattery and Stelck 392). The main question considered by the judge was whether or not Pritchard, who belonged to "a class of people commonly known as 'Indian' but are not treaty Indians, do not live on a reserve and are not Indians as defined in the *Indian Act*" (393) could still have a legal right to hunt, as contained in s.8(1) of the Saskatchewan Game Act. The judge in the initial case took a broad view, stating that "the accused, being of that race and ancestry of Indians is an Indian as contemplated in the Game Act, and I find him not guilty of the charge" (396). This case, and its appeal, is noteworthy because the defendant did not have to prove a particular lifestyle. The judge in the *Pritchard* decision was not concerned by the fact that the defendant's father, George Pritchard Sr., "owns seven quarters of land and rents four quarters and the accused lives with him" (392). Nor did this appear to be a problem for the Crown prosecutors, who did not raise the issue in court. Equally interesting, this decision was not used in subsequent cases regarding these matters.

  R. v. McPherson (1994; 1992) was a different story. This is the first case occurring after the Constitution Act and the *Sparrow* decision of 1990,[8] both of which "raised the stakes" for how the courts would consider Métis rights challenges that came before them. In the original case, two Manitoba Métis men, McPherson and Christie, were charged with and convicted of hunting moose out of season on unoccupied crown land. Both men argued that s.35 (of the Constitution Act of 1982) recognized and protected their Aboriginal right to hunt. In the initial decision the judge noted that both men grew up in relative poverty and had a close connection to the land. The judge also noted that the Métis were "really one extended family [who] lived mostly off the land, were very, very poor and often went hungry...[Henry Christie] also spoke Cree at home and he stated that he lived in the same way as the treaty kids" (*R. v. McPherson*, 1992: 147). The judge further observed "Métis people living off the land were treated with discretion" by enforcement officers who recognized the need for Métis men to feed themselves and their families even though there existed no policy allowing for unrestricted hunting (*R. v. McPherson*, 1992: 150). This early case established the importance, in the court's eyes, of living "close to the land" as proof of an Aboriginal right to hunt. In this particular case, while the conservation expert "shuddered at the possibility of having.... uncontrolled Métis hunters," he felt that "if the number of Métis hunters was restricted to those who *truly lived off the land* and who had continuously exercised that right to date, the impact may be acceptable" (*R. v. McPherson*, 1992: 148, emphasis added). Thus they are also defined with the concept of conservation in mind. The conservation expert's "shuddering" encapsulates the reasoning behind the whole lifestyle argument—we may not know what exactly a Métis looks like, but we *do* know what a moose looks like, and the provincial government-Crown's argument is that letting Métis hunt "willy-nilly" will decimate the moose population.

Soon after the *McPherson* decision, *R. v. Ferguson* (1994; 1993) was the first court case to make a fuller comment on lifestyle criteria as a means of evaluating the cultural "authenticity" of the defendant. However, it still deals with living an authentic Indian lifestyle, rather than a Métis lifestyle. Ferguson was an older Native man, charged under Alberta Provincial Wildlife regulations with hunting without a license and unlawful possession of wildlife. He had been hunting moose on unoccupied Crown land for food purposes. In his decision, the judge stated that the defendant had been born and grew up in an isolated community in northern Alberta as a "non-treaty Indian"; in other words, he followed "the Indian mode of life" (*R. v. Ferguson*, 1993: 152). The evidence indicates that Ferguson's first language was Cree and that he spoke only Cree until attending school. The community in which he lived was entirely Cree speaking, food was obtained by hunting and gathering, and the usual Cree customs were followed with respect to philosophy of life and lifestyle (although what exactly these Cree customs consisted of were not defined in the decision). According to Justice Goodson's calculations, Ferguson's genealogy made him "one-half Indian racially" and that, "the defendant is an Indian in terms of culture" (*R. v. Ferguson*, 993: 152). The judge ended his decision by stating "it is difficult to imagine a more basic Aboriginal right than the right to avoid starvation by feeding oneself by the traditional methods of the community" (1993: 156). The Crown appealed this decision (1994). They argued that the respondent's lifestyle in his later years disqualified him from the "Indian mode of life" he had followed in his younger days. In other words, the Crown argued that because Ferguson "ran tractors and built roads" he wasn't really an Indian anymore, at least according to legal criteria. Despite this, the appeal court upheld the original decision.

The *Ferguson* case established a "Métis" right to hunt—but only in Alberta. In Saskatchewan, a number of cases have formalized the right both to hunt and fish. Métis defendants in these cases attempted to win these rights by proving that though they might not call themselves Indians they lived similar enough lifestyles to be considered Indians for the purposes of the alleged activities. Until recently, the Crown has not admitted this defence. One case that has changed this is *R. v. Laliberte* (1996), tried in the Provincial Court of Saskatchewan. The agreed facts of the case were that the defendant was hunting for food, and that "hunting, as well as trapping, fishing and gathering of wild edible plants is a defining feature of the Métis culture" (*R. v. Laliberte*, unreported: 5). The judge decided that, despite the strong evidence provided by the accused's counsel about the ambivalence between Indian and Métis identities, he felt bound by a higher court's decision in an earlier case (*R. v. Laprise*) and convicted Laliberte. In doing so, however, he strongly urged an appeal, revealing the deep ambiguity in his mind about the ability of existing Métis case law to deal fairly with Métis claims. Although Laliberte was convicted and the case was not appealed, it represented progress for the Métis. For the first time, the judge questioned the historical differentiation between Métis and Indians, and the courts accepted new and more sophisticated types of historical evidence derived from the records of the scrip and treaty commissions that dotted the Canadian landscape in the late-nineteenth and early twentieth century.

These preceding cases establish only a Métis right to hunt—or at least, the right of those Métis who live like Indians. *R. v. Morin & Daigneault* (1998; 1996) extended these rights, establishing a Métis right to fish. The defendants were two Métis men from Turner Lake, an isolated northern Saskatchewan community. They were charged with a variety of offences under the Saskatchewan Fishery Regulations. The basic question before the trial judge was: "did the Accused have an Aboriginal right to fish?" (*R. v. Morin & Daigneault*, 1996: 157). In ruling that they did, the judge noted that the people of Turner Lake had lived off the land since the early 1800s and that fish had always comprised an important part of their diet. The judge stated that "the contemporary lifestyle of the Métis in the area was described by both defendants.... [and] that they preferred to live on 'bush food'... [b]ush food is of course the product of hunting, fishing and trapping" (*R. v. Morin & Daigneault*, 1996: 167–8). In addition, the judge recited historical information illustrating that "the impression given to the Indian and Métis population was that you had to make a choice and it made little difference whether you were Indian or Métis and whether you took treaty or scrip" (*R. v. Morin & Daigneault*, 1996: 171).[9] In fact the judge actually entitled a section of his decision "Indian or Métis—is there a difference?" (1996: 174). The Crown appealed this decision on more technical grounds, but the appeal court judge agreed with the provincial court decision, arguing that the Métis in that area did possess an Aboriginal right to fish for food.

John Grumbo (*R. v. Grumbo*, 1998; 1996), a Métis man, was charged under several sections of the Saskatchewan Wildlife Act with possession of wildlife taken by an Indian. Grumbo's nephew, a treaty Indian, had given him two deer, and Grumbo's possession of the deer contravened the Wildlife Act, s.31, s.32(1). In his decision, the judge was careful to note that Grumbo described himself as "a non-status Indian, a non-treaty Indian and a Métis" (1996: 122). He had not spent one day in school, could not read or write, but spoke English, Cree, Saulteaux, French, and some Sioux. The judge was struck by the fact that Grumbo had hunted all his life—he killed deer, rabbits, ducks, geese, partridge, and prairie chickens (*R. v. Grumbo*, 1996: 124). In reference to his self-identity, Grumbo stated that "[y]ou can go to any white place and you are dark. Naturally they are not going to call you a Métis. You're automatically Indian" (1996: 125). The importance of the Grumbo case is the Crown's admission for the first time that the Métis in Saskatchewan should be considered Indians for the purposes of the 1867 British North America (BNA) Act. While the Crown was willing to make this admission, they fell back on the argument that Indians in s.91(24) of the 1967 BNA Act were not the same as those of the Natural Resources Transfer Agreement. The Court of Queen's Bench judge sided with the Métis, arguing that the Crown had failed to prove that Grumbo was not an Indian. Grumbo was acquitted. The Saskatchewan Court of Appeal upheld this decision but ordered a new trial to determine who a "Métis such as the respondent" was (*R. v. Grumbo*, 1998: 184). This case was not appealed further—the Crown "stayed" the charges, meaning they would not pursue them further.

In southern Manitoba in 1994, a group of Métis hunters were charged with unlawfully hunting deer out of season on unoccupied Crown land, contrary to s.26 of the Wildlife Act, R.S.M. 1987 (*R. v. Blais*, 1998; 1997). The crux of the defence argument was that their Métis status exempted them from the provisions of this Wildlife Act, at least for subsistence purposes. They were found guilty, and this was upheld upon appeal. This case is particularly important, for two reasons. First, it takes place in what is conventionally understood to be the historical heartland of the Métis—near Red River—but this very fact was used to disqualify the defendants. The judge ruled, essentially, that any reference to Indians within the meaning of the Indian Act of the day had no reference to the Métis people—Métis are *not*, according to the presiding judge, Indians. The second reason this case is important is because of the evidence used to disqualify Blais. The judge noted that the Crown cross-examination revealed that Mr. Blais "had employment as hotel owner, as a consultant, as a real estate broker, and that he has worked for the railway" (*R. v. Blais*, 1997: 121). He went on to observe that all three of the accused "are reasonably well established in contemporary society. Certainly they did not appear to fall within the category of Métis [in other court cases where]… the Métis individuals before the court were following lifestyles which kept them 'close to the land'" (1997: 122). This case is on appeal to the Manitoba Court of Appeal, having passed through the Manitoba Provincial Court and the Court of Queen's Bench of Manitoba.

Conclusion: Beyond Lifestyle

These court decisions show that the concept of "lifestyle" has figured prominently in the Canadian provincial courts' consideration of Métis hunting and fishing rights, particularly where the defendants convincingly argue they live an "Indian" lifestyle. However, a recent decision in Ontario may signal a change in how the courts are examining the issue of Métis hunting and fishing rights in central Canada. In Sault Ste. Marie, Ontario, a father and son were charged under s.46 and s.47(1) of the Ontario Game and Fish Act for shooting a bull moose without a proper licence. The son affixed a handwritten tag with his Métis Local number, in place of a licensed tag. At the time, the son was in possession of an Ontario Métis and Aboriginal Association card, and he claimed the card gave him fishing, hunting, trapping, wild rice harvesting, and timber rights. The reason given by the defendant for claiming these rights was "to preserve [his] Aboriginal heritage and the right to harvest natural resources that [his] family has done since time immemorial" (*R. v. Powley*, 1999: 157).

The case was won, not by proving their Indianness or "living an Indian mode of life," but through solid historical evidence that documented a historical Métis presence in the particular area. The judge stated that "it is clear from the totality of the historical documentation and evidence in connection thereto that the Métis people were a recognizable group that was closely associated with the local Indians. The Métis had created a distinctive lifestyle that was recognized by others" (1999: 169). He ruled that to engage in traditional rights and to be considered a Métis, the individual had to (1) be of Aboriginal ancestry, and have a genealogical connection to the historical Métis society, (2) must self-identify as Métis, and (3) must be accepted as Métis by a Métis community (*Powley*, 1999: 168). Upon appeal, the superior court judge accepted this definition, adding however, that ancestral family mentioned in the first part of the trial judge's definition did not necessarily have to be genetic (*R. v. Powley*, 2000: 44).[10]

The idea of race is strongly embedded in the modern world and does its "work" through stereotypes, which construct very narrow ranges of images about particular communities. These racial stereotypes, often embedded in relationships of great inequalities, result in binary images between "colonizers" and those who resisted "colonization," between traditional and modern. In the context of Métis hunting and fishing court cases, these stereotypes play themselves out through judicial decisions. Judges hold stereotypical views about what it means to live a "traditional" lifestyle, stereotypes that Indians themselves are not required to live up to. This means that the Métis have had to prove they live "close to the land," despite more than two hundred years of fur trade history that would suggest a strong commercial aspect to their culture. *R. v. Powley* is the first case to deliberately set into motion a process for defining who a Métis person is and that includes consultation from the Métis communities themselves. It is to be hoped that this direction will continue as it allows for a more relevant definition of what it means to be Métis.

Endnotes

[1] I have chosen the French spelling of Métis for this paper. Readers should remember that this spelling does not limit the discussion to those people of only Aboriginal-French ancestry. It also includes those of Aboriginal-Scots ancestry, the Grande Cache Métis, and today, others of mixed blood who don't fit contemporary legal definitions of Indian.

[2] "Whitestream," a term coined by Denis (1997), refers to a Canadian society that is mainly "structured on the basis of the European, 'white,' experience" (13), despite the fact that it is not solely composed of those experiences.

[3] By "real" I mean a point of view that sees race as having definable and specific characteristics that can be identified and categorized culturally, phenotypically, or psychologically.

[4] In fact, as will be discussed later, one hundred years ago there wasn't necessarily a distinct, hard line to be drawn between "Indian" and "Métis" communities.

[5] We should also note, however, that the *Powley* decision was able to move beyond this lifestyle criteria by virtue of a later court decision, *Delgamuukw v. The Queen* (1997), which modified what the Métis defendants had to prove to pursue a successful claim.

[6] These trial excerpts are taken from the court case information, zip-filed at the Métis Nation of Ontario's Web site, http://www.metisnation.org.

[7] Although the Crown in the *Grumbo* (1996) decision has acknowledged that the Métis are to be understood as Indians, in the context of the decision this was still understood as granting a subsistence right. See also Clem Chartier, "'Indian': An Analysis of the Term Used in Section 91(24) of the British North America Act, 1867," *Saskatchewan Law Review* 43 (1978–79): 36–80.

[8] *R. v. Sparrow* was a 1990 Supreme Court of Canada decision that "fleshed out" the meaning of Aboriginal rights. Sparrow set new parameters for interpreting Aboriginal rights and called for a "liberal and generous" interpretation of them.

[9] During the treaty and scrip commissions, those who wanted to be "Indians" surrendered their Aboriginal title and took treaty entering into a band list. Those who wished to be "Métis" surrendered their title through scrip, a coupon entitling them to 240 acres of land or $240.

[10] This decision was taken from the Métis Nation of Ontario's Web site, located at http://www.metisnation.org. as file:///GI/writings/Powley-SCJDecision.htm

Works Cited

Andersen, C. "Governing Aboriginal Justice in Canada: Constructing Responsible Individuals and Communities through 'Tradition.'" *Crime, Law and Social Change* 31 (1999). 303–26.

Aylward, C. *Canadian Critical Race Theory.* Halifax: Fernwood Publishing, 1999.

Bell, C. *Alberta's Métis Settlement Legislation: An Overview of Ownership and Management of Settlement Lands.* Regina: Canadian Plains Research Centre, 1994.

Berkhofer, R. *The White Man's Indian: Images of the American Indian from Columbus to the Present.* New York: Random House, 1978.

Blaut, J. *The Colonizer's Model of the World: Geographical Diffusionism and Eurocentric History.* New York and London: The Guilford Press, 1993.

Brown, J. *Strangers in Blood: Fur Trade Company Families in Indian Country.* Vancouver: University of British Columbia Press, 1980.

_____. "Linguistic Solitudes and Changing Social Categories." *Old Trails and New Directions: Papers of the Third North American Fur Trade Conference.* Ed. C. Judd and A.J. Ray. Toronto: University of Toronto Press, 1980.

Canada Sessional Papers. Annual Reports for the Department of the Interior, 1885–1887. Detailed Statement of claims of the Half-Breed Commission.

Canadian Centre for Justice Statistics. *Profile of Courts in Canada 1997.* Ottawa : Statistics Canada, 1998.

Culhane, D. *The Pleasure of the Crown: Anthropology, Law and First Nations*. Burnaby: Talonbooks, 1998.

Denis, C. *We Are Not You: First Nations and Canadian Modernity*. Peterborough: Broadview Press, 1997.

Ens, G. *Homeland to Hinterland: The Changing Worlds of the Red River Metis in the Nineteenth Century*. Toronto: University of Toronto Press, 1996.

Fitzpatrick, P. *The Mythology of Modern Law*. London and New York: Routledge, 1992.

Flanagan, T. *Métis Lands in Manitoba*. Calgary: University of Calgary Press, 1991.

Foster, J. "Some Questions and Perspectives on the Problem of Métis Roots." *The New Peoples: Being and Becoming Métis in North America*. Ed. J. Peterson and J. Brown. Winnipeg: University of Manitoba Press, 1985.

Francis, D. *The Imaginary Indian: The Image of the Indian in Canadian Culture*. Vancouver: Arsenal Pulp Press, 1992.

Giraud, M. *The Métis in the Canadian West*. Trans. George Woodcock. Edmonton: University of Alberta Press, 1986.

Green, J. "Exploring Identity and Citizenship: Aboriginal Women, Bill C-31 and the Sawridge Case." Ph.D. diss., University of Alberta, 1997.

Hall, S., ed. *Representation: Cultural Representations and Signifying Practices*. London: and Thousand Oaks, CA: Sage in association with the Open University, 1997.

Hamilton, A.C. and C.M. Sinclair. *The Report of the Aboriginal Justice Inquiry of Manitoba. Volume 1: The Justice System and Aboriginal People*. Province of Manitoba, 1991.

Hunt, A. *Explorations in Law and Society: Toward a Constitutive Theory of Law*. New York: Routledge, 1993.

McCormick, P. *Canada's Courts*. Toronto: James Lorimer & Company, Publishers, 1994.

Nicks, T. and K. Morgan. "Grande Cache: The Historic Development of an Indigenous Alberta Métis Population." *The New Peoples: Being and Becoming Metis in North America*. Ed. J. Peterson and J. Brown. Winnipeg: University of Manitoba Press, 1985.

Peterson, J. "Many Roads to Red River: Métis Genesis in the Great Lakes Region, 1680–1815." *The New Peoples: Being and Becoming Métis in North America*. Ed. J. Peterson and J. Brown. Winnipeg: University of Manitoba Press, 1985.

Ray, A. *Indians in the Fur Trade: Their role as Hunters, Trappers and Middlemen in the Lands Southwest of Hudson Bay, 1660–1870*. Toronto: University of Toronto Press, 1974.

Ross, R. *Dancing with a Ghost: Exploring Indian Reality*. Markham: Octopus Publishing Group, 1992.

_____. "Dueling Paradigms? Western Criminal Justice versus Aboriginal Community Healing." *Continuing Poundmaker and Riel's Quest: Presentations Made at a Conference on Aboriginal Peoples and Justice.* Ed. R. Gosse, J. Youngblood, and R. Carter. Saskatoon: Purich Publishing, 1994.

_____. *Returning to the Teachings: Exploring Aboriginal Justice*. Toronto: Penguin Books, 1996.

Royal Commission on Aboriginal Peoples. *Restructuring the Relationship.* Five Volumes. Ottawa: Minister of Supply and Services, 1996.

Said, E.W. *Culture and Imperialism*. New York: Knopf, 1993.

_____. *Orientalism*. New York: Vintage Books, 1979.

Slattery, B. and S. Stelck. "*R. v. Pritchard* [1971]." *7 Canadian Native Law Cases*. Saskatoon: University of Saskatchewan Native Law Centre, 1988. 391.

Sprague, D. *Canada and the Metis, 1869–1885*. Waterloo: Wilfrid Laurier University Press, 1988.

Stanley, G. *The Birth of Western Canada: A History of the Riel Rebellions.* Toronto: University of Toronto Press, 1960.

Stoler, A.L. *Race and the Education of Desire: Foucault's History of Sexuality and the Colonial Order of Things*. Durham: Duke University Press, 1995.

Taylor, J. "A Historical Introduction to Métis Claims In Canada." *Canadian Journal of Native Studies* 3.1 (1983): 151–69.

Tough, F. *'As Their Natural Resources Fail': Native Peoples and the Economic History of Northern Manitoba, 1870–1930*. Vancouver: University of British Columbia Press, 1996.

Van Kirk, S. "*Many Tender Ties": Women in Fur Trade Society, 1670–1870.* Winnipeg: Saults & Pollard Ltd, 1980.

Weber, M. *Economy and Society: An Outline of Interpretive Sociology.* Ed. G. Roth and C. Wittich. New York: Bedminster Press, 1968.

Wolf, E. *Europe and the People Without History*. Los Angeles: University of California Press, 1982.

Young, R. *Colonial Desire: Hybridity in Theory, Culture and Race*. London and New York: Routledge, 1995.

Legal Cases Cited

Delgamuukw v. *The Queen* (1997) *S.C.R.* 1010 (S.C.C.)

R. v. *Blais* (1998) 4 *C.N.L.R.* 103 (Man. Q.B.).

_____. (1997) 3 *C.N.L.R.* 109 (Man. Prov. Ct.).

R. v. *Ferguson* (1994) 1 *C.N.L.R.* 117 (Alta. Q.B.).

_____. (1993) 2 *C.N.L.R.* 148 (Alta. Prov. Ct.).

R. v. *Gladstone* (1996) 4 *C.N.L.R.* 65 (S.C.C.).

R. v. *Grumbo* (1998) 3 *C.N.L.R.* 172 (Sask. C. A.).

_____. (1996) *C.N.L.R.* 122 (Court Q.B.).

R. v. *Howse* (2000) B.C.J. (B.C.P.C.).

R. v. *Laliberte* (1996) *unreported* (Sask. Prov. Ct.).

R. v. *Laprise* (1978) 6 *W.W.R.* 85 (Sask. C.A.).

_____. (1977) 3 *W.W.R.* 1977 (Sask. Q.B.).

R. v. *Marshall* (1999) *S.C.C.* File No.: 26014 (Sept. 17th, 1999).

R. v. *McPherson* (1994) 2 *C.N.L.R.* 137 (Man. Q. B.).

_____. (1992) 4 *C.N.L.R.* 144 (Man. Prov. Ct.).

R. v. *Morin & Daigneault* (1998) 1 *C.N.L.R.* 182 (Sask. C.B.)(indexed as
      R. v. *Morin*).

_____. (1996) 3 *C.N.L.R.* 157 (Sask. Prov. Ct.).

R. v. *Powley* (2000) *O.J. No. 99* (Ont. Superior Court)

_____. (1999) *C.N.L.R.* 153 (Ont. Prov. Ct.).

R. v. *Pritchard* (1972) 32 *D.L.R.* (3d) 617 (Sask. Q.B.).

_____. (1971) *Unreported* (Sask. Prov. Ct.)

R. v. *Sparrow* (1990) 3 *C.N.L.R.* 160 (S.C.C.).

Jacob

Maria Campbell

Maria Campbell is a Métis writer, filmmaker and teacher. She is currently working on a play and completing a Masters thesis at the University of Saskatchewan.

My people were Cree Michif speakers and in older times, English was a third (often a fourth) language and very few people spoke it. Those who spoke English spoke it in the dialect and rhythm of their communities. Jacob is presented in the dialect and rhythm of my community, and in the same way the late Old Gabriel Vandal told it. I put it on paper in this way to honour him and the old men of our people who never allowed "dah Anglais to be dah boss over dem," not even in the use of the English language. Gabriel did not speak "proper English" but he treated it with respect thus making it "work" for him. Hi hi ni moosoom, ni gran pere. Ki nah nah skoom tin.

Mistupuch he was my granmudder.
He come from Muskeg
dat was before he was a reservation.
My granmudder he was about twenty-eight when he
marry my granfawder.
Dat was real ole for a woman to marry in dem days
But he was an Indian doctor
I guess dats why he wait so long.

Ooh he was a good doctor too
All the peoples dey say dat about him.
He doctor everybody dat come to him
an he birt all dah babies too.

Reprinted from *Stories of the Road Allowance People* (Penticton, BC: Theytus Books, 1994). Published with permission of the author and Theytus Books.

Jus about everybody my age
my granmudder he birt dem.

He marry my granfawder around 1890.
Dat old man he come to him for doctoring
and when he get better
he never leave him again.
Dey get married dah Indian way
an after dat my granfawder
he help him with all hees doctoring.
Dats dah way he use to be a long time ago.
If dah woman he work
den dah man he help him an if had man he work
dah woman he help.
You never heerd peoples fighting over whose job he was
dey all know what dey got to do to stay alive.

My granfawder his name he was Kannap
but had whitemans dey call him Jim Boy
so hees Indian name he gets los.
Dats why we don know who his peoples dey are.
We los lots of our relations like dat.
Dey get da whitemans name
den no body
he knows who his peoples dey are anymore.

Sometimes me
I tink dats dah reason why we have such a hard time
us peoples.
Our roots dey gets broken so many times.
Hees hard to be strong you know
when you don got far to look back for help.

Dah whitemans
he can look back tousands of years
cause him
he write everything down.
but us peoples
we use dah membering
an we pass it on by telling stories an singing songs.
Sometimes we even dance dah membering.

But all dis trouble you know
he start after we get dah new names
cause wit dah new names
he come a new language an a new way of living.
Once a long time ago
I could'ave told you dah story of my granfawder Kannap
an all his peoples but no more.
All I can tell you now
is about Jim Boy
an hees story hees not very ole.

Well my granmudder Mistupuch
he never gets a whitemans name an him
he knowed lots of stories.
Dat ole lady
he even knowed dah songs.
He always use to tell me
one about an ole man call Jacob.

Dat old man you know
he don live to far from here.
well hees gone now
but dis story he was about him when he was alive.

Jacob him
he gets one of dem new names when dey put him in dah
residential school.
He was jus small boy when he go
an he don come home for twelve years.

Twelve years!
Dats a long time to be gone from your peoples.
He can come home you know
cause dah school he was damn near two hundred miles
away.
His Mommy and Daddy dey can go and see him
cause deres no roads in dem days
an dah Indians dey don gots many horses
'specially to travel dat far.

Dats true you know
not many peoples in dem days dey have horses.
Its only in dah comic books an dah picture shows dey
gots lots of horses.
He was never like dat in dah real life.

Well Jacob him
he stay in dat school all dem years an when he come
home he was a man.
While he was gone
his Mommy and Daddy dey die so he gots nobody.
An on top of dat
nobody he knowed him cause he gots a new name.
My granmudder
he say dat ole man he have a hell of time.
No body he can understand dat
unless he happen to him.

Dem peoples dat go away to dem schools
an come back you know dey really suffer.
No matter how many stories we tell
we'll never be able to tell
what dem schools dey done to dah peoples
an all dere relations.

Well anyways
Jacob he was jus plain pitiful
He can talk his own language
He don know how to live in dah bush.
Its a good ting da peoples dey was kine
cause dy help him dah very bes dey can.
Well a couple of summers later
he meet dis girl
an dey gets married.

Dat girl he was kine
an real smart too.
He teach Jacob how to make an Indian living.
Dey have a good life togedder an after a few years
dey have a boy.
Not long after dat
dey raise two little girls day was orphans.

Jacob and his wife dey was good peoples
Boat of dem dey was hard working
an all dah peoples
dey respec dem an dey come to Jacob for advice.

But dah good times dey was too good to las
coause one day
dah Preeses
dey comes to dah village with dah policemans.
Dey come to take dah kids to dah school.

When dey get to Jacob hees house
he tell dem dey can take his kids.

Dah Prees he tell him
he have to lets dem go cause dats the law.
Well dah Prees
he have a big book
an dat book he gots dah names
of all dah kids
an who dey belongs to.

He open dat bok an ask Jacob for his name
an den he look it up.
"Jacob" he say
"you know better you went to dah school an you know
dah edjication hees important."

My granmudder Mistupuch
he say Jacob he tell that Prees
"Yes I go to dah school
an dats why I don wan my kids to go.
All dere is in dat place is suffering."

Dah Prees he wasn happy about dat
an he say to Jacob
"But the peoples day have to suffer Jacob cause dah Jesus he suffer."

"But dah Jesus he never lose his language an
hees peoples" Jacob tell him.
"He stay home in hees own land and he do hees
suffering."

Well da Prees him
he gets mad
an he tell him its a sin to tink like dat
an hees gonna end up in purgatory for dem kind of
words.

But Jacob he don care
cause far as hees concern
purgatory
he can be worse den the hell he live with trying to
learn hees language and hees Indian ways.

He tell dat Prees
he don even know who his people dey are.
"Dah Jesus he knowed his Mommy and Daddy"
Jacob he tell him
"and he always knowed who his people dey are."

Well
dah Prees he tell him
if he wans to know who hees peoples dey are
he can tell him dat
an he open in dah book again.

"Your Dad hees Indian name he was Awchak"
dah prees he say
"I tink dat means Star in your language.
He never gets a new name cause he never become a
Christian."

Jacob he tell my granmudder
dat when da Prees he say hees Dad hees name
his wife he start to cry real hard.

"Jacob someday you'll tank the God we done dis."
dah Prees he tell him
an dey start loading up dah kids on dah big wagons.
All dah kids dey was crying an screaming
An dah mudders
dey was chasing dah wagons.

Dah ole womans
dey was all singing dah det song
an none of the mans
dey can do anyting.
Dey can
cause the policemans dey gots guns.

When dah wagons dey was all gone
Jacob he look for hees wife but he can find him no
place.
An ole woman he see him an he call to him
"Pay api noosim"
"Come an sit down my granchild I mus talk to you.
Hees hard for me to tell you dis but dat Prees
hees book he bring us bad news today.
He tell you dat Awchak he was your Daddy.
My granchild
Awchak he was your wife's Daddy too."

Jacob he tell my granmudder
he can cry when he hear dat.
He can even hurt inside.
Dat night he go looking
an he fine hees wife in dah bush
Dat woman he kill hisself.

Jacob he say
dah ole womans
dey stay wit him for a long time
an dey sing healing songs an dey try to help him
But he say he can feel nutting.
Maybe if he did
he would have done dah same ting.

For many years Jacob he was like dat
just dead inside.

Dah peoples dey try to talk wit him
but it was no use.
Hees kids dey growed up
an dey come home an live wit him.

"I made dem suffer" he tell my granmudder
"Dem kids dey try so hard to help me."

Den one day
his daughter he get married an he have a baby.
He bring it to Jacob to see.
Jacob he say
he look at dat lil baby
an he start to cry and he can stop.
He say he cry for himself an his wife
an den he cry for his Mommy and Daddy.
When he was done
he sing dah healing songs dah ole womans
dey sing to him a long time ago.

Well you know
Jacob he die when he was an ole ole man.
An all hees life
he write in a big book
dah Indian names of all dah Mommies and Daddies.
An beside dem
he write dah old names and
dah new names of all dere kids.

An for dah res of hees life
he fight dah government to build schools on the
reservation.
"The good God he wouldn of make babies come
from Mommies and Daddies"
he use to say
"if he didn want dem to stay home
an learn dere language
an dere Indian ways."

You know
dat ole man was right.
No body he can do dat.
Take all dah babies away. Hees jus not right.
Long time ago
dah old peoples dey use to do dah naming
an dey do dah teaching too.

If dah parents dey have troubles
den dah aunties and dah uncles
or somebody in dah family
he help out till dah parents dey gets dere life work
out.
But no one
no one
he ever take dah babies away from dere peoples.

You know my ole granmudder
Mistupuch
he have lots of stories about people like Jacob.
Good ole peoples
dat work hard so tings will be better for us.
We should never forget dem ole peoples.

Celestial and Social Families of the Inuit

Karla Jessen Williamson.

Karla Jessen Williamson was born in Appamiut, Greenland where she received her primary education. She attended high school in Denmark and, after moving to Canada, received a BA and MA from the University of Saskatchewan. She is completing her Ph.D. at the University of Aberdeen, UK, studying Inuit gender relations and how Inuit women in post-colonial Greenland Inuit communities gain status through genderless empowerment. She is Executive Director of the Arctic Institute of North America-University of Calgary. Takujumaarivagit—I'll meet you in the future.

Seqineq Aningaarlu: The Sun and the Moon—Sister and Brother

There is a story of how the moon and the sun came into being.[1] Once in an Arctic village, people were getting very impatient due to the persistence of one particularly hard winter. The village members reached the point of "dimming the oil lamps," the old games where members of the village satisfied their amorous desires. When the lamp flames were dancing their luminescent light again, people laughed their tensions away, and got on with the hardship of living the winter through—laughing and reminiscing about their lusts and what they lead to.

On one occasion of dimming the flames a young, unmarried woman noticed that one man persistently chose her as a partner. On each occasion she became more and more suspicious about the identity of the young, unknown lover. Her thoughts were unsettling ones, and as she found no peace, she decided to authenticate her anxieties. She had to find out who this person was. At the next dimming of lights, she brushed her hand under the cooking pot and brushed the soot on the face of the young man as he made love to her. When the lights went back on, she confirmed her suspicion. The young man was her brother!

Out of shame, outrage and self-loathing she ran out of the house and into the darkness. As she ran out, she dipped a torch into the oil barrel and lit it, then left the community, never to return.

Seeing his sister fleeing from him, the young man picked up a torch and in his haste did not dip it thoroughly into the oil. He ran after her as fast as he could. Both ran further and further from the settlement, she with a fully lit torch and he with a dimly lit torch. As they ran, they rose from the ground so high that only their lights could be seen. She, with her fully lit torch, became the magnificent sun, while he, with his torch only half-lit, became the moon. They are worlds opposite to one another and will never meet again.

Eskimos, Esquimaux, Eskimos, Eskimoer, Eskimos, Eskimuut, Eskimos, Eske'k

The term *Eskimo* was used to refer to Indigenous people living along the Arctic sea coasts. In Mi'kmaq the word *Eske'k* is anything raw, not cooked, and the Mi'kmaq believe that the word Eskimo is derived from a Mi'kmaw expression to describe their observations of the people from the north who ate raw fish and meat (Battiste, personal communication). I do not have any problems with that description, since I take great pleasure in submitting myself to the good will of the animals, all their soul, and gifts the land has granted us when we eat raw meat. We eat raw meat only from animals of the far north, those that have not been manipulated by human beings. These animals are, in our minds, self-determining free beings who fully enjoy a good life and who provide us with the means of life and enrichment of our souls. Their presence materializes our mutual relationship with the habitat.

The problem with the term *Eskimo* arises because most writings, some scientific but largely popular literature, tend to depict the Eskimos stereotypically as relatively unintelligent, as invalidated "Stone Age people," ever smiling in their horribly "unforgiving" environment and greatly maladjusted to the changing social realities of the Western world.

Over the many years of my formal education, I undertook a lot of self-evaluation to overcome the burdensome stereotyping of the Eskimo depicted through such writing. I felt Inuit were frozen into images of primitiveness, simplemindedness, and childlike character. Lately, I have begun to recognize the discourse on Inuit and on other indigenous groups written from European point of view, which has a "historical-tunnel vision" (Blaut 1993: 5). This discourse suggests that many non-European cultures "are not intelligent, not as honorable, and ... not as courageous as Europeans: God made them inferior" (3). The gathering of scientific knowledge has often been subject to European manipulation that trivialized Indigenous peoples' economic, cultural, and spiritual lives as a justification for colonization and cognitive assimilation (Battiste, "Micmac Literacy"). So, when reading about "The Eskimos," be aware of assimilationist discourse and find ways of overcoming it. A substantial amount of the writing about the Eskimos omitted real Inuit perspectives and was uncritically predicated upon assumptions directly stemming from Eurocentric, paternalistic, patronizing, and belittling paradigms; it was, at the very least, colonialist. Furthermore, the Christian doctrine played a great role in discounting other ways of being.

As a child I was sent to spend a fair amount of time with my older out-of-town relatives. When my settlement was closed down by the Danish and Greenlandic authorities, my parents had decided to move to a bigger town. My paternal and maternal families also lived in two smaller towns as a result of the closing down of small settlements. I spent much time with my dearest relative, my maternal grandmother, who told me stories like the one I just told you, even when I was a very young child. I remember my first impression of the Seqineq and Aningaaq (the sun and the moon) story—a clear image of the tail of a falling meteorite as the two ran away from their settlement. I was for a long time very satisfied knowing that the sun and the moon were siblings. This image was even more strongly imprinted in my mind as an *ullorissap anaa*, waste material of a star that penetrated the earth's atmosphere and spumed all over the horizon one day when my whole family was out picking berries. How beautiful and powerful both sun and moon are.

Inuit Nunaat: Diversity of the Inuit

We call ourselves Inuit, which means "the human beings"—*Inuk* for one person. All human beings are "inuit"; it is only recently that the term has become politicized and used for people of "Eskimoic" background. As Inuit, we have come to realize that we are the luckiest of all peoples to be born on our *nuna*—our land. While there is warfare, political unrest, and great human suffering around the world, on our land we found peace, contentment, and a good life. Obviously, this can only be gained by a deep understanding of the reciprocal relationship with the land and its riches. For us, the land is a soul enriching totality, which by its own integrity has allowed human existence. The allowing of human life on *nuna* is premised by a strong sense of affinity with all other beings. A relationship with the land, the animals, and their souls has assured the Inuit a sustainable way of life over the last four or five millennia. This relationship has given us a strong sense of identity, one solidly bonded with the land. The sense of belonging to the land of our birth remains remarkably significant and very few Inuit have contested this by moving away from their place of birth.

Let me share a number of terms relating to the Arctic environment. *Ukiortartoq*—the habitat, or land, winters; *Aajuitsoq*— the habitat, or land, never melts; and today you see variations of the word *nuna* as more and more recognition of the Inuit is given on the new maps. Nunavut is just the latest, replacing the colonial Northwest Territories as the name for the Inuit homeland in Canada. Inuit of Arctic Quebec call their homeland Nunavik. *Qalasersuaq*—the Big Navel of the World—is a name in Greenlandic for the North Pole. Unlike the many dismissive terms used to describe the Arctic ("barren lands," "Arctic wastelands," "Arctic desert," "harsh, unforgiving environment," "bitter climate") our expressions praise our land for its immense beauty and its generosity. To the Inuit, nobody owns the land, the land owns itself, and animals on land, sea, and air are perfectly capable of living without the interference of human beings. For us, the land is a forgiving, soul enriching totality, which by virtue of its own integrity has allowed human existence.

Today, Inuit live under four nation states: Russia, the United States, Canada, and Denmark. In terms of the totality of human history, including that of the Inuit, these nation states are relatively new constructs, and there is no doubt that these will alter over time as it is the nature of human behaviour to change. In the furthest western part of Inuit habitat, on the easternmost peninsula of Siberia, live the Chukchi. Yupiit, Aleut, and Inupiaat enjoy life on the coastal areas of Alaska. Inuvialuit occupy the MacKenzie Delta and Beaufort Sea areas of the Northwest Territories in Canada (now Nunavut). Further east, Inuinnaat (named "Copper Eskimos" by recent non-Inuit explorers) cherish their quality of life. All around Hudson Bay, Baffin Island, Quebec, and the Labrador coastal areas, the people call themselves Inuit. The northernmost people of the world are the Inughuit of northwestern Greenland. Along the west Greenland coast we call ourselves Kalaallit, (*Kalaaleq* for one person). I believe the word *kalaaleq* is a misnomer, a mispronunciation of a "Careler"—an inhabitant of Carelen, which was once believed to an extension of the northern cape area of Scandinavia. Iit, the most eastern group of the Inuit, live in eastern Greenland.

When I came to Canada I was struck by the fact that my Danish/ Greenlandic education had done me a disservice by neglecting to tell me about "Edmonton Eskimos." I thought they must be modern-day Canadian Inuit, whose migration had not yet been documented because it was so recent! Ach! I only later realized that the "Edmonton Eskimos" were a Canadian football team. Nevertheless, Inuit love travelling, and some day new tribes will be created.

Each one of the Inuit groups has a distinctive dialect and cultural ways, since distances between the groups are great. Traditionally there would have been minimal contact between the various groups unless they lived in close proximity. Each group was self-sufficient in terms of their own needs and freedom; they enjoyed self-determination since there was no state intervention, instead they owed their lives to their families, community, and the good will of the animals and the land. As a result of the influence of colonial laws, culture, state borders, and government structures that modern Inuit have assimilated into their way of life, the distinctions between the various groups are now greater. For example, the Kalaallit of west Greenland have become Danified in lifestyle, and in the organization of their political structure and bureaucracy. The Inupiaat of Alaska are quite American in their approach to life and their political organizations. Canadian Inuit have adopted southern Canadian ways. As a result of colonization, each of the groups have internalized in varying degrees nationalistic sentiments and are proud to be members of nation states. This sentiment has particular significance in relationship to attainment of self-government within each nation state.

Would you believe that the sun and the moon were actually siblings? I looked around and found my siblings playing around me, all of them totally happy in their being the embodiment of sun and moon. I remember feeling awed about the sister and the brother becoming lights in the form of the sun and the moon. On each sunny day we were blessed by her sisterly warmth and stunning light, enjoying her luminance during summers, in the pre-autumn days, then in full autumn-time, then during brilliant winter sunny days after the sunlight comes back, continuing through blindingly bright early spring sunny days, and then in the true spring days when she is rushing the snow off the rocky outcrops of the land.

On each clear night, we were liberated from ghostly shadows on the land when good light from the moon illuminated. His light was ever so welcome during the wintertime, as his presence was totally lacking in the summer.

Sister—brother, brother—sister, taking turns to give light; how perfect life was.

Exploration of the Inuit World View

Since the expansion of western European peoples to the rest of the world, much fascination has been accorded the "Eskimos." Going to school, and becoming assimilated into a non-Inuit world in the process, I craved formal information about my own cultural background. After all, getting to know one's own culture was believed to be an emancipatory process through which one could freely explore future possibilities. My own travel back in time through written documents became more and more blurred, and I came to realize how written documentation can distort the actuality of the Inuit way of life. Gregory Cajete, a Pueblo, says that Indigenous student experience is "wrought with contradictions, prejudice, hypocrisy, narcissism, and unethical predisposition" (19), and I have no doubt that my own reading experience could have encased me in a self-fulfilling prophesy of conflict, frustration, and feelings of alienation. However, I was able to work beyond these feelings.

Coming from shamanic traditions, I appreciated the "self-actualization" process encouraged through graduate studies, and I started to explore my "inner space synonymous with the soul, the spirit, the self [and] the being" (Ermine 103). I was fortunate I came to my studies at a time when other scholars had taken up the call to move away from "ethnocentric" writing toward a more realistic portrayal of the peoples inhabiting this world. Some of these intellectuals have become friends, and they have given me courage to explore my understanding of the Inuit world view.

Using aspects of linguistics that indicate that languages are social constructs of epistemological knowledge, I understood that by analyzing the structure of any language, I might gain insight into ways world views are expressed. I started to look into how we as Inuit understood the way in which this world came to be. I realized the significance of the word *pinngortitaq*, which is used in reference to the biblical Creation story. One day, I was struck by the fact that the Christian missionaries must have adopted Indigenous terms already in existence to convey their particular religious teaching. So here began my exploration.

Kalaallit in Greenland call the earth *pinngortitaq*. If we break this word-complex down, we see that "pi-" (the root of the word) means "to realize / to objectify" in English; "nngor-" (infix) "making of," and "-titaq" (suffix) "the process of becoming." The term refers to an objectification, and shows the Inuit perception that the world has come into existence through spontaneous actualization. Rather than believing in human-like gods, we believe in non-identifiable forces that create life and life forms. The word *pinngortitaq* suggests that creative life forces came together. The fact that these forces became integrated may be coincidental, but each of these forces is life ordaining and in combination the creative possibilities are enormous. We believe that all beings in this world are manifestations of these integrating, life-ordaining forces, and each one of them is to be respected for its own engagement of these forces. They deserve to be recognized for their distinct, mystic quality ordained by the life forces.

In light of this concept, attempts to create some other form of order—hierarchical, linear, causal, evolutionary, human versus animals, rock versus sea, animate versus inanimate, man versus woman—become irrelevant and meaningless. Coming from an animalistic belief system, we tend to see life in all objects—animate and inanimate. We think that whatever the objects are and however they appear (as air or as a sea, rock, tree, or insect)—are to be respected for their own quality because each being is the epitome of these life-ordaining forces. This we call *inua*—the essence. For example, we can talk about *orpiup inua*—essence of tree; *qaqqap inua*—essence of mountain; *immap inua*—essence of a sea, and as human beings we cannot presume to be more nor less than any objects or beings around us (Fitzhugh and Kaplan). As much as a piece of rock is a manifestation of the objectified actualization of this world, as human beings we have to realize that we are a mere human manifestation of that objectification—just one of many. The Yupik scholar Oscar Kawagley explains:

> The creative force as manifested is more profound and powerful than anything the human being can do, because in it is the very essence of all things… all creatures, including humans are born equal. This does not imply that all functions or jobs of the creatures are equal, but hold that each does its job equally well. (18)

While exploring original creation stories, I came upon Edna Ahgeak MacLean's writing. An Inupiaq from Alaska, she analyzed the term for sun—*seqineq*:

> The stem of word is "seqi-" which in English means "to splatter, to splash outwards" and the ending of the word "-neq"… indicates the result or end product of an activity.… According to the Inupiaq legend there was darkness before there was light. This was the time when humans did not age. The Raven-spirit… secured the land and the source of light from an old man and his wife and daughter. Light appeared only after the Raven-Spirit stole the source of light from them. As he was fleeing, the Raven

Spirit dropped the source of light which then exploded and dispersed units of light throughout existence. (168)

Dr. MacLean goes on to argue that the Big Bang theory is supported by ancient Inuit thinking.

The Big Bang theory is a relatively recent Western theory about the origin of the universe that, as MacLean notes, shares some common descriptions the Inuit description on the origin of the universe. The Inuit concept was developed over the last four or five thousand years without the aid of costly sophisticated technology for taking measurements and making calculations that Western scientists pride themselves on using. Instead Inuit have created a way of life in accordance with *pinngortitaq* and have enjoyed their lifestyle, cherishing wisdom gained over the years. They are awed by and mindful of the essence each of the objects revealed in manifestations of the creative life forces, and it is out of this reverence that their stories were told.

The sun and the moon were sister and brother. How could a brother do this to his own sister? Is it not... what is the word... incest? What kind of sick story is this? Why should a child be lured into such a story so full of sexuality? How shameful! There is something really unsettling about this story.

Inuit Intellect

The story of the creation of the sun is just one of the many objectifications in relation to *Silarsuaq*, the universe, the source of the intellect. *Sila* is the root of the word, which Inuit use to refer to air, weather, intellect, knowledge, integratedness, wisdom, and the external. *Sila* is one of the life-giving force that makes "anything and everything possible on this earth" (Ermine 110). I describe this force as a "power which controlled all life... which enfolds all the worlds and invests all living organisms" (Williamson 1992, 22). *Sila* is a

> force that gives all the living beings air to breathe, and intelligence. With every breath people and animals take, air becomes transformed into energy to be used for intelligence, because as much as there is no life without air, without it there is no intelligence either. (24)

This life-giving energy gained from the *sila* is pervasive, encompassing, and distributed to all organisms on earth, and distributed according to the distinct needs of each of the beings. Fish need it, rocks need it, animals need it, human beings need it, land needs it. However, all these fish, rocks, animals, everything on earth have their own special powers different from that of human beings. The challenge to human beings is to learn that which the animals and other beings already know and as holders of self-conscious knowledge, only one of the many forms of intelligence found in the world, human beings have yet to solve the minimal truths of the creation.

The sun and the moon violated a social taboo and banished themselves for their actions, or at least the sun had the courtesy to leave in the first place. How disgusted she must be about herself. The brother must be a sick person to inflect such hurt on his own sister. It is a good thing "that the two would never meet" again. How could anyone overcome such shame, and look so brilliant as the two do?

The Inuit and the Colonizers

Qallunaat is the term we use for colonizers. Interestingly, both Canadian Inuit and Kalaallit use exactly the same words to describe their respective colonizers: in Greenland the word usually refers to Danes, while in Canada it refers to southern Canadians or any non-Inuit. In some parts of Alaska the word *Kassak* (Fienup-Riordan) is used in reference to the earlier Russian invaders, a Yupik-style word for Kozaks. *Qallunaat* denotes "white people," but does not in any way refer to colour. In many ways it refers to eyebrows. When Qallunaat started to travel the Arctic seas and lands, it was in their attempt to reach the lands of spices and silks—China, Japan, India, and surrounding areas—that they got lost. It is no wonder their brows frowned as they realized the slim possibility of reaching their goal. Many of the Arctic "explorers'" accounts of their voyages through the Arctic seas tell of hardship after enormous hardship, causing, no doubt, a lot of unrestrained frowns, and the bushing and brushing of eyebrows in all directions. Hence, the name Qallunaat: people with discernible eyebrows. When trading was introduced, we shopped for *qallunaamerngit*—goods ranging from buttons, materials, guns, sugar, flour, tea, coffee.

The extensive expeditionary search for the elusive Northwest Passage was later replaced by whaling expeditions from the south. In all Arctic waters the great whales were pursued by non-Inuit so vigourously they are now in danger of extinction. The oil from whales lit and heated European homes for nearly a century. The next Qallunaat visitors to the Arctic were fur-traders. There were never enough Arctic fur-bearing animals that could be trapped to fulfill the Qallunaat fashion mania for fur coats and hats. During the trapping era, missionaries also came to the Inuit lands, converting Inuit into various denominations of Christianity. Today the insatiable power quest of the Qallunaat is expressed through ongoing exploration for the non-renewable oil and mineral resources found under the sea and land, a land now depicted as "the last frontier" (Berger).

Gender, Naming, and Inuit

Each one of these waves of visitors, including scientists who believed they were outside traditional colonial attitudes, consisted mainly of males, and it was as though southerners sent their single males to undertake some kind a test for bravery and travel in the far north was only for testosterone-filled bodies. It was not until recently that females dared to travel to the far north to nurse or teach. Interestingly, most of these southerners remain visitors; to this day there are few from the south who settle for good in the far north. As one of my friends in Iqaluit pointed out, not too many Qallunaat get buried there.

Most of the male Qallunaaq visitors interpreted the Inuit societies as male dominated. After all, Inuit societies are based on hunting on land and sea, and the hunters are the ones who bring in the food. But as a child growing up as a Kalaaleq I never really felt any sense that males' were regarded as having exceptional status, and as a mature female, I began to look into Inuit gender relations.

Gender equality is expressed through an understanding of *sila* (intellect), which by its ordination of life grants the bearer undeniable autonomy. *Sila*, one of the life forces, is indivisible, and discussing gender in that context becomes frivolous and senseless. Applying spiritual terms to our mundane daily lives means that Inuit do not secularize their cosmology. This is immediately apparent in the Inuit naming system.

Genderless personal empowerment is conveyed through androgynous names, where gender does not play any significant role in bestowing names. What matters is what Guemple describes as "the entry of a relatively indestructible spiritual substance, a 'soul'" (27) and once given, the individual is accorded reverential respect.

For the Inuit a name is a soul and a soul is a name. This life-giving entity comes directly from the universe *silarsuaq*—the home of all souls, the settling of eternal life. Our bodies are temporary vehicles of the real matter that exists beyond this material world. One British scholar, after studying the naming system in Greenland, concluded that this temporary embodiment really is a form of recharging of souls (Nutall). Our names are the bridges, connections with our past, with the animals, the land, and the ever-existing universe, validating our presence in this world.

Another scholar working in other parts of the Arctic wrote:

> Inuit foetus is considered as a miniature human endowed with consciousness and will, but psychologically fragile, unstable, susceptible, and versatile, characteristics shared with the spirits of the dead and with animals, as well as with supernatural beings.... Endowed with hypersensitivity, it hears, understands, smells, and sees... that which humans cannot see, smell, hear, or understand, the exception of course, being the shaman. (D'Anglure 83)

This perception extends to all newborn animals because to us they are just entering this world, still carrying with them unknown powers and qualities from elsewhere—some aspects to be cherished, others to be feared. One cannot underestimate the quality and strengths of other beings, particularly those in the newly born state. Rasmussen, one of the earliest Arctic ethnographers, explains:

> Everyone on receiving a name receives with it the strength and skill of the deceased namesake, but since all persons bearing the same name have the same source of life, spiritual and physical qualities are also inherited from those who in the distant past once bore the same name. The shamans say that sometimes, on their flights, they can see, behind each human being, as it were a mighty procession of spirits aiding and guiding, as the rules of life are duly observed; but when this is not done... then all the invisible guardians turn against him as enemies, and he is lost beyond hope. (58–9)

So it is that each name represents a soul and the present bearer is a namesake of someone who has passed away. Because the name represents a soul, one's soul identity can be traced to a soul kinship system. Not only are we members of our biological extended family, but through our names and therefore souls we enter into membership of other families in the Inuit communities.

Names are to be reckoned with because they represent elements in the universe as well as the name of a previous soul. For that matter, the bearer of a name also tried to behave well to invest his or her quality in the name in the hope that others will be given one's name in the future and thereby pass along desirable qualities associated with the person. Names are, therefore, part of the life-giving force and obviously could not be divided by gender. In fact, until recently, Inuit names were shared across gender. An Inuk woman can indeed be male through her name, as a man could be a woman through his name.

I remember, when I started to become aware at the age of three or four, my pride in being my own two cousins. I was named after my paternal aunt's two daughters who died before my birth. I also bear the name of a caring wife of an old man, the name of a mother of a disabled young man, and the name of the sister of a woman who to this day calls me her beloved sister. I am in fact six people through my various names and in their physical absence, I celebrate with my name-sakes' living families some of the events of their past lives, such as their birthdays and the days my namesakes died, and I try to visit the various families during my namesakes' important days to give presence of their beloved dead. These activities may seem complicated and confusing to non-Inuit, but as I said earlier, our families become extended through the naming system. Such confusion may further be intensified as Inuit widely practice open adoption to this day. My own paternal grandmother was adopted by her mother's husband who was not my grandmother's biological father. We loved him as much as my grandmother did, and she, through many gestures, affection-ately thanked him for a good life. As part of our homage to him my youngest sister was named after him. I named my own son after this man, and both of them represent our cherished great-grandfather, Aata Tubbia. Through names, I and others can trace soul-scapes of other people in our communities.

The Inuit naming system also illustrates the ways in which the culture has accommodated Christianity. Assimilation of various religious practices has led the Inuit into interesting new hybrids of Christianity, and heated debates about the influence of Christi-anity can be heard among the young people today. Much criticism is possible concerning the negative influence the missionaries had on Inuit cultures, but we also have to appreciate that belief systems such as Christianity provide hope and stability to individuals suffering when cultures are in flux. Regardless of the particular Christian denomina-tion, the ancient naming system is very much intact. One may have a baptismal name, used for official state purposes, and one may also have Inuktitut names for community and family use. One may think that the androgynous names would not be appropriate to-day because Christian names are based on gender. Although Inuit names have become gender specific through Christianity, most of the Christian names can accommodate cross-genderization. Hans can easily become Hansigna, Robert becomes Roberta, Charles becomes Charlene, John becomes Joelene. Thus the genderless naming practice continues among Christian Inuit. I know very few Inuit children who have been given names simply because the parents liked the name or thought it was "fashionable."

I suppose that the moon also did have feelings, however sick he must be to do this to his own sister. He loved her as anyone can love. He desired and loved her enough to give up his life in his community. There must be something to learn from this story. I guess I have been conditioned to support the victim, and my bias in that regard has been too strong to understand the position of the moon. There is so much abuse in many communities—physical, psychological, and indeed sexual. Sexual abuses? What can be learnt from this story? The sun and the moon committed a travesty but managed to overcome their personal tragedies by becoming magnificent beings in the universe. Can this be true for mundane human beings? Can people who have suffered greatly overcome their problems and become great not only for themselves but for the community?

Inuit Construction of Gender

There are many different beliefs about how a foetus becomes a boy or a girl, for example, establishment of gender may be the result of a family's wish to have a boy or a girl. But in my experience, each child regardless of his or her sex was appreciated and seen as a gift of life. Prior to the acceptance of the Christian belief systems, Inuit did not have any notion of "illegitimacy"; a child came to this world already endowed with its own autonomy. As an Inuit parent, you do not "own" your child; the child owns herself or himself. Today, some of the old belief system is still practised in combination with a modern way of life.

Recognized gender identity starts to be inculcated in children soon after birth. The gender of the child is constantly mentioned and greeted with great enthusiasm and delight by the parents of a child. Young children's genitalia are discussed openly and freely by the closest relatives, since these are manifestations and symbols of the creative life forces expressed in womanhood and manhood. This continues until the children start to become self-conscious, whereupon this practice diminishes as the child develops cognitive *sila*, or at this point *isuma* - reasoning (Briggs). At the same time, children are given incremental responsibilities that relate to their gender roles in the Inuit community. Little boys are given tasks related to *angutit* (men's) work and these tasks increase in difficulty as they grow older. In the same way, little girls are given *arnat* (women's) work. Usually, each child is praised for a good job, and a big fuss is made over the smallest accomplishment. Taking away responsibilities from a child for a wrongdoing is seen as one of the most severe forms of punishment in a child's development.

Children's development is evaluated on the basis of how they combine their physical growth with the psychological, cognitive and the spiritual aspects of life. Too many demands by a child for personal attention, whether they take the form of too many questions, nosiness, or tantrums is much discouraged.

Gender-based division of labour is usually apparent and held to be a necessary adjustment to life on *nuna*—the land. The division of labour does not in any way diminish the validation of individual human existence provided through the life forces. Gender-based division of labour is seen to be a valued social practice necessary for the enjoyment of the products of the life forces available in the habitat. *Arnaassuseq* (femaleness) and *angutaassuseq* (maleness) are real manifestations of humanity and their distinctive qualities are highly cherished. Inuit have strongly defined expectations of how men ought to behave and present themselves: as strong and appreciative of their own maleness. Most of all, as Inuit women, we like to see the willingness of Inuit men to invest their energies into sensible and sensitive use of the surroundings—the land and the animals—to the extent that this use meets the needs of family and community and is mindful of the spiritual realities. Likewise, Inuit hold strongly defined expectations of how women ought to behave: as strong and sensitive to the needs of family and community, and mindful of the inter-relationship of these to the forces of life. Couples recognize the qualities of their partners and each develop in a manner complementary to the relationship. As an Inuk woman in Pangnirtung, Baffin Island expressed it, "the Inuktitut way of living is to respect your man and the man respects you" (Williamson 1992, 125).

The possibilities of switching gender roles are not necessarily exceptional and doing this is not disparaged: women may hunt and men carry out women's tasks. These arrangements depend on the individual relationship and the responsibilities partners have within their families.

Another way of developing gender identity is through the instilling of terms related to kinship. The terms for kinship membership are gender based. At birth a child will be called *panik* or *ernik* (daughter or son, respectively) by the parents. The hierarchical order of siblings is also explicit in kinship terminology. Such terms as *angaju, nuka* are based on same sex sibling relationships, one the older and one the younger. *Naja* (a younger sister of a male), *aleqa* (an older sister of a male), *anik* (an older brother of a female), *aqqalu* (a younger brother of a female) are used in reference to the speaker's relationship to a sibling.

This explicit and extensive system continues to all other family relationships where for example one might be an *atsa*—paternal; *aja*—maternal; or *ukuaq*—aunt-in-law. Or one might be an uncle, through the paternal side—*akka*; through the maternal side—*anga*; or in-law—*ningaa*. So it goes on. One never loses opportunities to understand one's own gender in an Inuit community.

Maybe there is more to life than the black and white we have been taught to see. Life is not black and white. Society is not simply made up of victims and victimizers. How can we learn from one another?

Inuit Language—Inuktitut

As suggested earlier, if language is seen as a social construction of epistemological knowledge, and if a rational explanation of the world can be derived from analyzing the structure of any language, one can then understand how the Inuktitut language reinforces the importance of deep appreciation of humanity. Like many other Indigenous languages, Inuktitut omits genderization and emphasizes the existence of a broader universalized social truth: namely, we all comprise humanity. It de-emphasizes the dichotomy of gender relations. As the Canadian cultural linguist Louis-Jacques Dorais explains: "for the Inuit, language cannot be divorced from the cosmic order. Without it, [the language] there would be no life and death, no day and night, and even no difference between men and women" (186).

I have already shown how through the Inuit language the theory of the origins of the universe can be traced. To the Inuit, words have metaphysical and magical powers (Williamson 1974), and the power of the word is considered tremendous (Berthelsen 343). William Ermine in "Aboriginal Epistemology" writes, "our languages reveal a very high level of rationality that can only come from an earlier insight into power" (107–8).

Like any other intelligent people, Inuit enjoy the flexibility, expediency, accuracy, and delivery of both concrete and abstract thought through their language, Inuktitut. The oral tradition of legends and myths that comprise the Inuit world view had great importance in transmitting the Inuit culture and psyche (Berthelsen 343) and reflects values and what is of significance in who we are. Too few people are aware of the Inuits' great love for poetry and creative prose. I remember my husband telling about an Inuk friend of his who felt he could not let a day go by without composing "a breath" of poetry. Inuktitut words comprise word-roots, infix, and suffixes. Some of the words can be long and might appear to have no specific order, grammatically speaking.

MacLean argues this flexible arrangement is a perfect illustration of Inuit theory of the origin of the universe:

> The concept of interdependence stands out in the structure of the Inupiaq and Yupik languages. Each word has a marker which identifies its relation to the other words in the sentence. There is no set order of words in a sentence, just as there is no way of determining what will happen next in nature. Man cannot control nature. (MacLean 164)

In Inuit sentence structure a listener cannot determine whether it refers to a man, a woman, or other being by the suffix alone. The listener has to determine this in relation to the context of the conversation. Context is always vital, and this goes back to the placing of value on all beings, where each has equal rights to exist on individual terms.

During the assimilationist era, most Indigenous people around the world experienced great devaluation by the colonialist cultures of Indigenous cultural knowledge and language. Inuktitut was no exception partly because languages based on oral traditions were challenged by the assumptions of the superiority of written forms. Schools and churches operating residential schools played a highly influential role in eliminating Indigenous languages. These efforts now threaten the Inuvialuktun and Inuinnartun dialects in northern Canada. Today, attempts are being made to keep various forms of Inuktitut alive in most parts of all Arctic countries. Language is the heart of a people and, as shown earlier, contains their values, and cosmic and social knowledge. Each of the Inuit languages has its own way of conveying some truth of human nature and must be respected for what it is.

A number of orthographies have been introduced to the Inuit by the missionaries. The eastern Canadian Inuit were introduced to syllabics, a form of shorthand writing that symbolizes the sound of the language. Syllabics were introduced late in the last century through the church, and they use the system effectively for written language. Syllabics have become very much a part of the Canadian Inuit identity, and are used in all sorts of media. Greenland Inuktitut—Kalaallisut— has been more standardized because German missionaries introduced the Roman alphabet in the middle of the last century. In the western Canadian Arctic and Alaska, Roman letters have also been adopted for writing dialects. Compared to many other Indigenous people, most Inuit live relatively isolated lives away from non-Inuit communities. They remain the majority in their own communities. Due to this, most eastern and central Arctic and Greenland homes speak Inuit dialects and are keeping the language alive.

I have referred to the various nations that Inuit live under today. Most Inuit youth today are more multilingual since most schooling is in the colonizer's language and the Inuktitut dialect is learned at home. In places such as Quebec, in addition to English, French has become widely used by the Inuit. It is not uncommon to meet educated trilingual Inuit individuals. At the same time, one can meet Inuit people barely able to speak broken Inuktitut and a broken second language.

Big Bang theory, Chaos theory, Black Hole, Adam and Eve, evolution... who knows the answer to life? What do we, as human beings, know about the rest of the universe? How intriguing it is to get to know some inkling of answers through these various thoughts on the beginning of life. There must be many more other travels. Concerning this, an esteemed Utoqqartaq (an elder) once told me Inuit have thought... that the universe, which was made a very long time ago, will never come to an end unless it has reached the satisfaction of achieving its final fate.... Everything has its end. Animals and human beings have been made simultaneously; they would not become extinct until their purpose of existence has reached its fulfilment. They will not reach the point of extinction, unless that point has reached itself. That is how they are together, they are made together. For me, this was a profound revelation about the understanding of the continuum of the life forces and their endless creative manifestations elsewhere in the silarsuaq (the universe). These forces may in different compositions create very different qualities of life.

How Is This Translated into Modern Inuit Life?

Substantial parts of the Inuit languages are still intact, but threatened by the intrusion of European cultures through state intervention—through the administration of people's lives, through schools, churches, hospitals, housing, commerce, and technology. As a circumpolar population, the Inuit have been divided between Russia, the United States, Canada, and Denmark. Each of these nations has been setting up extensive infrastructures that govern most parts of Inuit life.

I fully endorse the call for a continuing search for appropriate academic paradigms to studying social constructions across cultures (Mackie; Bodenhorn; Klein and Ackerman). At the same time there is a need for a new discourse that empowers the Indigenous societies. As I said earlier, much Western scientific knowledge-gathering and analysis have contributed to the invalidation of Indigenous ways of knowing and have not always been in the best interests of the Indigenous populations around the world. There is indeed a need for solid Indigenous paradigms to be developed to evaluate the present social structures imposed upon Indigenous populations, beyond mere ontological studies.

Such an endeavour will be complicated by the introduction of Aboriginal self-government by nation states today. The introduction of self-government will not necessarily contribute to Indigenous peoples' knowledge about and ability to govern themselves. Aboriginal self-governments are attained through negotiation with the nation state and are premised on Western forms of governing. The challenge of Aboriginal self-government is the coordination of Aboriginal values and norms with the existing structures. Today, Greenland's Home Rule (Aboriginal self-government) is much more responsive and sensitive to the previous colonizers way of governing, than with meeting the needs of the people socially, culturally, and spiritually. Through all of the modern trends, ideologies, and socio-political complexities, there is to be found among Inuit a traditional intellect-respecting egalitarianism whereby the people reassert their full status, power, and prestige by adjusting and using their sophisticated contemporary understanding of their real identity.

I heard the story of Seqineq and Aningaaq (the sun and the moon) many times and love the story as it keeps on revealing new sides to my travels to the inner world of humanity. You will also realize that there are a number of different stories relating how the sun and the moon came about, even among different groups of the Inuit. In my mind, it is a good thing that the two are a sister and a brother: after all we know so little about the universe. What do you think? Qujannamiik, nakormiik, qujanaq—"thank you"—in various Inuktitut dialects.

Endnote

[1] Storytelling is a means to connect the listener to the universe, to the past, to the present, and to the future; it establishes a relationship to the souls and minds of human beings, animals, and the land. In Inuit societies, adults are not to impose their own values on the developing minds of listeners, and stories reflect this principle. Parents recognize that each child is uniquely gifted, and the manifestations of giftedness are acknowledged according to each characteristic.

As a child growing up in such a social environment, one is left to think for oneself. This is not an easy process because there are usually no guidelines on to how to arrive at conclusions or to know if the conclusion arrived at was a correct one, if indeed there is a correct one. The conclusions one makes are all relative and changeable according to the circumstances, and the flexibility of some of these stories still amazes me.

Works Cited

Battiste, Marie. "Micmac Literacy and Cognitive Assimilation." *Indian Education in Canada*. Ed. J. Barman, Y. Hebert, and D. McCaskill. Vancouver: University of British Columbia Press: Vancouver, 1986. 23–44.

_____. Personal communication, April 12, 2000.

Berger, T. Northern Frontier Northern Homeland (Vol.1). Minister of Supply and Services Canada, 1977.

Berthelsen, Christian. "Greenlandic Literature." In *Arctic Languages: An Awakening*. Ed. Dirmid R.F. Collis. Paris: The United Nations Educational, Scientific and Cultural Organization, 1990. 343–53.

Blaut, J.M. *The Colonizer's Model of the World*. New York: The Guild Ford Press, 1993.

Bodenhorn, Barbara. "I'm Not the Great Hunter, My Wife Is. Inupiat and Anthropological Models of Gender." *Etudes/Inuit/ Studies* 14.1–2 (1990): 55–74.

Briggs Jean L. *Never in Anger*. Cambridge, MA: Harvard University Press, 1971.

Burch, Ernest S. Jr. and Walter Foreman. *The Eskimos*. Norman: University of Oklahoma Press, 1988.

Cajete, Gregory. *Look to the Mountain: An Ecology of Indigenous Education*. Durango: Kivaki Press, 1994.

Condon, Richard G. *Inuit Youth: Growth and Change in the Canadian Arctic*. New Brunswick: Rutgers University Press, 1988.

D'Anglure, Bernard Saladin. "From Foetus to Shaman: The Construction of an Inuit Third Sex." *Amerindian Rebirth: Reincarnation Belief Among North American Indians and Inuit*. Ed. Antonia Mills and Richard Slobodin. Toronto: University of Toronto Press, 1994. 82–106.

Dorais, Louis-Jacques. "The Canadian Inuit and Their Language." *Arctic Languages: An Awakening*. Ed. Dirmid R.F. Collis. Paris: The United Nations Educational, Scientific and Cultural Organization, 1990. 185–289.

Duran, Eduardo and Bonnie Duran. *Native American Post Colonial Psychology*. Albany: State University of New York Press, 1995.

Ermine, William. "Aboriginal Epistemology." *The Circle Unfolds*. Ed. Marie Battiste and Jean Barman. Vancouver: University of British Columbia Press, 1995. 101–12.

Fienup-Riordan, Ann. *Eskimo Essays. Yup'ik Lives and How We See Them*. New Brunswick and London: Rutgers University Press, 1990.

Fitzhugh, William W. and Susan Kaplan. *Inua, Spirit World of the Bering Sea Eskimo*. Washington: National Museum History by Smithsonian Institution Press, 1982.

Guemple, Lee. "Gender in Inuit Society." *Women and Power in Native North America*. Ed. Klein, Laura F. and Lillian A. Ackerman. Norman and London: University of Oklahoma Press, 1995.

Hall, Judy, Jill Oakes, and Sally Qimmiu'naaq Webster. *Sanatujut. Pride in Women's Work*. Hull: Canadian Museum of Civilization, 1994.

Kaliss, Tony. "What Was the 'Other' That Came on Columbus' Ships?" *The Journal of Indigenous Studies* 3.2 (1996). 27–42.

Kawagley, Oscar. "A Yupiaq World view: Implication for Cultural, Educational, and Technological Adaptation in a Contemporary World." Master's thesis, University of British Columbia, 1993.

Klein, Laura F. and Lillian A. Ackerman, Eds. *Women and Power in Native North America*. Norman and London: University of Oklahoma Press, 1995.

Mackie, Marlene. *Constructing Women and Men. Gender Socialization*. Toronto: Holt, Rinehart and Winston of Canada, 1987.

MacLean, Edna Ahgeak. "Culture and Change for Inupiat and Yupiks of Alaska." *Arctic Languages: An Awakening*. Ed. Dirmid R.F. Collis. Paris: The United Nations Educational, Scientific and Cultural Organization, 1990. 159–75.

Mikaere, Annie. "The Balance Destroyed: The Consequences from Maori Women of the Colonization of Tikanga Maori. Master's thesis, University of Waikato, 1995.

Ministeriet for Gronland. *Ordbogi. Kalaallisuumit-Qallunaatuumut*, 1977.

Nutall, Mark. *Arctic Homeland: Kinship, Community and Development in Northwest Greenland*. Toronto: University of Toronto Press, 1992.

Sioui, Georges. *For an Amerindian Autohistory: An Essay on the Foundations of Social Ethic*. Montreal and Kingston: McGill-Queen's University Press, 1992.

Wenzel, George. *Animal Rights Human Rights: Ecology, Economy, and Ideology in the Canadian Arctic*. Toronto: University of Toronto Press, 1991.

Weyer, E. *The Eskimo: Their Environment and Folkways*. Hamden, CT: Archon Books, 1962.

Williamson, Karla Jessen. "The Cultural Ecological Perspectives of Canadian Inuit: Implication for Child-rearing and Education." Master's thesis, University of Saskatchewan, 1992.

Williamson, Robert G. *Eskimo Underground: Socio-cultural Change in the Central Arctic*. Uppsala: Institutionen for allman och jamforende etnografi vid Uppsala Universitet, 1974.

*Challenging
the Past*

Old World Law and
New World Political Realities

Olive Patricia Dickason

Olive Dickason grew up in northern Manitoba and was for many years a journalist with various newspapers, winding up on the Globe and Mail. *She subsequently became a Professor of History and taught at the University of Alberta. She is Professor Emeritus, University of Alberta, an Adjunct Professor, University of Ottawa, and continues to work as an historical consultant, researcher, and writer. In 1992 she was elected Métis Woman of the Year by the Women of the Métis Nation of Alberta.*

The expansion of Europe's geographical horizons during the fifteenth and sixteenth centuries also saw a widening of legal horizons as a host of new considerations complicated debates on Roman and canon law that had been going on for centuries.[1] These debates had been increasing in intensity with the rise of nation states during the Renaissance. Now, with the discovery that the world was larger and more complex than Europeans had ever imagined, legal issues took on unforeseen dimensions. If those aspects of divine, human, and natural law, which were classified as the "law of nations," had been important before, they now became crucial, particularly where sovereignty was concerned. This is evident in the works of Dominican Francisco de Vitoria (1480?–1546), primary professor of sacred theology at the University of Salamanca; Alberico Gentili (1552–1608), regius professor of civil law at the University of Oxford; and Hugo Grotius (Huigh de Groot, 1583–1645), jurist and diplomat, who published his epoch-making *De jure belli ac pacis* in 1625. These men are generally credited with laying the basis for international law as we know it today; in fact, however, they are only the best known of the many who were involved. All attempted to fit the new realities of the Americas into the European legal traditions that had been evolving since the days of the Roman empire.

Principal points at issue were the legitimacy of authority, and the rights of Christians compared to those of non-Christians. The first point concerned the legal system inherited from the old Roman empire— was it a universal expression of law, and if so, how did the rights of newly discovered peoples and nation-states in America relate, if at all, to those of Europe? As for the second point, while there was disagreement about the extent to which Christians held priority over non-Christians, European monarchs continued to act on the assumption, as they had done during the days of the Crusades, that they were within their rights if they wished to claim lands not under the control of a Christian prince. If they encountered resistance, they assumed the right, particularly if they had papal sanction to evangelize, to attack, and to conquer. The Americas offered previously undreamed-of opportunities to work out these assumptions in the field.

Dividing the Unknown World

Columbus had no sooner reported his epoch-making landfall than Spain moved to establish its claim to these new lands. There was some urgency about this, as Portugal was also in the running. According to Columbus, these strange regions abounded in wealth and were inhabited by peoples who wore no clothes and whose only weapons were stone—pointed spears and arrows. Columbus foresaw no difficulty in transforming these people into Spanish subjects, or perhaps enslaving them. When Spain brought pressure to bear on the Spanish pope Alexander VI (in office 1492–1503) to recognize its claims, the pope tempered his response by making provision at the same time for the imperial claims of Portugal. He did this in his 1493 bulls by dividing between the two powers the right to evangelize in this newly discovered world. Alexander's line of demarcation may not have satisfied either power, but it paved the way for them to settle their differences in the Treaty of Tordesillas in 1494, which moved the line 300 leagues to the west. Thus the line placed the Americas in the Spanish zone of influence, except for Brazil, which fell to the Portugese.

While there was much criticism of the papal action in regard to its temporal aspects, no one at the time challenged its spiritual basis. After the rise of Protestantism, the grant to Spain and Portugal would be justified on the grounds that the New World had been revealed to a Catholic power. This was cited as proof positive that Roman Catholicism was the true faith, as God was thus indicating the type of Christianity He wanted taught to these strange peoples.[2]

France, a growing continental power, found the bulls galling to her national pride: by what right was she, a Catholic power, excluded from the New World? To make matters worse, the division had been accomplished without even consulting her.[3] Such indignation was compounded by the immensity of the gift to the Spanish and Portuguese, once it was definitely established that the new lands were continents and not just islands. "*Je ne puis pas croire,*" complained cosmographer André Thevet (1516/17?–1592), "*que le Pape ait accordé toute ceste longue terre depuis un Pole jusques à l'autre, veu qu'elle suffiroit à une cinquantaine de Roys Chrestiens.*" ("I cannot believe that the pope has granted this length of territory stretching from one pole to the other, which is sufficient for fifty Christian kings.")[4] France was not to be confined to Europe, an anonymous pamphleteer proclaimed. "*Il faut que les Barbares esprouvent à l'avenir la douceur de sa domination, et se polissent à son exemple.... Nous sommes dans un siècle où tout ce qui est grand, tout ce qui est beau, tout ce qui est utile pour l'Etat, s'entreprend et s'execute.*" ("In the future the barbarians must experience the advantages of her [France's] domination, and civilize themselves following her example.... We are in a century when everything that is great, everything that is beautiful, everything that is useful for the State is being undertaken and put into effect.")[5] Antoine de Montchrestien (ca. 1575–1621), dramatist and economist, was just as vehement, claiming that if anyone had the right to civilize the non-Christian world it was the French, known for the glories of their arts and civilities; besides, it was really they who could bring true Christianity to the New World: "*quoy que les aultres prétendent.*"[6] The flood of such sentiment all but drowned out the few voices that asserted old arguments and raised awkward questions about Amerindian sovereignty and proprietary rights.

Rights of Christians Versus Non-Christians

European jurists had long been divided about the infidel's right to sovereignty in his national life and to property in his personal life. The moderate position had been championed by Pope Innocent IV (in office 1243–1254), who defended the right of all rational creatures to hold property and upheld the legitimacy of the non-Christian ruler's power.[7] But if such a ruler had Christian subjects whom he was abusing, then Innocent held that the pope, by virtue of his universal authority over all men, would have the power to depose him. In other words, a just and sufficient cause was needed to legitimately deprive a non-Christian ruler of his *dominium*. This argument was to provide the Dominican "Apostle to the Indians," Bartolomé de Las Casas (1474–1556), with some of his most effective ammunition in his defence of New World peoples.[8]

The principal opposing position was championed by Henry of Susa, Cardinal of Ostia (d. 1271); it became known as the Ostiensian (or Hostiensian) doctrine.[9] Henry had maintained that there was no legitimate secular power outside of the church; that heathens had lost their right to political jurisdiction and to worldly possessions when Christ had become king of the earth. He held that Jesus had transferred His temporal and spiritual dominion to Peter and hence to the Pope.[10] In practical terms this meant that a people without a knowledge of the Christian God could retain their lands only with the approval of the Church. The pope had the right to appoint a Christian ruler to bring such people within the fold of the faith; however, the power of such a prince was defined as *politicum* and not *despoticum*.

Possession Since "Time Immemorial"

Quite apart from the religious issue, there was an important point in Roman law to consider. All the best legal authorities agreed that rights of discovery could only be invoked in the case of unoccupied territories, as set out in the code of Emperor Justinian I (483–565).[11] Jurists considered the continuous use and possession of land "from time immemorial" as a basis for title to be a self-evident rule of natural law. Since the newly discovered lands were irrefutably occupied, an alternative for Spain had been to obtain the right to evangelize.

One of the earliest voices in defence of title "from time immemorial" was that of a Scottish Dominican theologian at the Sorbonne, John Major (Mair, 1469–1550). Major denied the pope's temporal dominion of the world on the grounds that Jesus had declared that His kingdom was not of this world. Therefore temporal dominion (or title) lay not in faith, but in natural law, which gave the infidel as much right to his land as the Christian had to his. However, Christians had not only the right but the duty to preach the Gospel: if heathens resisted, then Christians had the right to resort to the use of arms. In such a case, Major argued, the pope could authorize the seizure of political power and the levying of tribute. As for Amerindians, "Those people live like animals... it is evident that some men are by nature free, and others servile. In the natural order of things the qualities of some men are such that, in their own interests, it is right and just that they should serve, while others, living freely, exercise their natural authority and command."[12]

Natural Law and Papal Power

More far-ranging was the stand taken by Vitoria, who is considered by many to have made the first major statement on aboriginal rights following Columbus' landfall. In a series of lectures delivered in 1532 under the overall title "De Indis et De Jure Belli Relectiones," he outlined his position on the bulls of demarcation, Spanish imperial claims, and the rights of Amerindians. He agreed with Major that the bulls had no legal validity, as "the Pope has no civil or temporal dominion over the earth"; nor did he have temporal power over Amerindians or other pagans.[13] Even if the pope had possessed such power, he could not transfer it.[14] Neither could the Spanish emperor claim to be the lord of the earth. Should he be granted such a position, that still would not entitle him "to seize the territories of the aborigines, nor to erect new rulers, nor to dethrone the old ones and capture their possessions."[15] The aborigines, he found, "undoubtedly had true dominion in both public and private matters, just like Christians, and that neither their princes nor private persons could be despoiled of their property on the ground of their not being true owners."[16] This line of reasoning reflected the majority opinion of jurists of the period; Vitoria's originality lay not so much in the principles he enunciated as in his application of them to the New World.[17]

But theory was one thing and practical politics another, and so Vitoria found it necessary to modify his position. Pressured by high officialdom, he qualified his position by supporting the doctrine of the Christian right to preach the gospel and to resort to force if the infidels refused to listen,[18] and even he claimed an exclusive right for Spain in this regard as one of the rights of discovery.[19] Vitoria now also found that discovery had given the Spanish the exclusive right to trade in the new lands they claimed, which could be supported by the use of arms, if necessary.[20] Further, Spaniards had the right and duty to intervene in Amerindian states to rescue people from such tyrannies as human sacrifice and cannibalistic rituals.[21] In other words, the propagation of Christianity could legitimately lead to the subjugation of Amerindians by Christian princes on civil as well as religious grounds so long as this was done for the benefit of Amerindians rather than of Spaniards.[22]

Justifying Intervention

Thus even Vitoria, for all his reservations on the subject, was led from accepting intervention for religious reasons to accepting it for secular purposes. No such circuitous approach was used by the learned lay jurist Juan Ginés de Sepúlveda (1490–1572), ardent apologist for the Spanish conquest. He had no doubts that it was necessary "to divide the Indians of the cities and fields among honourable, just and prudent Spaniards, especially among those who helped to bring the Indians under Spanish rule, so that they may train the Indians in virtuous and humane customs, and teach them the Christian religion…. In return for this, the Spaniards may employ the labour of the Indians in performing those tasks necessary for civilized life."[23]

Sepúlveda enunciated the theoretical and legal justification for what was actually happening in the New World. Even the hesitant Vitoria conceded that Amerindians could be considered unfit to administer a lawful state as "they have no proper laws nor magistrates, and are not even capable of controlling their family affairs; they are without any literature or arts, not only the liberal arts, but the mechanical arts also; they have no careful agriculture and no artisans; and they lack many other conveniences, yea necessaries, of human life."[24] This was reinforced, Vitoria thought, by the fact that Amerindians were by nature slaves "so they may be in part governed as slaves are"; also, "their food is no more pleasant and hardly better than that of beasts."[25]

The force of such sentiments was to prove more powerful than early canonical concern for human rights. For instance, even as it was argued that title to New World lands did indeed belong to its original inhabitants, it was also held to be legitimate to wage war on Amerindians who, in the words of Gentili, "practiced abominable lewdness even with beasts, and who ate human flesh, slaying men for that purpose…. against such men… war is made as against brutes."[26] Grotius would also concur that violations of the laws of nature, such as cannibalism, justified war: "the most just war is against savage beasts, the next against men who are like beasts."[27]

There were those, particularly among the missionaries, who claimed that Amerindian vices were being wildly exaggerated and that undesirable behaviour was no more prevalent among New World natives than among other peoples. In any event, such behaviour on the part of some did not justify depriving whole peoples of *dominium*. Besides Las Casas, an outstanding figure in this group was Alonso de la Vera Cruz (1507–1584), Augustinian missionary who became professor of theological law at the University of Mexico shortly after it was founded in 1551. Both of these men vigorously argued that Amerindians had been true lords of their lands since time immemorial, and that neither pope nor European monarch had any right under natural law to make grants of Amerindian lands without the express consent of the peoples whose territories were involved. Vera Cruz would modify this by accepting Vitoria's concession concerning the overriding right to propagate Christianity, which was not a compromise that Las Casas ever made. Another concession held that it was legitimate for Amerindians to ask for the protection of outsiders and in return to transfer their land rights if they so chose. [28]

As such rationalizations lent themselves only too easily to the justification of abuses in colonial procedures, which were very quickly evident, Pope Paul III (in office 1534–1539) was moved in 1537 to declare in his bull *Sublimis Deus Sic Dilexit* that Amerindians "were by no means to be deprived of their liberty or the possession of their property, even though they may be outside the faith of Jesus Christ."[29] But Charles V (Holy Roman Emperor, 1519–1539; as king of Spain, 1516–1556, he was Carlos I) saw this bull as a challenge to his authority, and so it was never publicized in his domains. Above all, it was not announced in New Spain, where the colonists were firmly convinced of their right to limit the liberty of the Amerindians and seize their property. The Spanish Crown's efforts to protect the rights of Amerindians were thus not only secondary to political considerations, they never matched the colonists' capacities to evade them. The abuses were such that a century later, in 1639, Urban VIII (pope, 1623–1644) decreed excommunication for those who deprived Amerindians of their liberty or property.[30] But such a threat was not as powerful as it would have been in 1493, as the process of secularization had been in the meantime reinforced by the Protestant Reformation. Other considerations were now in the forefront: in the words of Marc Lescarbot (ca. 1570–1642), the Paris lawyer who spent a year (1606–1607) at Port Royal in Acadia, "There is here no question of applying the law and policy of Nations, by which it would not be permissible to claim the territory of another. This being so, we must possess it and preserve the natural inhabitants."[31] On another occasion he was even more forceful: "*Que sert de prendre tant de peine pour aller à une terre de conquête, si ce n'est pour la posseder entierement. Et pour la posseder, il faut se camper en la terre ferme et la bien cultiver.*" ("What is the purpose in taking over a territory, if not to possess it entirely. And to do that, one must settle on the land and cultivate it.")[32]

Redefining Natural Law

Before Columbus, military conquest had been Europe's principal means of national aggrandizement. But in the Americas, only Mexico, Central America, and Peru possessed indigenous city-states that could be conquered militarily. For most of the Americas, other means had to be found to legitimize European expansion. Since the rights of discovery could only be claimed for unoccupied territory, as Vitoria had inconveniently pointed out, and since the Americas were obviously peopled, the nature of their habitation quickly came into question. The legal argument developed that since a large proportion of the aborigines followed a mobile lifestyle without settled abodes, "like beasts in the woods," they were not inhabitants according to European law, since they "ranged" rather inhabiting the land. In this interpretation, most of the Americas were legally *terra nullius*, "empty land," and thus subject to rights of discovery. A second legal phrase, *vacuum domicilium*, expressed another version of the same idea. According to these concepts it was reasoned that proprietary rights could only exist within the framework of law enacted by an organized state; the lands of prestate peoples without such statutory law were therefore legally vacant. In other words, habitation or occupation from "time immemorial" had no meaning unless validated by positive law, an interpretation that would have surprised Justinian's legal advisers.

Sir Thomas More (1478–1535) expressed a corollary to this idea in his *Utopia* when he wrote that the most just cause for war was "when any people holdeth a piece of ground void and vacant for no good nor profitable use, keeping others from the use and possession of it which nothwithstanding by the law of nature ought thereof to be nourished and relieved."[33] Justification for claiming possession of land in the Americas eventually received its legal formulation by Emerich de Vattel (1714–1767) in his *Le droit des gens* in 1758. According to the Swiss jurist, Amerindians' "Uncertain occupancy of these vast regions can not be held as a real and lawful taking of possession; and when the Nations of Europe, which are too confined at home, come upon lands which the savages have no special need of and are making no present and continuous use of, they may lawfully take possession of them and establish colonies in them."[34] Vattel justifies this argument by saying that God intended the land to be farmed (the type of farming practised by many Amerindians was not seen as "true" agriculture).[35]

Means of Possession

Colonizers soon discovered another justification for their takeover of Amerindian lands: it was, they proclaimed, "full recompense" for bringing the Christian message to the New World.[36] In other words, it was fair exchange to take Amerindian lands in return for preaching the gospel.[37] This popular belief drew a rebuke from the English divine, Samuel Purchas (1577–1626), who had inherited the geographer and historian Richard Hakluyt's (1552–1616) monumental project of publishing accounts of voyages of exploration. Purchas observed tartly:

> It was barbarous Latine to turn fides into feodum… to dispossess Barbarians of their Inheritance, and by their want of Faith to increase our fees of Inheritance… Christ came not to destroy the Law but to fulfill it…[38]

Purchas, like Vitoria, would later qualify his opinion, even as he steadily maintained that it was not "lawful for Christians to usurpe the goods and lands of Heathens…." The turning point was the bloody attempt of the Amerindians to drive the English out of Virginia in 1622. After that, Purchas found that he agreed with his countrymen on one point when he wrote that: it was the duty of humans to make the earth productive. If land was not being cultivated, then it could be taken without injustice to anyone, "especially where the people is wild, and holdeth no settled possession in any parts."[39]

Following another lead indicated by Vitoria, trade also was used as a means of peaceful occupation: in 1698, Francis Nicholson, governor of Virginia 1698–1705, urged a policy of furnishing "the inland Indians with goods in such quantity and so cheap that they may take the trade from the French, as the French do, and build vessels upon their lakes."[40] Similar sentiments were expressed by Richard Coote, Earl of Bellomont, Governor of New York, New Hampshire, and Massachusetts 1697–1700.[41]

Purchase became a favourite means of winning Amerindian acquiescence to the takeover of their lands. Introduced by the Dutch and quickly picked up by the English, these "purchases" involved an exchange of goods for the land received. The value of the goods used for these transactions bore no relation to the value of the land received, not even in the terms of the day. These agreements were ambiguous in the sense that they recognized Amerindian proprietary right while sidestepping that of sovereignty. It was partly to avoid this ambiguity that the French never resorted to purchase.[42]

The European view of such arrangements, that they involved an absolute surrender to title and use of the land involved, was not shared by Amerindians. They regarded such purchases as merely conveyances of residence and subsistence rights for as long a time as the interested parties were satisfied with the terms. Hence the Amerindians considered it quite within their rights to return later to ask for additional payments, giving rise to the derisory epithet, "Indian giving."[43]

A religious literary figure such as the Huguenot pastor Urbain de Chauveton (ca. 1540–1614) might insist on the theoretical right of each man to live in liberty and to be free from the danger of assault from his neighbour,[44] or Louis XIV might instruct a Governor of New France that the Amerindians were not to be disturbed in the peaceful possession of their lands for the convenience of Frenchmen,[45] but there the matter rested as far as French law was concerned. The French never recognized either Amerindian sovereignty or proprietary rights as such, but only the latter as they were granted, either directly or indirectly, from the French King.[46] Consequently, in the France of the sixteenth and seventeenth centuries, as in the England of the same period, there had not been any great debate on aboriginal rights in relation to official policy, as there had been in Spain.

Possession, by whatever means, coupled with the divine mandate to convert the heathen, gave European monarchs the right, at least in their own eyes, to make grants of New World lands to their own subjects or to whomever they chose. These grants were often lavish, and nearly always drawn up in ignorance of the geography concerned. Not infrequently boundaries overlapped, leading to disputes that reached the violence of civil war, as happened in Acadia during 1635–1650. At other times two different monarchs granted the same land, again as happened in Acadia, when James I (1566–1625) in 1621 honoured one of his favourites, Sir William Alexander (ca. 1577–1640, Earl of Stirling), by granting him Mi'Kmaq, territory the French considered to be theirs. Armand-Jean Du Plessis, Cardinal, and Duc de Richelieu, principal minister to Louis XIII (1624–1642), did not think all of North America north of New Spain too large a territory for the operations of the Company of One Hundred Associates when he established it in 1627. Similarly, when Charles II (1630–1685) issued the charter for the Hudson's Bay Company in 1670, he granted that enterprise those lands draining into the Bay without having any clear idea of their extent. In fact, they had all been previously included in Richelieu's charter to the Company of One Hundred Associates. The underlying assumption in all these cases was the same: if these lands were not under the clear and effective control of a Christian prince, then European monarchs had to right to ensure that this deficiency was rectified.

The Amerindians, for their part, had no doubts as to their sovereignty and the rights to their lands. One group, upon being informed of the papal donation, was reported to have replied that the pope was indeed liberal with that which belonged to others, and that the Spanish King must be a poor man as he had asked for land.[47] The French, in repeating such tales with obvious relish, were motivated less by concern about Amerindian territorial rights than they were by anti-

Spanish sentiment. Neither did the English display much sensitivity
on the issue: when New England Amerindians began to insist that
their lands were inalienable, the English regarded this as "insolent"
and observed that "nobody doubts but that the French missionaries
prompt'em to."[48] The incident not only indicates the growing restiveness of
the indigenous population at European infringements on their lands
but also the beginnings of French exploitation of that reaction as a
weapon against the English.

In 1721, Abenaki chiefs sent an ultimatum to Samuel Shute, governor of Massachusetts 1716–1727, in which they sought to curb further
English settlement in Abenaki lands east of the Connecticut River.[49]
The English responded by declaring war, which resulted in the defeat
of the Abenaki in 1725 and the loss of more land, but did not put an
end to Abenaki resistance. For example, Atecouando of Odanak (also
known as Jérome; he flourished between 1749–57) in 1752 confronted
the British who were surveying Abenaki lands without the Natives'
permission: "We forbid you very expressly to kill a single beaver
or to take a single stick of wood on the lands we live on. If you
want wood, we will sell it to you, but you shall not have it without
our permission."[50] There are many more examples of such stands by
early Amerindian leaders. The French also encountered such attitudes.
In one instance, at Louisbourg, the Mi'Kmaq found it necessary to
remind them that the only rights the French had in Acadia, in
Mi'Kmaq eyes, were those of the enjoyment and use of the land
without destroying, damaging, or diminishing it. In law this is known
as usufruct.

For the Amerindians, the problem was essentially one of power.
When the English claimed suzerainty, or sovereignty, over the Iroquois
in 1698, a proud chief could reply, "We are masters of our own lands";
an Ojibwa headman, Minweweh (ca. 1710–1770), could tell Alexander
Henry (1739–1824) at Michilimackinac in 1761, "Englishman, although
you have conquered the French, you have not conquered us. We are
not your slaves. These lakes, these woods and mountains, were left us
by our ancestors. They are our inheritance; and we will part with them
to none."[51] But neither Minweweh nor the comparatively well-organ-
ized Iroquois possessed either the political hegemony or the technology to defend their rights over the long term, although they could and
did become skilful bargainers in the short term. They were further
handicapped by their social philosophy on two other counts. First of
all, it called for the sharing of land and its resources, which had led
them at first to welcome Europeans.[52] By the time they realized their

error, the tide of the European invasion was already irreversible. Secondly, the social fragmentation that had been so successful as a technique for survival under pre-contact conditions became an instrument for Amerindian subjugation with the arrival of the Europeans. Throughout the Americas, Europeans had found it comparatively easy to divide and conquer.

Thus, in this new order of things, the classical legal principle that first occupants were true owners of the land was lost. By redefining "occupancy" and "habitation," Europeans nullified what had once been considered to be a self-evident principle of natural law. In doing so, they ushered in a new era of colonialism.

Endnotes

[1] This paper is a reworking, with additional material, of my article, "Renaissance Europe's View of Amerindian Sovereignty and Territoriality," *Plural Societies* 8.3–8.4 (1977): 97–107. It was published in French, under the title "La loi dans l'Ancien Continent et les réalités politiques du Nouveau Monde," in *Cahiers d'histoire* (Université de Montréal) 13.2 (1993): 75–86.

[2] Gaspard de Saulx, "Memoires" (1509–1573), in *Collection complètes des memoires relatif à l'histoire de France*, ed. Claude Bernard Petitot, (Paris, 1819–1826) 23:238–9.

[3] Jean Alfonce (Jean Fonteneau), "La Cosmographie avec l'espère et regime du soleil et du nord," in *Recueil de Voyages et de Documents pour servir à l'histoire de la geographie depuis le XIIe jusqu'à la fin du XVIe siècle*, ed. Ch. Schefer and Henri Cordier (Paris: Ernest Leroux, 1904) 83.

[4] André Thevet, *La Cosmographie Universelle* (Paris: Guillaume Chaudiere, 1575), 965. All the translations from French are mine.

[5] *Relation de l'Etablissement de la Compagnie françoise pour le commerce des Indes Occidentales* (Paris: Sebastian Cramoisy, 1565) 1.

[6] Antoine de Montchretien, *Traicté de L'Oeconomie politique*, (s.l.n.d.) 270.

[7] Innocent IV, *Commentaria super libros quinque Decretalium...* (Frankfort, 1570). This was a gloss of Innocent III's decretal of 1200, *Quod super his*. St. Thomas Aquinas has also been much cited in support of this view, but his writings are equivocal.

[8] Bartolomé de las Casas, *De Regia Potestate* (Madrid: Consejo Superior de Investigaciones Científicas, 1969) 22, 55–6.

[9] Henricus de Segusia, *Hostiensis.... in primum[-sextum] Decretalium librum commentaria....* 4 vols. (Venice, 1581). See also James Muldoon, "*Extra ecclesiam non est imperium*, The Canonists and the

Legitimacy of Secular Power," *Studia Gratiana* 9 (1966): 553–80; and John of Paris, *On Royal and Papal Power*, trans. J.A. Watt (Toronto: Pontifical Institute of Mediaeval Studies, 1971).

[10] Henry Folmer, *Franco-Spanish Rivalry in North America 1524–1763* (Glendale, Ca: A.H. Clark, 1953), 21. Las Casas took strong exception to this position. Cf. *De Regia Potestate*, 30. The Hostensian position was implicity supported by both John Hus and John Wycliffe when they held that legitimate *dominium* could not be exercised without divine grace, which in effect deprived non-Christians of the right to rule. See Kenneth J. Pennington, Jr., "Bartolomé de Las Casas and the Tradition of Medieval Law," *Church History* 39.2 (1970): 156.

[11] Justinian's *Corpus Iuris Civilis* (Body of Civil Law), comprised the Codex, Digest (Pandects), Institutes, and Novels. The rights of discovery are dealt with in the Institutes 2.1.12.

[12] P. Laturia, *Major y Vitoria ante la Conquista de America, Estudios Ecclesiasticos* (Madrid, 1932), appendix. Also, J.H. Parry, *The Spanish Theory of Empire in the Sixteenth Century* (Cambridge: Cambridge University Press, 1940), 16–18. Major's ready acceptance of the bestiality of Amerindians would later draw a stinging rebuke from Las Casas. See Bartolomé de Las Casas, *Apología*, trans. and ed. Angel Losada (Madrid: Editoria Nacional, 1975) 373–5.

[13] Francisco de Vitoria, *De Indis et de Jure Belli Relectiones*, ed. Ernest Nys, "On the Indians," II.3 and II.6, in *The Classics of International Law*, gen. ed. James Brown Scott (Washington, D.C.: Carnegie Institution of Washington, 1912). Etienne Grisel discussed Vitoria's thought in "The Beginnings of International Law and General Public Law Doctrine: Francisco de Vitoria's De Indiis prior," in *First Images of America*, ed. Fredi Chiappelli(Los Angeles: University of California Press, 1976) I:305–25.

[14] Vitoria, "On the Indians," II.3.

[15] Ibid., II.4

[16] Ibid., I.24.

[17] Grisel, "Beginnings of International Law," 323–4.

[18] Vitoria, "On the Indians," III.12.

[19] Ibid., III.10.

[20] Ibid., III.3 and III.7; III.12.

[21] Ibid., III.15. Vitoria also argued that the King of Spain would have the right to intervene and compel obedience if the French people refused to obey their king. (Ibid., II.7).

[22] Ibid., III.16.

[23] Cited by J.H. Parry, "A Secular Sense of Responsibility," *First Images*, I: 293.

[24] Vitoria, "On the Indians," III.18.

[25] Ibid.

[26] Alberico Gentili, *De Jure Belli* (1612), trans. John C. Rolfe (Washington: Carnegie Institution, 1933), bk. 1, ch. 25, 122.

[27] Grotius, Hugo. *Law of War and Peace (De Jure Belli ac Pacis, 1625)*, trans. Francis W. Kelsey, (Washington: Carnegie Institution, 1911; reprint, Indianapolis: Bobbs-Merrill, 1925), bk.2, ch.20, s.XL, 506.

[28] A leading spokesman for this position was Thomas Gage (1597–1655), a Dominican of Irish origin at one point in the service of Spain. See his *Nouvelle relation contenant les voyages de Thomas Gage dans la nouvelle Espagne....*, trans. Sieur de Beaulieu Huës O'Neil, 2 vols. (Paris: G. Clouzier, 1676) I:Epistre.

[29] Lewis Hanke, "Pope Paul III and the American Indians," *The Harvard Theological Review* 30 (1937): 72.

[30] Ludwig Pastor, *The History of the Popes* (London: K. Paul, Trench Trubner, 1923–1953) 29:262.

[31] Lescarbot, *The History of New France*, ed. W.L. Grant (Toronto: The Champlain Society, 1907–1914) I:17.

[32] Jean de Léry, *Histoire d'un voyage fait en la terre du Bresil* (Lausanne, Impr. Réunies, 1972) 298.

[33] *More's Utopia and a Dialogue of Comfort* (London: Dent; New York: Dutton, 1955), 70; cited by Robin Fisher, *Contact and Conflict* (Vancouver: University of British Columbia Press, 1977), 104, who also notes that this position was supported by John Locke in his *Second Treatise of Government*. For the view that Amerindians ranged the land like wild beasts, see Ralph Horton, "The Relations Between the Indians and the White in Colonial Virgina," (master's thesis, University of Chicago, 1921), 20; and Francis Jennings, "Virgin Land and Savage People," *American Quarterly* (October 1971): 519–41.

[34] Emer de Vattel, *The Law of Nations or the Principles of Natural Law*, trans. Charles G. Fenwick (Washington, D.C., 1902; reprint, New York, 1964), 85. There were contrary views. Francis Bacon, for one, wrote, "I like a *Plantation* in Pure Soile...where People are not *Displanted*, to the end, to *Plant* in Others. For else, it is rather an Extirpation, then a *Plantation*." "Of Plantations," in *Essays or Counsels, Civill and Morall....*, (London, 1625) 204.

[35] Even today, anthropologists refer to early Amerindian agriculture as "horticulture."

[36] George Peckham, "A True Report of the late discoveries, and possession taken in the right of the Crowne of England of the Newfound Lands" (1583), in Richard Hakluyt, *The Principall*

Navigations Voiages and Discoveries of the English Nation, ed. D.G. Quinn and R.A. Skelton, 2 vols. (Cambridge: Cambridge University Press, 1965; first published 1589) II:705–6. See also Robert Gray, *A Good Speed to Virginia* (1609), ed. Wesley F. Craven (New York: Scholar's Facsimile, 1937) B1 verso, C3 passim; and Fred M. Kimmey, "Christianity and Indian Lands," *Ethnohistory* 7 (1960): 44–61.

[37] Fred M. Kimmey, "Christianity and Indian Lands," *Ethnohistory* 7 (1960): 44–60.

[38] Samuel Purchas, *Hakluytus Posthumus or Purchas His Pilgrimes* (Glasgow: MacLehose, 1905–1907) I:42.

[39] Ibid., 19: 222–223.

[40] "Governor Nicholson to Council of Trade and Plantations, 20 August 1698," *Calendar of State Papers, Colonial Series, America and West Indies, 27 October 1697–31 December 1698* (London: His Majesty's Stationery Office, 1905) 392.

[41] Ibid., 547–8.

[42] Earl Edward Muntz, "Race Contact, A Study of the Social and Economic Consequences of Contact Between Civilized and Uncivilized Races" (Ph.D. diss., Yale University, 1925), 81. This was published in 1927.

[43] Allen W. Trelease, "Indian Relations and the Fur Trade in New Netherland, 1609–1664" (Ph.D. diss., Harvard University, 1955), 48.

[44] Nicolas Le Challeux, *Brief discours et histoire d'un voyage de quelque François en la Floride....*, Revue et augmentee de nouveau par M. Urbain de Chauveton (Geneva, 1579) 7–8.

[45] "Instructions pour le Sieur de Courcelle au sujet des indiens, 1665," *Collection de Manuscrits contenant lettres, memoires et autres documents historiques relatif à la Nouvelle-France*, 4 vols. (Québec, 1883–1885) I:175.

[46] George F.G. Stanley, "The First Indian 'Reserves' in Canada," *Revue de l'Histoire de l'Amérique française* 4 (1950): 209.

[47] Franciso López de Gómara, *Histoire generalle des Indes Occidentales....*, trans. M. Fumée (Paris: Michel Sonnius, 1569) 233.

[48] Sister Mary Anna Joseph (Mary Genevieve Hennessey), "French and English Pressures on the Indians of Acadia and Eastern New England" (Master's thesis, University of New Brunswick, 1962): 94.

[49] *Massachusetts Historical Society Collections*, second series, 8 (1826), 260, Eastern Indians' letter to the Governor, 27 July 1721.

[50] *Dictionary of Canadian Biography* III, s.v. "Atecouando." This chief is not to be confused with the earlier one of the same name, who

flourished in 1701–26. Among Amerindians, it was a general custom to attach certain names to certain positions.

[51] Francis Parkman, *The Conspiracy of Pontiac* (Toronto: George N. Morang and Co., 1907) I: 329.

[52] *Indians Without Tipis: A Resource Book*, ed. D. Bruce Sealey and Verna J. Kirkness (Vancouver, BC: W. Clare, 1973), frontispiece.

Fur Trade History as an Aspect of Native History

Arthur J. Ray

A Professor of History at the University of British Columbia, Arthur J. Ray has written or co-authored a number of books on the fur trade. More recently he has turned his attention to treaties, particularly the comparative history of Aboriginal and treaty rights litigation in Australia, Canada, New Zealand, and the United States, and together with Frank Tough and J.R. Miller recently published Bounty and Benevolence: A Documentary History of Saskatchewan Treaties. *He has also been an expert witness in a number of trials, among them the* Delgamuukw, *and* Powley *cases.*

Howard Adams, among others, has made the point that the dominant white Euro-Canadian culture has projected racist images of the Indians that "are so distorted that they portray natives as little more than savages without intelligence or beauty."[1] He argued further that the Indians "must endure a history that shames them, destroys their confidence, and causes them to reject their heritage."[2] There is a great deal of truth in Adam's statements, and clearly a considerable amount of historical research needs to be done to correct these distorted images. One important aspect of any new meaningful Indian history necessarily will be concerned with the involvement of the Indian peoples in the fur trade and with the impact of that

This article was originally published in *One Century Later: Western Canadian Reserve Indians since Treaty 7*, edited by Ian A.L. Getty and Donald B. Smith. Reprinted with permission of the author.

participation upon their traditional cultures as well as those of the European intruders. Work in this area will be important not only because it holds a potential for giving us new insights into Indian history, but also because it should serve to help establish Indian history in its rightful place in the mainstream of Canadian historiography. As some of Canada's most prominent historians have emphasized, the fur trade was a moulding force in the economic, political, and social development of Canada,[3] and the Indian peoples played a central role in this enterprise. For these reasons Indian history should not simply be devoted to recounting the manner in which the aboriginal peoples of Canada were subjugated and exploited, but it must also consider the positive contribution that the Indian peoples made to the fur trade and, hence, to the development of Canada. If this positive contribution is recognized, it should help destroy some of the distorted images that many Canadians have of Indians and their history.

Given that fur trade history and Indian history are inextricably bound together, several questions immediately arise. How much attention have historians devoted to the roles that the Indians played in the fur trade in the considerable body of fur trade literature that already exists? What images of the Indian peoples emerge from this literature? What aspects of Indian involvement have yet to be explored fully?

Until relatively recently the Indian peoples have not figured prominently in works dealing with the fur trade.[4] Rather, they generally appear only as shadowy figures who are always present, but never central characters, in the unfolding events.[5] In part, this neglect appears related to the fact that historians have been primarily concerned with studying the fur trade as an aspect of European imperial history or of Canadian business and economic history.[6] And, reflecting these basic interests, the considerable biographical literature that fur trade research has generated deals almost exclusively with Euro-Canadian personalities.[7] Relatively few Indian leaders have been studied to date.[8]

Although the tendency to consider the fur trade primarily as an aspect of Euro-Canadian history has been partly responsible for the failure of scholars to focus on the Indians' role in the enterprise, other factors have been influential as well. One of the basic problems with most studies of Indian-white relations has been that ethno-historians and historians have taken a retrospective view. They see the subjugation of the Indian peoples and the destruction of their lifestyles as inevitable consequences of the technological gap that existed between European and Indian cultures at the time of contact.[9] From this technological-determinist perspective, the Indian has been rendered as an essentially powerless figure who was swept along by the tide of European expansion without any real hope of channelling its direction or of influencing the character of the contact situation. The dominance of this outlook has meant that in most fur trade studies the Indian has been cast in a reflexive role. Reflecting this perspective, until recently most ethno-historical research has been approached from an acculturation-assimilation point of view. The questions asked are generally concerned with determining how Indian groups incorporated European technology as well as social, political, economic, and religious customs into their traditional cultures.

While also interested in these issues, historians have devoted a considerable amount of attention toward outlining the manner and extent to which Euro-Canadian groups, particularly missionaries and government officials, helped the Indians to adjust to the new socio-economic conditions that resulted from the expansion of Western cultures into the new world.[10] Often historical research has taken a certain moralistic tone, assuming that members of the dominant white society had an obligation to help the Indians adopt agriculture and European socio-economic practices and moral codes, so that the Indian peoples could fit into the newly emerging social order.[11] Thus, historians who undertake these types of studies are frequently seeking to determine whether or not the traders, missionaries, and government officials had fulfilled their obligations to help "civilize" the Indian.

Granting that much good work has been done in the above areas, it is my opinion that many new insights into Indian history can be obtained if we abandon the retrospective, technological-determinist outlook and devote more attention to an examination of Indian involvement in the fur trade in the context of contemporary conditions. Such an approach would necessarily recognize that the nature of the trading partnerships that existed between Indian groups and various European interests changed substantially over time and place, making it difficult, frequently misleading, and certainly premature, given the amount of research that still needs to be done, to make any sweeping statements at this time about the nature of Indian-white relations in the context of the Canadian fur trade.

In order to pursue this work effectively, two courses of action need to be followed—one is not currently popular, and the other is extremely tedious. First, students of Indian history need to abandon the assumption that the Indians were ruthlessly exploited and cheated in all areas and periods by white traders. At present this is a very popular theme for both Indian and liberal white historians. All of us have heard the story many times of how the Indians sold Manhattan Island for a few pounds of beads, and we have been informed of the many instances when Indians parted with valuable furs for trinkets and a drink. But, why are we never informed of what the Indians' perceptions of trade were? It may well be that they too thought they were taking advantage of the Europeans. For example, in 1634, when commenting on Montagnais beaver trapping in eastern Canada, Father Le Jeune wrote:

> The Castor or Beaver is taken in several ways. The Savages say it is the animal well-beloved by the French, English and Basques,—in a word, by the Europeans. I heard my [Indian] host say one day, jokingly, *Missi picoutau amiscou*, "The Beaver does everything perfectly well, it makes kettles, hatchets, swords, knives, bread; and in short, it makes everything." He was making sport of us Europeans, who have such a fondness for the skin of this animal and who fight to see who will get it; they carry this to such an extent that my host said to me one day, showing me a beautiful knife, "The English have no sense; they give us twenty knives like this for one Beaver skin."[12]

While there is no denying that European abuses of Indians were all too common, there are several things wrong with continually stressing this aspect of the fur trade and Indian history. As the previous quote suggests, it gives us only half the story. Of greater importance, by continually focusing only on this dimension of the trade, we run the serious risk of simply perpetuating one of the images in Indian historiography that Adams, among others, most strongly objects to, namely, the view that the Indians were little more than "savages without intelligence." It also glosses over a fundamental point that must be recognized if the Indian is to be cast in an active and creative role. We must not forget that the Indians became involved in the fur trade by their own choice. Bearing that in mind, an objective and thorough examination of the archival records of the leading trading companies, admittedly a wearisome task, gives considerable evidence that the Indians were sophisticated traders, who had their own clearly defined sets of objectives and conventions for carrying on exchange with the Europeans.

This can be demonstrated by following several lines of inquiry. One of these involves attempting to determine the kind of consumers the Indians were at the time of initial contact and how their buying habits changed over time. Probably one of the most striking pictures that emerges from an examination of the early correspondence books of the

Hudson's Bay Company is that, contrary to the popular image, the Indians had a sharp eye for quality merchandise and a well-defined shopping list. In short, they were astute consumers and not people who were easily hoodwinked.

If this is doubted, the early letters that the traders on Hudson Bay sent to the governor and committee of the Hudson's Bay Company in London should be read carefully. A substantial portion of almost every letter deals with the subject of the quality of the company's trade goods and with the Indians' reactions to it. Not only do these letters reveal that the Indians could readily recognize superior merchandise, but they also indicate that the Indians knew how to take advantage of the prevailing economic situation to improve the quality of the goods being offered to them. The following quote, typical of those that were written in the period before 1763, demonstrates the point and at the same time indicates one of the problems that is associated with carrying on research of this type. On 8 August 1728, Thomas McCliesh sent a letter from York Factory to the governor and committee in London informing them:

> I have sent home two bath rings as samples, for of late most of the rings [which] are sent are too small, having now upon remains 216 that none of the Indians will Trade. I have likewise sent home 59 ivory combs that will not be traded, they having no great teeth, and 3900 large musket flints and small pistol flints, likewise one hatchet, finding at least 150 such in three casks that we opened this summer which causes great grumbling amongst the natives. We have likewise Sent home 18 barrels of powder that came over in 1727, for badness I never saw the like, for it will not kill fowl nor beast at thirty yards distance: and as for kettles in general they are not fit to put into a Indian's hand being all of them thin, and eared with tender old brass that will not bear their weight when full of liquid, and soldered in several places. Never was any man so upbraided with our powder, kettles and hatchets, than we have been this summer by all the natives, especially by those that borders near the French. Our cloth likewise is so stretched with the tenterhooks, so as the selvedge is almost tore from one end of the pieces to the other. I hope that such care will be taken so as will prevent the like for the future, for the natives are grown so politic in their way of trade, so as they are not to be dealt by as formerly… and I affirm that man is not fit to be entrusted with the Company's interest here or in any of

their factories that does not make more profit to the Company in dealing in a good commodity than in a bad. For now is the time to oblidge [sic] the natives before the French draws them to their settlement.[13]

From McCliesh's letter one gets the impression that few of the goods on hand were satisfactory as far as the Indians were concerned. Taken out of context, comments of this type, which are common in the correspondence from the posts, could be construed to indicate that the governor and committee of the Hudson's Bay Company hoped to enhance their profits by dealing in cheap, poor quality merchandise whenever possible. However, such a conclusion would distort the reality of the situation and overlook important developments that were underway in the eighteenth century. If one examines the letters that the governor and committee sent to the Bay during the same period, as well as the minutes of their meetings in London and correspondence with British manufacturers and purchasing agents, other important facts emerge.

These other documents reveal that from the outset the governor and committee were concerned with having an array of the types and quality of goods that would appeal to the Indians. From the minute books of the company we learn that in the earliest years of operations the London directors relied heavily upon the experience and judgement of Pierre-Esprit Radisson to provide them with guidance in developing an inventory of merchandise that would be suitable for their posts in Canada. Radisson helped choose the patterns for knives, hatchets, guns, and so forth that manufacturers were to use, and he was expected to evaluate the quality of items that were produced for the company.[14] The governor and committee also sought the expertise of others in their efforts to maintain some quality control. For instance, in 1674 they attempted to enlist the services of the gunsmith who inspected and approved the trade guns of the East India Company.[15] They wanted him to evaluate the firearms that the Hudson's Bay Company was purchasing.

In their annual letters to the posts on the Bay, the governor and committee generally asked the traders to comment on the goods that they received and to indicate which, if any, manufacturer's merchandise was substandard. When new items were introduced, the directors wanted to know what the Indians' reactions to them were.

The question that no doubt arises is, if the governor and committee were as concerned with the quality of the products they sold, as suggested above, then why was there a steady stream of complaints back to London about their goods? Before a completely satisfactory answer to this question can be given, a great deal more research needs to be done in these records. However, several working hypotheses may be put forth at this time for the sake of discussion and research orientation. In developing its inventory of trade goods, the Hudson's Bay Company, as well as other European groups, had to deal with several problems. One of these was environmental in character. Goods that may have been satisfactory for trade in Europe, Africa, or Asia, often proved to be unsuitable in the harsh, subarctic environment. This was especially true of any items that were manufactured of iron. For example, one of the problems with the early flintlocks was that the locks froze in the winter.[16]

The extremely cold temperatures of the winter also meant that metal became brittle. Hence, if there were any flaws or cracks in the metal used to make mainsprings for guns, gun barrels, knives, hatchets, or kettles, these goods would break during the winter. In this way the severe environment of the subarctic necessitated very rigid standards of quality if the goods that were offered to the Indians were going to be satisfactory. These standards sorely tested the skills of the company's suppliers and forced the company to monitor closely how the various manufacturers' goods held up under use.

Besides having to respond to environmental conditions, the traders also had to contend with a group of consumers who were becoming increasingly sophisticated and demanding. As the Indians substituted more and more European manufactures for traditional items, their livelihood and well-being became more dependent upon the quality of the articles that they were acquiring at the trading posts. This growing reliance meant that the Indians could no longer afford to accept goods that experience taught them would fail under the stress of hard usage and the environment, since such failures could threaten their survival. It was partly for these reasons that the Indians developed a critical eye for quality and could readily perceive the most minute defects in trade merchandise.

Indian groups were also quick to take advantage of competitive conditions. They became good comparison shoppers and until 1821 used European trading rivalries to force the improvement of quality and range of goods that were made available to them. For example, during the first century of trade on Hudson Bay, the Indians frequently brought to Hudson's Bay Company posts French goods that they judged to be superior to those of English manufacture. The Indians then demanded that the Hudson's Bay Company traders match or exceed the quality of these items or risk the loss of their trade to the French. Similar tactics were used by the Indians in later years whenever competition was strong between Euro-Canadian groups. Clearly such actions were not those of "dumb savages," but rather were those of astute traders and consumers, who knew how to respond to changing economic conditions to further their own best interests. The impact that these actions had on the overall profitability of the trade for Euro-Canadian traders has yet to be determined.

The issue of profits raises another whole area of concern that is poorly understood and should be studied in depth. To date we know little about how the economic motivations of the Europeans and the Indians influenced the rates of exchange that were used at the posts. In fact, there is still a great deal of confusion about the complicated system of pricing goods and furs that was used in Canada. We know that the Hudson's Bay Company traders used two sets of standards. There was an official rate of exchange that was set by the governor and committee in London that differed from the actual rate that was used at the posts. Of importance, the traders advanced the prices of their merchandise above the stated tariff by resorting to the use of short measures. Contemporary critics of the Hudson's Bay Company and modern native historians have attacked the company for using such business practices, charging that the Indians were thereby being systematically cheated, or to use the modern expression, "ripped off."[17] But was this the case? Could the company traders have duped the Indians over long periods of time without the latter having caught on? Again, common sense and the record suggest that this was not the case.

The traders have left accounts of what they claimed were typical speeches of Indian trading leaders. One central element of all of these addresses was the request by these leaders that the traders give the Indians "full measure and a little over."[18] Also, the Indians usually asked to see the old measures or standards. Significantly, the Indians do not appear to have ever challenged the official standards, while at the same time they knew that they never received "full measure." What can we conclude from these facts?

In reality, the official standards of trade of the Hudson's Bay Company, and perhaps those of other companies as well, served only as a language of trade, or point of reference, that enabled the Indians and the traders to come to terms relatively quickly. The traders would not sell goods at prices below those set in the official standard. The Indian goal, on the other hand, was to try to obtain terms that approximated the official rate of exchange. An analysis of the Hudson's Bay Company post account books for the period before 1770 reveals that the company traders always managed to advance prices above the standard, but the margin of the advance diminished as the intensity of French opposition increased.[19] And even under monopoly conditions such as existed in western Canada before the 1730s, the Hudson's Bay Company traders were not able to achieve an across-the-board increase that exceeded fifty percent for any length of time.[20] This suggests strongly that the Indians successfully used competitive situations to improve the terms of trade and that they had their limits. If prices were advanced beyond a certain level, the Indians must have perceived that their economic reward was no longer worth the effort expended, and they broke off trade even if there was no alternative European group to turn to.

These remarks about the *overplus* system apply to the period before 1770. What we need to know is the extent to which the Indians were able to influence the rates of exchange during the time of bitter Hudson's Bay Company and North West Company rivalry. A preliminary sample of data from that period suggests their impact was much greater and that the range of price variation was much more extreme than in the earlier years. Similarly, it would be helpful to have some idea what effect the re-establishment of the Hudson's Bay Company's monopoly after 1821 had on trade good prices and fur values in western Canada. Being able to monitor prices under these contrasting conditions would enable us to obtain some idea of how the Indians were coping with the changing economic situation and how their responses influenced the material well-being of the different tribal groups.

Although this sample of the early accounting records shows that the Indians were economic men in the sense that they sought to maximize the return they obtained for their efforts, the same documents also indicate that, unlike their European counterparts, the Indians did not trade to accumulate wealth for status purposes. Rather, the Indians seem to have engaged in trade primarily to satisfy their own immediate requirement for goods. On a short-term basis their consumer demand was inelastic. In the early years this type of response was important in two respects. It was disconcerting to the European traders in that when they were offered better prices for their furs, the Indians typically responded by offering fewer pelts on a per capita basis. This type of a supply response was reinforced by gift-giving practices. Following the Indian custom, prior to trade tribal groups and the Europeans exchanged gifts. As rivalries for the allegiance of the Indians intensified, the lavishness of the gifts that the traders offered increased.

The ramifications that Indian supply responses to rising fur prices and to European gift-giving practices had for the overall conduct of the fur trade have yet to be fully explored. Clearly the costs that the Europeans would have had to absorb would have risen substantially during the periods when competition was strong, but to date no one has attempted to obtain even a rough idea of the magnitude by which these costs rose during the time of English-French or Hudson's Bay Company-North West Company rivalry. Nor has serious consideration been given to the manner in which such economic pressures may have favoured the use and abuse of certain trade articles such as alcohol and tobacco.

Concerning the use of alcohol, the excessive consumption of this drug was an inevitable consequence of the manner in which the economies of the Indian and European were linked together in the fur trade and of the contrasting economic motives of the two groups. As rivalries intensified, the European traders sought some means of retaining their contacts with the Indians, while at the same time keeping the per capita supply of furs that were obtained at as high a level as was possible. However, in attempting to accomplish the latter objective, the Europeans faced a number of problems. The mobile life of the Indians meant that their ability to accumulate material wealth was limited, especially in the early years when the trading posts were distant from the Indians' homelands. And, there were social sanctions against the accumulation of wealth by individual Indians.[21] To combat these problems, the traders needed to find commodities that could be transported easily or, even better, consumed at the trading post.

Unfortunately, alcohol was ideal when viewed from this coldly economic perspective. It offered one of the best means of absorbing the excess purchasing power of the Indians during periods of intensive competition. Furthermore, alcohol could be obtained relatively cheaply and diluted with water prior to trade.[22] Hence, it was a high profit trade item, an article that helped the traders hold down their gift-giving expenses, and it could be consumed at the forts. Given these characteristics, the only way that the abusive use of alcohol in trade could have been prevented in the absence of a strong European or native system of government was through monopoly control.

The traditional Indian consumer habits and responses to rising fur prices were important in another way. They were basically conservationist in nature although not intentionally so. By trapping only enough furs to buy the goods they needed in the early years, the pressures that the Indians exerted on the environment by their trapping activities were far less than they would have been had the objective

been one of accumulating wealth for status purposes. If the latter had
been the primary goal, then the Indians would have been tempted to
increase their per capita supply of peltry as fur prices rose, since their
purchasing power was greater.

In light of the above, the period between 1763 and 1821 is particularly
interesting and warrants close study. During that period Euro-Canadian
trading rivalries reached a peak, and one of the consequences of the
cut-throat competition that characterized the time was that large
territories were over-hunted and trapped by the Indians to the point
that the economies of the latter were threatened.[23] The question is
had the basic economic behaviour of the Indians changed to such an
extent that it facilitated their over-killing fur and game animals? Or,
was the heavy use of addictive consumables such as alcohol and
tobacco a major factor in the destruction of the environment?

Yet another aspect of the fur trade that has received too little attention
is the connection that existed between the European and eastern
North American markets and the western Canadian operations of
the trading companies. It needs to be determined how prices for trade
goods and furs in these markets, as well as transportation costs,
influenced rates of exchange at the posts. For instance, it has become
popular to cite cases where European traders advanced the prices of
certain articles by as much as 1000 percent over what it cost the
companies to buy them in Europe. Similarly, accounts of occasions
when the Indians received a mere pittance for valuable fur[24] are
common. But it is rarely reported, and indeed it is generally not
known, what percentage of the total gross revenues of a company
were made by buying and selling such items. Nor is it known if losses
were sustained on the sales of other commodities. Equally important,
there is not even a rough idea of what the total overhead costs of
the companies were at various times. Hence, their net profit margins
remain a mystery, and what was considered to be a reasonable profit
margin by European standards in the seventeenth, eighteenth, and
early nineteenth centuries is not known. Answers to all of these
questions must be found before any conclusions can be reached
about whether or not the Indian or the European trader was being
"ripped off."

And indeed, the Indian side must be considered when dealing with
this question and when attempting to understand how the trading system responded to changing economic conditions. Even though Harold
Innis pointed out that Indian trading specialists played a crucial role in
the development and expansion of the fur trade, a common view of the

Indians in the enterprise is still one that portrays them basically as simple trappers who hunted their own furs and accepted whatever prices for these commodities that the traders were willing to give them. The fact of the matter is that the records show that in the period before 1770, probably 80 percent of all of the furs the Europeans received in central Canada came from Indian middlemen who acquired their peltry through their own trading networks.

Furthermore, these middlemen charged the Europeans substantially more for these furs than they had paid to obtain them from the trapping bands with whom they dealt. In turn, the middlemen advanced the prices for their trade goods well above the levels they had been charged by the Europeans, sometimes by margins of almost 1,000 percent.

These practices of the Indian middlemen raise a difficult question. If the Indians were not engaged in the trade to accumulate wealth, as suggested earlier, then why did the middlemen advance their prices to the extent that they did? Did their price levels simply enable them to maintain a material standard that they had become accustomed to? Before this question can be answered, a great deal more needs to be known about the problems that the Indian middlemen had to cope with in their efforts to acquire and transport goods and furs. A clearer understanding of their motives for engaging in the trade is also required. For example, why did some Indian groups quickly assume the middleman role while others were apparently content to continue as trappers? How did middlemen groups fare, economically, in comparison with trapping groups?

The Indians played a variety of other roles in the fur trade. They served as provision suppliers, canoe builders, canoe and boat men, and farm labourers around the posts, to name only a few. The Indians quickly assumed these roles as economic conditions changed, rendering old positions obsolete and opening up new opportunities.

This brings to mind another broad research area that should be explored more fully than it has been to date. It deals with determining how the various Indian groups perceived and responded to changing economic situations. Work in this area would serve to destroy another distorted image that many Euro-Canadians have of Indian societies, namely, the view that these societies are rigid and incapable of responding to change. Historically there is little evidence to support such a notion for the period before 1870. While the fur trade was a going concern and the Indians were not tied to the reserves and shackled with bureaucratic red tape, they made many successful adaptations to new circumstances. More needs to be written about this aspect of Indian history. If this work is done, perhaps a picture will emerge that shows the Indians to be innovative, dynamic, land responsive people, whose creativity and initiative have been thwarted in the post-treaty period.

In conclusion, this paper has focused upon the early phases of the western Canadian fur trade, and the discussion has been restricted primarily to the economic dimension of trade. However, this restriction is justified because many of the problems of Indian-white relations are rooted in the past. Also, many of the distorted images that Euro-Canadians currently hold regarding Indians, thereby causing problems in the relationships between the two groups, have been generated and perpetuated by the manner in which the fur trade history has been written. Correcting these images requires starting at the beginning, and it is not simply a matter of rewriting what has already been done. New research has to be conducted in the various archival collections across the country and records that have received little attention to date, such as accounting records, need to be exhaustively explored. In conducting this research and presenting our results, the urge to over-compensate for past wrongs and inaccuracies by placing the Indian on a pedestal must be resisted. If the latter course of action is taken, a new mythology that will not stand the test of time will be created. Even more serious, it would probably serve only to perpetuate the warped images that such research set out to destroy because it would fail to treat the Indians as equals, with their own cultures and sets of values. Finally, if one of the objectives of studying the fur trade is to attempt to obtain a better understanding of Indian-white relations, it must be based on solid objective historical research.

Endnotes

I would like to thank Charles A. Bishop, SUNY-Oswego, James R. Gibson and Conrad Heidenrich, York University, and Carol Judd, Ottawa, for commenting on earlier drafts of this paper. The author, of course, is responsible for this paper.

[1] Howard Adams, *Prison of Grass* (Toronto: New Press, 1975) 4 1.
[2] Ibid., 43.
[3] The most notable example was probably Harold Innis. See H. A. Innis, *The Fur Trade in Canada* (1930; reprint, New Haven: Yale University Press, 1962) 386–92.
[4] See, for example, Innis, *The Fur Trade*; A. S. Morton, *The History of the Canadian West to 1870–71*, 2nd ed., (Toronto: University of Toronto

Press, 1973); and E. E. Rich, *The Fur Trade and the Northwest to 1857* (Toronto: McClelland & Stewart, 1967).

[5] C. Jaenen, *Friend and Foe* (Toronto: McClelland & Stewart, 1976) 1–11.

[6] Innis and Rich deal extensively with the fur trade as an aspect of imperial history. See Innis, *The Fur Trade*, 383; and Rich, *Fur Trade and Northwest*, xi and 296. Several corporate histories have been written. See as examples, L. R. Masson, *Les Bourgeois de la Compagnie du Nord-Ouest*, 2 vols. (1889–90; reprint, New York: Antiquarian Press, 1960); E. E. Rich, *The History of Hudson's Bay Company 1670–1870*, 2 vols. (London: Hudson's Bay Record Society, 1958–59); and W. S. Wallace, *Documents Relating to the North West Company* (Toronto: Champlain Society, 1934).

[7] One of the problems, of course, is that biographical details regarding Indian personalities are few. The historical record often does not provide information regarding births, deaths, and family relationships of Indian leaders.

[8] There are some notable exceptions such as Dempsey's study of Crowfoot and Sluman's of Poundmaker. See H. Dempsey, *Crowfoot: Chief of the Blackfoot* (Edmonton: Hurtig, 1972), and N. Sluman, *Poundmaker* (Toronto: McGraw-Hill Ryerson, 1967).

[9] This point of view was perhaps most strongly expressed by Diamond Jenness. See Diamond Jenness, "The Indian Background of Canadian History," National Museum of Canada Bulletin No. 86 (Ottawa: Department of Mines and Resources, 1937), 1–2; and Diamond Jenness, *Indians of Canada*, 6th ed. (Ottawa: National Museum of Canada, 1963), 249. See also George F. Stanley, "The Indian Background of Canadian History," *Papers* (Canadian Historical Association, 1952) 14.

[10] A notable example of this interest as it pertains to western Canada is the early work of Frits Pannekoek: see "Protestant Agricultural Missions in the Canadian West in 1870" (M.A. thesis, University of Alberta, 1970). More recently, Pannekoek has begun to consider the divisive role these groups played in terms of race relations in western Canada. See Frits Pannekoek, "The Rev. Griffiths Owen Corbett and the Red River Civil War of 1869–70," *Canadian Historical Review* 57 (1976): 133–49.

[11] A notable exception to this viewpoint is that expressed by Stanley in 1952. He pointed out that programs oriented towards assimilating the Indians into the dominant white society lead to cultural extinction of the former group. This is offensive to any people having a strong sense of identity. See Stanley, 21.

[12] R. G. Thwaites, ed., *The Jesuit Relations and Allied Documents,* vol. 6 (New York: Pagent Book Company, 1959), 297–9.

[13] K. G. Davies, ed., *Letters from Hudson Bay, 1703-40* (London: Hudson's Bay Record Society, 1965) 136.

[14] E. E. Rich, ed., *Minutes of the Hudson's Bay Company, 1671–74* (Toronto: Champlain Society, 1942) 26–7, 58–9.

[15] Ibid.

[16] A. J. Ray, *Indians in the Fur Trade* (Toronto: University of Toronto Press, 1974) 75.

[17] For example, in the eighteenth century Arthur Dobbs charged that the company advanced the prices of its goods above the Standards of Trade to such an extent that it discouraged the Indians from trading. Arthur Dobbs, *An Account of the Countries Adjoining to Hudson's Bay in the Northwest Part of America* (London, 1744), 43. More recently the company has been attacked for its pricing policy by Adams, *Prison of Grass*, 24.

[18] C. E. Heidenreich and A. J. Ray, *The Early Fur Trade: A Study in Cultural Interaction* (Toronto: McClelland & Stewart, 1976) 82–3.

[19] A. J. Ray, "The Hudson's Bay Company Account Books As Sources for Comparative Economic Analyses of the Fur Trade: An Examination of Exchange Rate Data," *Western Canadian Journal of Anthropology* 6.1 (1976): 44–50.

[20] The principal exception was at Eastmain where the prevailing rates exceeded the fifty percent markup level from the late 1690s until about 1720. However, it should be pointed out that French opposition was relatively weak in this area. See Ray, "Hudson's Bay Company Account Books," 45–50.

[21] For example, one of the virtues of Indian leaders was generosity. And, generalized reciprocity or sharing was practiced amongst band members. These values and practices served to discourage any individual, regardless of his position, from accumulating wealth in excess of that of his kinsmen.

[22] Generally, alcohol was diluted with water by a ratio of one-quarter to one-third at the Hudson's Bay Company posts in the eighteenth century. See Davies, *Learn from Hudson Bay*, 268.

[23] Ray, *Indians in the Fur Trade*, 117–24.

[24] Adams, *Prison of Grass*, 51; and Susan Hurlich, "Up Against the Bay: Resource Imperialism and Native Resistance," *This Magazine* 9.4 (1975): 4.

The Woman Who Married a Beaver:

Trade Patterns and Gender Roles in the Ojibwa Fur Trade

Bruce M. White

Bruce White is an historical anthropologist who is currently writing a book on the Ojibwe-European fur trade in the Lake Superior region from 1650 to 1900.

Introduction

In 1904, Kagige Pinasi (John Pinesi), an Ojibwa (Anishinaabe)-French man living at Fort William on the north shore of Lake Superior, told the anthropologist William Jones a story about a young woman who married a beaver. With blackened face she went to fast for a long time during a vision quest. She saw a person in human form who spoke to her. He asked her to come live with him. She did and eventually agreed to marry him. She was well provided with food and clothing and soon gave birth to four children.[1]

She soon noticed something very odd that led her to realize for the first time that she had married a beaver. From time to time the woman's husband or children would leave with a human being who appeared outside their house. "And back home would they always return again. All sorts of things would they fetch—kettles and bowls, knives, tobacco, and all the things that are used when a beaver is eaten; such was what they brought. Continually they were adding to their great wealth." They would go to where the person lived and the person would kill the beavers. Yet the beavers

This article was originally published in *Ethnohistory* 46:1 (Winter 1999): 109–47. Reprinted with permission of the author.

were never really killed. They would come back home again with the clothes and tobacco that people gave them. The beavers were very fond of the people and would visit them often. The woman herself was forbidden to go by her husband, but this is what she heard.

Eventually the woman's husband died and she returned to live with human beings. She lived a long time after that and often told the story of what happened while she lived with the beavers. She always told people that they should never speak ill of a beaver or they would never be able to kill any: "If any one regards a beaver with too much contempt, speaking ill of it, one simply [will] not [be able to] kill it. Just the same as the feelings of one who is disliked, so is the feeling of the beaver. And he who never speaks ill of a beaver is very much loved by it; in the same way as people often love one another, so is one held in the mind of the beaver, particularly lucky then is one at killing beavers."

Referring to stories like this one, the philosopher Jean-François Lyotard wrote that such accounts are a succinct record of the beliefs of the societies in which they are told. "What is transmitted through these narratives," Lyotard wrote, "is the set of pragmatic rules that constitutes the social bond." He noted that such stories "recount what could be called positive or negative apprenticeships." They tell of the success or failure of a hero, whose adventures define a society's "criteria of competence" and delineate a range of possible actions for members of the society.[2]

A primary purpose of such accounts is educational. Ojibwa elders told stories like this, usually in winter, to teach young people about the world while entertaining them.[3] As such, these narratives are also a useful way for outsiders to learn about the people's world view and understand their view of their history.[4] Kagige Pinasi may have had a variety of reasons for wishing to instruct the anthropologist William Jones by telling him this story. Jones' biographer, Henry M. Rideout, spoke of the informant as "an old chief" and an experienced trapper who made Jones examples of animal traps. He told Jones a number of odd experiences he had had while hunting and trapping with his sons. He also recounted, for Jones' transcription, more than fifty stories, which Jones praised for their artistry. Jones wrote that the man developed a fondness for him—the anthropologist was of Fox and British-American ancestry—and tried to convince him to "come and live here, take to myself a wife, and be one of the people." Telling Jones this story of a kind of intermarriage may have been a form of subtle encouragement.[5]

Beyond Kagige Pinasi's own personal motives, this story is, like all Ojibwa stories, interesting on many levels. It instructs young people, especially girls, on the importance of the vision quest, the means through which an Ojibwa person obtained a relationship with powerful beings who would be helpful to her and could chart a unique course for her life. Further, it is a basic description of and commentary on the co-operative arrangements that many Ojibwa people believed existed between different kinds of beings in the world. Ojibwa people who hunted, fished, or gathered plants had to be aware of their reciprocal obligations with the natural world and give back something to the animals, fish, or plants from which they harvested. In taking small plants in the woods, or bark from the trees, people often left a gift of tobacco. After a bear was killed, they held an elaborate ceremony of thanks and gave presents to the bear. The beaver story shows that reciprocity was necessary to keep the system operating. Without gifts and respect, animals would not be so helpful to humans. They would hold themselves back and not allow themselves to be used by people. Without gifts and respect, the system would cease to function.[6]

Ojibwa people also applied the principle of reciprocity to their dealings with people, including non-Indians. In their earliest interactions with the French and the British, the Ojibwa made use of the same gifts, ceremonies, and words that they used in dealing with animals, plants, and other beings.[7] The logic of approaching Europeans in this way was solid: interaction with Europeans was important because of the valuable technology they brought with them. Reciprocity was necessary to keep the system operating. Without gifts and respect, Europeans would not be so helpful to Indian people. They would withhold their technology from Indian people. Without gifts and respect, the system would cease to function.

Dealing with animals differed, of course, from dealing with Europeans. The Ojibwa quickly worked out a variety of strategies that were specific to the newcomers. For example, they gave different things. The story of the woman who married the beaver describes a reverse fur trade. In the European fur trade, Indian people gave furs in return for tools, kettles, and tobacco, but this story tells of a relationship in which people gave tools, kettles, and tobacco to beavers in return for the animals' furs.

There is yet another striking feature of the story: it delineates an intermediary role for women in the interaction between people and animals, suggesting a role for women in the interaction between the Ojibwa and Europeans. This story is not an origin tale.[8] It does not describe the beginnings of the reciprocal arrangement between people and animals. For the people in the story, the relationship was a well-established, functioning system. Yet the story explains the system and how it works through the experiences of a woman. If the story was intended to teach, in Lyotard's words, "positive or negative apprenticeships" there was clearly a special message in it for young women about what was possible. Women, it would appear, have power to cross boundaries, explaining one world to another, in this case through a marriage relationship. This power had implications for the workings of the fur trade.

Gender and Fur Trade Historiography

Many accounts of the fur trade imply that trade took place mainly between native and European men, with women playing an adjunct role. Until recent years, few studies of the fur trade mentioned women specifically. Harold A. Innis, in his major economic study, *The Fur Trade in Canada*, seldom spoke of gender. Although he noted that "the personal relationship of the trader to the Indian" was essential under "conditions of competition," he did not discuss the role that intermarriage played between male traders and native women in the trade.[9] Historian Arthur J. Ray, in several major studies, explored the coming together of native people and Europeans in the fur trade. In one book he analyzed "the set of institutions which developed as a compromise between the customs and norms of traditional Indian exchange and those of European market trade." However, he failed to consider in his detailed work any differing impact that men and women may have had upon this composite trade.[10]

More recently, the historian Richard White has examined the accommodation between native people and Europeans in a complex set of relationships that took place in what he called a cultural, social, and political "middle ground" of the Great Lakes of the seventeenth and eighteenth centuries. White argued that the "fur trade proper is merely an arbitrary selection from a fuller and quite coherent spectrum of exchange that was embedded in particular social relations."[11] White wrote mostly of the role of diplomacy in native-European interactions—diplomacy in which women apparently had a smaller role than men—and emphasized the role of men as speechmakers, negotiators, and warriors. Nonetheless, White referred at many points in his study to the role of women in trade. For example, in describing a speech by a Potawatomi man in Montreal, White noted that the man was representing, in part, the women in his community who "by implication, were a major force in exchange." Similarly, White wrote that much of the "petty trading" of French traders in native villages was "probably with women." But neither point was developed in detail.[12]

The major work on the differing roles of men and women in the fur trade has come, not surprisingly, from the research of women historians and anthropologists. Anthropologist Jennifer Brown, in her 1980 study *Strangers in Blood*, examined the dynamics of Canadian fur-trade societies established within the institutional frameworks of the North West and Hudson Bay Companies. She showed the joint effect of native and European cultures on the available roles for men and women and the formation of trade cultures and institutions.[13]

Feminist historian Sylvia Van Kirk, in *Many Tender Ties* also emphasized the Canadian fur trade in her look at the roles of women in fur-trade society. She stated that her study "supports the claims of theorists in women's history that sex roles should constitute a category of historical investigation" because the experience of women "has differed substantially from that of their male counterparts." She suggested that "the lives of both sexes must be examined if we are to fully understand the dynamics of social change."[14] Van Kirk emphasized the role of native women as "women-in-between," a situation "which could be manipulated to advantage." She stated that native women in general may have had a vested interest in promoting cordial relations with the whites and that "if the traders were driven from the country, the Indian women would lose the source of European goods which had revolutionized their lives." She argued that native women sometimes received better treatment and had more influence at the trading post than in native villages. She suggested that they had a more sedentary life and had more help in doing their work when married to a trader. All of these facts may have led some women to choose new roles from among those available to them.[15]

Jacqueline Peterson's influential 1981 dissertation, "The People in Between," took another look at men and women in the fur trade. She examined Indian-white marriages and the formation of a mixed-blood people in the Great Lakes between the seventeenth and nineteenth centuries. Peterson viewed the culture of the Great Lakes fur-trade communities as a "unique lifeway—an occupational subculture" that gave birth to a people who would later be called the Métis. In particular, Peterson explored the key role played by native women in these communities, as social, economic, and cultural intermediaries between Europeans and native societies.[16]

Despite these broad examinations of the roles of women in the fur trade, detailed and focused studies of gender relations in the Ojibwa fur trade have yet to be done. Discussion of the role of Ojibwa men and women in the fur trade has come largely in the context of ethnographic and historical studies of Ojibwa women. In such work, the differing roles of men and women in relation to the fur trade have been interpreted in light of theories about the autonomy and power of Ojibwa women—the control of women over their own activities and the power they exerted in the society as a whole.[17]

Pioneering work was done by the anthropologist Ruth Landes in her book *The Ojibwa Woman,* a classic study based on fieldwork in northwestern Ontario in the 1930s. Although often interpreted as a contemporary description of the roles of Ojibwa women, the work was to a large extent historical. It contained stories of women's lives— told to her by her informant Maggie Wilson—dating back to the mid-nineteenth century, a period during which the fur trade continued to be a major influence on Ojibwa society.[18] In this study, Landes provided a rich view of Ojibwa women's lives, including examples of women who had significant roles as hunters, warriors, and healers. Landes, however, appeared to believe that these women were exceptions to the rule that women and their accomplishments were devalued or simply ignored in modem Ojibwa society. She noted, for example, that men's work was considered "infinitely more interesting and honorable" than women's work and spoke of "men's supremacy" in Ojibwa society.[19] In a brief discussion of the fur trade, Landes suggested that women had little role in trading either in the 1930s or earlier. She noted that Ojibwa men had learned to barter furs and meat "which they had secured in hunting," since they, "rather than the women, possessed the material desired by the Whites."[20]

Landes' comments on Ojibwa gender roles, if not the examples she gave, seemed to imply that a devaluation of women was ingrained in Ojibwa society and would have been present during the fur-trade era and perhaps even earlier. Anthropologist Eleanor Leacock took issue with at least one aspect of this implication in a 1978 article. Writing about the Ojibwa and other "egalitarian band societies," Leacock stated that nothing in the structure of such societies "necessitated special deference to men." Leacock took particular issue with Landes' conclusions about the Ojibwa, asserting that Landes exhibited a "lack of a critical and historical orientation toward her material" as well as a "downgrading of women that is built into unexamined and ethnocentric phraseology." In keeping with a Marxist approach to the topic, Leacock suggested that the situation of women in egalitarian societies often changed when the products of labour began to be treated as commodities in trade with Europeans. Women became dependent on men only when the trade made men's products more "commercially relevant" than their own.[21]

More recent studies have echoed such views. In her analysis of the responses of Great Lake native women to Christian missionaries and to the fur trade, Carol Devens wrote that before contact with Europeans, Ojibwa society had a gender balance upon which the communities depended. This balance was disrupted by European missions and trade. The trade, in particular, acted as a "catalyst for modification in social structures throughout native bands." Devens argued that the trade favoured "intensive production in order to accumulate and then exchange surplus goods." Disruption of native gender roles occurred because "French traders wanted the furs obtained by men rather than the small game, tools, utensils, or clothing procured or produced by women." She suggested that "most of the items given in exchange by the French were tools and weapons intended to facilitate trapping." This caused "daily and seasonal life" of native communities to "revolve around the trade." Women became "auxiliaries to the trapping process" rather than "producers in their own right." Devens wrote that the fur trade led to a decrease in women's "direct contribution to the community welfare."[22]

The basic argument advanced in slightly different ways by Landes, Leacock, and Devens is that women had little direct role in the fur trade. Leacock and Devens argued that this lack of participation and authority in making decisions about an increasingly important economic endeavour led to a devaluation of women in Ojibwa society. The basis of this change, they suggested, was that men were the primary traders because the product of women's labour was not in great demand in the trade.

In fact, this theory has yet to be thoroughly demonstrated using the records of the fur trade. A major problem with doing so is simply that the sources used to describe the trade are marred by misconceptions about the roles of women in native societies. This point was made by Priscilla K. Buffalohead in a 1983 study of the roles available to Ojibwa women during the fur-trade era. Buffalohead noted that the common view in earlier sources on the Ojibwa was that native men were lazy and native women were overworked "drudges." Buffalohead pointed out that many eighteenth- and nineteenth-century sources on the Ojibwa viewed men's and women's roles from the point of view of European beliefs about the desirable roles for men and women. These beliefs made it difficult to accurately gauge Ojibwa people's own beliefs about the autonomy of women and their value to their society. The derogatory statements by European men about native women are sometimes wrongly seen as descriptive of Ojibwa beliefs or social structures, providing unwarranted support for a belief that the fur trade led to a devaluation of Ojibwa women.[23]

Buffalohead's work dealt with the explicit beliefs about those who reported on Ojibwa women and their role in society. Just as problematic was the frequent lack of mention of women in the narratives of European interactions with the Ojibwa. Based on the evidence of many written sources, one might assume that the Ojibwa were a people entirely without women. Thomas Vennum, Jr., in his study of the use of wild rice among the Ojibwa, provided an example of this problem. He quoted a 1804–5 journal of François Victoire Malhiot, a North West Company trader at Lac du Flambeau (Wisconsin). In a translation of the original French, Malhiot stated that on 10 September 1804, a leader named L'Outarde, or Goose, "started yesterday with his young men to gather wild rice at [Trout Lake], where his village is."[24]

Without other evidence, this passage might be interpreted to suggest that gathering wild rice was a band activity, led by a male leader and carried out by his "young men," or followers. Vennum noted, however, that such a statement "should be taken to mean that the band went to establish its rice camps, and not that the men were the harvesters." Vennum based his conclusions on more recent ethnographic and historical evidence, the preponderance of which suggests that women, rather than men, managed and did most of the wild-rice harvesting until the twentieth century. While the wild-rice harvest was under way, Vennum noted, men were more generally involved in fishing and hunting geese.[25]

Using ethnographic materials in this way is a technique that has been called "upstreaming." The term was initially used by the anthropologist William Fenton, in an influential 1952 essay on the training of "historical ethnologists." Fenton argued that "major patterns of culture tend to be stable over long periods of time," so that it was possible to proceed "from the known to the unknown, concentrating on recent sources first because they contain familiar things, and thence going to earlier sources." Fenton noted, however, that it was important to show a preference for those sources in which the descriptions of the society ring true at both ends of the time scale."[26]

As Fenton went on to state, ethnographic sources from the nineteenth and twentieth centuries and earlier accounts were all historical sources. They were all the product of points of view and perspectives, which must be considered in evaluating the information they contain. In arguing in favour of upstreaming, Fenton was reacting against those who assumed "acculturation" or inevitable change of native cultures in the face of European cultural conquest. Although the concept of acculturation has become less accepted, a related view—which should perhaps be called "downstreaming"—persists. This is the belief that lacking detailed written documentation, the cultural attributes of native people in the nineteenth and twentieth centuries cannot be assumed to have existed earlier.[27]

The assertion that seventeenth-century native people shared cultural values, gender relations, or social organization with nineteenth-century native people simply because they shared languages or tribal names is one that sometimes needs to be demonstrated, given the many social, economic, and political changes that took place in the Great Lakes in those two hundred years. On the other hand, to presume that there was no similarity in culture between such groups is equally problematic. In fact, many aspects of seventeenth- and eighteenth-century Ojibwa history may be totally inexplicable without the guidance from later ethnographic sources.[28] To insist too strictly on the primacy of early French or British documents is to suggest that native people of more recent times have nothing useful to say about their own past. It can also lead to ignoring, as the earlier documents often do, the role of native women, simply because they are not mentioned in documents written by European men, who recorded only interactions with native men.

Ethnographic sources can and should be used to pose questions about earlier events and patterns, to investigate what is said, and often more important, what is not said in earlier historical documents. The rich works of Johann George Kohl, Frances Densmore, M. Inez Hilger, and Ruth Landes, all of which are cited in this article, describe the lives, skills, and beliefs of Ojibwa women in more detail, providing some alternative explanations that avoid the value judgments inherent in many historical sources. Perhaps more than anything, such ethnographic work suggests the need to acknowledge individual experience and motives in the interpretation of historical documents. When interacting with Europeans, Ojibwa men and women were presented with new situations, ones that involved the application and alteration of culturally received ideas. In many ways these new situations provided more rather than fewer opportunities for men and women. Evidence from the fur trade illuminated with the knowledge gained from later ethnographic work demonstrates that Ojibwa men and women had many ways to participate in the fur trade. As I argue, the nature of the possibilities available to both Ojibwa men and women calls into question the belief that the trade provided a mechanism for transforming an earlier egalitarian society into one in which men dominated women.

Gendered Patterns of Trade

Pierre Radisson and his brother-in-law Médard Chouart des Groseilliers spent the winter of 1659–60 in the region south of Lake Superior, living among a mixed group of Huron, Ottawa, Ojibwa, and later, Dakota. For a period of time they lived at an unnamed village by a lake. The cultural identity of the inhabitants is not altogether clear from the narrative, though they may have been Ojibwa speakers. Radisson stated on his arrival: "We destinated [presented] three presents, one for the men, one for the women, and the other for the children—to the end that they should remember that journey, that we should be spoaken of a hundred years after, if other Europeans should not come in those quarters and be liberal to them, which will hardly come to passe." Each present was in fact a group of presents:

> The first [for the men] was a kettle, two hatchets [tomahawks], and six knives, and a blade for a sword. The kettle was to call all nations that weare their friends to the feast which is made for the remembrance of the death; that is, they make it once in seaven years; it's a renewing of friendship…. The hattchets were to encourage the yong people to strengthen themselves in all places, to preserve their wives, and show themselves men by knocking the heads of their ennemyes with said hattchets. The knives were to show that the French were great and mighty, and their confederats and friends. The sword was to signifie that we would be masters both of peace and of wars, being willing to help and relieve them and to destroy our ennemyes with our arms.

> The second gift [for the women] was 2 and 20 awls, 50 needles, 2 gratters [scrapers] of castors, 2 ivory combs and 2 wooden ones, with red painte [vermilion], 6 looking-glasses of tin. The awls signifieth to take good courage that we should keepe their lives and that they with their husbands should come down to the French when time and season should permit. The needles for to make them robes of castor because the French loved them. The two gratters [scrapers] were to dress the skins; the combs [and] the paint to make themselves beautifull; the looking-glasses to admire themselves.

> The third gift [for the children] was of brasse rings, of small bells, and rasades [beads] of divers colours, and given in this manner. We sent a man to make all the children come together. When they were there we throw these things over their heads.

You would admire what a beat was among them, everyone striving to have the best. This was done upon this consideration, that they should be always under our protection, giving them wherewithal to make them merry and remember us when they should be men.[29]

Radisson and Groseilliers were seeking to encourage native demand for European goods and to encourage participation in the fur trade. Their gifts communicated what they sought to accomplish, as well as their understanding of native culture. Clearly, not all of their gifts were to the point. The gift of the tools of adornment to the women, for example, ignored the fact that, as many later sources suggest, Ojibwa men were as much concerned with such things as Ojibwa women.[30] Similarly, though the kettle may have been intended to symbolize the feast of the dead in which men may have been instrumental, kettles came to be used more often by women in cooking, making maple sugar, and parching wild rice.[31]

On the other hand, as indicated by the gifts of hatchets, usually called tomahawks, to the men and awls and scrapers to the women, the Frenchmen clearly understood some aspects of the gendered division of labour among the Ojibwa. On the simplest level, as recorded in a variety of later sources, men hunted, trapped, and went to war, and women gathered rice, made maple sugar, gardened, fished, processed a variety of foods, built bark houses, and wove mats. In doing these things, both men and women, as Buffalohead put it, "clearly managed and directed their own activities." Even in co-operative work, there was a division of labour. For example in the making of birchbark canoes, men shaped ribs and thwarts, while women sewed the panels of bark to the framework.[32]

The tools used to perform these tasks symbolized, for the Ojibwa, the gendered nature of the activities.[33] Frances Densmore wrote of the Ojibwa custom of burying with people who died a variety of tools that would be useful to them on the journey of death: "A pipe and tobacco pouch, with flint, steel, and punk were buried with a man and, if he were a good hunter, his gun might be placed beside him. A woman's favorite ax or pack strap might be buried with her."[34] Similarly, writing in 1836, the French ethnographer Joseph N. Nicollet stated that tools like this were a means of teaching children about gender. When a male child was born, men in the village would sing and dance around the family's house, firing shots. Then they would enter the house and give the child a small rifle carved out of wood, a leader saying: "I found your rifle. It seems you did not take good care of it. We bring it back to you. Here it is. Indeed, you must hunt to survive and you must defend yourself when the enemy strikes. Keep it safely." Similarly when a female child was born, women in the village would dance, each one with a hatchet, "singing and dancing around the lodge and making gestures of women busy chopping wood." Then they would give the child a little wooden hatchet, saying: "We found your hatchet. It appears you did not take good care of it. We bring it back to you. Here it is. Indeed, you must chop wood to stay warm, and chop more wood to fortify your lodge should the enemy attack."[35]

In many ways, this picture of the gendered nature of Ojibwa labour and the manner in which traders like Radisson and Groseilliers accommodated it accords with the views of Leacock and Devens. The gift of awls and scrapers could be seen as bearing out Devens' suggestion that French gifts were intended to encourage trapping. The only outstanding question would appear to be whether or not this encouragement actually made changes in Ojibwa gender and subsistence patterns as all labour became geared to the production of furs.[36]

The problem with this view of Ojibwa participation in the fur trade, however, is that it is simplistic, revealing nothing of the complex nature of the far trade, a trade that provided varied opportunities for direct participation by both men and women. Gifts such as these were not representative of the entire relationship between Ojibwa and European traders, either in 1659 or for the next 250 years. From the seventeenth century on, the fur trade was important to the Ojibwa, who had a continuing, though variable, interest in obtaining European merchandise to use in their daily lives, in hunting, cooking, and religious ceremonies.[37] Trade goods offered material benefits, increased status, and much more. But from the beginning, traders accommodated Ojibwa demand by bringing a rich assortment of goods, including cloth, blankets, utensils, tools, silver jewellery, thread, and beads. In return, traders needed more from the Ojibwa than furs. They also needed a rich variety of products that only women could provide. All these factors meant that both Ojibwa men and women had a variety of roles to play and methods of exerting power and influence over the trade process.

The major role of women in the fur trade was not evident in the earliest years of French-Ojibwa interaction, when canoe-loads of people from the western Great Lakes went east to Montreal to trade their furs with the French. It may be that women were involved in these expeditions, although most accounts suggest that the participants were mainly men.[38] Later, however, when the location of trade shifted to native villages, at the time of Radisson and Groseilliers, women became crucial to the trade.

In the context of the trading post and the village, Ojibwa men and women had distinct and often different relationships with traders. The fur trade was never simply an exchange of furs for trade goods. It included a variety of other kinds of transactions. Traders needed to get food from native people; without it, they could not survive the winter in the western Great Lakes. They simply could not bring in or collect enough food to feed themselves, while at the same time carrying on the fur business. At the same time, as described later in more detail, traders needed a variety of native-manufactured supplies. The multifaceted nature of this trade meant that native people interacted with traders in many ways.

The varied interactions of Ojibwa men and women with traders were manifested in the complex set of trade patterns that made up a complete trading year. In the eighteenth century, a trading year in a Southwestern Ojibwa community would begin with the arrival in the fall of the trader with a new supply of goods. Once established in a fort or trading house, he gathered members of the community and gave and received ceremonial gifts. Goods such as clothing and utensils designed to help the Ojibwa survive the winter were then given out on credit, and customers went on their fall and winter hunts. The trader often purchased supplies of wild rice for his own survival and in some cases hired a hunter and his family to provide him with meat during the winter. Later, the trader or his men might visit native families to collect the furs they produced. Similarly, native people might revisit the trading post bringing in furs. In such circumstances, there could be further gifts and further credit. At the end of the trading year in the spring, before the trader's departure, certain goods were traded in direct exchanges and there might be concluding gifts and ceremonies.[39]

Gift, barter, and credit transactions were differentiated in a variety of ways. One means of differentiation was simply the way in which both parties spoke about them. Both traders and customers gave speeches in which they explained what they expected of their relationship as a whole and what they expected of any particular transaction. The temporal and seasonal context was also important. Gifts began the trading year, cemented other exchanges, and ended the year.[40] Credit was largely given in the fall. Direct exchanges of furs for merchandise took place in late winter or in the spring.

Another means of differentiating these various transactions was in the trade goods and native products. Evidence suggests the existence of spheres of exchange, or categories of trade goods subject to different rules and procedures.[41] For example, cloth goods and alcohol were defined and treated in strikingly different ways in the trade context. Alcohol, whether brandy, high wines, or rum, had some obvious culturally defined characteristics in the fur trade as well as native-European diplomacy.[42] Among traders in the Lake Superior region in the late eighteenth and early nineteenth centuries, alcohol in the form of rum or brandy was chiefly given to native people in two kinds of transactions: as gifts and in exchange for food. The trading ceremonies at the beginning and end of the year, and on the repayment of debts, usually featured gifts of alcohol. The food on which the trader depended, such as wild rice, game, and maple sugar, was often obtained with liquor.[43] By contrast, cloth, clothing, and blankets were mainly exchanged in the context of credit/ debt transactions or in direct exchange for furs and possibly for supplies. Thus, contrary to the usual picture of the fur trade, the bulk of furs received by traders was not actually obtained in barter. Rather, the furs were received as repayment for credit granted in the fall, in the form of cloth, tools, and utensils.

Trade transactions were not only differentiated by time and type of trade merchandise, but also by gender. The full extent of men's and women's participation in the trade among the Ojibwa is difficult to document. No complete sets of account books have been found that fully record all aspects of any trader's business. If account books existed in which each type of trade transaction was noted, as well as the gender of the person who participated, it would be possible to determine what percentage of each transaction was carried on by men or by women. Unfortunately, this is not possible. The historian must rely on trade narratives that are incomplete, leaving out important pieces of information. Some traders say almost nothing about women. Others mention them in passing, referring to them in generic fashion, using terms such is "a widow" or simply "a woman " or by their relationship to male Ojibwa. Because of this, scholars may assume that, without contrary evidence, all named persons in traders' narratives are men. This may not always be a safe assumption.[44] Nor is it safe to assume that because a particular trader never mentions women, he never had dealings with them.

Despite these problems, some conclusions can be drawn about the role of women in the trade. Men appear to have been the most frequent participants in trade ceremonies, as they were in other kinds of non-trade-related diplomacy. Leading men in the community gave speeches and sometimes, especially at the beginning of the trading year, presented gifts of furs or food. In return, they were given gifts of liquor, which they appear to have shared with men and women alike. It was also on such occasions that leading men were presented with chief's coats and other symbols of their role in the trade and in the community. Sometimes they were "made chiefs," that is, given status by the trader that they did not actually have in the community. It should be noted that the skillful leader—one who understood the need of leaders to give things away in order to increase their own status in the community—often gave away the clothing and other symbols of power given them by traders.[45] Such gifts may have gone to women as well as men. In any case, trade ceremonies also involved more general gifts to men and women in the community. Alexander Henry, the younger, a North West Company trader on the Red River in 1800, made this clear in his account of the transactions that took place on his arrival in the region of trade. On 21 August of that year, he presented several male community leaders with scarlet laced coats, laced hats, red feathers, white linen shirts, leggings, breech cloths and flags, as well as tobacco and alcohol. A few weeks later, in addition to unspecified goods on credit to the amount of twenty skins' worth each to a number of individuals, he also gave "an assortment of small articles gratis, such as one Scalper, two Folders, and four Flints [apiece to the men], [and to the] Women, two awls, three needles, one seine of net Thread, one fi[r]e steel, a little Vermilion, and a half f[atho]m of Tobacco."[46]

It is usually asserted that men were the primary traders of furs. This is hard to document, given the fact that few furs were actually traded directly. Instead, as noted, they were exchanged in credit/debt transactions. Traders seldom listed the goods they gave out on credit or even to whom credit was given, though usually traders recorded debts in the names of men.[47] It is impossible to know whether women or men chose the goods given out in this fashion. It could be argued that even if the credit was granted to the hunters or trappers who were expected to produce the furs, this does not preclude the possibility that women were involved in the choice of goods or that men discussed with their wives what the wives or children needed for the winter. Given the documented concern of Ojibwa people for their families, it is hard to picture Ojibwa men who acted like mythical "economic men" in the theoretical sense, maximizing their own self-interest at the expense of their families.[48] This would, perhaps, have been productive for them in the short run, but would have lowered their status in the community.[49]

As for the repayment of the debts during the winter, a variety of people could be involved, including the hunter or trapper, his children, and his wives or female relations. Often the trader would be notified that a particular group of trappers had produced some furs.[50] He would then send off his men to pick them up. Subsequently, the hunter or other members of the family would be given a gift of alcohol in some form, which would, again, be shared among men and women.[51] It should also be noted that there were occasions when women traded furs directly.[52] While men were the primary hunters and trappers in Ojibwa communities, women processed the furs, a fact that would have given them greater authority in deciding what would happen to the furs as well as the opportunity to trade them.

The occasional role of women in bartering furs was part of a larger role in bartering. Food was an important part of women's trade. They supplied wild rice and maple sugar, both of which were mainstays for the trader. As noted, the characteristic return for such items of food was liquor. However, there were exceptions to this pattern. For example, food was sometimes traded for a variety of trade goods other than liquor, especially in times of scarcity. Michel Curot, a young clerk trading along the St. Croix River in 1803–04, for example, stated that because food supplies were scarce during the winter, traders were paying blankets for wild rice. In other years, this was an unusual transaction and after paying a two-and-a-half-point blanket to one woman in late February 1804, Curot felt obligated to explain: "I resolved to give the blanket, having only a single fawn of rice for provisions." Normally such a blanket was worth three beaverskins or more. He went on to describe the failure of his men to obtain fish to feed them.[53]

Wild rice was important not only as a trade item to be consumed by traders while living in an Ojibwa village near the Great Lakes, but also as an important way to feed brigades travelling further west. One account of large-scale trading of wild rice suggests something of women's power in the trade and in the Ojibwa community. The British trader Alexander Henry, the elder, went west of Lake Superior for the first time in 1775. When he reached Lake of the Woods, he and his men received a warm welcome:

> From this village we received ceremonious presents. The mode with the Indians is, first to collect all the provisions they can spare, and place them in a heap; after which they send for the trader, and address him in a formal speech. They tell him, that the Indians are happy in seeing him return into their country; that they have been long in expectation of his arrival; that their wives have deprived themselves of their provisions, in order to afford him a supply; that they are in great want, being destitute

of every thing, and particularly of ammunition and clothing; and what they most long for, is a taste of his rum, which they uniformly denominate milk.

The present, in return, consisted in one keg of gunpowder, of sixty pounds weight; a bag of shot, and another of powder, of eighty pounds each; a few smaller articles, and a keg of rum. The last appeared to be the chief treasure, though on the former depended the greater part of their winter's subsistence.

In a short time, the men began to drink, while the women brought me a further and very valuable present, of twenty bags of rice. This I returned with goods and rum, and at the same time offered more, for an additional quantity of rice. A trade was opened, the women bartering rice, while the men were drinking. Before morning, I had purchased a hundred bags, of nearly a bushel measure each. Without a large quantity of rice, the voyage could not have been prosecuted to its completion. The canoes, as I have already observed, are not large enough to carry provisions.[54]

There was a great deal more going on in this encounter than is evident in Henry's description. In this trading encounter, men played their usual ceremonial role, describing what it was they sought from the traders. Their words, along with their "ceremonious presents," suggest that their aim was to establish a continuing relationship, one that would ensure them of a supply of merchandise, not just a one-time interaction. Unfortunately, Henry was only passing through. The ceremony did not initiate a full year's worth of credit, debt, trade, and gift.[55] Instead, the only native product to be traded was wild rice, a product largely harvested by women and, for trading purposes, under their control. Given the limited nature of the encounter and the need, and the pressing schedule of the trader, these women had the power to obtain not just alcohol, but, apparently, a full range of goods. This interaction differs strikingly from the picture of women made powerless by a trade that had no need for what they controlled, the picture suggested by Ruth Landes in her study done 160 years later in the very same region.[56]

Women's role in the trade was evident in relation to other resources. Canoes—the product of both men's and women's labour—were often traded by women and were a useful way to obtain a full range of trade goods. In one case, a woman at Fond du Lac traded Curot a small canoe in return for two capots, a two-and-a-half-point blanket, and two pots of mixed rum. Together this was worth more than ten beaverskins.[57] Supplies for maintaining canoes were also produced by women. In early April 1804, Curot and his men left their Yellow River wintering post to camp out on the St. Croix River. Curot's canoes were badly in need of repair and the trader sent off one of his men with ruin and cloth "to hire the women to make gum that I absolutely need, since we cannot make use of any of our canoes without it filling immediately." It was not until 1 May that Curot was able to purchase gum from a woman named La Petite Rivière, or Little River, in return for a three-point blanket, generally worth three or four beaverskins. Curot obtained birchbark and *wadab*, the spruce roots used for tying panels of bark, from an unidentified person—possibly from Little River—in return for some jewellery, and the next day his men were able to repair the canoes. They finally set off for Grand Portage the following day.[58] Little River, who was unusual in being identified by her own name, also tanned three deerskins in return for two pairs of wool leggings, which together were worth four beaverskins.[59]

Considering their role in trading a wide variety of food and supplies, it may be that women were more often involved in direct trade than men. Curot's journal provides some statistical evidence on this point. As suggested by the examples given here, Curot not only used his journal as a way of recording a narrative of trade activities, but also for recording specific trade transactions. While he was generally vague about the quantity of goods given on credit—usually recording only the name of the person given credit—he was more specific about direct trade. Throughout the pages of the journal, Curot recorded sixty-four separate transactions that were clearly examples of direct trade. Of these, nineteen involved men and twenty-two involved women. In addition, there were twenty-three transactions in which the gender of the person trading was not evident. Given the frequency with which Curot named the male Ojibwa with whom he traded, and the fact that most of the men had received credit from him, it is very likely that most of the anonymous trade transactions were also examples of trade with women. This suggests that the vast majority of Curot's direct trade transactions were with women.[60]

Beyond these opportunities for women to trade their own products for a wide range of goods, some women took part in the ceremonial trading roles of giving and receiving gifts and getting credit, the more typical role of men. A prime example was Netnokwa, the Ottawa mother of the adopted white captive, John Tanner, who lived with her family among Ojibwa west of the Red River around 1800. On the occasion of trading with one trader, according to Tanner, Netnokwa "took ten fine beaver skins, and presented them to the trader. In return for this accustomed present, she was in the habit of receiving every year a chief's dress and ornaments, and a ten gallon keg of spirits."[61] Around the time described in the narrative, Charles Chaboillez, a North West Company trader, stated that on arriving in the region of the Red River, he exchanged presents with and gave credit to the "Old Courte Oreille [Ottawa] & Two Sons." This was clearly a reference to Netnokwa, her son, and her adopted son, Tanner. Later, Chaboillez stated that he gave her a present of rum and tobacco, "to encourage her to return" with furs and other products, a suggestion of her primary role in trading.[62] How typical Netnokwa was of other women in the community in which she lived is not clear. Laura Peers pointed out that "while Netnokwa was an exceptionally strong and charismatic woman... her influence was presumably neither unprecedented nor unparalleled."[63]

There were various explanations for Netnokwa's participation in trade rituals more frequently undertaken by men. For one thing, when she and her family were coming west several years before, Netnokwa's husband had died. Death or illness of a husband and other emergencies appear to have been important reasons for women to undertake activities that were normally the work of men, as it would have been for men to undertake the work of women on occasion. Ruth Landes argued that women were "reserve material" capable of doing men's work when necessary for survival. In fact, though Landes gave many examples of women who hunted, traded, and went to war when they had to, she could provide only one example of a woman who resisted doing men's work when left alone by the death of her husband.[64]

In the case of Netnokwa, however, her transcendence of usual gender roles was evident even before her husband's death. As an older woman who had been married to a younger husband with two other wives, Netnokwa was, according to Tanner, considered to be the head of the household, even before his adopted father's death. Tanner stated that Netnokwa was seventeen years older than her husband, was an accomplished trader, and was owner of most of the family's wealth. Tanner said, perhaps exaggerating, that she was "notwithstanding her sex..., regarded as principal chief of the Ottawwaws," and that "whenever she came to Mackinac, she was saluted by a gun from the fort." Perhaps most significant of all—in terms of Ojibwa and Ottawa culture—Netnokwa was, as described by Tanner, a person of strong spirituality, and she used her power to aid her sons in hunting.[65]

Dreams and visions were often cited as providing authorization for Ojibwa men and women to transcend the gendered division of labour. Despite the tendency of scholars to analyze gender roles based on material factors, including participation in the fur trade, power in an Ojibwa community was never purely material, and even material power was usually seen as having a nonmaterial basis. Gwen Morris, in a remarkable recent study of women in Ojibwa society, notes that women, on the beginning of menstruation, were seen as having a unique source of power, made clear by its perceived danger to men.[66] Beyond that, as recounted in the story of the woman who married the beaver, girls fasted at puberty, seeking to gain a continuing relationship with a being who could help them in their lives. Having this relationship—especially when it was renewed from time to time through ceremony and further visions and dreams—helped men in important activities like hunting and war. For women, such a relationship might aid them in activities usually described as women's work.[67] Similarly, as Morris notes, such dreams and visions could help define a particular and unique course for their lives that transcended their own gender. This may have been the case with Netnokwa, whose spirituality was evident in her actions, though her own puberty visions were never recorded.[68]

Thus, despite the existence of a well-understood division of labour, described as rigid in many generalized descriptions of the Ojibwa, the more recent ethnographic evidence suggests that the Ojibwa gave cultural acceptance to those who violated the usual gender roles, and who demonstrated competence brought about by spiritual aid.[69] Such cultural acceptance suggests that many Ojibwa saw creative, dynamic women forging a unique course as having a beneficial effect on their communities. This is also evident in a major aspect of the roles of women in the fur trade, as the wives of traders. As I show, this unique role—one that Ojibwa men could not fill—had a major social and economic impact on the trade.

Fur-Trade Marriages

Claude-Charles Le Roy, *dit* Bacqueville de La Potherie, stated that in the late seventeenth century the Dakota, residing in what is now north-central Minnesota, made an alliance with the Ojibwa, then living mainly at the eastern end of Lake Superior, based on a desire for European trade goods. Because they "could obtain French merchandise only through the agency of the Sauteurs," they made "a treaty of peace with the latter by which they were mutually bound to give their daughters in marriage on both sides. That was a strong bond for the maintenance of entire harmony."[70] The agreement appears to have been encouraged by the French diplomat Daniel Greysolon, *Sieur* du Lhut, who, in mid-September 1679, convened a meeting of representatives from various "nations of the north," including Dakota, Assiniboine, and probably Ojibwa at Fond du Lac, the present site of Duluth. He later wrote: "I was able to gain their esteem and friendship. In order to make sure that the peace was more durable among them, I found that the best way to cement it was by bringing about reciprocal marriages. I was not able to do this without great deal of expense. During the following winter, I brought them together again in the woods where I was, so that they could hunt together, feast, and by this means, create a closer friendship."[71]

Among the Ojibwa, marriage was defined by the decision of two parties, sometimes through the intercession of parents or other relations, to sleep, live, and carry on their day-to-day lives together. Although the event was not marked by the ceremonies with which Europeans were familiar, it could involve ceremonial exchanges of gifts."[72] From the point of view of the native community, marriages between traders and native women could help achieve the important aim of ensuring a steady supply of merchandise. Ties of affection could increase the likelihood that a trader would return to the community in future years and that he might be more generous with gifts and in the rates exacted for direct exchange.

Historian Jacqueline Peterson wrote that "tribal people, throughout the fur trading era, saw intermarriage as a means of entangling strangers in a series of kinship obligations. Relatives by marriage were expected not only to deal fairly, but to provide protection, hospitality, and sustenance in time of famine." Peterson stated that "in addition to assuming positions of economic and political leverage, traders' wives used to advantage their symbolic status as links between two societies by serving as spies, interpreters, guides, or diplomatic emissaries."[73]

Early accounts of encounters between Ojibwa women and traders did not always clarify the political, social, or economic implications of what took place, making it difficult to interpret the behaviour described. Pierre Radisson, in his description of what preceded the gift-giving ceremony south of Lake Superior in 1659, noted: "The women throw themselves backwards upon the ground, thinking to give us tokens of friendship and of welcome."[74] What actually happened is not clear. Radisson may have exaggerated to impress and amuse his English patrons, as is the case with many portions of his narrative. Assuming there was a kernel of truth in the description, however, Radisson was obviously not convinced of the validity of this gesture. He may have thought it a little odd. The point of view of the native people involved is not recorded, yet the desire of people in a society to use sexual relations as a means of establishing long-term relationships between themselves and people of another society who had something to offer was a rational strategy, one that has been described in many parts of the world.[75]

Similarly, in the aforementioned account of trading rice with women at Lake of the Woods, Alexander Henry stated: "When morning arrived, all the village was inebriated; and the danger of misunderstanding was increased by the facility with which the women abandoned themselves to my Canadians. In consequence, I lost no time in leaving the place." Apparently, for Henry the sexual overtures of the women were a potential cause of jealousy and complication, due to his fear that the behaviour of these women would result in violence on the part of Ojibwa men. Henry does not make clear who these women were or even whether they were married. However, it is possible that their overtures were not, from the Ojibwa point of view, dangerous in that sense but were rather actions sanctioned by the community for the purpose of establishing long-term trade. In fact, it may have been that long-term entanglement, not sexual jealousy, was what Henry feared, since he hoped to travel much further west.

Whether or not the strategy succeeded in the case of the people described by Henry or Radisson is not known. However, there were many cases of marriage between Ojibwa women that did accomplish this purpose and enabled long and peaceful trade. Benjamin G. Armstrong, a trader among the Ojibwa in the 1840s who was married to a daughter of Chief Buffalo of La Pointe, stated that when a trader came into an Ojibwa community to trade, people would at first have nothing to do with him, except in a small way, so that they could gauge his honesty. "If satisfied on these points, the chiefs would together take their marriageable girls to his trading house and he was given his choice of the lot." If the trader made a choice, trade would begin right away. If not, he was compelled to move on his way and trade elsewhere, because the band would not trade with him "unless he took one of their women for his wife." As Peterson stated, this description "seems overly rationalistic." However, she stated that in such cases Indian wives "served as the cement between a band and a trader with long-range expectations."[76]

For fur traders, their wives or the wives of their employees could prove to be useful socially and economically. The evidence suggests that leading traders often married the daughters of Ojibwa leaders, although it is sometimes hard to say which came first.[77] In marrying a leader's daughter, a trader gained a powerful ally among his Indian customers. Since the authority of a leader was in part the result of extended kin ties, the trader may have formed ties with a large number of people. The leader's influence over kin and non-kin alike depended also on his persuasive oratory.[78] Thus, through marriage, the trader gained an alliance with a man of demonstrated ability to influence his fellows. The father-in-law could become, in a sense, an economic agent for the trader, useful in persuading the people to be friends and clients.

Simon Chaurette, a head trader for the North West, XY, and American Fur Companies, mostly at Lac du Flambeau, between 1795 and the early 1820s, was married to the daughter of Keeshkemun (Sharpened Stone or La Pierre à Affiler), an important leader who was a member of the Crane clan. According to François Victoire Malhiot, a rival trader in the region in 1804–05, Keeshkemun was allied in trade terms with Chaurette, although this alliance did not lessen the trader's obligation to give gifts and fulfill other native expectations of him. As for Keeshkemun's daughter, little has been written about her. Mostly she is identified in trade documents by the name of her husband or father. However, American Fur Company documents show that a woman named Keenistinoquay (or Cree Woman), identified as Chaurette's wife, was so important to the company's operation at Lac du Flambeau that she was employed as a trader there from 1819–21, receiving an average of more than $200 per year, around half of her husband's yearly salary.[79]

Another trader who benefited from a connection to a prominent native family was Charles Oakes Ermatinger, who, from a base at Sault Ste. Marie, shipped goods to trading posts south and west of Lake Superior from 1800 to the mid-1820s. Ermatinger married Charlotte, the daughter of Kadowaubeda, or Broken Tooth, a member of the Loon clan and a civil leader described by Henry R. Schoolcraft, an Indian agent and a noted writer on Ojibwa culture, as "patriarch" of the region around Sandy Lake and the upper Mississippi, the area of Ermatinger's trade. After her husband's retirement in the 1820s, Charlotte went to live with him and her children in Montreal, where she spent the rest of her life.[80]

Important traders like Chaurette and Ermatinger were not the only members of their companies married to native women. It is apparent from accounts of stable trading posts south of Lake Superior in Wisconsin and Minnesota that some fur company outfits were linked to the Indian community from top to bottom of the trade hierarchy, meaning that fur companies had access to an extensive kinship network.[81]

Because traders were unsystematic in recording genealogical information about themselves and their employees, it is not always possible to pin down the parameters of these networks. However, the unofficial and supposedly non-economic network that existed around each trading post was probably as important to companies as was the network of suppliers and shippers through which they obtained their supplies of trade goods. As Jennifer Brown suggested in her study of Hudson Bay Company and North West Company social life, women associated with the trading post could provide a more certain food supply.[82] When the North West Company wintering partner John Sayer was stationed on the St. Croix River, his Ojibwa wife went to the sugar bush in 1803 and 1804 to process maple sugar for their food supply.[83] When food was scarce at the trading post, traders were sometimes fed by their wives' families. On 17 March 1804, George Nelson wrote: "Brunet with my permission goes with his family to his father in law's lodge, as we have nothing here to eat. I give him a little ammunition & a few silverworks to trade provisions—for we have now nothing else to trade. We subsiste upon indian Charity."[84]

Beyond providing food, native women and the trade kinship networks served as a source of information for traders as much as for Indian people. In 1804, Michel Curot learned that one Ojibwa family did not want to give their furs to the opposition North West trader because the man was out of rum. Curot said he had heard it from the wife of his man Savoyard, who had in turn heard it from the wife of the North West trader's clerk.[85]

Some fur companies had economic reasons for encouraging such marriages. If the employee himself was responsible for the expense of a wife, he would take more of his wages in goods purchased from his employer, thus effectively discounting the company's wage burden. In August 1799, Alexander Mackenzie wrote to John Sayer, the head of the Fond du Lac department, giving him a reading on the financial health of Sayer's outfit: "Were it not that Men Spend their Wages and the extraordinarily high price of Bears and Beaver, it would be to us a losing business. With these advantages there will be very little profit this last year."[86]

A few years later, after leaving the North West Company to head the rival XY Company, Mackenzie took a different point of view, at least according to George Nelson. Nelson told in his journal and reminiscences of an incident that occurred in the fall of 1803 when he was a young man, working as Simon Chaurette's clerk for the XY Company in northern Wisconsin. Assigned to act as Nelson's guide was an

Indian the traders called "le Commis" (the clerk) because "formerly traders would give him about a 9 gallon keg of rum & other things and send him trading among or with the other Indians. He was always sure to make good returns." The Commis had a teenage daughter. Very early in the fall the man decided that eighteen-year-old Nelson should marry her. Nelson suspected that Chaurette—or as he spells the man's name, Chorette—was behind it. "This old fellow either took a fancy for me, or Chorette took a fancy for my little wages. I believe both to be the case."[87]

Chaurette was not working on a salary for the XY. Instead, he had a three-year agreement with the company that stated that he would be furnished goods at $37\frac{1}{3}$ percent above Montreal prices. In addition, he would be furnished with whatever number of men he needed to carry on the trade. Also, it appears that Chaurette was liable for the men's wages. This meant that it would be to his own advantage to pay wages in goods valued above what he paid for them, since this would reduce the monetary cost of the wages. Nelson recalled later that Chaurette told him to give the men "what they might ask for, as it was for his own interest that they should take up their wages & even more in goods, liquor, tobacco, or any other such articles as we had on board our canoe."[88]

Nelson's suspicions increased when Chaurette kept encouraging him to marry, saying that "it would not require much money to cloath only a woman." For many days Nelson resisted, in part because he expected that the head of the XY company, Alexander Mackenzie, would not approve—though he later recalled that he himself, "to tell the truth, was far from averse to it." Finally after he and the Commis had separated from Chaurette and were on their way to their wintering grounds, the Indian made Nelson an offer he could not refuse. He told Nelson that if the young man would not marry his daughter, he, the Commis, would let Nelson find his way by himself. Although there were several company employees with Nelson, the Commis was the only person who knew how to get where they were going. Nelson and his men depended "entirely upon what the old man and his friends whom he kept with him, could procure us." So Nelson agreed. Later he recalled: "I think I still see the satisfaction, the pleasure the poor old man felt. He gave me his daughter! He thought no doubt that it would be the means of rendering him happy & comfortable in his old days."[89]

This account demonstrates the various material expectations that the people involved brought to such marriages. Chaurette hoped it would simply mean more debts against Nelson's wages. The Commis thought a connection with a fur-trade clerk would help provide support for himself and his family. Nelson married so that he could get to his wintering ground and perform his duty, in addition to what he admitted was "above all the secret satisfaction at being *compelled...* to marry for my safety." As Nelson expected, Mackenzie disapproved of the marriage. He withdrew Nelson from the district the following summer and sent him to the Lake Winnipeg area. Nelson's wife left him at Grand Portage that summer to live with another company employee, an interpreter.[90]

Whether Mackenzie's disapproval was based on moral grounds or not, there were, even from the point of view of the administrator, good reasons for opposing marriages between Indian women and company employees. For example, if the company was in any way responsible for feeding a trader and his family, the cost could perhaps outweigh the benefits of this extra expenditure of wages. Michel Curot stated that in the XY Company's St. Croix River valley outfit in 1803–04, married men received double the customary ration of one pint corn or wild rice to each man per day.[91]

Furthermore, what if the employee's expenditure of his wages far outweighed what was coming to him for years to come? This factor became especially important after the coalition of the XY and North West Companies in 1805, when a surplus of men were working at wages driven higher by competition. How could one dismiss an employee who had a large debt? It may have been for this reason that the North West Company at its annual meeting at Fort William in July 1806 announced a new policy about the marriages of its employees: "It was suggested that the number of women and Children in the Country was a heavy burthen to the Concern & that some remedy ought to be applied to check so great an evil, at least if nothing effectual could be done to suppress it entirely—It was therefore resolved that every practicable means should be used throughout the Country to reduce by degrees the number of women maintained by the Company." It was decided that henceforth no partner, clerk, or engagé be allowed to marry any Indian woman or at least take her "to live with him within the Company's Houses or Forts & be maintained at the Expences of the Concern." The company did, however, allow traders to marry the daughters of other traders.[92]

The implication of some accounts of marriages arranged by traders and the parents of native women is that women were passive objects like the furs, food, and merchandise exchanged in the fur trade. This does not appear to have been the case of Nelson's wife, who dissolved the relationship easily, and it is open to question whether this was the case with most such marriages. To be effective in achieving the purposes native communities might envision for such marriages, women could not be passive. They had to exert influence and be active communicators of information. Further, there is evidence that marriages were not simply arranged by male and female elders in communities. Rather they were embraced by many women themselves as a way of achieving useful purposes for themselves and for the communities in which they lived.

Marriages between traders and native women were based on a variety of factors, not just material motives. Jacqueline Peterson, in her study of Great Lakes Métis society, suggested that marriages with fur traders took exceptional women, people with unusual ambitions, influenced by dreams and visions—like the women who became hunters, traders, healers, and warriors in Ruth Landes' account of Ojibwa women. One example Peterson gave was Oshahgushkodanaqua, a woman from the western end of Lake Superior who married the Sault Ste. Marie trader John Johnston in the 1790s.[93] Oshahgushkodanaqua was the granddaughter of Mamongeseda (Big Foot or Big Feet), a La Pointe leader noted for his prowess in war and diplomacy. One of Mamongeseda's daughters—one source suggests her name was Obernaunoqua—was the wife of John Sayer, who was in charge of the entire Lake Superior area for the General Company of Lake Superior and the South in the 1780s and the North West Company from 1794 to 1805. One of Mamongeseda's sons, Waubojeeg (White Fisher), also based at La Pointe, was as renowned in war and diplomacy as his father. Waubojeeg was the father of Oshahgushkodanaqua.[94]

Oshahgushkodanaqua's marriage was preceded by a dream during the vision quest she undertook at puberty. She told the story many years later, after her husband's death, to a visiting British writer named Anna Jameson. The story of the dream has some interesting parallels to the story of the woman who married the beaver.

According to Jameson, Oshahgushkodanaqua fasted "according to the universal Indian custom, for *a guardian spirit.*" She went to a high hill and built a lodge of cedar boughs, painted herself black, and then began to fast.

She dreamed continually of a white man, who approached her with a cup in his hand, saying, "Poor thing! why are you punishing yourself? why do you fast? here is food for you!" He was always accompanied by a dog, which looked up in her face as though he knew her. Also she dreamed of being on a high hill, which was surrounded by water, and from which she beheld many canoes full of Indians, coming to her and paying her homage; after this, she felt as if she were carried up into the heavens, and as she looked down upon the earth, she perceived it was on fire, and said to herself, "All my relations will be burned!" but a voice answered and said, "No, they will not be destroyed, they will be saved"; and she *knew it was a spirit,* because the voice was not human. She fasted for ten days, during which time her grandmother brought her at intervals some water. When satisfied that she had obtained a guardian spirit in the white stranger who haunted her dreams, she returned to her father's lodge.[95]

Some time after this dream, John Johnston appeared at her parents' home at Chequamegon to trade for furs. He asked the woman's father, Waubojeeg, for her hand in marriage. Her father at first was scornful of Johnston because he did not believe the trader was seeking a long-term relationship. He told Johnston to return to Montreal in the spring and if he still wished to marry her, he could come back to Lake Superior and marry her, "according to the law of the white man *till death.*" Johnston returned to Lake Superior and the marriage was arranged.

The young woman, however, was not keen on the idea and took some persuasion to stay with her husband. Given the possibilities for dissolving marriage among the Ojibwa, this fear may have been due in part to Johnston's insistence on marriage until death. Once she consented, however, the couple remained married for thirty-six years.[96] All evidence suggests that she served an important and influential role in relations between her people and her husband, who was an important trader in the Lake Superior region from the 1790s to the 1820s. According to Jameson, Oshahgushkodanaqua throughout her life carried on a variety of subsistence activities characteristic of Ojibwa women—activities that would have been advantageous for her husband's business. She sugared every year and fished. In addition, Jameson noted, in words that could have appeared in one of Ruth Landes' accounts of remarkable women, that "in her youth she hunted, and was accounted the surest eye and fleetest foot among the women of her tribe."[97]

Later in her life, Oshahgushkodanaqua also taught Ojibwa and Ojibwa culture to her children and to visitors to the region, including her son-in-law, Henry R. Schoolcraft. Her career transcended the fur trade, lasting into an era when Ojibwa people had need for intermediaries who would help them in dealings with the U.S. Government. All in all, Oshahgushkodanaqua actively made use of the situation in which she found herself.[98]

It should be said that Oshahgushkodanaqua's interpretation of the experience may have evolved over the years. It may have been coloured by the death of her husband. It may have been shaped by her Christian conversion, as suggested by some of the imagery and wording in the story. On the other hand, her experience bears the clear imprint of Ojibwa culture. The vision quest, though an apparently solitary endeavour pursued by young people, was shaped in part by the Ojibwa educational process, including the telling of stories, some of which, in Oshahgushkodanaqua's case, may have resembled the story of the woman who married the beaver. The process of seeking a vision was also usually supervised by adults, who encouraged certain desirable results.[99]

It may be that in this way, Oshahgushkodanaqua's experience was shaped by community needs. Her story contains the suggestion that a marriage with an outsider could be of benefit to the woman's relations, that there was some social purpose in undertaking a marriage with such a person who could provide something useful to the community. She felt some fear about the risks involved to herself and her community, but in the long run, the marriage was a good one. In her life she achieved a great deal.

All of these elements were found, too, of course, in the story of the woman who married the beaver, a story which tells a great deal about how the Ojibwa community did honour to women who followed unique destinies. The nature of the message communicated by the story can be seen by comparing it to another of Kagige Pinasi's stories, a humorous tale about a young man named Clothed-in-Fur, a trickster-like figure, who marries, in turn, a wolf, a raven, a porcupine, a Canada Jay, a beaver, and finally a bear. Most of the marriages are unsuccessful, due to drawbacks Clothed-in-Fur finds in the various wives: the wolf could not carry heavy loads, and the raven was a bad cook and a poor housekeeper, for example. But in the course of the story, Clothed-in-Fur learns valuable lessons on how to treat with respect the bones of animals he kills so that the animals will come back to life. There is another version of this same story, collected by Schoolcraft. In this version, the young man marries a nighthawk, a marten, a beaver, and a bear. The story ends with the man's bear-wife giving herself up to a hunter to be killed. The man spoke to the hunter and gave him important instructions about the proper way to treat bears: "You must… never cut the flesh in taking off the skin, nor hang up the feet with the flesh when drying it. But you must take the head and feet, and decorate them handsomely, and place tobacco on the head, for these animals are very fond of this article, and on the *fourth day* they come to life again."[100]

Both of these versions have a humorous tone, as the hapless hero discovers the identity, drawbacks, and faults of each marriage partner. The serious portion of the story is in its instructions about the treatment of animals, comparable in some ways to the injunctions given in the story of the woman who married the beaver. In telling the latter story, however, Kagige Pinasi had something more in mind than entertaining and instructing about the proper treatment of animals. There was an important message about women. In particular, this is revealed in a description of the woman's discovery by the trappers who found her in the beaver lodge many years after her marriage. Hearing her voice calling to them, they broke open the beaver lodge, and one of them reached in his hand and touched her, "whereupon he found by the feel of her that she was a human being; all over did he try feeling her, on her head; and her ears, having on numerous ear-rings, he felt. And when he had forced a wide opening, out came the woman; very white was her head. And beautiful was the whole mystic cloth that she had for a skirt; worked all over with beads was her cloak; and her moccasins too were very pretty; and her ear-rings she also had on; she was very handsomely arrayed."[101]

This key description captures something of the awe with which the woman was viewed, in the story and by the storyteller. Her white hair, beaded clothing, and earrings were all symbols of power, spiritual and material, and the honour she would have in an Ojibwa community. Unlike the man who married the beaver, the birds, the bear, and the other animals, the woman who married a beaver is an object of respect and reverence.[102]

This story, together with the other accounts given here, can serve as a guide to interpreting experiences and events, suggesting other ways of looking at them and providing Ojibwa alternatives to scholarly scenarios. Far from being beasts of burden, subsidiary to interactions with outsiders, Ojibwa women were central to the process, honoured for the role they played. The way in which these and other women used their relationships with outsiders for their own benefit, the benefit of the communities, or of their husbands—and in the process influenced the patterns of interaction with outsiders—must be evaluated based on all the available details, on a case-by-case basis. It would be wrong to see in any of the women described here a single set of motives or a single path for Ojibwa women.[103] Nonetheless, it is only by considering all the available Ojibwa models of women's roles as warriors, shamans, wives, suppliers of food, traders, intermediaries, brokers, and teachers, that one can hope to understand the role of Ojibwa women in the fur trade.

Conclusion

The fur trade is sometimes seen simply as an exchange that took place between men of European and native cultures. However, an examination of the trade among the Ojibwa of Lake Superior shows that women and men both participated in the trade. They also had different opportunities, different expectations, and different roles to play. As acknowledged by traders in their gift giving and trade, men and women sought a different assortment of trade goods. Women also played an important role in providing the resources that were their responsibility in native life: wild rice, maple sugar, and a variety of vital supplies necessary for the function of trade. While most women did not usually participate in trade ceremonies or receive credit from traders, they were able to trade the products of their labour for goods they needed. Finally, women also could serve as a vital link between their communities and European traders by marrying traders. Such marriages could ensure a steady supply of merchandise for a community by providing an incentive for traders to return to the communities from which their wives came and, possibly, by increasing their generosity toward their wives' relations. Although such marriages were encouraged and often arranged by men, women were not mere objects to be exchanged. The value of such marriages to a native community could only be achieved if women exercised influence on the trader and served to increase the flow of information and merchandise in both directions.

The challenge of examining the differing roles of Ojibwa men and women in the fur trade means using both early documents and later ethnographies in an ongoing creative process. This process may not always provide a satisfying narrative of exactly what occurred in the past, but it does reveal a catalogue of possible roles for men and women, roles that they may have assumed at various times in the past.

The multiple nature of the fur trade and of Ojibwa women's roles in relation to that trade suggests that the theories of Landes, Leacock, and Devens need revision. The fur trade provided more than a few opportunities for Ojibwa women. While the fur trade was important to native communities, both men and women had distinct and powerful roles to play in relation to a trade that was never simply one of furs for merchandise. Women had many opportunities to trade food, supplies, and on occasion, furs, to obtain what they needed and wanted from traders.

This does not deny the possibility that there may have been particular situations in which women had fewer opportunities to trade the products of their work for the things that they needed. With the improvement of transportation methods and the growth of white population centres in the Great Lakes, traders may have been able to bring better supplies of food, allowing them to trade for furs more exclusively. It should be noted, however, that while later fur traders may have had less use for Ojibwa women's food and supplies, there was a contemporaneous growing market for maple sugar, wild rice, and berries among lumbermen, settlers, and city people, which may well have provided greater opportunities for women than before. This was certainly the case along the Minnesota frontier in the late nineteenth century.[104]

The extent to which Ojibwa women's power and status in their own communities may have changed since contact with Europeans remains to be demonstrated. A major problem with describing the course of changes in Ojibwa society in the last four hundred years is the difficulty of reconstructing Ojibwa gender relations in the era prior to European contact using only documents that resulted from that contact. Analysis of the changes in Ojibwa society in the era of the fur trade also requires care, especially if it is based on documents that interpret Ojibwa gender from a European point of view of how men and women should live their lives. Scholars must take into account some of the Ojibwa beliefs about women's power and the accounts of individual women's lives and dreams discussed here. Though the Ojibwa did have a distinct division of labour, one that may have changed at various times in response to interaction with Europeans, women could make a distinct course for themselves through their spiritual power.

One way or another, however, care should be taken in attributing the condition of Ojibwa society and culture in the late twentieth century to the effects of the fur trade. To do so is to ignore the effects of treaties, a declining land base, limitation of opportunities to use natural resources, pervasive mass media, urbanization, and poverty, all of which have occurred in the years since the decline of the fur trade.

Further work is needed on the gendered patterns of the fur trade among the Ojibwa. It is important to take a fresh look at all primary sources to consider the gender dimensions of every transaction involving traders and native people, reading between the lines when necessary. Whether or not such an examination will suggest alterations in existing theories about gender and about other aspects of the impact of the fur trade on the Ojibwa, it will provide a richer view of the fur trade itself.

Endnotes

The inspiring work and teaching of Janet D. Spector influenced the approach taken in this article. I would like to thank the participants in the 1994 "Crucibles of Cultures"—a conference in New Orleans sponsored by the Institute of Early American History and Culture—for their comments and suggestions, in particular Christine Heyrman, Lucy E. Murphy, Neal Salisbury, Fredrika Teute, and Richard White. Subsequently, I received many helpful comments and encouragement from Jennifer Brown, Priscilla K. Buffalohead, Sharon Doherty, Laura Peers, and several anonymous reviewers. Peggy Hadid provided much appreciated help in searching for published literature on this topic. Finally, I am especially grateful to Gwen Morris for her detailed and generous critique of the essay, and for the provocative and suggestive nature of her own work on women in Ojibwa society. Portions of the article were written while I was a participant in the John Tanner Project. I would like to thank John Fierst, Lacey Sanders, and John Nichols for their encouragement and inspiration."

[1] William Jones, *Ojibwa Texts*, Publications of the American Ethnological Society, vol. 7. part 2, ed. Truman Michelson (Leyden: E.J. Brill, Limited; and New York: G.E. Stechert & Co., Agents, 1919) 251–57. For further information on Kagige Pinasi (Forever-Bird) or John Pinesi, see Jones, *Ojibwa Texts*, vol. 7, part I (Leiden, 1917), xvii; and Henry M. Rideout, *William Jones: Indian, Cowboy, American Scholar, and Anthropologist in the Field* (New York: Frederick A. Stokes Company, 1912) 98, 110–11. The story of the woman who married a beaver is reprinted in Thomas W. Overholt and J. Baird Callicott, *Clothed-in-Fur and Other Tales: An Introduction to an Ojibwa World View* (Washington: University Press of America, 1982) 74–5.

[2] Jean-François Lyotard wrote of what he called "popular stories" in *The Postmodern Condition: A Report on Knowledge*, trans. Geoff Bennington and Brian Massumi (Manchester: Manchester University Press, 1984) 20, 21.

[3] Overholt and Callicort, *Clothed-in-Fur*, 26.

[4] Overholt and Callicott use the stories to help explain Ojibwa worldview on pages 24–29.

[5] Rideout, *William Jones*, 98, 109–11. Notes entitled "Penessi goes hunting" are found in the William Jones Papers, American Philosophical Society, Philadelphia.

[6] For a discussion of these beliefs and their bearing on the fur trade, see Bruce M. White, "'Give Us a Little Milk': The Social and Cultural Meaning of Gift Giving in the Lake Superior Fur Trade,"

Rendezvous: Selected Papers of the Fourth North American Fur Trade Conference, 1981, ed. Thomas C. Buckley (St. Paul, MN: The Conference, 1984) 187–8.

[7] Bruce M. White, "Encounters with Spirits: Ojibwa and Dakota Theories about the French and Their Merchandise," *Ethnohistory* 41 (Summer 1994): 376 –81; B. White, "'Give Us a Little Milk,'" 187–92; Richard White, *The Middle Ground. Indians, Empires, and Republics in the Great Lakes Region, 1650–1815* (Cambridge and New York: Cambridge University Press, 1991) 95, 112–14.

[8] On Native American origin tales, see Stith Thompson, *The Folktale* (1946; reprint, Berkeley, CA, and Los Angeles: University of California Press, 1977) 303.

[9] Harold A. Innis, *The Fur Trade in Canada: An Introduction to Canadian Economic History* (1930; rev., Toronto: University of Toronto Press, 1956) 40.

[10] Arthur J. Ray and Donald B. Freeman, *"Give Us Good Measure":* *An Economic Analysis of Relations Between the Indians and the Hudson's Bay Company.* (Toronto: Toronto University Press, 1978), xv. See also Arthur J. Ray, *The Indians in the Fur Trade: Their Role as Hunters, Trappers, and Middlemen in the Lands Southwest of Hudson Bay, 1660–1870* (Toronto: Toronto University Press, 1974), which also lacks a detailed discussion of the role of gender in the fur trade.

[11] R. White, *Middle Ground,* 94, 105.

[12] Ibid., 74, 130. White's primary discussion of women in the book concerns sexual and marriage relations between Frenchmen and Indian women, 60–75.

[13] Jennifer Brown, *Strangers in Blood: Fur Trade Company Families in Indian Country* (Vancouver: University of British Columbia Press, 1980).

[14] Sylvia Van Kirk, *"Many Tender Ties": Women in Fur-Trade Society, 1670–1870* (1980; first American edition, Norman, OK: University of Oklahoma Press, 1983) 5.

[15] Ibid., 75–7, 80. See also Sylvia Van Kirk, "Toward a Feminist Perspective in Native History," *Papers of the Eighteenth Algonquian Conference,* ed. William Cowan (Ottawa: Carleton University, 1987) 377–89.

[16] Jacqueline Peterson, "The People in Between: Indian-White Marriage and the Genesis of a Métis Society and Culture in the Great Lakes Region, 1680–1830" (Ph.D. diss., University of Illinois at Chicago Circle, 1981), 2. An important chapter of Peterson's dissertation, from the point of view of trade patterns, was published as "Women Dreaming: The Religiopsychology of Indian-White Marriages and the Rise of a Métis Culture," *Western Women: Their Land, Their*

Lives, ed. Lillian Schlissel, Vicki L. Ruiz, and Janice Monk (Albuquerque: University of New Mexico Press, 1988) 49–68.

[17] For a discussion of the varying themes covered in the study of gender among Native American groups, see Patricia Albers, "From Illusion to Illumination: Anthropological Studies of American Indian Women," *Gender and Anthropology: Critical Reviews for Research and Teaching,* ed. Sandra Morgen (Washington, DC: American Anthropological Association, 1989) 137–48.

[18] The stories in Ruth Landes' book refer to Ojibwa people going to war against the Sioux or Dakota, suggesting this was a part of people's lives at the time, though Landes acknowledged that war between the two groups had not existed in at least fifty years. Landes, *The Ojibwa Woman* (1938; reprint, New York: W. W. Norton & Company, 1971) 4, 17, 132, 133, 141, 143, 149, 162, 163, 171. Maggie Wilson (see vii) was of Cree descent but spoke Ojibwa, had married an Ojibwa man, and had lived all her life among the Ojibwa.

[19] Ibid., 131, 137. On the range of roles available to women, see 135–71.

[20] Ibid., 134. Landes noted, however, that "today when rice and berries and maple sugar are commanding some white attention, the women also are learning to function as dealers."

[21] Eleanor Leacock, "Women's Status in Egalitarian Society: Implications for Social Evolution," *Current Anthropology* 19 (June 1978:) 249–52, 254, 255. Another useful critique of Landes' work appears in Sally Cole, "Women's Stories and Boasian Texts: The Ojibwa Ethnography of Ruth Landes and Maggie Wilson," *Anthropologica* 37 (1995): 3–25, especially 13, 17, 21. Harold Hickerson, who largely ignored gender in his influential work on the Ojibwa, appears to have agreed with the theory that the fur trade devalued women's roles. In one of his last published works, a study of "fur trade colonialism," he argued that among the Huron, the fur trade inevitably led to a decline in women's roles and importance. He suggested that men naturally assumed the major role in dealing with traders. Hickerson, "Fur Trade Colonialism and the North American Indians," *Journal of Ethnic Studies* 1 (Summer 1973): 15–44.

[22] Carol Devens, *Countering Colonization: Native American Women and Great Lakes Missions, 1630–1900* (Berkeley: University of California Press, 1992) 13, 14, 15–16, 17, 18.

[23] Priscilla K. Buffalohead, "Farmers, Warriors, Traders: A Fresh Look at Ojibway Women," *Minnesota History* 48 (Summer 1983) 237. One nineteenth-century example is Peter Grant, "The Sauteux Indians

about 1904," *Les Bourgeois de la Compagnie du Nord Ouest*, ed. Louis F. R. Masson, (1890; reprint, New York: Antiquarian Press, 1960) 2: 321. Grant stated that Ojibwa women, "for all their work and devotion, are regarded by the men little better than slaves to their will, or mere beasts of burden for their conveniency."

[24] Thomas Vennum, Jr., *Wild Rice and the Ojibway People* (St. Paul: Minnesota Historical Society Press, 1988), 108, 109. The translation is from R. G. Thwaites, ed., "A Wisconsin Fur Trader's Journal, 1804–5," *Collections of the State Historical Society of Wisconsin* 19 (1910): 197.

[25] Vennum, 108, 109. It should also be noted that François Victoire Malhiot in his original journal used the term *gens* to refer to L'Outarde's followers, a word that could be translated as "people" or even "band." Even this translation, however, may imply a more important role for men in ricing than is warranted. See Malhiot journal, 15 (10 September 1804), McGill University Libraries, Rare Books and Special Collections.

[26] William Fenton, "The Training of Historical Ethnologists in America," *American Anthropologist* 54 (3): 333, 335.

[27] Ibid., 333. R. White, at the beginning of *The Middle Ground*, wrote that "the technique of using ethnologies of present-day or nineteenth-century Indian groups to interpret Indian societies of the past" had a "bias toward continuity" that he tried to avoid. (xiv). Skepticism toward continuity in the analysis of Native American history is sometimes allied with the application of globalizing theories, as in Carol I. Mason, "Indians, Maple Sugaring, and the Spread of Market Economies," *The Woodland Tradition in the Western Great Lakes: Papers Presented to Elden Johnson* ed. Guy E. Gibbon (Minneapolis: Department of Anthropology, University of Minnesota, 1990) 37–43.

[28] Even scholars who argue for radical change in Native American cultures due to contact with Europeans often make use of later ethnographic works as evidence for their understanding of aboriginal culture. See, for example, Calvin Martin, *Keepers of the Game: Indian-Animal Relationships and the Fur Trade* (Berkeley: University of California Press, 1978) 72, a work that relies heavily on the twentieth-century ethnography of A. Irving Hallowell.

[29] Quotations, with modernized orthography and paragraph breaks added, are from Pierre Radisson, *Voyages of Peter Esprit Radisson, Being an Account of His Travels and Experiences Among the North American Indians, From 1652 to 1684* (Boston: Prince Society, 1885, 199, 200. Grace Lee Nute convincingly dates these events to 1659–60. See Nute, *Caesars of the Wilderness: Médard Chouart, Sieur des Groseilliers and Pierre Esprit Radisson, 1618-1710* (1943; reprint, St. Paul: Minnesota Historical Society

Press, 1978) 58, 62. The term *destinated* is a borrowing by Radisson of the French verb *destiner*, meaning "to intend something for someone or for some use," though in this context, "present" may be a better translation. Such borrowings from French were typical of Radisson's narrative.

[30] On Ojibwa facial adornment in the nineteenth century, see Johann Georg Kohl, *Kitchi-Gami: Life Among the Lake Superior Ojibway* (1960; reprint, St. Paul: Minnesota Historical Society Press, 1985) 18.

[31] Among Eastern groups, kettles clearly had an important symbolism in the feast of the dead, which may explain Radisson's reference here. See Laurier Turgeon, "The Tale of the Kettle: Odyssey of An Intercultural Object," *Ethnohistory* 44 (Winter): 11. Harold Hickerson gives an analysis of the Algonquian feast of the dead, with occasional reference to the roles of men and women, in Hickerson, "The Feast of the Dead among the Seventeenth-Century Algonkians of the Upper Great Lakes," *American Anthropologist* 62 (1960): 90. The uses of kettles in various activities among the Ojibwa are described in Vennum, 118–19; Alexander Henry, the elder, *Travels and Adventures in Canada and the Indian Territories* (1809; reprint, New York: Garland, 1976) 149.

[32] Buffalohead, "Farmers, Warriors, Traders," 238. Landes, *Ojibwa Woman*, 125, noted that there was a similar division of labour in the manufacture of cradleboards.

[33] Ivan Illich, in an illuminating definition, wrote in *Gender* (New York and Toronto: Pantheon Books, 1982) 99, that "gender not only tells who is who, but it also defines who is when, where, and with which tools and words; it divides space, time and technique." The gendered nature of material culture is of special interest to some archaeologists. For a discussion that focuses in particular on Dakota women's use of awls and other tools of native and European manufacture, see Janet D. Spector, *What This Awl Means: Feminist Archaeology at a Wabpeton Dakota Village* (St. Paul: Minnesota Historical Society Press, 1993), including 30–9. See also Spector, "Male/Female Task Differentiation among the Hidatsa: Toward the Development of an Archeological Approach to the Study of Gender," *The Hidden Half: Studies of Plains Indian Women*, ed. Patricia Albers and Beatrice Medicine (University Press of America: Lanham, MD, and London, 1983) 77–99.

[34] Frances Densmore, *Chippewa Customs* (1929; reprint, St. Paul: Minnesota Historical Society Press, 1979) 74.

[35] Joseph N. Nicollet, *The Journals of Joseph N. Nicollet: A Scientist on the Mississippi Headwaters*, ed. Martha Coleman Bray (St. Paul: Minnesota Historical Society, 1970) 181–2.

[36] It should be noted, however, that each item on the list would clearly be useful for other activities aside from preparing furs for trade. In fact, preparation of furs for use as clothing probably involved more scraping than preparing furs for trade, especially once traders no longer put a premium on beaver pelts that had been worn as beaver robes. See M. Inez Hilger, *Chippewa Child Life and Its Cultural Background* (1951; reprint, St. Paul: Minnesota Historical Society Press, 1992) 129–33; Densmore, *Chippewa Customs*, 31, 163–5; Clayton, "The American Fur Company: The Final Years" (Ph.D. diss., Cornell University, 1964) 96, 101, 108, 109; Ray and Freeman, *Give Us Good Measure*, 159.

[37] The argument here is in favour of a desire for and an interest in European merchandise, not necessarily a complete dependence upon it. For a longer discussion of the multiple nature of this interest in merchandise, see B. White, "Encounters with Spirits," 376–81. For one trader's account of Ojibwa interest in merchandise, see Henry, *Travels and Adventures*, 196. For a discussion of "dependency" in relation to Great Lakes Indian groups, see R. White, *Middle Ground*, 482–6.

[38] For accounts of expeditions to Montreal, see Nicolas Perrot's account in *Indian Tribes of the Upper Mississippi Valley and Region of the Great Lakes*, ed. Emma H. Blair (Cleveland: The Arthur H. Clark Company, 1911)1: 175, 210–20. In an earlier period, around 1609, Algonquin men and women from the upper Ottawa River, perhaps related to Great Lakes Algonquin peoples, did travel together to trade with the French in Montreal. See Bruce G. Trigger, *The Children of Aataentsic: A History of the Huron People to 1660* (1976; reprint, Kingston/Montreal: McGill-Queen's University Press, 1987) 249. See also a nineteenth-century account of a seventeenth-century Ojibwa husband and wife travelling east to discover the French, cited in B. White, "Encounters with Spirits," 373.

[39] Bruce M. White, "A Skilled Game of Exchange: Ojibway Fur Trade Protocol," *Minnesota History* 50: 229–40.

[40] Ibid., 231–4.

[41] On the concept of spheres of exchange, see Fredrik Barth, *The Role of the Entrepreneur in Social Change in Northern Norway* (Bergen, Norway, 1963), 10; Paul Bohannan and George Dalton, eds., *Markets in Africa* ([Evanston IL]: Northwestern University Press, 1962) 3.

[42] B. White, "'Give Us a Little Milk,'" 191–2.

[43] B. White, "A Skilled Game of Exchange," 235.

[44] Ojibwa women's names often, though not always, have the suffix -*ikwe* at the end, which is the Ojibwa word for woman. See John D. Nichols and Earl Nyholm, *A Concise Dictionary of Minnesota Ojibwe*

(Minneapolis and London: University of Minnesota Press, 1995), 64. English or French translations of such names may not always have included this portion of the name. On Ojibwa naming practices, see Hilger, *Chippewa Child Life*, 35–9.

[45] On the generosity of Ojibwa leaders, see Kohl, *Kitchi-Gami*, 66.

[46] *The Journal of Alexander Henry the Younger 1799–1814*, ed. Barry M. Gough (Toronto: Champlain Society, 1988–1992) 1: 26, 53. These entries correspond to 48, 111, in the original journal transcript in the Public Archives of Canada, Ottawa.

[47] Traders mentioned credit books or ledgers in their narrative journals, but none have been found for this period. Even credit books, however, do not make clear the role of the hunter's family in choosing the goods received on credit. For an analysis of a credit book from a later period, one kept using pictographic symbols, see George Fulford, "The Pictographic Account Book of an Ojibwa Fur Trader," *Papers of the Twenty-third Algonquian Conference*, ed. William Cowan (Ottawa: Carleton University, 1992) 190–217.

[48] Illich, Gender, 9–11; Lionel Robbins, *An Essay on the Nature and Significance of Economic Science* (1931; reprint, London: Macmillan, 1952) 94–9.

[49] On Ojibwa attitudes toward generosity, see Kohl, *Kitchi-Gami*, 66.

[50] For examples of women notifying the trader of available furs and other items, see Michel Curot's journal, 8 (22 September 1803) 19 (13 November 1803).

[51] Curot journal, 10 (13 October 1803), (14 October 1803), (24 October 1803), original in Masson Collection, Public Archives of Canada. A garbled translation of this narrative was published as "A Wisconsin Fur-Trader's journal, 1803–4," *Collections of the State Historical Society of Wisconsin* 20 (1911): 396–471.

[52] Some examples of direct trade of furs by women in Curot's journal include 23 (2 December 1803), 32 (9 February 1804).

[53] Ibid., 3 (17 and 18 August 1803), 6 (12 September 1803), 9 (4 and 5 October 1803), 13 (24 October 1803), 18 (10 November 1803), 21 (22 and 23 November 1803), 23 (2 December 1803), 28 (17 December 1803), 29 (December 23 1803), 32 (9 February 1804), 33 (20 February 1804), 41 (18 March 1804), 47 (15 and 16 April 1804).

[54] Henry, *Travels and Adventures*, 243–4.

[55] There are many examples in trade literature of food gifts to initiate the trading year. See B. White, "'Give Us a Little Milk,'" 187, 193.

[56] As quoted earlier, Landes did acknowledge that women learned how to trade when their food was in demand outside their communities. Landes, *Ojibwa Woman*, 134.

[57] Curot journal, 3 (17 August 1803). The estimate of the value of these goods is based on values found in accounts kept by Malhiot, originals in Rare Books and Special Collections, McGill University Libraries.

[58] Curot did some trading and collecting furs during the period when he was camped on the St. Croix River. Curot journal, 46 (7 April 1804), 47 (15 April 1804), 50 (8-10 May 1804). See also 5 (5 September 1803), in which it is noted that David can go nowhere because of a lack of gum for his canoe. On *wadab*, see Nichols and Nyholm, *Concise Dictionary*, 113; Densmore, *Chippewa Customs*, 150.

[59] Curot journal, 47 (15 April 1804).

[60] Figures on trade transactions were compiled from the Curot journal by the author.

[61] John Tanner, *A Narrative of the Captivity and Adventures of John Tanner* (1830, reprint, New York: Garland, 1975) 64, 69, 70, 75, 78, 101–2.

[62] Harold Hickerson, ed., "Journal of Charles Jean Baptiste Chaboillez," *Ethnohistory* 6 (1959): 275, 299, 374.

[63] Laura Peers, *The Ojibwa of Western Canada* (St. Paul: Minnesota Historical Society Press, 1994) 56–7. For other examples of powerful Ottawa woman involved in trading, see David Lavendar, *The Fist in the Wilderness* (Albuquerque, NM: University of New Mexico Press, 1964; reprint, 1979) 264–5.

[64] Landes, *Ojibwa Woman*, 162–3, 169, 173, 176, 177. Men also may have occasionally performed duties assigned to women, in the absence of their wives. See Tanner, *Narrative*, 56.

[65] Tanner, *Narrative*, 36, 37, 39, 40. Tanner demonstrates Netnokwa's ability as a trader in the transaction through which she obtained him from his original captors. On her dreams used to help her sons in hunting, see 52, 72.

[66] Gwen Morris, "Gifted Woman Light Around You: Ojibwa Women and Their Stories" (Ph.D. diss., University of Minnesota, 1992) 50–8.

[67] Landes, *Ojibwa Woman*, 20; Kohl, *Kitchi-Gami*, 126–8.

[68] Such visions or dreams were not usually discussed casually. See Kohl, *Kitchi-Gami*, 203.

[69] Landes *Ojibwa Woman*, 156–62, 165; Kohl, *Kitchi-Gami*, 125, 126, 128.

[70] Blair, *Indian Tribes*, 1: 277. On Ojibwa-Dakota intermarriage in the region of the St. Croix River, see William Warren, *History of the Ojibway People* (1885; reprint, St. Paul: Minnesota Historical Society Press, 1984), 164.

[71] Author's translation from Pierre Margry, *Découvertes et etablissements des français dans l'ouest et dans le sud de l'Amerique septentrionale* (New York: AMS Press, 1879–88; reprint, 1974), 6: 32.

[72] For descriptions of marriage customs, see Densmore, *Chippewa Customs*, 72–3; Hilger, *Chippewa Child Life*, 158–60; Grant, "The Sauteux Indians," 320.

[73] Peterson, "The People in Between," 71, 88.

[74] Radisson, *Voyages*, 199.

[75] Marriage as a means of preserving or gaining power was, of course, a long tradition among European nobility.

[76] Benjamin G. Armstrong, *Early Life among the Indians: Reminiscences from the Life of Benj. G. Armstrong* (Ashland, OR: Press of A. W. Bowron, 1892) 101–2; Peterson, "The People in Between," 89.

[77] It is sometimes unclear whether the extensive influence of the Ojibwa leader made the trader successful, or whether traders backed with large capital helped increase the renown of Ojibwa leaders. This is an area that needs further research.

[78] For a discussion of oratory and other leadership qualities, see James G. E. Smith, *Leadership Among the Southwestern Ojibwa* (Ottawa: National Museums of Canada, 1973) 17.

[79] Malhiot journal, 6 (5 August 1804), 27 (4 February 1805); 27 (4 February 1805); George Nelson journal, 16 (7, 8, and 14 November 1803–4), original in Metropolitan Toronto Public Library; *Warren, History of The Ojibway People*, 48, 192, 318, 325, 372–77; Bruce M. White, *The Fur Trade in Minnesota: An Introductory Guide to Manuscript Sources* (St. Paul: Minnesota Historical Society, 1977) 38, 45, 375. Even more distant Indian-trader kinship was still useful. According to Warren, 302, trader Michel Cadot, at Lac du Flambeau in the 1780s, derived benefits from the intercession of his wife's uncle. Warren does not give the name of this man, but it may be Keeshkemun.

[80] B. White, *Fur Trade in Minnesota*, 41; Lawrence Taliaferro journal, 8 (9 October 1827): 92, Minnesota Historical Society; Thomas L. McKenney and James Hall, *The Indian Tribes of North America, With Biographical Sketches and Anecdotes of the Principal Chiefs*, ed. Frederick Webb Hodge, (Edinburgh: J. Grant, 1933–1934) 2: 316–19; Kohl, *Kitchi-Gami*, 147–8; Henry R. Schoolcraft, *Personal Memoirs of a Residence of Thirty Years with the Indian Tribes on the American Frontiers* (Philadelphia: Lippincott, Grambo and Co., 1851), 293. Information on Charlotte, sometimes listed as Charlotte Kattawabide, after her father, is found in Montreal Protestant church registers, compiled in MG19, A2, series 4, Public Archives of Canada, Ottawa, ON. Charlotte died on 9 July

1850 at the age of seventy-five. See also the Ermatinger family history in MG25, G38, Public Archives of Canada.

[81] For examples, see Malhiot Journal, 32 (12 April 1805), 33 (26 April 1805), 34 (18 May 1805); Curot journal, 2 (14 Auguit 1804), 16 (4 November 1804),17 (6 November 1804); Nelson journal, 25 (13 March 1804).

[82] Brown, *Strangers in Blood*, 81.

[83] On Sayer's wife making sugar, see Curot journal, 39 (8 March 1804); John Sayer journal, erroneously printed as that of Thomas Connor in Charles M. Gates, ed., *Five Fur Traders of the Northwest* (1933; reprint, St. Paul: Minnesota Historical Society, 1965), 270 (1 March 1805); Nelson journal, 25. See also Douglas A. Birk, ed., *John Sayer's Snake River Journal, 1804–1805: A Fur Trade Diary From East Central Minnesota* (Minneapolis: Institute for Minnesota Archaeology, 1989) 49.

[84] Nelson journal, 25.

[85] Curot journal, 51 (15 May 1804).

[86] W. Kaye Lamb, ed., *The Journals and Letters of Sir Alexander Mackenzie* (Cambridge: Published for the Hakluyt Society at the University Press, 1970) 495.

[87] Nelson journal, 3.

[88] Ibid., 1.

[89] Ibid., 7, 8; George Nelson reminiscences, 36, also in the Metropolitan Toronto Public Library.

[90] Nelson journal, 33–4; Nelson reminiscences, 36.

[91] Curot journal, 2 (14 August 1804), 21 (22 November 1803).

[92] W. Stewart Wallace, ed. *Documents Relating to the North West Company* (Toronto: The Champlain Society, 1934) 210–11.

[93] The Ojibwa name Oshahgushkodanaqua, spelled in various ways, was translated by the woman's son-in-law, Henry R. Schoolcraft, as "Woman of the Green Valley." See Schoolcraft, *Personal Memoirs of a Residence of Thirty Years with the Indian Tribes on the American Frontiers* (Philadelphia: Lippincott, Grambo and Co., 1851), 431, 662, 676. It may be that the name is a garbled misspelling of some combination of the Ojibwe words for green (*ozhawaawashko-*, the lexical prefix for green or blue, occurring on verbs and on some nouns and participles), prairie or plain (*mashkode*) and woman (*ikwe*). See Nichols and Nyholm, *Concise Dictionary*, xii, 64, 78, 111.

[94] Charles H. Chapman, "The Historic Johnston Family of the 'Soo,'" *Michigan Pioneer and Historical Collections* 32 (1903): 305–43. On 341, in letter six of a series of autobiographical letters written by John Johnston, there is reference to Mamongeseda's daughter as being "a Mrs. Jayer." However, an examination of the original letter (filed with

the first letter of the series, 14 January 1828) in the Henry R. Schoolcraft Papers, Library of Congress, Washington, DC, suggests that the name should really be read as Sayer. On John Sayer, see Douglas A. Birk, "John Sayer and the Fond du Lac Trade: The North West Company in Minnesota and Wisconsin," *Rendezvous: Selected Papers of the Fourth North American Fur Trade Conference, 1981,* ed. Thomas C. Buckley, 51–61. For the name of Sayer's wife, see Thomas L. McKenney, *Sketches of a Tour to the Lakes* (1827; reprint, Minneapolis: Ross & Haines, 1959) 485.

[95] Anna Jameson, *Winter Studies and Summer Rambles in Canada* (London: Saunders and Otley, 1838) 3: 211–14.

[96] Jameson, *Winter Studies,* 210–211; Chapman, "The Historic Johnston Family," 308, 313.

[97] Jameson, *Winter Studies,* 217.

[98] Chapman, "The Historic Johnston Family," 308, 313; Philip Mason, ed., *The Literary Voyager or Muzzeniegun* (Lansing: Michigan State University Press, 1962) xxv, xxiii.

[99] On the cultural nature of dreams experienced during vision quests, see Radin, "Some Aspects of Puberty Fasting Among the Ojibwa," *Museum Bulletin* 2: 69–78; "Ojibwa and Ottawa Puberty Dreams," *Essays in Anthropology: Presented to A. L. Kroeber in Celebration of His Sixtieth Birthday, June 11, 1936,* ed. Robert H. Lowie (Berkeley: University of California Press, 1936) 233–64. Landes, *Ojibwa Woman,* 9–10.

[100] Jones, *Ojibwa Texts,* vol. 7, part 2, 207–41; Henry R. Schoolcraft, *Schoolcraft's Indian Legends From Algic Researches,* ed. Mentor L. Williams (1956; reprint, Westport, CT: Greenwood Press, 1974) 87–91.

[101] Jones, *Ojibwa Texts,* vol. 7, part 2, 256.

[102] The word used by Kigage Pinasi for "mystic cloth" was *manidowagin,* sometimes translated as "spirit skin," a term sometimes used to refer to the woolen cloth brought initially by French traders. Similarly, his word for beads was manidōminäsa or "spirit seeds." See Jones, *Ojibwa Texts,* vol. 7, part 2., 256. Both terms reflect the early wonder of the Ojibwa at European technology. For a discussion of these words and the beliefs behind them, see B. White, "Encounters with Spirits," 397 fn. 11, 398 fn. 12. Landes' informant described a woman with strong ability as a "sucking doctor" in similar fashion: "She dressed in red, green, blue, yellow, black, and wore beads of all colours and different kind of ribbons in her hair, and a feather sticking on her head, and earrings, and beaded moccasins, and her face was painted." See Landes, *Ojibwa Woman,* 158.

[103] As Ruth Landes noted in writing of women who tested the flexible boundaries of Ojibwa gender roles: "It cannot be assumed that one woman's motivations are similar to those of other women" (*Ojibwa Woman*, 148). Landes also noted, "The important factor is that a girl grows up seeing these unconventional possibilities about her, and sees them easily accepted" (140).

[104] Maude Kegg, growing up around 1900 near Mille Lacs Lake, Minnesota, stated: "That's the way they made their living, selling berries and buying lard, flour, sugar, whatever they needed." See Kegg, *Portage Lake: Memories of an Ojibwe Childhood* (Edmonton: University of Alberta Press, 1991) 47. Early examples of Indian people selling game, wild rice, and maple sugar in early Minnesota communities are described in Marjorie Kreidberg, *Food on the Frontier: Minnesota Cooking from 1850–1900* (St. Paul: Minnesota Historical Society Press, 1975) 15–16, 18, 199.

Louis Riel: A Debate

Louis Riel: Hero of His People?

Ron Bourgeault

Ron Bourgeault teaches in Indian Studies and sociology at the University of Regina and is the author of several articles on Louis Riel and the Métis.

In her recent Statement of Reconciliation with Aboriginal Peoples of Canada, Jane Stewart, Minister of Indian Affairs, lamented the execution of Louis Riel. She said the federal government wanted to acknowledge his contribution to Canadian history. While the government did not make a commitment to specific action, there are indications it may declare Riel a Father of Confederation, or grant him a posthumous pardon, or both. Ottawa's proposed intention to rehabilitate Riel was immediately criticized by some pundits as an expression of historical revisionism.

Why is Ottawa so concerned at this particular time with rehabilitating Riel, and also with apologizing to the Indian and Métis peoples for past treatment? There are many questions concerning past government actions, and whose interests they were serving. Why did the "rebellions" of 1869–70 and 1885 occur in the first place? Why was Riel charged with treason and hanged? These and other questions must be answered before Riel can be raised to his rightful place in history.

While I intend to argue in favour of the rehabilitation of Riel, my argument is not an endorsement of Ottawa's proposed intention, how-

This debate was originally published as "Louis Riel: Hero of His People or Villain of History?" in *NeWest ReView* (April/May 1998): 13–16. Published with permission of the authors and *NeWest ReView*.

ever it may be expressed. In order to clarify matters, I will identify some of the more important issues raised by critics of Ottawa's announcement, most notably Thomas Flanagan who, in a series of media commentaries, clearly articulated his opposition to any rehabilitation of Riel.

Flanagan said that declarations that the hanging of Riel was unjust, and that the distribution of lands to the Métis was fraudulently administered by Ottawa in the interests of speculators, were historical falsehoods. Yet these points have been verified by Métis historians, including this writer, and supported by Métis political organizations.

What, then, is the true historical record?

Flanagan and others say Riel, a religious fanatic who twice declared independence and committed a treasonous act of rebellion against the Canadian state, was justly hanged. They say he should not be elevated to the lofty position of Father of Confederation.

The struggle of the Métis (and Indians) with Riel in 1869–70 was similar to that of the Mestizos, Mullatos, and Indians with Simon Bolivar in Latin America at the turn of the century. They were national-democratic struggles, the culmination of many previous rebellions against colonialism, and were as much an internal civil war as they were external, anti-colonial conflicts. Afterwards, Ottawa imposed on the Métis and Indian peoples in Western Canada policies similar to what the British imposed on the African peoples in Southern Africa.

It is too convenient to dismiss Riel as a religious mystic and political fanatic. There is much more to him than this simple categorization. Riel was first and foremost a 19th century liberal-democrat, though also influenced by Roman Catholicism. On his return to the Red River, he inherited a tradition of secular liberal-democratic ideals and a political struggle that went back to the free trade battles of the 1840s. The economy of the Red River colony in the 19th century was mercantilist, a mixture of semi-feudal land ownership and some free enterprise commerce, all under the monopoly control of the Hudson's Bay Co. (HBC). The colony was divided on racial lines, creating a hierarchy with power in the hands of the British (HBC).

In the 1840s, a burgeoning, mostly Métis, merchant and working class, looking to Britain and the 1840s revolutions in Europe, was exposed to the secular ideas of European liberalism. They began to think in terms of free enterprise capitalism, responsible self government, and nationalism. They wanted uncontrolled access to European and American markets for their produce, an end to HBC monopoly control of the local economy, including tariffs, free hold land ownership and control of the local colonial state by liberal-democratic institutions. The

British resisted and resorted to a military dictatorship to maintain control. Moderate Métis elements collaborated, supported by the churches. The stage was set for a civil war in 1869–70.

The "rebellion" of 1869–70 was a continuation of this struggle. Riel and his working class supporters feared that British colonialism would be replaced by Canadian colonialism if the Red River colony and outlying territory was incorporated into Canada without the creation of democratic institutions. They believed the whole legacy of political and economic controls, along with the racist social structure, would be reproduced under Canadian rule.

The colony was divided. Ottawa's *agent provocateurs* encouraged the divisions. One group, which included some Métis, wished to declare independence and negotiate democratic institutions and eventual entry into Canada. Others, including some Métis, were in compliance with Ottawa's policy of direct rule.

These internal divisions rooted in class interests were simultaneously acted out on one level as an anti-colonial war, and on another as an internal civil war. Riel's demand for liberal-democratic institutions and directly allotted individual land ownership, all negotiated and embedded in the Manitoba Act, was a concession Ottawa didn't wish to make.

What became of the Métis lands? Ottawa systematically went about undermining the provisions of the Manitoba Act. A.G. Archibald, the first lieutenant-governor of Manitoba, reported to Ottawa that the grants took too much land out of commercial speculation. The Manitoba Métis Federation has proven conclusively through painstaking research that Ottawa conspired with land speculators to deprive the Métis of their land. Landless Métis were then forced to emigrate to the Northwest Territories, thereby shifting the population balance in favour of the incoming Canadian settlers. The democratic institutions provided for in the Manitoba Act applied to those settlers, as they were property owners.

I documented almost every Métis scrip given out in the NWT in 1885 and 1900, and the same holds true. Basically, the institutions that are now major Canadian banks were the ones that profited greatly. They organized in concert with Ottawa to set a monopoly price of twenty-five cents an acre per scrip (scrips were given out in 160- and 80-acre denominations, and dominion lands were set at one dollar an acre). The scrips were then applied to homestead lands and sold to incoming settlers at anywhere from eight to twelve dollars an acre. The same banks would then give loans with interest to the settlers. Métis scrips were also used to purchase coal fields in southern Alberta, pre-emption rights on settled land, timber leases and mineral deposits. The major banks made millions of dollars. This is why the Métis never got their lands.

The rebellion of 1885 was a revolt against Ottawa's displacement of Indian and Métis. I suggest it was fought as bloody putsch by Riel and the Métis, knowing there could be no victory. In the case of the Indian peoples, it was a revolt against the total destruction of their societies, a policy that was implemented by Ottawa with the Indian Act, and a reservation system designed to turn the majority population into a minority.

Undoubtedly, Riel was in intellectual conflict within himself, particularly as he had to come to terms with the agenda of advanced capitalism in western Canada toward marginalized peoples. Riel was a modernist in the tradition of 19th century liberalism. He understood the inevitability of the encroaching economic system and tried to incorporate Indian and Métis interests into it for their betterment. His personal conflict was a struggle to synthesize outdated, semi-feudal religious dogma with current liberal-democratic ideals. His liberalism became radical as he challenged the agenda of the Canadian state, and his Christianity dissenting as he dealt with the rigidity of the Roman Catholic Church and its relationship to the state. In fact, his Christianity was far more ecumenical than that of the churches. Riel became what may be considered an early liberation theologist.

So, what does one say about the recent statement of reconciliation and the possible rehabilitation of Riel?

The statement, made by Indian Affairs Minister Jane Stewart, is basically Ottawa's response to the Royal Commission on Aboriginal Affairs. It is not a major break with Ottawa's aboriginal policy since the white paper of 1969, which is the integration of aboriginal peoples into Canadian society and economy through social policy spending, dissolving the old colonial institutions of segregation (Indian Act and reservation system), land claims, and collaborative participation of the aboriginal policy organizations.

To what extent Ottawa will implement all the recommendations remains to be seen, but I don't think it is very likely since their national policy is directed at managing an economy and society based upon high levels of under employment and unemployment, with a marked decrease in social spending. With this in mind, I think the real federal government strategy is to negate the notion that past treatment of indigenous peoples is responsible for today's inequities. In that way, and with participation from the political organizations, the government can control an increasingly dispossessed aboriginal population. This is the intent behind the statement of reconciliation and the proposed rehabilitation of Riel. It is propaganda for illusional reform.

While I support the rehabilitation of Riel, I think his real politics will remain buried in moral accolades from Ottawa about mistakes and misunderstandings. He may be elevated, but only if the politics can be effectively controlled. There will not be any admission from Ottawa of the historic role of the state in conquest, or whose interests were being served then, as today. Riel committed no crime other than being a democrat, Christian, and an integrationist. For that, he was killed.

Louis Riel: A Debate

Louis Riel: Exoneration at Last?

Tom Flanagan

Tom Flanagan is a Professor of Political Science at the University of Calgary. He is the author of three books on Louis Riel; the one most relevant to this article is Riel and the Rebellion: 1885 Reconsidered. *His most recent publication is* First Nations? Second Thoughts.

Preston Manning says Louis Riel is a bridge-builder and a proto-Reformer. Jane Stewart, the Minister of Indian Affairs, says she's sorry about Riel's execution and adds that the government will try to honour his place in Canadian history. That might mean a posthumous pardon, or perhaps a declaration that Riel was a Father of Confederation. Either step would be a big mistake.

Let's look at the pardon issue first. Riel was hanged after being convicted of treason. The historical record is clear that he provoked the Northwest Rebellion of 1885 for his own purposes. He was irritated because the government had refused to accede to his secret demands for money for himself. True, the Métis of the Saskatchewan Valley had grievances involving river lots and land scrip, but the federal government was well on the way to dealing with these. Riel resorted to arms precisely because a successful resolution of the Métis complaints would have undercut his position of leadership.

This debate was originally published as "Louis Riel: Hero of His People or Villain of History?" in *NeWest ReView* (April/May 1998): 13–16. Published with permission of the authors and *NeWest ReView*.

At this point in his life he saw himself as the divinely inspired voice of the Holy Spirit, called to regenerate a sinful world. He styled himself the "Prophet of the New World," and he planned to establish an exotic version of Roman Catholicism in North America, with the French-Canadian Métis playing the role of Chosen People. Métis land claims were only a small factor in his grandiose scheme of world renewal.

His rebellion cost dozens of lives and millions of dollars in property damage. The ensuing reaction also took away the political influence that the Métis had enjoyed in the Northwest up to that time. Minister Stewart is right that his death was a sad event, but that does not mean that it was unjust. We wouldn't hang a Louis Riel today because we have abolished capital punishment, but it was the accepted retribution in his day for what he had done. Riel himself set the standard when he had Thomas Scott executed by firing squad in the earlier rebellion in Manitoba.

Calling Riel a Father of Confederation rests on a certain view of his role in the Manitoba Rebellion of 1869–70. It is not quite as misguided as the demand for a posthumous pardon, but it is still bad history.

After purchasing Rupert's Land from the Hudson's Bay Company in 1869, Canada planned to govern its new acquisition as a territory because this enormous expanse of territory was so thinly inhabited. The only civilized settlement was at Red River, and that had only 12,000 people. Territorial status was not intended to be a permanent arrangement; just as in the United States, the advance of settlement would have led to the conversion of territories into self-governing provinces.

Enter Louis Riel with his demand for immediate provincial status. In order to bring the Rebellion to a close, the federal government finally accepted this demand, but with severe qualifications. It made Manitoba an undersized, "postage stamp" province, deprived of control over public lands and natural resources. Without a normal tax base, Manitoba was in financial difficulty from the beginning; and it became the prototype for Saskatchewan and Alberta as second-class prairie provinces—a situation that persisted until the Natural Resource Transfer Agreement of 1930.

Riel's Rebellion also led to needless linguistic, religious, and racial hostility in Manitoba. Prior to 1870, French and English, Catholics and Protestants, Indian, Métis, and whites had managed to get along tolerably well in the Red River colony. By tarnishing the French, Catholics, and Métis as rebels, the Rebellion provoked suspicion on the part of the new immigrants—most of whom were English, Protestant, and white—flooding into the province.

This is not to defend any intolerance that the newcomers exhibited; it is merely to point out the obvious, that Riel's rash uprising made things far worse than they needed to be. Maybe we should not judge Riel too harshly. He was, after all, only twenty-five years old when he started the Red River Rebellion. But forgiving Riel's immature judgment does not mean we have to pretend a hotheaded young man was a great statesman.

The manipulation of Riel's image also raises important contemporary considerations. Canada is negotiating or litigating hundreds of aboriginal land claims. Most of these are Indian claims, but Métis leaders are also launching their own cases. Such claims depend crucially on the exact reconstruction of history. To ignore the historical record in an attempt to rehabilitate Louis Riel will set a precedent for these claims that will prove costly for Canadian taxpayers.

The ulterior motive for rehabilitating Louis Riel is to build support for the view that, in Lloyd Axworthy's words, "promises were made to the Métis that were not kept." The alleged breach of faith has to do with 19th century Métis land grants about which most Canadians know very little.

When Manitoba became a province in 1870, the Manitoba Act set aside 1.4 million acres of land for distribution to "the children of the half-breed heads of families." Each child got 240 acres. Subsequent legislation gave the Métis adults in Manitoba scrip worth $160, with which they could buy Dominion Lands at a dollar an acre. After some delay, the government made similar grants to the Métis of Saskatchewan, Alberta, and part of the Northwest Territories. Adults got scrip for $160, and children scrip for $240, redeemable in Dominion Lands. All these grants of land and scrip were legally rationalized as being "expedient, towards the extinguishment of the Indian title," which the Métis had presumably inherited from their Indian forebears.

Métis organizations in the prairie provinces now say that fraudsters tricked their ancestors out of their benefits. Either the Métis never got the land and scrip in the first place; or—in the alternative, as lawyers say—if they did get it, they received no enduring benefit because the government allowed them to sell their land and scrip to speculators for derisory amounts of money. Although historically false, both theories are politically useful, allowing Métis organizations to claim that their people still possess unextinguished aboriginal title to western lands.

The long-term strategy of these organizations is to use both litigation and negotiation to force the federal government to take responsibility for the Métis. They want the same things that status Indians have now—a land base, trust funds, a registry, federal financial support, a Métis Act, and a declaration that they are Indians in the sense of section 91(24) of the Constitution Act of 1867.

If this scenario comes to pass, it is bound to be expensive for taxpayers. Parliament appropriates over six billion dollars a year for approximately 550,000 registered Indians. How much more will it cost to accord parallel treatment to the 210,000 people who called themselves Métis in the 1996 census? And how many additional people with some Indian ancestry will claim Métis status if federal payments are on the table?

Ironically, the Métis, although not as prosperous as the Canadian average, are already better off than Indians by any objective indicator. The Report of the Royal Commission on Aboriginal Peoples showed that the Métis have higher average income and educational attainment, and lower rates of unemployment and welfare dependency than Indians do. They are better off because they have been treated since Confederation not as dependent wards of the Crown but as citizens with the same rights and duties as everyone else.

Indeed, the available statistics underestimate how well the Métis are doing because they apply only to those who designate themselves Métis in the census. There are also hundreds of thousands, probably millions, of people with Indian ancestry who simply call themselves Canadians and whose demographics are similar to national norms—a great but lamentably uncelebrated success story of Canadian history.

Creating a federally funded Métis status will benefit the Métis politicians, lawyers, and administrators who will manage the programs. But over the long run it will make ordinary Métis people worse off by inducing them to become administered clients of the state rather than self-supporting citizens.

Granting Louis Riel a posthumous pardon or declaring him to be a Father of Confederation will be a crucial step in the wrong direction. It will inevitably be interpreted as a statement that Riel's Rebellions were not the psychodrama of a self-styled prophet, but justified attempts at redressing grievances. The grievances are historically fictional, but, if validated by Riel's rehabilitation, they will become politically real. And at that point, how will our politicians resist taking further steps to create official Métis status?

Finally, to their great credit, both the governing Liberals and the Reform opposition have come out strongly against the right of Quebec, or of any province, to separate unilaterally from Canada. But unilateral declarations of independence (UDI) were Louis Riel's stockin-trade. He announced UDI not once, but twice, first in Manitoba in 1869, then in Saskatchewan in 1885. In view of the coming struggle over the independence of Quebec, does the government really want to canonize Canada's foremost practitioner of UDI?

The Five Treaties in Saskatchewan: An Historical Overview

The events of the relationship between First Nations and the newcomers are recorded and represented quite differently in the two cultures. They use different methods, different forms, and different contexts. The purpose of this section is to provide an overview of those past events and experiences from the perspective of the First Nations and the perspective of the newcomers. Because many people know little about the treaties in Saskatchewan, this section provides an overview of the main events leading up to treaty-making and the important understandings about the nature of the treaty relationship. In setting out the histories of the treaty relationship, it is essential to respect the perspectives of both parties. Relying on one perspective alone would lead to an incomplete and unbalanced understanding of the treaty relationship.

Written History—Western Concepts

Although the history of the soldiers, traders and settlers who came to North America is different from that of First Nations, it would be unwise to typecast the two as polar opposites. It is true that Europeans relied much more on written documents for an account of past events, although at the time of treaty-making much of the population was still illiterate. But it was also the case that oral history, unwritten conventions and creation stories influenced Western concepts of history. They still do. For example, although we have the *Constitution Act, 1867* (formerly

This article is from *Statement of Treaty Issues: Treaties as a Bridge to the Future* (Saskatoon: Office of the Treaty Commissioner, 1998). Presented to The Honourable Jane Stewart, Minister of Indian Affairs and Northern Development and Chief Perry Bellegarde, Federation of Sasatchewan Indian Nations by The Honourable Judge David M. Arnot, Treaty Commissioner for Saskatchewan, October 1998.

known as the *British North America Act*) and the Charter of Rights and Freedoms, much of our constitution remains unwritten, as does that of Great Britain. Similarly, often the "corporate memory" of an organization is not in its formal reports but in its customary practices and in the oral history of its long-term employees.

Non-Aboriginal history is rooted in Western scientific methodology, which is focused on objectivity. The observers attempt to insulate themselves from their own values, norms, cultures and traditions, in order that their recording of events will be as "value-free" as possible. The observers are to distance themselves in time from the events being described, as well as from their readers. In the Western tradition, then, history is to be purely secular, dividing what is scientific from what is religious or spiritual. As part of Western "value-free" scientific methodology, there is an emphasis on scholarly documentation and written records, with detailed citation of original source material.

Despite the attempts at objectivity, Western history is not simply a neutral description of a series of events. It is influenced by the values and ideas of the era in which it was written. For example, the human being is the focus of attention in the Western humanist intellectual tradition. It is often the story of man "conquering" new territories, of "harnessing" nature, of "triumphing" above all other creatures. The human being is portrayed as the most highly evolved form of life, which all other life forms must serve.

In the western European and non-Aboriginal Canadian tradition, history is often conceived of as linear in nature, with events marching through time, from past, to present, to future, a conception influenced by notions of social progress and evolution. From this perspective, it follows that societies evolve, grow, and progress from one stage to the next. Societies which were industrialized, literate, and urbanized, with well developed market economies were believed to be superior to those that were not. This led social reformers in the Western tradition to want to help raise the less fortunate groups to their own level.

Because Western history is aware that the interpretation of events in a particular era is encased in the ideas and philosophy of that time, it is constantly rejecting earlier interpretations of past events. The interpretation of Western history evolves: it recognizes the limitations of its past interpretations. Thus, the earlier view that some societies are at a "higher" stage of development than others is now discredited, replaced with a perspective that looks at societies as different but equal. Western history will continue to evolve, such that its interpretation of treaty history in this document will no doubt be challenged in the future.

Since all history is imbued with values, however, be they from western humanism or the spirituality of First Nations, this affects not only what is recorded—whether orally or in writing—but also how it is recorded. This point was reinforced in the research commissioned by the Office of the Treaty Commissioner, when the researchers conclude that:

> Nevertheless, the documentary records connected to treaty-making events strongly indicate that the written version of any treaty text is an incomplete and inadequate representation of the understandings and agreements made at treaty talks.[1]

It is important in addressing this history, therefore, to look at all sources of information, written and oral, if we are to understand the different perspectives of the treaty partners. All of these sources are required to develop a complete and balanced history of the treaty relationship.

Oral History—First Nations' Concepts

First Nations' Elders say that oral history begins with the Creator. The nature of the relationship that the First Nations had with the Creator is expressed by the Cree term, *Nista Mee Magan* which Elder Jacob Bill describes as meaning:

> ...the one who first received our ways - ways that we use to communicate with our Creator and His Creation... Nations that were here first were given a way to pray... when a person is praying, he thinks about the first generation of First Nations... there he has a sense of identity and recognition and prays to them for help [with his prayers]... We remember the first born in our prayers because they were the ones who first received the blessing from the Creator.[2]

Elders informed the Exploratory Treaty Table that contained within First Nations' oral history are the laws given by the Creator. A fundamental law that respects the sacredness of these Creator-made laws is the requirement that one cannot embellish, add to, or change these laws. The Elders who informed the Exploratory Treaty Table qualified their statements in two ways. Firstly, they identified the source of their knowledge and secondly, they repeated only that which they heard, no more and no less. The parties have agreed that further research is required on the protocols and methodology of oral history research in Saskatchewan.

Oral history preserves traditions, transfers knowledge, and records events. The Elders describe the process as very rigorous and disciplined and as one which emphasizes the requirement for preserving accuracy, precision and procedural protocols. This procedural and substantive knowledge is passed from one generation to the next. The process of preserving and transferring traditional laws and procedures is a solemn obligation and serious commitment. It is a life-long endeavour that select individuals accept. Speaking at a Treaty Elders' Forum in 1997, Elder Norman Sunchild of the Thunderchild First Nation explained it this way:

> Our Old Ones spent their lifetime studying, meditating, and living the way of life required to understand those traditions, teachings and laws in which the treaties are rooted. In their study, they rooted their physical, and spiritual beings directly on Mother Earth as a way of establishing a "connectedness" to the Creator and his creation. Through that "connectedness," they received the conceptual knowledge they required, and the capacity to verbalize and describe the many blessings bestowed on them by the Creator. They were meticulous in following the disciplines, processes, and procedures required for such an endeavour.[3]

The First Nations' perspective about the treaties and the treaty relationship begins with the fundamental relationship between the Creator and the First Peoples. Elders informed the Exploratory Treaty Table that to understand the treaties and the treaty relationship one must have some understanding of the First Nations' spiritual traditions. This is because the spiritual traditions contain the First Nations' world views, customs, and laws that are reflected in and are a fundamental component of the treaties and the treaty relationship.

This belief system contains a number of sacred ceremonies, practices, and customs that show respect for the relationship between the Creator and the individual. The nature of a ceremonial lodge and the encampment surrounding the lodge both serve as affirmative statements of the unity of the First Nations with their Creator and their spiritual institutions. The oneness of the First Nations' citizen with the Creator is extended to the spiritual, social and political institutions of their Nations. The circle is a statement of allegiance, loyalty, fidelity and unity by both the nation and its citizens.[4] The doctrine of relationships and the laws of relationships are part of the circle.

First Nations believe principles of good relations were amongst the Creator's first gifts.[5] According to the elders, the Creator established various types of relationships including blood relatives, relatives by marriage, and relatives through traditional adoption. Certain words and phrases in the First Nations' languages contain the concepts of how First Nations would live together and build relations among themselves, and with others such as with the Crown and her subjects. In Cree these concepts include: *Askeew Pim Atchi howin* (making a living off the land); *Wah kooh toowin* (laws of familial relationships and the respective duties and responsibilities); *Meyo Weecheh towin* (principles of good relations); and *Wi Taski Win* (living together on the land in harmony). The concepts and principles of good relations expanded the circle to include family, community, and other First Nations, and beyond that to relations with the newcomers. These principles embodied the essential elements for constructing good relations. There were also well established spiritual traditions, which became an essential part of creating diplomatic and trade relations with the Europeans.

The view of Creator-made relations carried through into First Nations' relations with the Europeans upon their arrival and into the period when treaties were concluded. Elders continue to explain that these first principles of good relations underlying Treaty remain today embodied in the unalterable foundation of the relationship established between Treaty First Nations and the Crown. Understanding the treaties and treaty relationship therefore requires a look at the histories of both parties to the treaties.

At the time of treaty-making, First Nations looked to their spiritual traditions for guidance and strength. Elders today invariably emphasize the significance of these traditions. In both eras these traditions, beliefs and ceremonies are central to the survival of First Nations as distinct peoples. Elders reaffirm the First Nations' belief that the starting point for discussions about treaties lies in the relationship that was established with the Creator at the beginning of time.[6] When relations were formed, they were seen as spiritual undertakings, made before and with the Creator. For this reason the treaties and the treaty relationship were regarded as unalterable arrangements of the highest order. The nature of these undertakings was inviolably sacred and therefore cannot be breached.[7]

Many Elders who provided First Nations oral history to the Exploratory Treaty Table emphasized that treaties are about the concepts of sharing, generosity, love, and kindness—that is, treaties are about, in Cree, *Askee Pim Atchi Howin, Wah kooh toowin, Meyo Weecheh towin,* and *Wi Taski win.* By using the pipe, the Crown was seen to acknowledge these concepts, and to accept the responsibilities of coming into the land as a brother or cousin. "[the Queen had] offered to be our Mother and us to be her children and to love us in the way we want to live."[8]

Both parties had committed themselves to a mutual life-giving relationship. The nature of the treaty relationship between the parties is familial as well. In an interview on December 21, 1997, Elder Simon Kytwayhat stated:

> when our cousins, the Whiteman, first came to peacefully live on these lands *"wetaskematchik"* with the indigenous people, as far as I can remember, Elders have referred to them as *kitchewamnouwahk* [our first cousins]. It was a traditional adoption in itself. I have heard [from my elders] that the Queen came to offer a traditional adoption to us as our mother. "You will be my children," she had said.[9]

First Nations' Diplomacy Prior to European Contact

North America was home to hundreds of distinct First Nations, differing greatly in their political organizations, economic and social systems, and environments. First Nations communities ranged from being large populated centres to smaller communities of farmers, hunters, and fishers. Some communities were dispersed and autonomous while other First Nations were organized into vast confederacies.[10] As distinct as they were, First Nations were able to work cooperatively and respected differences. Diversity of language and culture did not prevent First Nations from developing shared diplomatic protocols which allowed for a free flow of trade on a continental scale. The fur trade adopted the east-west routes that had been established by First Nations long before European arrival.

First Nations generally shared a common approach to alliance-building. Alliances were often modelled on the family unit and were solidified and maintained through arranged marriages, adoption, or the exchange of gifts. The family circle expanded to accommodate the allied Nations, and those new members of the alliance assumed kinship roles such as *brother to brother,* and *cousin to cousin.* Each role carried certain responsibilities. Overall, the family model implied a spirit of mutual respect, generosity, responsibility and non-interference. Through family-based alliances, First Nations gained opportunities to share each other's resources and knowledge. Each nation could safely travel, visit, and trade in the territories of its allies, and rely on the nexus of extended family for economic assistance in times of need and military defence in times of conflict. First Nations were able to build beneficial alliances without constraining their autonomy and their way of life. First Nations viewed this approach to alliance-building as a fundamental aspect of their traditional law. Similar to "natural law" in European jurisprudence, First Nations traditional law is a gift of the Creator.

First Nations modelled their societies after ecosystems where all species co-exist in a dynamic equilibrium. They feed one another, and are fed, in ongoing relationships. If something in the ecosystem changes, relationships adjust. In the same way, making alliances created new relatives, and brought new people into the territory, requiring adjustments in relationships with their ecosystem including the buffalo, the moose, the beaver, the eagle and all other creatures. Within this spiritual and legal framework, from the perspective of Treaty First Nations, sharing the land was a profoundly serious procedure that required consideration of all interested parties.

European Diplomacy

Treaty-making in the Old World was developed to achieve a number of purposes – to achieve military alliance, to promote peace, to develop trade, to provide for safe conduct, and to determine terms of surrender following war, among other reasons. Treaty-making in Europe can be traced back to the days of the Roman Empire, when Rome used the treaty instrument to form alliances for mutual defence and trade. The promise of safe conduct for its merchants, together with protection from the armies of its treaty partners, enabled an already powerful empire to further expand. After the breakup of the Roman Empire, the Church was able to maintain a certain degree of order throughout Europe by linking powerful families through marriage and by mediating territorial disputes. Treaties for military surrender were common during this period.

By the 1200s, Italian city-states began to negotiate trade treaties with Islamic rulers in North Africa and the Middle East. By 1450, Portugese explorers established trade treaties with West Africa. Treaties became the accepted means of acquiring trade monopolies in newly explored or "discovered" countries, and of protecting these economic interests against those of rival European nations. Trade treaties were eventually made throughout south and southeast Asia, Africa, and North and South America by Great Britain, France, Spain, Portugal, the Netherlands, and other European mercantile powers.

Throughout the period of European exploration and settlement of the Americas, European powers continued to use treaties as instruments to promote peace, to secure military alliances, and to negotiate peace following periods of conflict. These, together with the trade treaties, formed a consistent tradition of European treaty-making which influenced

British officials, and later Canadian officials, at the time of treaty-making with First Nations.

Early Trade Relations

In western Canada, First Nations relations with Europeans were forged with the expansion of the fur trade. In order to secure successful, long-term commercial relations, institutions and practices emerged to accommodate the sharply different diplomatic, economic, political and social traditions of the two parties. These institutions and practices from the fur trade were carried over to the treaty-making era in Saskatchewan, and incorporated into the treaty relationship. A better understanding of the numbered treaties in Saskatchewan can be achieved by understanding the context of early compacts between First Nations and the early trading companies.

The process of establishing trade relations involved the application of longstanding European practices to newly explored regions. Early trade relations in the west were conducted through a number of chartered trading companies. The Virginia Company and Hudson's Bay Company were entrusted with the earliest British efforts to secure permanent footholds in North America through the establishment of these trade relations. These trading companies were quasi-sovereign, and usually had the power to wage war and to conclude treaties, on their own account and for the benefit of their flag. The ways in which the trading companies and First Nations conducted their affairs set precedents that were followed at subsequent treaty negotiations between the Imperial British Crown and First Nations. The largest and most prominent was the Hudson's Bay Company (HBC), which was granted a monopoly of trade in all the land traversed by rivers running into Hudson Bay. The huge charter territory, first called Rupert's's Land, eventually became the prairie provinces and the Northwest Territories. Shortly after the founding of the Hudson's Bay Company in 1670, some First Nations became involved in the fur-trade by travelling to York Factory.[11]

In establishing trade relations, the Hudson's Bay Company followed the precedent set by the French in New France, by accommodating the customs of First Nations as much as possible. Although Charles II had granted the HBC the equivalent of freehold tenure (similar to full ownership) to all lands draining into Hudson Bay, the directors of the HBC still considered it prudent to obtain the consent of the First Nations to build trading posts and to conduct trade in their territories. In 1680, the directors of the HBC wrote to John Nixon, their governor in James Bay, and informed him:

There is another thing, if it may be done, that we judge would
be much for the interest & safety of the Company, That is, In
the several places where you are or shall settle, you contrive
to make compact with. The Captns. or Chiefs of the respective
Rivers & places, whereby it might be understood by them that
you had purchased both the lands and rivers of them and that
they had transferred the absolute propriety to you, or at least
only freedome of trade, and that you should cause them to do
some act wch. By the Religion or Custome of their Country
should be thought most sacred to them for the confirmation
of such Agreements.[12]

Despite the grant of Rupert's Land, the HBC thought that it would
be prudent to obtain the approval of First Nations to occupy
portions of First Nations traditional territories.[13] The trading
companies knew that to establish good relations, they would
require a level of understanding and a demonstration of respect
for the traditions and practices of First Nations.

HBC agents gradually built a network of alliances with First Nations
throughout Rupert's Land. First Nations' protocols were borrowed,
adapted, and to some extent standardized. Alliances were created and
renewed annually. The process involved ceremonies such as smoking
the sacred pipe, the exchange of gifts that symbolized good will, and
arranged marriages.[14] An example of the protocol is the sacred pipe
ceremony which was conducted in the greatest solemnity before trading
actually occurred. The conducting of the ceremony signified that good
relations were established, and that the First Nations were treated with
respect. In some instances some First Nations might leave the pipe with
their new trading partner. There is some indication that if proper protocol
and conduct was not displayed by a trading company, then the First
Nations would indicate their displeasure by taking the pipe with them
thereby signifying an end to the trade agreement.[15]

The gift exchange that was part of this process also had ceremonial
significance. Every member of the First Nations trading party
would contribute to the collective giveaway ("*Puc ci tin assowin*"
in Cree).[16] *Puc ci tin assowin* is a ceremony of mutual benefit in that
the First Nations' expect to receive good will and spiritual blessing
in return.

It was also customary for trading companies to present medicines to
the First Nations' medicine men. This conduct displayed the willingness
of the Company to share its medicines in order to help First Nations deal
with new sicknesses they were unaccustomed to combating.[17]

HBC representatives wore uniforms to signify their authority, and distributed uniforms to First Nations chiefs in order to acknowledge their leadership positions and to win their loyalty.[18] The research commissioned by the Office of the Treaty Commissioner summarized the significance of these practices:

> Significantly, all of the major components of this pre-trade gift-exchange ceremony, the [pipe ceremony], the presentation of outfits of clothing to Aboriginal leaders, and the distribution of food, were carried over into the treaty-making process in the late nineteenth century. Promises to give medicine (in time of need) were incorporated into treaties.[19]

From the earliest days of the fur trade, credit was extended to First Nations by the HBC. Trappers would be outfitted with a supply of goods as credit against their next year's return. The HBC sponsorship of First Nations' trappers was family-like in practice, with credit freely extended in times of need, analogous to sharing amongst family in First Nations' communities. If poor hunts, outbreaks of disease, or other events resulted in a shortfall, lines of credit were normally extended over two or more years, or written off altogether. The credit system provided a safety net for First Nations who became increasingly reliant upon European goods.[20] While the Company aimed to make a profit, it was acutely aware that its most important asset was the loyalty and trust of First Nations.

In the early 1800s, as the depletion of wildlife and rapid spread of contagious diseases decimated First Nations, the HBC took further measures to protect its interest by administering vaccinations and giving relief and medicine to the elderly and destitute. Investing in First Nations' means of livelihood, and providing sustenance in hard times, was in keeping with First Nations' principles of good relations.[21] The research commissioned for the Exploratory Treaty Table summarizes the impact of this custom:

> Thus, before 1870 the economic safety net remained in place for the HBC's Aboriginal customers in the form of a debt system (to address the short-term problems which its able-bodied clients faced from time to time earning their livelihood) and in the form of sick and destitute relief (for the chronically infirm). As well, whenever the local hunts failed, the company supplied food (rations).[22]

Maintaining good relations and good will was the key to success for the trading companies. However, external pressures and forces required a new kind of relationship. Although the HBC had been content to limit its charter rights to freedom of trade for two centuries, land speculators began to take an interest in Rupert's Land by the 1860s. This placed the HBC in an awkward position. Any change in its policy towards First Nations could have destabilized the frontier at a time when Canada's western settlements were still small, and vulnerable not only to resistance by First Nations but to American encroachments as well.

Treaties Prior to Canadian Confederation

In 1763, when New France fell to British forces, Britain was confronted with the twin challenges of winning the trust and friendship of France's First Nations allies, and of dealing with the restiveness of its own indigenous allies over the incursion of American colonists on their lands. In the summer of that year, a widespread war led by Odawa Chief Pontiac engulfed the American interior.[23] This led the British to adopt a comprehensive and enforceable policy, and to issue a royal proclamation declaring the terms of this policy. Under British legal principles, prerogative instruments such as a royal proclamation have the force of statutes of a legislature or parliament in regions that do not have representative legislative bodies, as was the case in British North America in 1763. To create greater certainty and avoid conflict, that proclamation set out terms and a defined process in its bid for obtaining access and title to First Nations' lands:

> And whereas it is just and reasonable, and essential to Our Interest and the Security of Our Colonies, that the several Nations or Tribes of Indians, with whom We are connected, and who live under Our Protection, should not be molested or disturbed in the Possession of such Parts of Our Dominions and Territories as, not having been ceded to, or purchase by Us, are reserved to them, or any of them, as their Hunting Grounds.[24]

The proclamation, in the name of King George III, went on to forbid private individuals to purchase any lands from the Indians, and set out a procedure requiring the voluntary cession of Indian lands to the Crown in a public assembly of the Indians concerned.[25] The British Crown thus established its precedent for mutual agreement or treaty, and a binding procedure for the acquisition of First Nations' lands according to British law.

The first treaty between the First Nations and the Crown in what is now western Canada was the Selkirk Treaty of 1817. The intention of the Selkirk Treaty was to secure a tract of land adjacent to the Red and

Assiniboine Rivers for Scottish settlers in exchange for an annual present of tobacco as *quit rent* to chiefs and warriors of the Saulteaux and Cree Nations.[26] Medals and the HBC company flag, together with rum and other goods, were also exchanged as part of the relationship. In the late 1860s, when the proposed sale of Rupert's Land to Canada became widely known, the status of title to the lands in the Red River Settlement as established in the Selkirk treaty became controversial. This uncertainty eventually led to the negotiation of new arrangements reflected in numbered Treaties 1 and 2 in 1871.[27]

Some precedents for the numbered treaties of the prairies can be found in the Robinson Treaties of 1850 in what is now Ontario. By the late 1840s the Province of Canada had issued several leases to mining companies in Ojibway territory without obtaining the First Nation's consent. In 1846, Chief Shingwak addressed the Governor General in Montreal, seeking money for Ojibway lands and a share of the benefits, since the First Nations had previously leased lands to mining companies on their own:[28]

> Can you lay claim to our land? If so, by what right? Have you conquered it from us? You have not, for when you first came among us your children were few and weak, and the war cry of the Ojibway struck terror to the heart of the pale face... Have you purchased it from us, or have we surrendered it to you? If so, when? And how? And where are the treaties?[29]

In 1849 an armed party of Indians and Metis seized the Quebec Mining Company property at Mica Bay.[30] In order to quell the conflict and to obtain access to mining, to provide for settlement north of the Great Lakes, and to assert British jurisdiction in the face of American incursions in the area, the Crown sent Commissioner William Robinson to make treaty with the First Nations of Lakes Huron and Superior. The Robinson Superior and Robinson Huron Treaties of 1850 provided the Ojibway with a share of revenues from the exploitation of resources in their territories, and annuities, or cash payments, were to increase as revenues increased. Reservations of land for the Ojibway were also secured, as were traditional and commercial hunting, fishing and harvesting in their traditional territories.[31] The research commissioned for the Exploratory Treaty Table summarized Commissioner Robinson's approach as follows:

> In short, Robinson... claimed it was a win-win proposition (to use a modern expression) for Native people. They would be able to continue their traditional subsistence and commercial fishing, hunting, trapping, and other economic pursuits, but

with the benefit of expanded commercial opportunities for the fruits of their labor and more competitive prices for the Euroamerican goods they wanted.[32]

The precedents of annuities, hunting, fishing and harvesting on traditional lands, and reserve lands were to find their way into the numbered treaties. There were also differences of interpretation about the treaty provisions concerning land. The written text of the Robinson treaties describes the agreement as a total surrender of territory, terminology that First Nations stated had not been agreed to in the negotiations. From the Ojibway perspective, the treaties involved only a limited use of their land for the purposes of exploiting minerals.[33] Land title disputes continued long after the conclusion of the Robinson treaties and the numbered treaties.

Post-Confederation Treaties

After Confederation in 1867, Canada focused on settling the prairies, and treaty commissioners were instructed to "establish friendly relations" with the Indians, through treaty or other means to enable "...the flow of population into the fertile lands that lie between Manitoba and the Rocky Mountains."[34] In devising a format for new treaties in Rupert's Land, Canada was informed by two streams of diplomatic precedent. One was the practice established between the First Nations and the HBC. Many of these diplomatic protocols were carried over into the negotiation of Canada's post-Confederation treaties, such as the use of the sacred pipe, formal exchanges of gifts and the distribution of uniforms, medals, and flags. Canada was also mindful of another stream of precedent: Crown treaties concluded with First Nations east and north of the Great Lakes prior to Confederation, to which we have just referred.

In 1869-1870, the Dominion acquired Rupert's Land from the HBC without the knowledge of the First Nations. First Nations were angered by reports that the HBC had "sold" what they considered to be their First Nations' lands to the Dominion, and conflict followed. Surveyors were stopped and settlers turned back. This action frustrated settlement, as well as the second objective of the Crown, which was peace and security in the west.

As historian John Tobias points out, this aspect of the history is often ignored:

> ...the treaty process only started after Yellow Quill's Band of Saulteaux turned back settlers who tried to go west of Portage la Prairie, and after other Saulteaux leaders insisted upon

enforcement of the Selkirk Treaty or, more often, insisted upon making a new treaty. Also ignored is that fact the Ojibway of the North-west Angle [Treaty 3] demanded rents, and created fear of violence against prospective settlers who crossed their land or made use of their territory, if Ojibwa rights to their lands were not recognized. This pressure and fear of resulting violence is what motivated the government to begin the treaty-making process.[35]

Canada was also facing external pressures. The government was conscious of the expansionist pressures in the United States to extend the American border northward into Canada. The Canadian government also feared that an alliance of First Nations on both sides of the international border in the prairie region would build up against the Crown. Both the Canadian government and First Nations were aware of the Indian Wars in the United States, and the heavy human and financial costs they exacted. During those Indian Wars, the budget of the U.S. Department of War exceeded that of the entire Dominion of Canada.[36]

First Nations were beginning to suffer severe hardship from the impact of settlement and commercial harvesting of buffalo and other wildlife, and were also growing anxious over the security of their way of life and their means of livelihood. First Nations' objectives were related to their land, and their livelihood, and to dealing with deteriorating economic and health conditions in their communities brought about by declining wildlife populations and fur prices, diseases and contact with growing numbers of settlers. They also wanted peace and recognized the importance of securing additional means of livelihood while protecting their way of life. They were hopeful that their objectives would be addressed through a treaty relationship.

As early as 1857, Chief Peguis had been concerned about the impact of settlement before the end of HBC rule. In a letter to the Aborigines Protection Society in England, in that year, he asked that:

> before whites will be again permitted to take possession of our lands, we wish that a fair and mutually advantageous treaty be entered into with my tribe for their lands.[37]

The objective of mutual advantage was repeated by Chief Mawedopenais during the negotiation of Treaty 3 in 1873:

> All this is our property where you have come.... This is what we think, that the Great Spirit has planted us on this ground where we are, as you were where you came from...

Our hands are poor but our heads are rich, and it is riches that we ask so that we may be able to support our families as long as the sun rises and the water runs...

The sound of the rustling of the gold is under my feet where I stand; we have a rich country; it is the Great Spirit who gave us this; where we stand upon is the Indians' property, and belongs to them.

It is your charitableness that you spoke of yesterday—her Majesty's charitableness that was given you. It is our chiefs, our young men, our children and great grand children, and those that are to be born, that I represent here, and it is for them that I ask for terms. The white man has robbed us of our riches, and we don't wish to give them up again without getting something in their place.[38]

Commissioner Alexander Morris also urged the Chiefs and Headmen to look to the future. He stated, "I only ask you to think of yourselves, and your families, and for your children and children's children."[39]

The commissioned research summarizes the Crown's objectives in the treaty-making process. Each of the numbered treaties began by stressing:

...the desire of Her Majesty to open up for settlement, immigration, and such other purposes as to Her Majesty may seem meet, a tract of country bounded and described as hereinafter mentioned; and to obtain the consent thereof of her Indian subjects inhabiting the said tract; and to make a treaty and arrange with them so that there may be peace and good-will between them and Her Majesty, and between them and Her Majesty's other subjects; and there her Indian people may know and be assured of what allowance they are to count upon and receive from Her Majesty's bounty and benevolence.[40]

In effect, as this language indicates, the Crown's objectives for the treaty-making process were opening areas of settlement in exchange for the Crown's bounty and benevolence, and thereby ensuring peace and good will.[41]

Treaties 1, 2, and 3 were concluded in 1871–1873 with the Cree and Ojibway of Manitoba and northwestern Ontario. Treaty 1 was concluded at the HBC post Lower Fort Garry, and Treaty 2 at Manitoba House post in August of 1871, while Treaty 3 was negotiated at the

Northwest Angle near Lake of the Woods in 1873. The written terms of Treaty 1 require First Nations to maintain peace amongst each other and with settlers and to avoid interference with property of the Crown and the Crown's subjects.[42] The text of Treaty 2 and subsequent treaties added that First Nations were to obey the law, maintain peace and order between themselves and other Indian tribes, and assist in bringing to justice any Indian offending the treaty or the law. The Crown proposed reserving land for the exclusive use of First Nations, and this provision is reflected in all numbered treaties. First Nations were also free to choose whether to continue hunting, or to take up farming on a reserve. Lieutenant-Governor Archibald, who negotiated Treaties 1 and 2 on behalf of the Crown, emphasized during the meetings that First Nations "would not be compelled to settle on reserves and that they would be able to continue their traditional way of life and hunt as they always had."[43] Annual distributions of money, ammunition, twine and other items were also promised, much like the annual provisions that HBC formerly provided to some of the First Nations. Many of these same features appear in the written text of Treaties 4, 5, and 6.

The Prairie Treaties of Saskatchewan—Treaties 4, 5 and 6

Prairie Treaties 4, 5, and 6 were negotiated in 1874, 1875, and 1876 respectively. The situation for First Nations prior to treaty negotiations was similar to the experience of First Nations in Treaties 1, 2, and 3. In Treaty areas 4, 5, and 6, deteriorating buffalo herds, declining fur prices, and new diseases deepened the hardships of First Nations. Canada was also anxious about the Cree and Blackfoot alliance which had been made in 1871 after many generations of conflict. From the Crown's perspective, accelerating settlement along the Saskatchewan River and its tributaries was regarded as necessary to demonstrate its sovereignty, and this required obtaining access to the remaining agricultural lands on the prairies. Treaties 4, 5, and 6 were concluded with these objectives in mind.[44]

Negotiations for Treaty 4, also known as the Qu'Appelle Treaty after the place where it was concluded, involved the Cree and Saulteaux Nations. *Kakiishiway* (Loud Voice) spoke for the Cree, while *Mee-may* (Gabriel Cote) and *Otahaoman* (The Gambler) led the Saulteaux. Principal negotiators for the Crown were Alexander Morris, a lawyer and Lieutenant-Governor of Manitoba and the North-West Territories, and David Laird, Minister of the Interior and Superintendent General of Indian Affairs, in the Alexander Mackenzie federal government.[45]

For the first four and one-half days of preliminary discussions, the Saulteaux negotiators refused to engage in substantive negotiations because they were upset that land, which they regarded as their territory, was "sold" to the Dominion of Canada without their consent. Through the transfer of Rupert's Land in 1870, Canada had purchased the HBC's claims and interests for 300,000 pounds.[46] The Gambler articulated this concern:

> I have understood plainly before what he (the Hudson Bay Company) told me about the Queen. This country that he (H.B.Co.) bought from the Indians let him complete that. It is that which is in the way.

> The company have stolen our land. I heard that at first. I hear it is true. The Queen's messengers never came here...

> The Company have no right to this earth... The Indians were not told of the reserves at all. I hear now, it was the Queen gave the land (to the HBC). The Indians thought it was they who gave it to the Company... The Indians did not know when the land was given [to the company].[47]

The oral history of Treaty 4 First Nations in Saskatchewan is consistent on two points regarding the status of land ownership: the land was to be shared; and the newcomers had only a limited right to use that shared land. Elder Danny Musqua, a descendent of one of the Saulteaux leaders, spoke to the Exploratory Treaty Table on this issue:

> Through the whole process there was never an understanding that they were going to surrender totally and give up totally the resources that were on those lands... Never at anytime did we understand... that we were giving up anything more that the depth of a plow.[48]

This is in sharp contrast to the written text of Treaty 4 which uses the words:

> The Cree and Saulteaux tribes of Indians, and all other the Indians inhabiting the district hereinafter described and defined, do hereby cede, release, surrender and yield up to the Government of the Dominion of Canada for Her Majesty the Queen and her successors forever, all their rights, titles and privileges whatsoever to the lands included with the following limits...[49]

The Crown was interested in acquiring unencumbered land to enable it to open up the west for settlement and, in return, was willing to provide certain benefits to First Nations.

In the oral history of Treaty First Nations, it was clearly understood that if the First Nations agreed to share the land, the Queen would see that their needs were met, and the Queen's power and authority would protect the First Nations from encroachment by settlement. A caring relationship was emphasized by which the Indian Nations' way of life would be safeguarded and the parties would mutually benefit.[50]

Treaty 4 First Nations were interested in acquiring the benefits of European technology—"the cunning of the white man" as Morris termed it—in order to adapt to drastically changing circumstances. A poignant account was given by Saulteaux Elder Danny Musqua in May 1997. His grandfather had been at Treaty 4 as a young boy, and observed that an elderly Saulteaux inquired about the "learned man" who was taking notes for the Treaty Commissioners. On being told that this was a learned man, the Saulteaux exclaimed, "that is what I want my children to have. That kind of education is what my children must have."[51] In addition to farming provisions, Treaty 4 also provided for education and support for continued hunting and fishing. As in earlier treaties, provisions for annuities, flags, suits and medals were included in the treaty.

Treaty 5, also known as the Lake Winnipeg Treaty, was concluded in 1875 between the Swampy Cree and others and the Crown as represented by Commissioner Morris. It covers part of the Manitoba Interlake, the lower Saskatchewan River, and the Canadian Shield country around Lake Winnipeg. Negotiations were held at Berens River, Norway House and Grand Rapids.

For the Crown, the coming of the steam boat to the Lake Winnipeg waterway would require a treaty to deal with navigation and to make arrangements so that "settlers and traders might have undisturbed access to its waters, shores, islands, inlets and tributary streams."[52] First Nations knew that steamboats would disrupt their lives. In 1874, Chief Rundle and several other leaders wrote to Alexander Morris noting the increased population density on their land and the threat to its carrying capacity. They also inquired into the possibility of relocating to good farming country, and noted that nearly two-hundred of their people would be thrown out of employment when tripping to York Factory ceased.[53] Livelihood was a critical concern for the First Nations in this territory.

The terms of Treaty 5 were similar to those of Treaties 3 and 4, although fewer benefits accrued to the Treaty 5 First Nations. Instead of one square mile of land (640 acres) per family of five, Treaty 5 received only 160 acres per family of five.[54] The reasons for this are unknown. There was concern among the First Nations about the location and size of reservations, but the matter was left to be dealt with in the future. The Cree were assured, however, that they would be able to continue to hunt and trap as before on their traditional territories.[55] Annuities, medals and suits of clothing were presented, and promises of tools and implements for agriculture, and promises of education were made. Other provisions included ammunition, twine and nets for fishing and the prohibition of alcohol.

Treaty 6 was negotiated at Fort Carlton and Fort Pitt in 1876 between the Plains Cree, Willow Cree and other bands, and the Crown as represented by Alexander Morris. As early as 1871, some Cree Chiefs of the Plains had requested consultations with government representatives. HBC Chief Factor W.J. Christie assisted *Weekaskookeensayyin* (Sweet Grass) in the writing of a letter to Lieutenant-Governor Archibald:

> Great Father, I shake hands with you and bid you welcome. We heard our lands were sold and we did not like it; we don't want to sell our lands; it is our property, and no one has a right to sell them...

> Our country is getting ruined of fur-bearing animals, hitherto our sole support, and now we are poor and want help—we want you to pity us. We want cattle, tools, agricultural implements and assistance in everything when we come to settle—our country is no longer able to support us.

> Make provision for us against years of starvation. We have had great starvation the past winter, and the small-pox took away many of our people, the old, young and children.

> We want you to stop the Americans from coming to trade on our lands, and giving firewater, ammunition and arms to our enemies the Blackfeet.

> We made a peace this winter with the Blackfeet. Our young men are foolish, it may not last long.

> We invite you to come and see us and to speak with us. If you can't come yourself, send some one in your place.

> We send these words by our Master, Mr. Christie, in whom we have every confidence. That is all.[56]

At this time the Cree on the Plains were also agitated by the presence of surveyors of the Pacific Railway and the construction of telegraph lines through their territories. Lieutenant Governor Morris responded to the Cree Chiefs by giving them assurances that Commissioners would be sent to negotiate a treaty with them.[57]

In August, 1876, Alexander Morris was sent to negotiate with the Cree at Fort Carlton. Morris' report in December, 1876 recounted the elaborate ceremonies that preceded the treaty negotiations. The Union Jack was hoisted, and the Crees assembled with the accompaniment of beating drums, singing, dancing and the discharge of fire-arms. The Cree Chiefs advanced in a semicircle, with men on horseback galloping in circles, shouting, singing and discharging fire-arms. The pipe ceremony was conducted, the pipe was extended to the Treaty Commissioner who stroked the pipe. After the pipe ceremony was concluded, the Cree were "satisfied that in accordance with their custom [the Treaty Commissioner] had accepted the friendship of the Cree nation."[58]

By 1876 the buffalo were in serious decline and the Cree were recovering from a smallpox epidemic of a few years earlier. Anger over the sale of Rupert's Land remained an issue in the discussions around Treaty 6, as it had been at Treaty 4. First Nations also stressed the necessity of education and agriculture to establish new means of ensuring an adequate livelihood for future generations. In response to pressure at Fort Carlton, Morris made a number of concessions. He offered to increase the number of cattle and farm implements the government would provide, and to make $1,000 available every spring for three years to assist in buying provisions while planting the ground.[59] First Nations looked to the Government of Canada to outfit them for farming, just as they had looked to the HBC to outfit them for trapping.

Alexander Morris' report stressed the Queen's offer of protection and benevolence, and made a point of including promises of emergency relief in the event of famine and pestilence, and a medicine chest at the house of each Indian Agent. Morris promised that the Crown would see to Indians' welfare even better than had the HBC, that their existing way of life would not be disturbed, and they would be provided the means of adopting agriculture if they wished. As the commissioned research concluded, the Cree and Saulteaux were seeking a partnership with Canada to obtain protection that was equivalent to what they had become accustomed to receive in their mercantile relationship with HBC:

> Thus, from the First Nations perspective, Treaty Six would have many symbolic parallels to the older unwritten accords they had forged with the company. Treaty coats were the equivalent of captain's coats; annuities and other recurring allowances recalled the annual gift of the fur trade; and government commitments to provide relief, medical aid, and education served the same ends as the HBC's practice of providing liberal credit to the ablebodied and aid to the elderly, sick and destitute.[60]

The Northern Treaties of Saskatchewan—
Treaties 8 and 10

Treaty 8 territory extends across the Athabasca and Peace River districts into northern British Columbia. In the late 1880s the Cree and Dene within this area sought treaty.[61] First Nations in the region were experiencing falling fur prices, starvation, and miners encroaching on their lands. Three consecutive years of severe winter conditions contributed to the hardship First Nations had encountered prior to treaty negotiations. Father G. Breynat wrote from Fond du Lac about the plight of these people in the winter of 1898–99:

> Dogs died of hunger, and people had no more transportation. Some of the people walked to the village for three days without food... some arrived with hand and nose frozen... Influenza followed famine...[62]

However, until gold was discovered in the Klondike in 1897, the Crown was slow to respond to the plight of First Nations. With the discovery of gold in Alaska, miners and prospectors flooded the various routes through British Columbia and Alberta, searching for gold along the way. In the absence of a treaty relationship, hostile relations developed between the First Nations and the miners. An excerpt from the 1899 Annual Report of the North-West Mounted Police (NWMP) reflects on the environment of the times:

> Mr. Fox (the post manager) informs me that the Indians here at first refused to allow the whitemen to come through their country without paying toll... They threatened to burn the feed and kill the horses; in fact several times fires were started, but the head men were persuaded by Mr. Fox to send out and stop them.
>
> There is not doubt that the influx of whites will materially increase the difficulties of hunting by the Indians, and these people, who, even before the rush, were often starving from their inability to procure game, will in future be in much worse condition... They are very likely to take what they consider a just revenge on the whitemen who have come, contrary to their wishes, and scattered themselves over their country. When told that if they started fighting as they threatened, it could only end in their extermination, the reply was, we may as well die by the white men's bullets as of starvation.[63]

The NWMP, the trading companies, and the churches all suggested treaties should be negotiated to address these problems.

Treaty 8 was the first major treaty to be negotiated following the Rebellion of 1885. In 1899, the commissioners travelled to meet the Cree and Dene people of northern Saskatchewan, Alberta and British Columbia and of the Northwest Territories south of the Hay River and Great Slave Lake. Treaty Commissioner J.A.J. McKenna initially questioned the appropriateness of setting aside reserves in the north, recognizing that the Indians did not form large tribal organizations but rather lived dispersed on the land, and would probably resist centralization.[64] Because the territory was perceived to be of little value to the Crown, Commissioner McKenna assumed treaty would not result in any significant change to the First Nations' way of life.

However, First Nations had considerable apprehension that their way of life would be threatened and their livelihood would be curtailed. First Nations in the north wanted to hunt, fish, trap and gather as they had for hundreds of years. As Martin Josey, a Denesuline Elder from Fond du Lac stated in November 1997:

> ...we want to ensure that our abilities to carry on with our way of life over our lands will always be there, and always be protected for the future generations. But you did not buy that from us, you have to remember that.... Our people were assured that was not to be, that our way of life would always continue, as well our ability to hunt, harvest the resources off our land, would be protected for all further generations. That is what I remember the Elders speaking about when I was young.[65]

This reluctance was reported by Father Lacombe 100 years ago, to the Secretary of Indian Affairs in 1898:

> ...the Northern native population is not any too well disposed to view favourably any proposition involving the cession of their rights to their country.[66]

Being assured that they would be retaining their way of life was the key to persuading the First Nations to accept Treaty 8.

In response to their concerns, the Crown solemnly assured the First Nations that they be as free to hunt and fish after the treaty as they would be if they never entered into treaty, that the treaty would not lead to any forced interference with their mode of life, that it did not open the way to the imposition of any tax, and that there was no fear of enforced military service.[67]

Treaty 8 extends into the northwest part of present day Saskatchewan in the area surrounding Lake Athabasca. Treaty 8 was drafted based on the provisions of the prairie treaties, some of which were completely unsuitable in the north, such as those relating to livestock, farming equipment and the amount of land set aside for reserves. Other provisions included the right to pursue hunting, trapping, and fishing throughout their territories, to reserve land collectively or in severalty, to annuities, to famine relief, a silver medal, a suitable flag, a suit of clothing, and the salaries of teachers.

Treaty 10 was the last of the numbered treaties in Saskatchewan. Interest on the part of the First Nations in a treaty in that region of northeastern Saskatchewan was expressed as early as 1883.[68] First Nations in that region were interested in a treaty relationship as established by other First Nations as a way of accessing support from the Crown. First Nations beyond treaty territory were treated differently from First Nations with treaty. Those without treaty relied solely upon the generosity of the government to provide aid in the time of need.[69]

In 1905, the issue of treaty was reassessed by the Crown because the creation of the Province of Saskatchewan extended far beyond existing treaty limits. The Crown entered into negotiations on Treaty 10:

> In view of the fact that the boundaries of the newly organized province of Saskatchewan extend far beyond the present treaty limits, I would suggest that measures be taken to bring the remainder of the Indians within the said boundaries into treaty...[70]

The text of Treaty 8 was later presented to the First Nations in the northeast region of Saskatchewan in 1906 as a draft of Treaty 10. Discussions were held in the late summer at Ile à la Crosse, Portage la Loche, and Buffalo Narrows. During Treaty 10 negotiations, Treaty Commissioner J.A.J. McKenna told the First Nations that the Crown's objective was to do for them, what had been done for other Treaty Nations when trade and settlement began to interfere with First Nations' way of life.[71]

First Nations held concerns about their way of life and livelihood similar to those expressed during the negotiations of Treaty 8. They expressed concern about the restrictive and confining nature of the reserve system, and did not want reserve creation to impede their traditional way of life. McKenna assured First Nations that "the same means of earning a livelihood would continue after the treaty was made as existed before it,"[72] and the Crown would assist them in times of real distress, and would help support the elderly and indigent; "I guaranteed that the treaty would not lead to any forced interference with their mode of life."[73] Verbal assurances were given by Commissioner McKenna that education and medical assistance would be provided to the First Nations.[74]

Protecting the way of life and securing livelihood was the focus and primary concern for First Nations of Treaties 8 and 10. Both treaties contained a formula for setting aside reserves, although this was left as an option for First Nations to exercise in the future, and no surveys were immediately undertaken.

Post Treaty-Making Period

Since the conclusion of the numbered treaties, First Nations experienced a series of problems with the implementation of what they understood they had agreed to at treaty-making. The post-treaty era is complex and multi-faceted. Problems with implementation arose for a number of reasons and treaty implementation remains a complex issue today. Our purpose in this section is not to describe and analyze all problems arising in the post-treaty era, but rather to acknowledge a number of significant factors which have influenced the development of First Nations' communities and First Nations' relations with the Government of Canada.

In the 1880s, First Nations on reserves experienced severe poverty and malnutrition because of the depletion of animals and the erosion of their way of life, in addition to ration cutbacks by Indian Affairs, especially following the 1885 Rebellion. There were numerous petitions by First Nations demanding adequate food and medicines, and a number of confrontations, such as the Yellow Calf incident at Sakimay First Nation in Treaty 4 in 1884.[75] In February of 1884, amidst extreme famine, some two dozen armed men on the Sakimay reserve demanded bacon and flour from Indian Agent Hilton Keith. When Agent Keith refused to provide food, the party stormed the warehouse, took provisions, and then barricaded themselves in the building. Louis O'Soup, a Saulteaux spokesman, met with Assistant Commissioner Hayter Reed and Mounted Police Inspector R.B. Deane a few days later, and said:

> If he were allowed to starve he would die, and if he were doomed to die he might as well die one way as another...

> Their women and children were starving and that the men... would not allow themselves to be arrested—that they would fight to the death—that they were well-armed and might as well die than be starved by the government.[76]

The First Nations considered the stored provisions to be theirs as a result of the treaty promises, to be used by them in times of need.

Similar incidents took place in Treaty 6 region. First Nations leaders sought the famine relief and schools as promised in the treaty. In 1884, leaders from Fort à la Corne and the Battleford and Carlton regions met with Indian Agent Ansdell Macrae. Macrae reported to Indian Commissioner Edgar Dewdney on his meeting. The Chiefs told Macrae that wild oxen were given to them, rather than tame cattle, and these should be replaced, as should the cows and horses. The wagons broke down because they were poorly made. They received none of the clothing promised, nor any of the schools, nor any of the agricultural machinery, nor the medicine chests. The charitable aid promised was insufficient. The chiefs said that these grievances had been made again and again without effect, and they were glad that the young men had not resorted to violence.[77]

In Treaty 10, there was a general fear that the treaty would curtail hunting and fishing activities and that the rivers and lakes would be monopolized or depleted by external commercial fishing. Contrary to the guarantee given by Commissioner McKenna, "that the treaty would not lead to any forced interference with their mode of life," the Dene experienced constraints on their hunting, fishing, and trapping activities because of provincial government regulations.

In the recent past, a number of studies have focused on the effects government policies and legislation have had on First Nations' cultures, governments and way of life.[78] For example, the Royal Commission on Aboriginal Peoples concluded that the present and historic relationship between Treaty First Nations and the Government of Canada is severely strained[79] due in large part to the fact that the Government of Canada did not enact laws pertaining to treaty implementation after it concluded treaties with First Nations. According to the Royal Commission:

> In the absence of effective laws to implement treaties, the federal Indian administration fell back on the *Indian Act*. As time went on basic treaty provisions such as annuities were provided for in the *Indian Act* to enable the federal government to deliver them. Although it does not recognize, affirm or otherwise acknowledge treaties, the *Indian Act* continues to be the only federal statute administering to Indians generally, including those with historical treaty agreements.[80]

Before Confederation in 1867, the colonial government developed policies that guided its relations with First Nations people in Upper and Lower Canada. After the conclusion of the numbered treaties, the federal government relied on the existing Indian Department with all its pre-existing policies to deal with First Nations. While Indian policies had developed in eastern Canada before the numbered treaties were concluded, these policies later evolved and extended west to First Nations in the Treaty 4, 5, 6, 8 and 10 territories.

The *Indian Act* played a dominant role in the lives of First Nations people and has had an impact upon the present relationship between First Nations and the Government of Canada. Indian policy was designed with the objectives of protection, civilization and assimilation of First Nations people. Included in the *Indian Act* and subsequent amendments were considerable powers allocated to the Superintendent General of Indian Affairs. The Department of Indian Affairs directed operations in the administration of local affairs – local Indian Agents exercised significant powers in the internal affairs of First Nations' communities.[81] Indian policies evolved since the creation of a colonial Indian Department in 1755 and, after confederation in 1867, policies specifically dealing with protection, civilization and assimilation were consolidated under the *Indian Act* in 1876.[82] After 1876, the *Indian Act* was applied throughout the western numbered treaty regions.

Assimilation policies and procedures were designed to replace traditional First Nations' governments and way of life with western lifestyles, governments and economies.[83] In advancing the process of assimilation, the government embarked upon a number of initiatives to encourage new economic, political and cultural transitions. In 1876 and 1880, a new elective system of government was introduced in the west to replace traditional forms of First Nation's government.[84] The Band Council system of government was introduced and rules and regulations on membership, elections, leadership and Band Council responsibilities were intended to replace traditional political activity.[85] After 1883, federally funded industrial and residential schools were introduced in what is now Saskatchewan.[86] These schools, which were created to educate Treaty First Nations children, isolated them from their families, communities and cultures. Through a period of tutelage, residential and industrial schools were intended to equip youth with knowledge and skills that were premised upon European values and behaviours.[87]

Assimilation policies towards First Nations continued throughout the first half of the 20th century. One widely held notion that formed the basis for Indian policy in western Canada was that of the "vanishing race."[88] Duncan Campbell Scott, Superintendent General of Indian Affairs, echoed this sentiment to Parliament in 1920:

> Our object is to continue until there is not a single Indian in Canada that has not been absorbed into the body politic and there is no Indian Question.[89]

It was believed that the First Nations' way of life would not endure in a new society and the approach was to ensure that First Nations assimilate into non-Aboriginal society.

Between 1895 and 1914, new restrictions included in Section 114 of the *Indian Act* prohibited First Nations' spiritual expression by banning or regulating ceremonies, dance, singing, and dressing in ceremonial regalia.[90] Following the 1885 North West Rebellion, added restrictions were put in place when the pass system was introduced. First Nations people were required to obtain consent from an Indian Agent to leave their reserves, although restrictions varied from community to community. The pass system restricted the mobility of First Nations and obstructed their ability to pass freely across the border to the United States, participate in ceremonies outside the reserve, and congregate with First Nations from other Bands.[91]

After the introduction of the pass system and new restrictions included in Section 114 of the *Indian Act*, a number of Chiefs protested the banning of their ceremonies as an abrogation of treaty promises. In 1897, Chief Thunderchild and a number of his Band members were convicted on charges of holding a giveaway ceremony and were sentenced to two months imprisonment.[92] Chief Thunderchild's Treaty Six medal was also confiscated, despite his loyalty to the government during the 1885 Rebellion. In 1914, Chief Thunderchild submitted a letter that challenged the local Indian Agent's refusal to allow his Band members to travel to a sundance being held on another reserve:

> When the law was first made here I listened to the true law. The man that I made the bargain with [was] the queen's serv-ant. When he was first going to look over us he said, I show our God what I am now doing it is true, there is no fooling about it. I am not going to stop your manners. You will have in you[r] future your dance. Your people around Battleford would like to assemble for a sundance and another thing that was said is your farming you will have your own food that is to say all the ... animals. It makes all the Indians think very much of that as they are now forbidden to kill anything. I was told there is going to be a sundance in Poundmaker. The in-spector told me that no people could go to it but them. You will let me know if this is true as soon as you can...[93]

First Nations leaders expressed their frustration with these new policies and the lack of success in their new economic pursuits. While agriculture was presented as a new form of economic activity during treaty making, the Chiefs grew increasingly frustrated with economic interference from the Indian Department. Many reserves were simply not suitable for agriculture and Chiefs and Councillors found it difficult to acquire the necessary implements for farming.[94]

Despite the problems encountered during the post-treaty era, First Nations' leaders continued to advocate for treaty implementation. Many members of the First Nations' communities also continued to maintain ties to their traditional way of life. The political leadership of Treaty First Nations has evolved and survived along with the spiritual, cultural and social systems inherent within First Nation communities. In turn, policies of the federal government have also evolved and changed over time.[95] Today, the Treaty First Nations in Saskatchewan, in partnership with the Governments of Canada and Saskatchewan, have initiated dialogue and are building upon their common understandings about the treaty relationship.

Endnotes

[1] Frank Tough, J.R. Miller, and Arthur J. Ray, "Bounty and Benevolence: A Documentary History of Saskatchewan Treaties" (unpublished report for the Office of the Treaty Commissioner, Saskatoon, Saskatchewan, March 15, 1998) 400.

[2] Elder Jacob Bill, Pelican Lake First Nation, at an Elders meeting with Harold Cardinal, Walter Hildebrandt, FSIN, and the Office of the Treaty Commissioner, Saskatoon, Saskatchewan, 10–11 January 1998. Translated from Cree to English.

[3] Elder Norman Sunchild, Thunderchild First Nation, Treaty Elders' Forum, Jackfish Lake Lodge, 12–14 November 1997. Translated from Cree to English.

[4] Harold Cardinal and Walter Hildebrandt, "My Dream: That We Will Be One Day Clearly Recognized as First Nations" (draft report for the Office of the Treaty Commissioner, Saskatoon, Saskatchewan, March 1, 1998) 16.

[5] Cardinal and Hildebrandt, 16–19.

[6] Cardinal and Hildebrandt, 6. For a history of First Nations in Canada generally, see Olive Patricia Dickason, *Canada First Nations: A History of Founding Peoples from Earliest Times* (Toronto: McClelland & Stewart, 1992). Chapter 4.

[7] Elder Jimmy Myo, Moosomin First Nation, Treaty Elders' Forum, Nekaneet Recreation Center, Saskatchewan, 22–4 May 1997, explained the nature of the consequence as the Cree term *pastahowin*: "we have laws as Indian people and those laws are not man-made, they were given to us by God. In my law, if you [breach a sacred undertaking] even if no other human being is aware of it, you will always carry that for the rest of your life.... The amount we do not pay for here on earth, when we die we will pay for it."

[8] Elder Alma Kytwayhat, Makwa Sahgaiehcan First Nation, interviewed by FSIN on December 21, 1997, Saskatoon, Saskatchewan. Translated from Cree to English.

[9] Elder Simon Kytwayhat, Makwa Sahgaiehcan First Nation, interviewed by FSIN on December 21, 1997, Saskatoon, Saskatchewan. Translated from Cree to English.

[10] Russel L. Barsh, "The Nature and Spirit of North American Political Systems," *American Indian Quarterly* 10.3 (1986): 181–98.

[11] Tough et al., 7.

[12] Cited in Tough et al., 8.

[13] Tough et al., 8.

[14] Ibid., 10.

[15] Ibid., 17.

[16] Ibid., 11.

[17] Ibid., 16.

[18] Ibid., 13.

[19] Ibid., 17.

[20] Ibid., 18.

[21] Cardinal and Hildebrandt, 19–21.

[22] Tough et al., 23.

[23] Royal Commission on Aboriginal Peoples, *Report of the Royal Commission on Aboriginal Peoples*, vol. 1 (Ottawa: Minister of Supply and Services Canada, 1996), 115; see also Tough et al., 58.

[24] As cited in the *Report of the Royal Commission on Aboriginal Peoples*, vol. 1, 116.

[25] Tough et al., 59–60.

[26] See Tough et al., 36–55.

[27] *Report of the Royal Commission on Aboriginal Peoples*, vol. 1, 160–1.

[28] Tough et al., 63–5; see also James Morrison, "The Robinson Treaties of 1850: A Case Study" (research study prepared for the Royal Commission on Aboriginal Peoples, 1993). This study provides an account of the treaty negotiations from both the Crown and the Indian perspective.

[29] As cited in the *Report of the Royal Commission on Aboriginal Peoples*, vol. 1, 158.

[30] Tough et al., 65–7.

[31] Ibid., 77–8.

[32] Ibid., 77.

[33] *Report of the Royal Commission on Aboriginal Peoples*, vol. 1, 158–9.

[34] Tough et al., 117.

[35] John L. Tobias, "Canada's Subjugation of the Plains Cree, 1849–1885," *Sweet Promises: A Reader on Indian-White Relations in Canada*. Ed. J.R. Miller (Toronto: University of Toronto Press, 1991) 212–40.

[36] Jill St.Germain, "A Comparison of Canadian and American Treaty Making Policy with the Plains Indians, 1867–1877" (M.A. thesis, School of Canadian Studies, Carleton University, 1998).

[37] Great Britain, *Report of the Select Committee on the Hudson's Bay Company* (1857) 445.

[38] The *Manitoban*, as cited in Alexander Morris, *The Treaties of Canada with the Indians of Manitoba and the North-West Territories Including the Negotiations on Which They Were Based* (Saskatoon: Fifth House Publishers, 1991), 59–62. Emphasis in original document.

[39] The *Manitoban*, as cited in Alexander Morris, 61.

[40] See Morris, Treaty No. 1, 313–14; Treaty No. 2, 317; and Treaty No. 3, 321 for almost identical wording.

[41] Tough et al., 110–11.

[42] Ibid., 111–12.

[43] *Report of the Royal Commission on Aboriginal Peoples*, vol. 1, 164.

[44] Treaty No. 7 with the Blackfoot Confederacy is not included: Treaty No. 7 boundaries are essentially within the present-day province of Alberta. It was negotiated by the same Crown team, however, with the same aims and similar results.

[45] Tough et al., 199.

[46] Tough et al., 203; see also Morris, 81–2, and report of proceedings in Morris, 99–107.

[47] Report of proceedings in Morris, 99–104.

[48] Elder Danny Musqua, Keeseekoose First Nation, Treaty Elders' Forum, Nekaneet Recreation Centre, Saskatchewan, 22–4 May 1997.

[49] Treaty No. 4 in Morris, 331.

[50] *Report of the Royal Commission on Aboriginal Peoples*, vol. 1, 167–8.

[51] Elder Danny Musqua, *supra* note 48.

[52] Morris, 143–4.

[53] Tough et al., 231.

[54] *Report of the Royal Commission on Aboriginal Peoples*, vol. 1, 168.

[55] Tough et al., 246.

[56] W.J. Christie quoted in Morris, 170–1.

[57] The Hon. David Mills quoted in Morris, 172.

[58] Morris, 183; see also Tough et al., 254.

[59] Tough et al., 261–2.

[60] Ibid., 280–1.

[61] Ibid., 302.

[62] Cited in Tough et al., 293.

[63] Canada, *Sessional Papers* (Annual Report of the North-West Mounted Police, Paper No. 15, 1899), 13.

[64] Public Archives of Canada (PAC) RG10 Vol. 3848, File 75236-1. J.A.J. McKenna to Clifford Sifton, Ottawa, 17 April 1899.

[65] Cardinal and Hildebrandt, 38.

[66] Cited in the *Report of the Royal Commission on Aboriginal Peoples*, vol. 1, 171.

[67] Tough et al., 313.

[68] Ibid., 321.

[69] Ibid., 325.

[70] Cited in Tough et al., 326.

[71] PAC RG10, vol. 4009, File 241, 209-1 18 January 1907; cited in Tough et al., 340.

[72] PAC RG10, vol. 4009, File 241, 209-1 18 January 1907; cited in Tough et al., 341.

[73] PAC RG10, vol. 4009, File 241, 209-1 18 January 1907; cited in Tough et al., 342.

[74] Tough et al., 343–4.

[75] Tough et al., 356–7; see also Isabel Andrews, "Indian Protest Against Starvation: The Yellow Calf Incident of 1884," *Saskatchewan History* 28.2 (1975); Sarah Carter, *Lost Harvests: Prairie Indian Reserve Farmers and Government Policy* (Montreal & Kingston: McGill-Queen's University Press, 1990) 121–2..

[76] Tough et al., 357.

[77] Ibid., 372–5.

[78] See Sarah Carter, *Lost Harvests: Prairie Indian Reserve Farmers and Government Policy*; Helen Buckley, *From Wooden Ploughs to Welfare: Why Indian Policy Failed in the Prairie Provinces* (Montreal & Kingston: McGill-Queen's University Press, 1992); A.C. Hamilton and C.M. Sinclair, *Report of the Aboriginal Justice Inquiry of Manitoba* (Winnipeg: Province of Manitoba, 1991); and the *Report of the Royal Commission on Aboriginal Peoples*, vols. 1–5.

[79] *Report of the Royal Commission on Aboriginal Peoples*, vol. 1, 7.

[80] *Report of the Royal Commission on Aboriginal Peoples*, vol. 1, 177–8; Chapter 9 of the Report provides a detailed description of the evolution of Indian policies and legislation in Canada, including the Indian Act. It should be noted, however, that Section 88 of the Indian Act provides for the primacy of treaty rights over provincial laws.

[81] *Report of the Royal Commission on Aboriginal Peoples*, vol. 1, 281 and 297–8. Some examples of the powers of Indian Agents in the late

1890s include directing the farming operations on reserves; allocating passes for First Nations people wanting to leave reserves for specific periods of time; administering relief to the people in the community; ensuring the rules of the Department were followed, for example, ensuring children attended residential schools and regulating the sale of livestock, implements, and other forms of revenue; presiding over elections on reserves; and acting in the capacity of justices of the peace.

[82] John Leslie and Ron Macquire, "The Historical Development of the Indian Act" (Treaties and Historical Research Centre, DIAND, 1979) 2–20; 23–35; 71–6.

[83] *Report of the Royal Commission on Aboriginal Peoples*, vol. 1, 274–5; *Report of the Aboriginal Justice Inquiry of Manitoba*, 121–3.

[84] The Indian Act, 1876. S.C. 1876, c.18. (39 Vict.); the Indian Act, 1880. S.C. 1880, c.28. (43 Vict.); See also W. Daugherty and Dennis Madill, "Indian Government Under Indian Act Legislation, 1868–1951" (Treaties and Historical Research Center, DIAND, 1980).

[85] *Report of the Royal Commission on Aboriginal Peoples*, vol. 1, 275–6; see also J.L. Tobias, "Protection, Civilization, Assimilation: An Outline History of Canada's Indian Policy," *Sweet Promises: A Reader on Indian-White Relations in Canada,*. Ed. J.R. Miller (Toronto: University of Toronto Press, 1991).

[86] J.R. Miller, *Shingwauk's Vision: A History of Native Residential Schools* (Toronto: University of Toronto Press, 1996), 105; see also J. Barman, Y. Herbert and Don McCaskill. *Indian Education in Canada: The Legacy* (Vancouver: University of British Columbia Press, 1986) 90–2.

[87] *Report of the Royal Commission on Aboriginal Peoples*, vol. 1, 335; see also Katherine Pettipas, "Severing the Ties That Bind: The Canadian Indian Act and the Repression of Indigenous Religious Systems in the Prairie Region" (Ph.D. diss., University of Manitoba, Winnipeg, Manitoba, 1989) 176–9.

[88] D. Jenness, *Indians of Canada* (Ottawa: National Museum of Canada, 1960), 264.

[89] Cited in the *Report of the Royal Commission on Aboriginal Peoples*, vol. 1, 183.

[90] Pettipas, 220–6, 233–60; see also *Report of the Royal Commission on Aboriginal Peoples*, vol. 1, 291–3.

[91] The pass system was introduced as a policy and was often implemented at the discretion of the Indian Department officials. The pass system was never legislated through Parliament and was later phased out during the 1920s and 1930s. In the aftermath of the 1885 Rebellion, if a Band was considered disloyal, the people would most

often face the harsher application of the pass system while the "loyal" Bands were rewarded. See John L. Tobias, "Canada's Subjugation of the Plains Cree, 1849–1885"; Laurie Barron and James B. Waldram, eds., *1885 and After: Native Society in Transition*, 1986; and Norma Sluman and Jean Goodwill, *John Tootoosis: Biography of a Cree Leader* (Ottawa: Golden Dog Press, 1982).

⁹² Pettipas, 248–9.

⁹³ Cited in Pettipas, 268–9; also in "Chief Thunderchild to the Department of Indian Affairs" (PAC RG10, Vol. 3,826, File 60, 511-4, Part 1, 4 June 1914).

⁹⁴ Carter, 115.

⁹⁵ Federal government policies and constitutional amendments, especially those introduced in the last two decades, have moved to address many of the issues that have troubled the relationship between Canada and First Nations. These initiatives include the comprehensive and specific land claims processes; Sections 25 and 35 of the Constitution Act, 1982 (as amended), which addresses aboriginal and treaty rights; treaty land entitlements, which address unfulfilled promises of land; self-government negotiations; the Statement of Reconciliation, which includes a response to the residential school system policy; and "Gathering Strength—Canada's Aboriginal Action Plan" the most recent federal government policy statement. Although progress is being made, much remains to be done.

Federal Government Policy and the "National Interest"

Menno Boldt

Menno Boldt, a retired Professor of Sociology from the University of Lethbridge, has researched and worked with Indigenous peoples for more than twenty-five years in both personal and professional capacities. The book from which this article is drawn was nominated for the John Porter Award.

For officials at the Department of Indian Affairs and Northern Development (DIAND), the 1960s began as just another decade of smug bureaucratic arrogance wedded to ignorance about their Indian wards. Cultural assimilation was still considered a "progressive policy," and both politicians and bureaucrats were blissfully optimistic about the progress being made in that direction. Statistics showed increases in the number of Indian children receiving post-elementary schooling; federal programs to relocate Indians from reserves (and federal responsibility) to urban centres (and provincial responsibility) were deemed to be progressing at a satisfying pace; Indian friendship centres were springing up in cities to facilitate Indian relocation from reserves; there were illusions of viable economic development on reserves; studies on Indians were being commissioned and "solutions" and new ideas were being presented (e.g., the Hawthorn Report);[1] Indian leaders were learning how to function in colonial political and bureaucratic structures; DIAND was in full control of Indians and land reserved for Indians. In short, everything was humming along smoothly for Indian Affairs.

This article is a portion of a chapter entitled "Policy," from *Surviving As Indians: The Challenge of Self-Government* by Menno Boldt, (Toronto: University of Toronto Press, 1993). Reprinted with permission of the publisher.

But following the 1968 federal election, Pierre Elliott Trudeau, the liberal-democrat, burst upon the Canadian scene and DIAND's blissful world was shattered forever. Full of "just society" idealism and fervour, Trudeau was determined to make a difference. As a liberal, he "knew" what was right and good for Indians—to become "Canadians as all other Canadians." But, as a democrat, he was bound to consult Indians before implementing his solutions. Thus, in the year leading up to the 1969 White Paper on Indian Policy, DIAND bureaucrats, under marching orders from their political "masters," had to leave their comfortable offices and scurry into the remote corners of Canada, where the reserves are located, to engage Indians in "consultations" about their future.

For Indians, this was a radically new experience. Never before had the princely mandarins from Ottawa deigned to solicit their views in such a diligent fashion. The effect of the consultation process on Indian leaders was remarkable. It raised their expectations, inspired new ideas, charged their emotions, and unleashed a tremendous pan-Indian dynamic that irrevocably changed Indian-Canadian relationships. Most consequential of all, it raised in Indian leaders a profound sense of individual and collective empowerment and political efficacy—something they had never experienced before. Later, this sense of empowerment was translated into political protest when the contents of the White Paper on Indian Policy were revealed in the fall of 1969, and Indian leaders discovered that the "consultations" had been a total sham. None of their expressed interests, rights, needs, and aspirations had been heeded. The shock of this discovery transformed their characteristic posture of subordination and passiveness into such a fierce resistance that, in 1971, the government retracted the White Paper.

The unity and intensity of Indian opposition to the White Paper caught Canadian government officials off guard and sent them reeling in confusion. So decisive was the Indian triumph that for a full decade (the 1970s) the Canadian government lost its will and capacity to make "Indian policy." DIAND became bogged down in a muddle of defensive strategies: to lower Indian expectations (e.g., on sovereignty); to neutralize Indian demands (e.g., on aboriginal rights); to diffuse Indian energies (e.g., by proposing amendments to the Indian Act); to divide Indians (e.g., by making them compete for scarce funds); and to devitalize Indian leadership (e.g., by co-optation). Only in the 1980s did the government recover its balance sufficiently to again undertake new policy initiatives uniquely affecting Indians. These new initiatives included the Parliamentary Task Force on Indian Self-Government

(Penner Report) in 1982; the sections 25, 35, and 37 amendments to the Constitution Act in 1982 and 1983; the First Ministers' Conferences on aboriginal matters in 1983–7; the Ministerial Task Force on Program Review (Nielsen Report) in 1986; and the Indian Self-Government Community Negotiations policy statement in 1986. By the 1990s, the government was on a policy-making "roll" as it announced the Royal Commission on Aboriginal Peoples and the Aboriginal Constitutional Process.

What goals does the Canadian government harbour for Indian peoples in its recent spree of policy initiatives? In this article I review and analyse the goals of government policies towards Indians in Canada. I take the position that "Indian policy" provides too limited a framework for understanding the conduct of Indian affairs in Canada; that the conduct of Indian affairs can be understood only as part of a much broader policy-making process in the Canadian polity, economy, and society. This broader policy-making process which impacts on Indians is identified here as the actualization of the "national interest." I begin my discussion with an elaboration of the "national interest" as a policy paradigm for understanding the conduct of Indian affairs in Canada.

The "National Interest"

The Canadian "national interest" is an artificial construct, a device of the reigning Canadian "establishment" for asserting its political, economic, and social hegemony over the Canadian nation. It is used to create the illusion that there exists a national homogeneity of interests, and that government policies are designed to promote these interests. Thus, it serves to legitimate government policies. But, clearly, the "national interest" is not arrived at by any rational calculations referenced to the "national good" as defined by the majority of Canadians. More often than not, assessments and definitions of the "national interest" are made behind closed doors—political, bureaucratic, and corporate—where only the voices of the powerful are heard.

The "national interest" is not a well-defined or precise notion. Commonly, it denotes no more than the convergent or mediated interests of the powerful as arbitrated by the federal cabinet. Nonetheless, the "national interest" is an overwhelming and permanent force in Canadian policy development; it will not be denied, and it affects Indian interests in profound ways. For purposes of analysing its impact on Indian policy we must look to prevailing economic, political, and social priorities as defined by the Canadian government. Some current "national interest" priorities that can be seen to impact on the conduct of Indian affairs are national unity (i.e., resolving federal-provincial constitutional disputes and conciliating differences with Quebec), the national debt (i.e., controlling or "capping" government expenditures), and resource development (i.e., removing legal constraints to corporate exploitation of oil, mineral, logging, and hydro potential).

In the following pages, I evaluate "the national interest" as a force in Indian affairs from the perspective of Indian interests, Indian influence, and the role of Canadian politicians and bureaucrats; and in terms of "sidestream" effects.

Indian Interests

Implicit in the "national interest" policy paradigm as presented here is the thesis that all Canadian government policies, whether they are "Canadian" policies or "Indian" policies, will subordinate, if not sacrifice, Indian interests to Canadian interests. This "national interest" imperative relative to Canada's conduct of Indian affairs was already in evidence in Canada's founding charter. Although section 91 (24) of the British North America Act, 1867, which created special federal government legislative authority over Indians and lands reserved for Indians, has been construed as policy in the Indian interest— specifically, to protect Indians from provincial and private exploitation—the facts don't support this construction. If the primary rationale for section 91 (24) was to protect Indians, why did the Canadian government use its authority under this section to cede large areas of Indian land to provinces and private enterprises without Indian consent, and far below their market values? Arguably, section 91 (24) has afforded some incidental protection to Indians, but the primary reason it was enacted in 1867 was to serve the fledgling "national interest" by creating central federal control and jurisdiction over Indians and their territories, thereby facilitating coordination of Indian policy with national military, settlement, and economic policies.

One merit of the "national interest" policy perspective is that it exposes more fully the extent to which Indian interests, rights, needs, and aspirations are prey to government policy designs. Under section 91 (24) of the BNA Act the Canadian government is declared to be the sole trustee of Indians and lands reserved for Indians. Legally and morally, trusteeship implies that the federal government has an obligation at all times to act in the best interest of Indian peoples. This comprehensive obligation goes beyond the limited concept of the government's "trust" or "fiduciary" responsibility recently addressed by the courts (i.e., issues of government responsibility for competent and honest management of Indian resources and affairs, including legal liability for misuse of Indian funds and unauthorized leasing, taking, or selling of Indian land and water). The Canadian government's trust responsibility requires it, at all times, to act in the best interest of Indians within the total "Canadian policy" framework and not just with respect to "Indian" policies. In other words, the government's trust responsibility goes beyond an obligation merely to avoid iniquitous "Indian" policies. It includes an obligation to ensure "Canadian" policies do not deliberately, or even inadvertently, sacrifice Indian interests to the Canadian interest. But, as author and executor of the Canadian "national interest," the government is in an ongoing fundamental conflict-of-interest position vis-à-vis Indian interests.

In this regard, "Indian policy" has always been a misnomer. We can reasonably infer from "Canadian policy" that it is designed to serve some sort or segment of "Canadian" interest. But we can never infer from "Indian policy" that it is designed to serve any "Indian" interests. On the contrary, "Indian policy" has always been, and is today, a design for sacrificing Indian interests for the general "Canadian good," that is, the "national interest." Such was the case with the Indian Act (a policy for government control), the treaties (a policy for acquiring Indian lands), extending the vote (a policy for undermining Indian nationhood), education (historically a policy of "civilization," i.e., assimilation; however, recently, when the government faced a fiscal crunch, a redefined "national interest" dictated a policy of capping funding for Indian post-secondary education). All of these "Indian policies" were formulated with primary reference to the "national interest," not with reference to the interests, rights, needs, and aspirations of Indian people. In short "Indian policy" has historically served as a metaphor for the Canadian "national interest." Nowhere is the "national interest" written more explicitly and unambiguously than in "Indian policy."

The "national interest" policy imperative has extended even to creating appropriate Indian stereotypes to rationalize and justify the "Indian policies" designed to serve the "national interest." When the "national interest" dictated the taking of Indian lands, the Indian was given the image of a "heathen," implying an ignorant, cruel, dirty, immoral, lazy, subhuman species. This image was elaborated and validated with gruesome fictional accounts of Indian cruelty, treachery, and perversity. Such a subhuman species could have no moral claim or legal title to land that God created for his children. This Indian stereotype justified both military and missionary actions against Indians—genocide and ethnocide.

When the "national interest" imperative required that Indians should be removed from their ancestral lands to make way for settlers and business enterprise, the image of Indians was transmuted from heathen into a childlike people, ignorant, naive, and vulnerable to exploitation, debauching by alcohol, and abuse by unprincipled European traffickers. Such a people heeded government protection, and thus the reserve system was introduced, along with the Indian Act.

When the "national interest" imperative prescribed that Indians should be "Canadians as all other Canadians," they were given the image of a racial minority group, of disadvantaged citizens suffering from multiple burdens of segregation, prejudice, discrimination, inequality, and lack of individual rights. This set the scene for the 1969 White Paper that identified their special status, their aboriginal rights, and their land claims as the "cause" of all their disadvantages, and sought to terminate these elements of the aboriginal heritage.

A recent instance of a Canadian policy initiative premised on sacrificing Indian interests to the "national interest" imperative occurred during negotiations leading up to the ill-fated Meech Lake Accord. The "national interest" called for Quebec to be brought into the Canadian constitutional framework. The "trade-offs" that occurred in the Quebec-Canada conciliation process at Meech Lake resulted in the adoption of an agenda that effectively removed aboriginal self-government from the program of constitutional reform and gave approval to an amending formula that empowered each province to veto any constitutional amendment on Indian government. Had the Meech Lake Accord been enacted, these "deals," which were struck in the "national interest," would have effectively ruled out, for all time, any possibility of Indians achieving meaningful self-government.

One reason why Indian interests are readily subordinated or sacrificed to the "national interest" is that government officials generally construe those interests as being inimical to the "national interest." This tendency has been most evident when dealing with Indian economic interests such as land rights, hunting, and fishing. But it is also evident in the political realm when Indians make claims to self-government, treaty rights, special status, and so on. Such claims are always interpreted by Canadian politicians and bureaucrats as threatening Canadian political sovereignty and integrity.

The Penner Committee Report (discussed later in this article) stands as an exception to the Canadian government's historical practice of subordinating Indian interests to the "national interest."

This committee of Parliament worked diligently to understand Indian interests, rights, needs, and aspirations. While it did not give Indian interests full equality to the "national interest," it made a praiseworthy attempt to develop a policy framework for *reconciling* some key Indian interests with the "national interest." This report was relegated to the wastebaskets of the bureaucracy. Its fate serves to confirm the assertion that the Canadian government is unwilling to fulfil its fiduciary responsibility to Indians. When Indian interests compete with the "national interest," Canadian politicians will always subordinate or sacrifice them.

Subordination of Indian interests to the "national interest" has also been effected through judicial decisions. Jurisprudence relating to Indian rights and claims has been shaped by the "national interest"; that is, Canadian judges make their decisions with reference to the "national interest" and the "national interest" always prevails over Indian interests in all decisions of consequence. Indians have learned from experience that the courts are not above compromising historical moral and legal commitments to Indians, if necessary, to protect the "national interest." To cite one example among many, in *Simon* v. *The Queen* (1985)[2] the Canadian Supreme Court ruled that, under section 88 of the Indian Act, when the terms of a treaty come into conflict with federal government legislation, the latter prevails. Leon Mitchell cites cases in which the federal court has ruled that the Canadian government holds the authority to unilaterally alter Indian treaty rights when it enters into an agreement with a province, if the federal-provincial agreement contains terms that require the restriction of Indian rights as set out in a treaty.[3]

For more evidence of judicial subordination of Indian interests to the Canadian "national interest," Indians can point to judicial rulings in regard to the Migratory Birds Convention Act, the Jay Treaty, and the decisions reached in *Sikeyea* v. *The Queen* (1964), *The Queen* v. *George* (1966), and *Daniels* v. *White and The Queen* (1968).[4] All of these decisions, made in the "national interest," violated treaty covenants and Canadian moral and legal commitments to Indians in favour of the "national interest." In these and other cases (e.g., the *Sparrow* decision), Canadian courts have consistently held that the government, acting in the "national interest," has the sovereign power to regulate and extinguish aboriginal rights. The courts need not act intrusively to serve the "national interest." They merely take creative advantage of the obscure and vague wording in the constitution, the treaties, the laws, and the agreements. Lower-court judges who aspire to make decisions on Indian rights that will survive the appeal process need only apprehend where the "national interest" lies, and then artfully exploit any legal vagueness to construct a ruling (preferably worded in high-sounding language) to serve the "national interest."

To sum up, Indian interests are always either subordinated or sacrificed to promote the "national interest." When the "national interest" requires fiscal retrenchment, then Indian program budgets are capped. When the "national interest" requires a federal-provincial constitutional accord, then Indian self-government is removed from the constitutional agenda. When the "national interest" dictates a recon-ciliation with Quebec, then the federal government's fiduciary responsi-bility for Indians in Quebec is abdicated. When the "national interest" dictates resource development, then aboriginal title is extinguished.

Indian Influence

Canadian policymaking is always a complex political process of mediation among a variety of concerns and interests. A partial listing of these concerns and interests includes: international political and economic forces, federal-provincial mandates, cabinet priorities, economic and social exigencies, political partisanship and ideological values, regional concerns, inter-departmental rivalries, public expectations, interest-group pressures, legislative and judicial precedents, and resistance to change—a virtual snarl of competing concerns and interests. In this snarl, Indian concerns and interests have a low ranking. This has been the case ever since confederation when Indians became superfluous to Canadian military and economic concerns.

Unless confronted with an "Indian crisis," the time of Parliament and of Cabinet is deemed too valuable to take up for a concentrated examination of Indian interests, rights, needs, and aspirations. Argu-ably, the 1969 White Paper on Indian policy and the Penner Report stand as exceptions to this rule. But neither of these initiatives culmi-nated in policy. The 1969 White Paper was recanted, and the Penner Report was shelved. More typically, when Canadian politicians, individually and collectively, assess national priorities, they are swayed by bigger, richer, more cohesive, more influential, and more compatible constituencies that come well ahead of Indians. Indians fall at the margin, if not outside the periphery, of Canadian politicians' consciousness and concerns. This was exemplified, recently, during deliberations around the Free Trade Agreement. Indian interests, rights, needs, and aspirations were not even mentioned by Canadian politicians in the debate on this historical agreement.

Although the Canadian government, mainly out of guilt, occasionally surrenders some power to Indians, and Indian leaders are getting better at frustrating Canadian politicians when they ignore Indian interests, nonetheless, the fact is that Indians lack the mechanisms and resources to penetrate the closed political, bureaucratic, and corporate doors behind which the "national interest" gets defined. Even when they are admitted into the "inner circle," their voices are lost in the snarl of competing concerns and interests. For example, in 1975 the federal government sought to place its relations with Indians on a better footing by creating the Joint Cabinet/National Indian Brotherhood Committee as a joint policy-formulating experiment. But three years later the experiment was terminated without having produced a single joint policy agreement.[5] A similar lack of results marked the four First Ministers' conferences that were held to deal with aboriginal constitutional matters.

The conventional means for a minority group to advance its interests—that is, by intense and targeted involvement in the political process—has not worked for aboriginal peoples. They have not been able to translate their electoral potential into political influence. For example, in the 1988 national election there were twenty-four electoral ridings in which the number of eligible aboriginal voters exceeded the margin of victory by the successful candidate.[6] Arithmetically, aboriginal voters could have decided the election outcome in most of these ridings. More than half the time in the past three decades this number of ridings could have determined which political party would form the government. For most ethnic minorities in Canada such political potential would translate into significant political muscle. But, in the case of aboriginal peoples, their potential electoral power has proved inconsequential. The reasons for this are twofold: aboriginal people, emotionally and intellectually, have not "accepted" Canadian citizenship, thus they tend to have a very low voter turnout, and those who vote seem uninterested in voting as a block. Consequently, Canadian politicians, with few exceptions, simply disregard the Indian vote. The effect is that, politically, Indians are consigned to a status of "citizen-minus."

Some Indian leaders have advocated greater involvement by their people in the various levels of federal, provincial, and municipal government, by voting and by standing for election. Others have proposed formation of an independent aboriginal peoples' party to encourage aboriginal peoples to elect aboriginal representatives to the various levels of government. Still others have championed the notion of "proportionate assured representation," that is, a fixed number of aboriginal seats in the provincial and federal legislatures and in the Senate. The Royal Commission on Electoral Reform and Party Financing (1990) asked Indian leaders across Canada for their reaction to the idea of a constitutionally guaranteed number of seats in Parliament for aboriginal people. The chairman of the commission noted that, if aboriginal people were represented in Parliament according to their percentage of the Canadian population, they would have ten sitting members. Given the closeness of Canadian elections since 1957, ten aboriginal members voting as a block could have held the balance of power in Parliament more than half the time. While these ideas are under continuing discussion, as yet none has achieved widespread support among Indians, and none has been officially adopted as a policy priority by major Indian organizations. One underlying reason for the lack of interest is that Indians are chary of being identified as Canadian citizens. Participation in Canadian politics is viewed by many to be in conflict with their claims to historical aboriginal nationhood.

The matter of Indian representation in Canadian legislatures raises a large unanswered question: Would the Canadian "establishment," and Canadians generally, tolerate a political system or situation that might give Indians a parliamentary "balance of power"; are they prepared to tolerate more than a token Indian influence in Canadian politics? Based on past behaviour it is highly unlikely that Canadian legislators would constitutionally guarantee to Indians enough seats to give them a potential "swing vote" in Parliament. Indian leaders claim, already, to have evidence of provincial governments gerrymandering electoral boundaries to reduce the number of Indian electors in northern provincial constituencies where they have a potential swing vote in provincial elections.

The lack of Indian influence in shaping the "national interest" is not attributable to a lack of public forums or media channels to present their issues and views to the Canadian public. Indian leaders regularly have access to the Canadian public, and on a number of occasions they have gained international attention for their grievances. But such approaches have not proved very fruitful as avenues of political influence in shaping the "national interest." The Canadian government ignores such initiatives, or it neutralizes them with counter-claims, more "studies," new committees, deceptive rhetoric, and empty gestures, or it co-opts Indian leadership. However, one notable exception to this generalization occurred on 23 June 1990, when

Elijah Harper, lone Indian member of the Manitoba legislature, used procedural tactics to block Manitoba's ratification of the Meech Lake Accord. Because the Accord required the ratification of all ten provincial legislatures, Harper single-handedly killed the Accord. This is not to say that Harper dispatched the "national interest" imperative in Canadian constitutional development, but he did temporarily frustrate it—an epic achievement, all things considered.

Politicians and Bureaucrats

The broader "national interest" policy perspective on the conduct of Indian affairs helps us to answer [the applied anthropologist] Sally Weaver's question: "Why in the new [Mulroney] government, is a minister [Crombie] unable to implement his own priorities when they have prime-ministerial and [Indian] constituency support?"[7] When considered within a "national interest" policy paradigm, the influence and philosophies of individual government officials, even the most senior officials, are marginal to the conduct of Indian affairs. From time to time, senior officials in government (e.g., Chrétien, Penner, Crombie, and Nielsen), holding distinctive personal philosophies, briefly figure prominently as champions of particular "Indian policy" designs. And, because the conduct of Indian affairs sometimes appears to conform to the personal philosophy articulated by such officials, the appearance is of causal antecedency (especially if the philosophy is articulated by the Minister of Indian Affairs). But it is a mistake to posit a causal link between the personal philosophies of senior government officials and "Indian policy."

As I have already said, in the snarl of competing concerns and interests out of which Canadian government decisions emerge, Indian policy is always shaped by the political, economic, and social imperatives of the evolving "national interest." Personal philosophies about how Indian affairs should be conducted, even if they are the philosophies of cabinet ministers, count for little. Such is especially true in the case of the DIAND, which, as a department, occupies one of the lowest rungs in the government hierarchy and where the tenancy of ministers is too brief for their personal philosophy to take root as "departmental" philosophy. At best, their ideas briefly become part of the political discourse on the future of Indians. Therefore, it is of small consequence whether a minister of the DIAND is "friendly" or "hostile" to the Indians' interests. In either case, the "national interest" prevails over their personally held priorities and philosophies.

Moreover, being "successful politicians," cabinet ministers are well aware of the folly of advocating policies that run counter to the "national interest." Thus, in respect to fundamentals, Crombie and Nielsen, although they represented profoundly different philosophic and value orientations, both pursued Indian policies that were essentially consistent with what has been acknowledged as being in the "national interest"; that is, both advocated devolution of responsibility under a municipal style of "Indian government" with limited *delegated* (not inherent) powers; both sought to restrain government spending by advocating greater Indian responsibility and accountability (self-reliance); and both advocated restructuring Canadian-Indian relationships to bring jurisdictional arrangements more into conformity with the constitutionally mandated roles of federal and provincial governments as these apply to Canadian citizens generally.

Media reporters with a need to simplify complex policy processes typically emphasize the personalities, personal philosophies, and ideologies of DIAND ministers and senior bureaucrats in their interpretation of Indian policy. Some scholars have made similar analyses. However, in the course of four First Ministers' Conferences on aboriginal matters over a period of five years, the policy positions of the federal government and of the various provinces at the constitutional negotiating table did not change on any one of the fundamental issues that were under contention with aboriginal representatives (e.g., Crown sovereignty and Crown land title). Yet, during this period we witnessed a turnover of federal and provincial government officials that resulted in virtually a new slate of prime minister, premiers, and political parties they represent, and the bureaucrats who advise them. This suggests that Indian policy positions derive from a "higher source" than the personal philosophies and values of prime ministers, premiers, cabinet ministers, or senior bureaucrats. That higher source I submit here is the "national interest."

"Sidestream" Effects

Most members of the Canadian government will admit that government policies affecting Indians have at times been misguided, but none would agree that they were deliberately malicious. All would say they want a better life for Indians. How is it, then, that a government comprised of such well-intentioned people can foster policies that created and continue the horrendous conditions that prevail in all Indian communities? One common tendency among Indian leaders is to attribute such problems to officialdom's ignorance about Indians.

While the charge of official ignorance is well founded, the "ignorant politician/bureaucrat" rationale is not an adequate explanation for the Indian condition. This is evident on reserves where administration of programs and services has been substantially transferred from DIAND to band/tribal councils and their bureaucrats. Conditions on these reserves have not improved measurably.

If the horrendous conditions of Indians is not comprehensible as a product of sinister intentions, or lack of concern, or political and bureaucratic ignorance, then how do we explain these conditions? I have already proposed that, significantly, these conditions are a consequence of the government's subordination and sacrifice of Indian interests to the "national interest" imperative. In this section I propose that these conditions are also attributable to unpremeditated "sidestream" consequence of "Canadian policies" that are designed to serve the "national interest." An example of such a sidestream consequence can be observed in the Canadian government's 1988 policy announcement of fiscal restraint. One of the "casualties" of this "Canadian policy" of fiscal restraint was funding for Indian post-secondary education. There were no sinister intentions behind this policy, nor did it uniquely sacrifice Indian interests to the "national interest." But, the sidestream effect of the "Canadian policy" was that Indians, who are already at an enormous disadvantage vis-à-vis Canadians, were further victimized.

The "sidestream" reality of the "national interest" in government thinking could not have been more explicitly enunciated than was done by the Honourable Bill McKnight, erstwhile minister of DIAND, when, on 26 October 1988, he explained to Canadians why it was so important to bring Canada's northern comprehensive aboriginal claims process to a quick conclusion. His explanation and rationalization emphasized two "national interest" imperatives: the first "national interest" theme was resource development—"the most dramatic step to date in this comprehensive claims process was taken when agreements-in-principle were signed... for managing and regulating onshore oil and gas development"[8]—and the second, the consolidation of Canada's Arctic sovereignty—"By resolving once and for all the claims of Native Northerners, we make the strongest possible statement for our continuing, responsible sovereignty throughout the area."[9] The interests, rights, needs, and aspirations of the aboriginal peoples with whom the government was negotiating the aboriginal claims, and for whom the minister carried a fiduciary responsibility, were incidental; they were relegated to the "sidestream" of these two "national interest" rationales for concluding the agreement.

Another example of the "sidestream" fact in Canadian policy can be discerned in the government's abjuration of its historical policy of Indian cultural assimilation. Until the 1960s the Canadian government considered cultural assimilation to be a progressive Indian policy. The subsequent change in this policy came not as a response to Indian interests, rights, needs, and aspirations, but as a sidestream effect of Canada's policy of bilingualism and multiculturalism—a policy designed to serve the "national interest" by conciliating Quebec separatists without offending other immigrant groups in Canada. Had the policy of bilingualism and multiculturalism been referenced to Indian interests, rights, needs, and aspirations it would have included the "original peoples" as one of the "founding nations" along with the English and French. It would not have lumped, as it does, Indians with the "other" immigrant minorities.

Aboriginal leaders are not unaware of the sidestream effects of Canadian policy. The United Native Nations of BC and the Native Council of Canada were reacting to anticipated sidestream policy effects on their members when they supported the BC government in its suit against the federal government's decision to impose a cap on its transfer payments to that province. In an affidavit filed with the BC Court of Appeal, these two aboriginal groups asserted that a limit on the federal government's contribution to British Columbia under the Canada Assistance plan (a 50-50 federal-provincial cost-sharing scheme that covers welfare and social programs) would have a disproportionately negative impact on Natives because about 60 percent of Native people living away from reserves depend on provincial social assistance. In their written argument they asserted that the limitation on transfer payments "will make it difficult if not impossible for the province to accommodate the needs of aboriginal people living off the reserve."[10]

So long as Indians remained solely a federal responsibility, they were somewhat shielded from the sidestream effects of provincial policies. But, with the entrenchment of their aboriginal rights in the Constitution Act, 1982, and with the growing involvement of the provinces in Indian affairs, it is inevitable that, in future, Indian interests will become increasingly vulnerable to "provincial interests" and to the sidestream effects of provincial policies designed to serve those interests.

Summing up, in my analysis to this point I have considered the Canadian government's conduct of Indian affairs within a "national interest" policy paradigm. Despite its vagueness, the "national interest" imperative provides a valid policy paradigm for under-standing the conduct of Indian affairs because it carries a constant and consequential impact on Indians, even when turnover in governments occurs. Successive Canadian governments have evidenced different styles and philosophies, but all have conducted Indian affairs to serve the "national interest"; that is, all Canadian governments, of whatever party stripe, have consistently subordinated Indian interests to the Canadian "national interest" in their development of policy. None has developed policies with primary or coequal reference to Indian interests, rights, needs, or aspirations. The grounds for this assertion will become more evident as my analysis continues.

Institutional Assimilation

The power-sharing formula worked out by the Fathers of Confederation in 1867 gave the provinces jurisdiction over education, health care, civil and property law, resource development, municipal institutions, and sales tax. It mandated the federal government to take charge of virtually everything else. But, under section 91 (24) of the British North America Act, Indians were assigned a "special status" that gave the federal government exclusive jurisdiction over "Indians, and land reserved for Indians." For the past half-century the most persistent aspect of Canada's policy towards Indians has been to attenuate the "special status" of Indians under section 91 (24). Attenuation of Indian special status is deemed to be in the "national interest" because of the troublesome political-economic-legal liability incurred by Indian claims to aboriginal rights, treaty rights, land title and sovereignty, and by the spiralling costs of maintaining a complex of separate federal political, economic, legal, and bureaucratic structures and programs to serve Indians.

Consequently, the Canadian government has placed Indian special status under assault from all sides. The most insidious and perilous assault on Indian special status is concentrated on the institutional assimilation of Indians, that is, the progressive incorporation of Indians into the political, legal, social, and economic institutional framework of Canadian society. The ultimate goal is the elimination of all institutional arrangements that set Indians apart from Canadians. For public consumption—Indian, Canadian, and international—this policy initiative is presented by the Canadian government as having the goal of moving Indians from their colonial status of collective subordination to equality through desegregation of institutional arrangements. But, in fact, institutional assimilation can be regarded as the "final assault" in the Canadian government's historic campaign to "civilize" Indians Or, using Trudeau's euphemism, to make them into "Canadians as all other Canadians."

Although the federal and provincial governments have conflicting perspectives as to what ought to be the constitutional mandates of their respective institutions, there is no fundamental disagreement between them over the goal of institutional assimilation of Indians. Both levels of government are fully committed to the goal of incorporating Indians into the prevailing federal and provincial political, legal, social, and economic institutional framework. Provincial governments have already cooperated extensively with the federal government in the institutional assimilation of Indians by negotiating bilateral agreements under which the provincial institutions provide education, health, welfare, economic development, and other services to Indians.

Despite the federal government's horrific record of betrayed trust, paternalism, mismanagement, and so on, Indians consider the transfer of responsibility for services to their communities from federal to provincial jurisdiction as a worrisome trend. This attitude derives from a deep concern by Indians that their special status and their aboriginal and treaty rights will be jeopardized if they come under provincial jurisdiction. The Assembly of First Nations has characterized the federal government's policy of transferring its constitutional responsibility for Indians to the provinces as inviting the "wolves to tend the sheep."[11]

The Canadian government's approach to institutional assimilation of Indians is multifaceted. Next, I briefly elaborate on three of the main strategies of the Canadian government: structural integration, constitutional normalization, and individualization.

Structural Integration

Structural integration has reference to the elimination of all segregated Indian institutional structures. This objective is being achieved through a two-phase government strategy. In the first place, traditional Indian social systems (e.g., traditional forms of self-government, redistribution and sharing, custom, and spirituality) were displaced by forcibly imposing Euro-Western political, economic, legal, and social structures and norms on Indian communities. Initially, these imposed structures were segregated from prevailing Canadian institutional structures, and placed under the control of the DIAND. While this segregated arrangement shielded Indians from the full force of cultural assimilation, it also served the important function of schooling them in how to function within Canadian models of institutional structures.

In the second, and current, phase of structural integration, the Canadian government is deliberately phasing out the DIAND, the Indian Act, and the segregated system of institutional structures for Indians, and is progressively incorporating Indians into prevailing federal and provincial institutional structures.

A specific instance where the Canadian government has carried structural integration into the second phase is in education. During the first phase, Indian children were forcibly enrolled in segregated federal Indian schools where they were educated according to Canadian curricula and standards. In the second phase, the federal government closed many Indian schools and entered into negotiated agreements with the provinces for provision of education to Indian children in provincial schools. Already, more than half of school-age Indian children have been transferred to provincial school systems. Under such agreements most Indian children will soon be fully assimilated into the Canadian educational system.

The Canadian government's objective of structural integration is being facilitated by Indian migration to urban centres. Prior to the Second World War, virtually all Indians lived in reserve communities, and the federal government dealt with them as a collectivity through segregated institutional structures. Today, more than a third of all Indians live in urban centres, and they are being assimilated, as individuals, into provincial institutional structures. This enormous and accelerating shift of the Indian population to urban centres has been deliberately facilitated by the federal government in order to expedite the structural integration of Indians. To this end, the federal government has instituted a number of assistance programs to lure Indians into leaving the reserve, such as offering them relocation and housing grants. A more reprehensible federal government tactic, also purposed to expedite the structural integration of Indians, has been to allow some federal services on reserves (e.g., schools, housing, health services) to deteriorate to such a point that Indians are compelled to leave the reserve and accept provincial services.

Historically, structural segregation of Indians derived from their special status, and has buttressed it. Therefore, the Canadian government's strategy of progressive structural integration has the effect of undermining the Indians' historical claims to special status.

Constitutional Normalization

Since the Second World War, the federal government has given a high priority to the "constitutional normalization" of Indian status, that is, to vitiating the historic constitutional anomaly of section 91 (24) that assigned exclusive jurisdiction over Indians to the federal government. The goal is to bring Indian status into broad conformity with prevailing federal and provincial constitutional mandates as these apply to Canadians generally. That is what Trudeau had in mind when he introduced the 1969 White Paper. More recent evidence for this idea can be found in "Federal-Provincial Memoranda of Agreements"—bilateral accords for the "normalization" of the delivery of services and programs to Indians. Additional evidence can be inferred from the Nielsen Report recommendation that Indian special status should be diminished by ending their exclusive relationship with the federal government.[12]

From time to time the courts have facilitated the process of constitutional normalization with rulings that broaden the application of provincial jurisdiction over Indians. The courts have done so with reference to section 88 of the Indian Act, which subjects Indians to provincially enacted "laws of general application," with some exceptions. With the courts' sanction, section 88 has been used by the federal and provincial governments as a license to erode Indian special status under section 91 (24) by expanding provincial legislative jurisdiction over Indians. Interpretations of section 88, as to which provincial laws are "laws of general application" and therefore applicable to Indians, represent a value judgment made by the courts. The history of judicial interpretation of section 88 reveals a consistent pattern of incremental expansion of the powers of the provinces over Indians; that is, the extent to which provincial laws of general application apply to Indians is constantly being broadened by the courts.

A more subtle but nonetheless consequential actuation of the idea of constitutional normalization can be found in section 35 (2) of the Constitution Act, 1982. Here Indians have been lumped together and equated with Metis in the constitutional definition of "aboriginal peoples." This idea was first floated by Jean Chrétien (then minister of the DIAND) during the parliamentary debates on the 1969 White Paper. Chrétien asserted that the problems of Indians could not be solved separately from those of the Metis. He offered no explanation why the legal distinction between the two groups rendered the problems of both groups intractable to improvement. With the benefit of hindsight, it is evident that Chrétien's statement signalled an emerging government policy designed to blur and undermine the special status of Indians by joining them with the Metis. The Metis do not come under section 91 (24) of the BNA Act, or under the Indian Act, or under the DIAND; they have neither treaties, nor a constitutionally grounded land base, nor a trust relationship with the federal government; they are accepted as full "provincial citizens." In short, the Metis meet Trudeau's "Canadians as all other Canadians" standard. By equating the constitutional status and rights of Indians with those of the Metis ("Canadians") the governments of Canada have created the "vagueness" that opens the door for the courts to bring Indians into conformity with prevailing federal and provincial constitutional mandates.

A most damaging implementation of the idea of constitutional normalization occurred when full Canadian citizenship and the franchise were thrust upon Indians by a unilateral declaration of the Canadian government. This constitutional "right" was not sought by Indians and, quite contrary to democratic theory, was proclaimed without Indian consent. In effect, the right to vote in Canadian elections was imposed on Indians in the "national interest," to affirm Canadian sovereignty over Indians. The Canadian government touts its extension of the franchise to Indians as an "enlightened" democratic act done in the interest of Indians, but this act holds significant adverse implications for Indian special status. Bringing Indians into the Canadian political system has had the effect of subjecting them to a process of socialization that promotes intrinsic individualism ("one person, one vote"), and it functions to channel Indians' opposition to Canadian policies through the ballot-box, where they have little influence. Moreover, it lends symbolic legitimacy to the fiction that Indians have given democratic consent to Canadian sovereignty and citizenship, and that their primary commitment is to the Canadian regime. Thus, it undermines Indian claims to "peoples' rights" under the U.N. charter.

Individualization

In the wake of independence movements by colonized third-world nations following the Second World War, the Canadian government came under growing domestic and international pressures to decolonize the Indian peoples within its borders. In this regard, the government had two options: it could grant "peoples' rights" to Indians (i.e., the path of self-determination) or it could impose "individual rights" on them (i.e., the path of institutional assimilation). The Canadian government, with the consent of the provincial governments, has opted to decolonize Indians by imposing individual rights. Trudeau's 1969 White Paper represents a failed "Indian policy" approach to this goal; Trudeau's Charter of Rights and Freedoms is serving as an effective "Canadian policy" approach to achieve the same end.

Canada's rationale for choosing "individual rights" over "peoples' rights" as the pathway to Indian decolonization rests partly on the premise that the concept of "peoples' rights" deviates fundamentally from the Western-liberal principle underlying Canadian democracy that there must be no inequalities among citizens based on racial or ethic status. As already noted, the most influential Canadian advocate of this Western-liberal principle, Trudeau, viewed Indians as a disadvantaged racial minority, and he attributed this disadvantage to their special status, which he saw as engendering a racial psychology against Indians. It is worth noting here that, although the Metis do not have a special status, they are no less victims of racism. Clearly, the Canadian racism towards Indians is not explained by Indian special status. Rather, it is a consequence of how the Canadian government has chosen to define Indians (and Metis). Indians (and Metis) are victims of racial discrimination because, historically, the Canadian government has defined Indians (and Metis) in terms of racial, rather than cultural, criteria. If we take the experience of the Metis as an indication, removing special status from Indians and providing them with individual rights will not change the racial psychology of Canadians towards Indians.

Thus, one is forced to conclude that there is a much more weighty consideration than "Western-liberal principles" that underlies Canada's bias in favour of individual rights over peoples' rights as its design for decolonizing Indians. Aboriginal rights, treaty rights, self-determination, land claims, resource claims, reparation claims, and many other troublesome demands by Indians are made in the name of their historical special status. By imposing the Western-liberal principle of individual rights, that is, making Indians into "Canadians as all other Canadians," the governments of Canada can legally void most problematic Indian rights and claims because these rights and claims have no application to Indians as individuals. Clearly, the "national interest" rather than any idealistic commitment to Western-liberal principles is what drives all eleven governments in Canada to assert that decolonization must proceed with reference to the individualistic Charter of Rights and Freedoms, and not by Indian self-determination.

Consistent with this strategy, the Canadian government, in its public policy on Indian status, insists on defining Indians as a minority group, rather than as a "people." A particular example of this perspective can be noted in Canada's observance of the U.N. Convention on the Elimination of all Forms of Racial Discrimination (1969). This convention requires that appropriate measures be undertaken to secure the advancement of disadvantaged racial or ethnic groups. To the degree Canada has made gestures to fulfil its obligations to Indians under this convention, it has done so within the concept of *individual* rights, not "peoples' rights." The declared official Canadian policy is to liberate Indians from their underprivileged "minority group" condition through equality of *individual* opportunity.

To sum up, the imperative of the "national interest" is dictating Canadian policies designed to attenuate Indian special status even though Indians consider this to be contrary to their interests rights, needs, and aspirations. The government's design for achieving the end of Indian special status is through institutional assimilation, and its strategies are "structural integration," "constitutional normalization," and "individualization." Already the government has made great progress on all three fronts, and perhaps the process has already moved beyond the point of no return.

Pan-Indianism

Pan-Indian political mobilization in Canada occurred as a sidestream effect of colonial political, legal, and economic policies. By defining culturally diverse Indian tribes/bands as a single legal category and by imposing uniform colonial policies and structures on them (e.g., the Indian Act, the reserve system, and the DIAND), the Canadian government created a shared experience, circumstance, and condition for all Indians. Moreover, the residential school experience, to which most Indians were subjected, gave them a common language, which greatly facilitated the emergence of the pan-Indian movement. However, it took the 1969 White Paper on Indian Policy to precipitate the Indians' commonalities and discontent into a significant pan-Indian political movement. The "consultation process" mandated by Trudeau to legitimate the 1969 White Paper engendered a feeling of empowerment among Indian leaders, and the subsequent sense of betrayal the White Paper policy evoked among all Indian leaders served to raise their consciousness about their shared colonial experience, circumstance, and condition. The frequent meetings also made them aware of their cultural commonalities, which helped to draw them together in a spiritual cause. In effect, the 1969 White Paper brought to an end a century during which the Canadian government successfully fragmented Indians into hundreds of isolated communities. The post-1969 period saw a proliferation of pan-Indian organizations—provincial, regional, national, treaty, women, youth—all devoted to the purpose of representing and promoting their shared interests and goals, and building collective strength. The most prominent pan-Indian organization is the Assembly of First Nations, the national organization that represents status Indians in Canada.

However, while regressive Canadian Indian policies created shared interests and a common cause for Indians, they have not provided an effective glue for pan-Indian unity. Pan-Indian unity is tenuous and elusive. The reasons for this are several: there exists no historical cultural or social community at the pan-Indian level; there is no tradition of large-scale political and cultural cooperation among most Indian bands/tribes; there exist profoundly diverse, often conflicting, political and economic interests among band/tribes that cause factionalism. Moreover, pan-Indian leaders operate at a considerable social distance from the "grass roots" constituency they are supposed to represent. In the absence of a strong connection with their constituency, pan-Indian leaders have their primary affiliation with other Indian leaders. This has led to a pattern of decision making based on "leadership consensus" and the advice of professional consultants. This approach to decision making tends to neglect the immediate day-to-day needs and interests of "grass roots" Indians. In consequence pan-Indian leadership functions without a mass following.

In an effort to close the gap between themselves and the grass-roots constituency, pan-Indian leaders have made moves to restructure their organizations to give direct representation to band/tribal councils through their respective chiefs. The Assembly of First Nations comprises over six hundred chiefs. And, in an effort to generate wider appeal and commitment from their putative constituency, pan-Indian leaders have emphasized popular ideological issues of pan-Indian concern, such as sovereignty and aboriginal and treaty rights. Moreover, they have sought out high-profile international and national forums in which to confront and oppose the Canadian government on these ideological issues—at the United Nations, The Hague, the U.K. House of Lords, the First Ministers' Conferences, and so on. But the chiefs are not "grass roots" Indian people and, despite the popular ideological issues to which pan-Indian leaders give emphasis, the gap between themselves and the "grass roots" Indians has not been bridged.

The Canadian government's treatment of the pan-Indian movement is revealing. When the government believed that pan-Indian organizations could be used to control Indians and to give legitimacy to its Indian policies, it volunteered generous funding, and created "joint" committees made up of senior government officials and pan-Indian leaders, moves that were designed to co-opt pan-Indian leaders onto the "government team." However, as events unfolded and some pan-Indian leaders took strong public stands against its policies, the federal government expediently shifted its focus and funding away from pan-Indian organizations and processes to local band/tribal councils and initiatives. This created a divisive competition between band/tribal councils, and national Indian organizations, for political influence and government funding. The government's strategy caused pan-Indian leaders to lose control of their "troops," so to speak. And it significantly diminished their capacity to oppose federal and provincial government policies that are contrary to the Indian common interests.

Most recently, the Canadian government, now intent on forging a constitutional deal that will bring Quebec into the Canadian family and fearing that pan-Indian leaders might find a way to sabotage the process (as they did in the case of the Meech Lake Accord), has expediently sought a rapprochement with pan-Indian leaders. Government funds to pan-Indian organizations are flowing freely again; pan-Indian leaders have the ear of the prime minister and cabinet ministers again; Indian leaders are being co-opted onto high-level committees and commissions again; the government is offering pan-Indian leaders another fifteen minutes of fame and fortune.

In retrospect it can be seen that government policy towards the pan-Indian movement was never motivated to enhance the movement's capacity to advance Indian common interests, rights, needs, and aspirations. Consistently, the government's policy was designed to "use" the pan-Indian movement to advance the "national interest."

Endnotes

[1] H.B. Hawthorn, ed., *A Survey of Contemporary Indians of Canada*, 2 vols. (also known as "The Hawthorn Report" (Ottawa: Department of Indian Affairs, 1966–7).

[2] *Simon* v. *The Queen* [1985] 2 SCR, 387 23 ccc (3d) 238.

[3] Leon Mitchell, "Indian Treaty Land Entitlement in Manitoba," in *Governments in Conflict: Provinces and Indian Nations in Canada*, ed. J. Anthony Long and Menno Boldt (Toronto: University of Toronto Press, 1988), 134.

[4] *Sikyea* v. *The Queen* 2 SCR 387, 23 ccc (3d) 238; *The Queen* v. *George* 3 ccc 137; *Daniels* v. *White and The Queen* 1968 SCR 517.

[5] Sally M. Weaver, "The Joint Cabinet/National Indian Brotherhood Committee: A Unique Experience in Pressure Group Relations," *Canadian Public Administration* 252 (Summer 1982): 211–39.

[6] *Globe and Mail*, August 18, 1984.

[7] Sally M. Weaver, "Indian Policy in the New Conservative Government, Part 2: The Nielsen Task Force in the Context of Recent Policy Initiative," *Native Studies Review* 22 (1986): 32.

[8] The Honourable Bill McKnight, Minister of DIAND, "Notes for Remarks to the 11th Northern Development Conference," Edmonton, Alberta, October 26, 1988: 8.

[9] Ibid. 13.

[10] *Globe and Mail*, May 18, 1990.

[11] Assembly of First Nations, Press Release, 18 April 1985.

[12] Government of Canada, "Improved Program Delivery: Indians and Natives," Vol. 12. Ministerial Task Force on Program Review, The Honourable Erik Nielsen, Deputy Prime Minister, chair (Ottawa: Supply and Service Canada, 1985).

Challenging the Present – Looking to the Future

The *Delgamuukw* Decision and Oral History

Peter R. Grant and Neil J. Sterritt

Peter Grant, a senior partner in Hutchins, Soroka & Grant in Vancouver, was legal counsel for the Gitksan and Wet'suwet'en in the Delgamuukw case at trial before the British Columbia Supreme Court and before the British Columbia Court of Appeal; he was counsel for the Gitksan in the appeal of the Delgamuukw case to the Supreme Court of Canada.

Neil Sterritt was research director for the Gitksan in the 1970s, president of the Gitksan-Wet'suwet'en Tribal Council from 1981 to 1987, and an expert witness in the Delgamuukw case. He is the principal of Sterritt Consulting Ltd. in Hazelton, British Columbia, and offers advice and other services to First Nations. He learned the territories first hand and on the land from the hereditary chiefs, beginning as a child, and continues to learn and study them to this day. He is a member of the Gitksan Nation.

Introduction: Government Policy and the Gitksan and Wet'suwet'en Claim

In November 1977, the Gitksan and Wet'suwet'en Hereditary Chiefs presented their declaration of their Aboriginal title to about 58,000 square kilometres of territory in northwestern British Columbia to the Minister of Indian and Northern Affairs, the Honourable Hugh Faulkner, at Kispiox, British Columbia, amidst tremendous celebration. For the Gitksan and the Wet'suwet'en this was viewed as Crown recognition of Aboriginal title and the negotiation of a fair treaty. Six years later, the same Gitksan and Wet'suwet'en Hereditary Chiefs made a firm decision to take the issue of their Aboriginal title to their territory to the courts for recognition. This decision began the process that culminated in the Supreme Court of Canada in 1997 when that Court handed down a judgment known as the *Delgamuukw* decision. It addressed a number of important issues, one of which we will examine in detail later in this paper: the treatment of oral history in court. But what led the Gitskan and Wet'suwet'en to pursue their Aboriginal land title through the courts?

In order to understand the reasons why the Gitksan and Wet'suwet'en Chiefs decided to go to court in 1984, it is necessary to consider the evolution of Canada's policies with respect to recognition of Aboriginal title.

In 1969, eight years before Canada accepted the Gitksan and Wet'suwet'en claim for treaty negotiations, the current Prime Minister, the Honourable Jean Chrétien, who was then the Minister of Indian Affairs produced a White Paper announcing that, although Aboriginal peoples claimed Aboriginal title, those claims were too vague to be accepted.

Prime Minister Pierre Trudeau explained on August 8, 1969, in Vancouver, British Columbia, that the White Paper was his government's response to demands by Aboriginal peoples:

> ...aboriginal rights, this really means saying, "We were here before you. You came and you took the land from us and perhaps you cheated us by giving us some worthless things in return for vast expanses of land and we want to re-open this question. We want you to preserve our aboriginal rights and to restore them to us." And our answer-it may not be the right one and may not be one which is accepted but it will be up to all of you people to make your minds up and to choose for or against it and to discuss with the Indians-our answer is "no."[1]

In 1973, the Supreme Court of Canada rendered a split decision in the appeal of *Calder* v. *Attorney-General of British Columbia* as to whether the Nisga'a held Aboriginal title to their territory. In the case under appeal, British Columbia argued that Aboriginal title had been extinguished because the pre-Confederation (1871) colony of British Columbia had passed 13 Land Ordinances in the 1850s and early 1860s allowing white settlers to acquire lands in the Colony. These pre-Confederation Ordinances made no mention of Aboriginal title or stated any intention to extinguish Aboriginal title. In fact, they reflected the subsequent position of British Columbia for 100 years (until *Calder*) that there was never Aboriginal title in British Columbia.[2]

Six of seven Supreme Court judges in *Calder* found that the Nisga'a had Aboriginal title. Having said this, three of those judges then found that the Aboriginal title had been extinguished, by the pre-Confederation Land Ordinances, and three found that it had not been extinguished.

As a result of the Supreme Court of Canada majority decision in *Calder* that the Nisga'a had Aboriginal title to their territory, the Government of Canada reversed the position espoused by Trudeau in 1969 and implemented a policy of negotiating treaties with those Aboriginal peoples who had not yet entered into treaty. This was referred to as the "Comprehensive Claims" policy. The subsequent 1977 celebration in Kispiox was the presentation by Gitksan and Wet'suwet'en of their Aboriginal title for the purpose of these treaty negotiations.

However, the comprehensive claims policy was extremely limited. First, Canada would negotiate only six comprehensive treaties in Canada at one time. Therefore, the Gitksan and the Wet'suwet'en, along with many other Aboriginal groups in British Columbia, were far down the list. Second, the federal government would negotiate only one claim in British Columbia, and they were in the process of negotiating the Nisga'a claim. The most serious impediment, however, was that the Government of British Columbia, which was recognized by Canada as having control over the lands and resources at stake, refused to participate in these treaty negotiations because it continued to maintain that there was no Aboriginal title in British Columbia and, therefore, there was nothing to negotiate.

In short, nothing happened to advance the Gitksan and Wet'suwet'en treaty negotiation between 1977 and 1984 because the governments refused to enter into negotiations. British Columbia maintained the position that its argument in *Calder* had been successful and that Aboriginal title in British Columbia had been extinguished, even though there was a split decision in the Supreme Court of Canada.

The Gitksan and the Wet'suwet'en continued to research in preparation for treaty negotiations. This included collecting oral histories and researching historical records to support their claim to the title to their territory. Unfortunately, no matter how much research and preparation the Gitksan and the Wet'suwet'en conducted, they were unable to get to the negotiating table with either government.

Many Gitksan chiefs and elders expressed increasing concern with the refusal of the Crown to negotiate. As a result, there were a series of meetings in the fall of 1983 and the early spring of 1984, leading to the decision to proceed with a court action to establish once and for all that the Gitksan and the Wet'suwet'en held Aboriginal title to their territory. The Gitksan and the Wet'suwet'en developed their own claim and, as far as they were concerned, their Aboriginal title was nothing short of a right of ownership and jurisdiction over their territories. On October 22, 1984, the two leading Chiefs in the court action, the Gitksan Chief Delgamuukw (the late Albert Tait) and the Wet'suwet'en Chief Gisday Wa (Alfred Joseph) filed B.C. Supreme Court Action No. 842 in the courthouse at Smithers, British Columbia. This was the commencement of the most extensive Aboriginal title lawsuit in the history of Canada, and one of the most extensive Aboriginal title lawsuits throughout the Commonwealth.[3]

The Gitksan and the Wet'suwet'en decided to maintain control of the case throughout. As a result, they wanted the trial judge to hear evidence from several Gitksan and Wet'suwet'en chiefs with respect to their territories. The Gitksan and the Wet'suwet'en have an internal system of governance under which they have different House groups. Each House holds one or more territories. Within each House there is a head chief and a number of wing chiefs, as well as the members of the House. The lawsuit was brought by the head chief of each House acting on behalf of one or more Houses: there were 69 House chiefs who were individual plaintiffs. They represented their own House and, in some cases, closely related Houses. This was an extremely different process from *Calder*, in which the case was brought forward by the Nisga'a Tribal Council and not directly by the hereditary chiefs.

Preparation for Trial and the Courts' Decisions

The *Delgamuukw* case was complex from the beginning. The Province of British Columbia hired Russell and DuMoulin, one of the largest law firms in Vancouver to act in its defence. This is the law firm that the presiding judge in the Delgamuukw case, Honourable Allan McEachern, belonged to prior to his appointment as Chief Justice of the British Columbia Supreme Court in 1979. British Columbia also applied to have Canada joined as a defendant. The Gitksan and the Wet'suwet'en decided to proceed only against the province because the province stated it had control over the lands and resources, and it was also the party that refused to enter into treaty negotiations. The case began in the British Columbia Supreme Court and there were six interim appeals to the British Columbia Court of Appeal involving complex points of law and procedure.[4] There were extensive oral discoveries and commission evidence of several elders whose health was so fragile that it would have been risky to have them wait for trial in order to testify in court.[5]

After three years of preparations, the case commenced on May 11,

1987, in Smithers, British Columbia. The two chiefs, Gisday Wa and Delgamuukw, spoke at the opening. Delgamuukw stated:

> My name is Delgam Uukw. I am a Gitksan Chief and a plaintiff in this case. My House owns territories in the Upper Kispiox Valley and the Upper Nass Valley. Each Gitksan plaintiff's House owns similar territories. Together the Gitksan and Wet'suwet'en Chiefs own and govern the 22,000 square miles of Gitksan and Wet'suwet'en territory.
>
> For us the ownership of territory is a marriage of the chief and the land. Each chief has an ancestor who encountered and acknowledged the life of the land. From such encounters came power. The land, the plants, the animals and the people all have spirit-they all must be shown respect. This is the basis of our law.[6]

With these opening comments and a detailed opening statement that took an entire day, the Gitksan and the Wet'suwet'en Aboriginal title lawsuit commenced. The trial took over three years. Although the trial judge, Justice McEachern, was appointed Chief Justice of the British Columbia Court of Appeal during this time, he continued to sit as the trial judge until the trial was completed. There were over 367 trial days. As well, there were over 50 witnesses who testified out of court and whose evidence was relied upon in the case. A critical distinction between *Delgamuukw* and other cases was that *Delgamuukw* was founded first and foremost on the evidence of the Gitksan and the Wet'suwet'en people themselves. The case concluded on June 30, 1990. The judge reserved until March 8, 1991, and on that day he reviewed the main categories of evidence and pronounced his judgment.

The trial judgment is over 400 pages long. Justice McEachern found that the Aboriginal title was extinguished on the basis of the British Columbia Colonial Land Ordinances relied upon by the Province. He found that if there were any Aboriginal rights or Aboriginal title, they were limited to a declaration that the Gitksan and the Wet'suwet'en "have a continuing legal right to use unoccupied or vacant Crown land in the territory for Aboriginal sustenance purposes, subject to the general law of the Province."[7]

However, the plaintiffs' appealed Justice McEachern's judgment to the British Columbia Court of Appeal. At this point a significant change occurred: while the parties were waiting for the trial court decision, the provincial government, as a result of the uncertainty with respect to Aboriginal title lands throughout the province, agreed to set up a task force to make recommendations for a treaty negotiation process.

The British Columbia Task Force provided a series of recommendations and, just prior to the *Delgamuukw* decision in the British Columbia Supreme Court, in March 1991, the British Columbia government agreed to participate in treaty negotiations. Soon after this decision a New Democratic Party government was elected in British Columbia. This government changed legal counsel and the Provinces' position in Court. They agreed that Aboriginal title had not been extinguished. The Court of Appeal appointed the previous law firm of Russell and DuMoulin, as *amicus curiae* to argue extinguishment. The Provinces' new position, however, sought to limit Aboriginal rights, so that most rights were extinguished by post-confederation legislation.

Between May 4 and July 3, 1992, the British Columbia Court of Appeal sat for 39 days and heard arguments on the appeal. Judgment was rendered almost one year later on June 25, 1993. Five judges of British Columbia Court of Appeal unanimously overturned the trial judge's decision that Gitksan and Wet'suwet'en Aboriginal title had been extinguished by the Colonial Land Ordinances. However, they split three to two as to what the Aboriginal rights were. The majority judgment by Justice MacFarlane (which two other judges agreed with) held:

> All of the plaintiffs' aboriginal rights were not extinguished before 1871.
>
> The plaintiffs, being Gitksan and Wet'suwet'en persons, have unextinguished non-exclusive aboriginal rights, other than a right of ownership or a property right, in an area of the approximate size shown on Map 5, a copy of which is attached. Such rights are of a *sui generis* nature. The exact territorial limits within which such rights may be exercised, if not agreed to by the parties, shall be those designated by the trial judge in reference to Map 5. The scope, content and consequences of such non-exclusive aboriginal rights of use and occupation, including the effect of s.35 of the *Constitution Act, 1982* on grants or renewals of grants, licences, leases or permits respecting any resources within the area shown on Map 5, are left to be determined in trial proceedings properly framed to deal with such issues.[8]

The Gitksan and Wet'suwet'en appealed to the Supreme Court of Canada. The provincial Crown cross-appealed with respect to the Court of Appeal's ruling that the province had no power to extinguish Aboriginal title after British Columbia joined Confederation in 1871.

At this time, Canada and British Columbia encouraged the Gitksan and the Wet'suwet'en to enter into treaty negotiations, and in June

1994 they agreed to put the appeal in abeyance and to give the treaty negotiation process a chance. But in 1996 the provincial government walked away from the negotiations because the Gitksan maintained that their Aboriginal title included rights to all the resources and, as a result, the appeal to the Supreme Court of Canada was revived. The appeal was argued in June 1997 and the Supreme Court of Canada's decision was rendered December 11, 1997.

The Supreme Court of Canada decided that the case had to be sent back for a new trial because the right of Aboriginal title was a collective right and not based on House groups of an individual nation. However, the court also held that Aboriginal title was an exclusive right and made a series of findings with respect to the importance of Aboriginal title and the obligations of the Crown when dealing with Aboriginal title. For example, the Supreme Court of Canada swept away the minimalist interpretation of Aboriginal rights in Canada as consisting of nothing more than traditional hunting, fishing, and gathering on a "non-exclusive basis": the Supreme Court of Canada held that Aboriginal title is a property interest that has "economic value" and any infringement of the right must be compensated. It rejected the concept of Aboriginal title as a minor "usufructary" right, that is, a right to use the resources with no title to the land.

The Supreme Court of Canada has made it clear that Aboriginal title is "exclusive" and the Aboriginal people who hold title have rights to the resources. The Court also established the scope of Aboriginal title and how to prove Aboriginal title. Furthermore, the court found that at the very minimum, the Crown has a duty to consult with the Aboriginal people who hold Aboriginal title before it interferes with Aboriginal title lands by taking or selling the resources. The involvement of First Nations in access to resources has become a serious issue, both in British Columbia and on lands in other provinces that are not subject to treaty. If anything, the *Delgamuukw* decision in the Supreme Court of Canada has motivated both the Governments of Canada and of British Columbia to intensify their efforts at negotiating treaties with First Nations in British Columbia. This, ultimately, was the goal of the Gitksan and the Wet'suwet'en.

The *Delgamuukw* decision has been referred to as one of the most important decisions in Canadian history.[9] This paper concentrates on only one aspect of the Supreme Court of Canada's judgment: the impact of the *Delgamuukw* decision on the treatment of oral history in court.

The Supreme Court of Canada Decision in *Delgamuukw:* Recognition of Oral History as Valid Evidence

What is revolutionary about the *Delgamuukw* decision for British Columbia is that the provincial government was clearly told by the highest court in the land that it is time to address the longstanding issue of Aboriginal title and to stop denying that Aboriginal title exists in British Columbia. The decision also makes Aboriginal title easier for First Nations to prove than was previously assumed. The Supreme Court of Canada also clearly stated that the rules of evidence must be interpreted so as to allow Aboriginal history to be given the same weight as Euro-Canadian history.

The Supreme Court of Canada's determination that Aboriginal title has not been extinguished is a reason for the federal and provincial governments to negotiate in good faith to arrive at modern-day treaties with First Nations. But if and when Aboriginal people are forced to go to the courts to defend their Aboriginal rights or to prove their title, they will be able to rely on the Supreme Court of Canada's ruling that oral history passed down from generation to generation is relevant and compelling evidence.

Oral History Is as Valid as Written History

The Gitksan and the Wet'suwet'en made a significant decision early in the development of the *Delgamuukw* case. They took a risk and for the first time entered the court to give their own information in their own voices, so that their histories could be heard by the court and used as a basis for the recognition of their rights. In 1997, the Supreme Court of Canada rejected a narrow approach to evidentiary rules, which would preclude Aboriginal people from demonstrating the importance of their territory to the court through their oral histories.

The Supreme Court of Canada held that the trial judge was wrong when he accepted oral evidence but attached no weight to it. Chief Justice Lamer's directive on this issue could not be clearer:

> Notwithstanding the challenges created by the use of oral histories as proof of historical facts, *the laws of evidence must be adapted in order that this type of evidence can be accommodated and placed on an equal footing with the types of historical evidence that courts are familiar with,* which largely consists of historical documents (emphasis added).[10]

The Supreme Court of Canada overturned the trial judge's findings of fact, which the British Columbia Court of Appeal had declined to do. This part of the Supreme Court of Canada decision is noteworthy because, ordinarily, appeal courts consider only whether the trial judge made an error with respect to the law and its interpretation. Appeal courts ordinarily accept a trial judge's determinations of fact based on the evidence heard at trial, unless there is a "palpable and overriding error" in the assessment of the facts.

Since the *Delgamuukw* decision is the leading authority on the reliance on oral history in Aboriginal rights cases, it is worth considering the principles by which the evidence was assessed by the trial judge and which the Supreme Court of Canada rejected.[11]

The Gitksan and Wet'suwet'en Evidence: The Peoples and Their Claim

The Gitksan and the Wet'suwet'en live in the Nass, Skeena, Babine, and Bulkley River watersheds in northwestern British Columbia. They are two separate peoples with very different languages but their territories adjoin one another; at one place, Hagwilget, which is near New Hazelton, they live together.

The Gitksan and the Wet'suwet'en peoples are divided into four and five clans respectively. Each clan is divided into House groups made up of people who share maternal ancestors. The House groups are the owners of specific areas of land under traditional law.

The Gitksan and Wet'suwet'en Hereditary Chiefs, both individually and on behalf of their houses, claimed the territories of 51 houses, amounting to about 58,000 square kilometres. They asked the court to declare that they had both ownership of and jurisdiction over these lands.

The evidence at trial showed that the Gitksan and the Wet'suwet'en had their first contact with Europeans no earlier than 1820, when fur traders arrived in their territory. Great Britain did not properly establish its claim to sovereignty over British Columbia any earlier than 1846, when it entered into the Oregon Boundary Treaty with the United States. Since that time, no treaty had been entered into by Britain or Canada with the Gitksan and the Wet'suwet'en because the government of British Columbia steadfastly refused to acknowledge that any Aboriginal rights existed in the province, except for a brief period in the 1850s when Governor James Douglas entered into treaties with certain tribes on Vancouver Island.[12]

The Evidence at Trial

The Gitksan and Wet'suwet'en Hereditary Chiefs told the trial judge in their opening statement that "The challenge for this Court is to hear this evidence, in all its complexity, in all its elaboration, as the articulation of a way of looking at the world which pre-dates the Canadian constitution by many thousands of years."[13]

Both the Gitksan and the Wet'suwet'en have a system of oral histories. These oral histories include Gitksan *adaawk* and Wet'suwet'en *kungax*,[14] which are recounted within their respective House groups and the histories and stories they contain are described in major feasts such as those held after a pole-raising. The first part of the Supreme Court of Canada's ruling on oral histories in *Delgamuukw* addressed the adaawk and kungax.

Delgamuukw, then also known as Ken Muldoe, the second of three chiefs to carry that name during the case, is the Gitksan chief whose House owns territories in the Upper Kispiox and Upper Nass Valley. The Gitksan chief explained his traditional power to the court in their opening statement on March 11, 1987, in the following way:

> My power is carried in my House's histories, songs, dances and crests. It is recreated at the Feast when the histories are told, the songs and dances performed, and the crests displayed. With the wealth that comes from respectful use of the territory, the House feeds the name of the Chief in the Feast Hall. In this way, the law, the Chief, the territory, and the Feast become one. The unity of the Chief's authority and his House's ownership of its territory are witnessed and thus affirmed by the other Chiefs at the Feasts.
>
> By following the law, the power flows from the land to the people through the Chief; by using the wealth of the territory, the House feasts its Chief so he can properly fulfil the law. This cycle has been repeated on my land for thousands of years. The histories of my House are always being added to. My presence in this courtroom today will add to my House's power, as it adds to the power of the other Gitksan and Wet'suwet'en Chiefs who will appear here or who will witness the proceedings. All of our roles, including yours, will be remembered in the histories that will be told by my grandchildren. Through the witnessing of all the histories, century after century, we have exercised our jurisdiction.[15]

For the Gitksan, the adaawk describe the ancient migrations of a House, its acquisitions and defence of its territory and major events in the life of the House. The adaawk also describe its spirit power. Thus, the adaawk are based on real events and represent Gitksan oral history, even though supernatural elements may be included in the narrative.

Between 1973 and the trial in 1987, with the help of the elders the entire Gitksan territory had been mapped, from near the head of the Skeena River through two-thirds of the Nass River watershed. The elders have been able to tell where the events in the adaawk occurred, connecting historic events with geographic features and telling the Gitksan place names.

The *Delgamuukw* case was founded on the integrity of Gitksan and Wet'suwet'en history and culture, especially the feast system, with its oral history and the place names that are similar to the two cultures. Archaeology, anthropology, geology, and other disciplines were used to uphold what the Gitksan and Wet'suwet'en had to say.

The trial judge had heard evidence by some three dozen Gitksan and Wet'suwet'en in court, and fifteen Gitksan and Wet'suwet'en elders testified by way of commission evidence out of court. Almost all of these elders have now died. In addition, 53 affidavits were filed in which Gitksan and Wet'suwet'en witnesses described the intricate details of the territories that had been passed on to them by their grandparents. As the late Gwisgyen (Stanley Williams) stated, he could not talk about a territory unless he walked that territory. He described 26 territories that his elders had taken him to in the 1920s and 1930s.

The Gitksan and Wet'suwet'en plaintiffs in this case not only brought forward extensive evidence of the oral histories that had been documented as early as 1915 and were testified to by Chiefs at trial in 1987–1989, they also did independent scientific testing of a major landslide in the location in which an oral history described a supernatural event. That event was dated at over 3,500 years ago. This is the first time oral histories had actually been dated by independent scientific evidence.

The adaawk that referred to this event was recorded in 1936. This oral history described detailed reference to laws, ranked chiefs, crests and totems, medicines, technology for harvesting and processing resources and manufacturing tools and weapons, elaborate dances, costumes and festivals, and trade with the coast, and is in a temporal sequence after the narration of the Mountain Goat adaawk in which feasting is described.

Witnesses who testified during the trial also the adaawk and described in detail locations where the adaawk took place. For example, Chief, Tenimgyat (Art Matthews, Jr.) described an adaawk that occurred hundreds of years before contact throughout which there is a detailed description of his House territory where the grizzly bears were being hunted. Precise evidence showed where this territory is located in the far west of Gitksan territory, northwest of Terrace, which borders on the territories of the Tsimshian and the Nisga'a.

Finally, the Gitksan also had the benefit of an extensive record of oral histories that had been collected between 1915 and 1955 by the famous ethnologist Marius Barbeau and by a Tsimshian named William Beynon. These oral histories included statements by chiefs and elders of the ancient histories of the Gitksan going back 10,000 years with the ending of the last ice age.

The same oral histories collected by Barbeau and Beynon had been relied on by the Nisga'a in the *Calder* case. The late Wilson Duff, an anthropologist who taught at the University of British Columbia and who had spent a year studying the Barbeau-Beynon records, gave expert evidence in the *Calder* case on Nisga'a possession of the Lower Nass Valley. In his testimony in that case, Duff described the oral histories collected by Barbeau and Beynon as a "great, abundant body of unpublished anthropological and historical material" consisting of "hundreds and hundreds of pages of anthropological information and family traditions and narratives having to do with the Nishga and the Gitksan people," which had "provided me with the detailed information upon which I make these statements."[16]

The trial judge in the *Delgamuukw* case conceded: "The evidence is intensely detailed, which is why, in part, this judgment is so inordinately long."[17] The problem was not in the length of the judgment but the way in which Justice McEachern evaluated this evidence.

The Trial Judge's Rulings on Evidentiary Issues: The Reliability of Oral History

First, it should be noted that Justice McEachern, the trial judge, indicated the following as one of his first findings of fact, apparently based on records from early European contact: "The evidence suggests that the Indians of the territory were, by historical standards, a primitive people without any form of writing, horses, or wheeled wagons."[18] The trial judge then proceeded to reject the oral histories of the Gitksan and Wet'suwet'en in spite of their large number and their length and detail. He ruled that he could not attach any independent weight to them for the following reasons:

Except in a very few cases, the totality of the evidence raises serious doubts about the reliability of the adaawk and kungax as evidence of detailed history, or land ownership, use or occupation.

First, I am far from satisfied that there is any consistent practice among the Gitksan and Wet'suwet'en Houses about these matters. The early witnesses suggested that the adaawk are well formulated and the contents constantly sifted and verified. I am not persuaded that this is so. There is evidence that an adaawk is seldom told at feasts; that some chiefs never tell their adaawk; that some chiefs never tell them outside their Houses; that there is little likelihood of dissent; and that the verifying group is so small that they cannot safely be regarded as expressing the reputation of even the Indian community, let alone the larger [non-Indian] community whose opportunity to dispute territorial claims would be essential to weigh.

Secondly, the adaawk are seriously lacking in detail about the specific lands to which they are said to relate....

[Thirdly,] [t]hese adaawk are sprinkled with historical references making them suspect as trustworthy evidence of pre-contact history. They refer to such matters as guns, moose, the Hudson's Bay Company and other historic items.[19]

In the end, the trial judge decided: "I am unable to accept adaawk, kungax, and oral histories as reliable bases for detailed history, but they could confirm findings based on other admissible evidence."[20]

The Gitksan and Wet'suwet'en pointed out to the British Columbia Court of Appeal that despite these comments, the trial judge was willing to conclude that in pre-contact times "slavery and starvation was not uncommon, wars with neighbouring peoples were common."[21] Oral histories provided the only possible source of such information. How could it have been that oral histories were both ancient and accurate when they refer to Indian slavery, starvation, and war, but suddenly became recent and untrustworthy when they refer to Indian territories and political authority?

With respect to the independent scientific testing that indicated a major landslide over 3,500 years ago at Seeley Lake and where a Gitksan adaawk described a supernatural event, the plaintiffs argued that this link by date and description corroborated Gitksan presence within the heart of their territory for millennia. Furthermore, they argued that the adaawk demonstrated elaborate institutions and highly developed technology for harvesting and processing resources. While the trial judge did not reject this evidence, he decided it was not necessary to rely on it either.[22] The result was to ignore the value of the scientific evidence as independent confirmation of the accuracy of the oral histories in their description of major historical events and of the antiquity of the Gitksan presence in their territories as an organized society. The trial judge's rejection of the oral histories effectively made the Gitksan and Wet'suwet'en peoples without history before the first European records in the 1820s.

The Gitksan and Wet'suwet'en oral histories are unusual in that there are great numbers of them and they are very detailed. They have been accepted as reliable and used by anthropologists and archaeologists. However, Justice McEachern rejected this evidence and did so by applying a test of his own devising.

The "Long, Long Time" Test

The trial judge invented a new test for proving the existence of Aboriginal rights, namely, that they had to be proven to have been exercised for a "long, long time" prior to the assertion of sovereignty by the British.[23]

But as the Gitksan and Wet'suwet'en argued in the British Columbia Court of Appeal, there are no living witnesses to the time long before sovereignty and there were obviously no Europeans present to make written records.

The trial judge rejected all anthropological evidence as unnecessary,[24] and he suggested that archaeological evidence was unhelpful because any Aboriginal people could have created the remains.[25] He concluded that the post-contact historical records from which pre-contact "minimal levels of social organization" could be inferred were "equivocal" when it came to proving land ownership.[26]

If the Supreme Court of Canada had not overruled the trial judge's decision that these oral histories were entitled to little or no weight, it is doubtful that any Aboriginal people in Canada could have relied on their oral history to establish the existence and character of their pre-contact societies.

The Application of the Reputation Evidence Rule

The trial judge in *Delgamuukw* accepted arguments by the Crown that a rule of English common law about "reputation evidence" used to prove English land title was the type of evidence required for the Gitksan and Wet'suwet'en to prove their Aboriginal title.

In law, the hearsay rule provides that the only statements admissible as evidence are those made by a witness called to testify at trial; statements made by those who are not present but which are merely repeated by a witness are to be excluded as hearsay.[27] If there were no exceptions ever made to this rule, it would obviously be difficult to introduce evidence about historical facts not recorded on paper.

However, one of the exceptions to the hearsay rule is that the court may hear declarations made by individuals relating to the reputation of rights or interests that affect the community as a whole. A traditional example would be the land boundaries of a town.[28] That is, the location of a town boundary can have a reputation and in a dispute involving them, evidence regarding the boundary-based on what has been known for a long time (i.e., the reputation) can be used to prove the boundary. Based on the reputation evidence exception, the trial judge decided to admit into evidence the Gitksan and Wet'suwet'en oral history.[29]

The province countered the reputation evidence with an argument that could be referred to as the "Shelford Defence" in honour of Cyril Shelford, a former Social Credit cabinet minister in the British Columbia government. Mr. Shelford, who was raised on the shores of Ootsa Lake south of Burns Lake, testified at the trial that when he was growing up he had Aboriginal friends; they did not tell him Indian names for the lakes and mountains and they did not tell him Indian oral histories. The apparent point of this evidence was to show that the Gitksan and Wet'suwet'en did not tell to the world their oral histories and, therefore, the "reputation" of that evidence was so limited as not to have any weight. In fact, a number of Gitksan and Wet'suwet'en witnesses carefully explained that their oral histories or adaawk could be told only in the feast hall. The trial judge relied on the limited exposure and the sacred significance of the oral histories as grounds to deny them any independent weight or value.[30]

The trial judge also questioned the usefulness of these special oral histories because "the verifying group is so small that they cannot safely be regarded as expressing the reputation of even the Indian community."[31] As for the territorial affidavits (written statements confirmed by oath), the trial judge recognized that they were "the best evidence the appellants could adduce on the question of internal boundaries."[32] Yet he still rejected this evidence as also not complying with the reputation exception to the hearsay rule.

The provincial and federal governments had adopted a "divide and conquer" defence on this point. They obtained statements from neighbouring First Nations that their claims conflicted with those of the Gitksan and Wet'suwet'en. The federal government also disclosed extracts of their land claims files to show overlapping land claims by other Aboriginal groups.

This evidence, *without a single witness from a neighbouring Aboriginal nation*, was then relied upon to argue that the Gitksan and Wet'suwet'en had not demonstrated a broad enough "reputation" to establish the external boundaries of their territory. Notwithstanding the speculative nature of this argument with no proper evidentiary basis, the argument was accepted by the trial judge.[33]

An additional attack on the Gitksan and Wet'suwet'en reputation evidence argued that it was not admissible under the exception to the hearsay rule because the reputation evidence was developed during the heat of litigation, which might have tainted its accuracy.[34] At trial, the provincial government's lawyers cross-examined several of the Gitksan and Wet'suwet'en witnesses about their knowledge of the decision to make the land claim in 1977 and the decision to go to court in 1984. They argued that the evidence of territorial boundaries was developed after the plaintiffs knew that they were involved in this lawsuit. The trial judge accepted this objection to the evidence.[35]

Fortunately for the Aboriginal peoples of Canada, the Supreme Court of Canada also rejected this argument. In fact, Canada's highest court laid the responsibility for the failure to address the issue of Aboriginal title squarely with British Columbia:

> Casting doubt on the reliability of the territorial affidavits because land claims have been actively discussed for many years also fails to take account of the special context surrounding aboriginal claims, in two ways. *First, those claims have been discussed for so long because of British Columbia's persistent refusal to acknowledge the existence of aboriginal title in that province until relatively recently,* largely as a direct result of the decision of this Court in *Calder, supra.* It would be perverse, to say the least, to use the refusal of the province to acknowledge the rights of its aboriginal inhabitants as a reason for excluding evidence which may prove the existence of those rights (emphasis added).[36]

The Supreme Court of Canada's Instructions: The Use of Oral History

The Courts have traditionally not allowed evidence that did not fit one of the hearsay exceptions. However, on the issue of Aboriginal oral history as evidence, the first principle laid down by the Supreme Court of Canada is that a trial court must "appreciate the evidentiary difficulties inherent in adjudicating aboriginal claims, when, first applying the rules of evidence and, second, interpreting the evidence before it."[37] The Supreme Court of Canada mandated this "unique approach" because it held that the Canadian legal system must accommodate the Aboriginal perspective in order for there to be fair adjudication of claims to Aboriginal rights and title.[38] Aboriginal peoples' oral histories must be "placed on an equal footing" with other historical documents.[39]

The Supreme Court of Canada explained why the trial judge was wrong to give oral history no independent weight and to hold that it could only be useful insofar as it confirmed other evidence found in historical documents prepared by Euro-Canadians. Chief Justice Antonio Lamer wrote:

> I fear that if this [the trial judge's] reasoning were followed, the oral histories of aboriginal peoples would be *consistently and systematically undervalued by the Canadian legal system...* (emphasis added).[40]

It is not only Justice McEachern's approach to oral history that has "consistently and systematically undervalued" the traditions of Aboriginal peoples. This comment also certainly applies to the treatment of Aboriginal land rights by the governments of British Columbia since the end of the 1860s. The Supreme Court of Canada has clearly and unequivocally directed that the Crown respect both the oral histories of Aboriginal peoples and their underlying land rights.

The oral histories of the Gitksan and Wet'suwet'en that were accepted by the Supreme Court of Canada were not limited to ancient histories, such as the Gitksan adaawk and the Wet'suwet'en kungax. The Supreme Court of Canada also ruled that the evidence of the individual territorial holdings was extremely relevant to the collective claims of the Gitksan and the Wet'suwet'en.

Even for Aboriginal peoples who do not have a similar formalized oral history, the principles set out by the Supreme Court of Canada under the heading "Recollections of Aboriginal Life" recognizes the importance of testimony by living witnesses regarding their ancestors' use of the territory. Justice McEachern had held that this testimony could only prove, at best, use of the land by their ancestors "for the past 100 years or so." He ruled that the evidence was not precise enough with respect to land use by more distant ancestors "far enough back in time to permit the plaintiffs to succeed on issues such as internal boundaries."[41]

Chief Justice Lamer held that the trial judge had been wrong to attach so little value to these recollections:

> In my opinion, the trial judge expected too much of the oral history of the appellants, as expressed in the recollections of aboriginal life of members of the appellant nations. He expected that evidence to provide definitive and precise evidence of pre-contact aboriginal activities on the territory in question. However... this will be an almost impossible burden to meet. Rather, *if oral history cannot conclusively establish pre-sovereignty... occupation of land, it may still be relevant to demonstrate that current occupation has its origins prior to sovereignty* (emphasis added).[42]

In other words, Canadian courts must be prepared to assume that the earliest Aboriginal land use recorded by living memory resembles their land use in the period before that time.

This is a critical finding for those Aboriginal nations in eastern Canada where the assertion of sovereignty may have been much earlier than 1846. The evidence of live witnesses regarding "current occupation" may establish the origin of that occupation pre-sovereignty. This can be done through the use of the historical record established after contact in combination with the Aboriginal oral historical record. This is also critical for the interpretation of treaties as the Aboriginal oral history can demonstrate the Aboriginal understanding of what the historical treaties meant.

Finally, the Supreme Court of Canada overturned the trial judge's ruling on the territorial affidavits filed as evidence of the boundaries for the lands the Gitksan and Wet'suwet'en used and owned. As described above, the trial judge refused to admit the affidavits as reputation evidence because their contents were known only to the Gitksan and Wet'suwet'en communities and because they had been prepared at a time when land claims were already the subject of active discussion.

The Supreme Court of Canada emphasized that the trial judge failed to adapt the rules of evidence to the "difficulties inherent in adjudicating aboriginal claims."[43] First, it held that Aboriginal land claims have a "reputation" even if Euro-Canadians have not heard of it:

> The requirement that a reputation be known in the general community, for example, ignores the fact that oral histories, as noted by the Royal Commission on Aboriginal Peoples, generally relate to particular locations, and refer to particular families and communities and may, as a result, be unknown outside of that community, even to other aboriginal nations.

Second, the Supreme Court of Canada held that evidence cannot be excluded just because it is part of a contested Aboriginal land claim:

> Excluding the territorial affidavits because the claims to which they relate are disputed does not acknowledge that claims to *aboriginal rights, and aboriginal title in particular, are almost always disputed and contested.* Indeed, if those claims were uncontroversial, there would be no need to bring them to the courts for resolution (emphasis added).[44]

The Supreme Court of Canada pointed out that a community's oral history remains admissible even if it is widely discussed and close to the date of a trial, because "it must remain alive through the discussions of members of that community."[45]

The Test for Proving Aboriginal Title

The *Delgamuukw* decision is also important because it contains the Supreme Court of Canada's test for proving Aboriginal title. Only a brief summary is possible here but, as we have seen, the Aboriginal people's oral history will be a crucial part of proving its claim.

In order to establish a claim to Aboriginal title, an Aboriginal people asserting the claim must establish that it occupied the lands in question at the time at which the Crown asserted sovereignty over the same land, a date which will usually be later than first contact with Europeans. Occupancy by the Aboriginal people will be proved by physical occupation, such as the construction of dwellings, the cultivation of fields, or the regular use of land for hunting or fishing. In measuring the extent to which land was occupied, the courts will have to consider both the people, with respect to its size, lifestyle, and material and technological resources, and the character of the land itself. In addition, the Supreme Court of Canada held that, "if, at the time of sovereignty, an aboriginal society had laws in relation to land, those laws would be relevant to establishing the occupation."[46]

Since it will often be difficult to provide definitive proof of occupation before contact with Euro-Canadians and their record-keeping, Aboriginal people will be allowed to provide evidence of their occupation in the present as proof of their occupation before sovereignty, so long as some indication exists of continuity with occupation before sovereignty. In addition, the fact that the use of land had changed since contact will not defeat a claim to Aboriginal title, "as long as a substantial connection between the people and the land is maintained."[47]

Conclusion

Dora Wilson, whose Gitksan name is Yagalahl, was one of two individuals appointed to monitor the *Delgamuukw* case at trial on behalf of the hereditary chiefs. A month after the trial judge handed down his decision in 1991, she said:

> To me it was a sad day when I heard that decision. And yet in a way I was happy because in a way it was a victory. A victory in a way that yes, our oral history was slammed around as we were witnesses on the witness stand, but we have it written in black and white now for anyone to see in those transcripts, in those 374 volumes of transcripts. In all of the commissioned evidence, all of those affidavits-it's there written, and that is something that the Gitksan and Wet'suwet'en people have done to further this fight for recognition. And I think that it doesn't matter how long it takes; we are not finished yet.[48]

On December 11, 1997, the Gitksan and Wet'suwet'en people were told by the Supreme Court of Canada that their efforts to disclose their most sacred oral histories, their adaawk, and their effort to disclose to a Canadian court the intricacies of their social organization and their legal system had not, in the final analysis, been futile.

The Supreme Court of Canada in *Delgamuukw* certainly demonstrated how an "honourable" approach to the oral history of Aboriginal peoples may be adopted:

> ...oral histories were of critical importance to the appellants' case. They used those histories in an attempt to establish their occupation and use of the disputed territory, an essential requirement for aboriginal title. The trial judge, after refusing to admit, or giving no independent weight to these oral histories, reached the conclusion that the appellants had not demonstrated the requisite degree of occupation for "ownership." Had the trial judge assessed the oral histories correctly, his conclusions on these issues of fact might have been very different (emphasis added).[49]

The Supreme Court of Canada could not have been clearer in the mandate it has given to the lower courts of this country when they address issues of Aboriginal rights and title. Courts of Canada are to recognize and rely upon oral history in Aboriginal evidence and give it equal weight to "written history." The instructions from the Supreme Court of Canada are not limited to oral histories. The Court has provided direction to the lower courts with respect to all types of evidence necessary to properly adjudicate Aboriginal claims:

In cases involving the *determination of aboriginal rights,* appellate intervention [with findings of facts] is also warranted by the failure of a trial court to appreciate the evidentiary difficulties inherent in adjudicating aboriginal claims when, first, applying the rules of evidence and, second, interpreting the evidence before it (emphasis added).[50]

The outstanding question is whether the Crown will try to minimize the value of oral history when prosecuting Aboriginal people with respect to hunting and fishing rights or challenging the proof of Aboriginal title.

The alternative for the Crown is to recognize that it has been directed by the court to uphold the honour of the Crown in dealing with Aboriginal nations. If the Crown realizes and recognizes these factors, it will accept oral histories and oral evidence of Aboriginal witnesses as having the same validity as written histories.

Aboriginal nations in British Columbia have fought for recognition of their title ever since the first colonial government felt secure enough to try to deny this title in the face of the law. The Supreme Court of Canada has now given the Crown a clear direction that its past denials were wrong. Canada now has the chance truly to be a leader in the world in the recognition of the rights of its first peoples.

Endnotes

[1] Prime Minister Trudeau, "Remarks on Aboriginal and Treaty Rights," in *Native Rights in Canada,* 2nd edition, ed. Peter A. Cumming and Neil H. Mickenberg (Toronto: Indian-Eskimo Association of Canada/General Publishing, 1972), 332.

[2] *Calder* v. *Attorney-General of British Columbia,* [1973] *Supreme Court Reports* 313. The extinguishment theory advanced by the Province in *Calder* was argued again in *Delgamuukw* and was accepted by the trial judge. However, it was rejected by all five judges of the British Columbia Court of Appeal and that rejection was confirmed in the Supreme Court of Canada.

[3] *Delgamuukw* v. *British Columbia,* [1997] 3 S.C.R. 1010, reversing (1993), 104 *Dominion Law Reports* (4th) 470 (British Columbia Court of Appeal), varying [1991] 3 *Western Weekly Reports* 97 (British Columbia Supreme Court). All references to the Supreme Court of Canada's judgment, hereinafter, *Delgamuukw* (S.C.C.), are to the paragraphs, which are the same in all reported versions; all references to the trial judgment, hereinafter, *Delgamuukw* (B.C.S.C.), are to the *Western Weekly Reports* version.

[4] Two of the more unusual appeals were against a direction by Justice McEachern that four cases involving Aboriginal title would be heard at the same time. These included cases involving Meares Island off Vancouver Island and another case respecting Aboriginal title in the Fraser Canyon. The Court of Appeal said this should not occur even though a trial judge has control over his procedure. Justice McEachern stated he did not understand this decision and tried to join the cases a second time which required a second appeal to the British Columbia Court of Appeal. The remaining appeals to the British Columbia Court of Appeal were equally difficult procedural battles.

[5] Discoveries are oral questioning of the appointed parties by the lawyers. Commission evidence is the recording of evidence outside of the case. Here, commission evidence was of elders who were found to be too ill to testify in court. This evidence was video taped.

[6] Gisday Wa and Delgam Uukw, *The Spirit in the Land: Statements of the Gitksan and Wet'suwet'en Hereditary Chiefs in the Supreme Court of British Columbia, 1987–1990* (Gabriola, BC: Reflections, 1992), 7.

[7] *Delgamuukw* (B.C.S.C.), 476.

[8] *Delgamuukw* (B.C.C.A.), 547.

[9] *Globe and Mail*, 12 December 1997.

[10] *Delgamuukw* (S.C.C.) at para. 87.

[11] This paper is a legal analysis but the trial judgment's treatment of oral history has also been analyzed from an anthropological perspective. See for instance: Julie Cruikshank, "Invention of Anthropology in British Columbia's Supreme Court: Oral Tradition as Evidence in *Delgamuukw v. B.C.*" B.C. *Studies* 95 (1992), 25; Dara Culhane, *The Pleasure of the Crown; Anthropology, Law and First Nations* (Vancouver: Talon Books, 1998), Part IV.

[12] *R. v. White and Bob*, (1964), 50 *Dominion Law Reports* (2d) 613 (British Columbia Court of Appeal), affirmed (1965), 52 *Dominion Law Reports* (2d) 481 (Supreme Court of Canada).

[13] Gisday Wa and Delgam Uukw, *The Spirit in the Land, supra*, 36.

[14] *Adaawk* are Gitksan oral histories passed from generation to generation in the feast hall. They describe how territory was acquired, the wearing of crests and identify the House names. *Kungax* are Wet'suwet'en songs that have similar content. They are sung in the Wet'suwet'en feast halls.

[15] Gisday Wa and Delgam Uukw, *The Spirit in the Land, supra*, 7–8.

[16] *Calder, supra*, 365.

[17] *Delgamuukw* (B.C.S.C.), 116.

[18] *Delgamuukw* (B.C.S.C.), 141.

[19] *Delgamuukw* (B.C.S.C.), 180, 181.

[20] *Delgamuukw* (B.C.S.C.), 204.

[21] *Delgamuukw* (B.C.S.C.), 126.

[22] *Delgamuukw* (B.C.S.C.), 192.

[23] *Delgamuukw* (B.C.S.C.), 388.

[24] *Delgamuukw* (B.C.S.C.), 172.

[25] *Delgamuukw* (B.C.S.C.), 182.

[26] *Delgamuukw* (B.C.S.C.), 140, 383.

[27] John Sopinka *et al.*, *The Law of Evidence in Canada* (Toronto: Butterworths, 1992), 155–58

[28] Ibid., 216–219.

[29] *Delgamuukw* (B.C.S.C.), 175.

[30] *Delgamuukw* (B.C.S.C.), 383, 438.

[31] *Delgamuukw* (B.C.S.C.), 181, cited in *Delgamuukw* (S.C.C.) at para. 97.

[32] *Delgamuukw* (B.C.S.C.), 438.

[33] *Delgamuukw* (B.C.S.C.), 440–441.

[34] Sopinka, *The Law of Evidence in Canada, supra,* 220.

[35] *Delgamuukw* (B.C.S.C.), 169, 438–441.

[36] *Delgamuukw* (S.C.C.) at para. 106.

[37] *Delgamuukw* (S.C.C.) at para. 80.

[38] *Delgamuukw* (S.C.C.) at para. 82.

[39] *Delgamuukw* (S.C.C.) at para. 8.

[40] *Delgamuukw* (S.C.C.) at para. 98.

[41] *Delgamuukw* (B.C.S.C.), 177, cited in *Delgamuukw* (S.C.C.) at para. 100.

[42] *Delgamuukw* (S.C.C.) at para. 101.

[43] *Delgamuukw* (S.C.C.) at para. 105.

[44] *Delgamuukw* (S.C.C.) at para. 106.

[45] *Delgamuukw* (S.C.C.) at para. 106.

[46] *Delgamuukw* (S.C.C.) at para. 148.

[47] *Delgamuukw* (S.C.C.) at para. 154.

[48] Dora Wilson-Kenni, "Time of Trial: The Gitksan and Wet'suwet'en in Court" *B.C. Studies* 95 (1992), 10–11.

[49] *Delgamuukw* (S.C.C.) at para. 107.

[50] *Delgamuukw* (S.C.C.) at para. 80.

The Aboriginal Voice in the Canadian Unity Debate

Ted Moses

At the time this speech was delivered, Ted Moses was the Ambassador to the United Nations, Grand Council of the Crees. He is now Grand Chief of the James Bay Cree.

One of those old unforgotten animosities between colonial rivals has been brought back to life in the Province of Quebec. Some people want to settle old scores and rearrange history so that it will come out better for them the second time around. I am not speaking about the Indians, the Aboriginal peoples. It is not our fight. We would have good reason to try to remake history. After all, this entire continent was once ours. We lost it through a process of dispossession achieved through legal artifice, starvation, disease, transmigration, relocation, and genocidal extermination.

Certainly, if anyone should want to "correct" history, it should be the Native peoples. Everyone admits that we were grievously wronged. We are the survivors of a massive and intentional genocide. My one preoccupation is this: We will never let it happen again. You may have heard other survivors express the same idea. Now, I am extremely vigilant about my human rights. This is the reaction of my culture to its history. Knowing this, you will be in a better position to understand how we Crees come to be involved in the so-called Canadian unity debate.

This article was originally given as a speech to the Canada Seminar, Native American Program, Weatherhead Center for International Affairs, Harvard University. April 20, 1998. Published in the *Native Studies Review*, 12:2 (1999). Reprinted with permission of the *Native Studies Review* and the author.

We live in a territory we have always called Eeyou Istchee on the eastern side of James Bay and Hudson Bay. This was part of the territory that was given by Great Britain to the Hudson's Bay Company in the seventeenth century for fur exploitation. It was historically never a part of Quebec or of any French colonial possessions in North America. It was sold by the Hudson's Bay Company to become part of the Dominion of Canada in 1867 as part of Rupert's Land. Quebec also became part of Canada in the same period, giving up any pretensions to colonial ties to France or to a separate sovereign capacity. All of this, however, took place without the knowledge of the Crees. We continued to live in Eeyou Istchee

Meanwhile, in Europe papers were being signed and sealed, peace treaties were being negotiated, our lands were being bartered and exchanged. But we did not know, and our consent was never sought, offered, or received. Then in 1898 and 1912 the Parliament of Canada approved legislation whereby Rupert's Land was partitioned and divided among the provinces of Alberta, Saskatchewan, Manitoba, Ontario, and Quebec. And so without our knowledge or consent Eeyou Istchee became part of the Province of Quebec, and we Crees were passed along to Quebec with the land.

We want you to know some of our history because I understand that representatives of the separatist government in Quebec have come here to speak, to give you their view of history. They no doubt told you that Quebec has a right to independence based upon the principles of fairness, democracy, the right to self-determination, cultural identity, and the right to nationhood. They no doubt made this out to be a struggle between what both the federal government and the provincial government call the "two founding peoples" of Canada— the French and the English. The persistence of this idea of "two founding peoples" is strange. This idea is part of the legal myth upon which both the United States and Canada are based—the principle of *terra nullius*, literally, empty land. When the colonists arrived at our land they claimed it in the name of their sovereign. Of course we were here, but they did not ask if it was ours. From a European legal point of view America was virgin, unpopulated territory. We had no papers to prove title. We had no recognized monarch to assert sovereignty. We did not count.

Our rights are enshrined in the Canadian Constitution, and yet the Prime Minister of Canada and most of the provincial premiers refer over and over again to the "two founding peoples" of Canada, the French and the English. They speak of "English Canada" and "French

Canada." They never refer to "Aboriginal Canada." In many ways we still do not count. But look at a map of Canada. Over most of the Canadian territory, square mile by square mile, Aboriginal people make up the majority of the inhabitants. The non-Aboriginal population lives in a narrow strip just north of the United States border. They live in urban centres. We Aboriginal people are the ones who occupy, care for and still use the vast territory itself.

The Crees never wanted to become part of the Canadian unity debate. Notwithstanding all that has been done to us, all we have lost, everything that has been taken away—our lands, our forests, our animals—it is not the Crees who want to separate and break up Canada. No, it is certain politicians who claim to represent one of the "two founding peoples" who now want to "correct" their history. One would think under the circumstances that these would be the very people who could best understand the situation of the Aboriginal peoples. Who better than citizens who claim to be oppressed to understand others who have suffered oppression?

Among ordinary people in Quebec who are asked "If the Quebecois have a right to self-determination don't the Crees and the other Aboriginal peoples in Quebec also have this right?" Most answer that the Aboriginal peoples do have at least the same right. This is so logical and self-evident as to be undeniable to fair-minded people everywhere. On the other hand, fairness and logic do not lead to the preferred solution for those who want a separate and sovereign Quebec. To them, the Crees and other Aboriginal peoples in Quebec are a major obstacle because any arguments that can be made to support the case for the self-determination of Quebec can be made, even more strongly, for the self-determination of the Aboriginal peoples in Quebec.

Now place the Aboriginal peoples in the current context where the political leadership is claiming the right for Quebec to unilaterally separate from Canada and to take the Aboriginal peoples with them out of Canada, with or without our consent. In international law this threat by the present Government of Quebec to forcibly separate us from Canada, if need be, strengthens our right to exercise self-determination. It threatens to subject us directly to the reintroduction of a colonial relationship—to deny self-determination in its most basic form. As a result, there is a real divide here between most people in Quebec, who are willing to trust the Aboriginal peoples to make our own choices about our future, and the high profile separatist leaders such as Premier Lucian Bouchard who by political necessity must promote a double standard—

self-determination for Quebec but not for the Crees, independence for Quebec but local self-government for the Crees, official language status for the French language but not for the Cree language, ownership of resources for Quebec but not for the Crees, control over the environment for Quebec but not for the Crees.

While most Quebecois might understand the blatant inequality in these separatist double-standards, they may be unwilling to forsake their aspirations for independence to satisfy moral objections. It becomes particularly difficult when we Crees ask the Quebec separatist leaders to justify in law and equity the positions they have taken. How can you insist on one standard of rights for yourselves, we ask, and yet be willing to subject the Aboriginal peoples to lower human rights standards? This question has been put to these separatist leaders time and time again, in speeches, in books, in interviews, and we have never had a real answer. Is it because of our race, we ask, that you derogate from our human rights? Is it because we are Indians that our rights are subservient to yours?

We have heard all kinds of slippery nonsense. Separatist leaders have said, "only governments have the right of self- determination." They have said that international law does not recognize the right of self-determination for Indigenous peoples, that international law does not recognize Aboriginal peoples as "peoples" within the meaning of the international human rights instruments. When the Crees suggested that Quebec was practising a "racist double-standard" we were accused of making inflammatory remarks, "insulting the Quebec people," and "attacking Quebec." At one point a member of the Quebec provincial cabinet actually wrote to the federal government asking that sedition laws be applied against Cree Grand Chief Matthew Coon Come for a speech he made in the United States accusing the Quebec government of a "double-standard based upon race." Quebec somehow manages to portray itself as an aggrieved party suffering under the arbitrary and unfair rule of the federal government in "English Canada."

Imagine what this is like for us. Over all but a few years of my lifetime, many prime ministers of Canada have come from Quebec. Quebec has three judges on the Supreme Court. Several federal cabinet ministers are from Quebec. Quebec controls education, environment, land, resources, immigration, and most other jurisdictions. Quebec has it own civil law, court and prison system, its own police force, its own cultural entities, and its own territory over which it has jurisdiction. Would it not be nice if the Aboriginal peoples could have such power, influence, and wealth—we, the original peoples living in their own country where we have always lived? Could it be, I have to ask, that our rights are so easy to ignore because all the jurisdiction and wealth has been already split between those two founding peoples—the French and the English? Where do the Indians, the Aboriginal peoples, and the Cree in particular fit into this equation?

Here I have to return to the Canadian Constitution again. As I mentioned, the rights of the Aboriginal peoples of Canada are enshrined in the Constitution. Our aboriginal and treaty rights have special constitutional recognition and protection. We also have rights embodied in international human rights law and specific rights that derive from aboriginal treaties. In Canada, the Aboriginal peoples are the only peoples for which Parliament has direct responsibility. In a way, this is how we Crees got into the unity debate. We know that in law the federal government has the fiduciary duty and obligation to protect our rights. We assumed, therefore, that the federal government would intervene at some point to tell the separatist authorities that administer the Province of Quebec that they can not forcibly remove the Crees and the Cree Territory from Canada into an independent Quebec State.

The federal government said nothing of the kind. Instead, under pressure from the separatists, the federal government has been afraid to make the least mention of any obligations it has to defend the rights of the Aboriginal peoples in Quebec. To make matters worse the federal government for many years pursued a policy at the United Nations and in the international community to deny the recognition of the rights of Indigenous peoples in international law. While the very real threat of Quebec separatism was gaining strength in Canada with the election of the Bloc Quebecois as the official opposition in the House of Commons and the election of the Parti Quebecois as the government in Quebec, Canada was arguing at the United Nations and at the Organization of American States that there was a danger of Indigenous insurrection if Indigenous peoples were to be recognized as having the rights of "peoples" under the international human rights Covenants. Canada, with a representative of the separatist government in Quebec sitting at the same desk in the United Nations, encouraged other States to reject the use of the term "peoples" as applied to the world's Indigenous peoples.

I am the Crees' ambassador at the United Nations, and I objected to Canada's position. I raised the Quebec secession issue and asked that Canada not weaken the Crees' claim to have the right to remain in Canada if Quebec were to secede from Canada. I pointed out that Indigenous peoples need to be able to invoke the right of self-determination in such circumstances; that Canada's position at the United Nations actually went against Canada's national interests. Immediately after I made this statement [1991], I was approached by a Canadian diplomat who told me that the Canadian ambassador in Geneva wanted to see me. I went to see Ambassador Gerald Shannon who redressed me for raising the Quebec secession issue at the United Nations. He told me that I was making Quebec secession an international issue!

It became apparent at this time that it was the Crees, and only the Crees, who were raising fundamental rights issues in regard to possible Quebec secession. Amazingly, none of this was being discussed in the rest of Canada. We asked the federal Government of Canada to make a positive assertion concerning the rights of the Aboriginal peoples in Quebec, who, after all, in the event of separation, would lose all of their constitutional guarantees and their treaty rights. We thought: here we are, the only peoples under the direct protection of parliament; there is a strong movement to take us out of Canada—surely Canada should say something! It was the Crees who went to the United Nations and to Washington, DC to speak. We were severely criticized in the Quebec media for everything we said. It was the Crees who raised the possibility of a unilateral declaration of independence (UDI). Editorialists in Quebec called us fanatics—the little boy who cried wolf. We pointed out the inherent racism in the separatist policy. It was the Crees who explained that Quebec was planning a *coup d'état* against the constitution.

It stayed this way right up to the 1995 Quebec referendum. But we were ready. We held our own Cree referendum voting 97% in favour of remaining in Canada if Quebec attempted to take the Crees and Cree Territory out of Canada without Cree consent. We approached federal ministers and even Prime Minister Chrétien to obtain some assurance that our concerns would be met. We received only the most superficial and patronizing responses. The government was looking after everything, we were told. The "no" side would prevail in the Quebec referendum. We were told not to worry.

We made two successive submissions to the Royal Commission on Aboriginal Peoples asking that it give priority to considering the federal government's fiduciary obligations to Aboriginal peoples in the context of secession. The Royal Commission refused. The co-chairman, a Quebec judge, said the question was too hypothetical. Our sources in the Commission told us that the judge considered the Quebec issue a "bombshell" and would not dare touch it. It was only when all of the Quebec Aboriginal chiefs directly prevailed upon the

Royal Commission and demanded their involvement that a study was initiated. Nothing, however, appeared in the Commission's final report. The Aboriginal issues involved with Quebec secession were too dangerous and it was censored.

Meanwhile the federal government and the Quebec government took no official notice of the Cree referendum or any of the other strong and well publicized Aboriginal referendums, which showed that the Aboriginal peoples living in Quebec wanted to remain in Canada. On the same day that the Cree referendum results were announced, the separatists leaked a federal government Privy Council Office policy paper on Aboriginal self-determination, Quebec secession, and the Crees. The federal government quickly authenticated their leaked document and made no effort to repudiate it. The federal document the separatists wanted to headline demonstrated that the most senior levels of the Government of Canada were preparing to abandon the Aboriginal peoples in Quebec if secession were to occur. Privy council officials argued that Aboriginal peoples did not have the right of self-determination in international law. They took issue with the Crees' assertion that forcible inclusion of the Crees in a separate Quebec would be a fundamental violation of our rights. They disputed the binding nature of the federal government's fiduciary obligations to Aboriginal peoples. They doubted whether we would be able to have the Canadian federal courts enforce the federal government's treaty obligations to us. And if all of this were not enough, they pointed out that after Quebec independence we Crees would be the inhabitants of a foreign country. Canada, they claimed, would have no fiscal obligations to us anymore, since we would not be within its jurisdiction. Canada would therefore avoid the cost of respecting its obligations to us.

I could clearly see why the separatists wanted the public to know what the federal government thought about the rights of the Aboriginal peoples in Quebec. There had just been a poll that showed support for the independence of Quebec would drop significantly among people who were planning to vote "yes" in the Quebec referendum if either the federal government or the United Nations endorsed the arguments the Crees had been making about their rights.

We had just published the book *Sovereign Injustice: Forcible Inclusion of the James Bay Crees and Cree Territory into a Sovereign Quebec* (Grand Council of the Crees of Quebec, 1995), a legal study about Aboriginal rights in the context of Quebec secession. The book was well received in the international legal community and was being widely cited. The separatist authorities in the Quebec government and in the federal parliament had made no attempt to answer the legal and moral arguments set out in that book. They needed something to counter the effect of our book, and to reduce the effect of the Cree referendum results. What could be better than the federal government's own secret policy document which showed that federal officials considered the Aboriginal peoples to be a greater threat to Canada's future than the separatists themselves? I was not surprised when I saw the secret Privy Council Office document. It endorsed views that were entirely consistent with Canada's policy on Aboriginal issues in the international community. According to this view, we Indians and not the separatists were the enemies of Canada. The real danger to Canada, it was argued, was the threat of Aboriginal self-determination. The very same arguments were now coming from the separatist government in Quebec and from the federal government in Ottawa. It did not matter that we had been fighting for our right to stay in Canada while almost everyone in the federal government had been silent. Apparently, the overt threat against the unity of Canada from the separatists was more acceptable than the idea that somehow we Crees had secret plans to declare our independence if only we could persuade Canada to recognize our right to self-determination.

The secret Privy Council Office document concluded that the Crees would have no right to separate from an independent Quebec. Canada readily endorsed this view. In 1993 a Canadian diplomat at the United Nations Human Rights Summit in Vienna explained to the press that Canada could not support the Indigenous peoples' right to self-determination in the Vienna Declaration because the Crees might use this right to separate from an independent Quebec. We have always been very clear about our position. We have always recognized that it would not be wise to become parties to the old struggle between the former colonial masters of North America. Our interest is to protect and promote the rights of the Crees and the other Aboriginal peoples. We have stated many times that we do not oppose the secession of Quebec if it can be accomplished without affecting our rights.

The Crees have a relationship with Canada that we would like to preserve. We realize that Canada has not been a responsible fiduciary on our behalf, but we would nevertheless like to improve our relationship and reach true reconciliation with Canada. Unfortunately, from our perspective Canada seems to have regarded the Aboriginal peoples as adversaries. Our relationship with Quebec seems no better. Quebec views the Crees as obstacles to its own development and the assertion of its sovereignty over the northern part of the province.

Neither Quebec nor Canada have respected their treaty obligations to the Crees. Given the fact that the present constitutional order in Canada provides more checks and balances than would exist in a sovereign unitary Quebec, our preference for the status quo and thus Canadian unity has been persuasive, as it has been for most of the Aboriginal peoples in Quebec.

Quebec's overtures to us have always been contradicted by the unilateral and draconian manner in which Quebec conducts its daily business with the Aboriginal peoples. The ethnic nationalism that guides Quebec separatist aspirations carries strong racist overtones that are particularly abhorrent to the Aboriginal peoples. If Quebec politics and politicians can ever overcome this, our relationship could change. Of course the separatist argument that Quebec can unilaterally and forcibly include the Aboriginal peoples does not help. The Cree approach in this and many other issues has been to turn to the law. It was on this basis that we made arguments before the United Nations Commission on Human Rights in 1992, and I have referred already to our legal study entitled *Sovereign Injustice*. Our arguments are reiterated in our most recent publication, entitled *Never Without Consent: James Bay Crees' Stand Against Forcible Inclusion into an Independent Quebec* (Grand Council of the Crees, Toronto: ECW Press, 1998).

It is only somewhat ironic that it is the Aboriginal peoples of Canada who are insisting on law and order and the Constitution. In the lead-up to the 1995 Quebec referendum the federal government was unwilling to discuss legal and constitutional issues, and certainly not the legal and constitutional rights of the Aboriginal peoples in Quebec. Quebec makes all kinds of legal claims in support of its unilateral right to independence, but absolutely refuses to engage in a serious moderated discussion of legal claims. The separatists claim that they will not be bound by legalities and the Canadian Constitution. They insist on their "democratic" right to determine their own future. This should not, they say, be subject to any decisions made in the rest of Canada, and should not be subject to the Canadian Constitution. It most certainly should not be determined by the courts. Recourse to the courts, they argue, would be "undemocratic." On the other hand, when we the Crees and other Aboriginal peoples in Quebec argue that we also have the right to choose for ourselves, and that we also have the democratic right to our own referendum, that old double-standard is invoked once again: the choices made by the Crees and other Aboriginal peoples must be drowned within the vote of the entire Quebec population. When the then premier of Quebec, Jacques Parizeau, made his famous speech conceding defeat in the 1995 referendum he said, "It is true we have been defeated, but basically by what? By money and the ethnic vote."

After this racist remark, the federal government's reluctance to submit the legal and constitutional arguments to a test underwent a dramatic reversal. This very close, highly contested and statistically suspect referendum genuinely frightened the federalists. In a panic, the federal government immediately rushed two resolutions through Parliament. One recognized Quebec as a "distinct society," the other gave Quebec a veto over future constitutional amendments. The federal government promised that these resolutions would become constitutional amendments at the first possible opportunity.

The Crees opposed these resolutions because they potentially derogate from the constitutional rights of the Aboriginal peoples. When we raised these objections at parliamentary hearings we were told by federal officials not to worry, although they conceded that our legal arguments were sound. We want to keep our promises to Quebec, they explained; we will deal with your rights later. However, at the same time that the federal government enacted these conciliatory resolutions they embarked upon a strategy to begin a public discussion of the contentious issues that had been considered taboo before the referendum. The big question, of course, is whether the provincial government in Quebec has the legal authority under the Canadian Constitution or in international law to make a unilateral declaration of independence. In Canada a question such as this can be put directly by the federal government to the Supreme Court of Canada in the form of a reference case (see Reference re: Secession of Quebec, [1998] 2 S.C.R., 217). The Crees had been hoping that the federal government would make a reference to the Supreme Court, and we had been making preparations for such an eventuality.

Separatist leaders in Quebec took positions on both sides of the legal issue. They argued that the Quebec National Assembly had the right under international law to unilaterally declare independence. They argued that the Aboriginal peoples could not separate from a separate Quebec. They argued that the Canadian Constitution protected the borders of Quebec until independence. After independence, they claimed, international law would protect the "territorial integrity" of a sovereign Quebec. When the federal government suggested a possible reference on these issues to the Supreme Court, the separatists were indignant with outrage. How could the judges of the Supreme Court overrule the democratic will of the Quebec People? These objections to the Supreme Court were made notwithstanding the fact that Quebec itself had brought to the Supreme Court of Canada a case against the harvesting rights of Aboriginal peoples (*R v. Côté*, [1996] 3 S.C.R., 672), where it claimed that Aboriginal rights did not exist in Quebec at all.

In September 1996 the federal government passed an Order in Council sending three reference questions on Quebec secession to the Supreme Court of Canada. The Quebec government objected and refused to participate. Its objection was supported by the Quebec Liberal Party. Huge rallies were held in Quebec against the Supreme Court. Pressured by this popular reaction, several federal members of Cabinet and even Prime Minister Chrétien conceded that the federal government would agree to the separation of Quebec if a clear majority of the Quebec population were to vote to separate on a clearly phrased question.

These concessions clearly troubled the Aboriginal peoples in Quebec. On what authority, we wondered, could the federal government make such a concession? What about our rights? What about the federal government's fiduciary obligations to Aboriginal peoples? What about the Constitution? And if these concessions were being made publicly, why ask the Supreme Court for answers? The federal government chose its questions very carefully. It completely avoided the question of its obligations to the Aboriginal peoples under the Constitution. The federal government asked the court whether Quebec could unilaterally separate from Canada, if Quebec had a right of self-determination under international law, and whether international law or domestic law would have paramountcy.

The federal government asked its former United Nations Ambassador, Mr. Yves Fortier, to argue its case for the Attorney General. Canada also invited Quebec to submit arguments. Quebec refused with great public indignity, so the Supreme Court appointed a well-respected separatist lawyer to act as an *amicus curiae*, or friend of the court, to argue Quebec's case. The Crees and three other Aboriginal organizations intervened along with several other groups and individuals. Canada argued that the court need look, and should only look at a very narrow question. Does a provincial legislature have the power under the Constitution to unilaterally separate from Canada? The Crees' intervention examined the reference questions in a broader context. We argued that Quebec could not unilaterally separate because the unilateral nature of the secession would violate the principle of Cree and Aboriginal consent.

We sought to demonstrate that the rights of the Aboriginal peoples would be seriously violated by unilateral secession. We also sought to show that our human rights, our treaty rights, and our aboriginal rights were highly relevant to the reference questions, and that the federal government had fiduciary obligations to the Aboriginal peoples in Quebec it had to respect in the context of secession.

The federal government had hoped to keep a tight lid on the scope of the reference case, but it was clear as soon as the intervener's factums had been filed that this would not be possible. The federal government's second reply factum instructed the court to avoid the Aboriginal issues completely. Canada assured the court that it did indeed take the interests of the Aboriginal peoples seriously, but it suggested that the court not consider the issues raised by the Aboriginal interveners. It advised the court that these issues were far beyond the scope of the reference questions.

Everything I have described so far was done through written submissions leading up to a dramatic and historic week of oral submissions which recently took place before the full court in Ottawa. The Crees' oral submission was straightforward. We maintained that Quebec could not secede unilaterally without violating our right of self-determination. Such a violation, we told the Supreme Court, would be an act of colonialism against the Crees. Colonialism is one of the explicit rights violations in international law that provides justification for a people to exercise their own right of secession. By forcibly including the Crees in a separate Quebec, Quebec would be forced to relinquish the Cree Territory, Eeyou Istchee. Cree consent is required.

For most of the week the court listened to the various submissions. The federal lawyer reiterated his position that the federal government would accept Quebec secession if a significant majority were to approve a clear question on secession.

The *amicus* made the novel argument that Quebec need only gain effective control over the Quebec Territory in order to achieve independence. He called this the principle of "effectivity"—control the territory, displace the federal authorities, and insist on the territorial integrity of the territory that Quebec would claim. The justices listened. They showed no expression, no reaction to anything that was said. They asked no questions. Then, at the end of the third day, they told the lawyers that they would ask questions the following day and want answers.

If these questions are any indication of what the justices of the Supreme Court are thinking, I think we can look forward to a very interesting judgment indeed. I can tell you this—everyone agreed that the federal lawyer and the *amicus* were caught off guard and rattled by the questions. "On what ground," the chief justice asked the federal lawyer, "is Ottawa constitutionally permitted to concede, as it has done here, that the people of Quebec have the ultimate right to decide their own political future? Does such a concession by Ottawa in a judicial context like this one have any binding legal effect?" This was the very same question an Aboriginal chief had asked a few months before in a public letter to a member of the federal cabinet—a letter that was never answered. We had also wondered, how could the federal government concede our rights unilaterally? Where did it get the authority to do this? The government's answer was that the concession to Quebec was a matter of "policy," and that it did not create a right to secede outside of the constitutional process. The essential question was never answered.

After several more questions the chief justice dropped his bombshell, the very same one that the Royal Commission on Aboriginal Peoples had gone to such lengths to avoid. Canada was asked: "What is your position with regard to the fiduciary duty owed to the First Nations peoples if there should be a UDI (unilateral declaration of independence)? Do you consider your obligations to extend to consideration of territorial claims of First Nations Peoples?" Mr. Fortier, the federal lawyer, told the court that Canada had already answered these questions in its factum to the Court. Canada's position, he said, was that the Aboriginal rights issue should not form part of the case. Canada would respect its fiduciary obligations to the Aboriginals, and that was the end of it.

This did not satisfy the justices who could see that a very important question was being evaded by the Canadian government. Mr. Justice Peter Cory, who had not said a word for the entire week, then asked how the Aboriginal issue could be left out. "It seems to me, Mr. Fortier," he observed, "that's an essential and integral part of the response to the question. This is perhaps the group that is most vulnerable and most affected." Mr. Fortier squirmed and waffled, instructing the court once again to avoid the Aboriginal rights question. Under pressure he conceded that is was "essential" to keep in mind the constitutional guarantees and special Aboriginal and Treaty rights. Nevertheless, he stressed again the court need not address such issues in their ruling.

The court was being given a first-hand example of Canada's questionable respect for its constitutional obligations to the Aboriginal peoples. The chief justice wryly observed: "You're saying, Mr. Fortier, we should have it in our mind but not talk about it." The courtroom burst into laughter.

Editors' note: On August 24, 1998 the Supreme Court ruled that Quebec cannot secede from Canada without Canada's consent. At the same time, it required Canada to negotiate in good faith if Quebec voters, by a clear majority, voted for secession in a fair referendum. The three questions the court considered were (1) Does Canadian law allow Quebec to secede from Canada unilaterally? (2) Does international law allow Quebec to secede unilaterally? (3) If there's a conflict between the two, which takes precedence? The court answered "no" to questions 1 and 2, and said question 3 is "a moot point."

Constitutionalizing the Patriarchy:

Aboriginal Women and Aboriginal Government

Joyce Green

Joyce Green teaches political science (with a special interest in Canadian politics, critical theory, and political economy) at the University of Regina. She is currently writing a book about citizenship and identity, focusing on Aboriginal women; with Cora Voyageur of the University of Calgary is conducting research on ethnic, gender, and class composition of candidates in the 1999 Saskatchewan election; and is also researching the contradictory impulses of decolonization of the state by transnational capitalists.

Foreword

C ontext is always important in understanding historic events. "Constitutionalizing the Patriarchy" was written shortly after the historic national referendum of 1992, when Canadians declined to endorse the package of proposed constitutional amendments known as the Charlottetown Accord. The Accord was a negotiated package ranging from institutional reform such as a transformed Senate and asymmetrical federalism, to new provisions for a social and economic framework for Canada, to Quebec-specific changes to federal processes and jurisdictions, to Aboriginal governance. The processes that resulted in the Accord were themselves reactions against the elite practices that produced the Meech Lake Accord, a failed constitutional amendment initiated in 1987. Canadians had been involved in public discussions

This article was originally published in *Constitutional Forum* 4:4 (Spring 1993): 110–20. Published with permission of the author.

leading up to the Charlottetown Accord, about the nature of Canadian federalism, Canadian citizenship, and the implications of the 1982 Charter of Rights and Freedoms, in an unprecedented manner. There was general agreement that many Canadians found intolerable the traditional practice of federalism and constitutional change as the prerogatives of governments and their elites.

It was in this climate of the demands for citizen participation in the process of constitutional reform that social movements, especially those representing marginalized sectors of society, asked for the opportunity to participate. The National Action Committee on the Status of Women, for example, presented a set of proposals on virtually every issue raised by both the Meech Lake and Charlottetown Accords. The Native Women's Association of Canada, the National Métis Women of Canada, and Pauktuutit developed positions on the Constitution and especially on the proposed constitutional recognition of the right of Aboriginal self-government. They brought to the debate analyses that were distinct from those brought by the male-dominated Aboriginal organizations that the federal and provincial governments were accustomed to dealing with. That is, women organized to bring a gendered analysis to what had traditionally been a male political preserve. "Constitutionalizing the Patriarchy" reviews the efforts of Aboriginal women's groups, especially those of the Native Women's Association of Canada, to participate in the consultations held by the Government of Canada with first ministers, their political and bureaucratic elites, and with the male-dominated national Aboriginal political associations.

Introduction

During the pre-Charlottetown Accord politicking, a tension became apparent between Aboriginal women represented by the Native Women's Association of Canada (NWAC) and the "male-stream"[1] Aboriginal organizations, particularly the "status" organization, the Assembly of First Nations (AFN). The AFN, Métis National Council (MNC), Native Council of Canada (NCC), and Inuit Taparisat of Canada (ITC) were given participant status in constitutional negotiations,[2] and lobbied successfully to have the matter of the explicit[3] inclusion of the inherent right of self-government in the Constitution to be settled during this "Canada Round." As part of this package, the AFN advanced the proposition that the *Charter of Rights and Freedoms* not apply to Aboriginal governments: in this it was apparently supported by the other Aboriginal organizations.

It is important to note that three broad-based national feminist organizations had asked for and been denied participant status in the negotiations. The National Action Committee on the Status of Women, NWAC, and the newly minted National Métis Women of Canada[4] all claimed that women's voices had to be explicitly included for the new constitutional package to adequately reflect Canadian / Aboriginal aspirations. They argued that their participation would provide content, context, and analysis not presented by the First Ministers and the favoured lobby organizations. The First Ministers and the Aboriginal lobby organizations declined to support the inclusion of these women's organizations.

When NWAC sought status at the constitutional table equivalent to that of the four included organizations, the federal government encouraged NWAC to work through the "male-stream" organizations to advance its interests rather than to promote them separately. NWAC attempted to do this; however, on some issues NWAC and these organizations, in particular the AFN, are in substantial opposition. This is particularly apparent where Native women identify a shared experience of oppression as women within the Native community, together with (instead of only as) the experience of colonial oppression as Aboriginals within the dominant society. Not for the first time,[5] the AFN sought to deny the reality of sex-based oppression in Aboriginal communities and to resist women's attempts to put these issues on the political agenda.[6]

The MNC similarly was criticized by Métis women for not incorporating women's agendas, and for not making space for women's voices at the table. Marge Friedel, speaking to the Royal Commission on Aboriginal Peoples on behalf of the Women of the Métis Nation of Alberta, said:

> Métis women firmly believe that for the constitutional process to reflect a true Métis women's involvement it must ensure that our voices are heard, that our experiences are understood and that our expectations are given a respectful and responsive hearing.... Aboriginal women have been and continue to be discriminated against by the unaccountable male dominated political organizations.[7]

NWAC raised three issues at variance with the Canadian and Aboriginal "male-stream" participants at the constitutional table. First, NWAC wished to be a full participant, with status equal to the other four Aboriginal organizations. In support of this, NWAC argued that it represented a constituency whose interests were not articulated by any of the other Aboriginal players, and whose interests were being negatively affected by negotiations. Second, NWAC wanted equal funding with which to advance its position. Third, NWAC wanted the Charter to continue to apply to constitutional Aboriginal governments, at least until an equally authoritative Aboriginal Charter, whose terms would protect women's equality rights, was in place.

NWAC was excluded from full participation in the constitutional negotiations, and from equal federal funding for the negotiation process. The process of exclusion of Aboriginal women by key players in the constitutional sandbox, with the tacit approval of all other players, is characteristically sexist, and indicative of political and policy hegemony by men. It is this process that is of primary interest here.

Ultimately the process excluded women *qua* women. That is, despite a significant court ruling[8] that the Charter rights of NWAC members were abrogated by the exclusionary process, despite the court's acknowledgement that the participant organizations, and particularly the AFN, acted in ways inimical to NWAC interests, and despite the court's acknowledgement that NWAC was the only valid voice of those interests, *nothing changed*. The select group of First Ministers and Aboriginal lobby organizations, exclusive of explicit women's representation, was not expanded.

Perhaps this result could have been predicted, based on the difficult and frustrating experience of women organizing to ensure protection for women's rights in the Charter in the 1980–1982 period. As Sue Findlay put it:

> The resistance of the state—including both federal and provincial governments—to consultations with feminists about ways to guarantee women's rights in the new Constitution was a stunning display of the limits of state commitment to actively promote women's equality.[9]

The political choreography of the state apparatus and the key players throughout the Charlottetown process was no less stunning. For Aboriginal and non-Aboriginal feminists alike, it seems a categorical rejection by the power-brokers of women's inclusion in the "unequal structure of representation."[10] This suggests the conclusion that the ideology of patriarchy is more fundamental to the premises on which the Canadian state is founded than is the principle of democracy.

The exclusion of Aboriginal women from the Charlottetown round has implications for all women, for the prospects for our inclusion in political processes, and for the unlikelihood, despite Charter guarantees, of a genuine societal accommodation of our interests. The state apparatus appears to be designed to maintain the existing power relations, not to integrate powerless groups like Aboriginal people or all women in some equitable fashion.[11] The case study of NWAC's experience suggests that even when we win (for example, the judicial decision that NWAC's Charter rights were offended by the exclusionary political process) we lose.

Aboriginal Feminism

The existence of a critical mass of Aboriginal women who identify as feminists—as evidenced by the viability of NWAC—is a relatively new phenomenon. Feminist identification and feminist analysis is weak within Aboriginal communities and organizations, and is not widespread among individual women. Indeed, Aboriginal women have been urged to identify as Aboriginal, in the context of the domination and exploitation by the newcomer community, to the exclusion of identification as women with women across cultures, and with the experience of exploitation and domination by men within Aboriginal communities. Nevertheless, many Aboriginal women from disparate contexts identify commonalities in the experience of being women and Native that are both dual oppressions[12] and a unique way of understanding the world.

Many Aboriginal women do not adopt the label "feminist." Reasons for this range from those shared with many non-Aboriginal women— that is, a misunderstanding of feminism as an alienating ideology that negates the possibility of male-female relationships and detracts from the value of the family—to a refusal to identify with what is seen to be a middle-class white women's movement that has no understanding of race oppression. This, however, is changing as more individual women and more organizations share an analysis that is characterized by Aboriginality and gender and, in the case of organizations, whose internal organization and political objectives and strategies are characteristically feminist.[13] By "characteristically feminist" I mean feminism composed of an action-oriented understanding of women's lives and experiences as politically and socially significant and, therefore, amenable to public policy and social transformation. A good example of this can be found in the presentation of the Manitoba Indigenous Women's Collective to the Royal Commission on Aboriginal Peoples:

> As Aboriginal women, we face discrimination and racism because we are Aboriginal and because we are women. We lack access to jobs, to support, to training programs, and to positions of influence and authority.... All across Canada, Aboriginal women are involved in the struggle for equal rights.[14]

The analysis of inequitable relations between men and women has much in common with the feminism of other Canadian women and provides a basis for solidarity between women's organizations.

Feminism has been represented by Aboriginal organizations and by many prominent male and female Aboriginal activists as undermining the "greater" objective of Aboriginal liberation: women have been assured that their needs, where they differ from those of the male-dominated political power structure, will be addressed by "traditional" mechanisms at some future point when Aboriginal governments have political, economic, social, and cultural power.

While NWAC does not use the language generally associated with feminist theory, it pursues woman-identified objectives in a manner that is characteristically feminist. Before Charlottetown, the most prominent of the issues NWAC pursued included the fight to end the sexist status provisions of the Indian Act and its internalization by some band governments, and the struggle for the recognition of violence against women and children as a reality and a high priority issue. NWAC articulates Aboriginal women's experiences by way of a uniquely Aboriginal feminist analysis. NWAC's own political rifts and liaisons indicate that this analysis is being tested by implementation.

By virtue of being a national voice of Aboriginal women as women, NWAC (and its sister organization, the National Métis Women of Canada) promotes gender equality. It does so by existing despite a hostile political environment, by offering women's analysis in a male policy arena, and by speaking for women's inclusion despite a climate of exclusion. NWAC's existence is an organized response by Aboriginal women to the sexism within male-dominated Aboriginal communities and organizations, and the failure of those organizations to respond to or to validate women's issues as defined by women's experiences. That is, NWAC's existence is a response to the political void left by the AFN and others.

Assimilating the Patriarchy

Most Aboriginal women acknowledge that traditional, that is, pre-contact, Aboriginal societies valued women and women's work.[15] However, the trauma of colonization and the realities of social change in contemporary societies have changed social roles and expectations. The European model of the patriarchal family is now the norm in most Aboriginal communities:[16] the dominant society's low valuation of women and women's work has been laid over Aboriginal values.

Combined with the social pathologies of wife assault, child abuse, and sexual abuse, contemporary Aboriginal societies often manifest the worst of the European patriarchy. According to the Canadian Panel on Violence Against Women, eight out of ten Aboriginal women experience physical, sexual, psychological, or ritual abuse, a rate twice as high as that in non-Aboriginal society.[17] Similar findings led other researchers to conclude that "[t]his sadly confirms the family unit as a place of danger and high risk, instead of security and protection."[18] In a client survey of Native women in Lethbridge, Alberta, of sixty-three respondents:

- 91% had personal experience with family violence
- 75% grew up as targets of family violence
- 46% identified alcohol as a factor in violence
- 29% experienced violence without the alcohol factor
- 70% suffered violence at the hands of relatives
- 50% were currently single
- 75% lived on monthly incomes of less than $1,100
- 50% were supporting children

The writers concluded that "[f]amily violence is a constant reality in the lives of urban Native women."[19]

Violence against women and children has become a primary concern for many Aboriginal women, and is viewed as a priority for the political agenda. Many women worried that male politicians would make decisions around constitutional renewal and Aboriginal government structures and processes without integrating women's agendas, or understanding women's reality. "As women, we're saying, you're [men are] making the decisions and you don't even know what the hell we need out here or what we want," said Lil Sanderson, an NWAC representative from La Ronge.[20]

This view was reiterated by Marilyn Fontaine for the Aboriginal Women's Unity Coalition in a presentation to the Royal Commission on Aboriginal Peoples. Fontaine stated that her organization had no confidence in the primarily male Manitoba Indian leadership:

> Aboriginal women have been reluctant in the past to challenge the positions taken by the leadership in the perceived need to present a unified front to the outside society which oppresses us equally.... However it must be understood that Aboriginal women suffer the additional oppression of sexism within our own community. Not only are we victims of violence at the hands of Aboriginal men, our voices as women are for the most part not valued in the male-dominated political structures.[21]

Fontaine declared that "the abuse and exploitation of women and children is a political issue of equal importance to achieving recognition [of the right] to govern ourselves."[22]

In an address to the Royal Commission on Aboriginal Peoples, Doris Young of the Indigenous Women's Collective said:

> We believe that we have the inherent right to self-government, but we also recognize that since European contact, our leaders have mainly been men. Men who are the by-products of colonization....[23]

A 1993 *Edmonton Journal* story featuring Chief Felix Antoine of Rosseau River proposing an amnesty for child and wife abusers illustrates some of the problems suggested by Fontaine, Sanderson, and others:

> By allowing them time to talk about their problems without fearing arrest, those who abuse their children or beat their spouses can work with others in the community and "begin to feel like a human being," he said.[24]

The chief was speaking to a Native task force investigating charges of political interference by chiefs in Native child welfare cases. Nothing was reported about the chief's concern with the safety and humanity of victims, nor of the responsibility of abusers. Indeed, one gets the sense from the article that the abusers *are* the victims.

Systemic violence has come to be understood as a political expression of issues of power and control. Violence is one measure of the crisis in Aboriginal communities, and women's experience as primary victims of that violence is a measure of women's political marginalization. The issue of violence against women and children is only beginning to be taken seriously by Aboriginal organizations and by some band councils. However, measurable response (such as programs for victims and batterers, and zero-tolerance of violence) to the issue is slow in coming. This is consistent with the slow response or non-response of existing Aboriginal politics to other issues identified by Aboriginal women.

Old Issues Never Resolved

In 1869, the federal government passed the first Indian Act by that name. The Indian Act defined who was an Indian, and in so doing, applied European notions of patriarchal social and family structure, and of legitimate birth. Indian women who married anyone other than a status Indian man lost their status; their children took the status or non-status of their fathers. This discriminatory provision persisted through a Supreme Court challenge[25] and in violation of international law,[26] until the Bill C-31 amendments to the Indian Act in 1985. The amendments were motivated by the Charter of Rights and Freedoms, which prohibits discrimination on the basis of sex, and under which the offensive provisions of the Indian Act would have inevitably been struck down.[27] While the discriminatory law no longer exists, its effects linger, a legacy of colonial legislation. Many band councils (also creations of the Indian Act) defend the old status provisions as "tradition," and are bitterly opposed to reinstatement.[28]

The refusal of many band councils to accept the legitimacy of women and children reinstated under the 1985 Indian Act revisions is another example of political intransigence on women's issues. The political marginalization of women as a consequence of Indian Act "status" provisions continues. The *de facto* opposition from many band governments prevents many reinstatees from exercising their *de jure* legislative and constitutional rights. "We're going to be left out for the rest of our lives," said Philomena Aulotte, who was one of a number of Indian women in Alberta who fought for years to have the old discriminatory section of the Indian Act struck down.[29] Now, eight years after the amendment, "C-31" people are finding the *real politik* remains a barrier to going home.

Much of NWAC's constituency are women who lost their status under the old Indian Act. Of those who are eligible for "reinstatement" as status Indians, 91,112 of 165,571 persons who have applied have been re-instated—at least on the federal membership list.[30]

However, "[i]n Alberta, it is estimated that less than two per cent of the 9,541 persons Indian Affairs has added to the membership lists of the 43 bands in the province have been accepted by the bands."[31] Many more wait for an inadequate bureaucracy to process their applications to recognize their constitutional rights.[32] And only 2 percent of reinstated displaced Native women have been able to return to their reserves since the 1985 amendments, due in large measure to the political and tactical opposition by band governments. This continued discrimination by bands invoking both tradition and the inherent right to control membership or citizenship has left many Native women skeptical of the ability and political will of future Aboriginal governments to respect women's rights. NWAC suggests Aboriginal women's distrust of Aboriginal governments is a consequence of the latter's demonstrated resistance to women's rights.

Some chiefs and status Indians from Alberta, led by Senator Walter Twinn, Chief of the Sawridge Band, are asking the Federal Court of Canada to declare the C-31 amendment to the Indian Act to be unconstitutional and contrary to the Charter. The *Twinn* case argues that only Indian bands, and not the federal Parliament, can say who can be on the membership list. The case, one of several court challenges to C-31 amendments, is expected to be heard in September 1993.

The (E)quality of Rights

The injustices experienced by Indian women at the hands of the Canadian government have, since the 1985 Indian Act amendments, been continued by some bands. Some women first stripped of their Indian political rights by discriminatory federal legislation find that they now are being prevented from exercising their rights by certain Aboriginal hard-liners. These women have no immediate recourse apart from appeal, through the Canadian legal system, on the grounds of infraction of their Charter and other rights. However, many bands and the AFN take the view that the Charter is itself an infringement on the inherent right of self-government. The pre-Charlottetown political discussions that included the AFN, other Aboriginal lobby organizations, and the First Ministers, while excluding Aboriginal women's organizations, sought to find consensus on the elements of self-government. One of the points on which consensus was ultimately achieved was the possibility of suspending the Charter in relation to traditional practices in the exercise of self-government.

The split over whether the Charter of Rights and Freedoms should apply to Aboriginal governments came early. In January of 1992 NWAC was reported to support the inherent right of self-government but, in opposition to the AFN, was insisting traditional Aboriginal government practices be subject to the Charter.[33] Further, NWAC did not support Aboriginal governments' access to s.33, the notwithstanding clause, fearing male-dominated Native governments would override women's equality rights.[34] NWAC was not standing alone on this issue: many feminists and other scholars of constitutional law agreed. Instructionally, within the Aboriginal feminist community there was solidarity on this point. Speaking to the Royal Commission on Aboriginal Peoples, Doris Young asserted: "We, therefore, want the Charter of Rights and Freedoms enforced in Aboriginal self-government until such time as when our own Bill of Rights is developed that will protect women and children."[35]

The Charter guarantees of equality rights were thought to be vulnerable to such an override, invoked to shield exercise of the inherent right and "tradition." Section 15(l), equal protection and benefit of the law regardless of (among other differences) gender, could conceivably be suspended by s.33. The existence of s.35(4) of the Constitution Act 1982 is no comfort: it guarantees Aboriginal and treaty rights equally to men and women, but it is not clear that s.15 would be considered to be a component of Aboriginal and treaty rights. Therefore, it is conceivable that an abuse of gender equality rights could be insulated from judicial remedy by invoking s.35 inherent rights as legitimating gender discrimination. This kind of constitutional possibility, together with the recent history around Indian Act status provisions, moved NWAC to insist on Charter application to Aboriginal governments.

At a Native women's constituent assembly in Toronto on January 19th, 1992, Jeanette Corbiere Lavell said that Native women need the Charter's protection because they have no other. Lavell had challenged the discriminatory membership provisions of the pre-1985 Indian Act in the Supreme Court of Canada, alleging it violated the Canadian Bill of Rights. In that decision, the Supreme Court ruled that, as all Indian women were treated the same way under the legislation, the legislation was not discrimination in law, and therefore was not in violation of the Bill of Rights. The National Indian Brotherhood and some bands intervened against Lavell at that time. Lavell pointed out it was a chief who initially appealed the Federal Court of Canada's favourable decision in her case.

Speaking of the situation of many women since the 1985 Indian Act amendments, Lavell pointed out:

> Many of the provincial and national First Nations political organizations, as we begin the transition to self government, have fought this legislation, Bill C-31, all the way, and many of our communities are still in effect refusing to implement it today.[36]

NWAC promptly found itself roundly criticized by other Aboriginal women for its position.[37] Women advocating the explicit protection of women's equality rights were attacked for undermining the greater cause of Aboriginal rights. Chief Wendy Grant of the Musqueum band, a regional vice-chief of the AFN, charged that "[d]ivision between First Nations people based upon the non-Native fascination with extreme individualism simply supports the assimilation of our people into the non-Native culture."[38] This debate continues. Over a year later in February 1993 in Vancouver, at the annual conference of the National Association of Women and the Law lawyer Nancy Sandy, speaking in place of Chief Grant, argued that First Nations do not need external agents telling them how to handle rights. Lawyer Teressa Nahanee argued that the collective right to self-determination is premised on individuals being able to express rights to self-determination. She went on to answer the charge of "extreme individualism" in this way:

> I think it is wrong to characterize the struggle by First Nations
> women for sexual equality rights as a struggle between indi-
> vidual versus collective rights. Why? The women have been
> trying since 1967 to erase the artificial, legal barriers which
> separate women from the collective.[39]

NWAC, representing a largely disenfranchised community, found itself
marginalized by the powerbrokers shaping the constitutional
discourse. NWAC wanted a role in the form of a seat at the discussion
table and funding for constitutional participation. It had been surviving
on grant money funnelled through the other organizations, primarily
the AFN. This had the effect of incorporating NWAC into the AFN in
terms of political access to the negotiation table, as well as with respect
to priority agenda items for discussion at those tables. NWAC took
the position that, by funding the AFN to promote its anti-Charter
position and by not funding NWAC, the government was "expressing
an unconstitutional preference for the promotion of views which will
lead to the extinguishment of Aboriginal women's equality rights."[40]

Unwilling to continue to engage in an apparently fruitless negotiation
process, NWAC initiated legal action against the federal government.
In a 1992 press release, NWAC said it had

> brought this action to demand recognition at the Constitu-
> tional negotiation table. NWAC also demands funding equal
> to that which is provided to the four recognized Aboriginal
> organizations beginning April 1, 1992. Without those two
> essential conditions, NWAC asks the Federal Court to prohibit
> the government of Canada from giving any funds to the four
> organizations participating in the Canada Round.[41]

Citing discrimination, NWAC asked the Federal Court of Canada to stop
disbursement of the federally allocated $10 million to AFN, NCC, ITC,
and MNC until NWAC was granted an equal share.[42] NWAC also argued
it was an infringement on women's freedom of expression for the federal
government to fund only male-dominated groups to speak on Aboriginal
issues in the Constitution, while refusing to fund NWAC.[43]

At the trial level, Mr. Justice Walsh decided that there was no sex
discrimination or infringement of freedom of speech in the federal
government's refusal to include NWAC in the talks. He wrote that

> to hold that freedom of expression creates a right for every-
> one to have a voice in these discussions would paralyse the
> process... With respect to discrimination as to sex the dispro-
> portionate funds provided for the [NWAC] results not from

the fact that they are women but from the unwillingness of the government to recognize that they should be considered as a separate group within the Aboriginal community from the four named groups ... I find nothing unfair or contrary to natural justice in the selection of the said four groups to represent the Aboriginals at this conference.[44]

NWAC appealed.

The "Canada Round": No Room for Women

As regards the constitutional specifics of the inherent right of self-government, NWAC wanted the Charter to apply, at least until an Aboriginal charter is developed. It argued that failing to apply the Charter to Aboriginal government could jeopardize Native women's equality rights. NWAC president Gail Stacey-Moore insisted that self-government must guarantee basic human rights.[45] AFN National Chief Ovide Mercredi argued that Aboriginal people want and need their own charter. Stacey-Moore responded that Aboriginal women want their human rights guaranteed one way or another.[46] At the same time, Mercredi told reporters questioning whether there was a rift between the AFN and Native women, "there's no issue here."[47] The AFN rejected the application of the Charter because it is "white"; its imposition would be a "continuation of imperialism, with one set of values imposed upon another culture," according to Mercredi.[48]

This is interesting, in light of the appeals Aboriginal peoples frequently make to the Universal Declaration of Human Rights and the Covenants on Economic, Social and Cultural Rights, and on Civil and Political Rights. The Charter reiterates many of the guarantees in the international instruments. The latter are taken to be universal standards for state behaviour. Presumably, Aboriginal governments would not be exempt nor would they want to be exempt from these standards.

In a July 8, 1992, letter to all First Ministers, NWAC President Gail Stacey-Moore wrote: "It is obvious from the 'deal' you have now concluded that in the absence of Aboriginal women at the table—women elected to represent the interests of women—that our issues are not dealt with fairly and justly."[49] On July 10, she wrote to AFN National Chief Ovide Mercredi: "If, as you have publically [sic] stated, the Assembly of First Nations represents Aboriginal women as well as Chiefs, we demand to know the basis for the decision to reject demands by Native women for entrenchment of their sexual equality rights."[50]

And the First Ministers were apparently as willing as Aboriginal leaders for Native women's rights to be put on the back burner. The text of the Premiers' unity proposal, printed in the *Globe and Mail* on July 10, 1992 commented:

> On gender equality, the chair… reported the agreement of the principles not to change s.35(4) already in the Constitution (guaranteeing Aboriginal and treaty rights equally to male and female persons) and to *add the issue of gender equality to the agenda of the future First Ministers' Conference (FMC) on Aboriginal matters* [emphasis mine].[51]

The National Action Committee on the Status of Women cited this deferral of a discussion of Aboriginal women's equality rights in its campaign to have the Referendum on the Charlottetown Accord defeated.[52]

The exemption of Aboriginal governments from Charter application raised the spectre of some Aboriginal governments invoking "inherency" and "tradition" to support various kinds of sex-based discrimination (such as in relation to membership). NWAC feared, with some justification, that the existing s.35(4) would not shield women in such situations. As Michele Landsberg wrote:

> Native women have good cause to fear the "collective rights" that the Aboriginal men are demanding. Nations around the world have used similar collective rights to suppress women's equality on grounds of "tradition, custom, and history."[53]

Reacting to the not unexpected betrayal by First Ministers and the Aboriginal organizations, Sharon McIvor, speaking for NWAC, said "this constitutional 'deal' wipes out the 20-year struggle by Native women for sexual equality rights in Canada."[54] McIvor said Native women would not be protected from "male-dominated" Native governments because gender equality provisions in the Charter would not apply to Aboriginal governments. She pointed out that existing Charter guarantees could be insufficient in any case, as Aboriginal governments could resort to s.33, the notwithstanding clause.[55] (For those who think McIvor overstates the danger of this, consider how many First Nations would like to invoke a legal or political override of the C-31 status provisions; and watch the *Twinn* case in the Federal Court of Appeal this fall.) NWAC continued to request a seat in future negotiations.

Interestingly, the Native Council of Canada had unsuccessfully pressed for changes to accommodate NWAC's concerns; it did not get support from the other Native organizations.

All for One and One for All: Feminist Solidarity

In its response to the Beaudoin-Dobbie Report,[56] the National Action Committee on the Status of Women (NAC) had served notice that it would be supporting NWAC in regard to applicability of the Charter and the principle that the notwithstanding clause not be available to Aboriginal governments. Subsequently, NAC support translated into solidarity with NWAC in opposing the Charlottetown Accord. "NAC strongly supports the (NWAC). We've agreed with them that they would take the lead on this issue—it's their issue—and we would back them," said then NAC president Judy Rebick.[57] In a position paper issued by NAC shortly after the publication of the Accord, NAC called the Accord "a bad deal for women." It went on to warn that "There is no guarantee of gender equality for Aboriginal women in the text and NWAC and the National Métis Women of Canada believe that their rights will be threatened under this self-government agreement."[58] In a special edition of *Action Now,* the NAC newsletter, NAC issued a call to members to vote no in the October 26th referendum and to engage in the "No" campaign because, among other reasons, "(The Accord) does not protect Aboriginal women under self-government."[59]

This support was a logical expression of NAC's commitment to accepting women's definitions of their realities. NAC's feminist analysis includes an identification as women, with an obligation of solidarity with other women, because of the shared experience of gender oppression regardless of race or caste.[60] As Mary Daly put it, "Sisterhood is the bonding of those who are oppressed by definition."[61]

Some observers sought to discredit the alliance as poorly conceived or politically opportunistic. However, NAC has a long history of supporting Aboriginal women's struggles, notably since 1972. Further, some activists in NWAC have also held NAC membership, and as full and influential participants at senior levels. For example, NWAC leader Gail Stacey-Moore has been co-chair of the NAC committee on Aboriginal women.[62]

On August 24, 1992, NAC and NWAC sponsored a meeting attended by over 150 leaders of women's groups from across Canada to discuss the constitutional proposals. The consensus of the groups was that the agreement threatened social programs and equality rights. By the end of the conference, and further to the decision by the Federal Court of Canada that the NWAC had suffered discrimination by its exclusion from the constitutional table, NAC had reaffirmed that position[63] and called upon the federal government to ensure that NWAC and the National Métis Women of Canada would get participant status in the pending First Ministers Conference.[64]

On August 26th, NAC sent a letter to Prime Minister Brian Mulroney asking for a "seat at the table," and:

(1) that the Prime Minister invite a delegation of Aboriginal women including NWAC and the National Métis Women of Canada "to sit as a full delegation at Thursday's meeting of First Ministers and in any future multilateral negotiations."

(2) that a delegation from the conference, organised by NAC, be given time on the agenda to present proposals and concerns and to discuss these with the First Ministers.[65]

Denied participation in discussions and negotiations, and faced with the prospect of constitutionally permissible discrimination if the Charlottetown package was adopted in its entirety, NWAC changed its strategy to obtaining a court injunction halting the constitutional referendum. The request by NWAC to halt the referendum was delayed until less than three weeks before the vote by Mr. Justice Yvon Pinard of the Federal Court of Canada, at the request of the AFN, which intended to intervene.

Invoking the Charter

On August 20, 1992, NWAC won the Federal Court of Appeal decision[66] ruling that its right to free speech had been violated by its exclusion from the constitutional talks. Mr. Justice Mahoney wrote:

> [I]t is in the interests of Aboriginal women that... they continue to enjoy the protections of the Charter.... The interests of Aboriginal women were not represented by the AFN... nor... the NCC and the ITC on this issue.... By funding the participation of the four designated organizations and excluding the equal participation of the NWAC, the Canadian government accorded the advocates of male dominated Aboriginal self-governments a preferred position... by including the AFN, an organization proved to be adverse in interest to Aboriginal women, while excluding NWAC, an organization that speaks for their interest, in a constitutional review process, the federal government restricted the freedom of expression of Aboriginal women in a manner offensive to ss.2(b) and 28 of the Charter.[67]

Making its case, NWAC documented that the organization had been ignored in its requests to participate, and alleged that the constitutional provisions on Aboriginal government did not protect Native women's equality rights. NWAC asked the court to "halt the referendum and prohibit other native groups from further constitutional talks with the federal and provincial governments."[68] However, the court said it had no power to order the federal government to invite NWAC to join the talks. No remedy was granted.

Well-Placed Distrust

When it was revealed on August 26th, the Charlottetown Accord, while not dealing with the issue of Native sexual equality, suggested it should be on the agenda for future Aboriginal constitutional conferences. Apparently the old boys had incorporated the premiers' earlier package of proposals with regard to deferring consideration of gender equality. This "wait your turn" approach to Aboriginal women's concerns did not sit well with NWAC, NAC, and many other social justice groups.

And then the political negotiations and legal haggling began. The Accord would be interpreted and implemented by means of legal text and political accords, which were being drafted in elite working groups behind closed doors. The legal text was not available to the public until a few days before the national referendum. NWAC was not alone in articulating anxiety about the process and the possible compromises that would be made behind the scenes: many "No" groups sprang up across the country to mobilize public rejection of the Accord.[69] Rumours abounded that the legal text substantiated NWAC's fears of political isolation and marginalization.

NWAC had expressed concern that its exclusion from the federal, provincial, and Native officials' ongoing discussions on a legal text of the political accord further jeopardized its position.[70] Subsequent events proved NWAC right. NWAC warned that the draft legal text contained changes that negated the guarantee in the political accord to have the Charter apply to Aboriginal governments.[71] Anne Bayefsky, a noted human rights scholar and legal adviser to NWAC, publicly charged that the draft legal text showed that Native womens' rights had been sold out.[72]

When the legal text was finally released, it proved those fears to be well grounded. The draft legal text of October 9, 1991, for example, provided for access by Aboriginal legislative bodies to s.33, the not-withstanding clause.[73] The draft legal text went on to entrench "the inherent right of self-government" as "one of three orders of government," that right to be exercised by "duly constituted legislative bodies... each within its own jurisdiction... to safeguard and develop their languages, cultures, economics, identities, institutions and traditions."[74] There was some concern that this provided a legal arsenal for such bodies to defend discriminatory policy by invoking the right to "safeguard and develop… tradition"; that is, to claim that exclusion of women in various circumstances was traditional and therefore justified.

Joan Bryden, writing for the *Calgary Herald*, reported that

> The consensus report says the Charter… will apply to Aboriginal self-government. But the draft legal text effectively negates that provision, adding a clause specifying that nothing in the charter abrogates or derogates from the inherent right to self-government or the rights of Aboriginal governments to protect native languages, cultures and traditions.
>
> It further amends the charter to ensure that Aboriginal governments do not have to be elected….[75]

Mary Eberts for NWAC argued for an injunction to stop the October 26 referendum outside of Quebec. NWAC alleged that it was wrongly excluded from constitutional talks leading to the Accord, and that the Accord threatened Native women's rights. The legal result, argued Eberts, "could allow male-dominated native self-governments to discriminate against women, using traditions to justify denying women the right to vote, band membership or even proper protection from sexual assault and other abuse."[76] By way of example, Eberts cited the judicial response to the defence of "tradition" to the gang rape of a 13-year-old Inuit girl:

> In the case, three Inuit men were given light sentences—that were eventually raised to four months in jail—because a judge ruled that under Inuit tradition a girl is ready for intercourse when she is 13.
>
> The girl became pregnant as a result of the rape but the judge said she suffered no harm because Inuit tradition accepts children born out of wedlock.[77]

The drafting of the Accord, and of the more specific political accords, and of the critically important legal text, was done with consultation with the four other Aboriginal organizations, but without NWAC. The referendum timetable clashed with the significant constitutional questions raised by NWAC in its largely successful appeal from the Federal Court decision. NWAC and political fellow-travellers could only interpret the process of constitutional evolution as willfully exclusionary of Aboriginal women, and as blind to the historical record of injustice to them at the hands of both Aboriginal and mainstream governments.

On October 26, 1992, Canadians overwhelmingly voted against the Charlottetown Accord. Analysts have suggested the rejection was more of the process that created it than of the package itself; most commentators were quick to say that of any component in the package, the Aboriginal government portion was perhaps the most supported and should survive despite the Accord's demise.

Expressing relief the day after the national rejection of the Charlottetown Accord, NWAC's regional executive director Sharon McIvor said "There are currently about five cases in Canada where women have taken their band councils to court because of sexual discrimination. Those cases could have been 'thrown into limbo' if the vote had gone Yes."[78]

This Is a Song that Never Ends

The Charlottetown Accord may be dead, but its issues have a life of their own. The Aboriginal desire for self-determination has not been satisfied by the political process that resulted in the failure of the Charlottetown Accord. Aboriginal governments of various descriptions hold the view that the inherent right to Aboriginal government is implicitly contained in s.35 of the Constitution Act 1982. Many intend to exercise that right, and allow the Canadian political and legal institutions to respond to direct political action asserting Aboriginal sovereignty.

Issues of Aboriginal government, shared bilateral and trilateral jurisdictions, land claims, treaty modernization, and constitutional renewal now exist in an apparent policy vacuum. The federal government, by way of its largely discredited "community-based self-government" initiative,[79] the Yukon government's land claims and band government initiatives, the Aboriginal government implications of Northwest Territories division, and provincial initiatives such as BC's promising Treaty Commission, all attempt to inject some policy parameters into this vacuum. All governments are mindful that they can no longer pretend the issue of a third order of government does not exist, or that it does not have compelling merit. But none seem to be willing to grapple with the concomitant issue of gender oppression within Aboriginal communities. Perhaps the issue is too close to home—for the sex oppression in Aboriginal communities is patterned on the sex oppression in Canada generally. Perhaps addressing the systemic gender oppression of Aboriginal women would logically lead to examining the oppression of non-Aboriginal women, and a host of discriminatory relationships. And perhaps white guilt is stifling any critique of Aboriginal social and political relations.

Aboriginal peoples, and especially some Indian bands, are not prepared to forgo self-government because of the referendum failure.

Some have declared their intention to assert their political autonomy, and to replace mainstream institutions with Aboriginal ones. Women's interests are not often central to the analysis of the new order. A case in point is illustrated by the current tensions at the Rosseau River Reserve in Manitoba.

The Manitoba chiefs have taken the position that gaming—gambling— is within the jurisdiction of Aboriginal governments. The potential creation of gaming establishments on-reserve offers economic benefits; similar establishments on American reserves have done much to improve reserve economies. However, the provincial government is not prepared to concede the jurisdiction, and Rosseau River decided to act in advance of any agreement, by setting up gambling machines on the reserve, without the requisite provincial permit. In accordance with the existing law, the RCMP removed the gambling machines, assisted by the tribal police. The tribal government responded by ordering the tribal police off the reserve. The police were replaced by a warrior society, also known as the Peacekeepers. The band council insists it has the right to jurisdiction in this matter.

On January 26, 1993, CBC Radio ran a story in which women from the reserve said they were worried about their safety and security in the wake of eviction of RCMP and tribal police by the band council. The women wished to be anonymous, out of fear of harrassment. Said one woman, "They (the band council and warriors) say they want to work with the women, but then they tell us to shut up." One woman's abusive former boyfriend, on probation for assaulting her, is a warrior. The women are afraid. They don't trust the warriors or the band council to guarantee their safety."[80]

On January 28, women from Rosseau River met with AFN National Chief Ovide Mercredi, to voice concerns about the handling of policing on the reserve and the safety of the community. The women told Mercredi that they feared for their safety: several had been threatened or had witnessed threats by the Warriors to those who supported the tribal police.[81] They told how one woman had been told to "leave the reserve if she knew what was good for her." Phil Fontaine of the Manitoba chiefs disagreed with the women's analysis: he argued this is part of self-government, and that self-government has its risks and they must be accepted.[82]

Even those Aboriginal women who have a political analysis of their experience as women in addition to their experience as Aboriginal women are intimidated by the process of activism. As I have written elsewhere,

Aboriginal organizations and many First Nations are bludg-eoning dissent with the argument that dissent on this matter undermines the political strength of the organizations; and is orchestrated by "white Toronto feminists," and that Indian women are not feminists and do not support feminism, i.e. equal rights; and that Indian government, returning to tradi-tional ways or basing processes on traditional values, will put something in place (but not the Charter) to ensure equality among citizens.

Aboriginal women are vulnerable to being branded as puppets of the "white" feminist movements, as being unAboriginal, if they speak up for women's participation and protection of women's rights in Aboriginal contexts. This kind of powerful silencing technique is familiar to women of all races. Sadly, it is often effective.[83]

Speaking of C-31, Nellie Carlson, a prominent activist for repeal of discriminatory sections of the Indian Act, said: "Indian women worked so hard to have that bill passed. We had no money; our lives were threatened, we were followed everywhere we went, our phones were tapped—that's how Indian women were treated for speaking out."[84]

Aboriginal feminists take great risks and display real courage in continuing their activism. This intimidation is shared by all feminists who find themselves targets of ridicule, marginalization, and other sanctions including physical assault. However, it is a more profound threat for Aboriginal women, because the attackers deny the validity of their analysis as authentically Aboriginal. It is a painful thing to be labelled as a dupe of the colonizing society for undertaking to name and change women's experience.

The single most influential factor determining the exclusion of NWAC from the constitutional arena was the collective refusal to see Aboriginal women's concerns (or, for that matter, other women's concerns) as distinct from and equally legitimate with Aboriginal men's concerns, and to see "male-stream" organizations as precisely that. Closely tied to this was the collective denial of the reality of the experience of the NWAC constituency—an experience of marginalization and persecution.

In terms of policy outcomes, it is important to remember that neither the court nor the political alliances and advocacy created a remedy for NWAC. Had the Charlottetown Accord been approved and implemented, NWAC's concerns would not have changed the Accord's composition.

No one speaking for NWAC, NAC, or the National Métis Women of Canada is opposed to constitutional affirmation of the inherent right of Aboriginal peoples to their own governmental powers. But the women's organizations do not accept that a choice must be made between justice for Aboriginal societies vis-à-vis the dominant society, and justice between Aboriginal women and men. As the late Sally Weaver wrote, "First Nations women have continued to pursue socio-economic equality in Canadian society, while simultaneously seeking their primary targets of equality of Indian rights and human rights for Indian women."[85] Liberation from colonialism will be of no assistance to Aboriginal women if sexism maintains a colonial relationship between Aboriginal men and women. So far Aboriginal organizations have been unwilling to be internally critical, to tolerate any criticism, or to accept responsibility for discriminatory behaviour and politics. In the wake of the Charlottetown fracas, the problem of sexism persists.

Once again, women who object to the exclusion of their interests as women are told that there is no issue, and that the political interests of the First Nations are served by denying women's issues. While male leaders speak for "their people," dissident women's voices are silenced. *La plus ça change, la plus la même chose.*

Endnotes

[1] This term was coined by feminist theorist Mary O'Brien to describe what are often represented as "main-stream" organizations but which in fact are culturally and structurally male, primarily staffed by males, and pursue a male-identified and priorized agenda.

[2] Commenting on behalf of the Women of the Métis Nation to the Royal Commission on Aboriginal Peoples, on May 11, 1992, Marge Friedel observed: "The Government of Canada treats these self-interest groups as though they are governments…. because these groups are treated like governments, they now believe that they are governments… this is totally unacceptable and somewhat ludicrous." Presentation to the RCAP, May 11, 1992.

[3] The argument was initiated and has been persuasively made by First Nations activists and the five national Aboriginal organizations during the constitutional negotiations under s.37 that the inherent right of self-government is implicit in s.35 of the Constitution Act (1982).

[4] Métis women formed the National Métis Women of Canada on October 26, 1991. Throughout the last round of constitutional negotiations the NMW operated with the financial assistance of NWAC and the Native Council of Canada. Formerly under the NWAC umbrella, the

NMW decided a parallel Métis-specific organization would better articulate the views of Métis women. In an interview with the writer in March 1993, Marge Friedel, President of the NMW, indicated the NWAC preoccupation with status issues was not shared by Métis women; however the two organizations have a good relationship and share many views on women's issues and on constitutional development relating to Aboriginal peoples. Because of the relatively greater prominence of NWAC, due in no small part to its longer presence on the political scene, it was a more significant player in the constitutional arena and so this paper focuses particularly on NWAC.

[5] *AG* v. *Lavell* and *Isaac* v. *Bedard*. [1974] S.C.R. 1349. The National Indian Brotherhood, the precursor of the AFN, had intervened against Jeanette Corbiere Lavell in her Supreme Court challenge of the discriminatory provisions of the Indian Act.

[6] R. Platiel, "Women Seek to Block Grants to Other Native Groups in Charter Fight," *Globe & Mail* (March 19, 1992).

[7] Presentation by Marge Friedel and Wendy Walker, on behalf of the Women of the Métis Nation to the Royal Commission on Aboriginal Peoples, May 1992.

[8] *Native Women's Association of Canada* v. *Canada* (1992). 4 C.N.L.R (F.C.A.).

[9] Sue Findley, "Facing the State: The Politics of the Women's Movement Reconsidered," in *Feminism and Political Economy: Women's Work. Women's Struggles*, ed. H.J. Maroney and M. Luxton (Toronto: Metheun, 1987), 31.

[10] Rianne Mahon, "Canadian Public Policy: The Unequal Structure of Representation," in *The Canadian State*, ed. L. Panitch (Toronto: University of Toronto Press, 1977) 165–98.

[11] Findlay, 31.

[12] Arguably a third experience common to Aboriginal women, poverty, creates a third oppression, that of class.

[13] For example, the Women of the Métis Nation in Alberta, the National Métis Women of Canada (NWAC) and the Manitoba Indigenous Women's Collective.

[14] Evelyn Webster, Vice-President, Indigenous Women's Collective of Manitoba, to the Royal Commission on Aboriginal Peoples, April 22, 1992.

[15] D. Hoffman, "A Call For a Return to Historical Values," *Saskatoon StarPhoenix* (September 19, 1992); "Equal, Respected, Revered. Historically, This is How Aboriginal Societies Viewed Women," *Saskatoon StarPhoenix* (ca. September 1992). See also Karen

Anderson, "A Gendered World: Women, Men and the Political Economy of the Seventeenth-Century Huron," in *Feminism and Political Economy: Women's Work. Women's Struggles*, ed. H.J. Maroney and M. Luxton (Toronto: Metheun, 1987), for a discussion of the differently gendered but equally respected roles of traditional Huron society; and NWAC's discussion paper "Matriarchy and the Canadian Charter," reviewing the traditional Iroquoian matriarchy.

[16] For example, T. Nahanee, "First Nations Government Without Women" (Presented to the National Association of Women and the Law, Vancouver, 20 February 1993) [unpublished].

[17] Hoffman, "A Call For a Return to Historical Values."

[18] B. Bastion, E. Bastien, and J. Wierzba, "Native Family Violence in Lethbridge," *Native Studies Review* 7 (1991): 139.

[19] Ibid., 146.

[20] Hoffman, "A Call For a Return to Historical Values."

[21] R. Platiel, "Aboriginal Women Challenge Leadership," *Globe & Mail* (April 24, 1992).

[22] Ibid.

[23] Indigenous Women's Collective of Manitoba, to the Royal Commission on Aboriginal Peoples, April 22, 1992.

[24] "Amnesty Proposed for Child Abusers," *Edmonton Journal* (June 25, 1993) A-11.

[25] *AG* v. *Lavell* and *Isaac* v. *Bedard.* [1974] S.C.R. 1349.

[26] Re *Sandra Lovelace.* United Nations Human Rights Commission 6-50 M 215-51 CANA. Canada was found to be in violation of s.27 of the Covenant on Civil and Political Rights.

[27] For a more thorough discussion of this issue, see J. Green, "Sexual Equality and Indian Government: An Analysis of Bill C-31 Amendments to the Indian Act," *Native Studies Review* 1 (1995); and K. Jamieson, *Indian Women and the Law in Canada: Citizens Minus* (Ottawa: Supply and Services, 1978).

[28] Nahanee: "Many of our First Nations people believe paternalism, patriarchy and patriarchal customs are the great traditions to which we will return once we have cast off our oppressors."

[29] Jack Danylchuk, "The Long Road Home," *Edmonton Journal* (January 30, 1993).

[30] Ibid.

[31] Jack Danylchuk, "Bands Challenge Legality of Amendment," *Edmonton Journal* (January 30, 1993).

[32] Nahanee: "50,000 people are still waiting, and some may pass on to that other life before ever having their right to membership recognized."

[33] R. Platiel, "Native Women to Challenge Proposal on Aboriginal Rights," *Globe and Mail* (January 17, 1992).

[34] Ibid.

[35] Indigenous Women's Collective of Manitoba, to the Royal Commission on Aboriginal Peoples, April 22, 1992.

[36] R. Platiel, "Aboriginal Women Divide On Constitutional Protection" *Globe and Mail* (January 20, 1992).

[37] Ibid.

[38] Ibid.

[39] T. Nahanee.

[40] R. Platiel, "Women Seek to Block Grants to Other Native Groups in Charter Fight."

[41] NWAC press release (March 18, 1992).

[42] R. Platiel, "Women Seek to Block Grants to Other Native Groups in Charter Fight."

[43] "Native Women Lose Bid for Spot at Talks," *Globe and Mail* (April 1, 1992).

[44] *Native Women's Association of Canada* v. *Canada* (1992), 68–69.

[45] S. Delacourt, "Self government Must Guarantee Basic Human Rights—NWAC President Gail Stacey-Moore," *Globe and Mail* (March 14, 1992).

[46] Ibid.

[47] Ibid.

[48] Hoffman, "A Call For a Return to Historical Values."

[49] NWAC correspondence to all First Ministers, signed by Gail Stacey-Moore, July 8, 1992.

[50] NWAC correspondence to AFN National Chief Ovide Mercredi, signed by Gail Stacey-Moore, July 10, 1992.

[51] "Text of Premiers' Unity Proposal," *Globe and Mail* (July 10, 1992).

[52] "NAC says NO to this Constitutional Deal," undated NAC publication circa September 1992.

[53] M. Landsberg, "Feminists Have Backed Native Women From Outset," *Toronto Star* (March 31, 1992).

[54] R. Platiel, "Native Women Fear Loss of Rights," *Globe and Mail* (July 13, 1992).

[55] R. Platiel, "Native Groups Disunited Over Gender Equality," *Globe and Mail* (20 July 1992).

[56] NAC's Response to the Report of the Special Joint Committee on a Renewed Canada, May 4, 1992, 6, 12, and 19.

[57] Landsberg.

[58] NAC Constitution Position paper, undated, circa September 1992.

[59] National Action Committee on the Status of Women, *Action Now,* September/October 1992.

[60] Speaking of the feminist response to constitutional change in the earlier Meech Lake fiasco, Donna Greschner spoke of the logic of support for Aboriginal women: "Taking the perspective of aboriginal women as the standard of assessment for constitutional proposals is consistent with the feminist method of looking to the bottom, of asking who is buried beneath the social heap, why and what can be done about it. At the least, constitutional change should meet the Rawlsian standards of not making worse the position of the worst-off" in her "Commentary" in *After Meech Lake: Lesions for the Future* (Saskatoon: Fifth House Publishers, 1991), 223.

[61] M. Daly, *Beyond God the Father: Toward a Philosophy of Women's Liberation* (Boston: Beacon Press, 1973) 59.

[62] Landsberg.

[63] "Conclusions of the Women's Constitutional Conference," NAC fax. August 25, 1992.

[64] R. Platiel, "Aboriginal Women Challenge Leadership": "In light of last week's court decision that the federal government had discriminated against the Native Women's Association of Canada by denying them a seat at the Constitutional table, participants called for a delegation of Aboriginal women, including representatives of [NWAC] and the National Métis Women, to be seated as full participants at the upcoming First Ministers' Conference."

[65] Correspondence from NAC President Judy Rebick to Prime Minister Brian Mulroney, August 26, 1992.

[66] *Native Women's Association of Canada* v. *Canada* (1992).

[67] Ibid., 72–73.

[68] Ibid.

[69] Apart from the NWAC-NAC alliance, there was no "No" coalition to oppose the Charlottetown Accord. It is as untrue as it is distasteful to suggest (as some commentators did) that "NAC is in bed with the Reform Party." There was a "Yes" coalition, however.

[70] "Judge Delays Attempt by Native Women to Halt Referendum," *Globe and Mail* (September 1992).

[71] Ibid.

[72] J. Bryden, "Secret Reports Show Unity Deal Reworked" *Calgary Herald* (September 19, 1992).

[73] "Draft Legal Text," a "best efforts" text prepared by officials representing all First Ministers and Aboriginal and Territorial Leaders, October 9, 1992.

[74] Ibid.

[75] Ibid.

[76] "Judge, Lawyer Disagree on Loss of Rights," *Calgary Herald* (October 15, 1992).

[77] Ibid.

[78] W. Dudley, "Natives Greet the Vote with Bitterness, Relief," *Calgary Herald* (October 27, 1992).

[79] A Federal Department of Indian and Northern Affairs policy initiative, this process is limited in access to a select number of bands, and in result, to a delegated municipal form of government within a legislated framework. Many First Nations, and the Assembly of First Nations, have criticized the "CBSG" process for being inadequate for real change, inappropriate for constitutional change affirming Aboriginal and treaty rights, and pernicious in that it potentially undermines more comprehensive political initiatives.

[80] CBC Radio News (January 26, 1993).

[81] "Native Women Fearful," *Globe and Mail* (January 29, 1993).

[82] CBC Radio news (29 January 1993).

[83] J. Green, "The Parthenogenic Child of the Fathers" (published as "A Comprehensive Analysis of the Charlottetown Accord") *The Womanist* 3 (1982).

[84] J. Danylchuk, "Sweet Taste of Victory Soured by Band Reaction," *Edmonton Journal* (January 30, 1993).

[85]"First Nations Women and Government Policy, 1970–92: Discrimination and Conflict'" in *Changing Patterns: Women in Canada*, ed. S. Burt, L. Code and L. Domey (Toronto: McClelland & Stewart, 1993) 128–9.

Aboriginal Women and Self-Government

Margaret A. Jackson

Margaret Jackson is a Professor in the School of Criminology at Simon Fraser University, BC, who teaches and conducts research in the areas of Aboriginal women and justice, violence against women and children, corrections, and criminal justice policy analysis.

It has been argued that the application of Canadian law is becoming more sensitized to questions of gender equality (Brockman and Chunn). However, the fear has been expressed that the increased emphasis on customary law that is expected to accompany movement toward Aboriginal self-government may not capture this trend. It is a "Catch 22" situation. The arguments of certain Aboriginal women's groups (for example, the Native Women's Association of Canada—NWAC) are resisted by other Aboriginal women's groups and other traditional First Nations groups (for example, the Assembly of First Nations—AFN), in part because it is felt that public examination of the issue might jeopardize hard-won steps toward self-government (Fleras and Elliott). Meanwhile, some have suggested that a return to customary law should not provoke any such concerns, since one of the goals of self-government is to create local community governance structures based on traditional Aboriginal values.

This article presents an overview of self-determination/self-government issues from the perspective of Aboriginal women. It is their voices that carve out the various positions taken, and it is their voices that policy makers and legislators must weigh. My purpose is to provide a summation and analysis of their perspectives. After establishing

This article was originally published in *Aboriginal Self-Government in Canada*, ed. John H. Hylton (Saskatoon: Purich Publishing Ltd, 1994), 180–98. Published with permission of the author.

the historical context, I present a selection of the positions held by Aboriginal women and an analysis of possible future policy directions.

A review of recent Canadian legal history provides the context for the discussion. It is not my intention to provide a legal analysis of the issues, since this has already been completed by Aboriginal women lawyers (Turpel; Monture-OKanee, "Reclaiming Justice"; Nahanee). Rather, I wish to describe the socio-legal policy context—the values in conflict, the stakeholders, and the earlier decisions that can bring us to an understanding of present positions.

The Policy Environment: Four Historical Junctures

Four important junctures in recent history have influenced the current policy environment pertaining to Aboriginal women and self-government/self-determination.[1] These are:

1. The repeal of section 12(1)(b) of the Indian Act in 1985;
2. The increasing cultural sensitivity shown by some judiciary in the early 1980s;
3. Entrenchment of the Charter of Rights and Freedoms in the Canadian Constitution in 1982; and
4. More recent constitutional talks that involved consideration of self-government for the Aboriginal Peoples.

Together, these developments have provided the triggering stimulus for the accommodation of Aboriginal women's interests and perspectives.

1. Repeal of Section 12(1)(b): Beginning of the Path?

The repeal of section 12(1)(b) of the Indian Act in 1985 was, perhaps, the first signal given to Aboriginal women in Canada that they could achieve some measure of self-determination.

The legacy of the 1876 Indian Act cannot be overemphasized here. The intent of the original act (and subsequent versions) was to regulate the use of reserve land and persons eligible to use reserve land (Moss). One consequence of the government's decision to "enfranchise" Aboriginal people under the act was to have them lose their Aboriginal status. There was the clear government intent to absorb all Indians into Canadian society, such that there would be no need to even have an Indian department (Moss).

The impact of government policy on Aboriginal women was particularly discriminatory because section 12(1)(b) took away their Indian status when they married non-Indian men. Penalties included deprivation of rights, such as employment and accommodation rights, ostracism, and exclusion from involvement in tribal life (Fleras and Elliott).

In the 1970s, one Aboriginal woman, Jeanette Lavell, lost her challenge of the Indian Act in the Supreme Court of Canada. According to NWAC (13), the then-existing Bill of Rights was "simply another statute which could not override another statute." In 1981, however, Sandra Lovelace, another Aboriginal woman, succeeded in having the United Nations Committee on Human Rights declare the Indian Act provision discriminatory. The Lovelace decision was considered a landmark case because there was a recognition of "a right for minority groups and their members to define themselves" (Moss 294). In 1985, after the Charter of Rights and Freedoms was entrenched in the Constitution, Mary Two-Axe Early, the founder of a group called Indian Rights for Indian Women, won a case similar to Lavell's in the Supreme Court. These events paved the way for Parliament to adopt Bill C-31, which returned Indian status to thousands of Aboriginal women.[2]

As a result of Bill C-31, 70,000 men, women, girls, boys, and old and young people were added to the federal Indian registry and band lists (NWAC). According to NWAC, the status Indian population grew from 360,000 to 487,000 in a little over four and a half years.[3]

2. Cultural Sensitivity in the Courtroom: Unequal Justice?

Ironically, the second force contributing to the modern Aboriginal women's movement has been the increasing sensitivity shown by the Canadian judiciary. This was especially evident in the Northwest Territories during the 1980s, where customary law was considered in the sentencing of some Aboriginal offenders. Here the policy focus shifts to the justice system. For Aboriginal women, concerns have arisen because Aboriginal offenders (for the most part male) have been treated unequally by the Canadian justice system in the name of fair justice, but the result has often been injustice for Aboriginal women.[4] One high-profile case illustrates the concerns.

A one-week sentence was handed down by a judge for three Inuit men accused of raping a thirteen-year-old girl. The trial judge reasoned that cultural factors should be taken into consideration. He noted that Inuit people do not regard having sex with a girl under fourteen as a crime. He stated:

> A culturation process does not include the term statutory rape, jailbait, and other terms suggesting prohibition. Rather the morality or values of the people here is that when a girl begins to menstruate, she is considered ready to engage in sexual relations. That is the way life was and continues to be in the smaller communities. (Jackson 6)

In passing sentence, the trial judge described the three accused as a credit to the community and to their country. He also noted they used no violence and pleaded guilty, thus relieving the victim from the ordeal of three separate trials.

Although the trial judge attempted to incorporate Aboriginal standards for acceptable behaviour into his decision, his efforts to be sensitive to the local culture were rejected on appeal. The Court of Appeal asserted that courts are responsible for maintaining the law established by the Parliament of Canada and not for upholding community standards of behaviour. The sentence was lengthened to four months. The appeal court decision implied that Aboriginal custom did not carry the same weight as Canadian law and, by extension, that Aboriginal Peoples were not equal to non-Aboriginal peoples.[5]

Aboriginal women are concerned about these types of decisions. They fear that the attendance to cultural context does not necessarily serve the interests of Aboriginal women and children. In this regard, family violence and sexual abuse are frequently cited. Aboriginal women argue that these kinds of crimes have no place in customary or in traditional law (Jackson).

Another layer of difficulty for the current policy debate is that there has been no holistic approach, either legally or politically, to the role of customary law in Canada. Some argue that little or no customary law has been received into Canadian law (Haveman), while others have suggested that it has been deformed when introduced into the non-Aboriginal court system.

Richstone has pointed out that once a non-Aboriginal standard is adopted to determine the validity of Aboriginal customary law, the essence of the customary law may be lost. A judge, for example, may employ classifications of thought that are alien to the original structure of the Aboriginal *lex loci*. Richstone cites the example of Judge Sissons' decision in the Northwest Territories. Judge Sissons implied that Inuit custom was acceptable under the common law, only because it complied with the requirements of English law.[6] The danger arises that when an unconscientious ethnocentrism deforms a customary law, a precedent is established based on this distortion, and future cases follow from it (Richstone).

Many Aboriginal people have expressed the concern that customary law can (and has) become distorted in the white man's courts. Therefore, they feel it must be applied in its traditional form and setting. They view this as one of the important goals of self-government.

3. Charter of Rights and Freedoms: Needed Safeguard for Self-Government?

The third historical legal factor important for the current discussion is the entrenchment of the Charter of Rights and Freedoms in the Constitution Act (1982). Groups such as NWAC have argued that any collective self-governing arrangement must have the equality provisions of the Canadian Charter (or a similarly focused document) structured into the agreement in order to protect Aboriginal women's individual rights (Platiel). It is reasoned that customary law has traditionally held collective interests above individual interests in structuring social, political, and economical programs for Aboriginal communities. In the translation of such collective social values into operational mandates, the concern is that the interests of individual Aboriginal women could be overshadowed. This has happened in the past, and some fear that without a Charter safeguard, it could continue in the future.

The Charter, and other key provisions of the Constitution, have important implications for both individual rights and for self-government. With respect to individual rights, several sections, including 7, 15, 28, and 35, have been the subject of recent controversy.

Section 7 reads:

> Everyone has the right to life, liberty, and the security of the person and the right not to be deprived thereof except in accordance with the principles of fundamental justice.

It has already been argued that attendance to customary law does not necessarily constitute a negation of section 7 of the Charter. Mr. Justice de Weerdt, in the Saila case, for example, maintained that the principles of fundamental justice were not affected by the imposition of a customary form of punishment.[7] Therefore, the courts could give legal expression to community values through their sentencing decisions.

The courts' discretionary powers in sentencing, however, appear to have limits. The traditional method of discipline—ostracism by the community—is a well-recognized means of dealing with offenders who do not uphold customary traditions. However section 15(1) would appear to constrain the court's discretion. Section 15(1) states:

> Every individual is equal before and under the law and has the right to the equal protection and equal benefit of the law without discrimination and, in particular, without discrimination based on race, national or ethnic origin, colour, religion, sex, age or mental or physical disability.

Judges who consider Aboriginal customs in their sentencing are not meting out the same justice as that given to "white men" who do not possess Aboriginal customs, even though the underlying rationale may be well intended.

The next relevant section is section 28. It states: "Notwithstanding anything in this Charter, the rights and freedoms referred to in it are guaranteed equally to male and female persons." Finally, section 35(4) states: "Notwithstanding any other provision of this act, the Aboriginal treaty rights referred to in subsection (1) are guaranteed to male and female persons." Thus, the Charter and the Constitution, and especially the above-noted sections, are at the basis of self-government discussions for many Aboriginal women.

There are other implications of the Charter for self-government. While NWAC supports the inherent right to self-government, it argues that it is an existing right within the context of section 35 of the Constitution Act. If self-government is an inherent right, NWAC reasons that the Aboriginal governments subsequently formed must not simply be the currently existing patriarchal forms of governance that were created by a "foreign government," that is, those created under the Indian Act. If it is not agreed that self-government is an inherent right (and thus falls outside of section 35), then it is argued that section 2 of the Charter and sections 7 to 15 do apply to all Aboriginal persons.

NWAC has expressed the fear that some Aboriginal groups could, if given the opportunity, suspend the sections of the Charter that protect the individual rights described above. This could come about if Aboriginal governments have the opportunity to employ the notwithstanding clause of the Constitution Act.[8] Groups such as the AFN have long resisted the application of the Charter.[9] They hold that individual rights cannot override collective rights and that "the Canadian Charter is in conflict with our philosophy and culture" (NWAC 9).

4. The Constitutional Talks and Self-Government: Transcending to a Rights Perspective?

The fourth factor influencing Aboriginal women's perspectives on self-government is the recent constitutional talks. The efforts of Elijah Harper, former Aboriginal member of the Manitoba Legislature, forced attention in the Constitutional talks on the Aboriginal reality in Canada. This was in dramatic juxtaposition to the Quebec francophone concerns. Harper's actions were the culmination of a desire for cultural autonomy that had been growing since at least the 1980s.

In 1984, Marie Smallface Marule, in her article "Traditional Indian Government: Of the People, By the People, For the People," reported that a delegation from the Union of British Columbia Indian Chiefs had travelled to the United Nations to present their case to the under-secretary general of Political Affairs, Decolonization, and Trusteeships. They questioned why the colonial situations in Africa and Asia were being examined, but not those of the Aboriginal Peoples in the Western Hemisphere. It was, interestingly enough, shortly after this issue came to the attention of the UN, that the Canadian government appeared willing to negotiate changes to the Canadian Charter of Rights and Freedoms that added protection for Aboriginal rights and freedoms.

In 1990, Mr. Harper blocked approval of the Meech Lake Constitutional Accord because of his concern that Aboriginal issues were not being addressed in the constitutional process. As described by Mary Ellen Turpel, the distinct society clause triggered a strong reaction from Aboriginal Peoples. She quotes from the prepared statement of the AFN:

> It perpetuates the idea of a duality in Canada and strengthens the myth that the French and English peoples are the foundation of Canada. It neglects the original inhabitants and distorts history. It is as if the peoples of the First Nations never existed. It suggests that historically and presently as well the French peoples in Quebec form the only distinct society in Canada. The amendment fails to give explicit constitutional recognition to the existence of First Nations as distinct societies that also form a fundamental characteristic of Canada. We were told for five years that governments are reluctant to entrench undefined self-government of Aboriginal peoples in the Constitution. Yet, here is an equally vague idea of a "distinct society" unanimously agreed to and allowed to be left to the courts for interpretation.

Later, in the "Canada Round" of constitutional talks, NWAC was not allowed to have a place at the federal government's constitutional talks along with other Aboriginal groups. NWAC appeared before the Federal Court of Canada on March 16, 1992, to argue that Aboriginal women were being denied the right to free speech as guaranteed under the Charter. The decision of the court was in their favour—a landmark ruling that further marked the legitimacy of the individual rights claims. In the decision, Mr. Justice Walsh stated that "NWAC is a bona fide, established and recognized national voice of and for Aboriginal women" (Nahanee 22). In essence, the court determined that the rights of the Aboriginal women (as represented by NWAC) had been violated by the Canadian government.

The more recent interventions by Aboriginal women in the self-government process have been described by one law professor at the University of Calgary (quoted in Mahoney) as a "women's version of Elijah Harper." Just as Mr. Harper was concerned that Aboriginal rights to self-government were not being attended to in the constitutional talks, Aboriginal women are arguing that their individual rights are not being attended to in the self-government discussions.

Aboriginal Women Speak

It has been fascinating to observe how strong the voices of Aboriginal women have become in the debates about self-government. Teressa Nahanee, among others, would surely argue that this was not an overnight discovery of tongue, since she herself has been speaking out since at least 1976. It is only recently, however, that public awareness has been raised and tentative listening has begun.

There is not a single Aboriginal women's voice. Rather, divergent opinions are being offered. In this section, therefore, a representation of these voices is presented. For Aboriginal women, the key issues of concern have been the Indian Act, representation in constitutional talks, and the protection of individual rights.

The repeal of section 12(1)(b) of the Indian Act was received with qualified optimism by many Aboriginal women, but the issue of sexual discrimination was not completely addressed by the repeal of that one section. The continued existence of the act is a matter of considerable concern, and most Aboriginal organizations view reform efforts to date as piecemeal (Moss).

According to Moss, it has generally been maintained by women's groups that current inequalities are a "federally created problem" and that the elimination of sex discrimination from the Indian Act is the government's responsibility (287). But, as Moss observes, there is no real evidence that the government is willing to reopen the act to grapple with residual sexual discrimination or with other difficult policy issues relating to Aboriginal status entitlement.

The act has become a symbol of the struggle between Aboriginal collective rights, and individual human rights. Moss argues that, at least to some extent, the debate illustrates the difficulty of applying externally developed human rights' norms to cultures that resist them on grounds of conflict with traditional mores. To a greater degree, however, the problem may lie in the threat posed by imposing externally developed norms, even if they are consistent with current cultural norms.

Moss suggests that one key to achieving balance between collective and individual rights would seem to lie in consultations with Aboriginal groups. However, this raises an important question: Who should be consulted? The representation issue has emerged as a focal point for the current debates.

Not all Aboriginal women's groups have felt adequately represented at the constitutional talks on self-government, although there has certainly been a range of opinion in this regard. Wendy Grant, a vice-chief of a Musqueam reserve in British Columbia, for example, has stated (First Nations Summit 1992) that the Assembly of First Nations does have appropriate representation of women: "If you look at the AFN right now, our percentage of elected women chiefs is close to the percentage of elected women in the House of Commons."[10]

She is concerned that the NWAC insistence on entrenchment of the Charter in any self-governing process would "jeopardize key elements of traditional Native government, law and society" (quoted in Scott).

Jennie Jack of the AFN supports Grant's collective rights perspective: "To say that male chiefs do not represent their constituency is to be disrespectful of all men and women within their communities who elect their leadership." (Quoted in Scott) She continues by stating that a more "collective" role is the appropriate one for Aboriginal women:

> Aboriginal women have always looked out for the greater good of all people—men, women, children, and elders—rather than worry about putting the women's issue first. It's basic survival, it has nothing to do (with) gender.

Bernice Hammersmith, in her article on Aboriginal women and self-government, takes a similar position. She believes Aboriginal women should not attempt to make their own voices heard in the public fora, but they should stay "back in their own nations, no matter how evil they think the situation is. It is only by dealing with real concerns at the local level that we will get back to the original values of our nations" (56).

These Aboriginal women appear unwilling to focus upon gender equality as an issue apart from self-government. The collective interest "of all people" is seen to be the appropriate emphasis. Therefore, the individual rights of Aboriginal women are not singled out for attention.

With respect to the individual or collective rights debate, there has also been a variety of opinions. For example, the Ontario Native Women's Association, representing about ten thousand women, was among several Aboriginal women's groups that felt that representation at the constitutional talks was not an issue. They took the position (quoted in Fine) that enough protection had already been incorporated into the wording of the Charlottetown Accord, and therefore, an entrenched Charter was not a necessary condition for approval.

Rosemary Kuptana , head of the Inuit Tapirisat of Canada, adopted a similar stance. She was quoted as saying: "We are satisfied that the equality rights of Aboriginal women are not prejudiced by the Charlottetown Accord" (Canadian Press).

Sheila Genaille, president of the Métis National Council of Women, strongly endorsed the Charlottetown Accord as well: "From a Métis perspective, the constitutional agreement in Charlottetown provides protection for Aboriginal women in future self-government agreements." She further stated that the notwithstanding clause of the Charter did not allow any government (Aboriginal or otherwise) to "shield themselves from the gender equality rights (section 28) of the Charter."

These diverse and influential Aboriginal women appeared to have no difficulty with an accord that did not absolutely entrench Charter rights in self-governing arrangements, that is, they were not concerned about the possibility that an Aboriginal government would use the notwithstanding clause of the Charter to "opt out." Therefore, what are the other Aboriginal women's groups, such as NWAC, concerned about? Why are they adamant about having a Charter safeguard? On the surface, it may appear ironic that the NWAC position demands the inclusion of certain elements of white man's law—the Charter—in the self-government exercise. There are important underlying issues that need to be explored in order to arrive at an understanding of the basis for these different positions.

An understanding of the different positions that Aboriginal women have adopted in relation to self-government requires an analysis of the objectives that Aboriginal women are seeking to attain. In addition to being able to define themselves as Aboriginal, many Aboriginal women are also expressing a need to define themselves as women. The issue is one of self-determination. In this regard, Monture-OKanee quotes Osennontion:

> The establishment, exercise and enforcement of government, is only one aspect of 'self-determination'. In our own language, we have a word that, of course, even better describes what we have been instructed to do. TEWATATHA: which best translates into "we carry ourselves"—a rather simple concept, some might say, but I think it says it all. ("Reflecting on Flint Woman," 16)

Monture-OKanee has difficulty with what she perceives to be the construction of woman as "other" in the line of questioning of Aboriginal feminist. She states that "when one gender is constructed as 'other', then the goal of equality will continue to be elusive" ("Reclaiming Justice," 9).

In her paper "Reclaiming Justice: Aboriginal Women and Justice Initiatives in the 1990's," Monture-OKanee describes a story told by Marie Wilson of the Gitskan Wet'suwet'en Tribal Council. Wilson likens the relationship between women and men to the eagle. An eagle soars to unbelievable heights and has tremendous power on two equal wings, one female and one male, that carries the body of life between them. In the same way, women and men are said to be balanced parts of the whole, yet they are very different from each other. They are not "equal," if equality is defined as being the same. Rather, equality in this case is the contribution of both wings to the flight.

Monture-OKanee examines the feminist mind and the perspective of Aboriginal women. While she finds a certain shared reality between the two approaches in thinking, she also finds differences. She makes reference to a Cree colleague, Winona Stephenson:

> I want to understand why feminists continue to believe in the universality of male dominance, the universality of sisterhood, and why they strive so hard to convert Aboriginal women. I want feminists to know why many Aboriginal women do not identify as feminist. I perceive two parallel but distinct movements, but there ought to be a place where we can meet to share, learn, and offer honest support without trying to convert each other. ("Reclaiming Justice," 27)

This points out an important additional layer in the debate. The emphasis Aboriginal feminists place on the gender equality component of self-government contrasts with the emphasis of Aboriginal women who do not approach self-government from a feminist perspective. Those, such as Monture-OKanee, who argue that racial and cultural inequality are as important as gender inequality, undoubtedly have a different perspective than feminists, such as Nahanee, who argue that the main concern for Aboriginal women relates to the gender issue and the protection of individual rights.

Monture-OKanee has challenged the feminist point of view:

> Feminist thought can inform attempts to understand Aboriginal women's reality. But, feminism must be seen as only one tool which may or may not accurately inform our developing understanding. ("Reclaiming Justice," 28)

Similarly, Lillian Head has commented:

> Women are often the most oppressed in any marginalized group. Moreover, relationships that women seem to have with the land, Mother Earth, are very special. As Indigenous women we can't belittle the feminist movement because they too are going through struggles. Different women's groups are going through different experiences in terms of being oppressed by patriarchal societies. (Clark 48)

In contrast, feminist arguments have been advanced by NWAC member Teressa Nahanee and others. In her paper, "Dancing with a Gorilla," Nahanee takes a feminist-legal theory approach. While her starting point is one that Monture-OKanee and Head would agree with—that Aboriginal women need to be included in the consultation process—Nahanee focuses on justice issues, and, in particular, on the reality of sexual and physical abuse of Aboriginal women. She notes that "customary" sanctioning of sexual offenders has been ineffective in curbing sexual violence, and that customary cultural values—such as kindness, reconciliation, and family cohesiveness—may actually prevent Aboriginal women from officially reporting violence in the home. She traces much of the difficulty to the fact that males have almost total control in Aboriginal communities through band councils that, ironically, were first established under the Indian Act.[11]

Nahanee expresses concerns about the types of cases in the Northwest Territories, cited earlier, and those occurring more recently in British Columbia. She feels these cases indicate why "culturally sensitive" judicial decision-making is detrimental to Aboriginal women. Interestingly, her "feminist" resolution appears quite similar to Monture-OKanee's. She states: "There needs to be a return to traditional ways, healing circles, and a sharing of power between the men and the women" (9).

According to Nahanee, Aboriginal women want to revive traditions that recognize equally valued roles for both men and women. She fears, however, that men are not willing to share power in many situations. For instance, she notes that women are told that they cannot participate in sweat lodges and other ceremonies when they are menstruating because men are afraid of "women" power.

Nahanee traces the history of Indian sexual inequality from the Lavell case. For Nahanee, the challenge Lavell made to the Indian Act in 1970 was a challenge to the patriarchal state. The court decision in Lavell clearly underpins the social values of equality that Nahanee feels should remain foremost in the movement toward self-government.

The threats to equality, she believes, are very real. She notes that in the 1980s, the AFN and the Native Council of Canada both agreed that sexual discrimination should end; however, they felt that interim measures could be taken while further studies were pursued. The Native Women's Association of Canada, on the other hand, insisted that amendments to the Indian Act that would end discrimination should be brought forward immediately.

Other Aboriginal women and women's groups support the Nahanee/NWAC position. Winnie Giesbrecht, for example, president of the Indigenous Women's Collective of Manitoba, opposes self-government arrangements that do not have a guarantee of gender equality rights. She fears that Native politicians are no different from other politicians: "A politician is a politician. A politician is there for one reason—for themselves" (*Vancouver Sun*).

Freda Cooper, a fifty-nine-year-old Salish woman from Vancouver Island, takes the argument a step further. She questions the wisdom of returning to certain customary traditions. Pointing to a February 1992 BC Supreme Court decision, Cooper describes how a thirty-five-year-old Salish man was awarded $42,000 in damages for pain, suffering, and mental distress he suffered during his forcible initiation into the Coast Salish tradition of spirit dancing. She is also concerned about the protection of the Christian minority on reserves if there is a return to traditional spirituality.

It is clear that while Monture-OKanee is sensitive and appreciative of the feminist concerns about equality rights, she feels that this is only part of a larger rights issue. Her vision is for self-government based on Aboriginal values, not just values unique to Aboriginal women. She foresees a process by which both men and women undergo a healing process together in order to return to more traditional spirituality and self-determination. While Nahanee also sees the need for traditional healing, her emphasis is different. She does not want a return to customary law, if that means a return to the subservient role that Aboriginal women have been experiencing in Canada since the white society's patriarchal institutions distorted Aboriginal culture. She sees women in Canadian society engaging more fully in a participatory democratic system, and she sees a system that brings with it the safeguards of a Western legal system, including provisions of the Charter and the Criminal Code. She does not want this to be lost in the process of implementing self-government.

Like Monture-OKanee, Nahanee approaches the question of equality of rights from a human rights perspective. She argues that the Canadian government is racist in the way it deals with Aboriginals and that this constitutes a violation of the Universal Declaration of Human Rights. The difference between the two positions appears in how gender issues are collapsed into, or separated from, racial and cultural inequalities. The point has been made that the feminists appear to "lift away" the power issues from the larger question of Aboriginal self-determination.

Yet another perspective on the rights question is provided by Mary Ellen Turpel. She has suggested that a lot of the confusion about "Aboriginal rights" may emerge because of ambiguous definitions. The very expression "Aboriginal rights" cannot easily be translated into anything meaningful for many Aboriginal people. These are expressions that have been "thought up and imposed on those peoples by the same culture that brought us the 'rights category'" (Turpel 37). But, according to Turpel, these are incompatible with Aboriginal approaches to an everyday world based on land, family, social life, and spirituality.[12]

Conclusion

This analysis highlights a dilemma. There is, for many Aboriginal people, the hope that a fading cultural identity can be recovered and that a strong desire for self-government and autonomy can be achieved. At the same time, for many Aboriginal women, there is an interest in preserving and extending gender equality. Thus, a central issue for Aboriginal women concerns what a return to traditional customs would involve. Would it involve a return to the historical subservience of Aboriginal women to Aboriginal men, or would it involve the equality of power between Aboriginal men and women that existed earlier but was distorted by the imposition of European patriarchal law and practices?[13]

On the basis of the current review, it is apparent that there is a need to articulate which Aboriginal social values are to be given priority in the development of self-governing structures. Once these values have been articulated, their implications for self-governing policies, structures, and procedures can be more carefully examined.

Policy-making is concerned with competing values and the achievement of social purposes. Social policies seek to effect compromises between social values that are in tension (for example, individual rights versus collective rights). In the widest sense, social policy seeks to address the balance between fairness to the individual and the well-being of society as a whole (Ekstedt). In the self-government debates, we may ask: where is the balance to be struck? The Aboriginal Peoples must decide. It is important to get agreement on these underlying assumptions before proceeding to debate the form that specific self-governing structures should take. This is not a question of supporting or not supporting self-government. It is about getting the directions to self-government right, and about the need to have a map before starting the journey.

In some respects, Nahanee's stance, and the stance of Aboriginal women feminists, is less risky than the type of position adopted by Monture-OKanee. The latter position asserts that the unique Aboriginal way of being will, if allowed to develop, assure the protection of Aboriginal women. The former position is more skeptical. It asserts the necessity of a return to the unique Aboriginal way of being for healing, but the return requires an escort—the Charter. In this way, the journey can be observed by international bodies, such as the United Nations, as it twists and turns toward successful completion.

While difficult to judge, it may be that the harm done to customary Aboriginal ways of being is already too great for a return to spiritual balance without the imposition of structure and process. As Nahanee says, there are many Aboriginal people who are no longer in touch with their Aboriginal roots. What of the overwhelming proportion of Aboriginals who have become urbanized? What meaning does a healing circle have to someone born in a city where concrete, and concrete poverty, provide the surround?

It does appear that in both Nahanee's and Monture-OKanee's assessments, the debate needs to transcend self-government pragmatics to focus upon wider human rights issues if Aboriginal women are to have a stronger base from which to address their concerns.[14] An emphasis on social values, such as equality and freedom of speech, may be the better road to travel for at least two reasons:

1. It allows a wider support network to be accessed through international linkages, such as the UN Human Rights Sub-Committee on Indigenous Populations, and international and national women's groups, both feminist and otherwise; and

2. There is more certainty about how values such as equality and freedom of expression will be translated into policies and programs.

It is far less certain how the sometimes uncertain visions of the past, which may have become distorted by the dominant society, might affect women in the movement toward self-government.

The various positions taken by Aboriginal women and women's groups are not significantly different in their basic assumptions. For the most part, the social values they seek to entrench are the same: sexual equality, freedom of speech, to name two. The differences lie in the paths chosen to secure those values and in the speeds thought safest to achieve them.

At the present juncture, it is important to priorize the values themselves. This is an undertaking for all the Aboriginal Peoples and not just for Aboriginal women. The metaphor of the eagle flying should be kept in mind, not only for a vision of how Aboriginal men and women can work together, but also for a vision of how Aboriginal and non-Aboriginal peoples can work together. The eagle cannot fly with only one wing beating.

Endnotes

The author wishes to acknowledge the assistance of Jennifer Stevens, First Nations Law Program at the University of British Columbia, for providing relevant materials for this article and an initial discussion of its vision. As well, I appreciated receiving comments on an earlier draft from John Ekstedt, Al Patenaude, and Hannele Janti.

[1] Turpel makes a helpful distinction between self-government and self-determination. She feels that self-determination is the more hopeful concept. Quoting Deloria and Lytle (38), she notes: "Self-government... implies a recognition by the superior political power that some measure of local decision-making is necessary but that this process must be monitored very carefully so that its products are compatible with the goals and policies of the larger political power. (I)t implies that... people... are now ready to assume some, but not all, of the responsibilities of a new municipality."

[2] *Globe and Mail*, May 29, 1992.

[3] The effects of the repeal have not, however, been positive in every respect. Arlene Guerin of the Musqueam Band in British Columbia, for example, argues the repeal has left a legacy of other difficulties that now result in "splits" between husbands and wives over matters of property.

[4] Whatever the plight of the Aboriginal Peoples generally, the fate of Aboriginal women is even worse. In times of economic and social oppression, Aboriginal women rank among the most severely disadvantaged in Canada (Fleras and Elliott). Their social problems are worse because of poor housing, substance abuse, inadequate child-rearing conditions, and, most especially, because of physical and sexual abuse. These conditions result in "high rates of suicide, alcohol

dependency and neglect of children" (Fleras and Elliott 19).

[5] This perspective is substantiated with reference to how the Aboriginal Peoples have been treated until quite recent times. For example, numbers instead of names were assigned to Inuit involved in divorce cases (Crawford).

[6] See R. Noah Estate, (1961), 32 D.L.R. (2nd) 185, and R. Adoption of K., (1961), 32 D.L.R. (2nd) 686, Northwest Territorial Court.

[7] *Saila* v. *R.* (1984) C.N.L.R., Vol. 1, 173–81.

[8] Section 33 of the Charter allows federal and provincial governments to opt out of certain sections of the Charter if they deem it necessary.

[9] However, the AFN did support the Charlottetown Accord, which provided that Aboriginal self-government would have to comply with the Charter of Rights and Freedoms. But, once established, these governments would have the right to opt out of the Charter, just as provinces and the federal government do, through the use of a "not-withstanding" clause. The Accord was subsequently rejected by the Canadian people in a national referendum.

[10] In 1992, according to the *Montreal Gazette,* Saturday, March 28, 1992, there were 1,153,800 Natives in Canada, and 447,128 of these were women. Reserve populations totaled 155,989 men and 133,697 women. There were 603 bands and 60 female chiefs.

[11] As Palys observes, "(t)raditional forms of governance were undermined by a century of funding Band Councils, with the result that, in many communities, Band Councils and more traditional structures now conflict over funding and tribal policies" (6).

[12] In a similar vein, Monture-OKanee has pointed out that there is no word in Ojibwa for justice. Justice is a way of being that is learned from childhood and a process learned by example. She quotes Alex Denny: "Harmony, not justice is the idea." ("Reflecting on Flint Woman," 44).

[13] Some authors have suggested that in the "pre-white man's era," there was equality between Aboriginal men and women (Greschner 1992; Monture-OKanee, "Reclaiming Justice"). Others are more skeptical (see Van Kirk). The latter position holds that the imposed European patriarchy cannot explain the observed disparities that seem to have existed prior to the white man's emergence as a controlling influence.

[14] The present discussion does not intend to diminish the importance of balancing these concerns with the concerns that other Aboriginal women have expressed about the need for community, grassroots development.

Works Cited

Brockman, J., and D. Chunn, eds. *Investigating Gender Bias: Law, Courts, and the Legal Profession*. Toronto: Thompson Educational Publishing, 1993.

Clark, Donna. "Interview With Lillian Head." *Aquelarre*, 1992: 47–51.

Cooper, F. "Fearful Native Women Plead for Protection Against Ancient Rituals. *Vancouver Sun*, Monday, March 16,1992, p. A3.

Crawford, A. "Outside Law and Traditional Communities in the Northwest Territories." Paper presented to the Western Regional Science Association, San Diego, California, February 1985.

Ekstedt, J.W. "Canadian Crime Policy. *Canadian Criminology: Perspectives on Crime and Criminality*. Ed. M. Jackson and C. Griffiths. Toronto: Harcourt Brace Jovanovich, 1991.

Fine, S. "Native Women Aim to Block National Referendum in Court. *Globe and Mail*, Tuesday, October 13, 1992.

Fleras, A., and J.L. Elliott. *The Nations Within*. Toronto: Oxford University Press, 1992.

Genaille, S. D. "Metis Women Endorse Agreement. *Globe and Mail*, September 30, 1992.

Giesbrecht, Winnie. *Vancouver Sun*, February 12, 1992.

Greschner, D. "Aboriginal Women, the Constitution and Criminal Justice." *University of British Columbia Law Review* (Special edition) (1992): 338–59.

Guerin, Arlene. Personal communication, March 24, 1993.

Hammersmith, B. "Aboriginal Women and Self-government."*Nation to Nation: Aboriginal Sovereignty and the Future of Canada*. Ed. Diane Engelstad and John Bird. Concord, ON: Anansi Press, 1992, 53–9.

Haveman, P. "The Indigenization of Social Control in Canada." Paper presented at a conference sponsored by the Commission on Folk Law and Legal Pluralism, Vancouver, August 19–23, 1983.

"Indian Negotiators Say Deal Will Protect Native Women. *The Globe and Mail*, September 24, 1992.

Jackson, M. A. "Unequal Justice and the Law: Traditional Versus Customary Law. Montreal: Proceedings from the Canadian Law and Society Annual Meeting, 1985.

Little Bear, Leroy, Menno Boldt, and J. Anthony Long, eds. *Pathways to Self-Determination: Canadian Indians and the Canadian State*. Toronto: University of Toronto Press, 1984.

Mahoney, Kathleen.*The Globe and Mail*, Tuesday, October 13, 1993, p. A10.

Marule, Marie Smallface. "Traditional Indian Government: Of the People By the People, For the People. *Pathways to Self-determination: Canadian*

Indians and the Canadian State. Ed. Leroy Little Bear, Menno Boldt, and J. Anthony Long. Toronto: University of Toronto Press, 1984, 36–45.

Monture-OKanee, Patricia. "Reclaiming Justice: Aboriginal Women and Justice Initiatives in the 1990's." Paper presented to the Royal Commission on Aboriginal Peoples, Round Table on Justice Issues, Ottawa, November 25–27, 1992.

————. "Reflecting on Flint Woman." *First Nations Issues.* Ed. R. F. Devlin. Toronto: Emond Montgomery Publications Limited, 1991, 351–66.

Monture-OKanee, Patricia, and Mary Ellen Turpel. "Aboriginal Peoples and Canadian Criminal Law: Rethinking Justice." *University of British Columbia Law Review* (Special Edition) (1992): 239–77.

Moss, W. "Indigenous Self-government in Canada and Sexual Equality Under the Indian Act. *Queen's Law Journal* (1990): 15: 299–305.

Nahanee, T. "Dancing With a Gorilla: Aboriginal Women and the Charter." Paper presented to the Royal Commission on Aboriginal Peoples, Round Table on Justice Issues, Ottawa, November 25–27, 1992.

"Native Women Well Represented at National Constitutional Talks. *Kahtou News,* October 15, 1992. (Re: First Nations Summit).

Native Women's Association of Canada (NWAC). *Statement on the Canada Package.* Ottawa: Native Women's Association of Canada, 1992.

Palys, T. "Prospects for Aboriginal Justice in Canada." Unpublished manuscript, 1993.

Picard, A. "Native Women Cling to Charter: Won't Trade Rights for Unity Deal. *The Globe and Mail,* May 29, 1992.

Platiel, R. "Aboriginal Women Divided on Constitutional Protection." *Globe and Mail.* January 20, 1992.

Richstone, J. "The Inuit and Customary Law: Constitutional Perspectives." Paper presented at a conference sponsored by the Commission on Folk Law and Legal Pluralism, Vancouver, August 19–23, 1983.

Scott, S. "The Native Rights Stuff." *The Montreal Gazette,* Saturday, March 28, 1992, p. B5.

Turpel, Mary Ellen. "Aboriginal Peoples and the Charter: Interpretative Monopolies, Cultural Differences. *Canadian Human Rights Yearbook* 3, 1989.

Van Kirk, S. "Women in Between: Indian Women in Fur Trade Society in Western Canada. *Out of the Background: Readings on Canadian Native History.* Ed. R. Fisher and K. Coates. Toronto: Copp Clark Pitman, 1988 150–66.

York, G. "Support for Deal Growing Among Native Women. *Globe and Mail ,* October 9, 1992.

Honouring the Blood of the People:

Berry Fasting in the Twenty-First Century

Kim Anderson

Kim Anderson is a Cree/Métis writer and consultant. She lives in Guelph, Ontario, with her partner, David, and their two children. Her book A Recognition of Being: Reconstructing Native Womanhood *was recently published with Second Story Press (Toronto).*

It always starts with story.[1] Stories have that pervasive power to shape our lives, to craft our beliefs, to cast us in certain roles and plots that we act upon, sometimes consciously but often unconsciously.

Before getting into this descriptive text about the "berry fast," a puberty ceremony that is becoming increasingly popular among young women from various Indigenous nations in Canada and the United States, I would like to start with a story. To me, this story is an example of the kind of enlightenment we need to offer our girls. It was told to me by a Mohawk auntie, Sylvia Maracle, and is a shorter version of the stories that she relates to young women at the beginning of their year-long berry fast:

> It begins with the other world. It begins in our creation story. In that creation story they talk about a world where we lived, and where we seem to have had a parallel existence to here. Parallel, not the same. They say that even in that world, there were prophecies, and in that world they prophesied a time when a woman, a two-legged, would come here.
>
> The teaching for the berry fast centres around a part of the creation story that talks about this young man and this young woman who were raised by their parents and their grandparents

and their aunts and uncles and their clans. They were raised to be magnificent. Even when we do the teaching we talk about how they looked, and how that energy and shininess came to them.

They were at a ceremony one day in the longhouse, and they looked across the longhouse at each other and that spark flew. But in those days you didn't go and do anything about it. You went to your mother and to your grandmother. And your mother and your grandmother decided what was a good match. So these families had already been looking for this match for these young people, who knew their language, who knew their clan, who knew their songs, who knew the ceremonies, who had just been raised in the best of the world that they could have in that day.

It happened that their grandmothers knew each other from when they were young girls, and they were watching this non-verbal communication across the longhouse. Those old women started talking. They called their daughters over (the mothers), and they thought Yeah, these young people have been raised the same way. So the young couple were encouraged to dance and to see each other, and sure enough, a relationship was created. But they did everything right. They offered their tobacco, they waited the two years, and then they stood before the Creator. They made the commitment to each other.

That young man already had a job working for the people, and his job was taking care of the tree that is planted at the very centre of that world, and it is called the tree of life. And on that tree is every leaf, every blossom, every fruit, every root. Everything known to us now as human beings was on that tree. And his job was to care for that tree. To get up in the morning, to offer prayers, to sing that song, to remember, and then to take care of whatever needed to be taken care of.

He lived a ways away from the village where this tree was. It is normal that he would have gone to her place to live in those days, but the people decided that it was good that these two halves of this medicine wheel would be there and that tree would really then be provided for. So all the people got together and helped make this place for them, and that is where she moved.

They took care of that tree, and they laughed, and they had great joy, and they had a tremendous relationship. And they put down their tobacco; they offered tobacco to bring a new spirit into this world. They went through all of those cycles of ceremonies and they talked about how will we raise this child; how will we discipline this child—all these things that you need to do before you bring those spirits here.

So it happened that they were blessed and a spirit came to them. They say that the traditions that women have in childbirth today go back to that time; that we can trace them back to that time.

So she craved a particular root. And he being a really decent partner went to find her that root. He walked into the village, and he asked around, and he had tobacco. Nobody had that root for some reason. People thought they had it, but it wasn't there, it was gone. So he had to come back and he had to tell her, "I can't find the root." She said, "Oh, I really, really want it. I really crave this." But they went on, and they got up every morning and they did their duties and they cared for the tree and they did the things that they had to do.

As her pregnancy moved along, she began to crave this root more and more. Now she is saying, "If I don't have this root something is going to happen. I don't know what it is." And he said, "Well, you know there is a village that is four days away. I will go there, and I will see. I will take something to trade and I will get you that root, because my job is to help you, is to support you, is to provide for this child that we are having, and I will do anything that I have to do." Remember, he was raised the right way. These weren't just words. This was what he intended.

So he went off, and he was gone for those four days and four nights, and he came back and he told her that "The root is not there in that village. Nobody knows what has happened to that root." She said, "Oh no, I have to have it," so he told her, "Well, there is another village. It is seven days away, there and back, and I will go there." He reminded her, "You know, you have to take care of this tree," and she reassured him, "I will. I will."

He was starting to get a little worried about her, so he stopped off at his mother's and his mother-in-law's while going through the village, and he said, "I am worried about her. There is something that is different. She really craves this root and I am going to find this root, but can you check on her?"

So the old women came one day with their mothers. The grandmothers and the great-grandmothers of the child-to-be came to visit, and they saw that the young woman wasn't right. When they walked up, they saw her walking around this tree, and she was kind of digging a little bit under the tree. They thought, Ohh…

That is our sacred tree. We had better talk to her. And so they talked to her, and they said, "What are you doing out there digging?" She answered, "Well you know, I just need a little piece of that root. Something is going to happen to the baby." So they told her, "Nothing is going to happen to the baby. Your partner has gone to find that root. You need to cheer up. To be that magnificent one we know you to be." So she said, "Yeah, okay."

They went, and on the way back they said, "You know, we have to do something to bring up her spirits." They decided that they would make her a dress. A white buckskin dress, because women at that time sometimes feel that they are not attractive, and that the pregnancy is never going to be over.

Every day she would go out and she would dig a little bit. Because she said, I know that root is here. It may not be anywhere in the villages, but everything that is known to us is here at this tree. She started digging and digging and her man came back. He had been gone now seven days, and he couldn't find that root. He said, "They all said, "Yeah, I have it," and they all went to get it for you, but it is not there. It is gone. Nobody understands what is happening to this root."

She is beside herself now: "There is something wrong with our baby! There is something wrong! If we don't get this root, something is going to happen to our child..." And now he is frantic, because this is his beloved. He can't believe that this child that they have worked so hard for, and they have waited for, and they have got everything right for, is at risk. And he believes her, because she is carrying the child.

But he notices that she has been digging around the tree, and he says, "Hey, we have a really sacred duty here." He says, "I am going to go. There is a community that is going to take me twenty-eight days and nights to go to. And I am going to go there, but you can't dig up this tree." And she said, "No no, I know. Don't worry."

So he says, "Okay." And so he gets his pack together and his clothes, and he stops in the village again and he sees his mother and his mother-in-law, and he says, "Look, she is digging at that tree. She is absolutely consumed with the fact that there will be something wrong with her baby and I have to go." They tell him, "You have to go because you made a commitment when you stood beside her that when she needed medicine, that whatever she would need, you would provide for that, and that you would protect that life. So go. And we will check on her. We have just finished this magnificent dress for her."

They say that the colours on that dress are the colours that give us the rainbow. It had long fringes, and it was white buckskin, and it was beautiful. They took it to her, and she put it on and she felt better. She felt magnificent again. And so they thought, Oh we are so pleased. She is feeling much better. And when she walked, those fringes swayed just like when the wind goes in the tall grasses, and the sun reflected off it, and it was just a magnificent sight. She felt better, they felt better, so they went back to their village.

That woman felt really strong.

Strong enough to really dig for that root. So she went and she dug. Every day that is what she did. She dug all around, big holes at the bottom of that tree.

One day, she was looking through that hole and she could see this blue ball, way in the distance. When you are pregnant, as you know, you are not as graceful and lithe as you normally are. And so she tumbled. When I tell the young girls this story, I say, she came from way up there in the sky world to here—it was only water, this blue ball.

Here in this world, the heron is one of our sacred teachers because it is always standing looking up, to see what is going to come from that world. The heron knew the prophecy that the two-legged would come. The heron was looking and saying, "Someone is coming. We need to get ready."

So the first thing that they agreed to do was to send someone down to call the grandmother turtle to come up from the bottom of that water, so that there was some place for that woman when she came to land. The animals that are important, like the ducks and the geese and the loons—and what is the other water bird—oh the little sand pipers—snipes, some call them—they all flew together, and they locked their wings in such a way that it was a big blanket when they went up to meet her, and she landed on the backs of the birds. And so our blankets and our weaving, and the things that we do as women are so important because we catch those first ones, like we catch them just now.

They brought her and they laid her on the turtle's back. And the turtle said, "Where I come from, there is earth. There is soil. Someone has to go get it, because I can't go down there because I have to hold her."

So the beaver said, "I'll go. I am the biggest, I am the best in the water. I am the smoothest." And the beaver went. The beaver was gone a long time, and then his body floated up. He sacrificed himself for this two-legged, but he didn't have any of that soil.

So then next the otter goes. (You see where the clans start to come from?) Otter says, "I am fast. I am sleek. Beaver is too big. He can't do it. You need somebody like me." So he goes. He is gone even longer, but his body pops up and he has nothing.

There is this little wee humble one sitting there. The muskrat. The muskrat says, "Well my big brother can't do it, and my fancy magnificent fast brother can't do it, but I will try. Because someone has to go do this." So he is gone, and he is gone even longer. And he comes up, and he sacrifices his life, but there tucked on his stomach, in his paws, is that soil.

So the ones that are gathered around spread that out on the turtle's back. The birds are helping lift that woman, just hovering, and the water creatures spread it all out on the back of the turtle, and they lay her down. And when they lay her down, that one from the other world, the Great Mystery, the one who created even the sky world and all of these things, the one who created even the Creator, was watching. That one sent the rain. The Great Mystery sent the rain. That rain fell on her face, and it woke her up. And to this day, when rain falls on a woman's face, it wakes her up. It brings to her mind those things that she needs to understand.

So when that rain came, that Sky Woman, that first one who came here, said, "Oh, I am in a different place. But I am alive." She checked her baby, and her baby was alive. She put down her tobacco, and she started that first dance. That round dance. She sang that song to give thanks for being alive. And on that magnificent dress that her mother and her mother-in-law and her grandmother and her grandmother-in-law had made her, those fringes started to sway. Some of those first plants, those first medicines came because they were caught in those beautiful long fringes. Our young girls wear those beautiful long fringes to this day, to collect up that life.

She danced that dance, and in her dancing the Great Mystery made that land grow. Made that Turtle Island grow. That Turtle Island where we live. And on that Turtle Island there are the thirteen markings, the thirteen moons. The thirteen markings of the original peoples who were placed here, and how they were placed. So that woman knew that life was going to be coming *soon, and she had to get ready for that life to come. All those water animals helped her. So you see those are some of the first ones, and the first clans that we had.*

It came time for her to have that baby. That first one that was born in this world—that was a woman. So Sky Woman gave birth to Original Woman, the one who would become our mother the earth.

Those two women, they got along really well. That little one grew, and she had powers. She may not have had that root, but she had powers that were beyond our understanding. But like all young women, there is a time that they run into conflict with their moth-ers. It is not peaceful, the relationship always, between a mother and a daughter. And you know, when you are the only two in the world, it is a little bit hard to have that expression! But Sky Woman had been raised with everything. She knew all that we could know, and so she even knew that this time would come.

To my people, the reason that Niagara Falls is so important is that we believe that is where Original Woman went for her fast, to get over this time. In the berry fast, we give those girls aunties because they are at that time when it is going to be difficult. But this first one, she didn't have that opportunity. So she went off and she was taking that time away from her mother. And they were using their power to begin to fill in this world as we know it.

Original Woman went to sleep, and she had a visitor in the night. She didn't know who it was, but when she woke up there were two crossed arrows on her abdomen. One was really beautifully made, with beautiful feathers, and the head of it was notched. It was just a beautiful, beautiful arrow. But the other one was misshapen, and it didn't have nice colours on it. You don't even know if it would have flown anywhere. And it was crossed on her.

So she picked those arrows up. You know, the thing about fight-ing with your mother is that you still need her when you are concerned or worried or afraid. So Original Woman went to her mother, and she showed her. The mother looked, and she offered her tobacco and she prayed, and she told her daughter: "The west wind has come to visit you." Now many people tell this story with many nuances. But the way that I heard was "The west wind came to visit you and has brought you a child so that life would begin here."

Sky Woman raised Original Woman exactly the way that she had been raised. They talked to that unborn baby, and they sang to that baby. We should teach our young people to continue to sing and to talk to them and to read to them. To make sure they hear the voices of the ones who will be in their life.

Anyway, they would listen, and they heard two voices. At first, those voices were kind of weak and getting along, but as the pregnancy advanced, those voices would get louder. It sounded like they were arguing with each other. Finally one day they heard them. They heard these two voices, and one is saying, "No, this is the way to go. It is the natural way." And the other one said, "I am going out over here, it is shorter!" They are both arguing, and Sky Woman is getting worried. She is getting worried. She is thinking, I had an easy time with my child because I came from that other world. But this child is coming from this world....

So it came time to be born, and in the midst of the birth, there was a lot of confusion and a lot of noise and one baby came the way that we understand babies to be born today. What we consider the natural way, with the water flowing and then through the birth canal. But the other one, he came out his mother's left side, and he killed his mother. And the grandmother, in the confusion of this noise and her daughter dying and her grief, didn't know who was who. Which one came which way.

One was born smooth and beautifully coloured, and well shaped and well-mannered and calm. And the other was born what we call flinty. Misshapen and demanding and cantankerous and loud and everything. And we know from our traditions that, to this day, grandmothers favour the different one in the family. It doesn't matter how many she has, that one that is not exactly right is the one that the grandmother goes to. We know that from the beginning of time.

The mother died. Original Woman died, and it came time to bury that Original Woman. And from that Original Woman, the Iroquoian people believe that there were four sacred gifts. That from her head grew tobacco, and it is always tobacco that goes first. We always think things before we believe them, human beings. "Prove it to me. Show it to me, and then I will believe you." So tobacco grew from there. They say that from her abdomen, from her sacred space grew the corn beans and squash. The staple of the Iroquois food; that came from there. That from her feet grew the maple tree. And the maple tree is really important to us in that sweet water, that fresh water ceremony that represents all of the waters of the world, that maple. It changes colours, and it goes through the cycle like women, and it is the leader of the trees, because it shows them when to bud, when to leaf, when to colour, when to fall.

But from her heart grew the strawberry. Really one of the Creators' hearts' berry.

That strawberry is what we want to teach those young women about in the teaching and in the ceremony for the berry fast. We say that if we open up that strawberry that Original Woman gave us, we will see a circle inside, and that represents the circle of life. And if you look inside that strawberry, you will see a path, where people have come to join the circle. So we teach them about that. We teach them in the centre of that circle, in the strawberry, there is a sacred space. And that sacred space is inside them. We teach them that colour and the texture of the strawberry is the colour and the texture of the blood that flows from them, the colour of the people. It is the blood of the people. We teach them that the way that the seeds are around the berry, that they are really clustered in the beginning, like they are clustered inside her, and she doesn't share them. And then you will see them start to drop as she sacrifices each seed with each moon, until we get to the very top of the berry, and there are no more seeds, just like us, too, as women.

Then we talk to her about how that berry is connected to the stem, and how you really have to try to take it. The berry doesn't fall off. The berry doesn't just give it away for a ride to town on Saturday night. It has to be taken. And there is a process to do that. And it flowers before it is ready, and it shows you all those things. We teach them that the berry grows out. Even if you plant it up high, it will grow tendrils down to the ground, and it will hold the earth. Because it holds its connection to that Original Woman, just like we need them to do. To hold the earth. To be connected to her.

That berry grows in a family, just like she grows in a family. She is not alone. Berries grow in patches. You can't plant a single plant, and even if you plant a single plant, then your relations grow there, just like she does. And that berry has a cycle, just like she has a cycle. And how she will go through her life like a cycle. That berry is influenced not only by her mother, but by her grandmother, because it is the grandmother who decides when things are going to grow. And Sky Woman continues to do that.

In the rest of the teaching, we tell them that those twins who were born brought the differences to the world. As they grew into young men, that grandmother favoured that one that was different, and there was a lot of tension between them. Eventually it came to a point where there was a fight, and in the midst of that fight the grandmother was killed. And the smooth one, the one we call today Sonkwaiatison, who was given the task of finishing creation, he was so distraught that his grandmother never knew that he was the one that came the right way, the natural way. He wanted to remind the people that there was going to be someone who would always be watching them in those dark times, in those times of despair. And so he separated the head from his grandmother's body, and he placed it in the sky.

They say that the trail of blood that those young women sacrifice connects them to that moon, connects all of us to this day. And it is grandmother moon who uses that blood to mark the time when new life will come among us. It is she who makes the waters rise up. It is she who deals with our passions, and it is she who teaches those young girls to behave in such a way that they would not be embarrassed in front of their mothers. That is the ways of the right-handed twin. And that other one, the flinty twin, he was given the responsibility for the dark time. To use that porcupine quill, that embarrassment, those things our face gets red over, to try to continue his control and his fight with his brother about what is the natural way, and to get them off the path. And so when we are doing these teachings, we talk a lot to those young girls about saying no. Even in the ceremonial part when they have to refuse the berries, you hear them with little wee voices say, "no." And eventually by the fourth time, they are saying "NO." They are adamant about it.

So from that first gift of that Original Woman, that berry, that is the connectedness in the teaching for our young women. We talk about how we want to raise them in magnificence. About the conflicts that they will have in their life. About how they have aunties and grandmothers around them who will surround them with love, and who will protect them and teach them during this time. And they will become the magnificent women who can carry our nations.

As told by Sylvia Maracle
September 29, 1999

As a thirty-five-year-old Cree/Métis woman trying to sort through who I am and what kind of world I want to live in, I have spent many years trying to unpack the stories that have shaped my existence. I think I began this process in my adolescence, a period when many of us begin to question the stories that we have been told (either verbally or by witnessing them as they unfold around us). At this time, we begin to look for the stories that tell *our* truths. Issues of sexuality and gender are at the core of our adolescent self-definition, probably because it is the first time we consciously process what it means to be male or female, or that we think about how we are going to play out our sexuality as well as our gendered identities.

What are the kinds of stories we are currently telling our young people, and how do they help Aboriginal adolescents make sense of the adult world they are about to take their place in? How do we fit them into modern-day rites of passage? And what do they mean to girls, as opposed to boys? At one point while I was working on this article, I was sitting in front of a computer at the library, remembering my own adolescence. Without much notice, I found myself crying at the realization that my pubescence was checkered with feelings of fear, anger, and sadness. It occurred to me that these sensations had been *my* puberty rite, and that it is probably the rite of passage for many girls and women in our societies.[2] I had intellectualized this before, but suddenly my emotional intelligence made it clear how much we have lost and how much we need to work at rites of passage that are empowering for our young people.

I have recently come to recognize that, as an Aboriginal person, I am heir to a whole other set of stories, and as an Aboriginal female I have a duty to pass along those stories that will empower our young girls. Traditionally, every Aboriginal society had some way of recognizing the passage from childhood to adulthood. When the colonizer came, these ceremonies (like all our ceremonies) were forced underground or lost to the pressures of assimilation. Today certain rites of passage are now experiencing a rebirth in our communities, and they are being practised in such a way that they support the needs of contemporary Aboriginal youth. This article is about a group of women who have been telling Aboriginal girls a story of empowerment through the increasingly popular "berry fast," a ceremony that has been working its way both east and west from its origins in Ojibway country in Ontario and Minnesota. Writing about it is my way of passing it on.

Berry fasting requires the commitment of a few "aunties" who will guide pubescent girls through this year-long process. There are many women now doing this work; in this piece I will focus on the work being done by the storyteller in this article, Sylvia Maracle, a Mohawk from Tyendinaga First Nation (Ontario), and Gertie Beaucage, an Ojibway from Nipissing First Nation (Ontario). Both live in Toronto, and both work for the Ontario Federation of Indian Friendship Centres where I interviewed them in September, 1999. In addition to speaking to these women, I also interviewed six young women (aged thirteen to twenty-seven) who had been through a berry fast as well as one of their mothers.

In the early 1990s, Beaucage and Maracle began to get requests from young people who wished to learn about fasting. They responded by researching the traditions of berry fasting (which had begun to take root in some rural Ojibway communities), and soon after began to practise with a small group of girls, generally the daughters of women who were part of the organizational family where they worked. As they had both passed through adolescence in the 1960s (a time when Indigenous ceremony was still considered taboo), neither Maracle nor Beaucage had experienced a berry fast of the same nature as the one they now practice. Yet both had been through a version of it, as conducted by their respective grandmothers.

When she was thirteen, Sylvia Maracle had returned to her home community after having spent eight years as a ward of the Children's Aid Society. Her grandmother's concern for the young teen motivated her to call together thirty of the older women in the community. The intent was to offer guidance. Maracle remembers her grandmother having to put blankets on the windows as well as having to use kerosene lamps so that community members wouldn't accuse her of practising "witchcraft" in this late-night ceremony. She recalls sitting in the middle of the room and having to turn to face each of the "grannies," who then proceeded one by one to tell her what they believed she needed to know as she entered womanhood. "Some of those old ladies were pretty graphic," Maracle laughs, remembering the sex education she received at that time. Yet she also recalls that she received many teachings that, to this day, guide her in her work as a leader in the Aboriginal community.

Gertie Beaucage said that when she was seven years old, her grand-mother sent her out to pick berries with the instructions "Don't eat any of them." This was new for her, as she had always been allowed to eat as many berries as she wanted. When she returned with her basket full, (and eager to eat some of her berries), her grandmother took them from her and simply declared that she intended to make jam. Once finished, the jam was put away until wintertime, when it was given away to visitors. Beaucage recalls, "Making sure that I could see, she would pick up those berries in the jar and hand them to somebody and say, 'My granddaughter picked these berries in the summer, and I want you to have them.' And just gave them away on me." Beaucage reminisces, *I knew I would never see those berries again!* This cycle of the young girl picking berries and the grandmother giving them away went on for five years until one winter, Beaucage's grandmother opened a jar and told her, "You should eat these first, before we give the rest away." Beaucage concludes, "What I learned from that was that I didn't have to have everything that I saw. You know, it might have looked good, but I didn't have to have it. I might really want it, but if I had to do something else with it, I could put my own wants aside."

Maracle and Beaucage now conduct their own berry fasts, which include both Iroquoian and Ojibway tradition.[3] They do this work with the girls around the time of their first menstruation, an occasion that has always marked the passing from childhood to womanhood. The ceremony starts out with a big feast in the spring, where girls come together with their female family members as well as a number of women who are to play the traditional role of "auntie" to them. They are taken aside with one of the aunties, who teaches them how to make tobacco ties (offerings of tobacco wrapped in cloth), which they are to put out at a designated time each month, during their moon time (menstruation), the full moon, or whatever monthly time they choose. While they are making these ties, they are party to longer versions of the story that I have placed at the beginning of this article. The girls then hear from each of the aunties who have assembled, who encourage them and talk to them about some of the challenges they will face, both during the fast and as they enter the world as women. Maracle says this is the time when the aunties will talk about patience, sacrifice, respecting their bodies, and taking time to build relationships. They are then offered the berries four times, and each time they are required to say "no." They must then offer the berries to their mothers, a part of the ceremony which Maracle reports inevitably results in "great emotional outpourings" from the parents, who have to recognize that they are saying goodbye to the child, and letting her proceed on her journey towards womanhood. Thus begins a thirteen-moon (month) period during which the young women are expected to refrain from eating berries or berry products (including, for example, strawberry ice-cream or blueberry muffins). They are told not to dance during this period, not to date (or to have any type of sexual contact), not to step over men, nor to pick up babies. At the end of this period, they come back to the circle of aunties, and are sent out on the land for twenty-four hours to do a fast (no food and no water). When they come off the fast, they are bathed in cedar-drenched water, dressed in their finest (often regalia), and introduced as the new women of the community to the aunties and family members who are attending the ceremony.

In the "old days," the end of this ceremony might have signified that the young women involved were ready to take on the responsibilities (among others) of marriage and child rearing. What does this mean to Aboriginal teens today, and how does it prepare them for what they are about to face? Aboriginal youth, like any youth, have to negotiate peer pressure, rebellion, the discovery of their sexuality, and a changing sense of their place and purpose in the community. Alcohol, drugs, and suicide are some of the struggles that we are faced with in our communities as part of the fallout of colonization. Teen pregnancy rates are high, and youth now have increasing cause to worry about sexually transmitted diseases, such as AIDS. From the challenges presented by these issues, learning to say "no" is important, and many of the young women I interviewed indicated that this was the strongest lesson they took from the ceremony. They demonstrated how they had applied this teaching of "learning to say no" through numerous examples. Angeline,[4] a thirteen year old who had recently come off her berry fast, told me:

> It helps me. Before I knew people who would smoke or do this and that. Now that I have done [the berry fast], if I see them doing it, I can go and stand with them and I don't have to feel like I need to do it. Because I know that I don't have to, I don't need to, and I don't want to. So that kind of helped.

Angeline spoke repeatedly about the value of learning to "withdraw" from situations that are not healthy for her. The expectation that berry fasters will think about what they are eating for an entire year is useful in and of itself, as it gets the young women into the practice of thinking about what they are ingesting. In turn, it encourages them to take the time to consider *beforehand* how things might affect them. Some grannies talk to berry fasters about the need to consider everything that will enter their bodies throughout their lifetimes, "including the male sex organ."[5]

"Saying no" is thus an invaluable skill for youth as they encounter the inevitable pressures associated with sex, drugs and alcohol. It can also be vital as a tool of resistance against some of the dangers more commonly faced by girls and women. Thirteen-year-old Mary-Jane told me a story of how learning to "say no" had saved her from a volatile situation. She and her friends had been at a corner store in Toronto when a man tried to lure them into his apartment, with the request that they help him carry his bike up the stairs. The coercive and aggressive nature of this man's request had the girls grappling with whether to help him or not until Mary-Jane found the courage to say "no," something she credits to her berry fast. This story is but one manifestation of Sylvia Maracle's hope for such doubtful situations. She asks of the young women, "If nothing else, let auntie's words be in the back of your mind."

One young woman told me about how her berry fast had helped her to resist and eventually disclose that she was being sexually abused by a family member. Until that time, she had blocked out what had been happening to her at night. The berry fast made her realize that she needed to address the violation, and it gave her the framework to say "no" to the perpetrator. She further related, "When they told me those teachings, it also scared me, because I realized that what he was doing was to create life, and so I started saying 'no' to him, and doing everything I could to not let him do that to me."

As incest and family violence have been so predominant in recent Aboriginal history, the need to provide our young people with tools to resist abuse seems particularly relevant. "Saying no" is about making healthy choices, and significantly for girls, it lets them know that they *have* a choice. In a world where girls and women must face male dominance and violence on a regular basis, the berry fast helps girls to understand that they *can* exercise some control over situations in which they are vulnerable.

Self-discipline is another lesson that the young women referred to in their reflections on the berry fast. They talked to me about the discipline that they had learned from having to deny themselves a number of predetermined things over the course of a year. Simone, a sixteen year old who underwent the berry fast when she was twelve told me:

> Anything to do with my willpower, if people are trying to pressure me or something, or if I think I want to do something, I stop and think about it first. That is what I had to do with the berries. Everyone would offer me berries, and I would stop and think, *no I can't have them.*

Several of the girls talked about the sense of accomplishment that they had as a result of completing their fast. They concluded, "If I can do this, I can do other things." Some of them pointed out that this lesson translates, for example, to having the discipline to do school work or to pursue higher education.

Teachings about self-discipline were prominent in the understanding that Gertie Beaucage took from her own berry fast. She came away with a clear understanding that "You don't have to have everything you want right away, nor is everything you need always going to be easy to find." Beaucage believes this to be especially important in contemporary times, where, she points out "everything is instant." She recognizes that this is a particular challenge for urban adolescents, accustomed as they are to constant distraction and sensory overload. At the point when everything seems to be coming in at an uncontrollable pace, she advocates sitting down somewhere and contemplating what it feels like to deny yourself something. "To know that it is survivable," she explains.

Further to the pressing needs of urban youth, Beaucage told me "I think there is a sort of discipline that comes with having to sit on the earth and just listen to the earth's voice." This time of silence can provide youth with the space to listen to themselves and to analyze what they need to work on (rather than avoiding their issues by smothering them with distractions, be it loud music, overscheduled lives, or thoughtless consumerism). For young women who are finishing a year-long berry fast, time alone on the land might be spent thinking about what had been the most difficult aspect of it for them. (for example, no boyfriends, eating restrictions, or a more reserved social role). Beaucage encourages "learning what their own pressures are and how they are going to handle them." She concludes "We need disciplined people in our society. We need people in our society who know what is important to them, [who know] that you can survive and be self-determined and able to see a future."

Sacrifice and a sense of responsibility come to many of the girls who go through the berry fast. Carol explained to me that one of the lessons she took from her fast was that the sacrifice of not eating berries (nor wild meat in her case) was a way of giving thanks for the life that is constantly given to nourish us. The fast helped her develop a sense of responsibility based on the interconnected nature of all life forms in creation.

Some girls develop a sense of responsibility to their people. Angeline said she wanted to do her berry fast because

I wanted to know that I had accomplished something in the

eyes of the Native community. This is probably the first thing I have done for the whole Native community. All my years I have been doing swimming and soccer and schooling and stuff like that, so I was pretty happy with myself that I wanted to do something that was actually for the Natives.

She went on to say that she felt good when the aunties told her that "they were thankful because every time a girl goes out on a fast it makes the land greater and stronger and more spiritual."

Lisa took on the berry fast when she was twenty-six because she felt as though she was "stuck in the fast life," living life relatively free of responsibility and "still feeling like a kid." She told me she wanted to "learn how to be a productive woman for my people." Such feelings of responsibility and purpose are especially important to our communities, where youth suicide is among the highest in the world. Aboriginal youth need to have a sense of hope and a notion of where they fit into the future.

It is significant that the berry fast grounds this sense of responsibility in Aboriginal notions of womanhood. As the berry fast is a gender-based puberty rite, it validates the girls' existence not only as Native people nor as women, but as *Native women*. It allows them to see the critical role they play in creation, and this is achieved through the telling of female-centred creation stories, through the teachings about the sacredness of the berry, through the celebration of their menstruation. Brooklyn, a fifteen year old, says that when her peers began to menstruate she had an atypical approach. "I was so excited for them," she told me. "I said to them, 'Think about it, you can now give life to another person.' I talked to them about how that is so special." This contrasted with some of the feelings that her friends were experiencing, that they had met with "the curse."

The berry fast teachings can thus help girls to honour their particular abilities to create, and to make the connection to an understanding of their central role in shaping the future of our nations. Maracle and Beaucage have taught Brooklyn and other berry fasters that their cycles are a sacred gift that ties them to creation, and this power of the feminine can be applied in many ways. They teach girls that their responsibility is to "create and nurture." Beaucage states, "Even if you choose not to have kids, you have to create something, and whether that is a cleaner environment, a safer, more nurturing society, or a society that is able to sustain its future; whatever it is, you had better be there for the sake of creation." This teaches young women that they are partners with the Creator, something that gives them a sense of responsibility and purpose. For young women who are beginning to encounter their oppression as females, it gives them an alternative story. It is the difference between conceptualizing their bodies' cycles as *The Blood of the People*, as opposed to *The Curse*.

The berry fast offers an opportune time for girls to reflect on sex, sexuality, and relationships. The restrictions on dating and dancing are helpful because they suggest to girls that they don't need to build everything around a male partner, nor do they need to be thinking of themselves in a sexual way all the time. Lisa reflected on the value she discovered in female company and of examining her own behaviour:

> The teachings about self-respect and sexuality were the most significant to me. As a survivor of family violence and sexual abuse, I had internalized many false beliefs about men, myself, and sex. Many of these attitudes were even unknown to me until my fast. Now that I was a spectator at parties and nights on the town, I found myself reflecting on the feelings that I was experiencing. I felt foolish, I felt competitive, I worried that my value was lessened because I wasn't "out on the scene." It seems silly to me now, but I realized that the majority of my personal worth was coming from my sexual desirability. As I reflected on those issues, I was able to unravel years of self-abuse and begin to see myself as a strong woman with many skills that had value.

Lisa says that by spending time with other women, she began to see them "not as competitors but as helpers to each other."

Sylvia Maracle often talks to the young women directly about sex, as this is an ideal time to debunk some of the myths that females grow up with. Maracle can be as graphic as the old ladies who instructed her, but she offers this detail for a reason: "I want the young women to know about communication. I talk to them about getting ready for a relationship, if that is what they want to do. I would prefer them to talk about it, and it not just to happen. To have conversations about it, because it is a lot harder to hide stuff if you talk about it." Sitting in her office, listening to her so decidedly name some of those myths that we don't widely discuss as women, I was taken with the potency of this direct approach. She talks to the young girls about a young woman's information needs concerning sex. For example:

> Her feelings are just as intense as his, and if she is able to say "no" then there is no reason that he can't. She needs to understand that she has choice, that there is safe sex, that there are

all kinds of contraceptives and support. That this is a relationship. This is two halves of the medicine wheel. This is a fifty-fifty proposition, a fifty-fifty responsibility. Not ninety percent hers and ten percent his, and "Oh, this is comfortable for him and it is not for her." That it is fifty-fifty *and if she can look somebody in the eye and have the kind of conversation that I am having with you right now, then she must be ready to proceed.*

As I listened, I began think about how different we might be as women if we all had someone with the confidence and clarity of Maracle sit down with our thirteen-year-old selves and spell out our sexual authority. Certainly there would be less confusion, abuse, and trauma. With respect to two-spirited girls, a group who have even more cause to question themselves, Maracle stated that the teachings equally apply, because "it is about honesty and integrity in the relationship." She added, however, that aunties need to be reminded that they may have two-spirited girls in the ceremony, who may or may not have discovered this in themselves yet, and that we have more work to do to in terms of reclaiming tradition that is inclusive of everyone.

Finally, the berry fast is about creating a new kind of relationship between adult women and girls who are becoming women. The first and most profound relationship that is affected is the one between mother and daughter. On a purely logistical level, it offers the mothers and daughters a chance to go and do something together, be it picking berries, attending gatherings, or going to ceremony. The ceremony itself offers mothers a formal way to recognize that their child is moving on, and that they need to let go. Ann Chabot, the mother of one of the berry fasters I interviewed, told me, "It is a powerful lesson about how life goes on, and how all women come from little girls." Through the ceremony, she recognized that her daughter was no longer a "helpless little girl," and that she, as a mother, needed to create her boundaries about where, when, and how she was going to help her daughter in the future. Though the year-long fast and the night spent on the land (in which mothers often have a difficult time resisting the temptation to go out with their daughters), Chabot began to see an inner strength, confidence, and self-discipline in her daughter that she "never knew existed."

The berry fast gives girls the opportunity to join a community of women, and both mothers and daughters talk about the realization that they are "part of something bigger." The girls that I interviewed talked about how much they appreciated the support of all the older women who acted as aunties and grannies in their ceremony, and who will continue to guide them in their lives. Thus, it offers strong teachings and a positive forum for us to pass on our strength and knowledge as Aboriginal women and to reclaim those understandings that can get lost or distorted when we become immersed in the ugly realities of colonized lives.

As I was close to finishing this article, Gertie Mai Muise, a Mi'kmaq singer/hand drummer, (and the colleague who started me thinking about this subject), sent this remarkable reflection to me about her discovery of the berry fast. She wrote:

> I grew up in a community infested with male violence, sexual abuse, child abuse, wife battering and oppression of women. Women are poor and dependent on the men. The strong women were the ones who buried their own spirits before the men broke and buried it for them.
>
> With these broken spirits, the women in my community are like walking dead people. They taught me damage control— how not to be violently raped, how to avoid getting beaten, how to please the men so they would not be angered, how to go unnoticed in a crowd of them, how to stay out of their line of fire, how to accept a little mauling with my head down. That's what I was taught. I was never anything in my own right. It was always and completely in relation to men. Then here I am, among those survivors and these young women standing together, strong, as we were in this ceremony. I cried for days later as I moved through deep pain about all these experiences as a teenager. I cried for all those women back in my home community. I cried for me. I just cried. I was tremendously relieved. I was comforted in knowing that we were changing the face of Aboriginal women's history. That the women's suffering would be no more. It was like becoming liberated all over again. Amazing.[6]

Like Gertie Mai, my discovery of the berry fast has been a process of emotional recognition. I cried a lot while writing this article, as it has taken me through both grieving and celebration. I offer it in the spirit of sharing. Meegwetch.

Endnotes

[1] I wish to thank Gertie Mai Muise for giving me the idea to write this story.

[2] The disempowering aspects of my experience were linked to

an awareness that I was now open to all sorts of harassment from men; that as a thirteen-year-old female, I couldn't walk down the street and be sure that no one would stare at me, honk, make threatening overtures, or follow me. I saw no cause for celebrating my woman-hood—my period was just a "curse" that I would have to live with for another forty years, and motherhood seemed to be a way of keeping women from participating in the "real" world. Having a boyfriend seemed to imply that you had to become a little less smart, a little less outgoing, a little more submissive. These were the stories that I saw unfolding, and playing the female held no appeal for the girl that I was.

[3] The collaboration of these two women from different nations is an example of how our peoples can work together to conduct ceremonies that work in environments where many nations are represented (e.g., Toronto). Maracle and Beaucage use Iroquois stories (creation story, teachings about berries) alongside Ojibway practices of berry fasting to create something that is fitting for the many girls they work with.

[4] I have used pseudonyms for all the young women I quote here.

[5] This was shared with me by Ojibway Grandmother Vera Martin. More information about her berry fast teachings are available in my book *A Recognition of Being: Reconstructing Native Womanhood* (Second Story Press).

[6] E-mail correspondence, Gertie Mai Muise to author, September 29, 1999.

From the Tribal to the Modern:

The Development of Modern Aboriginal Societies

David R. Newhouse

David Newhouse, an Associate Professor in the Department of Native Studies and Administrative Studies Program at Trent University, is an Onondaga from the Six Nations of the Grand River. He is conducting research into the changes he sees occurring in Aboriginal societies, trying to help Aboriginal people see that "we are more than the sum of our problems, that we are a thinking people pushing the bounds of tradition." He gardens on a drumlin.

Introduction

In the early part of its work, the Royal Commission on Aboriginal Peoples released a series of questions and research issues that it felt needed to be answered in the course of its work. In reading them, I was struck by the breadth of the questions that were to be addressed. However, the more I thought about the questions, the more I became concerned about the underlying ideas that the Commission was using as a foundation for its work. It seemed to me that the Commission was struggling with some fundamental ideas about the nature of contemporary Aboriginal societies but that these were not visible or being openly discussed.

This lack of visibility and open discussion stimulated me to begin to think about the ideas are at play within contemporary Aboriginal societies. My interest is not in continuing to document the problems that are present within Aboriginal societies and with the relationship between Aboriginal societies and mainstream Canadians. Many others do that exceptionally well. Rather my interest is in looking at the ideas that animate actions within contemporary Aboriginal societies. It is my fundamental belief that ideas animate actions, that ideas drive action as much as our passions. Like Hegel, I believe that history is the history of ideas and that we move forward as a result of a complex interplay of ideas. In this article, I try to set out not so much ideas, but the context within which these ideas are being discussed, debated, examined, and acted upon, often indirectly. The context affects our translation of ideas into action.

The Report of the Royal Commission on Aboriginal Peoples (RCAP) is an excellent presentation of the political aspirations of most Aboriginal people in this country. It captured, in 4,000 pages, the desire of Aboriginal people for recognition as "distinct peoples" within the Canadian federation. It also outlined the broad parameters of how to develop and maintain this distinctiveness within Canadian political, social, and cultural institutions.

RCAP also told a familiar tale of marginalization, broken promises, failed attempts at assimilation, racism, exclusion—the now familiar tale of Indian-white relations over the course of the last few centuries. Many, if not most, Canadians are aware of, if not necessarily fully accepting of this story. Focusing on the political aspirations of Aboriginal peoples, however, masks some of the fundamental changes that have occurred in Aboriginal societies since 1969.

Post-1969 Aboriginal Society

I want to look at the post-1969 Aboriginal society because I believe that the period 1969–1972 was a critical and profound period in Aboriginal history. It is in this time period that we can begin to see the contours of modern Aboriginal society emerge and become more distinct.

In 1969, the government of Canada introduced, for public discussion: "A Statement of Indian Policy"—now commonly referred to by its generic name, the *White Paper*—an ironic name because it largely proposed that Indians should become, for all intents and purposes, white. The paper proposed a repeal of the Indian Act, the dissolution of Indian reserves, and the turning over of responsibilities for Indian affairs to provinces, among other things.

I am old enough to recall the buzz surrounding the government proposals. I recall listening to radio newscasts of the proposals, hearing the talk from members of my family (my father was a condoled chief in the Iroquoian confederacy) and neighbours. The initial reaction was fear: what's going to happen to us? How will we live? Where will we live? This fear gradually turned to anger and outrage: how can the government do this? How can they repudiate the treaties? How can they ignore our relationship with the Crown?

It is in this period that "modern Aboriginal society" has its roots. The introduction of the *White Paper* and the subsequent Indian response that led to its withdrawal was to have profound effects upon Aboriginal peoples' thinking. The late Sally Weaver, a professor of anthropology at the University of Guelph in Ontario, has written an excellent account of the politics of this period in a book entitled *Making Canadian Indian Policy: The Hidden Agenda 1968–1970.*

The *White Paper* still remains in many Indian peoples' consciousness and became over the next two decades the *de facto* standard against which all government policies were measured. In 1996, it was replaced by RCAP. We used to say: "Is this just the *White Paper* in disguise?" Now we say: "How does this accord with RCAP?"

Indian reaction to this event has led to profound changes in our conceptions of ourselves: *We have power, we can use it to influence government policy; we can use it to create change.* In 1969, self-government was not part of our everyday speech. In 1998, it is part of the language of the country.

Before proceeding too much further I want to give a quick history of the changes that have occurred since 1969. The *White Paper* galvanized the Indian community in a way that no other event had. There were changes afoot within North American society. In 1969, humans landed on the moon. This was the dawning of the "Age of Aquarius," which was to usher in a 1,000-year era of peace and love. Everywhere in North American, traditional ways of doing things, old power structures, were being challenged and anyone over thirty was not to be trusted. Given the interconnected nature of Aboriginal and North American society, it follows that there would be changes afoot in Indian-white relations as well.

The Indian Chiefs of Alberta issued their 1969 *Red Paper* in response to the *White Paper*. They rejected all that had been proposed. In 1972, the Manitoba Indian Brotherhood (MIB) issued their own response: *Whabung: Our Tomorrows.* This report called for a comprehensive approach to the development of Indian communities, to see them both as an economy and as a community central to Indian life. It called for development not to proceed in bits and pieces but according to a comprehensive plan on several fronts. There were three elements to this strategy:

1.   A plan to help individuals and communities recover from the pathological consequences of poverty and powerlessness.

2. A plan for Indian people to protect their interests in lands and resources.

3. A concerted effort at human resource and cultural development. The MIB plan had at its heart the idea that if change were to lead to increased self- sufficiency, it ought to be directed by Indian people themselves, so that Indians could consider both individual and communal interests.

Arguments supporting Aboriginal self-sufficiency and self-government continued to be put forward over the next decade. In 1977, Jack Beaver released his report on economic development, *To Have What Is Our Own*. He also argued for a policy of self-direction as the fundamental basis for economic development of Indian communities. In 1982, the *Penner Report on Indian Self-Government* advanced the same argument. In 1995, the Government of Canada announced that it would support the policy of the inherent right to self-government for Aboriginal peoples of this country. And in 1996 the Royal Commission on Aboriginal Peoples underlined the importance of this policy and made a central recommendation for the reconstitution of Aboriginal nations and their governments.

When we look around at our communities, these political achievements are still masked by the effects of poverty that we see in most places. In twenty-seven years, from the *White Paper* in 1969 to the Royal Commission in 1996, we have moved from an official government policy of termination and assimilation to a reluctant acceptance of the inherent right of self- government. This is a re-markable achievement in such a short time, and we often forget what we have achieved and how we have achieved it.

A quarter of a century after the release of the *White Paper*, it is hard to imagine what that world was like then. The National Indian Broth-erhood, now the Assembly of First Nations, was just starting. The word *Aboriginal* was not used to describe the original inhabitants of this land. The term *First Nation* did not exist. We talked of Indians and Eskimos and Métis and non- status Indians. Aboriginal rights were not part of the popular vocabulary nor was there any talk of government. Self-determination was the order of the day.

This twenty-five-year period has seen extraordinary political development:

- In 1971, the government of Canada was forced to withdraw its policy of termination after much public outcry.
- In 1975, the Dene Nation of the Northwest Territories have made their declaration of nationhood.
- In 1976, the government of Canada signed the first modern-day treaty with the Crees of Quebec that created a form of

self-government and gave them varying degrees of control over resources.

- In the early 1980s, the constitution of Canada was repatriated and was written to recognize Aboriginal peoples as including Indian, Inuit (formerly Eskimo), and Métis. The constitution also affirmed existing Aboriginal rights and called for a series of constitutional conferences between Canada, the provinces, and Aboriginal peoples to try and determine what these rights were and what self-government meant.
- In 1985, the House of Commons Special Committee on Indian Self- Government issued its report. It said that Indian people were nations before the arrival of Europeans and had a tradition of government that had been removed. It recommended that Indian self-government within the Canadian federation be supported. The government of Canada agreed.
- In the mid- and late 1980s, two rounds of constitutional discussions tackled the questions surrounding Aboriginal self-government. There were endless discussions of what it meant, how it should be recognized, how it should be implemented, and what powers they should have.
- In the early 1990s, the government of Canada agreed to divide the Northwest territories into two: the west, as yet unnamed and the east to be known as Nunavut, where the majority of residents are Inuk.
- And in the mid-1990s, the RCAP recommended that self-government within the Canadian federation should be implemented through the reconstitution of Aboriginal nations and their governments and the creation of a new relationship between Aboriginal peoples and Canada.

Between 1972 and 1996, there were hundreds of reports containing thousands of recommendations on what to do to improve the condition of Aboriginal peoples in Canada. An extraordinary level of attention has been paid to Aboriginal issues, and they are on the agenda of virtually every government agency. These political developments have been paralleled in other areas: the arts, health, and education, to name three.

In the visual arts, there is a recognized genre of art known as Aboriginal art. We have seen the development of the woodland school that has developed new forms of carving, painting, and pottery, based upon the work and techniques of Norval Morriseau. Other expressions of Aboriginal art include Inuit stone carving, Iroquoian soapstone, Haida masks, Miqmaq baskets, Ojibway quills, and postmodern Aboriginal expressionism found in the work of painters such as Carl Beam, Jane Ash Poitras. In the field of music, Aboriginal musicians have moved beyond Winston Wuttunnee and Buffy Sainte-Marie. Kashtin, Red Power, 7th Fire, Robbie Robertson, Shania Twain have all been successful in a highly competitive industry. *Aboriginal Voices Magazine* now prints the top ten albums in Indian country. In the literary arts there are also writers galore: Tomson Highway, Jeannette Armstrong, Scott Momaday, Sherman Alexie, Drew Hayden Taylor, and Thomas King. All are telling the story of the Aboriginal community.

In education, there is now one Aboriginal university and seventeen Aboriginal-controlled post-secondary institutes. The last federally run Indian residential school was closed in the mid-1980s, and all public schools on Indian reserves are now under Indian control.

In the area of health and healing, we have seen the emergence of a widespread healing movement that affects just about every Aboriginal person in this country, and Aboriginal health centres have been established in many locations across the country.

In large urban centres, there is an extraordinary array of service and cultural organizations serving large urban Aboriginal populations. There are now almost 130 Aboriginal Friendship Centres located all over the country. In response to the explosion of talent emerging the National Native Achievement Foundation, formerly the Canadian Native Arts Foundation, gives out awards each year for outstanding contributions to the life and culture of Aboriginal peoples.

There is a consistent theme in Aboriginal rhetoric: a strong and over-whelming desire to survive as distinct Aboriginal peoples. We have heard it over and over again throughout the years. And it is not my intent to suggest that things are good. They are not, but we have come a long way in twenty-five years, and we are laying a solid foundation upon which those who come after us can build. This, then, is the context of modern Aboriginality: confident, aggressive, assertive, insistent, desirous of creating a new world out of Aboriginal and Western ideas.

In 1992, I spent a week at the twenty-first Annual General Meeting of the National Association of Friendship Centres (NAFC) in Ottawa. There were about 350 people from across the country. Upon arrival, each participant was provided with a small bound book of about 200 pages containing an agenda for the three-day conference, minutes of the previous AGM, various reports from the Executive Committee and staff of the NAFC, reports on resolutions from past meetings and financial statements for the previous twelve months.

All material was available in the two official languages of Canada. The meetings were conducted primarily in English; however, delegates from Quebec spoke French. and interpretation was readily available and used frequently. A smattering of Aboriginal languages was used throughout the proceedings.

The meetings began each day at 9:00 A.M. (or close to that time) with a prayer by an Elder. Following this, the procedures committee reported on the agenda, the assembly adopted the agenda, various delegates made reports, and the assembly voted on motions. The constitution of the NACF was debated and changed. Discussions proceeded in an orderly fashion using a variant of Robert's Rules of Order. Recorders kept minutes that would later be transcribed and distributed far and wide. The meetings ended at 5:00 P.M. or thereabouts.

There were elections for a new executive committee and nominations were held for four positions: President, Vice President, Treasurer, and Secretary. Nominators spoke on behalf of their candidates citing the familiar litany of good deeds that the candidate could be expected to perform. Candidates stood and told stories about themselves, pledged to do their very best and to work on behalf of the members. Delegates voted by secret ballot, and each candidate selected a scrutineer to ensure that the process was fair. The Elections Committee announced winners, who promptly thanked everyone for their support and again pledged to do good work.

This process was repeated the next year. And the year after. And probably will be repeated for as long as the NAFC is in existence.

The previous summer, I had watched the first nationally televised meeting of the Assembly of First Nations and the leadership race, which ended with the election by democratic secret ballot of Ovide Mercredi as National Chief. Listening to and watching the convention, I was hard pressed to distinguish any significant difference in the proceedings and those of other televised leadership conventions.

I see this same electoral process in many Aboriginal communities and organizations across the country. Band Council elections proceed similarly unless the band has chosen to define and use a customary form of selection of a government. The idea of one citizen, one vote appears to be a widely held idea within Aboriginal societies, even if the effect of that idea is a continuation of kinship leadership patterns.

These meetings, which I give as examples, indicate the extent to which modern western European institutions, thought, and ways of doing things have influenced and continue to influence Aboriginal societies. I do not mean to say that Aboriginal communities do not do things according to Aboriginal custom but that Western ways of thought and doing things are becoming more prevalent and in some areas dominant. This process has been underway since first contact and has been speeding up over the last twenty years.

Aboriginal people have also entered mainstream organizations in unprecedented numbers over the last two decades. However, over the last ten years, many of these same people have also been attempting to relearn and reinterpret the ancient teachings of Elders. These people now think about and see the world in significantly different ways than their forefathers.

Factors Influencing Changes in Aboriginal Society

There are profound changes occurring within Aboriginal societies today. Many scholars have not detected them because they have focused much of their effort on an examination of the social problems and material poverty present within Aboriginal communities. A number of these scholars persist in seeing Aboriginal people as victims, a characterization that many Aboriginal people have adapted themselves. When scholars have attempted to explain the changes they see, they use words such as *revitalization, urbanization, acculturation, assimilation, dispossession.*

I do agree that all these changes are occurring, but I believe they do not describe the entire landscape. The processes made visible by these scholars focus on only one aspect of the changes, and it is important to fully understand what is occurring in order to develop further strategies for change or make decisions about future directions. These are the developments I see occurring around me:

1. **Urbanization:** The demographics of urban Aboriginal communities have reached a critical point where they can grow without additional migration from rural reserve-based communities.
2. **Institutionalization:** New social, economic, and political institutions are appearing at a rapid rate. These institutions either supplement or replace traditional kinship systems (primarily clans) within Aboriginal society. As individuals, communities, and governments attempt to solve the problems facing them, more and more specialized organizations are being established.
3. **Cultural identity reinforcement:** The deliberate and internally defined individual and collective identities based upon traditional cultural groups is reinforcing cultural identity.
4. **Retraditionalization:** A return to traditional world views, values, and customs is becoming the central aspect of Aboriginal life for many individuals.
5. **Textual transformation:** There has been an emergence of a textual mode of cultural transmission, which is beginning to supersede the ancient oral transmission, and the emergence of English as

the lingua franca among Aboriginal people is influencing modern Aboriginal life.

6. **Self-governance**: The assertion of individual and collective control over the structures and processes of everyday Aboriginal life is becoming increasingly common.

These six developments (among others) are influencing modern Aboriginal societies. These societies will be as different from the tribal societies of our ancestors as contemporary Europe is from the days of the Enlightenment.

Modern Aboriginal Societies

Modern Aboriginal societies will be a blend of modern Western and traditional Aboriginal societies. It can be no other way. The relatively small number of Aboriginal people (one million) living in Canada are surrounded by more than twenty-five million others. Education, the major cultural transmission process, currently presents aspects of both worlds: young people who live in the remotest communities learn their own history, cultural practices, and language from Elders, written curricula, and video images while listening to rap artists, watching *Beverly Hills 90210, Star Trek: The Next Generation*, and reading Superman and Batman comics. From a very young age, the current generation of Aboriginal youth have lived in this curious blend of two worlds. The process of cultural transfer from a large group to a smaller group is well documented. It adds nothing to say that the future will be a blend of the past. Instinctively, we know this. The trick is to identify the way in which the two worlds will blend together to see whether you get a bread or a cake. What will this new society look like?

Urban Based

It will be largely urban based. Between forty and sixty percent of all Aboriginal people live in urban centres in Canada, and the off-reserve population is forecast to increase over the next twenty-five years. As noted earlier, the urban population in many centres is now large enough to grow without additional migration from reserve or rural communities. There are now Aboriginal people who have lived for three generations in cities, that is, there are Aboriginal children who have not been born on a reserve or in rural community and who will never live there. Many of these people have little desire to return to a rural life, and their experiences of Aboriginal life will be much different from those of their parents and grandparents.

This is not to say that reserves or rural communities will not exist or cease to be places where people will want to live or will continue to live. There will always be people who choose to live on reserves for a variety of reasons. For many people, however, reserves will become a place to visit family on vacations or places where traditional ceremonies take place.

What does this mean? It means that the majority of Aboriginal people will not live close to the land and may not hold the same traditional emotional and spiritual views of it. It also means that many Aboriginal people will want to have access to the consumer goods and material life they see around them. Their connection to the lives as lived by their grandfathers will be tenuous. It may mean that an Aboriginal descent may become, for some people, a heritage rather than a way of life. It does mean that one will need to take extraordinary steps to ensure the survival of Aboriginal cultures, including languages and spirituality.

Institutions Appropriate to Aboriginal Culture

The central institutions of Aboriginal life will primarily be Western in nature with adaptations to ensure that they are appropriate to Aboriginal cultures. Family structures will continue their movement towards the small nuclear family; schools will be organized on the Western-based model and use Western curricula modified to reflect Aboriginal content and values; businesses will develop and be run both for profit and for social reasons; social institutions such as daycare or various health agencies to deal with the various needs of people will emerge. In short, the structures of everyday life will become more Western in nature, but they will operate using Aboriginal values.

For example, many organizations have blended the Western structure of a board of directors and various levels of staff with an Aboriginal decision making process based primarily on consensus. The Medicine Wheel, primarily a teaching tool, is being used in some places as the basis for organization structures, an approach to community development, or for the development of social services. In some communities, Aboriginal governments, based upon the Western democratic model, regularly elect only members of clans from which leaders have traditionally been chosen.

What does this mean? I believe that Aboriginal societies will come to rely upon organizations for meeting individual and collective needs as much as and in the same way Western society has. As traditional structures are replaced or adapted to modern organizations, Aboriginal communities will experience much debate and dissention over cultural interpretation and definition (cultural correctness) and proper control of these institutions. (There are many different interpretations of the Medicine Wheel, for example. Which one should be used?) Or in the area of self-government, one of the questions will be to whom should Aboriginal governments be accountable? And in what ways? Future developments are unlikely to be smooth or continuous.

Positive Self-Identity

Aboriginal individual and collective identities will be positive and self-constructed. Olive Dickason, a Métis scholar at the University of Ottawa, writes in the epilogue of her book *Canada's First Nations* (1992):

> If any one theme can be traced throughout the history of Canada's Amerindians, it is the persistence of their identity. The confident expectation of Europeans that Indians were a vanishing people, the remnants of whom would finally be absorbed by the dominant society, has not happened. If anything, Indians are more prominent in the collective conscience of the nation than they have ever been.

I believe there are two factors that will have a profound effect upon Aboriginal societies: the reinforcement of Aboriginal identities and the re-traditionalization of Aboriginal societies. These two processes are intertwined, hence it is difficult to talk about one without discussing the other. I think the crucial element linking the two is the regaining of the control of identity. Over the past 500 years, control over identity has been wrenched from the hands of Aboriginal communities and placed in the hands of non-Aboriginal politicians, teachers, and social workers. All have sought to define who Aboriginal people were and are.

It started with Columbus, who believed that he had reached India and insisted, despite knowledge to the contrary, that the people he encountered were Indians. Not only were Aboriginal people being defined by others but these definitions made it possible for others to make value judgements about Aboriginal people and found them wanting or lacking. Through that process, Aboriginal peoples lost knowledge of and faith in their own traditions but did not lose faith in their identities.

Within the Aboriginal community, over the past decade particularly, there has been a move to relearn the traditional ways and to move these ways back to the centre of Aboriginal life. This is a process some sociologists call "revitalization" and that I call "retraditionalization."

Revitalization gives the impression you are giving something a new energy. That is not the process that I believe is occurring today. Something new is being created and it requires a new word. What is occurring is that Aboriginal identity is being examined on both an individual and collective basis, and it is being deliberately reconstructed by Aboriginal insititutions, educators, communities, and band leaders to be as Aboriginal as possible. This examination has made Aboriginal societies think carefully about their assumptions, values, and ways of doing things.

For example, Aboriginal child care agencies are emerging in Ontario and Quebec. These are adaptations of modern structures that use Aboriginal values; in the area of justice, instead of a court-based punitive system, there are now experiments with Aboriginal systems, which use Elders as adjudicators and the focus of which is restoring the balance upset by the crime rather than punishing the offender. Native art has become a distinct discipline where Aboriginal artists are continually reinterpreting the world and creating new ways of seeing it.

This process of relearning and reinterpreting traditional ways has led to a rethinking of Aboriginal identities and to the development of new individual and collective identities. These identities are based on traditional cultural groupings such as Oneida, Mohawk, Sioux, Cree, or Ojibway rather than the generic "Indian" or "Aboriginal person."

The identities themselves are positive in nature rather than negative, that is, they define what is in isolation rather than what is not in reference to others. A Mohawk is a Mohawk. These positive statements provide a basis for dealing with others and the world. One can then be a Mohawk and be proud of it and wear the identity with dignity when one is aware of the long heritage and tradition of the name. This way of thinking about oneself, of constructing an identity, is modern and is now well accepted by modern societies.

I believe this means that Aboriginal people will approach the world with a new confidence and will want to be recognized and to live as Aboriginal people. These reconstructed identities will provide a solid foundation for experimentation and perhaps change. However, it will also mean a growing acceptance of the notion that there are a variety of ways to be Aboriginal without losing the essence of Aboriginality. This broader approach to Aboriginality will also mean a series of identity clashes between those who have constructed ideas about Aboriginal identities based upon narrow interpretations of tradition and custom.

Aboriginal Self-Governance

Self-governance will be a social and political reality. Self-governance is a broader concept than self-government. By self-governance, I mean that the major structures and processes of Aboriginal life will be largely under Aboriginal control and will influence identity, education, and government, to name a few important areas. Under self-governance Aboriginal individuals and communities, to the extent possible in a global village, will be able to direct and influence the development of their children, the education of their young, the development of their communities, and the care and tending of their spiritual lives.

I believe that this means there will be more organizations established to deal with the various needs Aboriginal societies want fulfilled. This has been the experience in the mainstream society, and I do not see anything indicating that this will not be true of Aboriginal societies as well.

A recent review of the Arrowfax directory of Aboriginal organizations indicated about 6,000 Aboriginal organizations, split evenly between the profit and not-for-profit sectors, including First Nations governments.

A Fundamental Change

Anthropologists, sociologists, politicians, and even perhaps historians have tended to see Aboriginal people as being swallowed up or completely acculturated. Most people, it would be safe to say, see only either one of two realities concerning Aboriginal people: a dusty rose-coloured, romantic, hazy picture build upon the notions of the "noble savage" or an impoverished people who are forever to be consigned to the margins of society and who will remain powerless to define a place for themselves in the world except as victim.

I agree that the predominant attitude towards Aboriginal people has been one of discrimination and prejudice. However, events of the last twenty years have demonstrated clearly that attitudes towards Aboriginal people are changing significantly, as have Aboriginal people's views of themselves.

The fundamental change in the last two decades has been the acceptance by both Aboriginal people and mainstream Canadians of the way in which traditional Aboriginal people have viewed them-selves and the resultant construction of new identities, not as victims or as noble savages or primitive beings but as, for example, as Cree, Ojibway, or Inuit who have dignity and knowledge and are deserving of respect and a place in contemporary society.

The ability to construct an identity for the self, either as an individual or as a collective, lies at the heart of modernity. I now see a group of people who are constructing a positive identity for themselves, who see themselves as an integral part of and contributors to the society around them.

The governments that are being reconstituted are also an example of the modern in Aboriginal society. For the most part, they are incorporating Western notions of liberal democracy with their ideas about individuality, individual freedom, preservation of human rights, limits on the role of governments, and the rights of all citizens to participate meaningfully in both the economic and political institutions of society.

The idea of one citizen, one vote gives to an individual a role and power that may be at odds the roles of individuals within traditional societies. These modern notions are being combined with Aboriginal notions of collectivism and the fundamental values of respect, kindness, honesty, sharing, and caring. Yet, despite these combinations, we still recognize the governments as Aboriginal and the people as Aboriginal. What has happened is that our notion of "Aboriginal" has changed and now incorporates features of both the traditional and modern worlds. What does the future hold?

The next twenty years is a critical time for Aboriginal individuals and communities. During this period, many basic structures and processes of Aboriginal life will be modified and placed under Aboriginal influence: Aboriginal governance will become a social and political reality. Much like the mainstream society, modern Aboriginal society will be a society of organizations. These institutions (political, education, cultural, spiritual) will then work to improve the quality of Aboriginal lives.

The creative and contemporary interpretation of Aboriginal culture as a process is at the heart of modernization. Aboriginal people want to interpret their culture in ways that best fit their everyday lives at the end of the twentieth century. We must recognize that Aboriginal cultures are not static: they do not exist under glass and are ever changing in response to influences from within and without.

As Aboriginal societies blend their traditions with western European ways, the processes and institutions that arise will be varied: no single model will occur or prevail. It is futile and misguided to think this will happen. The development of modern societies in the world has not resulted anywhere in a uniform set of institutions or structures for everyday life. I do not think that we can expect anything different within Aboriginal societies in Canada.

There are opportunities here for a new beginning. I remember reading in the *Dune* novels of Frank Herbert: "Beginnings are dangerous times. It is important to get the balance right." It is not my place to render a judgment about the process of modernization that is underway. I do not know if it is good or bad or if the balance is right. I do know that Aboriginal individuals and communities need to have control of the structures and processes of their everyday lives if they are to get the balance right. And we get the balance right through a process of open and informed critical discussion.

Works Consulted

Beaver, Jack. *To Have What Is One's Own: The Report of the National Indian Socio-Economic Development Committee.* Ottawa: National Indian Socio-Economic Development Committee, 1979.

Dickason, Olive. *Canada's First Nations: A History of Founding Peoples from Earliest Times.* Toronto: McClelland & Stewart, 1992.

Dyck, Noel. *What Is the Indian Problem: Tutelage and Resistance in Canadian Indian Administration.* St. John's, NF: Institute of Social and Economic Research, Memorial University, 1991.

Herbert, Frank. *The Notebooks of Frank Herbert's Dune.* Brian Herbert, ed. New York: Perigee Books, Putnam, 1988.

Indian Chiefs of Alberta. *Citizens Plus,* Indian Chiefs of Alberta, 1970.

Royal Commission on Aboriginal Peoples. *The Report of the Royal Commission on Aboriginal Peoples.* Ottawa: Canada Communications Group-Publishing, 1996.

Satzewich, Vic, and Terry Wotherspoon. *First Nations Race, Class and Gender Relations.* Toronto: Nelson, 1993.

Smith, Dan. *The Seventh Fire: The Struggle for Aboriginal Government.* Toronto: Key Porter, 1993.

Special Committee on Indian Self-Government. Chair, K. Penner. *Indian Self- Government in Canada, Report of the Special Committee on Indian Self-Government,* Ottawa, Queen's Printer, 1985.

Waubageshig. *The Only Good Indian: Essays by Canadian Indians,* Don Mills: New Press, 1970.

Weaver, Sally. *Making Canadian Indian Policy: The Hidden Agenda, 1968– 1970.* Toronto: University of Toronto Press, 1981.

Reflections on Urban Satellite Reserves in Saskatchewan

F. Laurie Barron and Joseph Garcea

F. Laurie Barron was a founding member of the Department of Native Studies at the University of Saskatchewan. As a Professor of Native Studies, he dedicated his life to Aboriginal issues through the education of students and the training of teachers in Native Studies. He passed away in January 2000.

Joseph Garcea is a Professor in the departments of Native Studies and Political Studies at the University of Saskatchewan. He is currently serving as Chair of the Task Force on Municipal Legislature Renewal in Saskatchewan.

Introduction

First Nations across Canada have opted for some novel, experimental initiatives designed to help them capitalize on the benefits of various economic and political developments without compromising Aboriginal and treaty rights. One such experiment is the creation of "satellite reserves."[1] Since the early 1980s in Saskatchewan, there has been a veritable explosion in their creation and this marks a major development both in Aboriginal affairs and in relations between First Nations and municipalities. Satellite reserves have been created in urban, rural, and northern parts of the province and accordingly, they can be grouped into three major categories: urban satellite reserves, rural satellite reserves, and northern satellite reserves.

As its name suggests, urban satellite reserves are located in urban areas either within or adjacent to the boundaries of existing urban municipalities. Under the federal Indian Act, they have the same legal status as Indian reserves found in the rural areas. In Saskatchewan, they are generally the creations of band councils that govern what might be termed "base reserves," "home reserves," or "parent reserves" in various parts of the province. The urban satellite reserves are controlled and administered by these Indian band councils either under their general bylaws or special bylaws established for its particular urban reserve.

Since the first urban satellite reserve was created in Prince Albert in 1982, at least one dozen other such reserves have been created in various urban centres in southern and central Saskatchewan. They include the cities of Prince Albert, Saskatoon, and Yorkton as well as the towns or villages of Fort Qu'Appelle, Meadow Lake, Lebret, and Duck Lake. In addition to these, a number of other urban satellite reserves in southern Saskatchewan are either in the planning stages or in the formal process of being created both in these communities and other strategically located urban centres. Generally these reserves entail either a single urban lot and the buildings located on it within a municipality's downtown or a small parcel of land of several acres in size located in a municipal commercial or industrial park.

The proliferation of satellite reserves in Saskatchewan during the past twenty years has not been restricted to urban areas. A substantial number of reserves in the southern and central parts of the province have also been created within the boundaries of rural municipalities. The processes and issues surrounding the creation of these particular reserves have not been dissimilar from those related to the creation of reserves in urban and northern municipalities. The notable difference has been the protracted controversy regarding what constitutes adequate compensation to rural municipalities for tax loss compensations stemming from the conversion of lands within the municipal boundaries to reserve status. This is an issue that has been addressed on a collective basis on behalf of the affected municipalities by the Saskatchewan Association of Rural Municipalities for nearly a decade. An agreement on a compensation formula for such municipalities was finally reached in the spring of 2000.[2]

The creation of satellite reserves within or adjacent to the boundaries of existing municipalities has also occurred in municipalities in northern Saskatchewan. The Amended Cost-Sharing Agreement component of the Treaty Land Entitlement Framework Agreement (TLFEA) signed in September 1992 between the federal, provincial, and more than two dozen First Nation governments stipulates that either parts, or all, of at least five small municipalities or quasi-municipalities in northern Saskatchewan are to be converted to reserves.[3] These include Deschambault Lake, Pelican Narrows, Sandy Bay, Denare Beach, and Southend.

Although all of these satellite reserve creation initiatives merit further analysis, the overarching purpose in this article is to shed some light on the creation, governance and management, value, and future of Indian urban satellite reserves in Saskatchewan. The central focus of this article is on four of the urban satellite reserves created in Saskatchewan during the past two decades in Prince Albert, Saskatoon, Fort Qu'Appelle and Yorkton.[4] The insights gained from the creation of these particular reserves have considerable relevance for understanding comparable aspects of other satellite reserves that have been created or are in the process of being created in urban, rural, and northern areas in Saskatchewan and elsewhere.

There are eight dimensions of Indian urban satellite reserves that merit attention: the policies by which they are created, the nature and dynamics of the processes by which they are created, factors facilitating their creation, their purpose, the places where they are created, their governance and management, their value, and their future. Each of these dimensions is discussed in turn below.

Policies for Creating Urban Satellite Reserves

The policy and process for creating reserves is outlined in two documents: the Treaty Land Entitlement Framework Agreement (TLEFA) and the federal Additions to Reserve Policy (ARP).[5] TLEFA is a $450-million province-wide land claims agreement signed in 1992 by the federal government, the province of Saskatchewan, and more than two dozen bands in the province. ARP is the official policy statement of the federal government applying to lands earmarked for reserve status, particularly as a result of specific land claims by Indian bands anywhere in Canada. Both represent a parallel formula meant to ensure, where possible, a harmonious process that addresses the concerns and interests of all levels of government. Once the band has acquired the land in question and petitioned to have it transformed into a reserve, the Indian band must negotiate agreements with municipalities (and in some instances with school boards) on the following matters:

(1) whether compensation will be paid for the loss of municipal property taxes and school levies once the land in question is removed from the public domain;

(2) the type and financing of municipal services to be delivered to the new reserve;

(3) bylaw compatibility between the municipality and reserve, particularly where reserve development has the potential to affect neighbouring municipal lands and residents; and

(4) establishment of a joint consultative process, especially a dispute resolution mechanism, for matters of mutual concern between the band and municipality.[6]

Both the TLEFA and the ARP stipulate that these matters must be negotiated in good faith, and where a municipality fails to do so in response to the reasonable proposals of a band, the federal government may proceed to create the reserve in question, notwithstanding the objections of the municipality. This is precisely what happened in the case of the first urban reserve in the province, the Opawakoscikan Reserve in Prince Albert. The final part of the reserve creation process is a federal Order-in-Council that, in only a few sentences, officially proclaims the existence of the new reserve. In effect, the Order-in-Council makes the urban satellite reserve subject to the Indian Act, conferring on them the same rights and liabilities as other reserves in Canada.[7]

Processes for Creating Urban Satellite Reserves

Although some of the urban satellite reserves were created under the federal government's ARP and others were created pursuant to Article 9 of the TLEFA, the basic nature of the process was essentially the same.[8] It was a relatively closed intergovernmental negotiation process in which the key protagonists were elected or appointed officials of First Nations, federal, provincial, and municipal governments. Although there were public consultations and discussions on the creation of urban satellite reserves, invariably the key decisions were made by government officials rather than by members of bands or the municipal electorate through plebiscites or referenda. The one exception was the use of a referendum in the process that led to the creation of the Star Blanket reserve in Fort Qu'Appelle. The town council held a referendum on a bylaw that would have required any agreements with First Nations leading to the creation of an urban reserve to be ratified by the electors in a subsequent referendum. The defeat of the referendum and the proposed bylaw, which was generally interpreted by some as a vote of confidence in the municipal council's ability to make the right decision and by others as a vote of support for the creation of the urban reserve, negated a direct role for the local electorate in the creation of that reserve.[9] The reserve creation process was also relatively closed and elite driven within the First Nation communities, as decisions on the creation of urban satellite reserves were made by the band chiefs and councils in consultations with elders, rather than by plebiscites or referenda.

The reserve creation process involves up to four interrelated sets of intergovernmental negotiations. Although number of sets of negotiations depends on the types of issues involved, invariably, two sets are common to all urban reserve creation processes. The first set of negotiations involves the First Nation and the federal government, and the second set involves the First Nation and the municipal governments. In some cases, however, there is a third set of negotiations involving First Nation and provincial governments, where provincial agencies have a stake or interest in the creation of the reserve. For example, various provincial agencies are interested in issues of rights-of-way for provincial utilities and other governmental agencies. A fourth set of negotiations may involve First Nation and school division governments on the issue of tax-loss compensation to the latter. Such negotiations with school divisions have been rather brief and limited in scope as First Nations have generally taken the position that unless their members use school services, they should not have to compensate school boards for tax losses resulting from the creation of urban satellite reserves. The Muskeg Lake Cree Nation, for example, took the position that if the school boards were not providing educational services to any First Nation members living on its urban satellite reserve, it did not warrant either tax-loss compensation or the payment of an educational service fee. It maintained that such compensation or fees for school boards would amount to double taxation because educational services to First Nation children living on reserves throughout the province are already funded via other means.

Beyond the negotiations described above, the level of direct involvement of federal and provincial governments in the creation of the various urban satellite reserves tended to vary considerably, depending on the extent to which their own interests were at stake and the extent to which the negotiations between First Nation and municipal governments were problematical. Generally both preferred to distance themselves from the negotiations between the First Nations and municipalities.[10] Only when First Nations and municipalities reached a significant impasse did the federal and, to a much lesser extent, provincial governments become involved by assuming the role of mediators or arbitrators.

The dynamics surrounding the creation of urban satellite reserves in southern Saskatchewan were far from uniform. In some cases the reserve creation process was controversial and confrontational—Prince Albert during the early 1980s and Fort Qu'Appelle in the early 1990s— in other cases it was non-controversial and cooperative—Saskatoon 1989, Yorkton 1996, and Prince Albert 1996.[11] In Prince Albert, the role of arbitrator was performed by the federal government when the Peter Ballantyne Cree Nation decided to proceed with the creation of the reserve over the objections of that municipality's mayor and council. There, the nature and extent of federal and provincial involvement in the reserve creation process was a highly contested issue, particularly because the dynamics surrounding the creation of urban satellite reserves at that time were highly controversial and confrontational. In some cases representatives of First Nations and various local authorities demanded the involvement of the federal and provincial government, and in other cases they demanded that those levels of government limit their involvement.

The principal differences in the dynamics arising from the creation of the urban satellite reserves were three inextricably related factors—governmental interests, race relations, and interpersonal relations between the negotiators. The perceptions of various governmental and non-governmental actors regarding the effect that the creation of a particular reserve is likely to have for their respective interests played an important role. In cases where a substantial number of municipal officials and non-governmental representatives in a given municipality viewed the creation of an urban reserve as beneficial to their individual and collective interests, there was no significant organized opposition to the creation of the reserve, and the process tended to be non-controversial and non-confrontational. Conversely, when a substantial number of those officials and representatives viewed the creation of a reserve as detrimental to their interests, there was some significant organized opposition to the creation of a reserve and the process tended to be controversial and confrontational.

Race relations, or more precisely racism, was the second significant factor that contributed to the dynamics surrounding the creation of urban satellite reserves.[12] Unfortunately, there has not yet been an empirically based assessment of the extent to which racism was a factor in the position that various governmental and non-governmental actors took regarding the creation of the urban satellite reserves. Nevertheless, anecdotal evidence from those involved in some negotiations suggests that racism was undoubtedly a factor in the decision of some members of municipal governments and some members of various municipalities to oppose the creation of urban satellite reserves. Moreover, this evidence suggests that for such members racist considerations prevailed over both any rational arguments supporting urban reserve creation or any economic calculations regarding the effects that the creation of a given urban satellite reserve would have on the material interests of either the municipality or individuals.

The third important factor that affected the dynamics surrounding the creation of urban satellite reserves were the interpersonal relations between elected and appointed First Nation and municipal officials involved in the negotiations. In cases where interpersonal relations were positive and there was a high degree of respect and trust among such officials, the nature of the dynamics of the negotiations were generally non-controversial and non-confrontational. Conversely, in cases where there was a low degree of respect and trust among them, controversy and confrontation prevailed.

Factors Facilitating Creation of Urban Satellite Reserves

The creation of urban satellite reserves in Saskatchewan was facilitated by five major factors.

Value of Properties

The first factor was the vision of various First Nation leaders who recognized the value that such properties could have for their governments, their entrepreneurs, their other members, and the entire Aboriginal community. Such leaders were very instrumental in the creation of such reserves. Without their vision, leadership and negotiating skills, it is doubtful that any urban reserve would have been created.

Treaty Land Claims Process

The second factor was the Indian treaty land claims processes. That process provided Indian bands not only with a reason to search for lands and properties that could be acquired but also with substantial financial resources with which to acquire and develop various parcels of real-estate in urban settings.[13]

Aboriginal Rights and Emancipation

The third factor arising from the first two is the effect of the Aboriginal rights and emancipation movement of recent decades. That movement has provided the impetus for the federal government to make three interrelated federal policy decisions that helped create urban satellite reserves. The first policy decision was to resolve outstanding Aboriginal land entitlement issue, the second policy decision was to dispose of surplus Crown properties, and the third policy decision was to offer surplus federal Crown land to First Nations in settling outstanding land entitlement cases. That particular arrangement occurred by mutual consent of federal and First Nations governments.

Changes in Federal Policy

The fourth factor, arising from the changes in federal government policy, was the availability of suitable public federal Crown properties for the creation of the first set of urban satellite reserves. Three of the four reserves that are the focus of this chapter were created on federal Crown properties: a former federal government residential school became the Opawakoscikan Reserve in Prince Albert; land that had been set aside for a federal penitentiary became the Muskeg Lake Nation's McKnight Centre reserve in Saskatoon; a post-office became part of the Star Blanket band's reserve in Fort Qu'Appelle. Recently, the Peter Ballantyne Cree Nation added to the Opawakoscikan Reserve in Prince Albert by acquiring some federal government land originally slated for residential housing development by Canadian Mortgage and Housing Corporation. By contrast, the reserve in Yorkton was created on a property that originally had been acquired from private interests by the Yorkton Tribal Council for its educational centre. The conversion of that property to an urban reserve proved beneficial for the Sakimay First Nation, the Yorkton Tribal Council, and those who work for both of them on that reserve.

There is an advantage in using federal Crown land to facilitate the creation of urban satellite reserves because under the current constitutional and statutory framework, the creation of such reserves does not entail a radical change in the fundamental nature of the relationship of the land vis-à-vis the municipality. Indeed, pursuant to the Indian Act the land is still technically federal Crown land that has been designated for a specific use—in this case, an urban satellite reserve—by a particular First Nation. The only major change from the conversion of the land to reserve status is that it allows the federal government to distance itself from its relationship with the municipality and other local authorities on most matters pertaining to a given parcel of land. After the conversion, the First Nation government, rather than the federal government, is the principal agent in dealing with the municipality. It is not surprising, therefore, that the types of arrangements related to land-use planning, sub-division infrastructure, property services, and taxation of properties or businesses on urban satellite reserves that have been negotiated between First Nations and municipalities are not significantly different than the arrangements that have existed between the federal government and various municipalities.

Urbanization of Aboriginal Population

The fifth important factor was the urbanization of First Nation members. The steady migration of Aboriginal people to urban areas, either on a permanent or temporary basis, in the past twenty years has created urban-based Aboriginal communities in need of various types of social and financial services. Another issue related to urbanization of First Nation members is that in the Aboriginal sector, as in the non-Aboriginal sector, there has been a centralization in urban regions of the province of both social and financial service organizations as well as political organizations. This has led many organizations to establish offices in centrally located urban centres in a given region because these centres have the requisite infrastructure to support their respective operations and meet the various needs of their employees, their clients, and those with whom they deal.

In summary, the creation of these reserves at this particular juncture in history can be attributed to the vision of strategic and progressive thinking of First Nations' leaders, the settlement of treaty land claims, the effect of Aboriginal politics on federal policies, the availability of federal Crown lands, and the need for social and financial services for Aboriginals who have migrated to urban areas in recent decades.

Purpose of Urban Satellite Reserves

The creation of Indian urban satellite reserves has been driven, above all else, by the First Nations' economic, social, cultural, and political development objectives. In terms of their economic objectives, First Nations' leaders view urban satellite reserves as instruments that can contribute to the economic development of their communities. The most significant of these objectives is achieving a higher level of economic self-sufficiency for First Nation communities and governments that will both reduce their dependence on federal government funding and provide them with additional resources to meet the basic needs and raise the standard of living of their members.

First Nations' also leaders view urban satellite reserves as instruments that can contribute to meeting the community and social service needs of their members both in urban areas and also on the parent reserves in rural areas. They recognize that satellite reserves in major urban centres are attractive as central and convenient locations for band councils, regional tribal councils, and provincial Indian umbrella organizations, such as the Federation of Saskatchewan Indian Nations, to establish some of their agencies involved in the delivery of social and educational services. The ability to offer community and social services from a central urban location has been an important consideration in the creation of most, if not all, such reserves.

It has been recognized that urban satellite reserves can contribute, in one of two ways, to various initiatives designed to aid the survival of First Nations' culture. First, they make it possible for First Nations to obtain and preserve lands whose traditional uses in the past give them an historical or cultural importance. Second, it makes it possible for them to obtain lands on which to establish educational and cultural centres devoted to the preservation and development of First Nations' culture. Regardless of their precise use, however, all urban satellite reserves have become important bases for and focal points of educational and cultural activity for First Nations. In this they help to facilitate on a daily basis the congregation of a critical mass of First Nations' people that is required to foster cultural interactions and experiences. They are a place for First Nations' members to meet, deliberate, operate, and interact as entrepreneurs, clients, educators, or students in a context that is infused with and sensitive to Aboriginal culture. None of the foregoing is to suggest that such a culturally infused and sensitive context could not be created in spaces and places that are not urban satellite reserves. Rather, urban satellite reserves provide one more such place and one in which First Nations people feel a special sense of ownership. This feeling, in turn, facilitates cultural expression more readily than is possible in places that either are not owned by First Nations or do not have the same cultural and political status or import of the urban satellite reserves.

Urban satellite reserves are also viewed as important instruments that can contribute to the political development objectives of First Nations on a practical and symbolic level. On the practical level, it is believed that they can contribute to political development in two important ways. First, most urban reserves have become the bases from which certain individual bands as well as regional tribal councils and provincial First Nations' organizations operate and conduct some of their political and governance activities. Second, some of them, and particularly those created for commercial purposes, are viewed as important sources of revenue, which First Nations hope will foster greater fiscal autonomy and, by extension, greater political autonomy from the federal government.

At the symbolic level they are important political symbols of the continuing pursuit of the First Nations' goal for the recognition and fulfillment of inherent and treaty Aboriginal rights. In other words, they are important symbols of the existence of treaty and non-treaty rights that Aboriginal people want recognized and exercised. One contentious issue in the creation of the various Indian urban satellite reserves has been the extent to which various Aboriginal rights ought to be recognized and exercised in the context of urban satellite reserves. However, urban satellite reserves are more than symbols of the existence of treaty and non-treaty rights; they are models that can be held up whenever anyone wishes to make the political argument that it is possible for two relatively autonomous governments (First Nation and municipal governments) to identify and agree on arrangements that will allow them to exercise their respective jurisdiction within the same area or locale without creating insurmountable inter-jurisdictional problems.

In theory, urban satellite reserves can be created for any purpose bands deem appropriate, subject to federal approval. To date, those that have been created in Prince Albert, Saskatoon, Fort Qu'appelle, and Yorkton have been designed either for commercial purposes such as banks and retail outlets or institutional purposes such as offices for various types of First Nation governmental organizations. Notable examples of reserves being used for institutional purposes of First Nation governmental organizations include the offices of the Federation of Saskatchewan Indian Nations (FSIN) and the Saskatchewan Indian Gaming Authority (SIGA) located in the McKnight Centre in Saskatoon, the Peter Ballantyne Cree Nation offices located on the Opawakoscikan reserve in Prince Albert, the Yorkton Tribal Council's Educational Centre located on the Sakimay reserve in Yorkton. Notable examples of reserves being used for commercial purposes are the McKnight Centre in Saskatoon and the Star Blanket reserve in Fort Qu'Appelle, both of which house branches of Peace Hills Trust, a financial institution whose core mission is to provide banking services for First Nations and their members. As can be seen, the Muskeg Lake Cree Nation's McKnight Centre provides both institutional and commercial space.

Generally urban satellite reserves in southern Saskatchewan have not been created for residential purposes although this has been contemplated, and bands have consistently insisted on their right to do so. However, to date such efforts have been met with some challenges and, in some cases, even resistance. In 1996, for example, the Muskeg Lake Cree Nation tried to purchase and convert a parcel of city-owned land in Prince Albert to reserve status for residential purposes, but those efforts were blocked largely by protests of residents living in what would have been the neighbouring residential subdivision.[14] Although housing in urban areas has become an important issue for some bands, real estate for commercial and institutional purposes remains the main incentive behind the creation of urban satellite reserves in Saskatchewan.[15]

Place of Urban Satellite Reserves

The choice of communities in which urban satellite reserves have been created is based on some strategic calculations by the band councils who create them. Prince Albert, Saskatoon, Fort Qu'Appelle, and Yorkton all exhibited three characteristics that made them attractive sites for urban satellite reserves. First, they are large and medium-sized municipalities in the province, deemed to be strategically located and relatively important regional economic and service centres for both Aboriginal and non-Aboriginal communities. Second, all have a relatively large Aboriginal population living in them or in the surrounding area. Third, all are located within the same region as the base reserves of the First Nations creating the urban satellite reserves. Indeed, generally they are located within commuting distance of those base reserves.

Within the urban communities, the urban satellite reserves are generally located near in one of two important areas: near service, commercial, or industrial subdivisions, or near residential areas. The Peter Ballantyne Cree Nation reserve in Prince Albert is located adjacent to a major hospital and the RCMP offices; the Muskeg Lake Cree Nation reserve in Saskatoon is located in commercial and industrial subdivisions adjacent to residential neighbourhoods; the Star Blanket reserve in Fort Qu'Appelle is located near a major commercial strip in the downtown area; the Sakimay reserve in Yorkton is on a major commercial strip on a main street. What these properties have in common is that they are located within a highly viable and upscale service, commercial, or industrial subdivision or area with strong current and future value. In short, they are located on what today and in the future constitute prime real estate, rather than real estate of nominal or declining value.

Governance and Management of Urban Satellite Reserves

Urban satellite reserves do not have a system of governance that is separate or distinct from that of their base reserves.[16] For governance purposes they are, in effect, satellites or extensions of the base reserves and as such fall within their jurisdictional ambit. In other words, the jurisdictional authority that band councils have over their parent reserves pursuant to the Indian Act also applies to their urban satellite reserves. The distinguishing characteristic of the governance of urban satellite reserves is that it involves a special interface or interaction with the neighbouring urban municipality, something that rarely exists in the case of the base reserves. The spatial relationship of urban satellite reserves and municipalities means that certain key elements of municipal governance such as planning and development bylaws; the delivery of water, sewer, and light services; and various financial arrangements may be subject to formal and informal intergovernmental agreements that generally are not part of the normal governance framework for their base reserves. The current intergovernmental agreements are producing models that may be adopted by and adapted to the needs of First Nations not only in creating other urban satellite reserves in the future but also in the case of base reserves and satellite reserves located near rural and northern municipalities.

The governance of the existing urban satellite reserves is not a contested issue because those created so far are designated for institutional and commercial purposes rather than residential purposes. It will be interesting to see what, if any, alternative intergovernmental arrangements will develop if urban satellite reserves designated for residential purposes are created in the future. What type of representation and governance would First Nations' members living on such reserves want? Would they be willing to exist under the current governance structure? Or would they want either special representation on the band council or a special council of their own?

Several interesting and innovative models have been developed for managing urban satellite reserves.[17] They include the band council model, the special committee of the band council model, and the special management board. Under the band council model, the urban reserve is managed by a band council operating as a committee of the whole. Under the special committee of the band council model, a special committee or sub-committee of elected officials is charged with the responsibility for managing the urban reserve but is responsible to the band council as a whole. Finally, under the special management board model, the reserve is managed by a management team consisting of band members and appointed (rather than elected) management specialists to the management board of the urban reserve. Regardless of which model is adopted, ultimate responsibility for the management of the urban reserve rests with the band council. Band councils have considerable discretion about which model they use to manage their respective reserves, subject to some constraints imposed by the Indian Act related to the management of Indian lands and business ventures. However, if such constraints are deemed to pose serious problems for the management of urban satellite reserves they will come under increasing scrutiny. This will generate an additional set of intergovernmental negotiations and politics, thereby further complicating the complex and multidimensional ones that already exist. Before a definitive assessment of the relative merits of the different governance and management models and the need for reform can be considered, additional analysis is needed.

Value of Urban Satellite Reserves

Urban satellite reserves will likely continue to have an important practical and symbolic value in the near future. Nevertheless, the creation of reserves involves some risk and potential problems. As noted earlier, they provide a practical value for Indian bands and tribal councils with important urban enclaves that are used both for institutional or administrative purposes and commercial purposes. Those used for institutional or administrative purposes provide a strategically positioned base within a given region where various Indian organizations can locate both their administrative offices and institutions used for delivering educational and social programs and services. Similarly, those used for commercial purposes provide the base from which First Nation organizations, entrepreneurs, and professionals are able to operate various commercial ventures. Regardless of whether they are used for institutional or commercial purposes, the strategic location of urban satellite reserves provide Indian bands and their members with important financial benefits.

The tax immunity status on urban satellite reserves minimizes their respective tax loads and theoretically maximizes the financial returns for any work or commercial transactions that take place on the reserve. Tax immunity, however, is not the only financial advantage that urban satellite reserves provide for First Nations. Equally important are the financial returns on their investments through rental income and escalating land values. Urban satellite reserves also provide First Nation governments that own such reserves with an important resource that they can use as leverage in negotiating special financial and commercial partnerships either with other First Nations and their respective companies, or anyone else.

In terms of symbolic value, urban satellite reserves serve several important functions beyond those discussed earlier. In some respects, these may well be as important, if not more important, than the practical functions. First and foremost, they are manifestations of Indian empowerment and emancipation within the Canadian polity that are clearly visible to members of the Aboriginal and non-Aboriginal communities alike both in urban and rural areas. More specifically, they are powerful symbols of the will and ability of Aboriginal communities to retain a place and a distinct presence within the Canadian polity.

Second, they are also symbols of the potential for harmonious coexistence of Indian and non-Indian communities within an urban area and have demonstrated the ability of the two communities to share a geographic space in a consensual and mutually beneficial fashion. All the urban satellite reserves created to date, including those created amidst considerable controversy and confrontation, have become important models of positive relationships that can be developed between Aboriginal and non-Aboriginal communities. The symbolic functions also contribute to an important educational function by providing Aboriginal and non-Aboriginal people with an invaluable education on Aboriginal rights. They are examples of the potential for positive relations not only between First Nation and municipal councils as political and corporate entities but also between their respective members as individuals, all of whom share common geographic, political, economic, and social spaces.

The foregoing assessment of the practical and symbolic value of urban satellite reserves is preliminary and tentative. The jury is still out on their precise value to date and what their value is likely to be in the long term.[18] Nevertheless, it is evident that the creation of such reserves is not without risks and potential problems. Another important consideration is the effect that urban satellite reserves are likely to have for base reserves. There is the possibility that these urban enclaves will become urban magnets drawing human and financial resources away from the base reserves to urban areas. What effect would the resulting loss of members from base reserves have both on the sense of community and the social and economic development initiatives therein? Consequently, as First Nations' leaders contemplate the creation of urban satellite reserves, they must keep two important questions in mind. Could the creation of urban satellite reserves result in a brain drain and a youth drain that will have an adverse affect on the social and economic development potential of base reserves, which are generally located in rural areas? If so, what must be done to ensure that this does not occur? If there is a population drain, will it occur in a way that will not cause undue hardships for those who remain on the rural reserves? Only when these and other related questions are answered can sound judgments be made on whether urban satellite reserves are positive or negative developments for a particular First Nation.

To date, however, there is no evidence to suggest that the creation of urban satellite reserves has accelerated the migration of Aboriginal people to urban areas. Much of that migration continues to occur as a result of forces present before the urban satellite reserves were created and that persist today. This is not to suggest that such a shift of human and financial resources is problematic; rather it is to suggest that no one should be surprised if such a shift begins to occur. Any analysis of this problem must also explore the issue of opportunity costs that result when resources that could be used for economic and social development on base reserves are directed toward the development and operation of urban satellite reserves. Equally important in such an assessment of the value of such reserves are various issues regarding the distribution of benefits, and particularly the question of who benefits from their creation.

The foregoing discussion of the value of urban satellite reserves highlights an important irony and a dramatic shift in attitude to the role of reserves. Whereas in the past reserves were seen as instruments of social segregation, economic marginalization, and oppression, today both urban and rural reserves are seen as instruments of social integration (rather than assimilation), economic development, and emancipation. This is because the new reserves in urban and rural areas are seen as places where First Nations people can expect to be seen and treated as "citizens-plus" rather than as "citizens-minus." In other words, they are seen as places in which Aboriginal peoples can exercise certain historic rights on an individual and collective basis, rather than places where they are denied those rights. As a result of this revitalized view of reserves, today they are no longer seen as instruments of oppressive apartheid. It is quite remarkable that we have reached a point in our history where the reserve system is being perpetuated rather than terminated both by First Nation governments and the federal government. In light of this development, everyone, particularly those who support the creation of such reserves, should do everything possible both now and in the future to ensure that these reserves will be integral components of a positive legacy. The urban satellite reserves must continue to include not only the economic, social, cultural, and political development of First Nations and the neighbouring municipalities but also must remain models of positive social relations between members of the Aboriginal and non-Aboriginal communities who share the urban space.

Future of Urban Satellite Reserves

What does the future hold for the existing urban satellite reserves? Will they flourish or fail? Will they be retained or will they be sold? What are the prospects for the creation of more urban satellite reserves in the future? Although any discussion of these questions must be circumstantial and speculative, it is useful nonetheless because it fosters thinking and broadens our understanding of the future implications of present day developments.[19]

The future of the existing Indian urban satellite reserves, both in terms of whether they will flourish or fail and whether they will be retained or sold, is largely a function of how successful they are in serving the economic, social, cultural, and political development interests or objectives of the First Nations that have established them. Furthermore, their success in serving such objectives depends on an interrelated set of factors. The first critical factor is how well they are managed; if they are managed effectively, they are likely to flourish; if they are not well managed they will flounder and possibly fail.

Quite apart from how well they are managed, there are some other factors that will have an effect on the future of the existing urban satellite reserves. The most significant factor for those urban satellite reserves used primarily for commercial or industrial purposes is the performance of the local and regional economies. The performance of those economies is likely to affect, among other things, the viability of the various commercial and industrial ventures and, by extension, the level of demand for use of the reserve land and the buildings located on it. If the economies perform well the demand will likely be high; if they perform poorly it will be low. Another major factor that will determine the success of urban satellite reserves is the availability and price of land in the surrounding area. If land is scarce and costly, the value of the reserves will increase and their continuance will be more assured.

For urban satellite reserves used exclusively or primarily for delivering social programs or services to the Aboriginal population, their proximity to clients and ability to adopt to changing social needs will be a factor in their future. Their social value will be closely tied to, among other things, the continuance of those programs or services, the size of the Aboriginal population in the urban and surrounding areas, and the proportion of the population that is in need of, or more importantly, uses those programs. If such social programs were terminated, or the size of the Aboriginal population and Aboriginal users of those programs were to decrease, the social value those urban satellite reserves would also decrease unless, of course, an alternative use was found for them.

Another factor that could have a significant effect on the future of existing urban satellite reserves are changes in federal policy either on a unilateral or negotiated basis regarding changes in tax immunity status of First Nations members operating commercial enterprises or working on reserves. Although the probability of such a change in the near future is remote, it is a possibility. If that status were to change, the maintenance of current urban satellite reserves and the creation of new ones would have to be evaluated more closely. After all, although it has not been the only factor or even the principal factor in the creation of the current reserves, their tax immunity status has made the creation of such reserves attractive. Furthermore, in spite of the fact that First Nations have somewhat compromised the absolute value of the tax immunity status by agreeing to pay service charges in lieu of property taxes, they have not negated it completely because First Nations' businesses located on urban satellite reserves do not have to pay corporate income tax and status Indians working there are do not have to pay personal income taxes. Tax exemptions for the sale of certain goods on reserves to status Indians that were introduced by the provincial government in its budget in 2000, can provide additional competitive advantages for such reserves.[20]

How likely is it that the existing reserves will be sold in the future? Unless they became unbearable financial drains for First Nations, it is unlikely that any of the existing urban satellite reserves will be sold in the future. There are several reasons for this. First, in most cases establishing them was, to say the least, a challenge. This is true regardless of whether the dynamics surrounding their creation was confrontational or non-confrontational. Hence, those who participated or witnessed their creation are not likely to be anxious to dispose of them. They realize the difficulties that may be encountered in replacing such valuable assets, especially as the amount of disposable federal Crown land in urban areas diminishes.

Second, as noted earlier, urban satellite reserves have an importance beyond their economic value; they have a highly important symbolic political value. Consequently, for First Nations to consider the sale of such lands, these lands would either have to achieve astronomical value or become an unbearable financial drain.

Third, because of First Nations' alienation from their traditional lands since the time of contact, they place a high value on their title to land and appreciate its importance. Fourth, under the current constitutional and statutory frameworks, the sale of the lands, like the creation of the urban satellite reserves, is not entirely in the hands of the First Nations. Pursuant to Section 91(25) of the Constitution Act, 1867 and the Indian Act, the federal government retains the same ultimate control over urban reserve lands as it does for traditional reserve lands in rural areas. Thus, while they may have considerable discretion in the use of the urban reserve lands, First Nations do not have the same level of discretion in disposing of these lands. Given the new relationship that First Nations have been developing with the federal government in recent years, however, the latter will be much more attuned and responsive to the preferences of the First Nations on such matters than it has been in the past. Consequently, First Nations will have considerable, if not exclusive, say in the sale of any reserve land in the future.

The more likely scenario for the future is a potential change in use of both the existing urban satellite reserves (and any others that might be created in the future) as First Nations attempt to maximize the benefits that they and their members derive from them. Such changes may include, for example, the establishment of different types of businesses on those reserves that are now used for commercial purposes, or the conversion of those that now serve largely institutional or administrative purposes to either commercial or residential purposes. More than the change in status, this will likely be at the heart of future debates related to urban satellite reserves.

Another possible scenario for the future is the potential expansion of both existing urban satellite reserves and any that may be created henceforth. The prospect of that occurring, of course, is a function of many of the same factors that have contributed to the creation of urban satellite reserves to date and might contribute to the creation of comparable reserves in the future. The one additional factor here will be the availability of the neighbouring properties for purchase by the First Nation(s) that own the extant urban reserve. There has been such an expansion in Prince Albert, and an expansion is also being contemplated in Fort Qu'Appelle.

Although the number of reserves created to date in Saskatchewan is relatively small, current indications are that more will be created in the future. The number, location, and type of reserves that will be created are a function of a number of interrelated factors. As is the case with the future of existing reserves, the prospect of the creation of more reserves hinges largely on how well they are perceived to serve various governmental and non-governmental interests. Again there are a number of factors to consider.

Changes in Economic Climate

First and foremost will be the calculations of various governmental stakeholders regarding the extent to which the creation of urban satellite reserves will serve their interests and objectives given an ever changing political economy. This includes the calculations of First Nation governments who must take the initiative in the reserve creation process, and the municipal, provincial, and federal governments who must, perforce, respond to those initiatives.

Societal Interests

The second critical determinant in the creation of more urban satellite reserves are societal interests, in both the Aboriginal and non-Aboriginal communities, that will impinge on the decisions of governmental stakeholders. Urban satellite reserves are not merely the product of remedial justice; to a large extent they are the products of *realpolitik* in which various non-governmental interests have a stake or at least a preference, and some might even say a prejudice, that will lead them to support or oppose the creation of such entities. Such considerations were clearly evident in the creation of the urban satellite reserves in Prince Albert, Saskatoon, Fort Qu'Appelle, and Yorkton, and there is very little reason to believe that similar types of considerations will not be evident in the creation of urban satellite reserves in the future. What remains to be seen is the extent to which such considerations will affect the number of reserves created and how they will do so. If the dynamics surrounding the creation of the urban satellite reserves are any indication, the effect of such interests is likely to be variable and case specific. About all we can say with any certainty at this point is that whereas governments will be considering what effect the creation of urban satellite reserves have on their organizational objectives, various non-governmental actors will be considering what effect they will have on their own material interests, both on a collective and individual basis.

Legacy

A third important factor in the creation of more reserves in the future, and one that is closely related to the first two, will be the legacy of the existing urban satellite reserves. The existing urban satellite reserves are, in effect, experiments. If they continue to prove that there are benefits to be derived from their existence, their long-term future will be more secure. Various governmental and non-governmental interests are monitoring these experiments closely to determine their value and the merits of developing more of them either in the same or in different urban municipalities. In monitoring their value, various governmental officials are paying particular attention to the extent to which such reserves are serving the objectives for which they were created. Although the real value of existing and new reserves is important in the calculations of governmental and non-governmental stakeholders when considering the creation of additional ones in the future, their perceived value is also important. The perception that urban satellite reserves provide tangible benefits that serve their objectives is as important as the reality that they are doing so. Such benefits can be either material or symbolic. If there are no such benefits seen accruing to existing reserves, then the likelihood of a new reserve being sought, supported, and approved diminishes significantly. The importance of the legacy of existing urban satellite reserves for the creation of more in the future, places an onerous burden both on First Nations and municipalities with such reserves to ensure that they work to create a positive image, positive relationships, and positive outcomes.

Availability of Resources

The availability of resources is a fourth factor that will influence the calculations of the value of creating more reserves in the future. Unless urban land is ceded to First Nations for free or at a nominal price as part of a land entitlement settlement, they will need financial resources to purchase land in urban areas. Furthermore, even if the land is ceded to First Nations as part of a land claims settlement process, either for free or at a very nominal price, in some cases substantial financial resources will still be needed to develop it for the designated use. In the case of undeveloped land it will require the development of the site and the infrastructure for basic services, but in the case of developed land it may only require the construction of new buildings or the renovation of existing ones. In all cases, however, resources will be required. The innovative financing arrangements that were used in the creation and development of some of the existing reserves provide useful examples for some bands on how to leverage the value of the property in obtaining outside resources for such purposes.

The First Nation governments that signed the TLEFA, as well as the various bands involved in the Specific Claims process, are particularly well positioned to continue to obtain land in urban areas and to have it converted to reserve status. The various compensation agreements concluded provides them with both the financial resources to purchase and develop land as well as the policy framework to facilitate its conversion to reserve status. Given those resources, the creation of urban satellite reserves in Saskatchewan is likely to continue at least until the TLEFA and the various Specific Claims agreements are implemented fully. Those agreements contain clauses permitting Indian bands to use money they received as part of their land settlement for the purpose of purchasing land in urban, rural, and northern municipalities. This land, subject to meeting certain conditions, can be converted to reserve status. Whether more reserves will be created after those agreements have been implemented, however, is a moot point. Given that social, cultural, and political development depends on economic development, and given the continuing trend of urbanization of Indians, there is little reason to believe that First Nations will stop purchasing lands in areas that offer them valuable economic opportunities or that they will not continue to opt for the creation of reserves.

Availability of Land

A fifth factor that will have a significant effect on the creation of urban satellite reserves in the future, as in the past, will be the availability of suitable land. Even if First Nations have the resources to obtain land, there must be land available. In an open market land will always be available at a certain price. This includes surplus federal Crown land; provincial Crown lands; other public lands owned by any public agency or local authority, such as universities, school boards, health boards, or municipalities, that they are willing to sell or cede to Indian bands for their use; privately owned land that First Nations can purchase; and land that some First Nations own but is not currently designated as a reserve.

Reserve Capacity

A sixth factor that will affect not only the creation of additional urban satellite reserves but also the precise location and viability of all such reserves is what might be termed the "reserve capacity" of various urban areas, that is, the capacity of a given urban area to sustain one or more urban satellite reserves. Those contemplating the creation of any urban satellite reserve, particularly one in an urban area that already has one or more, must consider whether the additional reserve will have an adverse affect on the other(s). This possibility raises several other related issues. Will the creation of more than one urban reserve in a given municipality have an a beneficial or adverse effect on each of them? Will the existence of more than one urban reserve in a given area lead to healthy competition and coordination that will make each of them more valuable and viable? Or will it lead to unhealthy competition and problems that will adversely affect the value and viability of any or all of them? Failure to recognize that the creation of additional urban satellite reserves in a given urban area may create problems for existing ones could have devastating consequences not only for the individual reserve initiatives but also for the relations between First Nations that undertake such initiatives.

Aboriginal Self-Government and Sovereignty

A seventh factor that will undoubtedly determine whether new urban satellite reserves are created in the future is the Aboriginal self-government and sovereignty issue. The further First Nations move along the self-government continuum toward sovereignty, the more contentious the creation of new satellite reserves in urban, rural, and northern areas is likely to become. This is because some levels of government may become increasingly concerned about the checkerboard effect that certain forms of sovereign self-governance may have on the territorial unity and integrity of the Canadian state.

Conclusion

As can be seen, the creation of more urban satellite reserves in Saskatchewan is a function of an array of factors. At the moment however, it is safe to say that there is no end in sight for the creation of these reserves. Indeed, at this point, it seems that it will not abate, and the full weight of the federal and provincial governments would have to be applied to halt the creation of more such reserves in this province.

What does the future hold in terms of the creation of urban satellite reserves in other jurisdictions in Canada? There is little reason to believe the urban satellite reserve phenomenon will be limited to Saskatchewan. Bands in other provinces will see the benefits of these reserves in Saskatchewan, and they will probably seek to establish some in their own region, either as part of land settlement agreements or some other development initiatives. The federal government would find it politically difficult, if not impossible, to deny comparable arrangements and opportunities to First Nations in other provinces. In particular, in light of the precedent it has set in Saskatchewan, it would find it difficult not to make surplus federal Crown land available to them for such purposes. To some extent other provincial governments would also find it politically difficult to deny or block comparable arrangements and opportunities to First Nations in their respective provinces. Saskatchewan's experience suggests that the strongest resistance to the creation of such reserves is likely to come from both municipal governments and various non-Aboriginal constituents who will tend to focus more on their potential problems than their potential benefits. To date the Saskatchewan experience suggests that the benefits outweigh the problems. It remains to be seen whether this will continue or whether it will change. For this reason the urban satellite reserve creation experiment in Saskatchewan merits further monitoring and analysis.

Endnotes

[1] For an overview of various reserve creation initiatives in various jurisdictions in Canada and the resulting relationships between municipal and First Nation governments involved in their creation see: Theresa Dust, *The Impact of Aboriginal Land Claims and Self-Government on Canadian Municipalities: The Local Government Perspective,* Toronto: Intergovernmental Committee on Urban and Regional Research, 1995.

[2] See Anne Kyle, "Indians Inch Toward Self-government: Agreement to Set Wheels in Motion for FSIN, Ottawa, Province to Negotiate Self-rule," *StarPhoenix* (Saskatoon), May 27, 2000; and Pamela Cowan, "FSIN, Province Reach 'milestone,'" *StarPhoenix* (Saskatoon) May 29, 2000.

[3] See *Amended Cost Sharing Agreement between Canada and Saskatchewan,* signed as part of the *Saskatchewan Treaty Land Entitlement Framework Agreement,* September 1992, 14–15.

[4] For a detailed analysis of the creation of the urban satellite reserves discussed in this article see F. Laurie Barron and Joseph Garcea, editors, *Urban Indian Reserves: Forging New Relationships in Saskatchewan.* (Saskatoon: Purich Publishing, 1999).

[5] See Canada, Saskatchewan and Entitlement Bands, *Saskatchewan Treaty Land Entitlement Framework Agreement,* September 22, 1992, 14–15; and Department of Indian and Northern Affairs Canada, "Additions to Reserved Policy/New Reserves Policy," *Land Management and Procedures Manual 1991,* Chapter 9, Part 1.

[6] These matters that must be negotiated are itemized both in Article 9.3.2.2 of the Additions to Reserves Policy, 1991, and Article 9.01(a) of the Saskatchewan Treaty Land Entitlement Framework Agreement, 1992. Copies of these particular articles can be found in Appendix 1 and Appendix 2 in Barron and Garcea, eds., *Urban Indian Reserves,* 302–305.

[7] For a detailed analysis of jurisdictional and legal issues related to the creation of urban satellite reserves see Kathleen Makela,

"Legal and Jurisdictional Issues of Urban Reserves in Saskatchewan," in Barron and Garcea, eds., *Urban Indian Reserves*, 78–95.

[8] For an analysis of the nature and dynamics of the processes surrounding the creation of these urban satellite reserves see Laurie F. Barron and Joseph Garcea, "The Genesis of Urban Reserves and the Role of Governmental Self-Interest," in Barron and Garcea, eds., *Urban Indian Reserves*, 22–52.

[9] Paul Crozier, "Council Meets on Petition," *Fort Qu'Appelle Times,"* November 2, 1993.

[10] For a discussion of this tendency by the federal and provincial governments see Barron and Garcea, eds. "The Genesis of Urban Reserves and the Role of Government Self-Interest," *Urban Indian Reserves*, 22–51.

[11] Ibid. For a detailed overview of these particular reserve creation initiatives see the following chapters in Garcea and Barron, eds., *Urban Indian Reserves* : The Peter Ballantyne Cree Nation, "The Opawakoschikan reserve in Prince Albert," 159–176; Denton Yeo, "Municipal Perspectives from Prince Albert," 177–187; Lester Lafond, "Creation, Governance and Management of the McKnight Commercial Centre in Saskatoon," 188–212; Marty Irwin, "Municipal Perspectives from Saskatoon," 213–230; Noel Starblanket, "An Aboriginal Perpective on the Creation of the Star Blanket First Nation's Reserves," 231–242; Harold Smith, "An Aboriginal Perspective on the Star Blanket Reserve in Fort Qu'Appelle," 243–252; and Sam Bunnie, "The Creation, Governance and Management of the Sakimay Reserve in Yorkton," 253–262.

[12] For a discussion of the race relations component of the reserve creation dynamics see Barron and Garcea, eds., *Urban Indian Reserves* "The Genesis of the Creation of Urban Reserves and the Role of Governmental Self Interest," 22–52.

[13] For a detailed overview of the relationship of the treaty land claims settlement process and the creation of urban satellite reserves see Peggy Martin-McGuire, "Treaty Land Entitlement in Saskatchewan: A Context for the Creation of Urban Reserves," in Barron and Garcea, eds., *Urban Indian Reserves:* 53–72.

[14] See Greg Urbanoski and Dave Burlinguette, "P.A. Chastized for its Attitude: Opposition to land sale under Fire," *Prince Albert Herald."* April 7, 1995; and Greg Urbanoski, "Crescent Acres Affair Déjà Vu All Over Again," *Prince Albert Herald*, April 8, 1995.

[15] See for example the efforts of the Muskeg Lake Cree Nation and the English River First Nation to acquire land in the Saskatoon

area for residential purposes as report in the following newspaper articles: Leslie Perreaux, "Band Eyes Residential Properties," *StarPhoenix* (Saskatoon), January 4, 1999; and Darren Bernhardt, "Saskatooon Land Becoming Hot Item for Indian Bands," *StarPhoenix* (Saskatoon), January 6, 1999.

[16] For a good overview of the governance and management of urban satellite reserves see the following chapters in Barron and Garcea, eds., *Urban Indian Reserves* : Lester Lafond, "Creation, Governance and Management of the McKnight Commercial Centre in Saskatoon," 188–212; and Sam Bunnie, "The Creation, Governance and Management of the Sakimay Reserve in Yorkton," 253–262.

[17] Ibid.

[18] For an excellent discussion of the potential promise and potential problems of urban satellite reserves see Barron and Garcea, eds., *Urban Indian Reserves*: Michael Gertler, "Indian Urban Reserves and Community Development: Some Social Issues," 263–279.

[19] This section on the future of urban satellite reserves is drawn from in Barron and Garcea, eds., *Urban Indian Reserves*: F. Laurie Barron and Joseph Garcea, "Conclusion," 291–297.

[20] For an overview of the potential implications of the Saskatchewan government's budgetary policy see the following: Betty Ann Adam, "Tax breaks threaten stores: Off-reserve stores say they can't compete thanks to new policy," *StarPhoenix* (Saskatoon), June 10, 2000. The budgetary policy has several key components:

1. The elimination of the provincial sales tax exemption for purchases made off-reserve by status Indians
2. The elimination of fuel and tobacco taxes for purchases made on-reserve by status Indians
3. PST tax-exemptions for purchases of status Indians on reserves
4. PST tax-exemptions for status Indians for purchases made in businesses within 10 kilometres of a reserve and for which status Indians make up at least 90 percent of the client base
5. PST tax-exemptions for businesses located at least 350 kilometres from communities with populations of 5,000 or more and which have status Indians making up at least 50 percent of their client base.

The State of Traditional Ecological Knowledge Research in Canada:

A Critique of Current Theory and Practice

Deborah McGregor

Deborah McGregor is an Anishnabe from Wiigwaskingaa (Whitefish River First Nation, Birch Island, Ontario). She is completing her Ph.D. in the Faculty of Forestry and teaches in the Aboriginal Studies Program, both at the University of Toronto. She also teaches at the Centre for Indigenous Environmental Resources in Winnipeg. The focus of her research, teaching, curriculum development, and consultancy is Indigenous knowledge in relation to the environment. She hopes to devote more energy to First Nations community work in the future.

Introduction

Traditional Ecological Knowledge, or TEK, is rapidly coming to be viewed as a valuable source of knowledge that may be useful in addressing many of the environmental problems now faced by our increasingly global community (Hunn 1993, 13). Until recently, TEK received little consideration as a potential contributor to environmental management and planning. Only in the last two decades has TEK begun to receive the widespread attention of academics as well as environmental managers working in government, industry, and consulting.

Interest in Indigenous peoples' knowledge and its applicability to environmental or resource management problems was sparked by the release of the Brundtland Report (WCED 1987). The Brundtland Report called for official recognition and protection of Indigenous peoples and their knowledge because of their ability to contribute to local, regional, and global sustainability (Higgins 323). Since the release of the Brundtland Report, other international conventions (such as the Convention on Biological Diversity resulting from the 1992 United Nations Conference on Environment and Development), which support this view, have been established. In addition, many Native and non-Native individuals have struggled on a practical level to promote appropriate representation of Indigenous people and their knowledge in an effort to contribute to sustainability in environmental management (Roberts 34).

TEK has grown into a significant field of study, with an emerging consensus among academics that Indigenous knowledge systems need to be taken seriously. TEK has also gained a foothold in some mainstream political and administrative frameworks in Canada, including federal environmental assessment processes and policy development for resource management in the Northwest Territories. Many individuals working in government, industry, or non-governmental organizations, who are involved in environmental and resource management issues, now feel compelled to incorporate TEK into their work (Lukey iii). Aboriginal people have also felt the pressure to "share" or "inform" outsiders about their cherished knowledge in an effort to protect their interests (for example, their land, traditional activities, and cultural and spiritual values).

Despite substantial interest in TEK and efforts to apply it to resource management over the last two decades, many fundamental questions remain outstanding. Issues include the definition of TEK, its meaning and application in environmental management, and of particular concern in this paper, the interest in and application of TEK by non-Native people and the impact of this situation on Aboriginal peoples. Much of the published literature on TEK is from the point of view of non-Aboriginal scientists and does little to reveal Indigenous points of view because the research has been inspired, conducted, and directed by non-Aboriginal people (AFN/ICC 1; McGregor, "An Evaluation" 1).

The basic question of who benefits from the burgeoning field of study has not been addressed satisfactorily. Such a question is difficult to answer, at least in a public or political arena. Both Aboriginal people and environmental managers are increasingly dissatisfied with how TEK is applied (Stevenson, "What Are We Managing" 161). Attempts to critically analyze the effectiveness or appropriateness of TEK research processes are often met with resistance. Interest in TEK for environmental or resource management often develops externally to Aboriginal communities and is thus driven by the motivation of external interests which may or may not have beneficial effects on such communities (AFN 4). This trend was noticed a decade ago by the Assembly of First Nations and the Inuit Circumpolar Conference in a document prepared for the Canadian Environmental Research Council. In it the authors state:

> What is now referred to as Traditional Ecological Knowledge (TEK) is a growing field of study in which Native People have been increasingly dominated by non-Native experts, analysts, and consultants. As a result, knowledge which could- and should-be used for the benefit of Native people and their communities (in accordance with their priorities and values), has tended to be defined and appropriated by non-Native researchers. (AFN and ICC 1)

More recently, Karen Roberts wrote:

> While there is a great deal of interest in and demand for traditional knowledge information, Aboriginal people are concerned about documenting and using the knowledge. All parties involved with a proposed project, except for the affected communities, seem to benefit from the use of traditional knowledge. For some Aboriginal people, documenting traditional knowledge means that they are being forced to play by the rules of the dominant culture. (116)

In theory, the notion of applying TEK to environmental and resource management is an excellent one. Current practice, however, is sorely lacking in appropriate methodology and causes "the role of Aboriginal and First Nations' peoples and their knowledge in environmental management to be diminished" (Stevenson, "What Are We Managing" 161). In many cases "traditional knowledge is often sidelined and neglected despite all the lip service that is paid to it" (Roberts 92).

There is a political correctness or trendiness about TEK research that apparently leads many of those promoting it to be less than introspective about the appropriateness of their actions. Such an unwillingness to accept Aboriginal insights into these matters only serves to ensure that TEK will remain a misunderstood concept. People want to use and study TEK, without asking whether or not such actions are appropriate.

In the following pages, some of these basic questions regarding TEK are explored. As well, important issues in relation to the origin and concept of TEK in environmental management in Canada are raised.

TEK as a Western Construct

The notion of TEK is a construct of modern western society, created in an attempt to define and capture another culture's knowledge. The chasm between the representation and represented is common in cross-cultural interactions, particularly where power imbalances characterize the relationship between two societies. The more powerful society can, and does, project its own version of the world onto the less powerful. Thus, one of the fundamental underlying problems with TEK is that although it claims to represent Aboriginal knowledge, it is itself not an Aboriginal concept.

Indigenous people from all over the world have knowledge that enabled sustainable living for thousands of years. However, such knowledge was never intended to be expressed as a discrete body of information. TEK is a prime example of the use and misuse of western science: though TEK purports to be "Aboriginal" knowledge, it is really an expression of western science rather than one based on the views and experiences of Aboriginal people. Although TEK researchers claim to be respectful of Aboriginal people, it is often experienced by Aboriginal people to be another form of research on them. Aboriginal people, their culture and knowledge, have become objects of study, and various methods of carrying out such study have been developed by Western scientists to achieve this goal (see Grenier). There are now many instances when even Aboriginal people, who themselves choose to conduct TEK research for environmental management, employ the methods developed and used by non-Aboriginal scientists (Brascoupe 11; Colorado 60; McGregor, "Aboriginal Knowledge" 26; Stevenson, "What Are We Managing" 163). This framework, from which TEK operates in Canada, perpetuates the same pattern of "discovery" and investigation that has characterized colonial history in North America. TEK is therefore symptomatic of the relationship that Aboriginal people have with their colonizers (McGregor, "Aboriginal Knowledge" 30; Wavey 16).

The current state of TEK assumes that the western scientific paradigm is the best model in which to seek, gather (document), and explain phenomena. The western scientific method is accepted as rational and objective, unlike other investigations or experiences of the world. However, Pamela Colorado argues that western science degrades Indigenous knowledge and methods, regarding them as primitive, archaic, and irrelevant (61). Over time, discrimination has become subtler, but it is still destructive.

History of TEK

Recognition that Aboriginal people "know," "understand," or "experience" the natural environment in a complex and systematic way began to appear with the observation by natural scientists that Indigenous peoples have names and classifications for different plants and animals in their environment (Berkes 1; Johnson 5). Of particular surprise to the scientists studying Indigenous people was the "discovery" that the categories and classifications developed by Aboriginal people closely approximated those of western scientists.

Systematic study of Indigenous knowledge of the natural environment by anthropologists began with the analysis of the terms that Indigenous people use to classify objects in their social and natural environments. The studies revealed that Indigenous people recognize natural classes of animals and plants, and that Indigenous people were apparently just as concerned with classifying plants and animals as western-trained natural and social scientists. Although narrow in focus and highly Eurocentric, the early studies of Indigenous knowledge did enhance the realization that Indigenous people "know" something about the environment (DCI, "Traditional Ecological Knowledge" 3; DCI, "Guidelines" 4).

Following this initial recognition, two major events led to a rapid rise in the study of Aboriginal people and their knowledge. The first was the public recognition of a global ecological crisis. This came with a growing understanding that science and technology were probably not going to be able to fix the problem, which led to today's environmental movement that grew out of the 1960s and 1970s. Further to this was the increasing belief that science and technology were also the *cause* of many of the environmental or ecological problems facing the global community (Clarkson, Morrissette, and Regallet 35; Deloria 19; Knudtson and Suzuki xxiii; Mander 382; Berry 58). Not surprisingly, alternatives to science, and any information that could be of value in dealing with this crisis, began to be explored by many environmental and non-governmental organizations as well as by governments and academics.

The second major event was the rise of Indigenous rights. Though Indigenous people had of course been struggling to assert their rights since contact, it was not until the 1960s and 1970s that "the writing on the wall" began to appear as far as colonial policies were concerned. Through increased Aboriginal organization and ability to function in western political arenas, the message became ever clearer: despite ongoing government attempts at assimilation, Indigenous people were never going to go away—far from it. Indigenous people all over the world continued to assert, ever more strongly, that they have rights and they wish to exercise these rights. Indigenous people demanded a voice in their future. They made it clear they want a say in what happens in their lives and what happens on their traditional territories. They also made it clear that over time their efforts to achieve their goals would only increase.

These two main events caused a shift from scholarly interest solely in Aboriginal environmental knowledge to that of applied research. Thus arose the interest in Traditional Ecological Knowledge and its application in environmental management. The interest of scholars turned to questions such as: "What ecological knowledge and practices did Indigenous people have that contributed to their sustainability?" and "How can these practices be applied to deal with larger environmental issues that affect the global community?"

In summary, it can be seen that the concept of TEK did not emerge out of Indigenous communities, but out of an academic community that studied Aboriginal people. Indigenous understanding of the environment or ecosystems became simply an interest of western-trained scholars. Such knowledge was not regarded as particularly useful until western society decided it was needed, but upon reaching this decision, western society gave it the label Traditional Ecological Knowledge. Thus TEK emerged out of a circumstance external to Indigenous communities.

Definitions of TEK: A Lack of Shared Meaning

Given TEK's history, it is understandable that Traditional Ecological Knowledge remains a difficult concept to define for both Native and non-Native people. To date no common meaning for the term has developed. This is true in spite of its apparent integration into environmental management regimes and specific projects in Canada. In the following section some of the key issues around defining the term are explored.

A Non-Native Term

As has been discussed, TEK is not a concept derived from First Nations. It is a term coined by academics to describe an aspect of Indigenous peoples' knowledge relating to the natural environment. First Nations have never been able to satisfactorily define their knowledge for outsiders, and why should they? Some Aboriginal people are now asking why they should continue to explain themselves and why they should attempt to define a western construct for western people. These are valid questions and not ones generally asked by proponents of TEK research.

A Native Perspective

Despite not having developed the concept of TEK itself, Indigenous people remain inescapably involved in participating in some form of TEK research. Western society, in its own right, has made it apparent that it is not going to give up on obtaining TEK (however defined) from Aboriginal people. Moreover, *if* TEK can be developed into an appropriate concept with accompanying respectful procedures, it could provide substantial opportunities for Aboriginal involvement in environmental management. It could assist First Nations in becoming equitably involved in shaping the decisions that affect them as well as those that affect the global environment. Indigenous people, though in many ways resentful of the "hype" surrounding TEK (Lukey 35), nevertheless feel bound to try and develop the concept into a meaningful and respectful process.

From an Aboriginal perspective, current working definitions of TEK, such as those employed by consultants, governments, industry, and other agencies, are unsatisfactory and inappropriate (AFN 1). Controversy regarding the use of TEK (and Aboriginal participation in resource or environmental management) has emerged as a direct result of this lack of shared meaning. Many Aboriginal people will use the term TEK for the sake of discussion or convenience (AFN 1). However, some First Nations organizations refuse to use the phrase and have instead put forward their own labels for this knowledge in an effort to move away from the label defined by western scholars. Terms such as *Indigenous knowledge* (see later section in this paper), *Indigenous science*, and *naturalized knowledge systems* have been suggested to describe the knowledge that First Nations people have of the environment.

So how *do* Aboriginal peoples view their knowledge? Though broad generalizations should be avoided, common themes emerge. For example, Aboriginal people tend not to separate out "environment" from the rest of everyday living (Clarkson, Morrissette, and Regallet 12). Traditionally, environmental considerations were an integral part of all community institutions and decision making. Environmental or ecological considerations were such a matter of course in daily living and thinking that Indigenous people did not think of these terms as discrete aspects (Gisday Wa and Delgam Uukw 30). Words such as *environmental* or *ecological* (constructs of western society) do not generally exist in Indigenous languages and are barely, if at all, translatable. Some Native people therefore feel it entirely inappropriate to attempt to separate out specifically environmental knowledge along the conceptual lines defined by non-Native people (see, for example, definitions of TEK presented by F. Berkes, 5; R. Berkes 3; Richardson 30; and Tsuji 284). Knowledge thus described is limited in definition and will be limited in its application.

Definitions of TEK: Attempts to Appropriately Define

Non-Native definitions of TEK vary from person to person, but tend to focus on knowledge or information of First Nations people about the local environment gained through many years of observation and experience. This Native experience with a particular ecosystem is passed on from generation to generation via the oral tradition.

Some researchers recognize the importance of the spiritual aspect of TEK as well the cultural and social context in which it finds meaning (Chapeskie 41; Grenier 46; Johnson 13; Stevenson, "What Are We Managing" 282). Most non-Native researchers seem to base their definition of TEK on ideas presented in Martha Johnson's *Lore: Capturing Traditional Ecological Knowledge* and many definitions found in the literature generally are variations of this. Although flawed, the definition offered in Johnson contains valid insights: "TEK is both cumulative and dynamic, building upon the experience of earlier generations and adapting to new technological and socio-economic changes of the present" (4). The idea that TEK is *dynamic knowledge* means that it changes over time; it is not static and is conducive to incorporating other forms of knowledge or information into its framework. TEK is thus able to find expression in new technology, such as geographic information systems (GIS) or other tools of western science, *without losing its essence*. TEK is a flexible system that can adapt to new challenges facing First Nations people; it is not stuck in the past.

A second important point made by Johnson is that TEK is not a homogeneous body of knowledge. Unlike western science, where all who learn it are taught the same basic information up to a point, TEK "varies among community members." Even among a single community, different individuals will hold different knowledge. Grenier also notes differences among community members, stating that variation can be due to a whole range of factors:

> age, education, gender, social and economic status, daily experiences, outside influences, roles and responsibilities in the home and community, profession, available time, aptitude and intellectual capacity, level of curiosity and observation skills, ability to travel and degree of autonomy and control over natural resources. (2)

Where Johnson's definition fails to accurately describe TEK is in its reference to TEK as a "body of knowledge" rather than a way of life. TEK in this sense is unfortunately reduced or removed from its whole (world view and context) and also from the people themselves. By doing this, it becomes possible to "extract," "tap into," "harvest," or "capture" TEK from First Nations people. (Hence, the title of such works as Johnson's *Lore: Capturing Traditional Environmental Knowledge* and Richardson's *Harvesting TEK*.)

First Nations people in Canada are not satisfied with these status quo definitions of Indigenous knowledge. A report from the Assembly of First Nations suggests

> Indigenous experts working in this area have made it clear that they do not find any current external expressions or definitions of Indigenous knowledge to be appropriate. These are seen as either self-serving, or to exclude certain essential elements—particularly those spiritual aspects which western scientists sometimes find difficult to digest. (AFN 1)

In response to this situation, some Native authors have put forth their own views of TEK. Linda Clarkson, Vern Morrissette, and Gabriel Regallet's *Our Responsibility to the Seventh Generation: Indigenous Peoples and Sustainable Development*, Duane Good Striker's "TEK Wars: First Nations' Struggles for Environmental Planning," and Winona LaDuke's "Traditional Ecological Knowledge and Environmental Futures" are examples. Although variations also occur among Native definitions of TEK, there are remarkable similarities. LaDuke's explanation fairly well summarizes the definitions of a number of Aboriginal thinkers. She states that TEK is "the culturally and spiritually based *way in which indigenous people relate* to their ecosystems" (emphasis added 128). TEK is thus more than an accumulation of other knowledge; it is a way of relating to Creation and all of its beings and forces. It is more than knowledge of a relationship; it is the relationship itself. TEK, from an Indigenous perspective, is an active, living thing; a way of being, a "verb," so to speak. TEK is best expressed in how you live and how you relate to Creation. TEK is doing! You cannot take the knowledge and ignore the people. In the absence of the people expressing, living, and doing, the knowledge loses much of its meaning. The potential for abuse of the knowledge becomes tempting and frequently occurs when extracted from the people. Indigenous definitions of TEK thus contrast sharply with the western concept of TEK as a noun, commodity, or product.

The inseparability of knowledge from the people is a key concept from an Aboriginal perspective. It must be considered, as Mark

Stevenson argues in *Traditional Knowledge and Environmental Management: From Commodity to Process*, that definitions that consider TEK only as a product "fail to consider that [TEK] exists within a larger framework of understanding and cultural context from which it cannot and should not be separated" (3). Stevenson further points out that TEK cannot be "divorced from the people who own and want to effectively control and apply this knowledge" (4).

Gathering and Documenting TEK

In Canada, the way in which TEK research is conducted and applied removes the holder from the knowledge and from its broader social and cultural context (Stevenson, "Traditional Knowledge" 4). Louise Grenier recognizes that Indigenous knowledge is an integrated body of knowledge, yet tends to be studied in discrete aspects (2). The strategy for TEK research that Grenier outlines in *Working with Indigenous Knowledge: A Guide for Researchers* continues to treat Indigenous peoples as objects of study. She points out that standard research methods are re-invented in order to ensure "cultural sensitivity and appropriateness"; however, this is not by any means a replacement for relating to Indigenous people as equals in environmental decision making. The research process makes some minor attempts to consider Indigenous people and their knowledge together (making people subjects!), yet the whole research process is geared toward separating the two and coming up with a final product: knowledge. The people are not included in the outcome. This is the current research paradigm! It is hardly based on equality, respect, or reciprocity.

What are the end results of this type of research? One result is that any textbook, report, or map produced as part of TEK research comes to replace the person or people (TEK holders) from whom the information was obtained. The holder of the book, text, or map then becomes the expert and the product may or may not be used to influence decision making. The Indigenous person (the true expert) becomes dispensable and has been effectively removed from any real decision making once the product has been acquired. This is wholly inadequate, offensive to many, and grossly misrepresents Indigenous people and their knowledge. In this system, Aboriginal people tend to be involved in TEK research only insofar as the "product" has been acquired. This process of TEK extraction, often called "integrating" TEK with western science, reinforces the exclusion of Aboriginal people from the decision-making process. Indigenous people, if they are lucky, can have input, but only into the making of a preliminary product. Instead of a person participating in the final decision making process, a text (or report or map) now does. The western scientific tradition views "knowledge as primarily valid only in literate forms" (Stevenson, "Indigenous Knowledge" 4). This means that others, who do not understand the context nor have ever experienced TEK or actually "know" it, now "own" it and can use it as they wish. To "scientize" or "textualize" TEK has meant that only those facts or data that make sense to scientists will be translated and used. "Text, rather than holders of knowledge, becomes the authoritative source" (Stevenson, "Indigenous Knowledge" 5).

This whole process, as Stevenson outlines, aims to take, "specific elements of TEK that are of interest to the conservation bureaucracy out of context and then insert them into the dominant framework of western scientific knowledge" ("Traditional Knowledge" 4). Thus, claims of integrating Indigenous knowledge into environmental management have been made, but this has not really been achieved; only fragments of TEK are ever used (Brubaker and McGregor 16; Stevenson, "Traditional Knowledge" 4).

Though Indigenous people must be involved beyond this level, the documenting of TEK remains a critical task, the importance of which has been well established. Most environmental practitioners agree that is important to gather and document TEK before the knowledge disappears, as the number of knowledge possessors (Elders and resource users) is dwindling. The urgency is also great because many people wish to use the knowledge in environmental management areas such as environmental assessment, forest management, and endangered species protection. However, documenting TEK is far from simple, for a variety of reasons, and this urgency to document often takes precedence over the appropriate process for doing so (McGregor, "Sources, Transmissions" 1; Stevenson, "What Are We Managing" 164).

Initially, what will be gathered and documented over the course of a given project will depend on how TEK is defined by those involved. This is problematic because, as outlined earlier, there is little consensus on what TEK means. The disparity in definitions is heightened by the difference in world views of the knowledge holders (e.g., Native Elders) versus the knowledge seekers (e.g., government or industry representatives). From a First Nations' perspective, a definition of TEK must be broad in order to do justice to its original scope and intent. From a western researcher's point of view, the more limited the definition, the easier it will be to gather, document, and apply TEK.

Despite such fundamental disagreements, gathering and documenting of TEK has been ongoing for some time. Participatory models of research are often utilized in the exercise. Though there have been attempts at improvements in methods, research and documentation procedures continue to be firmly rooted in the western scientific tradition. The information gained in this research process is then "integrated" or "incorporated" into the resource management plan or environmental assessment. To date there has been little formal assessment or evaluation of this method of documenting and integrating TEK. Mainstream processes are still viewed as the only legitimate frameworks from which to manage the environment, and the question of how TEK fits into such processes remains controversial.

It is important that researchers realize that the facts and data that TEK can provide exist within a much larger realm of knowledge. As is discussed later in this paper, some authors are now moving away from using the narrow term such as TEK to a broader and more holistic views that as that conveyed by the term "Indigenous Knowledge" (McGregor, "Indigenous Knowledge" 194; O'Meara and West 1–11; Stevenson, "Indigenous Knowledge" 281). In this context, TEK is seen as only one component of a vast collection of knowledge about living in harmony with the world. Currently, TEK is viewed only in small fragments by non-Native researchers because of the nature of western science, which likes to deal with (and arguably can *only* deal with) easily manageable facts and data. Broader ideas such as social, cultural, and spiritual aspects of life are not easily accommodated in western science, even in its own context, let alone in a cross-cultural setting. Therefore, that which is sought, gathered, and documented about TEK still tends to be data and facts. The AFN writes that "practices and facts have attracted the most external attention and… have become the main content of definitions by non-Indigenous scientists…. It is this apparent fixation upon facts and practices that has disenchanted Indigenous experts" (2).

The issue of integrating TEK into resource management planning is further complicated when one realizes the time and effort that go into acquiring such knowledge. It is unlikely that significant TEK will be gathered over the short life of a project, since it takes a lifetime to learn. A few interviews and a mapping exercise will not adequately represent what TEK actually means to the First Nations people affected by the project.

Much of the early work on TEK was conducted by natural scientists, anthropologists, and ethnobotanists (R. Berkes 1; F. Berkes 4;

Brascoupe 11; Johnson 5). The work was thus guided by the approaches, biases, and methods of these disciplines. Recently, a more interdisciplinary approach has begun to be utilized, involving a mixture of social and natural sciences. Research, undertaken for various reasons, includes land use planning, land claims, land use or occupancy maps, resource management, environmental assessment, or education, and the research approaches and methods continue to be variations of the standard social and natural science methods (see Grenier 54 for a list). This is largely an externally driven process, although more Aboriginal people are getting involved. Therefore the types of questions posed, and the goals and objectives identified are far more concerned with fitting into existing scientific (resource management), legal (land claims, environmental assessment), and political (resource development) frameworks than inquiring into how Aboriginal people wish to be involved in environmental decision making. This means that much of what is revealed in TEK research is that which is deemed important, relevant, or manageable by the dominant society. Some knowledge that is shared may be ignored, trivialized, or simply not accepted (McDonald 18; Stevenson, "What Are We Managing" 167).

Furthermore, TEK is, more often than not, sought, gathered, documented, studied, and utilized by outside interests under coercive circumstances. For example, in the case of an environmental assessment that will impact traditional territory, the Aboriginal community is usually threatened with some kind of external agenda such as the desire to undertake major resource development (e.g., construction of a hydroelectric dam). The community has no choice but to participate in the environmental assessment if they are to have any say at all. They are hardly in a position to do much else. More enlightened planners may wish to incorporate TEK into the planning process, yet planners have few if any skills in dealing with community knowledge. After all, they are worlds away from where it originates. In any case, the Aboriginal community has to come up with the knowledge, on cue. This is a highly coercive way to obtain information (data and facts) and solicit "active participation."

Application of TEK

TEK, or rather fragmented data based on TEK, has been applied in Canada under various mainstream institutional frameworks. Examples include environmental assessment, wildlife management, forest and land management, co-management agreements, and environmental policy. Most of the existing literature focuses on the environmental assessment context, especially now that the Canadian Environmental Assessment Act (CEAA) includes TEK as part of its regular planning process. Co-management (primarily for wildlife) is another area where literature on the integration of TEK exists.

A review of such literature reveals that there is little in the way of developing innovation or creativity as far as incorporation of TEK into mainstream processes is concerned. Many Native and non-Native researchers working in the field have observed the power imbalance that underlies the relationship between Native and non-Native society and how this affects the incorporation of TEK into resource management (Wolfe et al.; McGregor, "An Evaluation"; Chapeskie; AFN; Stevenson, "Indigenous Knowledge"). Application of TEK continues to amount to an attempt to "integrate" this knowledge into mainstream management regimes. First Nations tend to be "participants" in a larger, mainstream process (such as environmental assessment or co-management). Chapeskie writes of the situation in Northwestern Ontario, where "the state largely controls the conceptual framework in which co-management negotiations take place" (27). Stevenson reports some First Nations as describing co-management "as a process whereby, "'we cooperate, they manage'" ("Inuit and Co-management" 15). Peggy Smith also found that co- management agreements fall short of Aboriginal aspirations (Bombay 16).

The idea of "integration" of TEK into mainstream frameworks is coming under increasing fire from First Nations. For example, in the Assembly of First Nations' *The Feasibility of Representing Traditional Indigenous Knowledge in Cartographic, Pictorial or Textual Forms*, it is pointed out that "integration" is erroneously interpreted or carried out in practice as "assimilation," a policy that Aboriginal people have rejected for centuries. Integration "reflects a reductionist attitude, by representing Indigenous knowledge as a catalogue of facts, some of which may be deemed useful for inclusion in western knowledge systems" (6). This is not to say that First Nations in Canada have not gained a foothold in environmental management decision making by using TEK data or information to advance their interests. Many First Nations have participated in processes that have used TEK in some fashion. However, even for these First Nations, the current process will not remain satisfactory for long. In fact, it is First Nations' dissatisfaction with the status quo of TEK research, and their challenges to this process, that are further shifting the thinking about appropriate ways to relate to Indigenous people in Canada. The colonial, subordinate role just won't do! The overriding fact that Aboriginal people and their knowledge can contribute significantly to developing sustainable systems of environmental management remains without question in the minds of many (Bombay 17; Clarkson et al. 63; Nantel 5; Notzke 5; Smith, Scott, and Merkel v-1).

Beyond TEK: A New Terminology

As has been discussed, there remain significant difficulties with current definitions of TEK, no matter how well intentioned may be those attempting to apply it. There is a trend in Canada to try and address this issue by developing terminology that better reflects what Aboriginal people mean when they speak of their relationship to all of Creation. In Canada, it is becoming more common to refer to Aboriginal ideas regarding the environment and sustainability as "Indigenous Knowledge," instead of TEK (McGregor, "Indigenous Knowledge in Canada" 194). This term is, of course, just that: another term. However, it denotes a sensibility that recognizes the limitations of TEK and refuses to be bound by TEK's western-generated confines.

Indigenous knowledge is regarded by its promoters as a more acceptable term because it represents a much broader concept that is inclusive of all the components of knowing and living, which western-defined TEK excludes. Two primary examples of such inclusions are the fact that people and their knowledge are seen as inseparable (whereas TEK separates the knowledge from the people and their lives), and the idea that knowledge can be gained from interacting with dominant society, a fact of life for all Aboriginal people. Not separating the knowledge from the people helps ensure that the knowledge will retain its meaning; it is not removed from its intended context. Along with this is the fact that Indigenous knowledge does not involve the separation of "environmental" or "ecological" knowledge from other components. The people, their knowledge, and their land or environment are all indivisibly connected. To remove one from the other is to lose the meaning of each.

The acceptance into Indigenous knowledge of knowledge gained from interacting with dominant society is a critical divergence from the concept of TEK. This acceptance means that Indigenous knowledge is thus a "living," continuously evolving entity, in sharp contrast to the packaged, largely historical ("traditional") nature of TEK. Indigenous knowledge recognizes that Aboriginal culture still exists, though not exactly as it did before contact with Europeans. The fact that Aboriginal people have adapted significantly in order to continue existing alongside European society, and have even incorporated information and knowledge from this society into their own ways of knowing, does not make them any less Aboriginal. Aboriginal culture continues to exist; as with all cultures, it has simply changed over time.

This being the case, Indigenous knowledge includes various experiences of colonization as well as an understanding of the dominant society (Fitznor 28). Indigenous knowledge also includes aspects of western society (e.g., certain components of science) that may contribute to Aboriginal views of sustainability. Aboriginal people have always evaluated new knowledge, tools, and technology and determined its suitability for meeting Aboriginal goals (Couture 3, Brant-Castellano 47).

Any concept that has assisted Aboriginal people in surviving despite concerted efforts to the contrary deserves some attention. Indigenous knowledge teachings thus include Aboriginal peoples' understanding of how to survive the dominant society's efforts at assimilation and integration. Fitznor writes:

> Working with teachings automatically includes discussions about our personal and collective historic experiences with colonialism, racism, oppression, displacement, cultures, loss of Aboriginal languages, and experiences with residential schools among other things.... Understanding the dominant society becomes part of the traditional teachings: for example, when we note what happens when the Earth is not respected, or what happens when people are not respected. (28)

Non-Native society now forms a part of Aboriginal reality in Canada. Indigenous knowledge reflects this fact, particularly in terms of knowledge about the dominant society that will help to sustain First Nations' cultures. Indigenous knowledge is not limited to the time prior to contact: it includes interactions with other nations (international relations). Indigenous knowledge includes that which has happened to Native people and all we have participated in; it is our history, our present, and our future.

Indigenous knowledge involves not only understanding the dominant society but subsequently challenging it. As such, resistance forms an integral part of Indigenous knowledge. Indeed, many Native "environmental" success stories revolve around resistance to the dominant society (for example, Cree opposition to James Bay Hydroelectric Development, Haida opposition to logging on Haida Gwaii). Closely related to resistance is the reclamation of traditions, languages, lands, and other aspects of Native culture. Stevenson echoes writings of Colorado, which state that Indigenous knowledge systems need to be strengthened because of the impacts of colonization and the undermining of the knowledge over the last few centuries. Such strengthening will likely have a more positive effect on the long-term health of Indigenous knowledge than will simply gathering and documenting TEK.

Thus, if we are to begin to understand Indigenous knowledge, we must realize that such knowledge has to be experienced; one *does* Indigenous knowledge. It is alive and it changes. A hunter pointed out to me recently that Indigenous knowledge changes from day to day. The map, text, or report gained from any given TEK research exercise would be obsolete in a week. Maps, texts, or reports depict only a snapshot of time and a fraction of what there is to know. The bottom line is that if Indigenous people, and not simply fragments of their knowledge, are to be adequately represented, then the holders and practitioners of the knowledge must be involved in the decision making, not just in the information gathering.

Summary

The Aboriginal experience historically has been, and continues to be, described by western scientists and academics. This is as true in the environmental realm as it is in other aspects of society. How TEK is conceptualized, defined, gathered, documented, and applied is all derived from the framework of the dominant society. There is very little that is Aboriginal about it, except that Aboriginal people are the objects being studied.

It is a move forward that Indigenous people are viewed as having something to contribute to addressing global, regional, and local environmental problems. However, restricting this "something" to a convenient package, labelling it TEK, and forcing it to fit into western paradigms is hardly an appropriate process. It is one form of knowledge attempting to approach and frame another, with frequently disastrous effects. TEK is, therefore, perhaps not the best expression of western society's new-found respect for Indigenous knowledge; in fact, some Native people have argued it is really the same process of "discovery" and colonization that has plagued First Nations for five centuries (AFN 1; Wavey 16). Western society's lack of knowledge of Indigenous people is a significant barrier to understanding Aboriginal knowledge systems. How can you understand the knowledge when you don't know the people? From an Aboriginal point of view, the knowledge and people are inseparable (Brascoupe 8).

TEK, as it is generally presented, consists of the knowledge non-Aboriginal researchers *think* Aboriginal people possess, rather than the knowledge itself. This is especially problematic because researchers, having obtained some TEK, think they understand when they do not; they believe that their own research methods and applications are appropriate when they are not. The dominant Canadian society has difficulty dealing with Aboriginal people in equitable, respectful terms in any situation: how can it expect to understand Indigenous knowledge?

At least in the short term, TEK is likely to cause more confusion than that which already exists regarding Aboriginal relationships to the environment. This means TEK can (and has already begun to be) easily reduced to a stereotype: yet another external description of Native people. In an attempt to avoid misrepresenting Aboriginal people and their knowledge, many Native people object to using the term TEK to describe Aboriginal world views regarding the environment (Lickers in Lukey 37). An alternative term, "Indigenous Knowledge," is suggested as a broader, more inclusive, and more appropriate descriptor of Aboriginal knowledge systems. However, political realities will ensure that many Aboriginal communities adopt the term TEK in an attempt to further acceptance of their ideas. Just as with any other non-Aboriginal term applied to Aboriginal people (for example, Aboriginal rights), Native people have learned, and continue to learn, to work with the system to achieve their goals.

Where Do We Go From Here?

What is required in appropriate sharing and application of Indigenous knowledge is a functional relationship between Native and non-Native people based on mutual respect. Excluding Native people from the decision-making table in favour of "knowledge" as defined by western science is not an appropriate way to develop healthy relationships; in fact, it is an exploitative way to deal with Aboriginal people. Native people should be more than mere "participants," applauded for "cooperating" in a process that will not serve their interests in the long run (Stevenson, "Inuit and Co-management" 15).

The colonial attitudes and legal/political frameworks that support and reinforce current unbalanced relationships must be challenged. A major shift towards positive relationships with Aboriginal people in Canada is essential. Models for such relationships have been put forth by Aboriginal People since contact. One example is the "co-existence" model, which has been among First Nations people since time immemorial. Rather than continuing unsuccessful attempts to "integrate" the two knowledge systems (which amounts to assimilation of the less dominant system into the more dominant one), co-existence promotes the functioning of both systems side by side. In short, the two systems "agree to disagree," then work together to ensure that both systems can function equitably. The model of co-existence encourages equality, mutual respect, support, and cooperation. This model would require dissolving the power imbalance that still exists between Native and non-Native people—the relationship that keeps colonialism alive and well in Canada.

Co-existence is only one model; others must be explored. It is time to be creative.

Works Cited

Assembly of First Nations (AFN). *The Feasibility of Representing Traditional Indigenous Knowledge in Cartographic, Pictorial or Textual Forms.* Ottawa, ON: Assembly of First Nations, National Aboriginal Forestry Association and National Atlas Information Service, 1995.

Assembly of First Nations (AFN) and Inuit Circumpolar Conference (ICC). "Traditional Ecological Knowledge and Environmental Impact Assessment Process: A Preliminary Research Prospectus." Unpublished paper prepared for the Canadian Environmental Assessment Research Council, Ottawa, 1991.

Berry, T. *The Dream of the Earth.* San Francisco: Sierra Club Books, 1988.

Berkes, F. *Sacred Ecology: Traditional Ecological Knowledge and Resource Management.* Taylor and Francis: Philadelphia, 1999.

Berkes, R. "Traditional Ecological Knowledge in Perspective." *Traditional Ecological Knowledge: Concepts and Cases.* Ed. I Inglis., Ottawa: International Program on Traditional Ecological Knowledge and International Development Research Centre, 1993. 1–7.

Bombay, H. *Aboriginal Forest-Based Ecological Knowledge in Canada.* Ottawa: National Aboriginal Forestry Association, 1996.

Brant-Castellano, M. "Updating Aboriginal Traditions of Knowledge" *Indigenous Knowledge in Global Context: Multiple Readings of Our World.* Eds. G. Dei, B. Hall, and D. Golden-Rosenberg. Toronto: University of Toronto Press (in press).

Brascoupe, S. "Indigenous Perspectives on International Development." *Akwe:kon Journal* 9.2 (1992): 6–17.

Brubaker, D., and D. McGregor. "Aboriginal Forest-Related Traditional Ecological Knowledge in Canada." Unpublished paper from the 19th session of the North American Forest Commission, Villahermosa, Mexico, November 16–20. 1998.

Chapeskie, A. *Land, Landscape, Culturescape: Aboriginal Relationships to Land and the Co- Management of Natural Resources.* A Report for the Royal Commission on Aboriginal Peoples. Land, Resource and Environment Regimes Project, October 1995.

Clarkson, L., B. Morrissette, and G. Regallet. *Our Responsibility to the Seventh Generation: Indigenous Peoples and Sustainable Development*. Winnipeg: International Institute for Sustainable Development, 1992.

Colorado, P. "Bridging Native and Western Science." *Convergence* 21.2/3 (1988): 49–67.

Couture, J. "Native Studies and the Academy." *Indigenous Knowledge in Global Context: Multiple Readings of Our World*. Eds. G. Dei, B. Hall, and D. Golden-Rosenberg. Toronto: University of Toronto Press (in press).

Dene Cultural Institute (DCI). "Traditional Ecological Knowledge and Environmental Assessment." An unpublished paper submitted to the Canadian Environmental Assessment Research Council, Ottawa, ON, 1989.

_____. "Guidelines for the Conduct of Participatory Community Research to Document Traditional Ecological Knowledge for the Purpose of Environmental Assessment and Environmental Management." Unpublished paper submitted to the Canadian Environmental Research Council, Ottawa, 1991.

Deloria, V. *Red Earth, White Lies: Native Americans and the Myth of Scientific Fact*. New York: Scribner, 1995.

Fitznor, L. "The Circle of Life: Affirming Aboriginal Philosophies in Everyday Living." *Life Ethics in World Religions*. Ed. D. McCance. Atlanta: Scholars Press, 1998. 22–40.

Gisday Wa, and Delgam Uukw. *The Spirit in the Land: Statements of the Gitksan and Wet'suwet'en Hereditary Chiefs in the Supreme Court of British Columbia 1987–1990*. Gabriola, BC: Reflections, 1992.

Good Striker, D. "TEK Wars: First Nations' Struggles for Environmental Planning." *Defending Mother Earth: Native American Perspectives on Environmental Justice*. Ed. J. Weaver. Maryknoll, NY: Orbis Books, 1996. 144–152.

Grenier, L. *Working with Indigenous Knowledge: A Guide for Researchers*. Ottawa: International Development Research Centre, 1998.

Healy, C. 1993. "The Significance and Application of TEK. *Traditional Ecological Knowledge: Wisdom for Sustainable Development*. Eds. N. Williams, N. and G. Baines. Canberra: Centre for Resource and Environmental Studies, Australian Natural University: 21–26.

Higgins, C. "The Role of Traditional Ecological Knowledge in Managing for Biodiversity. *Forestry Chronicle* 74.3 (1998): 323–326.

Hunn, E. "What is Traditional Ecological Knowledge?" *Traditional Ecological Knowledge: Wisdom for Sustainable Development*. Eds. N. Williams, N. and G. Baines. Canberra: Centre for Resource and Environmental Studies, Australian Natural University, 1993. 13–15.

Johnson, M., ed. *Lore: Capturing Traditional Ecological Knowledge*. Hay River, NWT: Dene Cultural Institute; Ottawa: the International Development Research Center, 1992.

Knudtson, P., and D. Suzuki. *Wisdom of the Elders*. Toronto: Stoddart Publishing 1992.

LaDuke, W. "Traditional Ecological Knowledge and Environmental Futures." *Endangered Peoples: Indigenous Rights and the Environment*. Special issue of the *Colorado Journal of International Environmental Law and Politics*. Niwot, CO: University Press of Colorado, 1994. 126–148.

Lukey, J. "Native and Non-Native Perspectives on Aboriginal Traditional Environmental Knowledge." Faculty of Environmental Studies, Unpublished Masters major paper, Toronto: York University, 1995.

MacDonald, J. *The Arctic Sky: Inuit Astronomy, Star Lore, and Legend*. Toronto: Royal Ontario Museum; Iqaluit, NT: Nunavut Research Institute, 1998.

Mander, J. *In the Absence of the Sacred: the Failure of Technology and the Survival of the Indian Nations*. San Francisco: Sierra Club Books, 1991.

McGregor, D. "Aboriginal Knowledge and Western Science: A Clash of Worldviews, Paradigms, and Methods." Unpublished research paper. Toronto: Department of Anthropology, University of Toronto, 1995.

_____. "An Evaluation of Traditional Environmental Knowledge from an Aboriginal Perspective." Unpublished research paper. Toronto: Faculty of Forestry, University of Toronto, 1994.

_____. "Indigenous Knowledge in Canada: Shifting Paradigms and the Influence of First Nations Advocates." *Science and Practice: Sustaining the Boreal Forest. Proceedings of the 1999 Sustainable Forest Management Network Conference, Edmonton, Alberta, 14–17 February 1999*. Eds. T. Veeman, D. Smith, B. Purdy, F. Salkie, and G. Larkin. Edmonton: Sustainable Forest Management Network, 1999. 192–97.

_____. "Sources, Transmission, and Control of Natural Knowledge Systems in Aboriginal Communities." Unpublished Research

Paper. Toronto: Department of History, University of Toronto, 1995.

Nantel, M. "So As To Hold Many Sheep: Towards Culturally Appropriate GIS." Unpublished Masters major paper. Toronto: Faculty of Environmental Studies, York University, 1999.

Notzke, C. *Aboriginal Peoples and Natural Resources in Canada.* York University, Toronto: Captus University Publications, 1994.

O'Meara, S., and D. West, eds. *From Our Eyes: Learning from Indigenous Peoples.* Toronto,: Garamond Press, 1996.

Richardson, B. "Harvesting Traditional Knowledge." *Nature Canada* 22.4 (1993): 30–37.

Roberts, K. "Circumpolar and Aboriginal People and Co-management Practice: Current Issues in Co-management and Environmental Assessment." *Proceedings of a Conference for the Joint Secretary-Inuvialuit Renewable Resources Committee and the Arctic Institute of North America.* Calgary: University of Calgary, 1996.

Smith, P., G. Scott, and G. Merkel. *Aboriginal Forest Land Management Guidelines: A Community Approach.* Ottawa: National Aboriginal Forestry Association, 1995.

Stevenson, M. "Indigenous Knowledge in Environmental Assessment." *Arctic* 49.3 (1996.): 276–291.

_____. "Inuit and Co-management: Principles, Practices and Challenges for the New Millennium." Report prepared for the Inuit Circumpolar Conference, President's Office, Nuuk, Greenland, on the occasion of the NAMMCO International Conference, "Sealing the Future," St. John's, Newfoundland, 25–27 November, 1997.

_____. "Traditional Knowledge and Environmental Management: From Commodity to Process." *Celebrating Partnerships,* National Aboriginal Forestry Association Conference, Prince Albert, SK, September 14–18, 1998. Edmonton: Sustainable Forest Management Network.

_____. "What Are We Managing? Traditional Systems of Management and Knowledge in Cooperative and Joint Management" *Science and Practice: Sustaining the Boreal Forest. Proceedings of the 1999 Sustainable Forest Management Network Conference, Edmonton, Alberta, 14–17 February 1999.* Eds. T. Veeman, D. Smith, B. Purdy, F. Salkie, and G. Larkin. Edmonton: Sustainable Forest Management Network, 1999. 161–169.

Tsuji, L. "Loss of Cree Traditional Ecological Knowledge in the Western James Bay Region of Northern Ontario, Canada: A Case Study of the Sharp-Tailed Groups, *Tympanuchus Phasianellus phasianellus." Canadian Journal of Native Studies* 16.2 (1996): 283–292.

Wavey, R. "International Workshop on Indigenous Knowledge and Community-Based Resource Management: Keynote Address." *Traditional Ecological Knowledge: Concepts and Cases.* Ed. I. Inglis. Ottawa: International Program on Traditional Ecological Knowledge and International Development Research Centre, 1993. 11–16.

Wolfe, J., C. Bechard, P. Crizek, and D. Cole. "Indigenous and Western Knowledge and Resources Management System." Guelph: University of Guelph, University School of Rural Planning and Development, 1992.

World Commission on Environment and Development (WCED). *Our Common Future.* Oxford, UK: Oxford University Press, 1987.

The Issue of Biodiversity, Intellectual Property Rights, and Indigenous Rights

Priscilla Settee

A Cree Indian from northern Saskatchewan, Priscilla Settee is presently Director of the Indigenous Peoples Program with the Extension Division at the University of Saskatchewan. Her M.Ed. from the University of Manitoba focused on Indigenous knowledge in the sciences and intellectual property rights. She has been an advisor to the International Development Research Centre, worked on "Seeding Solutions," policy options for genetic resources, and is an active member of the Intersessional Working Group on Article 8(J) of the Convention on Biological Diversity.

Indigenous communities are currently besieged by a relatively new problem. The natural surroundings found on Indigenous reserves and territories are being sought as a new form of wealth by non-Indigenous people and corporate interests. Increasingly, scientists have come to recognize the plant wealth that exists largely within natural habitats and homelands of Indigenous peoples, who are becoming more concerned and vigilant about the disappearance of natural plant life and the destruction of the natural environment. *Biodiversity* is a word that had been adopted by ecologists, scientists, and others to describe the vast array of species on the planet. The many species of plants and their resources have value to Indigenous communities because of their intrinsic worth to community and the belief that biodiversity is common property. Because Indigenous peoples see the circle of life as interconnected and believe that one cannot separate the various forms of life—human, plant, or animal—for them biodiversity is life. Each of elements in the circle of life is dependent on one another; if one disappears or is damaged, all suffer. The attempts to claim rights to plants have created tremendous strains and tensions within communities. Added to this state of affairs is the concern over patenting plants thereby endangering biodiversity.

This article describes some of the complex problems related to the issues of Indigenous rights and threats to biodiversity, documents the Indigenous political response mounted to save Indigenous knowledge, and discusses some issues related to biotechnology and the support that Indigenous peoples have received from non-governmental international groups. Indigenous groups from various countries have expressed concern that non-Indigenous people want to exercise control over Indigenous plants and knowledge. My own response to this situation is to respect Indigenous peoples' knowledge and rights to the land; ultimately, for me, it is about Indigenous rights to self-determination.

Issues Surrounding Biodiversity

Dr. Vandana Shiva, a leading scholar of ecology, is director of the Research Foundation for Science, Technology and Natural Resource Policy in India. She has been a outspoken advocate and leader in the preservation of biodiversity within Indigenous communities. Shiva coined the term *biopiracy* when referring to the situation faced by Indigenous peoples and the loss of their communities' plant life. Biopiracy is simply the theft of intellectual property, theft of the knowledge Indigenous peoples have about the growth, habits, and pharmaceutical properties of plants. Shiva refers to this brand of piracy as the new *conquistador*, in order to draw a parallel between the early Spanish invaders who colonized Latin America in search of gold and other sources of wealth. According to Shiva, one reason the world's biodiversity is being destroyed is because of internationally financed megaprojects such as mines, dams, highways, and aquaculture. A second reason is because of what Shiva describes as the "Blue Revolution"—exploitation of ocean waters through intensive fish farming, which affects coastal areas rich in marine diversity. Here in Canada, for example, fish droppings from the confined areas where fish are farmed poison natural shellfish beds below, which has an impact on the biodiversity of the ocean.

The global push for homogeneity in forestry, agriculture, animal husbandry, and fisheries is yet another cause of the destruction of biodiversity. In the 1970s an attempt by the developed countries to increase crop production in underdeveloped countries became known as the Green Revolution. It replaced traditional agricultural practices with mechanized Western practices that deliberately replaced the biological diversity of many areas with biological monocultures and uniformity. Because most of the world's biodiversity exists in the tropical rainforests and the coral reefs in the southern hemisphere where Indigenous peoples predominantly reside, these people are severely affected. Although studies show that the northern hemisphere is comparatively poor in terms of biodiversity and crop germplasm, the genetic material found in seeds, it is nonetheless a global problem (Simpson 52). The erosion of biodiversity causes a chain reaction that destroys many species along the way. Shiva explains:

> Biodiversity erosion starts a chain reaction. The disappearance of one species is related to the extinction of innumerable other species, with which it is interrelated through food webs and food chains. The crisis of biodiversity, however, is not just a crisis of the disappearance of species, which serve as industrial raw material and have the potential of spinning dollars for corporate enterprises. It is, more basically, a crisis that threatens the life-support systems and livelihoods of millions of people in Third World countries. (66)

The concept of intellectual property rights (IPR) is central to any discussion of biodiversity. IPR is a Western capitalist concept that sees natural resources as valuable only because of their commercial worth. Intellectual property rights encompass indigenous art, biological and medical knowledge, literature, songs, poetry, environmental management practices, and ecological knowledge as well as other aspects of Indigenous cultural heritage (Simpson 55). Thus IPR suggests ownership, commodity production, and private property. As noted at the outset, Indigenous peoples believe that biodiversity is a communal resource and for people who believe this it is impossible to believe you can "own" plants. Shiva relates biodiversity to economic capital this way:

> Biodiversity carries the intelligence of three and a half billion years of experimentation by life-forms. Human production is viewed as coproduction and cocreativity with nature. IPR regimes, in contrast, are based on the denial of creativity in nature. Yet, they usurp the creativity of emerging indigenous knowledge and the intellectual commons. Further, since IPRs are more a protection of capital investment than a recognition of creativity per se, there is a tendency for ownership of knowledge, and the products and processes emerging from it, to move toward areas of capital concentration and away from poor people without capital. (67)

The privatization of plant knowledge is a serious matter for people who rely on their backyards for cures and foods and who turn to healers who may give their knowledge as gifts. In India this practice is referred to as *gyan daan*, the gifting of knowledge. Unlike Western medical practitioners who "sell" their knowledge in the form of services, Indigenous practitioners do not use their knowledge to amass private wealth. The West's monopolistic right to much of the world's biodiversity is achieved though the system of intellectual property rights, primarily through the use of patents. Anyone who has visited a health food store and paid for the products of tea tree oil, feverfew, and a host of other commodities will clearly see the monetary benefits accrued by companies involved in the plant industry.

According to Shiva an economic system that reduces all value to market prices and all human activity to commercial transactions is the root of biodiversity exploitation. This causes a serious clash of values between cultures that subscribe to this economic system and cultures whose traditions and world view are based on non-monetary values. While it is difficult to put a dollar figure to the diversity in the backyards of Indigenous peoples; some have estimated it to be in the billions of dollars:

> It is probably impossible to estimate the full market value of traditional knowledge, but it is certainly enormous and may increase as advances in biotechnology broaden the range of life forms containing attributes with commercial applications. By one estimate the market value of plant-based medicines alone (many of which were used first by indigenous peoples) sold in developed countries amounted to $43 billion in 1985. (Posey 34)

Posey (34) and Simpson (52) state that less than one percent is ever returned to the source community.

Two central issues are involved in ownership of plant knowledge: compensation for ancestral Indigenous knowledge and recognition of the contributions of ancestors in laying the foundations for modern scientific knowledge and advances. A starting point, according to Patel (307), is a review and recognition of Indigenous contributions to world development. Such contributions would include: the wheel, rudder, and compass, pottery, weaving, fire, domestication of animals, agriculture, irrigation, selection and conservation of seeds, metals, roads, carriages, arithmetic, astronomy, geometry, city planning, architecture, paper, water supply and drainage, printing, glass, gears, systems of state, and administration. Consideration of these contributions puts the development of science into a proper perspective:

Such a recognition immediately raises the question of the relation between the contributions of indigenous people and their rightful share in the much enlarged output of goods and services which, building upon these foundations, modern science and technology have made possible. (Patel 307)

Still another concern for Indigenous peoples is the exploitation of how knowledge is presented or used when it is removed from a culturally appropriate context and infused with market-driven approaches. This can be seen in the commercialization of echinacea that has developed in recent years. Echinacea is a native North American plant and its value and use have long been part of Indigenous knowledge. Yet it is the manufacturing companies profiting from this knowledge, not the Indigenous groups from whose territories the seeds and knowledge originated. For many reasons, the current legal and ethical ways of dealing with questions of economics and ownership have been inadequate and have little or no provision for sharing benefits with the users and keepers of plants and local knowledge. Of utmost importance to the traditional plant users is the assurance that ethical practices go beyond just the letter of the law to embody the spirit of traditional values and ethical exchange. Some feel that fundamental principles ensuring the protection of Indigenous cultural heritage are not reconcilable with those of intellectual property law:

In contrast to Western legal systems, indigenous cultural heritage cannot be owned or monopolized by an individual, just as it cannot be alienated, surrendered or sold on an unconditional basis. Rather, the cultural heritage of indigenous peoples is a collective right, and as such the responsibility for its use and management in accordance with indigenous laws and traditions is borne by the community as a whole. (Simpson 54)

It is not sufficient to view biodiversity as the only issue. Biodiversity is a Western legal concept that is not founded on respect for the rights of Indigenous peoples. According to Simpson,

[t]his emphasis on biological information partly reflects the large financial investments now being made by governments, and the pharmaceutical, agricultural, and cosmetic industries in biodiversity prospecting. Other contributing factors include the resources of environment organizations which have been directed at the conservation of biodiversity (and not always in a manner that respects the rights of indigenous peoples), the effects of the specialty area of study known as ethnobotany, the international demand for the products produced from

> biological resources which transfers enormous economic
> power to corporations dealing in these products, and the
> specialized structure of the law that protects ownership rights
> to biological and biochemical materials. (56)

The assurances that biodiversity will be protected must be critically examined to determine whose interests are being served. The cultural aspects inherent in Indigenous knowledge, as defined by Indigenous communities, and use of biodiversity must also be protected. Ultimately, however, it is not possible to separate cultural rights from rights to self-determination on Indigenous territories. This land issue is at the heart of the struggle of the world's Indigenous peoples.

Also at issue is the Western practice of patenting, a tool used to protect the intellectual property rights of monopolistic exploiters. In practice, it ensures that communal access to healing plants is destroyed and undermines a central value in Indigenous communities, the belief that the plants and their resources belong to the whole community. A patent is granted by the state to a person who invents something new or introduces a new innovation:

> This right is really granted not to promote any noble cause—
> for example, promotion of inventiveness, as has so often been
> argued by the advocate of the system. It is a monopolistic right
> to prevent, to restrain, to limit others from imitating, adapting,
> improving, producing, or using, even for public welfare and
> development, the patented produce or process, or both. (Patel
> 310)

Industrially advanced countries, such as Britain, France, Belgium, the Netherlands, Portugal, Spain, Italy, and Germany, have been the strongest advocates of IPR. They have imposed this system on southern countries in Asia, Africa, and South America. Patents translate into wealth and power for foreign transnational companies and have a tremendous negative impact in the biodiversity of southern countries. There are about four million patents in the world, which provide a source of wealth for foreigners conducting business in the Third World.

> In the comity of nations, the Third World accounts for 75 percent of
> world population, 20 percent of world income, 25 percent of world
> trade, and about 45 percent of world enrollment in higher
> education. But it owns less than even 1 percent of world
> patent grants. The patent system is quite clearly the most
> unequal and the most unjust of all the relationships between
> the developed and developing countries. (310)

According to Patel less than five percent of the foreign-held patents are actually used in southern countries.

In order to understand whose interests are protected by patents, it is important to know a bit of the background them. Patent law has a history that goes back to 1883, when the Paris Convention for the Protection of Industrial Property was established to serve as the international guardian of the patent system. In underdeveloped countries, the Paris Convention, which still exists, has been referred to as a country club that serves the interests of the rich and powerful countries at the expense of the poorer ones. The Convention has been revised six times since 1883, each revision strengthening the monopolistic rights of patent holders.

Recognizing the inherent biases of the patent system that they had inherited from colonial masters, many of the developing countries altered their patent laws during the 1970s. Those countries were Iraq, Sri Lanka, Thailand, and South Korea in Asia; Egypt, Nigeria, and Algeria in Africa; and Chile, Peru, Colombia, Ecuador, Bolivia, Venezuela, and Mexico in Latin America. According to Patel, India led the movement to challenge the patent laws by producing the Indian Patents Act of 1970. Until recently, this act served as a model for other developing countries. The Indian Patents Act reduced the scope, degree, coverage, and duration of the patent monopolies, but its central objective was to bend the Intellectual Property Rights system so that it more directly addressed the development needs of the Third World.

Realizing that they were losing power to the Third World, the First World launched a new offensive called the Uruguay Round. The talks at this Round reflected the serious universal economic, social, political, and environmental crisis humanity is facing. Even the First World is now facing severe loss of political and economic power, and many First World countries are experiencing domestic disarray because of rising unemployment, prolonged recession, falling rates of growth, and a decline in social services, even some social chaos in the form of strikes and public protests. The Uruguay Round, completed in 1993, was a last-ditch effort by the First World to maintain control of how development should take place in underdeveloped countries. Intellectual Property Rights was an important subject covered by the Uruguay document that was designed to force the Third World to its knees:

> Instead of promoting self-reliance, these provisions [of the Uruguay Round] open the way for control by transnational corporations of the Third World's domestic markets. Instead of giving developing countries freedom and flexibility to exclude sectors of strategic importance for national development

from patentability, they force them to patent everything, including agricultural and biogenetic innovation. (Patel 315)

The Uruguay Agreement obliges developing countries to extend patent protection to twenty years for products as well as processes. Compulsory licensing was practically abolished, and import monopolies were preferred over home patents. Third World autonomy was quashed and First World control was intensified:

Instead of promoting self-reliant national development, they [patents] serve private interests of foreign corporations. In short, they universalize the U.S. system of intellectual property rights, thereby constraining the national interests of the developing countries to decommercialize progressively the IPR system in order to accelerate their development. (Patel 315)

Before the Uruguay round was completed, and recognizing that the world's biodiversity is vital to humanity's economic and social development, the United Nations Environment Program (UNEP) convened an ad hoc working group of experts on biodiversity in 1988 to explore the need for an international convention on it. At the 1992 United Nations Conference on Environment and Development in Rio de Janeiro, the Convention of Biological Diversity (CBD) was adopted. The objectives of the Convention were set out in article 1 of the document:

1. conservation of biodiversity
2. the sustainable use of biodiversity components
3. fair and equitable sharing of benefits arising from genetic resources
4. appropriate access to genetic resources
5. transfer of technology
6. consideration of rights over genetic resources and technologies
7. appropriate funding.

The objectives of the CBD were an attempt by both the developed nations and Indigenous peoples to address some of the concerns of Indigenous peoples.

Indigenous Peoples Political Response

The CBD represents only a partial victory for Indigenous peoples, but since its drafting in 1992 a political response to the issues around biodiversity has grown. On the one hand, the CBD represents an historic milestone, which explores the possibilities of compensating Indigenous communities for their pre-industrial knowledge. It is also an historical first step in the conservation of biodiversity:

The Convention on Biological Diversity was inspired by the world community's growing commitment to sustainable development. It represents a dramatic step forward in the conservation of biological diversity, the sustainable use of its components and the fair and equitable sharing of benefits arising from the use of genetic resources, the sustainable use of its components, and the fair and equitable sharing of benefits arising from the use of genetic resources. (Convention of Biological Diversity 1)

On the other hand, the final draft of the CBD reflects compromises by each side, and it is those compromises trouble Indigenous peoples. To the uncritical eye the CBD seems like a good idea, but Indigenous peoples continue to raise voices of concern. At a 1990 conference of the International Alliance of Indigenous Tribal Peoples of the Tropical Rainforest (representing thirty-one Indigenous organizations in Latin America, Africa, Asia, and the Pacific), several concerns were expressed. First and foremost, it was recognized that the CBD is a tool of governments, designed with little input by Indigenous peoples. Further, it was felt that the Convention increases the power of states to control Indigenous lands and resources. As defined in the CBD, the term *indigenous* is limited to local settlements living in isolated conditions, which does not accurately reflect how and where the broad population of Indigenous peoples live. The CBD promotes development of areas designated as protected areas, but peoples affected have not been consulted. Another concern is that the Convention promotes and facilitates agreements between governments and bioprospecting companies in order to gain access to the genetic resources on Indigenous territories. And lastly, the Convention opens up the possibility of top-down projects that support biodiversity, that is, they will be imposed on local settlements. In addition to the United Nations' efforts, Indigenous peoples have been mobilizing to protect their communities' knowledge and land: "The CBD reaffirms a unilateral state sovereignty, which could easily be used by states to deny indigenous sovereign rights to our territories, lands and resources" (*Biodiversity Bulletin* 12).

Indigenous peoples have been meeting regularly at international forums to ensure the full recognition of their rights. Three key issues have been identified: (1) collective ownership of territories; (2) self-determination in the exercising of customary law according to social and cultural practices, including legal and political representation through Indigenous institutions; and (3) control of Indigenous knowledge. Access to Indigenous knowledge, innovation, or practices should not take place without prior and informed consent of those Indigenous peoples affected. Indigenous peoples must not be at the bottom of a benefit-sharing heirarchy. Sharing must be equal.

A number of declarations, treaties, and agreements, such as The Mataatua Declaration on Cultural and Intellectual Property Rights of Indigenous Peoples, Kari-Oca Declaration, and the Indigenous Peoples' Earth Charter (Appendices A and B) have been drafted that address Indigenous peoples and biological diversity, among other issues. However, many of these documents fail to address rights and may even set down laws that greatly affect Indigenous peoples. The agreements fall into three categories: legally binding agreements, Indigenous peoples' declarations, and soft law, documents that are not directly enforceable in courts and tribunals but may have an impact on international law. It is important to note, however, that no international law has supremacy over a national law. Thus in a dispute involving biodiveristy, regardless of the wording of an international binding agreement, Indigenous peoples cannot make a legal claim against a government based on those agreements (Rothschild 55).

One document offered as a model for Indigenous rights is the Draft Declaration on the Rights of Indigenous Peoples, established by the Working Group on Indigenous Populations in 1982. Participation in the working group is open to any Indigenous peoples and is comprised of Indigenous peoples, experts on various issues, and representatives from governments and intergovernmental institutions. According to Simpson the Declaration is a document that eloquently expresses the spectrum of rights of Indigenous peoples. It emphasizes the importance of self-determination for Indigenous peoples. It stresses individual and collective rights of Indigenous peoples to the ownership, use, and control of their homelands, territories, and natural resources:

> It is therefore important to locate the discussion of the recognition and protection of indigenous peoples' cultural and intellectual property in the context of formulated, identified, inherent rights as expressed in the Draft Declaration of the Rights of Indigenous Peoples. This reflects the fact that the protection of the cultural and intellectual property of Indigenous Peoples is connected fundamentally with the realization of their territorial rights and right of self-determination. (Simpson 49)

With regard to property and territorial rights, the Declaration emphasizes the requirements of participation, consultation, and prior informed consent to activities that will have an impact on Indigenous peoples and their lands. It addresses the issue of just and fair compensation in violations of human rights. The draft has been held up as a document that can address the issues of consent, appropriation of resources and biodiversity, and self-determination, but it has not been fully endorsed by various governments or by the United Nations.

Biotechnology and Biodiversity

Discussion of these international documents needs to be understood within the context of international trade agreements, such as the General Agreement on Tariffs and Trade (GATT), the North American Free Trade Agreement, and others. These trade agreements are opening the door on the distribution of genetically modified seeds and products and this has serious consequences for biodiversity. Because the CBD had Indigenous input and attempted to respond to their concerns, it may potentially benefit them. The GATT, however, has allowed no input from Indigenous peoples and threatens their rights to their own resources: "The GATT is a multilateral binding treaty that creates a free market trade system throughout the world, to be enforced by the World Trade Organization (WTO). GATT's main objective is to establish free trade by dismantling trade barriers" (Rothschild 60). The GATT allows transnational corporations to compete with local markets worldwide and to sell products at less than prices, thereby driving traditional farmers and local industries out of business. The Trade Related Intellectual Property Rights (TRIPS), obliges countries to pass intellectual property legislation and requires signatory countries to establish patent protection for biotechnological innovations:

> This threatens to commercialize Indigenous knowledge and genetic resources worldwide. For example, medicines derived from Indigenous medicinal plants will be patentable in all GATT signatory countries. Most southern countries have been given until the year 2000 to pass the new required IPR legislation. The "least developed countries" have until 2004. (Rothschild 60)

The United States, which is home to many of the world's transnational and biotechnology corporations, has forcefully pressured countries, through trade sanctions, to create laws that cover biotechnological innovation in accordance with the TRIPS. India, China, and others have been forced to produce patent compliance laws, and in the case of India, dismantles the Indian Patents Act of 1970.

Related to Indigenous peoples' concerns regarding the use of their knowledge, there is the problem of the biotechnology industry and its impact on Indigenous farmers. A recent innovation, called "terminator technology" by its critics, is an example. In March 1998, the United States Department of Agriculture and the Delta and Pine Land Company (an American cotton seed company) received a U.S. patent on a technique that genetically alters seeds, so that it will not germinate unless a chemical is applied.

> The seed-sterilizing technology threatens to eliminate the age-old rights of farmers to save seed from their harvest and it jeopardizes the food security of 1.4 billion people—resource poor farmers in the South—who depend on farm-saved seed. (RAFI Communique 1)

The technology will be used primarily in the southern hemisphere as a means of preventing peasants from saving seeds, which are sold by American seed corporations. Patents on the terminator technology have been applied for in close to eighty countries. Should this new technology be used, ultimately the multinational seed and agrochemical industry will have an unprecedented and dangerous capacity to control the global food supply. According to the 1998 Rural Advancement Foundation International (RAFI) Communique, the terminator technology could drive millions of farmers out of agriculture altogether and threaten world food security. These small farms grow fifteen to twenty percent of the world food and directly feed 100 million people in Latin America, 300 million in Africa, and 1 billion in Asia. RAFI is calling for a global ban on the terminator technology on the basis of public morality. Non-governmental organizations will urge the CBD to condemn the new technology as a threat to world food security and farmer's rights. It is little wonder that the critics of this lethal technology are alarmed by its threat to Indigenous farmers, food sources, and biodiversity.

An example of the type of control over now exercised over biodiversity can be seen in the conduct of the agrochemical conglomerate Monsanto. This company has diversified into genetic modification of seeds and recently took steps to prevent seed saving, so central to the continuation of a diverse plant culture and to the economic survival of Indigenous farmers. They are suing more than 100 U.S. soybean growers who have violated a licensing agreement on transgenic soybean seeds and have hired Pinkerton private police to identify unauthorized seed-saving in the United States.

The issue of biotechnology touches all the world's people, not just Indigenous peoples and farmers as food grown or prepared from genetically modified seeds comes on to the market. Tomatoes, for example, have been engineered for longer shelf life or for delayed ripening, and lettuce shapes have been engineered to fit the vegetable drawers in home refrigerators. Over half the soy crop comes from seeds genetically modified to prevent them from becoming damaged from herbicide use, yet it is an additive in almost sixty percent of the processed foods on the market (RAFI Communique 3). Currently Canadian supermarkets have over thirty genetically engineered foods on their shelves that have been approved by Health Canada. It is not a requirement that these foods be labelled that they are genetically engineered in order to warn potential buyers (B.C. Biotechnology Circle Fact Sheet, no date). Consumers who wish to avoid genetically altered products have to conduct their own research—a sometimes difficult or time-consuming task. The growing power of the biotechnology industry and its consequent effect on food production are reason for concern and Indigenous people are launching many defensive strategies to make consumers aware of some of the issues.

There is room for optimism, thanks to the Satyagraha principle of tribal people of India. The Karnataka State Farmers Association (KSFA), an organization representing 10 million Indigenous peasants, represents a ray of hope in a sometimes depressing global picture. The KSFA invoked the Satyagraha principle of standing up to injustices by putting into practice the principle of freedom through their daring acts of defiance. The KSFA successfully removed both Kentucky Fried Chicken (KFC) and Cargill Seed Company from Karnataka state because they were a threat to Indian small-scale farming autonomy as well as a threat to biodiversity in the whole of India. Both KFC and Cargill use highly mechanized methods of food and seed production, which undermines the small scale practices of the local farmers and ultimately the local economy. After numerous warnings to the managers of KFC and Cargill, the KSFA set fire to the offices of KFC and Cargill, after employees left work.

I have listed a number of concerns of Indigenous peoples with regard to the protection of their knowledge and intellectual property rights. I have described this struggle within a global context to try to convey the extent of their concerns. Indigenous peoples around the world are becoming more vigilant about ensuring their rights are protected. They are in a race against time to ensure that their rights to sovereignty are protected, and they are establishing their rights by organizing through international forums. This fight is also a race to save the resources and the biodiversity that has sustained their communities for millennia.

The threat to Indigenous resources and biodiversity comes from transnational corporations, which have swept into countries swiftly and ruthlessly; profits have come at the expense of the social and economic integrity of Indigenous communities. To date Indigenous communities have effectively used international networks in order to stop the misappropriation of their communities' natural resources and biodiversity. In many respects it is a David and Goliath situation but the communities are strengthened by their commitment to their traditions and culture and by the solidarity of the network of Indigenous global communities. Globalism can work both ways.

Works Cited

Convention on Biological Diversity, Text and Annexes. Geneva: The Interim Secretariat for the Convention on Biological Diversity, November, 1994.

Patel, Surendra J. "Can the Intellectual Property Rights System Serve the Interests of Indigenous Knowledge?" *Valuing Local Knowledge, Indigenous People and Intellectual*. Eds. Stephen B. Brush and Doreen Stabinsky. Washington, DC: Island Press, 1996. 305–22.

Posey, Darrell A. *Beyond Intellectual Property, Toward Traditional Resource Rights For Indigenous Peoples and Local Communities*. Ottawa: International Development Research Centre, 1996.

RAFI Communique. Winnipeg: Rural Advancement Foundation International, March/April 1998.

Rothschild, David. *Protecting What's Ours, Indigenous Peoples and Biodiversity.* Oakland: South and Meso American Indian Rights Centre, 1997.

Shiva, Vandana. *Biopiracy the Plunder of Nature and Knowledge*. Boston: South End Press, 1997.

Simpson, Tony. *Indigenous Heritage and Self-determination*. Copenhagen: International Work Group and Indigenous Affairs, 1997.

Appendix A

The Mataatua Declaration on Cultural and Intellectual Property Rights of Indigenous Peoples

In recognition that 1993 is the United Nations International Year for the World's Indigenous Peoples, the Nine Tribes of Mataatua, in the Bay of Plenty Region of Aotearoa New Zealand, convened the First International Conference on the Cultural and Intellectual Property Rights of Indigenous Peoples (12–18 June 1993, Whakatane).

Over 150 delegates from 14 countries attended, including indigenous representatives from Ainu (Japan), Australia, Cook Islands, Fiji, India, Panama, Peru, the Philippines, Surinam, USA, and Aotearoa.

The Conference met over 6 days to consider a range of significant issues, including the value of indigenous knowledge, biodiversity and biotechnology, customary environmental management, arts, music, language, and other physical and spiritual cultural forms. On the final day, the following Declaration was passed by the Plenary.

Preamble

Recognizing that 1993 is the United Nations International Year for the World's Indigenous Peoples;
Reaffirming the undertaking of United Nations Member States to:
 "Adopt or strengthen appropriate policies and/or legal instruments that will protect indigenous intellectual and cultural property and the right to preserve customary and administrative systems and practices."
—*Agenda 21*, United Nations Conference on Environment and Development (UNCED), (26:4b);
Endorsing the recommendations on Culture and Science from the World Conference of Indigenous Peoples on Territory, Environment, and Development, Kari-Oca, Brazil, 25-30 May 1992;

We

Declare that Indigenous Peoples of the world have the right to self determination, and in exercising that right must be recognized as the exclusive owners of their cultural and intellectual property;

Acknowledge that Indigenous Peoples have a commonality of experiences relating to the exploitation of their cultural and intellectual property;

Affirm that the knowledge of the Indigenous Peoples of the world is of benefit to all humanity;

Recognize that Indigenous Peoples are capable of managing their traditional knowledge themselves, but are willing to offer it to all humanity provided their fundamental rights to define and control this knowledge are protected by the international community;

Insist that the first beneficiaries of indigenous knowledge (cultural and intellectual property rights) must be the direct indigenous descendants of such knowledge; and

Declare that all forms of discrimination and exploitation of Indigenous Peoples, indigenous knowledge, and indigenous cultural and intellectual property rights must cease.

1. Recommendations to Indigenous Peoples

In the development of policies and practices, Indigenous Peoples should:

1.1   Define for themselves their own intellectual and cultural property.

1.2   Note that existing protection mechanisms are insufficient for the protection of Indigenous Peoples' intellectual and cultural property rights.

1.3   Develop a code of ethics which external users must observe when recording (visual, audio, written) their traditional and customary knowledge.

1.4   Prioritize the establishment of indigenous education, research, and training centres to promote their knowledge of customary environmental and cultural practices.

1.5   Reacquire traditional indigenous lands for the purpose of promoting customary agricultural production.

1.6   Develop and maintain their traditional practices and sanctions for the protection, preservation, and revitalization of their traditional intellectual and cultural properties.

1.7   Assess existing legislation with respect to the protection of antiquities.

1.8   Establish an appropriate body with appropriate mechanisms to:
    (a) Preserve and monitor the commercialism or otherwise of indigenous cultural properties in the public domain;
    (b) Generally advise and encourage Indigenous Peoples to take steps to protect their cultural heritage; and
    (c) Allow a mandatory consultative process with respect to any new legislation affecting Indigenous Peoples' cultural and intellectual property rights.
1.9   Establish international indigenous information centres and networks.
1.10   Convene a Second International Conference (Hui) on the Cultural and Intellectual Property Rights of Indigenous Peoples to be hosted by the Coordinating Body for the Indigenous Peoples Organizations of the Amazon Basin (COICA).

2. Recommendations to states, and national and international agencies

In the development of policies and practices, states, and national and international agencies must:

2.1   Recognize that Indigenous Peoples are the guardians of their customary knowledge and have the right to protect and control dissemination of that knowledge.
2.2   Recognize that Indigenous Peoples also have the right to create new knowledge based on cultural traditions.
2.3   Note that existing protection mechanisms are insufficient for the protection of Indigenous Peoples cultural and intellectual property rights.
2.4   Accept that the cultural and intellectual property rights of Indigenous Peoples are vested with those who created them.
2.5   Develop in full cooperation with Indigenous Peoples an additional cultural and intellectual property rights regime incorporating the following:
    (a) Collective (as well as individual ownership and origin-retroactive coverage of historical as well as contemporary works;
    (b) Protection against debasement of culturally significant items;
    (c) Cooperative rather than competitive framework;

(d) First beneficiaries to be the direct descendants of the traditional guardians of that knowledge; and

(e) coverage span.

Biodiversity and customary environmental management

2.6   Indigenous flora and fauna are inextricably bound to the territories of indigenous communities and any property right claims must recognize their traditional guardianship.

2.7   Commercialization of any traditional plants and medicines of Indigenous Peoples, must be managed by the Indigenous Peoples who have inherited such knowledge.

2.8   A moratorium on any further commercialization of indigenous medicinal plants and human genetic materials must be declared until indigenous communities have developed appropriate protection mechanisms.

2.9   Companies and institutions, both governmental and private, must not undertake experiments or commercialization of any biogenetic resources without the consent of the appropriate Indigenous Peoples.

2.10   Prioritize settlement of any outstanding land and natural resources claims of Indigenous Peoples for the purpose of promoting customary, agricultural, and marine production.

2.11   Ensure current scientific environmental research is strengthened by increasing the involvement of indigenous communities and of customary environmental knowledge.

Cultural objects

2.12   All human remains and burial objects of Indigenous Peoples held by museums and other institutions must be returned to their traditional areas in a culturally appropriate manner.

2.13   Museums and other institutions must provide, to the country and Indigenous Peoples concerned, an inventory of any indigenous cultural objects still held in their possession.

2.14   Indigenous cultural objects held in museums and other institutions must be offered back to their traditional owners.

3. Recommendations to the United Nations

In respect for the rights of Indigenous Peoples, the United Nations should:

3.1 Ensure that the process of participation of Indigenous Peoples in United Nations fora is strengthened so their views are fairly represented.

3.2 Incorporate the Mataatua Declaration in its entirety in the United Nations Study on Cultural and Intellectual Property of Indigenous Peoples.

3.3 Monitor and take action against any states whose persistent policies and activities damage the cultural and intellectual property rights of Indigenous Peoples.

3.4 Ensure that Indigenous Peoples actively contribute to the way in which indigenous cultures are incorporated into the 1995 United Nations International Year of Culture.

3.5 Call for an immediate halt to the ongoing Human Genome Diversity Project (HUGO) until its moral, ethical, socioeconomic, physical, and political implications have been thoroughly discussed, understood, and approved by Indigenous Peoples.

4. Conclusion

The United Nations, international and national agencies, and states must provide additional funding to indigenous communities in order to implement these recommendations.

June 1993

Appendix B

Kari-Oca Declaration and Indigenous Peoples Earth Charter

In Brazil, 1992, at the First World Conference of Indigenous People on Territory, Environment, and Development, nearly one thousand Tribal people from every part of the globe wrote and unanimously signed a 109 point Earth Charter called the Kari-Oca Declaration. This earth Charter was presented by Marcos Terena to the United Nations Conference on Environment and Development (the "Earth Summit" as a representation of the Indigenous Peoples' view of sustainable and humane life on earth. [From http://www.yakoana.com/earthchart.html]

Preamble

The world Conference of Indigenous Peoples on Territory, Environment and Development (25–30 May 1992)

The Indigenous Peoples of the Americas, Asia, Africa, Australia, Europe, and the Pacific, united in one voice at Kari-Oca Villages, express our collective gratitude to the Indigenous peoples of Brazil. Inspired by this historical meeting, we celebrate the spiritual unity of the Indigenous peoples with the land and ourselves. We continue building and formulating our united commitment to save our Mother the Earth. We, the Indigenous peoples, endorse the following declaration as our collective responsibility to carry our Indigenous minds and voices into the future.

Declaration

We, the Indigenous Peoples, walk to the future in the footprints of our ancestors.

From the smallest to the largest living being, from the four directions, from the air, the land, and the mountains, the Creator has placed us, the Indigenous Peoples, upon our Mother the Earth.

The footprints of our ancestors are permanently etched upon the land of our peoples.

We, the Indigenous Peoples, maintain our inherent rights to self-determination.

We have always had the right to decide our own forms of government, to use our own laws to raise and educate our children, to our own cultural identity without interference.

We continue to maintain our rights as peoples despite centuries of deprivation, assimilation, and genocide.

We maintain our inalienable rights to our lands and territories, to all our resources—above and below—and to our waters. We assert our ongoing responsibility to pass these on to the future generations.

We cannot be removed from our lands. We, the Indigenous Peoples, are connected by the circle of life to our land and environments.

We, the Indigenous Peoples, walk to the future in the footprints of our ancestors.

Signed at Kari-Oca, Brazil, on the 30th day of May, 1992

(Please note, for the purposes of the Declaration, and this statement, any use of the term "Indigenous peoples" also includes tribal peoples.)

Human Rights and International Law

1. We demand the right to life.
2. International law must deal with the collective human rights of Indigenous peoples.
3. There are many international instruments which deal with the rights of individuals, but there are no declarations to recognize collective human rights. Therefore, we urge governments to support the United Nations Working Group on Indigenous Peoples' (UNWGIP) Universal Declaration of Indigenous Rights, which is presently in draft form.
4. There exists many examples of genocide against Indigenous peoples. Therefore, the convention against genocide must be changed to include the genocide of Indigenous peoples.
5. The United Nations should be able to send Indigenous peoples' representatives in a peace-keeping capacity, into Indigenous territories where conflicts arise. This would be done at the request and consent of the Indigenous peoples concerned.
6. The concept of Terra Nullius must be eliminated from international law usage. Many state governments have used internal domestic laws to deny us ownership of our own lands. These illegal acts should be condemned by the world.
7. Where small numbers of Indigenous peoples are residing within state boundaries, so-called democratic countries have denied Indigenous peoples the right of consent about their future, using the notion of majority rules to decide the future of Indigenous peoples. Indigenous peoples' right of consent to projects in their areas must be recognized.
8. We must promote the term "Indigenous peoples" at all fora. The use of the term "Indigenous peoples" must be without qualifications.
9. We urge governments to ratify International labour Organisation (ILO) Convention 169 to guarantee an international legal instrument for Indigenous peoples (Group 2 only).
10. Indigenous peoples' distinct and separate rights within their own territories must be recognized.

11.   We assert our rights to free passage through state-imposed political boundaries dividing our traditional territories. Adequate mechanisms must be established to secure this right.

12.   The colonial systems have tried to dominate and assimilate our peoples. However, our peoples remain distinct despite these pressures.

13.   Our Indigenous governments and legal systems must be recognized by the United Nations, state governments, and international legal instruments.

14.   Our right to self-determination must be recognized.

15.   We must be free from population transfer.

16.   We maintain our right to our traditional way of life.

17.   We maintain our right to our spiritual way of life.

18.   We maintain the right to be free from pressures from multinational (transnational) corporations upon lives and lands. All multinational (transnational) corporations which are encroaching upon Indigenous lands should be reported to the United Nations Transnational Office.

19.   We must be free from racism.

20.   We maintain the right to decide the direction of our communities.

21.   The United Nations should have a special procedure to deal with issues arising from violations of Indigenous treaties.

22.   Treaties signed between Indigenous peoples and non-Indigenous peoples must be accepted as treaties under international law.

23.   The United Nations must exercise the right to impose sanctions against governments that violate the rights of Indigenous peoples.

24.   We urge the United Nations to include the issue of Indigenous peoples in the agenda of the World Conference of Human Rights to be held in 1993. The work done so far by the United Nations Inter-American Commission of Human Rights should be taken into consideration.

25.   Indigenous peoples should have the right to their own knowledge, language, and culturally appropriate education, including bicultural and bilingual education. Through recognizing both formal and informal ways, the participation of family and community is guaranteed.

26.   Our health rights must include the recognition and respect of traditional knowledge held by Indigenous

healers. This knowledge, including our traditional medicines and their preventive and spiritual healing power, must be recognized and protected against exploitation.

27. The World Court must extend its powers to include complaints by Indigenous peoples.

28. There must be a monitoring system from this conference to oversee the return of delegates to their territories. The delegates should be free to attend and participate in international Indigenous conferences.

29. Indigenous women's rights must be respected. Women must be included in all local, national, regional, and international organizations.

30. The above-mentioned historical rights of Indigenous peoples must be guaranteed in national legislation.

Land and Territories

31. Indigenous peoples were placed upon our Mother the Earth by the Creator. We belong to the land. We cannot be separated from our lands and territories.

32. Our territories are living totalities in permanent vital relation between human beings and nature. Their possession produces the development of our culture. Our territorial property should be inalienable, unceasable, and not denied title. Legal, economic, and technical back-up are needed to guarantee this.

33. Indigenous peoples' inalienable right to land and resources confirm that we have always had ownership and stewardship over our traditional territories. We demand that these be respected.

34. We assert our rights to demarcate our traditional territories. The definition of territory includes space (air), land, and sea. We must promote a traditional analysis of traditional land rights in all our territories.

35. Where Indigenous territories have been degraded, resources must be made available to restore them. The recuperation of those affected territories is the duty of the respective jurisdiction in all nation states, which cannot be delayed. Within this process of recuperation the compensation for the historical ecological debt must be taken into account. Nation states must revise in depth the agrarian, mining, and forestry policies.

36. Indigenous peoples reject the assertion of non-Indigenous laws onto our lands; states cannot unilaterally extend

their jurisdiction over our lands and territories. The concept of Terra Nullius should be forever erased from the law books of states.

37.   We, as Indigenous peoples, must never alienate our lands. We must always maintain control over the land for future generations.

38.   If a non-Indigenous government, individual, or corporation wants to use our lands, then there must be a formal agreement which sets out the terms and conditions. Indigenous peoples maintain the right to be compensated for the use of their lands and resources.

39.   Traditional Indigenous territorial boundaries, including the waters, must be respected.

40.   There must be some control placed upon environmental groups who are lobbying to protect our territories and the species within those territories. In many instances, environmental groups are more concerned about animals than human beings. We call for Indigenous peoples to determine guidelines prior to allowing environmental groups into their territories.

41.   Parks must not be created at the expense of Indigenous peoples. There is no way to separate Indigenous peoples from their lands.

42.   Indigenous peoples must not be removed from their lands in order to make it available to settlers or other forms of economic activity on their lands.

43.   In many instances, the numbers of Indigenous peoples have been decreasing because of encroachment by non-Indigenous peoples.

44.   Indigenous peoples should encourage their peoples to cultivate their own traditional forms of products rather than to use imported exotic crops which do not benefit local peoples.

45.   Toxic wastes must not be deposited in our areas. Indigenous peoples must realize that chemicals, pesticides, and hazardous wastes do not benefit the peoples.

46.   Traditional areas must be protected against present and future forms of environmental degradation.

47.   There must be a cessation of all uses of nuclear material.

48.   Mining of products for nuclear production must cease.

49.   Indigenous lands must not be used for the testing or dumping of nuclear products.

50.   Population transfer policies by state governments in our

territories are causing hardship. Traditional lands are lost and traditional livelihoods are being destroyed.

51.   Our lands are being used by state governments to obtain funds from the World Bank, the International Monetary Fund, the Asian Pacific Development Bank, and other institutions, which has led to a loss of our lands and territories.

52.   In many countries, our lands are being used for military purposes. This is an unacceptable use of the lands.

53.   The colonizer governments have changed the names of our traditional and sacred areas. Our children learn these foreign names and start to lose their identity. In addition, the changing of the name of a place diminishes respect for the spirits which reside in those areas.

54.   Our forests are not being used for their intended purposes. The forests are being used to make money.

55.   Traditional activities, such as making pottery, are being destroyed by the importation of industrial goods. This impoverishes the local peoples.

Biodiversity and Conservation

56.   The Vital Circles are in a continuous interrelation in such a way that the change of one of its elements affects the whole.

57.   Climatic changes affect Indigenous peoples and all humanity. In addition, ecological systems and their rhythms are affected, which contributes to the deterioration of our quality of life and increases our dependency.

58.   The forests are being destroyed in the name of development and economic gains without considering the destruction of ecological balance. These activities do not benefit human beings, animals, birds, and fish. The logging concessions and incentives to the timber, cattle, and mining industries affecting the ecosystems and the natural resources should be cancelled.

59.   We value the efforts of protection of the Biodiversity but we reject being included as part of an inert diversity which pretends to be maintained for scientific and folkloric purposes.

60.   The Indigenous peoples' strategies should be kept in a reference framework for the formulation and application of national policies on environment and biodiversity.

Development Strategies

61.   Indigenous peoples must consent to all projects in our territories. Prior to consent being obtained the peoples must be fully and entirely involved in any decisions. They must be given all the information about the project and its effects. Failure to do so should be considered a crime against the Indigenous peoples. The person or persons who violate this should be tried in a world tribunal within the control of Indigenous peoples set for such a purpose. This could be similar to the trials held after World War II.

62.   We have the right to our own development strategies based on our cultural practices and with a transparent, efficient, and viable management and with economical and ecological viability.

63.   Our development and life strategies are obstructed by the interests of the government and big companies and by the neoliberal policies. Our strategies have, as a fundamental condition, the existence of international relationships based on justice, equity, and solidarity between the human beings and the nations.

64.   Any development strategy should prioritize the elimination of poverty, the climatic guarantee, the sustainable manageability of natural resources, the continuity of democratic societies, and the respect of cultural differences.

65.   The Global Environmental Facility should assign at best 20 percent for Indigenous peoples' strategies and programs of environmental emergency, improvement of life quality, protection of natural resources, and rehabilitation of ecosystems. This proposal in the case of South America and the Caribbean should be concrete in the Indigenous development fund as a pilot experience in order to be extended to the Indigenous peoples of other regions and continents.

66.   The concept of development has meant the destruction of our lands. We reject the current definition of development as being useful to our peoples. Our cultures are not static and we keep our identity through a permanent recreation of our life conditions; but all of this is obstructed in the name of so-called developments.

67.   Recognizing Indigenous peoples' harmonious relationship with Nature, Indigenous sustainable development strategies and cultural values must be respected as distinct and vital sources of knowledge.

68. Indigenous peoples have been here since the time before time began. We have come directly from the Creator. We have lived and kept the Earth as it was on the First Day. Peoples who do not belong to the land must go out from the lands because those things (so called "development" on the land) are against the laws of the Creator.

69. (a) In order for Indigenous peoples to assume control, management and administration of their resources and territories, development projects must be based on the principles of self-determination and self-management. (b) Indigenous peoples must be self-reliant.

70. If we are going to grow crops, we must feed the peoples. It is not appropriate that the lands be used to grow crops which do not benefit the local peoples.
(a) Regarding Indigenous policies, state government must cease attempts of assimilation and integration.
(b) Indigenous peoples must consent to all projects in their territories. Prior to consent being obtained, the peoples must be fully and entirely involved in any decisions. They must be given all the information about the project and its effects. Failure to do so should be considered a crime against Indigenous peoples. The person or persons responsible should be tried before a world tribunal, with a balance of Indigenous peoples et up for such a purpose. This could be similar to the trials held after the World War II.

71. We must never use the term "Land claims." It is the non-Indigenous peoples which do not have any land. All the land is our land. It is non-Indigenous peoples who are making claims to our lands. We are not making claims to our lands.

72. There should be a monitoring body within the United Nations to monitor all the land disputes around the world prior to development.

73. There should be a United Nations conference on the topic of "Indigenous Lands and Development."

74. Non-Indigenous peoples have come to our lands for the purpose of exploiting these lands and resources to benefit themselves, and to the impoverishment of our peoples. Indigenous peoples are victims of development. In many cases, Indigenous peoples are exterminated in the name of a development program. There are numerous examples of such occurrences.

75.   Development that occurs on Indigenous lands, without the consent of Indigenous peoples, must be stopped.

76.   Development which is occurring on Indigenous lands is usually decided without local consultation by those who are unfamiliar with local conditions and needs.

77.   The Eurocentric notion of ownership is destroying our peoples. We must return to our own view of the world, of the land, and of development. The issue cannot be separated from Indigenous peoples' rights.

78.   There are many different types of so-called development: road construction, communication facilities such as electricity, telephones. These allow developers easier access to the areas, but the effects of such industrialization destroy the lands.

79.   There is a world-wide move to remove Indigenous peoples from their lands and place them in villages. The relocation from the traditional territories is done to facilitate development.

80.   It is not appropriate for governments or agencies to move into our territories and to tell our peoples what is needed.

81.   In many instances, the state governments have crated artificial entities such as "district council" in the name of the state government in order to deceive the international community. These artificial entities then are consulted about development in the area. The state government, then, claims that Indigenous peoples were consulted about the project. These lies must be exposed to the international community.

82.   There must be an effective network to disseminate material and information between Indigenous peoples. This is necessary in order to keep informed about the problems of other Indigenous peoples.

83.   Indigenous peoples should form and direct their own environmental network.

Culture, Science, and Intellectual Property

84.   We feel the Earth as if we are within our mother. When the Earth is sick and polluted, human health is impossible. To heal ourselves, we must heal the Planet, and to heal the Planet, we must heal ourselves.

85.   We must begin to heal from the grassroots level and work towards the international level.

86. The destruction of the culture has always been considered an internal, domestic problem within national states. The United Nation must set up a tribunal to review the cultural destruction of the Indigenous peoples.

87. We need to have foreign observers come into our Indigenous territories to oversee national state elections to prevent corruption.

88. The human remains and artifacts of Indigenous peoples must be returned to their original peoples.

89. Our sacred and ceremonial sites should be protected and considered as the patrimony of Indigenous peoples and humanity. The establishment of a set of legal and operational instruments at both national and international levels would guarantee this.

90. The use of existing Indigenous languages is our right. These languages must be protected.

91. States that have outlaws Indigenous languages and their alphabets should be censored by United Nations.

92. We must not allow tourism to be used to diminish our culture. Tourists come into the communities and view the people as if Indigenous peoples were part of a zoo. Indigenous peoples have the right to allow or to disallow tourism within their areas.

93. Indigenous peoples must have the necessary resources and control over their own education systems.

94. Elders must be recognized and respected as teachers of the young people.

95. Indigenous wisdom must be recognized and encouraged.

96. The traditional knowledge of herbs and plants must be protected and passed onto future generations.

97. Traditions cannot be separated from land, territory, or science.

98. Traditional knowledge has enabled Indigenous peoples to survive.

99. The usurping of traditional medicines and knowledge from Indigenous peoples should be considered a crime against peoples.

100. Material culture is being used by the non-Indigenous to gain access to our lands and resources, thus destroying our cultures.

101. Most of the media at this conference were only interested in the pictures which will be sold for profit. This is another case of exploitation of Indigenous peoples. This does not advance the cause of Indigenous peoples.

102. As creators and carriers of civilizations which have given and continue to share knowledge, experience, and values with humanity, we require that our right to intellectual and cultural properties be guaranteed and that the mechanism for each implementation be in favour of our peoples and studied in depth and implemented. This respect must include the right over genetic resources, genebanks, biotechnology, and knowledge of biodiversity programs.

103. We should list the suspect museums and institutions that have misused our cultural and intellectual properties.

104. The protection, norms, and mechanisms of artistic and artisan creation of our peoples must be established and implemented in order to avoid plunder, plagiarism, undue exposure, and use.

105. When Indigenous peoples leave their communities, they should make every effort to return to the community.

106. In many instances, our songs, dances, and ceremonies have been viewed as the only aspects of our lives. In some instances, we have been asked to change a ceremony or a song to suit the occasion. This is racism.

107. At local, national, and international levels, governments must commit funds to new and existing resources to education and training for Indigenous peoples, to achieve their sustainable development, to contribute and to participate in sustainable and equitable development at all levels. Particular attention should be given to Indigenous women, children, and youth.

108. All kinds of folkloric discrimination must be stopped and forbidden.

109. The United Nations should promote research into Indigenous knowledge and develop a network of Indigenous sciences.

Documents

Excerpts from the
Royal Proclamation of 1763

And whereas it is just and reasonable, and essential to our Interest, and the security of our Colonies, that the several Nations or Tribes of Indians with whom We are connected, and who live under our protection, should not be molested or disturbed in the Possession of such Parts of Our Dominions and Territories as, not having been ceded to or purchased by Us, are reserved to them or any of them, as their Hunting Grounds – We do therefore, with the Advice of our Privy Council, declare it to be our Royal Will and Pleasure, that no Governor or Commander in Chief in any of our Colonies of Quebec, East Florida, or West Florida, do presume, upon any Pretence whatever, to grant Warrants of Survey, or pass any Patents for lands beyond the Bounds of their respective Governments, as described in their Commissions; as also that no Governor or Commander in Chief in any of our other Colonies or Plantations in America do presume for the present, and until our further Pleasure be Known, to grant Warrants of Survey, or pass Patents for any Lands beyond the Heads or Sources of any of the Rivers which fall into the Atlantic Ocean from the West and North West, or upon any Lands whatever, which, not having been ceded to or purchased by Us as aforesaid, are reserved to the said Indians, or any of them.

And We do further declare it to be Our Royal Will and Pleasure, for the present as aforesaid, to reserve under our Sovereignty, Protection, and Dominion, for the use of the said Indians, all the Lands and Territories not included within the limits of Our Said Three New Governments, or within the Limits of the Territory granted to the Hudson's Bay Company, as also all the Lands and Territories lying to the Westward of the Sources of the Rivers which fall into the Sea from the West and North West as aforesaid;

And We do hereby strictly forbid, on Pain of our Displeasure, all our loving Subjects from making any Purchases or Settlements whatever, or taking Possession of any of the Lands above reserved, without our especial leave and licence for the Purpose first obtained.

And, We do further strictly enjoin and require all Persons whatever who have either wilfully or inadvertently seated themselves upon any Lands within the Countries above described, or upon any other Lands which, not having been ceded to or purchased by Us, are still reserved to the said Indians as aforesaid, forthwith to remove themselves from such Settlements.

And Whereas Great Frauds and Abuses have been committed in purchasing Lands of the Indians, to the Great Prejudice of our Interests, and to the Great Dissatisfaction of the said Indians; In order, therefore, to prevent such Irregularities for the future, and to the End that the Indians may be convinced of our Justice and determined Resolution to remove all reasonable Cause of Discontent, We do, with the Advice of our Privy Council strictly enjoin and require, that no private Person do presume to make any Purchase from the said Indians of any Lands reserved to the said Indians, within those parts of our Colonies where, We have thought proper to allow Settlement; but that, if at any Time any of the said Indians should be inclined to dispose of the said Lands, the same shall be Purchased only for Us. in our Name, at some public Meeting or Assembly of the said Indians, to be held for the Purpose by the Governor or Commander in Chief of our Colony respectively within which they shall lie; and in case they shall lie within the limits of any Proprietary Government, they shall be purchased only for the Use and in the name of such Proprietaries, conformable to such Directions and Instructions as We or they shall think proper to give for the Purpose; And We do, by the Advice of our Privy Council, declare and enjoin, that the Trade with the said Indians shall be free and open to all our Subjects whatever, provided that every Person who may incline to Trade with the said Indians do take out a Licence for carrying on such Trade from the Governor or Commander in Chief of any of our Colonies respectively where such Person shall reside, and also give Security to observe such Regulations as We shall at any Time think fit, by ourselves or by our Commissaries to be appointed for this Purpose, to direct and appoint for the Benefit of the said Trade:

And We do hereby authorize, enjoin, and require the Governors and Commanders in Chief of all our Colonies respectively, as well those under Our immediate Government as those under the Government and Direction of Proprietaries, to grant such Licences without Fee or Regard, taking especial care to insert therein a Condition, that such Licence shall be void, and the Security forfeited in case the Person to whom the same is granted shall refuse or neglect to observe such Regulations as We shall think proper to prescribe as aforesaid.

And We do further expressly enjoin and require all Officers whatever, as well Military as those Employed in the Management and Direction of Indian Affairs, within the Territories reserved as aforesaid for the Use of the said Indians, to seize and apprehend all Persons whatever, who standing charged with Treason, Misprisions of Treason, Murders, or other Felonies or Misdemeanors, shall fly from Justice and take Refuge in the said Territory, and to send them under a proper Guard to the Colony where the Crime was committed of which they stand accused, in order to take their Trial for the same.

Given at our Court at St. James's the 7th Day of October 1763, in the Third Year of our Reign.

GOD SAVE THE KING

Excerpts from
The British North America
Act, 1867

ANNO TRICESIMO ET TRICESIMO-PRIMO

VICTORIÆ REGINÆ.

CAP. III.

An Act for the Union of Canada, Nova. Scotia, and New Brunswick, and the Government thereof; and for Purposes connected therewith.

[*29th March* 1867.]

WHEREAS the Provinces of Canada, Nova Scotia, and New Brunswick have expressed their Desire to be federally united into One Dominion under the Crown of the United Kingdom of Great Britain and Ireland, with a Constitution similar in Principle to that of the United Kingdom:

And whereas such a Union would conduce to the Welfare of the Provinces and promote the Interests of the British Empire:

And whereas on the Establishment of the Union by Authority of Parliament it is expedient, not only that the Constitution of the Legislative Authority in the Dominion be provided for, but also that the Nature of the Executive Government therein be declared:

And whereas it is expedient that Provision be made for the eventual Admission into the Union of other Parts of British North America:

Be it therefore enacted and declared by the Queen's most Excellent Majesty, by and with the Advice and Consent of the Lords Spiritual and Temporal, and Commons, in this present Parliament assembled, and by the Authority of the same, as follows:

VI.—Distribution of Legislative Powers.

Powers of the Parliament

91. It shall be lawful for the Queen, by and with the Advice and Consent of the Senate and House of Commons, to make Laws for the Peace, Order, and good Government Of Canada, in relation to all Matters not coming within the Classes of Subjects by this Act assigned exclusively to the Legislatures of the Provinces; and for greater Certainty, but not so as to restrict the Generality of the foregoing Terms of this Section, it is hereby declared that (notwithstanding anything in this Act) the exclusive Legislative Authority of the Parliament of Canada extends to all Matters coming within the Classes of Subjects next hereinafter enumerated; that is to, say:— *LegislativeAuthority of Parliament of Canada*

1. The Public Debt and Property.

2. The Regulation of Trade and Commerce.

3. The raising of Money by any Mode or System of Taxation.

4. The borrowing of Money on the Public Credit.

5. Postal Service.

6. The Census and Statistics

7.   Militia, Military and Naval Service, and Defence.

8.   The fixing of and providing for the Salaries and Allowances of Civil and other Officers of the Government of Canada.

9.   Beacons, Buoys, Lighthouses, and Sable Island.

10. Navigation and Shipping.

11. Quarantine and the Establishment and Maintenance of Marine Hospitals.

12. Sea Coast and Inland Fisheries.

13. Ferries between a Province and any British or Foreign Country or between Two Provinces.

14. Currency and Coinage.

15. Banking, Incorporation of Banks, and the Issue of Paper Money.

16. Savings Banks.

17. Weights and Measures.

18. Bills of Exchange and Promissory Notes.

19. Interest.

20. Legal Tender.

21. Bankruptcy and Insolvency.

22. Patents of Invention and Discovery.

23. Copyrights.

24. Indians, and Lands reserved for the Indians.

25. Naturalization and Aliens.

26. Marriage and Divorce.

27. The Criminal Law, except the Constitution of Courtsof Criminal Jurisdiction, but including the Procedure in Criminal Matters.

28. The Establishment, Maintenance, and Management of Penitentiaries.

29. Such Classes of Subjects as are expressly excepted the Enumertion of the Classes of Subjects by this Act assigned exclusively to the Legislatures of the Provinces.

And any Matter coming within any of the Classes of Subjects enumerated in this Section shall not be deemed to come within the Class of Matters of a local or private Nature comprised in the Enumeration of the Classes of Subjects by this Act assigned exclusively to the Legislatures of the Provinces.

Excerpts from the Indian Act, 1876

An Act to Amend and Consolidate the Laws Respecting Indians

Whereas it is expedient to amend and consolidate the laws respecting Indians: Therefore Her Majesty, by and with the advice and consent of the Senate and House of Commons of Canada, enacts as follows:

1. This Act shall be known and may be cited as "*The Indian Act* 1876," and shall apply to all the Provinces, and to the North West Territories, including the Territory of Keewatin.

2. The Minister of the Interior shall be Superintendent-General of Indian Affairs, and shall be governed in the supervision of the said affairs, and in the control and management of the reserves, lands, moneys and property of Indians in Canada by the provisions of this Act.

Terms

3. The following terms contained in this Act shall be held to have the meaning hereinafter assigned to them, unless such meaning be repugnant to the subject or inconsistent with the context:

(1) The term "band" means any tribe, band or body of Indians who own or are interested in a reserve or in Indian lands in common, of which the legal tide is vested in the Crown, or who share alike in the distribution of any annuities or interest moneys for which the Government of Canada is responsible; the term "the band" means the band to which the context relates; and the term "band," when action is being taken by the band as such, means the band in council...

(3) The term "Indian" means

First. Any male person of Indian blood reputed to belong to a particular band;

Secondly. Any child of such person;

Thirdly. Any woman who is or was lawfully married to such person:

(a) Provided that any illegitimate child, unless having shared with the consent of the band in the distribution moneys of such band for a period exceeding two years, may, at any time, be excluded from the membership thereof by the band, if such proceeding be sanctioned by the Superintendent-General:

(b) Provided that any Indian having for five years continuously resided in a foreign country shall with the sanction of the Superintendent-General, cease to be a member thereof and shall not be permitted to become again a member thereof, or of any other band, unless the consent of the band with the approval of the Superintendent-General or his agent, be first had and obtained; but this provision shall not apply to any professional man, mechanic, missionary, teacher or interpreter, while discharging his or her duty as such:

(c) Provided that any Indian woman marrying any other than an Indian or a non-treaty Indian shall cease to be an Indian in any respect within the meaning of this Act, except that she shall be entitled to share equally with the members of the band to which she formerly belonged, in the annual or semi-annual distribution of their annuities, interest moneys and rents, but this income may be commuted to her at any time at ten years' purchase with the consent of the band:

(d) Provided that any Indian woman marrying an Indian of any other band, or a non-treaty Indian shall cease to be a member of the band to which she formerly belonged, and become a member of the band or irregular band of which her husband is a member:

(e) Provided also that no half-breed in Manitoba who has shared in the distribution of half-breed lands shall be accounted an Indian; and that no half-breed head of a family (except the widow of an Indian, or a half-breed who has already been admitted into a treaty), shall, unless under very special circumstances, to be determined by the Superintendent-General or his agent, be accounted an Indian, or entitled to be admitted into any Indian treaty.

(4) The term "non-treaty Indian" means any person of Indian blood who is reputed to belong to an irregular band, or who follows the Indian mode of life, even though such person be only a temporary resident in Canada.

(5) The term "enfranchised Indian" means any Indian, his wife or minor unmarried child, who has received letters patent granting him in fee simple any portion of the reserve which may have been allotted to him, his wife and minor children, by the band to which he belongs, or any unmarried Indian who may have received letters

patent for an allotment of the reserve.

(6) The term "reserve" means any tract or tracts of land set apart by treaty or otherwise for the use or benefit of or granted to a particular band of Indians, of which the legal title is in the Crown, but which is unsurrendered, and includes all the trees, wood, timber, soil, stone, minerals, metals, or other valuables thereon or therein.

(7) The term "special reserve" means any tract or tracts of land and everything belonging thereto set apart for the use or benefit of any band or irregular band of Indians, the title of which is vested in a society, corporation or community legally established, and capable of suing and being sued, or in a person or persons of European descent, but which land is held in trust for, or benevolently allowed to be used by, such band or irregular band of Indians.

(8) The term "Indian lands" means any reserve or portion of a reserve which has been surrendered to the Crown....

Reserves

4. All reserves for Indians or for any band of Indians, or held in trust for their benefit shall be deemed to be reserved and held for the same purposes as before the passing of this Act, but subject to its provisions.

5. The Superintendent-General may authorize surveys, plans and reports to be made of any reserve for Indians, shewing and distinguishing the improved lands, the forests and lands fit for settlement, and such other information as may be required; and may authorize that the whole or any portion of a reserve be subdivided into lots.

6. In a reserve, or portion of a reserve, subdivided by survey into lots, no Indian shall be deemed to be lawfully in possession of one or more of such lots, or part of a lot, unless he or she has been or shall be located for the same by the band, with the approval of the Superintendent-General:

Provided that no Indian shall be dispossessed of any lot or part of a lot, on which he or she has improvements, without receiving compensation therefor, (at a valuation to be approved by the Superintendent-General) from the Indian who obtains the lot or part of a lot or from the funds of the band, as may be determined by the Superintendent-General.

7. On the Superintendent-General approving of any location as aforesaid, he shall issue in triplicate a ticket granting a location title to such Indian, one triplicate of which he shall retain in a book to be kept for the purpose; the other two he shall forward to the local agent, one

to be delivered to the Indian in whose favor it was issued, the other to be filed by the agent who shall permit it to be copied into the register of the band, if such register has been established....

Protection of Reserves

11. No person, or Indian other than an Indian of the band, shall settle, reside or hunt upon, occupy or use any land or marsh, or shall settle, reside upon or occupy any road, or allowance for roads running through any reserve belonging to or occupied by such band; ...

Surrenders

25. No reserve or portion of a reserve shall be sold, alienated or leased until it has been released or surrendered to the Crown for the purposes of this Act.

26. No release or surrender of a reserve, or portion of a reserve, held for the use of the Indian, of any band or of any individual Indian, shall be valid or binding, except on the following conditions:

(1) The release or surrender shall be assented to by a majority of the male members of that band of the full age of twenty-one years, at a meeting or council thereof summoned for that purpose according to their rules, and held in the presence of the Superintendent-General or of an officer duly authorized to attend such council by the Governor in Council or by the Superintendent-General; Provided, that no Indian shall be entitled to vote or be present at such council, unless he habitually resides on or near and is interested in the reserve in question;

(2) The fact that such release or surrender has been assented to by the band at such council or meeting, shall be certified on oath before some judge of a superior, county, or district court or stipendiary magistrate, by the Superintendent-General or by the officer authorized by him to attend such council or meeting, and by some one of the chiefs or principal men present thereat and entitled to vote, and when so certified as aforesaid shall be submitted to the Governor in Council for acceptance or refusal;

(3) But nothing herein contained shall be construed to prevent the Superintendent-General from issuing a license to any person or Indian to cut and remove trees, wood, timber and hay, or to quarry and remove stone and gravel on and from the reserve; Provided he, or his agent acting by his instructions, first obtain the consent of the band thereto in the ordinary manner as hereinafter provided.

27. It shall not be lawful to introduce at any council or meeting

of Indians held for the purpose of discussing or of assenting to a release or surrender of a reserve or portion thereof, or of assenting to the issuing of a timber or other license, any intoxicant; and any person introducing at such meeting, and any agent or officer employed by the Superintendent-General, or by the Governor in Council, introducing, allowing or countenancing by his presence the use of such intoxicant among such Indians a week before, at, or a week after, any such council or meeting, shall forfeit two hundred dollars, recoverable by action in any of the superior courts of law, one half of which penalty shall go to the informer....

Management and Sale of Indian Lands

30. No agent for the sale of Indian lands shall, within his division, directly or indirectly, unless under an order of the Governor in Council, purchase any land which he is appointed to sell, or become proprietor of or interested in any such land, during the time of his agency; and any such purchase or interest shall be void;...

Management and Sale of Timber

45. The Superintendent-General, or any officer or agent authorized by him to that effect may grant licenses to cut timber on reserves and ungranted Indian lands at such rates, and subject to such conditions, regulations and restrictions, as may from time to time be established by the Governor in Council, such conditions, regulations and restrictions to be adapted to the locality in which such reserves or lands are situated....

Moneys

58. All moneys or securities of any kind applicable to the support or benefit of Indians, or any band of Indians, and all moneys accrued or hereafter to accrue from the sale of any Indian lands or of any timber on any reserves or Indian lands shall, subject to the provisions of this Act, be applicable to the same purposes, and be dealt with in the same manner as they might have been applied to or dealt with before the passing of this Act.

59. The Governor in Council may, subject to the provisions of this Act, direct how, and in what manner, and by whom the moneys arising from sales of Indian lands, and from the property held or to be held in trust for the Indians, or from any timber on Indian lands or reserves, or from any other source for the benefit of Indians (with the exception of any small sum not exceeding ten per cent, of the proceeds

of any lands, timber or property, which may be agreed at the time of the surrender to be paid to the members of the band interested therein), shall be invested from time to time, and how the payments or assistance to which the Indians may be entitled shall be made or given, and may provide for the general management of such moneys, and direct what percentage or proportion thereof shall be set apart from time to time, to cover the cost of and attendant upon the management of reserves, lands, property and moneys under the provisions of this Act, and for the construction or repair of roads passing through such reserves or lands, and by way of contribution to schools frequented by such Indians.

60. The proceeds arising from the sale or lease of any Indian lands, or from the timber, hay, stone, minerals or other valuables thereon, or on a reserve, shall be paid to the Receiver General to the credit of the Indian fund.

Councils and Chiefs

61. At the election of a chief or chiefs, or the granting of any ordinary consent required of a band of Indians under this Act those entitled to vote at the council or meeting thereof shall be the male members of the band of the full age of twenty-one years; and the vote of a majority of such members at a council or meeting of the band summoned according to their rules, and held in the presence of the Superintendent-General, or an agent acting under his instructions, shall be sufficient to determine such election, or grant such consent;

Provided that in the case of any band having a council of chiefs or councillors, any ordinary consent required of the band may be granted by a vote of a majority of such chiefs or councillors at a council summoned according to their rules, and held in the presence of the Superintendent-General or his agent.

62. The Governor in Council may order that the chiefs of any band of Indians shall be elected, as hereinbefore provided, at such time and place, as the Superintendent-General may direct, and they shall in such case be elected for a period of three years, unless deposed by the Governor for dishonesty, intemperance, immorality, or incompetency, and they may be in the proportion of one head chief and two second chiefs or councillors for every two hundred Indians; but any such band composed of thirty Indians may have one chief: Provided always, that all life chiefs now living shall continue as such until death or resignation, or until their removal by the Governor for dishonesty, intemperance, immorality, or incompetency.

63. The chief or chiefs of any band in council may frame, subject

to confirmation by the Governor in Council, rules and regulations for the following subjects, viz.:

(1) The care of the public health;

(2) The observance of order and decorum at assemblies of the Indians in general council, or on other occasions;

(3) The repression of intemperance and profligacy.

(4) The prevention of trespass by cattle;

(5) The maintenance of roads, bridges, ditches and fences;

(6) The construction and repair of school houses, council houses and other Indian public buildings;

(7) The establishment of pounds and the appointment of pound-keepers;

(8) The locating of the land in their reserves, and the establishment of a register of such locations.

Privileges of Indians

64. No Indian or non-treaty Indian shall be liable to be taxed for any real or personal property, unless he holds real estate under lease or in fee simple, or personal property, outside of the reserve or special reserve, in which case he shall be liable to be taxed for such real or personal property at the same rate as other persons in the locality in which it is situate.

65. All land vested in the Crown, or in any person or body corporate, in trust for or for the use of any Indian or non-treaty Indian, or any band or irregular band of Indians or non-treaty Indians shall be exempt from taxation.

66. No person shall take any security or otherwise obtain any lien or charge, whether by mortgage, judgment or otherwise, upon real or personal property of any Indian or non-treaty Indian within Canada, except on real or personal property subject to taxation under section sixty-four of this Act: Provided always, that any person selling any article to an Indian or non-treaty Indian may, notwithstanding this section, take security on such article for any part of the price thereof which may be unpaid.

67. Indians and non-treaty Indians shall have the right to sue for debts due to them or in respect of any tort or wrong inflicted upon them, or to compel the performance of obligations contracted with them...

Disabilities and Penalties

70. No Indian or non-treaty Indian, resident in the province of Manitoba, the North-West Territories or the territory of Keewatin, shall be held capable of having acquired or acquiring a homestead of pre-emption right to a quarter section, or any portion of land in any surveyed or unsurveyed lands in the said province of Manitoba, the North-West Territories or the territory of Keewatin, or the right to share in the distribution of any lands allotted to half-breeds,...

71. Any Indian convicted of any crime punishable by imprisonment in any penitentiary or other place of confinement, shall, during such imprisonment, be excluded from participating in the annuities, interest money, or rents payable to the band of which he or she is a member, and whenever any Indian shall be convicted of any crime punishable by imprisonment in a penitentiary or other place of confinement, the legal costs incurred in procuring such conviction, and in carrying out the various sentences recorded, may be defrayed by the Superintendent-General, and paid out of any annuity or interest coming to such Indian, or to the band, as the case may be.

72. The Superintendent-General shall have power to stop the payment of the annuity and interest money of any Indian who may be proved, to the satisfaction of the Superintendent-General, to have been guilty of deserting his or her family, and the said Superintendent-General may apply the same towards the support of any family, woman or child so deserted; also to stop the payment of the annuity and interest money of any woman having no children, who deserts her husband and lives immorally with another man.

73. The Superintendent-General in cases where sick, or disabled, or aged and destitute persons are not provided for by the band of Indians of which they are members, may furnish sufficient aid from the funds of the band for the relief of such sick, disabled, aged or destitute persons.

Evidence of Non-Christian Indians

74. Upon any inquest, or upon any enquiry into any matter involving a criminal charge, or upon the trial of any crime or offence whatsoever or by whomsoever committed, it shall be lawful for any court, judge, stipendiary magistrate, coroner or justice of the peace to receive the evidence of any Indian or non-treaty Indian, who is destitute of the knowledge of God and of any fixed and clear belief in religion or in a future state of rewards and punishments, without administering the usual form of oath to any such Indian, or non-

treaty Indian, as aforesaid, upon his solemn affirmation or declaration to tell the truth, the whole truth and nothing but the truth, or in such form as may be approved by such court, judge, stipendiary magistrate, coroner or justice of the peace as most binding on the conscience of such Indian or non-treaty Indian....

Intoxicants

79. Whoever sells, exchanges with, barters, supplies or gives to any Indian, or non-treaty Indian in Canada, any kind of intoxicant or causes or procures the same to be done, or connives or attempts thereat or opens or keeps, or causes to be opened or kept on any reserve or special reserve, a tavern, house or building where any intoxicant is sold, bartered, exchanged or given, or is found in possession of any intoxicant in the house, tent, wigwam or place of abode of any Indian or non-treaty Indian, shall, on conviction thereof before any judge, stipendiary magistrate or two justices of the peace, upon the evidence of one credible witness other than the informer or prosecutor, be liable to imprisonment for a period not less than one month nor exceeding six months, with or without hard labor, and be fined not less than fifty nor more than three hundred dollars, with costs of prosecution,—one moiety of the fine to go to the informer or prosecutor, and the other moiety to her Majesty, to form part of the fund for the benefit of that body of Indians or non-treaty Indians, with respect to one or more members of which the offence was committed: ... and any Indian or non-treaty Indian who makes or manufactures any intoxicant or who has in his possession, or concealed, or who sells, exchanges with, barters, supplies or gives to any other Indian or non-treaty Indian in Canada any kind of intoxicant shall, on conviction thereof, before any judge, stipendiary magistrate or two justices of the peace, upon the evidence of one credible witness other than the informer or prosecutor, be liable to imprisonment for a period of not less than one month nor more than six months, with or without hard labor, and in all cases arising under this section, Indians or non-treaty Indians, shall be competent witnesses: but no penalty shall be incurred in case of sickness where the intoxicant is made use of under the sanction of a medical man or under the directions of a minister of religion...

83. It shall be lawful for any constable, without process of law, to arrest any Indian or non-treaty Indian whom he may find in a state of intoxication, and to convey him to any common gaol, house of correction, lock-up or other place of confinement there to be kept until he shall have become sober; and such Indian or non-treaty Indian shall

when sober, be brought before any judge, stipendiary magistrate, or justice of the peace, and if convicted being so found in a state of intoxication shall be liable to imprisonment in any common gaol, house of correction, lock-up or other place of confinement for any period not exceeding one month. And if any Indian or non-treaty Indian, having been so convicted as aforesaid, refuses upon examination to state or give information of the person, place and time from whom, where and when, he procured such intoxicant and if from any other Indian or non-treaty Indian, then, if within his knowledge, from whom, where and when such intoxicant was originally procured or received, he shall be liable to imprisonment as aforesaid for a further period not exceeding fourteen days....

Enfranchisement

86. Whenever any Indian man, or unmarried woman, of the full age of twenty-one years, obtains the consent of the band of which he or she is a member to become enfranchised, and whenever such Indian has been assigned by the band a suitable allotment of land for that purpose, the local agent shall report such action of the band, and the name of the applicant to the Superintendent-General; whereupon the said Superintendent-General, if satisfied that the proposed allotment of land is equitable, shall authorize some competent person to report whether the applicant is an Indian who, from the degree of civilization to which he or she has attained, and the character for integrity, morality and sobriety which he or she bears, appears to be qualified to become a proprietor of land in fee simple, and upon the favorable report of such person, the Superintendent-General may grant such Indian a location ticket as a probationary Indian, for the land allotted to him or her by the band.

(1) Any Indian who may be admitted to the degree of Doctor of Medicine, or to any other degree by any University of Learning, or who may be admitted in any Province of the Dominion to practice law either as an Advocate or as a Barrister or Counsellor or Solicitor or Attorney or to be a Notary Public, or who may enter Holy Orders or who may be licensed by any denomination of Christians as a Minister of the Gospel, shall *ipso facto* become and be enfranchised under this Act.

87. After the expiration of three years (or such longer period as the Superintendent-General may deem necessary in the event of such Indian's conduct not being satisfactory), the Governor may, on the report of the Superintendent-General, order the issue of letters patent

granting to such Indian in fee simple the land which had, with this object in view, been allotted to him or her by location ticket.

88. Every such Indian shall, before the issue of the letters patent mentioned in the next preceding section, declare to the Superintendent-General the name and surname by which he or she wishes to be enfranchised and thereafter known, and on his or her receiving such letters patent, in such name and surname, he or she shall be held to be also enfranchised, and he or she shall thereafter be known by such name or surname, and if such Indian be a married man his wife and minor unmarried children also shall be held to be enfranchised; and from the date of such letters patent the provisions of this Act and of any Act or law making any distinction between the legal rights, privileges, disabilities and liabilities of Indians and those of Her Majesty's other subjects shall cease to apply to any Indian, or to the wife or minor unmarried children of any Indian aforesaid, so declared to be enfranchised, who shall no longer be deemed Indians within the meaning of the laws relating to Indians, except in so far as their right to participate in the annuities and interest moneys, and rents and councils of the band or Indians to which they belonged is concerned ...

92. Any Indian, not a member of the band, or any non-treaty Indian, who, with the consent of the band and the approval of the Superintendent-General, has been permitted to reside upon the reserve, or obtain a location thereon, may, on being assigned a suitable allotment of land by the band for enfranchisement, become enfranchised on the same terms and conditions as a member of the band; ...

93. Whenever any band of Indians, at a council summoned for the purpose according to their rules, and held in the presence of the Superintendent-General or of an agent duly authorized by him to attend such council, decides to allow every member of the band who chooses, and who may be found qualified, to become enfranchised, and to receive his or her share of the principal moneys of the band, and sets apart for such member a suitable allotment of land for the purpose, any applicant of such band after such a decision may be dealt with as provided in the seven next preceding sections until his or her enfranchisement is attained; and whenever any member of the band, who for the three years immediately succeeding the date on which he or she was granted letters patent, or for any longer period that the Superintendent-General may deem necessary, by his or her exemplary good conduct and management of property, proves that he or she is qualified to receive his or her share of such moneys, the Governor may, on the report of the Superintendent-General to that effect order

that the said Indian be paid his or her share of the capital funds at the credit of the band, or his or her share of the principal of the annuities of the band, estimated as yielding five per cent, out of such moneys as may be provided for the purpose by Parliament; and if such Indian be a married man then he shall also be paid his wife and minor unmarried children's share of such funds and other principal moneys, and if such Indian be a widow, she shall also be paid her minor unmarried children's share: and the unmarried children of such married Indians, who become of age during either the probationary period for enfranchisement or for payment of such moneys, if qualified by the character for integrity, morality and sobriety which they bear, shall receive their own share of such moneys when their parents are paid, and if not so qualified, before they can become enfranchised or receive payment of such moneys they must themselves pass through the probationary periods; and all such Indians and their unmarried minor children who are paid their share of the principal moneys of their band as aforesaid, shall thenceforward cease in every respect to be Indians of any class within the meaning of this Act or Indians within the meaning of any other Act or law.

94. Sections eighty-six to ninety-three, both inclusive, of this Act, shall not apply to any band of Indians in the Province of British Columbia, the Province of Manitoba, the North-West Territories, or the Territory of Keewatin, save in so far as the said sections may, by proclamation of the Governor-General, be from time to time extended, as they may be, to any band of Indians in any of the said provinces or territories....

Assented to 12 April 1876

Indian Act Amendments

Editors' note: The amendments to the Indian Act below show the increasingly repressive government policy.

1884 Indian Act Amendment: The Potlatch Law

"Every Indian or other person who engages in or assists in celebrating the Indian festival known as the "Potlach" [*sic*] or in the Indian dance known as the "Tamanawas" [*sic*] is guilty of a misdemeanour and shall be liable to imprisonment for a term of not more than six or not less than two months in any gaol or other place of confinement; and any Indian or other person who encourages, either directly or indirectly, an Indian or Indians to get up such a festival or dance, or to celebrate the same, or who shall assist in the celebration of same is guilty of a like offence, and shall be liable to the same punishment" (*Statutes of Canada* 1884, 47 Vic., c.27).

1895 Amendment to the Indian Act: Section 114

"Every Indian or other person who engages in, or assists in celebrating or encourages either directly or indirectly another to celebrate, any Indian festival, dance or other ceremony of which the giving away or paying or giving back of money, goods, or articles of any sort forms a part, or is a feature, whether such gift of money, goods or articles takes place before, at, or after the celebration of the same, and every Indian or other person who engages or assists in any celebration or dance of which the wounding or mutilation of the dead or living body of any human being or animal forms a part or is a feature, is guilty of an indictable offence."

1914 Amendment to the Indian Act: Section 149

Any Indian in the province of Manitoba, Saskatchewan, Alberta, British Columbia, or the Territories who participates in any Indian dance outside the bounds of his own reserve, or who participates in any show, exhibition, performance, stampede or pageant in aboriginal costume without the consent of the Superintendent General of Indian Affairs or his authorized Agent, and any person who induces or employs any Indian to take part in such dance, show, exhibition, performance, stampede or pageant, or induces any Indian to leave his reserve or employs any Indian for such a purpose, whether the dance, show, exhibition, stampede or pageant has taken place or not, shall on summary conviction be liable to a penalty not exceeding twenty-five dollars, or to imprisonment for one month, or to both penalty and imprisonment.

Editors' note: Duncan Campbell Scott (1862–1947) joined the Department of Indian Affairs in 1879 and was Deputy Superintendent from 1913–1932. This letter reflects the attitudes that informed policy during this period.

CANADA

DEPARTMENT OF INDIAN AFFAIRS

CIRCULAR   OTTAWA, 15th December, 1921.

Sir, -

It is observed with alarm that the holding of dances by the Indians on their reserves is on the increase, and that these practices tend to disorganize the efforts which the Department is putting forth to make them self-supporting.

I have, therefore, to direct you to use your utmost endeavours to dissuade the Indians from excessive indulgence in the practice of dancing. You should suppress any dances which cause waste of time, interfere with the occupations of the Indians, unsettle them for serious work, injure their health or encourage them in sloth and idleness. You should also dissuade, and, if possible, prevent them from leaving their reserves for the purpose of attending fairs, exhibitions, etc., when their absence would result in their own farming and other interests being neglected. It is realized that reasonable amusement and recreation should be enjoyed by Indians, but they should not be allowed to dissipate their energies and abandon themselves to demoralizing amusements. By the use of tact and firmness you can obtain control and keep it, and this obstacle to continued progress will then disappear.

The rooms, halls or other places in which Indians congregate should be under constant inspections. They should be scrubbed, fumigated, cleansed or disinfected to prevent the dissemination of disease. The Indians should be instructed in regard to the matter of proper ventilation and the avoidance of over-crowding rooms where public assemblies are being held, and proper arrangement should be made for the shelter of their horses and ponies. The Agent will avail himself of the services of the medical attendant of his agency in this connection.

Except where further information is desired, there will be no necessity to acknowledge the receipt of this circular.

Yours very truly,

134

The Treaties at Forts Carlton and Pitt, Number Six

A RTICLES OF A TREATY made and concluded near Carlton, on the twenty-third day of August, and on the twenty-eighth day of said month, respectively, and near Fort Pitt on the ninth day of September, in the year of Our Lord one thousand eight hundred and seventy-six, between Her Most Gracious Majesty the Queen of Great Britain and Ireland, by her Commissioners, the Honorable Alexander Morris, Lieutenant Governor of the Province of Manitoba and the North-West Territories, and the Honorable James McKay and the Honorable William Joseph Christie, of the one part, and the Plain and the Wood Cree Tribes of Indians, and the other Tribes of Indians, inhabitants of the country within the limits hereinafter defined and described, by their Chiefs, chosen and named as hereinafter mentioned, of the other part.

Whereas the Indians inhabiting the said country have, pursuant to an appointment made by the said Commissioners, been convened at meetings at Fort Carlton, Fort Pitt and Battle River, to deliberate upon certain matters of interest to Her Most Gracious Majesty, of the one part, and the said Indians of the other;

And whereas the said Indians have been notified and informed by Her Majesty's said Commissioners that it is the desire of Her Majesty to open up for settlement, immigration and such other purposes as to Her Majesty may seem meet, a tract of country, bounded and described as hereinafter mentioned, and to obtain the consent thereto of her Indian subjects inhabiting the said tract, and to make a treaty and arrange with them, so that there may be peace and good will between them and Her Majesty, and that they may know and be assured of what allowance they are to count upon and receive from Her Majesty's bounty and benevolence;

And whereas the Indians of the said tract, duly convened in council as aforesaid, and being requested by Her Majesty's Commissioners to name certain Chiefs and head men, who should be authorized, on their behalf, to conduct such negotiations and sign any treaty to be founded thereon, and to become responsible to Her Majesty for the faithful performance by their respective bands of such obligations as shall be assumed by them, the said Indians have thereupon named for that purpose, that is to say:—representing the Indians who make the treaty at Carlton, the several Chiefs and Councillors who have subscribed hereto, and representing the Indians who make the treaty at Fort Pitt, the several Chiefs and Councillors who have subscribed hereto;

And thereupon, in open council, the different bands having presented their Chiefs to the said Commissioners as the Chiefs and head men, for the purposes aforesaid, of the respective bands of Indians inhabiting the district hereinafter described;

And whereas the said Commissioners then and there received and acknowledged the persons so represented, as Chiefs and head men, for the purposes aforesaid, of the respective bands of Indians inhabiting the said district hereinafter described;

And whereas the said Commissioners have proceeded to negotiate a treaty with the said Indians, and the same has been finally agreed upon and concluded as follows, that is to say:

The Plain and Wood Cree Tribes of Indians, and all other the Indians, inhabiting the district hereinafter described and defined, do hereby cede, release, surrender and yield up to the Government of the Dominion of Canada for Her Majesty the Queen and her successors forever, all their rights, titles and privileges whatsoever, to the lands included within the following limits, that is to say:

Commencing at the mouth of the river emptying into the north-west angle of Cumberland Lake, thence westerly up the said river to the source, thence on a straight line in a westerly direction to the head of Green Lake, thence northerly to the elbow in the Beaver River, thence down the said river northerly to a point twenty miles from the said elbow; thence in a westerly direction, keeping on a line generally parallel with the said Beaver River (above the elbow), and about twenty miles distance therefrom, to the source of the said river; thence northerly to the north-easterly point of the south shore of Red Deer Lake, continuing westerly along the said shore to the western limit thereof, and thence due west to the Athabaska River, thence up the said river, against the stream, to the Jasper House, in the Rocky Mountains; thence on a course south-eastwardly, following the easterly range of the Mountains, to the source of the main branch of the Red Deer River; thence down the said river, with the stream, to the junction therewith of the outlet of the river, being the outlet of the Buffalo Lake; thence due east twenty miles; thence on a straight line south-eastwardly to the mouth of the said Red Deer River on the South Branch of the Saskatchewan river; thence eastwardly and northwardly, following on the boundaries of the tracts conceded by the several Treaties numbered Four and Five, to the place of beginning;

And also all their rights, titles and privileges whatsoever, to all other lands, wherever situated, in the North-West Territories, or in any other Province or portion of Her Majesty's Dominions, situated and being within the Dominion of Canada;

The tract comprised within the lines above described, embracing an area of one hundred and twenty-one thousand square miles, be the same more or less;

To have and to hold the same to Her Majesty the Queen and her successors forever;

And Her Majesty the Queen hereby agrees and undertakes to lay aside reserves for farming lands, due respect being had to lands at present cultivated by the said Indians, and other reserves for the benefit of the said Indians, to be administered and dealt with for them by Her Majesty's Government of the Dominion of Canada, provided all such reserves shall not exceed in all one square mile for each family of five, or in that proportion for larger or smaller families, in manner following, that is to say:—

That the Chief Superintendent of Indian Affairs shall depute and send a suitable person to determine and set apart the reserves for each band, after consulting with the Indians thereof as to the locality which may be found to be most suitable for them;

Provided, however, that Her Majesty reserves the right to deal with any settlers within the bounds of any lands reserved for any band as she shall deem fit, and also that the aforesaid reserves of land or any interest therein may be sold or otherwise disposed of by Her Majesty's Government for the use and benefit of the said Indians entitled thereto, with their consent first had and obtained; and with a view to show the satisfaction of Her Majesty with the behavior and good conduct of her Indians, she hereby, through her Commissioners, makes them a present of twelve dollars for each man, woman and child belonging to the bands here represented, in extinguishment of all claims heretofore preferred;

And further, Her Majesty agrees to maintain schools for instruction in such reserves hereby made, as to her Government of the Dominion of Canada may seem advisable, whenever the Indians of the reserve shall desire it;

Her Majesty further agrees with her said Indians that within the boundary of Indian reserves, until otherwise determined by her Government of the Dominion of Canada, no intoxicating liquor shall be allowed to be introduced or sold, and all laws now in force or hereafter to be enacted to preserve her Indian subjects inhabiting the reserves or living elsewhere within her North-West Territories from the evil influence of the use of intoxicating liquors, shall be strictly enforced;

Her Majesty further agrees with her said Indians that they, the said Indians, shall have right to pursue their avocations of hunting and fishing throughout the tract surrendered as hereinbefore described, subject to such regulations as may from time to time be made by her Government of her Dominion of Canada, and saving and excepting such tracts as may from time to time be required or taken up for settlement, mining, lumbering or other purposes by her said Government of the Dominion of Canada, or by any of the subjects thereof, duly authorized therefor, by the said Government;

It is further agreed between Her Majesty and her said Indians, that such sections of the reserves above indicated as may at any time be required for public works or buildings of what nature soever, may be appropriated for that purpose by Her Majesty's Government of the Dominion of Canada, due compensation being made for the value of any improvements thereon;

And further, that Her Majesty's Commissioners shall, as soon as possible after the execution of this treaty, cause to be taken, an accurate census of an the Indians inhabiting the tract above described, distributing them in families, and shall in every year ensuing the date hereof, at some period in each year, to be duly notified to the Indians, and at a place or places to be appointed for that purpose, within the territories ceded, pay to each Indian person the sum of five dollars per head yearly;

It is further agreed between Her Majesty and the said Indians that the sum of fifteen hundred dollars per annum, shall be yearly and every year expended by Her Majesty in the purchase of ammunition and twine for nets for the use of the said Indians, in manner following, that is to say:—In the reasonable discretion as regards the distribution thereof, among the Indians inhabiting the several reserves, or otherwise included herein, of Her Majesty's Indian Agent having the supervision of this treaty;

It is further agreed between Her Majesty and the said Indians that the following articles shall be supplied to any band of the said Indians who are now cultivating the soil, or who shall hereafter commence to cultivate the land, that is to say:—Four hoes for every family actually cultivating, also two spades per family as aforesaid; one plough for every three families as aforesaid, one harrow for every three families as aforesaid; two scythes, and one whetstone and two hayforks and two reaping-hooks for every family as aforesaid; and also two axes, and also one cross-cut saw, and also one hand-saw, one pit-saw, the necessary files, one grindstone and one auger for each band; and also for each Chief, for the use of his band, one chest of ordinary carpenter's tools; also for each band, enough of wheat, barley, potatoes and oats to plant the land actually broken up for cultivation by such band; also for each band, four oxen, one bull and six cows, also one boar and two sows, and one handmill when any band shall raise sufficient grain therefor; all the aforesaid articles to be given *once for all* for the encouragement of the practice of agriculture among the Indians;

It is further agreed between Her Majesty and the said Indians, that each Chief, duly recognized as such, shall receive an annual salary of twenty-five dollars per annum; and each subordinate officer, not exceeding four for each band, shall receive fifteen dollars per annum; and each such Chief and subordinate officer as aforesaid, shall also receive, once every three years, a suitable suit of clothing, and each Chief shall receive, in recognition of the closing of the treaty, a suitable flag and medal, and also, as soon as convenient, one horse, harness and waggon;

That in the event hereafter of the Indians comprised within this treaty being overtaken by any pestilence, or by a general famine, the Queen, on being satisfied and certified thereof by her Indian Agent or Agents, will grant to the Indians assistance of such character and to such extent as her Chief Superintendent of Indian Affairs shall deem necessary and sufficient to relieve the Indians from the calamity that shall have befallen them;

That during the next three years, after two or more of the reserves hereby agreed to be set apart to the Indians, shall have been agreed upon and surveyed, there shall be granted to the Indians included under the Chiefs adhering to the treaty at Carlton, each spring, the sum of one thousand dollars to be expended for them by Her Majesty's Indian Agents, in the purchase of provisions for the use of such of the band as are actually settled on the reserves and are engaged in cultivating the soil, to assist them in such cultivation;

That a medicine chest shall be kept at the house of each Indian Agent for the use and benefit of the Indians, at the discretion of such Agent;

That with regard to the Indians included under the Chiefs adhering to the treaty at Fort Pitt, and to those under Chiefs within the treaty limits who may hereafter give their adhesion hereto (exclusively, however, of the Indians of the Carlton Region) there shall, during three years, after two or more reserves shall have been agreed upon and surveyed, be distributed each spring among the bands cultivating the soil on such reserves, by Her Majesty's Chief Indian Agent for this treaty in his discretion, a sum not exceeding one thousand dollars, in the purchase of provisions for the use of such members of the band as are actually settled on the reserves and engaged in the cultivation of the soil, to assist and encourage them in such cultivation;

That, in lieu of waggons, if they desire it, and declare their option to that effect, there shall be given to each of the Chiefs adhering hereto, at Fort Pitt or elsewhere hereafter (exclusively of those in the Carlton District) in recognition of this treaty, so soon as the same can be conveniently transported, two carts, with iron bushings and tires;

And the undersigned Chiefs, on their behalf, and on behalf of all other Indians inhabiting the tract within ceded, do hereby solemnly promise and engage to strictly observe this treaty, and also to conduct and behave themselves as good and loyal subjects of Her Majesty the Queen;

They promise and engage that they will in all respects obey and abide by the law, and they will maintain peace and good order between each other, and also between themselves and other tribes of Indians, and between themselves and others of Her Majesty's subjects, whether Indians or whites, now inhabiting or hereafter to inhabit any part of the said ceded tracts, and that they will not molest the person or property of any inhabitant of such ceded tracts, or the property of Her Majesty the Queen, or interfere with or trouble any person passing or travelling through the said tracts or any part thereof; and that they will aid and assist the officers of Her Majesty in bringing to justice and punishment any Indian offending against the stipulations of this treaty, or infringing the laws in force in the country so ceded.

In witness whereof, Her Majesty's said Commissioners and the said Indian Chiefs have hereunto subscribed and set their hands, at or near Fort Carlton, on the day and year aforesaid, and near Fort Pitt on the day above aforesaid.

Scrip

By order of Governor-in-Council, James A. J. McKenna was appointed to be Scrip Commissioner to deal with Métis claims in the Treaty 10 region. Throughout the month, Treaties were signed at the same time as Scrip was issue—they are parallel processes in the month. All Métis residents were to receive Scrip for 240 acres or dollars. Scrip could only be redeemed for land at a Dominion Lands Office and only for lands open for homestead entry.

The following pages are reproductions of the applications for the Scrip documents and Scrip coupons for Baptise and Marie Anne Nawtamaugan (Nanotomaken), the couple in the photograph below.

Baptiste and Marie Anne Nawtamaugan at
Ile-à-la-Crosse, Saskatchewan, 1920
National Archives of Canada

Scrip Application Form A: Baptiste Nanotomaken (Nawtamaugan) residing in Isle à la Crosse in 1906.

Baptiste was born in Isle à la Crosse and has always lived here to his present age of 69 years. His father was known as Nanatomokan and was a half-breed. His mother, Catherine was also a half-breed. Baptiste has never applied for or received Scrip.

The following reproductions of scrip applications are from the National Archives of Canada, RG 15, DII Vol. 1361–62.

Scrip Application Form A, page 2.

Bastiste was married twice: his first wife, Elise Des Roches, died four years ago, and he is currently married to Marie Anne who was an orphan and is a half-breed. He had six children:

Joseph, 39 yrs—married
Baptiste, 34 yrs—married
Sophie, 36 yrs—wife of François Larivierre
Therese, 25 yrs—wife of Pierre Maurice
Sara, 23 yrs—unmarried
Celestine, 28 yrs—unmarried and Scrip issued on his own evidence

Scrip Application A-2: Marie Anne (wife of Baptiste).

Form A-2. *Allow not deliver rpmt* 2/2 *ISSUED*

HALFBREED CLAIMS COMMISSION.

TREATY 10.

Before James Andrew Joseph McKenna, of the City of Winnipeg, in the Province of Manitoba, Esquire, duly appointed and sitting as Commissioner at *Isle a la Crosse* in the Province of Saskatchewan, to investigate claims of Halfbreeds in the territory situated partly in the Province of Saskatchewan and partly in the Province of Alberta and lying to the east of the territory covered by Indian Treaty numbered 8, and to the north of the territories covered by Indian Treaties numbered 5 and 6, personally came and appeared *Baptiste nanatawman*

as witness in the Claim of *Marie anne – his wife* *unable to appear because of illness* and being duly sworn, deposes as follows—

Question 1. What relationship, if any, do you bear to the person making this claim?

Answer. — *Husband. Have known her from childhood*

Question 2. Where was said person born?

Answer. *Here*

Question 3. When?

Answer. *36 yrs ago*

Question 4. Where does said person reside and for how long?

Answer. *She was brought up by the mission here – and has lived here ever since I knew her.*

Question 5. What is the name of the father?

Answer. *Don't Know*

Question 6. Is he a Whiteman, a Halfbreed or an Indian?

Answer. *Don't Know*

Question 7. What is the name of the mother?

Answer. *Don't Known*

Question 8. Is she a Whitewoman, a Halfbreed or an Indian?

Answer. *Don't Know*

Question 9. Was, or is, the person on whose behalf this claim is made a member of an Indian Band?

Answer. *No*

Question 10. Did the said person ever receive land or scrip in extinguishment of Halfbreed rights? If so, when and where?

Answer. *No*

Question 11. Was an application for such land or scrip ever previously made by or on behalf of said person? If so, when and where?

Answer. *No*

Baptiste filled this application out for Marie Anne as she was unable to appear because of illness. Baptiste has known her since childhood and states she was born in Isle à la Crosse thirty-six years ago. Marie Anne was orphaned and brought up at the Mission here.

Scrip application Form A-2, page 2.

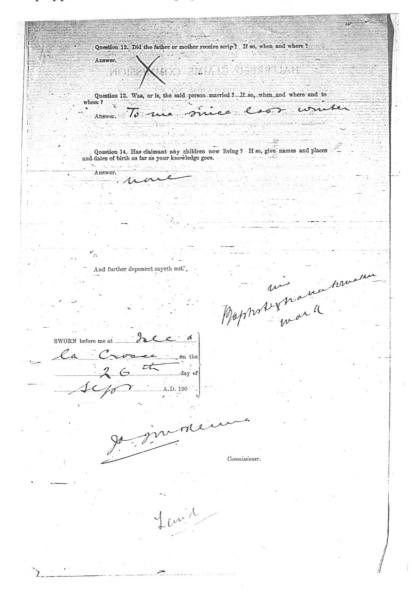

Baptiste does not know details about Marie Anne's family or whether anyone in her family had applied for Scrip or was a member of an Indian band. They have been married since last winter.

Scrip Application Form A-2: Magloire Maurice for Marie Anne who has no family relationship.

Magloire has known Marie Anne his whole life. Marie Anne was born at Island Lake near Buffalo Narrows about 35 years ago. She came from Island Lake as an infant. Because she was orphaned, she was taken in by the Mission and went to school there. She remained there until married. She has lived here ever since. Her father's name was Lafleur Daldonille, a Native probably with some white blood. Her Mother, Adeline Rabbit-Skin, was a Native. Magloire did not know if Marie Anne ever received Scrip or if she was a member of a band.

Scrip Application Form A-2, page 2.

Marie Anne's parents did not receive Scrip. Baptiste is her third husband—married last winter. Baptiste Charbois was her first husband and Alexis Sylvistre was her second husband. Magloire does not know if she has any living children.

Form A: Children from the Natomagan (Nawtamaugan) family
registered with the Catholic Mission at Isle à la Crosse, SK.

Four names are listed:

Sarah, b. 8 January 1884
Antoinette, b. 28 January 1902 (daughter of Sarah)
Marie Josephine, b 13 November 1905 (daughter of Sarah)
Cèlestine Mistkwatchàk, b. 20 January 1888

Scrip coupon for Baptiste Nanatomakan, son of Nanatomakan.

The following reproductions of scrip coupons are from the National Archives of Canada, RG 15, Vols. 1408 and 1410.

Second scrip coupon for Baptiste Nanatomakan, son of Nanatomakan.

Scrip coupon for Marie Anne Nanatomakan, wife of Baptiste Nanatomakan.

Statement of the Government of Canada on Indian Policy 1969

Introduced 25 June 1969

Foreword

The Government believes that its policies must lead to the full, free and non-discriminatory participation of the Indian people in Canadian society. Such a goal requires a break with the past. It requires that the Indian people's role of dependence be replaced by a role of equal status, opportunity and responsibility, a role they can share with all other Canadians.

This proposal is a recognition of the necessity made plain in a year's intensive discussions with Indian people throughout Canada. The Government believes that to continue its past course of action would not serve the interests of either the Indian people or their fellow Canadians.

The policies proposed recognize the simple reality that the separate legal status of Indians and the policies which have flowed from it have kept the Indian people apart from and behind other Canadians. The Indian people have not been full citizens of the communities and provinces in which they live and have not enjoyed the equality and benefits that such participation offers.

The treatment resulting from their different status has been often worse, sometimes equal and occasionally better than that accorded to their fellow citizens. What matters is that it has been different.

Many Indians, both in isolated communities and in cities, suffer from poverty. The discrimination which affects the poor, Indian and non-Indian alike, when compounded with a legal status that sets the Indian apart, provides dangerously fertile ground for social and cultural discrimination.

Editors' note: This document is oftenreferred to as the 1969 White Paper

In recent years there has been a rapid increase in the Indian population. Their health and education levels have improved. There has been a corresponding rise in expectations that the structure of separate treatment cannot meet.

A forceful and articulate Indian leadership has developed to express the aspirations and needs of the Indian community. Given the opportunity, the Indian people can realize an immense human and cultural potential that will enhance their own well-being, that of the regions in which they live and of Canada as a whole. Faced with a continuation of past policies, they will unite only in a common frustration.

The Government does not wish to perpetuate policies which carry with them the seeds of disharmony and disunity, policies which prevent Canadians from fulfilling themselves and contributing to their society. It seeks a partnership to achieve a better goal. The partners in this search are the Indian people, the governments of the provinces, the Canadian community as a whole and the Government of Canada. As all partnerships do, this will require consultation, negotiation, give and take, and co-operation if it is to succeed.

Many years will be needed. Some efforts may fail, but learning comes from failure and from what is learned success may follow. All the partners have to learn, all will have to change many attitudes.

Governments can set examples, but they cannot change the hearts of men. Canadians, Indians and non-Indians alike stand at the crossroads. For Canadian society the issue is whether a growing element of its population will become full participants contributing in a positive way to the general well-being or whether, conversely, the present social and economic gap will lead to their increasing frustration and isolation, a threat to the general well-being of society. For many Indian people, one road does exist the only road that has existed since Confederation and before, the road of different status, a road which has led to a blind alley of deprivation and frustration. This road, because it is a separate road, cannot lead to full participation, to equality in practice as well as in theory. In the pages which follow, the Government has outlined a number of measures and a policy which it is convinced will offer another road for Indians, a road that would lead gradually away from different status to full social, economic and political participation in Canadian life. This is the choice.

Indian people must be persuaded, must persuade themselves, that this path will lead them to a fuller and richer life. Canadian society as a whole will have to recognize the need for changed attitudes and a truly open society. Canadians should recognize the dangers of failing to strike down the barriers which frustrate Indian people. If Indian people are to become full members of Canadian society they must be warmly welcomed by that society.

The Government commends this policy for the consideration of all Canadians, Indians and non-Indians, and all governments in Canada.

Summary

1. Background

The Government has reviewed its programs for Indians and has considered the effects of them on the present situation of the Indian people. The review has drawn on extensive consultations with the Indian people, and on the knowledge and experience of many people both in and out of government.

This review was a response to things said by the Indian people at the consultation meetings which began a year ago and culminated in a meeting in Ottawa in April.

This review has shown that this is the right time to change long-standing policies. The Indian people have shown their determination that present conditions shall not persist.

Opportunities are present today in Canadian society and new directions are open. The Government believes that Indian people must not be shut out of Canadian life and must share equally in these opportunities.

The Government could press on with the policy of fostering further education; could go ahead with physical improvement programs now operating in reserve communities; could press forward in the directions of recent years, and eventually many of the problems would be solved. But progress would be too slow. The change in Canadian society in recent years has been too great and continues too rapidly for this to be the answer. Something more is needed. We can no longer perpetuate the separation of Canadians. Now is the time to change.

This Government believes in equality. It believes that all men and women have equal rights. It is determined that all shall be treated fairly and that no one shall be shut out of Canadian life, and especially that no one shall be shut out because of his race.

This belief is the basis for the Government's determination to open the doors of opportunity to all Canadians, to remove the barriers which impede the development of people, of regions and of the country.

Only a policy based on this belief can enable the Indian people to realize their needs and aspirations.

The Indian people are entitled to such a policy. They are entitled to an equality which preserves and enriches Indian identity and distinction; an equality which stresses Indian participation in its creation and which manifests itself in all aspects of Indian life.

The goals of the Indian people cannot be set by others; they must spring from the Indian community itself—but government can create a framework within which all persons and groups can seek their own goals.

2. The New Policy

True equality presupposes that the Indian people have the right to full and equal participation in the cultural, social, economic and political life of Canada.

The government believes that the framework within which individual Indians and bands could achieve full participation requires:

  (1) that the legislative and constitutional bases of discrimination be removed;
  (2) that there be positive recognition by everyone of the unique contribution of Indian culture to Canadian life;
  (3) that services come through the same channels and from the same government agencies for all Canadians;
  (4) that those who are furthest behind be helped most;
  (5) that lawful obligations be recognized;
  (6) that control of Indian lands be transferred to the Indian people.

The Government would be prepared to take the following steps to create this framework:

  (1) Propose to Parliament that the Indian Act be repealed and take such legislative steps as may be necessary to enable Indians to control Indian lands and to acquire title to them.
  (2) Propose to the governments of the provinces that they take over the same responsibility for Indians that they have for other citizens in their provinces. The takeover would be accompanied by the transfer to the provinces of federal funds normally provided for Indian programs, augmented as may be necessary.
  (3) Make substantial funds available for Indian economic development as an interim measure.
  (4) Wind up that part of the Department of Indian Affairs and Northern Development which deals with Indian Affairs. The residual responsibilities of the Federal Government for programs in the field of Indian affairs would be transferred to other appropriate federal departments.

In addition, the Government will appoint a Commissioner to consult with the Indians and to study and recommend acceptable procedures for the adjudication of claims.

The new policy looks to a better future for all Indian people wherever they may be. The measures for implementation are straightforward.

They require discussion, consultation and negotiation with the Indian people—individuals, bands and associations—and with provincial governments.

Success will depend upon the co-operation and assistance of the Indians and the provinces. The Government seeks this co-operation and will respond when it is offered.

3. The Immediate Steps

Some changes could take place quickly. Others would take longer. It is expected that within five years the Department of Indian Affairs and Northern Development would cease to operate in the field of Indian affairs; the new laws would be in effect and existing programs would have been devolved. The Indian lands would require special attention for some time. The process of transferring control to the Indian people would be under continuous review.

The Government believes this is a policy which is just and necessary. It can only be successful if it has the support of the Indian people, the provinces, and all Canadians.

The policy promises all Indian people a new opportunity to expand and develop their identity within the framework of a Canadian society which offers them the rewards and responsibilities of participation, the benefits of involvement and the pride of belonging.

Historical Background

The weight of history affects us all, but it presses most heavily on the Indian people. Because of history, Indians today are the subject of legal discrimination; they have grievances because of past undertakings that have been broken or misunderstood; they do not have full control of their lands; and a higher proportion of Indians than other Canadians suffer poverty in all its debilitating forms. Because of history too, Indians look to a special department of the Federal Government for many of the services that other Canadians get from provincial or local governments.

This burden of separation has its origin deep in Canada's past and in early French and British colonial policy. The elements which grew to weigh so heavily were deeply entrenched at the time of Confederation.

Before that time there had evolved a policy of entering into agreements with the Indians, of encouraging them to settle on reserves held by the Crown for their use and benefit and of dealing with Indian lands through a separate organization—a policy of treating Indian people as a race apart.

After Confederation, these well-established precedents were followed and expanded. Exclusive legislative authority was given the Parliament of Canada in relation to "Indians, and Lands reserved for the Indians" under Head 24 of Section 91 of the British North America Act. Special legislation—an Indian Act—was passed, new treaties were entered into, and a network of administrative offices spread across the country either in advance of or along with the tide of settlement.

This system—special legislation, a special land system and separate administration for the Indian people—continues to be the basis of present Indian policy. It has saved for the Indian people places they can call home, but has carried with it serious human and physical as well as administrative disabilities.

Because the system was in the hands of the Federal Government the Indians did not participate in the growth of provincial and local services. They were not required to participate in the development of their own communities which were tax exempt. The result was that the Indians, persuaded that property taxes were an unnecessary element in their lives, did not develop services for themselves. For many years such simple and limited services as were required to sustain life were provided through a network of Indian agencies reflecting the authoritarian tradition of a colonial administration, and until recently these agencies had staff and funds to do little more than meet the most severe cases of hardship and distress.

The tradition of federal responsibility for Indian matters inhibited the development of a proper relationship between the provinces and the Indian people as citizens. Most provinces, faced with their own problems of growth and change, left responsibility for their Indian residents to the Federal Government. Indeed, successive Federal Governments did little to change the pattern. The result was that Indians were the almost exclusive concern of one agency of the Federal Government for nearly a century.

For a long time the problems of physical, legal and administrative separation attracted little attention. The Indian people were scattered in small groups across the country, often in remote areas. When they were in contact with the new settlers, there was little difference between the living standards of the two groups.

Initially, settlers as well as Indians depended on game, fish and fur. The settlers, however, were more concerned with clearing land and establishing themselves and differences soon began to appear.

With the technological change of the twentieth century, society became increasingly industrial and complex, and the separateness of the Indian people became more evident. Most Canadians moved to the growing cities, but the Indians remained largely a rural people, lacking both education and opportunity. The land was being developed rapidly, but many reserves were located in places where little development was possible. Reserves were usually excluded from development and many began to stand out as islands of poverty. The policy of separation had become a burden.

The legal and administrative discrimination in the treatment of Indian people has not given them an equal chance of success. It has exposed them to discrimination in the broadest and worst sense of the term—a discrimination that has profoundly affected their confidence that success can be theirs. Discrimination breeds discrimination by example, and the separateness of Indian people has affected the attitudes of other Canadians towards them.

The system of separate legislation and administration has also separated people of Indian ancestry into three groups—registered Indians, who are further divided into those who are under treaty and those who are not; enfranchised Indians who lost, or voluntarily relinquished, their legal status as Indians; and the Métis, who are of Indian ancestry but never had the status of registered Indians.

The Case for the New Policy

In the past ten years or so, there have been important improvements in education, health, housing, welfare and community development. Developments in leadership among the Indian communities have become increasingly evident. Indian people have begun to forge a new unity. The Government believes progress can come from these developments but only if they are met by new responses. The proposed policy is a new response.

The policy rests upon the fundamental right of Indian people to full and equal participation in the cultural, social, economic and political life of Canada.

To argue against this right is to argue for discrimination, isolation and separation. No Canadian should be excluded from participation in community life, and none should expect to withdraw and still enjoy the benefits that flow to those who participate.

1. The Legal Structure

Legislative and constitutional bases of discrimination must be removed.

Canada cannot seek the just society and keep discriminatory legislation on its statute books. The Government believes this to be self-evident. The ultimate aim of removing the specific references to Indians from the constitution may take some time, but it is a goal to be kept constantly in view. In the meantime, barriers created by special legislation can generally be struck down.

Under the authority of Head 24, Section 91 of the British North America Act, the Parliament of Canada has enacted the Indian Act. Various federal-provincial agreements and some other statutes also affect Indian policies.

In the long term, removal of the reference in the constitution would be necessary to end the legal distinction between Indians and other Canadians. In the short term, repeal of the Indian Act and enactment of transitional legislation to ensure the orderly management of Indian land would do much to mitigate the problem.

The ultimate goal could not be achieved quickly, for it requires a change in the economic circumstances of the Indian people and much preliminary adjustment with provincial authorities. Until the Indian people are satisfied that their land holdings are solely within their control, there may have to be some special legislation for Indian lands.

2. The Indian Cultural Heritage

There must be positive recognition by everyone of the unique contribution of Indian culture to Canadian society.

It is important that Canadians recognize and give credit to the Indian contribution. It manifests itself in many ways; yet it goes largely unrecognized and unacknowledged. Without recognition by others it is not easy to be proud.

All of us seek a basis for pride in our own lives, in those of our families and of our ancestors. Man needs such pride to sustain him in the inevitable hour of discouragement, in the moment when he faces obstacles, whenever life seems turned against him. Everyone has such moments. We manifest our pride in many ways, but always it supports and sustains us. The legitimate pride of the Indian people has been crushed too many times by too many of their fellow Canadians.

The principle of equality and all that goes with it demands that all of us recognize each other's cultural heritage as a source of personal strength.

Canada has changed greatly since the first Indian Act was passed. Today it is made up of many people with many cultures. Each has its own manner of relating to the other; each makes its own adjustments to the larger society.

Successful adjustment requires that the larger groups accept every group with its distinctive traits without prejudice, and that all groups share equitably in the material and non-material wealth of the country.

For many years Canadians believed the Indian people had but two choices: they could live in a reserve community, or they could be assimilated and lose their Indian identity. Today Canada has more to offer. There is a third choice—a full role in Canadian society and in the economy while retaining, strengthening and developing an Indian identity which preserves the good things of the past and helps Indian people to prosper and thrive.

This choice offers great hope for the Indian people. It offers great opportunity for Canadians to demonstrate that in our open society there is room for the development of people who preserve their different cultures and take pride in their diversity.

This new opportunity to enrich Canadian life is central to the Government's new policy. If the policy is to be successful, the Indian people must be in a position to play a full role in Canada's diversified society, a role which stresses the value of their experience and the possibilities of the future.

The Indian contribution to North American society is often over-looked, even by the Indian people themselves. Their history and tradition can be a rich source of pride, but are not sufficiently known and recognized. Too often, the art forms which express the past are preserved but are inaccessible to most Indian people. This richness can be shared by all Canadians. Indian people must be helped to become aware of their history and heritage in all its forms, and this heritage must be brought before all Canadians in all its rich diversity.

Indian culture also lives through Indian speech and thought. The Indian languages are unique and valuable assets. Recognizing their value is not a matter of preserving ancient ways as fossils, but a ensuring the continuity of a people by encouraging and assisting them to work at the continuing development of their inheritance in the context of the present-day world. Culture lives and develops in the daily life of people, in their communities and in their other associations, and the Indian culture can be preserved, perpetuated and developed only by the Indian people themselves.

The Indian people have often been made to feel that their culture and history are not worthwhile. To lose a sense of worthiness is damaging. Success in life, in adapting to change, and in developing appropriate relations within the community as well as in relation to a wider world requires a strong sense of personal worth—a real sense of identity.

Rich in folklore, in art forms and in concepts of community life, the Indian cultural heritage can grow and expand further to enrich the general society. Such a development is essential if the Indian people are again to establish a meaningful sense of identity and purpose and if Canada is to realize its maximum potential.

The Government recognizes that people of Indian ancestry must be helped in new ways in this task. It proposes, through the Secretary of State, to support associations and groups in developing a greater appreciation of their cultural heritage. It wants to foster adequate communication among all people of Indian descent and between them and the Canadian community as a whole.

Steps will be taken to enlist the support of Canadians generally. The provincial government will be approached to support this goal through their many agencies operating in the field. Provincial educational authorities will be urged to intensify their review of school curriculae and course content with a view to ensuring that they adequately reflect Indian culture and Indian contributions to Canadian development.

3. Programs and Services

Services must come through the same channels and from the same government agencies for all Canadians.

This is an undeniable part of equality. It has been shown many times that separation of people flows from separate services. There can be no argument about the principle of common services. It is right.

It cannot be accepted now that Indians should be constitutionally excluded from the right to treated within their province as full and equal citizens, with all the responsibilities and all the privileges that this might entail. It is in the provincial sphere where social remedies are structured and applied, and the Indian people, by and large, have been non-participating members of Provincial society.

Canadians receive a wide range of services through provincial and local governments, but the Indian people and their communities are mostly outside that framework. It is no longer acceptable that the Indian people should be outside and apart. The Government believes that services should be available on an equitable basis, except for temporary differentiation based on need. Services ought not to flow from separate agencies established to serve particular groups, especially not to groups that are identified ethnically.

Separate but equal services do not provide truly equal treatment. Treatment has not been equal in the case of Indians and their communities. Many services require a wide range of facilities which cannot be duplicated by separate agencies. Others must be integral to the complex systems of community and regional life and cannot be matched on a small scale.

The Government is therefore convinced that the traditional method of providing separate services to Indians must be ended. All Indians should have access to all programs and services at all levels of government equally with other Canadians.

The Government proposes to negotiate with the provinces and conclude agreements under which Indian people would participate in and be served by the full programs of the provincial and local systems. Equitable financial arrangements would be sought to ensure that services would be provided in full measure commensurate with the needs. The negotiations must seek agreements to end discrimination while ensuring that no harm is inadvertently done to Indian interests. The Government further proposes that federal disbursements for Indian programs in each province be transferred to that province. Subject to negotiations with the provinces, such provisions would as a matter of principle eventually decline, the provinces ultimately assuming the same responsibility for services to Indian residents as they do for services to others.

At the same time, the Government proposes to transfer all remaining federal responsibilities for Indians from the Department of Indian Affairs and Northern Development to other departments, including the Departments of Regional Economic Expansion, Secretary of State, and Manpower and Immigration.

It is important that such transfers take place without disrupting services and that special arrangements not be compromised while they are subject to consultation and negotiation. The government will pay particular attention to this.

4. Enriched Services

Those who are furthest behind must be helped most.

There can be little argument that conditions for many Indian people are not satisfactory to them and are not acceptable to others. There can be little question that special services, and specially enriched services, will be needed for some time.

Equality before the law and in programs and services does not necessarily result in equality of social and economic conditions. For that reason, existing programs will be reviewed. The Department of Regional Economic Expansion, the Department of Manpower and Immigration, and other federal departments involved would be prepared to evolve programs that would help break past patterns of deprivation.

Additional funds would be available from a number of different sources. In an atmosphere of greater freedom, those who are able to do so would be expected to help themselves, so more Indians would be available to help those who really need it. The transfer of Indian lands to Indian control should enable many individuals and groups to move ahead on their own initiative. This in turn would free funds for further enrichment of programs to help those who are furthest behind. By ending some programs and replacing them with others evolved within the community, a more effective use of funds would be achieved. Administrative savings would result from the elimination of separate agencies as various levels of government bring general programs and resources to bear. By broadening the base of service agencies, this enrichment could be extended to all who need it. By involving more agencies working at different levels, and by providing those agencies with the means to make them more effective, the Government believes that root problems could be attacked, that solutions could be found that hitherto evaded the best efforts and best-directed of programs.

The economic base for many Indians is their reserve land, but the development of reserves has lagged.

Among the many factors that determine economic growth of reserves, their location and size are particularly important. There are a number of reserves located within or near growing industrial areas which could provide substantial employment and income to their owners if they were properly developed. There are other reserves in agricultural areas which could provide a livelihood for a larger number of family units than is presently the case. The majority of the reserves, however, are located in the boreal or wooded regions of Canada, most of them geographically isolated and many having little economic potential. In these areas, low income, unemployment and under-employment are characteristic of Indians and non-Indians alike.

Even where reserves have economic potential, the Indians have been handicapped. Private investors have been reluctant to supply capital for project on land which cannot be pledged as security. Adequate social and risk capital has not been available from public sources. Most Indians have not had the opportunity to acquire managerial experience, nor have they been offered sufficient technical assistance.

The Government believes that the Indian people should have the opportunity to develop the resources of their reserves so they may contribute to their own well-being and the economy of the nation. To develop Indian reserves to the level of the regions in which they are located will require considerable capital over a period of some years, as well as the provision of managerial and technical advice. Thus the Government believes that all programs and advisory services of the federal and provincial governments should be made readily available to Indians.

In addition, and as an interim measure, the Government proposes to make substantial additional funds available for investment in the economic progress of the Indian people. This would overcome the barriers to early development of Indian lands and resources, help bring Indians into a closer working relationship with the business community, help finance their adjustment to new employment opportunities, and facilitate access to normal financial sources.

Even if the resources of Indian reserves are fully utilized, however, they cannot all properly support their present Indian populations, much less the populations of the future. Many Indians will, as they are now doing, seek employment elsewhere as a means of solving their economic problems. Jobs are vital and the Government intends that the full counselling, occupational training and placement resources of the Department of Manpower and Immigration are used to further employment opportunities for Indians. The government will encourage private employers to provide opportunities for the Indian people.

In many situations, the problems of Indians are similar to those faced by their non-Indian neighbours. Solutions to their problems cannot be found in isolation but must be sought within the context of regional development plans involving all the people. The consequence of an integrated regional approach is that all levels of government—federal, provincial and local—and the people themselves are involved. Helping overcome regional disparities in the economic well-being of Canadians is the main task assigned to the Department of Regional Economic Expansion. The Government believes that the needs of Indian communities should be met within this framework.

5. Claims and Treaties
Lawful obligations must be recognized.

Many of the of the Indian people feel that successive governments have not dealt with them as fairly as they should. They believe that lands have been taken from them in an improper manner, or without adequate compensation, that their funds have been improperly administer, that their treaty rights have been breached. Their sense of grievance influences their relations with governments and the community and limits their participation in Canadian life.

Many Indians look upon their treaties as the source of their rights to land, to hunting and fishing privileges, and to other benefits. Some believe the treaties should be interpreted to encompass wider services and privileges, and many believe the treaties have not been honoured. Whether or not this is correct in some or many cases, the fact is the treaties affect only half the Indians of Canada. Most of the Indians of Quebec, British Columbia, and the Yukon are not parties to a treaty.

The terms and effects of the treaties between the Indian people and the Government are widely misunderstood. A plain reading of the words used in the treaties reveals the limited and minimal promises which were included in them. As a result of the treaties, some Indians were given an initial cash payment and were promised land reserved for their exclusive use, annuities, protection of hunting, fishing and trapping privileges subject (in most cases) to regulation, a school or teachers in most instances, and, in one treaty only, a medicine chest. There were some other minor considerations such as the annual provision of twine and ammunition.

The annuities have been paid regularly. The basic promise to set aside reserve land has been kept except in respect of the Indians of the Northwest Territories and a few bands in the northern parts of the Prairie Provinces. These Indians did not choose land when treaties were signed. The government wishes to see these obligations dealt with as soon as possible.

The right to hunt and fish for food is extended unevenly across the country and not always in relation to need. Although game and fish will become less and less important for survival as the pattern of Indian life continues to change, there are those who, at this time, still live in the traditional manner that their forefathers lived in when they entered into treaty with the government. The Government is prepared to allow such persons transitional freer hunting of migratory birds under the Migratory Birds Convention Act and Regulations.

The significance of the treaties in meeting the economic, educational, health and welfare needs of the Indian people has always been limited and will continue to decline. The services that have been provided go far beyond what could have been foreseen by those who signed the treaties.

The Government and the Indian people must reach a common understanding of the future role of the treaties. Some provisions will be found to have been discharged; others will have continuing importance. Many of the provisions and practices of another century may be considered irrelevant in the light of a rapidly changing society, and still others may be ended by mutual agreement. Finally, once Indian lands are securely within Indian control, the anomaly of treaties between groups within society and the government of that society will require that these treaties be reviewed to see how they can be equitably ended.

Other grievances have been asserted in more general terms. It is possible that some of these can be verified by appropriate research and may be susceptible of specific remedies. Others relate to aboriginal claims to land. These are so general and undefined that it is not realistic to think of them as specific claims capable of remedy except through a policy and program that will end injustice to Indians as members of the Canadian community. This is the policy that the government is proposing for discussion.

At the recent consultation meeting in Ottawa representatives of the Indians, chosen at each of the earlier regional meetings, expressed concern about the extent of their knowledge of Indian right and treaties. They indicated a desire to undertake further research to establish their rights with greater precision, elected a National Committee on Indian Rights and Treaties for this purpose and sought government financial support for research.

The Government had intended to introduce legislation to establish an Indian Claims Commission to hear and determine Indian claims. Consideration of the questions raised at the consultations and the review of Indian policy have raised serious doubts as to whether a Claims Commission as proposed to Parliament in 1965 is the right way to deal with the grievances of Indians put forward as claims.

The Government has concluded that further study and research are required by both the Indians and the Government. It will appoint a Commissioner who, in consultation with representatives of the Indians, will inquire into and report upon how claims arising in respect of the performance of the terms of treaties and agreements formally entered into by representatives of the Indians and the Crown, and the administration of moneys and lands pursuant to schemes established by legislation for the benefit of Indians may be adjudicated.

The Commissioner will also classify the claims that in his judgment ought to be referred to the courts or any special quasi-judicial body that may be recommended.

It is expected that the Commissioner's inquiry will go on concurrently with that of the National Indian Committee on Indian Rights and Treaties and the Commissioner will be authorized to recommend appropriate support to the Committee so that it may conduct research on the Indians' behalf and assist the Commissioner in his Inquiry.

6. Indian Lands

Control of Indian lands should be transferred to the Indian people.

Frustration is as great a handicap as a sense of grievance. True co-operation and participation can come only when the Indian people are controlling the land which makes up the reserves.

The reserve system has provided the Indian people with lands that generally have been protected against alienation without their consent. Widely scattered across Canada, the reserves total nearly 6,000,000 acres and are divided into about 2,200 parcels of varying sizes. Under the existing system, title to reserve lands is held either by the Crown in right of Canada or the Crown in right of one of the provinces. Administrative control and legislative authority are, however, vested exclusively in the Government and the Parliament of Canada. It is a trust. As long as this trust exists, the Government as a trustee, must supervise the business connected with the land.

The result of Crown ownership and the Indian Act has been to tie the Indian people to a land system that lacks flexibility and inhibits development. If an Indian band wishes to gain income by leasing its land, it has to do so through a cumbersome system involving the Government as trustee. It cannot mortgage reserve land to finance development on its own initiative. Indian people do not have control of their lands except as the Government allows, and this is no longer acceptable to them. The Indians have made this clear at the consultation meetings. They now want real control, and this Government believes that they should have it. The Government recognizes that full and true equality calls for Indian control and ownership of reserve land.

Between the present system and the full holding of title in fee simple lie a number of intermediate states. The first step is to change the system under which ministerial decision is required for all that is done with Indian land. This is where the delays, the frustrations and the obstructions lie. The Indians must control their land.

This can be done in many ways. The Government believes that each band must make its own decision as to the way it wants to take control of its land and the manner in which it intends to manage it. It will take some years to complete the process of devolution.

The Government believes that full ownership implies many things. It carries with it the free choice of use, of retention or of disposition. In our society it also carries with it an obligation to pay for certain services. The Government recognizes that it may not be acceptable to put all lands into the provincial systems immediately and make them subject to taxes. When the Indian people see that the only way they can own and fully control land is to accept taxation the way other Canadians do, they will make that decision.

Alternative methods for the control of their lands will be made available to Indian individuals and bands. Whatever methods of land control are chosen by the Indian people, the present system under which the Government must execute all leases, supervise and control procedures and surrenders, and generally act as trustee, must be brought to an end. But the Indian land heritage should be protected. Land should be alienated from them only by the consent of the Indian people themselves. Under a proposed Indian Lands Act full management would be in the hands of the bands and, if the bands wish, they or individuals would be able to take title to their land without restrictions.

As long as the Crown controls the land for the benefit of bands who use and occupy it is responsible for determining who may, as a member of a band, share in the assets of band land. The qualifications for band membership which it has imposed are part of the legislation— the Indian Act—governing the administration of reserve lands. Under the present Act, the Government applies and interprets these qualifications. When bands take title to their lands, they will be able to define and apply these qualifications themselves.

The Government is prepared to transfer to the Indian people the reserve lands, full control over them and, subject to the proposed Indian Lands Act, the right to determine who shares in partnership. The Government proposes to seek agreements with the bands and, where necessary, with the governments of the provinces. Discussions will be initiated with the Indian people and provinces to this end.

Implementation of the New Policy

1. Indian Associations and Consultation

Successful implementation of the new policy would require the further development of a close working relationship with the Indian community. This was made abundantly clear in the proposals set forth by the National Indian Brotherhood at the national meeting to consult on revising the Indian Act. Their brief succinctly identified the needs at that time and offers a basis for discussing the means of adaptation to the new policy.

To this end the Government proposes to invite the executives of the National Indian Brotherhood and the various provincial associations to discuss the role they might play in the implementation of the new policy, and the financial resources they may require. The Government recognizes their need for independent advice, especially on legal matters. The

Government also recognizes that the discussions will place a heavy burden on Indian leaders during the adjustment period. Special arrangements will have to be made so that they may take the time needed to meet and discuss all aspects of the new policy and its implementation.

Needs and conditions vary greatly from province to province. Since the adjustments would be different in each case, the bulk of the negotiations would likely be with the provincial bodies, regional groups and the bands themselves. There are those matters which are of concern to all, and the National Indian Brotherhood would be asked to act in liaison with the various provincial associations and with the federal departments which would have ongoing responsibilities.

The Government proposes to ask that the associations act as the principal agencies through which consultation and negotiations would be conducted, but each band would be consulted about gaining ownership of its land holdings. Bands would be asked to designate the association through which their broad interests would be represented.

2 Transitional Period

Government hopes to have the bulk of the policy in effect within five years and believes that the necessary financial and other arrangements can be concluded so that Indians will have full access to provincial services within that time. It will seek an immediate start to the many discussions that will need to be held with the provinces and with representatives of the Indian people.

The role of the Department of Indian Affairs and Northern Development in serving the Indian people would be phased out as arrangements with the provinces were completed and remaining federal Government responsibilities transferred to other departments.

The Commissioner will be appointed soon and instructed to get on with his work.

Steps would be taken in consultation with representatives of the Indian people to transfer control of land to them. Because of the need to consult over five hundred bands the process would take some time.

A policy can never provide the ultimate solutions to all problems. A policy can achieve no more than is desired by the people it is intended to serve. The essential feature of the Government's proposed new policy for Indians is that it acknowledges that truth by recognizing the central and essential role of the Indian people in solving their own problems. It will provide, for the first time, a non-discriminatory framework within which, in an atmosphere of freedom, the Indian people could, with other Canadians, work out their own destiny.

Excerpts from
the Canada Act, 1982

ELIZABETH II

Canada Act 1982

An Act to give effect to a request by the Senate and House of Commons of Canada

Whereas Canada has requested and consented to the enactment of an Act of the Parliament of the United Kingdom to give effect to the provisions hereinafter set forth and the Senate and the House of Commons of Canada in Parliament assembled have submitted an address to Her Majesty requesting that Her Majesty may graciously be pleased to cause a Bill to be laid before the Parliament of the United Kingdom for that purpose.

Be it therefore enacted by the Queen's Most Excellent Majesty, by and with the advice and consent of the Lords Spiritual and Temporal, and Commons, in this present Parliament assembled, and by the authority of the same, as follows:

Constitution Act, 1982 enacted

1. The *Constitution Act, 1982* set out in Schedule B to this Act is hereby enacted for and shall have the force of law in Canada and shall come into force as provided in that Act.

Termination of
power to legislate
for Canada

2. No Act of the Parliament of the United Kingdom passed after the *Constitution Act, 1982* comes into force shall extend to Canada as part of its law.

French version

3. So far as it is not contained in Schedule B, the French version of this Act is set out in Schedule A to this Act and has the same authority in Canada as the English version thereof.

Short title

4. This Act may be cited as the Canada *Act 1982.*

Schedule B
Constitution Act, 1982

Part I

Canadian Charter of Rights and Freedoms

Whereas Canada is founded upon principles that recognize the supremacy of God and the rule of law:

Guarantee of Rights and Freedoms

Rightsand
freedoms
in Canada

1. *The Canadian Charter of Rights and Freedoms* guarantees the rights and freedoms set out in it subject only to *such* reasonable limits prescribed by law as can be demonstrably justified in a free and democratic society.

Fundamental Freedoms

Fundamental
freedoms

2. Everyone has the following fundamental freedoms:
   (*a*) freedom of conscience and religion;
   (*b*) freedom of thought, belief, opinion and expression, including freedom of the press and other media of communication;

(c) freedom of peaceful assembly; and

(d) freedom of association.

Democratic Rights

Democratic rights
of citizens

3. Every citizen of Canada has the right to vote in an election of members of the House of Commons or of a legislative assembly and to be qualified for membership therein.

Maximum duration
of legislative bodies

4. (1) No House of Commons and no legislative assembly shall continue for longer than five years from the date fixed for the return of the writs at a general election of its members.

Continuation in
special
circumstances

(2) In time of real or apprehended war, invasion or insurrection, a House of Commons may be continued by Parliament and a legislative assembly may be continued by the legislature beyond five years if such continuation is not opposed by the votes of more than one third of the members of the House

Application where
numbers warrant

(3) The right of citizens of Canada under subsections (1) and (2) to have their children receive primary and secondary school instruction in the language of the English or French linguistic minority population of a province

　　(a) applies wherever in the province the number of children of citizens who have such a right is sufficient to warrant the provision to them out of public funds of minority language instruction; and

　　(b) includes, where the number of those children so warrants, the right to have them receive that instruction in minority language educational facilities provided out of public funds.

Enforcement

Enforcement of
guaranteed rights

24. (1) Anyone whose rights or freedoms, as guaranteed by this Charter, have been infringed or denied may apply to a court of competent jurisdiction to obtain such remedy as the court considers appropriate and just in the circumstances.

Exclusion of
evidencebringing
administration
of justice into
disrepute

(2) Where, in proceedings under subsection (1), a court concludes that evidence was obtained in a manner that infringed or denied any rights or freedoms guaranteed by this Charter, the evidence shall be excluded if it is established that, having regard to all the circumstances, the admission of it in the proceedings would bring the administration of justice into disrepute.

General

Aboriginal rights
and freedoms not
affected
by Charter

25. The guarantee in this Charter of certain rights and freedoms shall not be construed so as to abrogate or derogate from any aboriginal, treaty or other rights or freedoms that pertain to the aboriginal peoples of Canada including

(a) any rights or freedoms that have been recognized by the Royal Proclamation of October 7, 1763; and

(b) any rights or freedoms that may be acquired by the aboriginal peoples of Canada by way of land claims settlement.

Part II

Rights of the Aboriginal Peoples of Canada

Recognition of
existing aboriginal
and treaty rights

35. (1) The existing aboriginal and treaty rights of the aboriginal peoples of Canada are hereby recognized and affirmed.

Definition of
aboriginal peoples
of Canada

(2) In this Act, "aboriginal peoples of Canada" includes the Indian, Inuit and Métis peoples of Canada.

Guide to Critical Reading and Writing

Guide to Critical Reading: Analyzing Journal Articles

Frank Tough

Frank Tough, an historical geographer and researcher, is a Professor and Director of the School of Native Studies at the University of Alberta. He has been an expert witness in a number of treaty and Métis rights cases.

Information, ideas, and interpretations presented by published research in history and the social sciences are not always easy to understand. This guide provides a step by step approach to analyzing academic articles and readings so that so that students can get the most out of assigned readings, thereby improving their preparation for discussions, seminars, and written assignments. The information may be contained in a book, a chapter or portion of a book, or in a journal. Because articles published in academics journals represent a means of accumulating knowledge and research in a discipline, I will focus on this common form of academic communication. However, the following recommendations also apply to analyzing readings from books.

Journals provide a means for publishing up-to-date research and a forum for conflicting viewpoints about a topic. For students' essays and research, journal articles have several advantages over books, major studies, and monographs. Research published as an academic article tends to be more up-to-date than books because journals publish regularly and frequently. Because of space limitations, research presented in journals is usually concise. However, most academic

---

Published with permission of the author.

journals aim for a readership of professors and not undergraduate students, and this sometimes results in an incomplete elaboration of the main points. The following guide provides a means for improving reading and comprehension, and a method of critically examining published research. The ability to read this literature is a vital part of a university education.

An assigned reading may have to be read several times. But simply re-reading a difficult article over and over will not necessarily increase comprehension. Sometimes it makes sense to focus your efforts by concentrating on particular aspects of an article. The following points are designed to help you identify the focus of the articles, supporting data, and the significance of the conclusions.

Overview

On a first read of a difficult article, attempt to identify some of the general features of the article.
- What is the main thesis or argument?
- What academic discipline perspective does the author seem to employ (for example, History, Sociology, Native Studies)?
- Does the research make use of any particular frame of reference, research approach, or theoretical perspective?
- Does the article make reference to previous research or other studies? Does the author suggest that what is being presented contrasts or supports previous writers on the topic?
- Does the author define terms—are definitions made operational? Does the author use a lot of jargon?
- Do there appear to be any stated or unstated assumptions that affect the thesis?
- When was the article published?

Information, Data, and Methods

As an aid to understanding the main thesis, it helps to focus on the support for that thesis.
- What types of data and what types of sources are used? Primary—direct or firsthand sources or observation
  - archival research
  - published primary sources
  - interviews, surveys
  - oral history
  - government documents
  - numerical/statistical data
  - Internet.

Secondary—studies by other researchers on a subject
- books, monographs
- articles
- newspapers
- reports, studies
- theses
- Internet.

- Has the author gone out and collected information or has she used other people's research?
- If the article is largely historical in content, has the author presented new sources or has he used standard sources already used by other historians?
- Does the author explain her research methodology?
- Has the author analyzed the data (that is, used statistical techniques, mapping or diagramming, or textual analysis)?
- Is the information presented largely a descriptive account or is the article analytical? Is a particular theory being supported?
- Does the bibliography suggest that the author made use of current information at the time of publication?

Organization and Presentation

By attempting to identify the structure of an article, the main thesis may be better appreciated.

- Does the article's information appear to follow a logical sequence?
- What are the major points of the argument?
- Does the author make use of appropriate tables, maps, and diagrams to clearly present and summarize data?
- In developing an interpretation or argument, does the author present and deal effectively with counter arguments?
- Does the article present data that you feel contradicts the main argument?
- Does the information support the author's thesis?

Findings and Conclusions

Often a piece of published research is remembered only for its major findings or conclusion. Working back critically from the conclusion is another means to increase comprehension.

- What are the main findings? Are the author's claims contestable?
- Does the research engage in a debate or challenge commonly held views?
- Are the conclusions limited to a particular place or time period?
- Does the article take the findings and make conclusions that relate to our general knowledge and theory?

- Does the research alter our perspectives on an issue?
- Is the research relevant? Are the claims significant?

Not all these questions can be answered for each reading; however, these kinds of questions provide a general framework for approaching published academic writing. Familiarization with these questions before you read an article will assist in developing a systematic evaluation. After a few attempts and a little practice, rigorous critical evaluation skills will become second nature.

Preparation for each class discussion comes down to having a reasonable comprehension of the material. You may want to begin preparation with the "quick look over":

1. read the introduction, then
2. go to the first (topic) sentence of each paragraph
3. examine data presented as maps, tables, graphs, or charts
4. read the conclusion, and
5. examine the bibliography.

While this initial survey takes very little time, it can greatly increase comprehension. Do not expect 100 percent comprehension with only one reading. In preparing for seminars: make notes, and if there are problems prepare questions you would like answered, anticipate questions that will be asked in the seminar, and develop your viewpoint about the articles.

Guide to Critical Writing: Reviewing Articles and Books

Frank Tough

An important step in developing an individual writing style is the ability to critique published books and articles and to express these criticisms in a short review. This is a very different exercise than writing a "book report," which simply summarizes a book. A critical review provides a very brief summary of the main points of a piece of published research, but also seeks to evaluate the accuracy and validity of the research and to consider the contribution that a piece of academic writing has made to our knowledge of a topic. Thus, a critical review is not a blow-by-blow account of the contents of a book or an article, but an evaluation of published research.

Overview

Some steps required for reviewing published research (books, articles, reports):
- Read the book or article.
- Re-read the book or article.
- Devise a system of notation, make notes, and accurately record what you want to quote.
- React to the material: What do you like? What do you dislike? (If the research expresses a position with which you do not agree but is well documented, follow up—do some of your own research.)
- If you are reviewing a book, consult *The Book Review Digest* for summaries of published book reviews: How was the book received?
- Re-read certain sections. If data was presented as tables, graphs, charts, review this data again.

- Review footnotes and bibliography. Is the bibliography extensive? Is it up to date?
- Using your notes, construct an outline (introduction, summary, your critique, and conclusion). Pay close attention to the balance between summary of the article/book and your own reflections on its contents.
- Write a first draft, ideally leaving time for it to sit before writing a second draft.
- Proof your writing. Reading out loud can often catch problems.
- Turn in a final draft in a form that it can be read by your instructor.
- Reference your points taken from the text your are reviewing. There are two styles for doing this: Modern Language Association (MLA) and American Psychological Association (APA). Consult one of these guides to learn how to make citations.

Objectives or Aims

- What are the author's objectives/aims in presenting her research?
- Are these objectives clear?
- Does the author deliver on these objectives or does the research stray and drift from the aims?
- Does the author place the research into a context?
- Does the author seek to be original (break new ground), or reinterpret and redefine existing knowledge, or has he succeeded in getting something published on a safe topic that is already well known?
- Are the claims of the author contestable?

The stated objectives of a particular piece of writing compared to the results are an important discussion point. However, avoid the common mistake of redefining the author's objectives. This usually results in setting up a straw man that is easily knocked down. Such a tactic does not produce good critical writing. For example, if an author intended to examine Nishga-white relations in the twentieth century, it would be somewhat unfair to criticize the book for ignoring the demise of the Huron of central Canada in the seventeenth century. It is not really credible to criticize an author for failing to accomplish something she had no intention of doing. However, it is always valid to raise the issue of relevance of a particular piece of research.

Data and Sources

Closely examine the sources and types of data:

- Does the author rely on primary or secondary sources?
- Does she rely on other people's research?

- Is the argument well supported?
- Have new sources of data been brought to the reader's attention?
- Does the data say what the author claims?
- Are there sections of the argument that are based on emotions or conventional wisdom and not data?

Methods and Presentation

The method and the presentation are worth commenting on:
- What sort of "data processing" has the author done? Has he warned us about any problems or limitations of the data?
- How have numerical data (statistics) been used?
- Have arguments been reinforced with maps, tables, or graphs?
- Does the order and organization of information make sense?
- Are all statistics or direct quotations properly referenced?
- Could the data be verified?

Interpretation

- What sort of interpretation or conclusion does the author make about his research (or is the article simply long on facts and short on understanding)?

The above discussion of critical writing is not meant as a comprehensive formula. Many other questions can be asked and not all of the above points can relate to every piece of writing. Please note that critical reviews are not simply an exercise in negative commentary.

Critical reviews are generally short pieces of writing that take a long time to compose. Because reviews are concise, word choice is important. Words selected should be powerful and precise. But do not assume that the contrivance of a word processor's thesaurus will necessarily provide a reliable means to improve word choice. Learning to write critical reviews can be frustrating and difficult, but once accomplished, the task to do longer writing—essays or reports—can be made easier. Remember that writing is held to be an aid to clearer thinking.

The first step in a review, providing a summary, is straightforward. However, the important feature of a critical review—to examine closely a piece of research by an "expert" and then concisely express your reflections in a critical review—is a difficult, but essential step in developing a competent writing style.

Guide to Useful and Successful Seminar Presentations

Greater comprehension of readings of "the literature" can be achieved through active and participatory discussion. Good seminar presentations are not a mere regurgitation of an academic piece of writing. A lively and fruitful discussion—with elements of debate, disagreement, and discourse—should stem from a well prepared oral presentation. Thus student seminar presentation can achieve two important objectives:

- a clear and succinct presentation of a relevant reading that hereby
- provides the basis for a useful discussion.

Obviously, a stale, blow by blow regurgitation of what everybody has already read will do little more than take up the required time. The challenge of a presentation is to make a piece of academic writing interesting and relevant to your peers.

Preparation is essential. Know the material and know the limits of your comprehension. A well-written article should be reorganized for an oral presentation. Oral presentations are a public performance and rehearsing as part of your presentation makes sense. The main components of an oral presentation include:

Content highlights:

- author, title, year, background, theme
- main argument
- key data and supporting statements
- interesting points or new data.

Content highlights largely reflect the author's viewpoint. Provide a fair summary. This section of your oral presentation should not take more than half the allotted time of the presentation. Nor should organization of your summary of content slavishly follow the author's original structure. Set up a list of main points and present these points in descending order of importance.

For an oral presentation, a regrouping of information derived from written sources may make more sense.

Main concerns:

- your evaluation, general comments, questions provide a criticism or critique
- broaden the relevance of particular reading: does what the author says apply to other places and times?
- consider the relevance of the author's interpretation (to the

course, to an understanding of a world system, to contemporary struggles, towards a foundation for Native Studies).

Your concerns, criticism, and questions are a key part of an oral presentation. An evaluation provides original content to the presentation. Be critical without nit-picking. Critical evaluation of a reading will provide many opportunities for discussion, whereas a verbal precis, of even the most exciting reading, will be less successful at initiating a lively discussion.

Your original commentary should elucidate the reading in such a way as to foreshadow for the listener the points you intend to pursue in discussion.

Formulation of discussion points:

- clearly formulate key points from the content highlights and evaluation into questions for group
- relate content to other readings, course themes, and other sources of your knowledge.

Discussion might begin by throwing the presentation open to general questions before pursuing your prepared list of questions.

Some useful points about presentations:

- Make it clear to the listener when you are expressing your viewpoint and when the author's viewpoints are being expressed.
- Use your own words as much as possible. The effort required to rework an academic piece into your own words will lead to a higher comprehension.
- Use quotes sparingly and for effect.
- Remember that everyone has done the reading and therefore do not waste time by going into mundane details.
- Do not read the entire presentation, and when you do read, do not read in a monotone. Inflect your voice. Work from well-structured, point-form notes. Be familiar with your notes.
- Maintain contact with your listeners, and establish a presence that will lead to discussion. Speak clearly.
- Give consideration to possible aids such as blackboards, overhead projectors or photocopied handouts, but use aids to clarify not to confuse. Do not speak directly to blackboards. No offence is taken if you turn your back on a blackboard whilst speaking.
- Start and end with clarity and strength.
- Give careful consideration to your objectives: what do you want your listeners to get out of the presentation?
- Rehearse out loud and watch your time.
- Prepare a weekend in advance. This gives you time to fine-tune your presentation. Furthermore, early preparation can spare you the embarrassment of seeking an extension because of unforeseen events robbing your preparation time.

The ability to prepare and successfully deliver a clear oral presentation is a useful talent. Like writing, it develops such skills as critical evaluation, organization, and synthesis. Moreover, it is a skill that is often required in the real professional world. Discussions stemming from oral presentations will familiarize you with the literature, and the accumulative effect of a series of successful seminar presentations will provide a good foundation for oral work in other classes and in other areas of your life and future career.

Glossary

Glossary

The following definitions are intended as a guide, and readers should remember that many of the terms defined have more complex and multiple meanings than we are able to provide here.

Aboriginal peoples: The various Indian tribes indigenous to the Americas before the arrival of the Europeans or any persons descended from those first inhabitants. Indians, Inuit, and Métis are identified as the Aboriginal peoples of Canada in the Constitution Act of 1982, Sec. 35 (2).

Aboriginal people: The individuals belonging to the political and cultural entities known as Aboriginal peoples.

Aboriginal rights: Refers to rights deemed to be held by the Indigenous peoples of Canada by virtue of their ancestors' original and long-standing nationhood and their use and occupancy of land.

Acculturation: Learning, accepting, and adapting the cultural rules, values, and meanings of another society.

Adhesion: A chief who, on behalf of the people he represents, agrees to the terms and signs an already existing treaty, is said to have signed an adhesion to a treaty. In 1877, for example, Cree Chief Bobcat agreed to the terms of Treaty Six, which had been signed the previous year, and signed an adhesion to Treaty Six.

AFN: Assembly of First Nations.

Alternate funding arrangements (AFA): These are funding arrangements between the Department of Indian Affairs and a band or tribal council whereby the latter receive block funding for a designated period of time. The band can then allocate and manage the funds among programs and services at the band level. Some programs are excluded from the arrangements, which were first implemented in 1986. Participation is optional; the AFA provides some freedom from regular government controls, but bands are still accountable for funds.

Amicus curriae: An impartial advisor in a court of law. For example, a lawyer who files a brief or makes an oral argument before an appellate court

A number of terms in this glossary are from *Knots in a String: An Introduction to Native Studies in Canada* (2nd edition) by Peggy Brizinski. Reprinted with permission of the author.

on behalf of a person affected by or interested in a pending case but not actually party to it.

Annuity: An annual payment. Most treaties provided for annual payments, paid in perpetuity to each treaty Indian. An annuity paylist is the record of payment prepared each year, and lists each family receiving annuities.

Assimilation: Becoming part of another society, adapting to the society and taking on the characteristics of that society.

Band: A unit under the Indian Act for which land and monies are administered in common. Also a small group of people usually related by kin ties who live together. The band is egalitarian, individualistic, flexible, and often migratory. Leadership is based upon personality and competence.

Band membership: Band membership is determined by the Band Council and members are usually status Indians.

Bill C-31: In 1985, the Canadian government enacted Bill C-31 to reverse the detrimental effects of earlier legislation and redefined who is considered an Indian under the Indian Act. The legislation had three goals: 1) to ensure equality between men and women by removing blatantly discriminatory sections, 2) to restore Indian status and band membership to those who had lost them because of discrimination, and 3) to recognize the rights of the Bands to determine their own membership for the future. The *Act* created four new types of Indian: 1) status with band membership, 2) status without band membership, 3) non-status with band membership, and 4) non-status and non-band member. Persons who had lost status through marriage or enfranchisement, but not their descendants, could apply to have their status reinstated. The Act creates distinctions about how status is passed on.

Capitalism: An economic system characterized by open markets for buying and selling goods and by private or corporate ownership or control of the flow of money and profits in the markets. The system is usually stratified by class; the elite owners have more money and control than the lower classes. Also associated with an ethic of hard work and the accumulation of material goods.

Cession: When rights to a piece of land are given up or yielded to another party, as in a treaty.

Colonialism: The various economic, political, and social policies by which an imperial power maintains or extends its control over other areas or peoples.

Common law: Law based on custom and tradition, usually a law of general application to everyone. In other words, if a particular right is honoured in common practice, it may be put into law based on that custom or practice.

Comprehensive claims: Claims made to lands never ceded or surrendered by treaty or purchase; claims made to land on which Aboriginal rights were never extinguished and which Aboriginal people traditionally used and occupied.

Conveyance: Yielding rights to land in return for purchase. Lands conveyed by the Indians to the British were sold to the state for a cash payment.

COPE: Committee for Original Peoples' Entitlement. This is the political representation of the Inuvialuit of the western Arctic, and it succeeded in getting a land claims agreement for its people in 1984.

Core funding: Money given to an organization to cover its basic operating costs. Aboriginal organizations began getting core funding, primarily through the Secretary of State's office, in the 1970s.

Coureurs de bois: French for "woods runners." Young French men employed by the French trading companies in seventeenth to early eighteenth centuries, around the St. Lawrence-Great Lakes areas; they went among the Indians to trade for furs and other commodities.

Crown: This term denotes the British government, as led by the monarchy. When a document describes a particular role of the Crown, it means the role of the government representing the monarchy.

Culture: The collection of rules, values, and attitudes held by a society, which allows people to communicate, to interpret behaviour, and to attach shared meaning to behaviour and events.

Dene: The Athaspaskan-speaking peoples of northwestern Canada. This is their own name for themselves, "the people."

Denendeh: The name that the Dene proposed for their autonomous territory resulting from the division of the Northwest Territories. Although the federal government agreed with the idea of splitting the Northwest Territories, the Dene would not agree to extinguishment of Aboriginal title. As a result, negotiation of the Dene Metis Western Arctic Land Claim broke down in 1990.

DIAND: Department of Indian Affairs and Northern Development, the government department that was formerly named Indian and Northern Affairs Canada (INAC).

Diffusion: The spread of objects and ideas from one place to another by visiting, trade, migration, intermarriage, or conquest.

Enfranchisement: Occurs when a status Indian either gives up or loses his or her status. At different times in history, the Indian Act had many different ways for a status Indian to become enfranchised. For example, if any Indians wanted to go to university, become a minister, join the armed forces, vote, or own property they usually had to give up their status. If they were deemed to be responsible adults, Indian Affairs would allow them to become enfranchised and Canadian citizens. In the 1920s Indian Affairs was given the power to enfranchise people without their knowledge. Some Indians who volunteered for the World War I and II were unknowingly enfranchised. Up to 1985, any woman who married a non-status Indian automatically became enfranchised. The Department of Indian Affairs no longer has the power to enfranchise status Indians.

Entitlement: To acknowledge a claim or a right to something: a band is entitled to a certain amount of land according to the treaties. It may also refer to the allotment of reserve land due to a band under treaty; an outstanding entitlement means that the band did not get all the reserve land that it should have.

Entrench: To entrench Aboriginal rights in the Constitution means to make an amendment to the Constitution, which includes and defines those rights. They are then guaranteed unless the Constitution is changed to omit them. When they are guaranteed, federal and provincial legislation cannot take them away.

Ethnocentrism: To judge other people or groups by the standards and practices of one's own culture or group. Seeing one's group as best and judging others as inferior.

Ethnohistory: The study of the history of a particular group of people, using oral and written evidence, so that the historian can reconstruct what life was like at various stages of the society's history, and incorporate the point of view of members of the society. Loosely, ethnohistory is a combination of anthropology and history.

Eurocentricism: Label for all the beliefs that presume superiority of Europeans over non-Europeans.

Exogamy: A rule that one must find one's spouse from another group, such as another band or lineage.

Factor: The head trader and manager at Hudson's Bay Company posts.

Fee Simple: Refers to a form of title to land recognized by law. Under fee simple ownership, the owner can sell the property, use it to obtain loans, and generally use the property for his or her own interests.

Fiduciary: The meaning of the term "fiduciary" is embodied in the nation-to-nation treaty-making practice. It refers to a set of mutual obligations between the nations that were parties to the treaties. There is the agreement between the treaty parties to share a territory and its benefits, thereby establishing an irrevocable relationship of coexistence and partnership. These fiduciary principles serve as guides in cases where the relationship between the treaty parties becomes unbalanced and one nation becomes vulnerable to the power of the other. It is the view of Aboriginal groups in Canada that the Crown is under a fiduciary obligation to maintain a balanced relationship between itself and treaty nations. Otherwise, the Crown is compelled to implement measures to correct an imbalance in order to restore its relationship with treaty nations to a true partnership (RCAP, 1997).

First Nations: Usually used to refer to a politically autonomous band under the Indian Act, a nation of First Peoples.

FSIN: Federation of Saskatchewan Indian Nations.

Imperialism: A policy of seeking to extend control of a nation by acquiring new territory or dependencies especially when lying outside the nation's natural boundaries and extending control over the political or economic life of these other areas.

Identity: And individual, internal sense of identity by a person they labels himself or herself in relation to other people; also refers to an individual's sense of self-worth. We also "label" other people, assuming they have certain characteristics and qualities in relation to ourselves.

INAC: Department of Indian and Northern Affairs Canada, now known as Department of Indian Affairs and Northern Development (DIAND).

Indian: A term with many usages: could be a person of North American Indian ancestry, a status Indian under the Indian Act, or a treaty Indian.

Indian Act: Canadian legislation first passed in 1876 and amended many times since then; defines an Indian in relation to federal obligation; it sets out a series of regulations applying to Indians living on reserves.

Indigenous people: refers to all inhabitants indigenous to North America before contact with Euro-Canadians and their descendants.

Infrastructure: Underlying structure or arrangements. A community infrastructure includes its government and other organizations as well as community facilities such as health clinics, recreational complexes, roads, sewer and water systems, and schools. A developer who wants to locate a new manufacturing plant in a particular community may ask if the town has the infrastructure to accommodate more people moving into the community.

Inuvialuit: The Inuit people of the western Arctic, who live around the Beaufort Sea-Banks Island area.

ITC: Inuit Tapirisat of Canada. The umbrella organization representing the interests of Inuit people in central and eastern Arctic. It has branches concerned with land claims, Aboriginal rights and self-government, cultural programs, economic investments, research, and other areas.

Jurisdiction: Authority or power. The federal government has ultimate jurisdiction on reserves; its laws overrule those made by bands.

Justice system: The system of custom, law, courts, and corrections by which a society recognizes and deals with offences against society.

Language family: A group of languages that show some resemblances in vocabulary and grammar, and probably share a common ancestry.

Lineage: A group of people claiming kinship to each other through a line of descent from one ancestor, and who act upon those ties to form a social group. Matrilineal people claim descent through the female line, taking their name from their mothers, and patrilineal people claim descent through the male line. Some people claim descent from both, but may not recognize lineages as social groups.

Made Beaver: The standard of trade for the Hudson's Bay Company, equal to the market value of one prime winter beaver pelt.

Métis: Under the Canadian Constitution Act (1982), Métis are identified as one of the three Aboriginal peoples of Canada. The Métis are defined as people of mixed-blood ancestry, who self-identify as Métis and are accepted as such by Métis people. The term Métis has typically been used to describe the offspring of Indian-European unions in west-central North America. However, this geographic boundary excludes some historical Métis communities. Today the MNC additionally recognizes Métis individuals and communities in British Columbia, Labrador, and Ontario.

MNC: Métis National Council.

Myth: Collective cultural interpretations of the world and how it came to be, using narratives and symbols to convey meaning and entertainment.

NCC: Native Council of Canada.

Non-status Indian: An Indian person who is not registered as an Indian under the Indian Act, either because the individual or his or her ancestors were never registered, or because status was lost through marriage or other provisions of the Act.

Numbered treaties: Land cession treaties signed between 1871 and 1921, each numbered, throughout the North and West. The treaties conferred certain rights to both parties who signed. The Canadian government, for example, gained access to vast tracts of land, while the Indians gained annuities in perpetuity.

Nunavut: the formal name that the Inuit have for the new land and government of the eastern NWT, after division of the Northwest Territories April 1, 1999.

Order of Government: The federal and provincial systems are two different orders of government. They are set up in the Constitution so that each has certain powers and responsibilities, for example, provinces are responsible for education. A First Nations government would be a third order of government (in addition to provincial and federal ones). The powers of the third order would have to be laid out in relation to the first two orders, so that it is clear which responsibilities they have to their citizens.

Overplus: An extra margin of profit added to standard prices for trade items by Hudson's Bay Company factors to keep income above the costs of credit, gift exchange, and other business expenses. Sometimes accomplished by short measure, or giving out less of a trade item than the buyer paid for.

Peace and friendship treaties: Treaties that signified that the two parties would not make war on each other. In the eighteenth century peace and friendship treaties signed between the British and Maritimes Indians, there was no explicit mention of land or land rights.

Pemmican: Meat, often buffalo, that has been dried, pounded, and mixed with fat and berries; a lightweight, concentrated, long-lasting food source.

Perpetuity: The treaties were signed in perpetuity, which means either forever or as long as the treaties are deemed valid. Treaty commissioners promised that the provisions of the treaties would last "as long as the sun shines and the water flows."

Phenotype: Set of observable characteristics of individuals or groups as determined by genotype (genetic constitution of an individual) and environment.

Prehistory or protohistory: History before there were written records of it; we have only indirect evidence of prehistory. The prehistory of the Indians covers the period before explorers, fur traders, and missionaries began to record what Native life was like. Many people dislike the term, because it implies that "real" history took place only after contact.

Race: A way of describing human genetic variation. Most scientists reject the idea that there are clear-cut races of humans, since one physical type blends into another. General categories such as Mongoloid and Caucasoid are sometimes still used to understand variation, but the term race should be used with caution because cultural and racial characteristics are easily confused; for example, the people who make such statements as "Indians are lazy" and "White men are greedy" sometimes confuse race and culture by implying that all people with certain physical features share personality traits.

Revenue sharing: Many Native bands and governments desire to share in the revenues obtained from their lands. Indians on reserves get a share of revenues from their lands. Revenue is any form of income from an investment, such as rent, taxes, or royalties. Revenue sharing in land claims agreements may mean that Native claimants share in investment income from some categories of land included in the claim; this may substitute for cash compensation.

Scrip: A token or paper entitling the bearer to goods, money, or land. It is not itself considered currency.

Sovereignty: Ultimate jurisdiction or power. Claiming sovereignty for an Indian nation means claiming it has the right to rule itself without any external control.

Specific claims: Claims relating to lands entitled by treaties or any land cession arrangement. A specific claim might be one that states that the amount of land a band was entitled to under the treaty they signed was never provided. Specific claims also include loss of land under bureaucratic policy or practice, such as illegal surrenders.

State society: A sociological and anthropological term to describe a complex, highly institutionalized form of governance. A state society has centralized leadership, a bureaucracy, division of labour and economic specialization, institutionalized education and religion, and class divisions.

Status Indian: An Indian person who is registered as an Indian under the Indian Act and thus recognized by the federal government as an Indian and accorded the accompanying rights, benefits, and restrictions of the Indian Act and related policies.

Structural racism: A form of discrimination practised when institutions of society and the state systematically exclude a racial group from certain jobs or institutions. The former apartheid system of South Africa, where the law prevented black people from participating in government and from living in certain areas, is one of the most overt examples of structural racism in the twentieth century. Some writers suggest that economic discrimination against Native people has been "built into" the economic foundations of Canada since the fur trade.

Surrender of land: Under the Indian Act, there are provisions for surrender of reserve land for sale, leasing, or right-of-way. Some surrenders were conducted under pressure on the bands, or under questionable practice, and are the subject of claims today.

Suzerainty: The dominion of a suzerain (feudal overlord). A sovereign or a state which has power over another state. The subordinate state possesses its own ruler and has authority in its internal affairs but cannot act as an independent power.

Terra nullius: Land belonging to no one; empty, unpeopled land. The notion that no one owned the land before European arrival.

Transfer payments: Government-provided cash payments for specific purposes, often intended to alleviate poverty. Such payments include social assistance (welfare), old age pensions, disability pensions, and family allowances.

Treaty: A contract made between two parties, whereby each agrees to follow the terms. Treaties could involve peace agreements between the two parties, or an agreement to cede lands in return for certain rights and services. The legal status of treaties is still under debate.

Treaty Indian: An Indian person whose forefathers signed a numbered treaty in which land was exchanged for certain listed payments, such as money, tools, and health and educational benefits. The term is often used in the prairie provinces as synonymous with status Indians.

Tribe: This term is, very generally, used to designate a group of bands or villages claiming common language and ancestry, and recognizing some social and political ties—a tribal nation. The term is also used sometimes by anthropologists to label a type of society where special institutions, such as councils and war or religious societies, provide governing or organizing functions for the entire group of bands or communities. Tribal societies occasionally gathered for religion or warfare, and bands may have representatives on these pan-tribal organizations. This is a general type of society and few societies past or present fit it precisely.

Usufruct: A legal term relating to land ownership, which means that the occupant of the land has the right to enjoy, occupy, and use some of the resources, such as hunting and fishing, from the land, but without full ownership of the land as in fee simple title. Courts are increasingly recognizing only a usufructory title for Native claimants, meaning that Native people have little entitlement to mineral or forestry resources, for example.

Voyageurs: French and Métis men who transported goods and furs by canoe for the North West Company.

Index

Index

aajuitsoq, 128
Aboriginal Friendship Centres, 400
Aboriginal languages, *see also* Indigenous languages; teaching of, 19–20
Aboriginal people, *see also* First Nations; Indians; Indigenous peoples; Native people; and names of individual groups; perceptions regarding, 407–408; self-determination for, 316–17, 318–19, 320, 321, 325
Aboriginal rights, 292, 318; "long, long time" test, 304; in Quebec, 324; urban satellite reserves and, 416–17, 419–20; women's rights *vs.*, 338
Aboriginal title, *see also* Land; Gitksan people and, 291–92, 293–313; Nisga'a people and, 292–93; Wet'suwet'en people and, 291–92, 293–313
Aboriginal Women's Unity Collective, 334
academic freedom: Native Studies and, 15
adaawk, 300–301, 303–304, 312*n*.14
Adair, James, 45
Adams, Howard, 28, 29, 163
Additions to Reserve Policy (ARP), 412

adolescents, 384
agriculture, 47–48, 258, 470–71
Aleut people, 128
Alexander, Sir William, 156
Alexander VI, Pope, 148
Amherst, Lord Jeffrey, 45
Amin, Samir, 42–43
anthropology: Native Studies and, 22–23
Antoine, Felix, 335
Archibald, A.G., 224, 250
Armstrong, Benjamin G., 199
art, 399–98, 406
Assembly of First Nations (AFN), 286, *see also* National Indian Brotherhood; on federal-provincial responsibility, 280; on Indigenous knowledge, 444, 449; leadership conventions, 401; on self-government and women's rights, 329, 331, 337, 340, 347; on TEK, 438
assimilation, 70, 257; cultural, 265, 278; institutional, 279–81
Atecouando of Odanak, 157
Aulotte, Philomena, 336
Axworthy, Lloyd, 229

Bacqueville de la Potherie, *see* Le Roy, Claude-Charles
band councils, 257, 422–23
Barbeau, Marius, 302

Hakluyt, Richard, 155
halfbreeds, 48, 80–82, 91*n*.5, *see also* mixed race
Hammersmith, Bernice, 363
Harper, Elijah, 275, 360
Head, Lillian, 366
healing movements, 400
hearsay rule, 305
Henry, Alexander, the elder, 152, 193–94, 199
Henry, Alexander, the younger, 192
Henry, of Susa, 150
history: Eurocentric, 40–52; First Nations' concepts, 234–37; Indigenous Studies and, 29; Native Studies and, 20–21; objectivity in, 233; oral, *see* oral history; storytelling; subjective, 43–44; Western concepts, 232–34; written, 32, 48, 232–34; written *vs.* oral, 298–99
housing: on urban satellite reserves, 420–21
Hudson's Bay Company, 239–42; charter granted to, 156; Red River rebellion and, 223–24
hunting rights, 105–10

identity, 57–59, 80, 91*n*.5, 92*n*.11, 402, 405–406, 408, *see also* Indianness; Métis, 90–91*n*.5, 95–111; race and, 96–97
immigration, 47
income: gender and, 85; of Métis people, 230
Indian Act, 76, 78, 81, 106, 256–57, 258, 335–36, 498–509; amendments, 510; section 88, 282; section 12(1)(b), 356–57, 362
Indian agents, 262–63*n*.81

Indian Chiefs of Alberta. *Red Paper*, 397
Indian identity: Métis identity *vs.*, 96, 102, 108, 109, 111*n*.4
Indian Patents Act, 469
Indian people: appearance, 84–87
Indian policy: "national interest" *vs.*, 268–72
Indian Rights for Indian Women, 357
Indian status: Aboriginal women and, 335–37, 356–57; constitutional normalization of, 281–83; Indianness and, 87–88; loss of, 74–75, 79; marriage and, 78–79, 356–57; Métis people and, 74–75; Native women and, 91*n*.7
Indianness, *see also* nativeness; defined, 76–82; Indian status and, 87–88
Indians, *see also* Aboriginal people; First Nations; Native people; involvement in political process, 273–74; justice system and, 271–72
Indigenous knowledge, 450–52, *see also* Traditional Ecological Knowledge (TEK); traditional knowledge
Indigenous languages, 29, *see also* Aboriginal languages
Indigenous peoples, *see also* Aboriginal people; First Nations; Convention of Biological Diversity and, 466–67; intellectual property rights (IPR) and, 473–77; as objects of study, 445; TEK research and, 445–46
Indigenous Peoples' Earth Charter, 468, 478–88